MW00779826

LA VARENNE'S COOKERY

LA VARENNE'S COOKERY

THE FRENCH COOK
THE FRENCH PASTRY CHEF
THE FRENCH CONFECTIONER

François Pierre,
SIEUR DE LA VARENNE

LE CUISINIER FRANÇOIS
LE PASTISSIER FRANÇOIS
LE CONFITURIER FRANÇOIS

A modern translation and commentary by
TERENCE SCULLY

PROSPECT BOOKS
2006

First published in Great Britain in 2006 by Prospect Books,
Allaleigh House, Blackawton, Totnes, TQ9 7DL

BRITISH LIBRARY CATALOGUING IN PUBLICATION DATA:
A catalogue entry for this book is available from the British Library.

ISBN 1-903018-41-2

Typeset and designed by Terence Scully.

Printed and bound in Great Britain by The Cromwell Press, Trowbridge, Wiltshire.

Table of Contents

for *The French Cook,*
The French Pastry Chef
and *The French Confectioner*

The French Cook **129**

**Instructing on the Proper Manner of Preparing and Seasoning
Meats that are served in the four Seasons of the Year
at Great and Private Tables.**

The French Pastry Chef **375**

In which is taught the way of making every sort of Pastry,
very useful for every sort of Person
together with
the way to prepare every sort of Egg Dish
for lean and other days in more than sixty ways

The French Confectioner **485**

in which is taught how to make all sorts of confections,
dragées, liqueurs and pleasant beverages, along with
the Way of Folding Table Linen,
and of making all sorts of shapes with it.

Introduction

A. François Pierre, Sieur de La Varenne

(i) La Varenne: his life

François Pierre was born probably in or near Chalon-sur-Saône around 1615. In all likelihood he concluded his professional initiation as a cook in the kitchens of the Marquis d'Uxelles in his new Château de Cormatin.[1] Wherever he began his oral instruction and practical training in the craft of cookery he progressed through his apprenticeship and was probably admitted to the grade of master cook in the early 1640s.[2] He would die in the capital of his native Burgundy, Dijon, in 1678, after a life in which his professional activities garnered him a respect and reputation second to none in France, and that reached into most of the aristocratic kitchens in Europe. His book, *Le Cuisinier françois*, earned such popularity that sales exhausted an astounding 30 editions in 75 years.[3]

---

[1] The rebuilding of the Château de Cormatin was begun around 1616 by Antoine du Blé (1560–1616). Most of that structure still stands — though unfortunately not the south wing, collapsed in the nineteenth century, in whose basement the original kitchens were located. The Château at Uxelles had been poorly maintained and had become virtually uninhabitable by the second half of the sixteenth century; that property had been acquired by Pétrarque du Blé in 1560 along with the estate and title as part of an inheritance of his wife Catherine de Sercy. The fief of Cormatin had been in the Du Blé family since at least 1235.

[2] In his dedication at the beginning of the *Cuisinier françois* (1651) La Varenne writes that he has worked for the Marquis d'Uxelles for ten years and in that time learned the secrets of fine cookery.

[3] In their introduction to a recent reprint, *The French Cook, by François Pierre, La Varenne translated into English in 1653 by I.D.G.* (Lewes, East Sussex: Southover Press, 1999), Philip and Mary Hyman have counted "61 editions, the last of which was printed around 1754" (p. xii). On La Varenne the only biographic evidence, though it is perhaps none too firm, is quoted in the same place (p. xii): "Varenne, (Pierre) Châlonnais, vint s'établir à Dijon où il mourut en 1678 âgé de plus de 60 ans": Philippe Papillon, *Bibliothèque des auteurs de Bourgogne* (Dijon: P. Marteret, 1742), Vol. II, p. 342.

Furthermore La Varenne's book demonstrated its huge contemporary success by arousing, during those years of continual reprinting and long after
its author's death, a degree of jealousy within the fraternity, along with repeated efforts on the part of competitors to dethrone the reigning culinary
monarch. Over several generations the rivals, forever younger and forever
more inventive, did eventually prove successful. Perhaps despite himself
but indisputably, La Varenne was at the origin of a culinary awakening
in France, a vigorous efflorescence of creativity unlike any that has been
seen anywhere before or, even, since.

Who was this La Varenne, the man whose name became indelibly
identified with French classical cooking?

In the kitchens of the great in France it had long been customary
to dub the chief cook with a nickname. Some three centuries before, for
instance, at the close of the Middle Ages the chief cook of King Charles V,
one Guillaume Tirel, had acquired the name Taillevent or "Wind-Slicer":
we can imagine him regularly impressing his underlings by cleaving the air
with the swing of a huge chopping blade. In time that sobriquet displaced
the great cook's own name — except on legal documents and on his
tombstone, now hanging obscurely in the Museum of Saint-Germain-en-
Laye; it is immortally fused into the name of the old recipe collection he
adopted and refined: the *Viandier de Taillevent*.

At some stage in his own career, François Pierre was given or assumed
a nickname which, within his profession, had already been rendered moderately famous a generation or two before him. Toward the end of the
sixteenth century a certain Guillaume Fouquet (1560–1616) worked in the
kitchens of the sister of Henry IV of France, Catherine, Duchess of Bar.
Apart from those culinary duties Fouquet seems also to have served his
employer's brother, the King, by bearing personal messages, along with
the odd *billet doux* — all on behalf of his royal master. In faithfully
fulfilling this secondary function the cook saw bestowed upon him the
whimsical titles of cloak-bearer (*porte-manteau*), mail supervisor and, finally, Lord of the Game Preserve (or Wasteland: *Seigneur de la varenne*).
This last title likely derived from Fouquet's frequent need to eschew high-
ways while travelling from estate to estate, but rather to cross uncultivated
land — called *la garenne* in Old French — directly in the performance

of his royal assignments.[4] King Henry's amorous liaisons earned *him* the qualification of the *Vert Galant*.

François Pierre, the chief cook of the Marquis d'Uxelles, also became known, and eventually much better known, by the nickname of "Sieur de La Varenne." That is the form, and the only form, by which he is named as author on the title page of the book that embodies his life's work. In the case of François Pierre the reason for this sobriquet is not recorded. He may have been a descendent of the earlier La Varenne, and facetiously have claimed the title by right of inheritance. It is conceivable also that the Marquis likewise engaged in covert activities of a nature similar to those ardent pastimes for which the former King was known. François Pierre may have been employed, on the rare occasions the Marquis was in residence, to transmit clandestine messages privily across "the wild land" between his master and various aristocratic neighbours. It is worth keeping in mind that in any noble household of this and earlier periods the person in whom the lord placed — had of necessity to have — the most absolute and unquestioning trust was invariably his cook. It is entirely natural that royalty and nobility sometimes elevated their chief cook either by means of an actual title, as was the case of Charles V's Taillevent, or by conferring upon him a secondary and intimately ambassadorial role. This was simply a different form of confidence in the person who held his master's very health and welfare in his competent hands.

We know little of the life of François Pierre. In all likelihood he learned his trade by working at it. Somewhere, either in the Uxelles kitchen at Cormatin or elsewhere, he trained in the culinary craft of the time. He may have begun to earn his keep in life by doing a scullion's chores, scrubbing, hauling, stirring, kindling, stoking. Under the guidance of a master cook, he himself would have trained in all the tricks of the profession, learned all the standard culinary repertoire of the day, become imbued with all the inherent sense of obligation and honour that defines a great cook of any age. In time, in the faithful service of of the Marquis d'Uxelles, François Pierre distinguished himself to such a degree as master

---

[4] According to Agrippa d'Aubigné, a militant protestant, the earlier La Varenne was nothing more or less than a procurer (*pourvoyeur*) of mistresses for the apostate Henry IV.

cook that he rose to the rank of kitchen clerk[5] in the Uxelles' *hôtel* or household, an executive position in which he exercised authority over all kitchen activities and purchases. There can be little doubt that more than just professional competence was responsible for this elevation in post. It is fair to assume that the personality of François Pierre played a large part in the respect in which his master held him.

Kitchen Clerk to the Marquis d'Uxelles was no mean position for an untitled bourgeois such as François Pierre to have attained. Louis Chalon du Blé (1619–1658), Marquis d'Uxelles, was in fact one of significant aristocrats in France at a time when the monarchy was determined to restrict the power of the nobility quite severely.[6] He belonged to one of the first families of Burgundy and bore titles to estates in several localities around modern-day Chalon-sur-Saône: Marquis d'Uxelles, Baron of Cormatin, Lord of Buxy and of Tenarre. His wife, Marie de Bailleul (1626–1712) whom he married in 1645 several years after La Varenne began working for him, was an exceptionally refined, social, beautiful and literate person and undoubtedly exercised a strong influence upon the household of this military man.[7] For several generations by royal appointment the civil function of Lieutenant General of Burgundy had been

---

[5] La Varenne's title was *écuyer de cuisine*. Properly and originally an *escuyer* was a military term, identifying a warrior's "shield-bearer". By the seventeenth century, however, the sense of the word was no longer the English literal equivalent "squire" but rather "attendant" or "superintendent" (*préposé* in modern French). In his *Dictionarie of the French and English Tongues* (London, 1611) Cotgrave glosses the title *escuyer de cuisine* as "the clarke of a kitchin". That is how the contemporary English translator, I. D. G., handles La Varenne's qualifications on his own title page: "Monsieur De La Varenne, Clerk of the Kitchin to the Lord Marquesse of Uxelles" (see section D. ii (a), below).

[6] A very detailed biography of the Du Blé family as lords of Uxelles, and of Louis Chalon du Blé in particular, was established by Gabriel Jeanton and Jean Martin in "Le château d'Uxelles et ses seigneurs," *Annales de l'Académie de Mâcon. Société des arts, sciences, belles-lettres, agriculture et encouragement au bien de Saône-et-Loire*, 3rd series, vol. 12 (Mâcon: Protat, 1907), 157–392; the life of Louis Chalon is at pp. 291–298. In La Varenne's dedication of the *Cuisinier françois* his patron's name is typeset as "Messire Louis Chaalon du Bled". The family was native of a Mâconnais hamlet called Ublé: *villa Oblato* (canton of Cluny).

[7] Her father, Nicolas de Bailleul, was an outstanding figure in the capital himself: "Baron de Chaâteau Gontier, seigneur de Valtot, Soisy et Etiolles, il fut successivement conseiller au Parlement de Paris, maître des requestes, ambassadeur en Savoie, président au grand conseil, lieutenant civil en Paris, prévôt des marchands, chevalier

passed down from heir to heir in the Du Blé (or Du Bled) family, as well
as the rank of military Lieutenant General and the position "Bailiff" of
the nobility in Burgundy.[8] Locally he was (from 1629 at the age of 10!)
appointed Governor of both the city of Chalon and its Citadel. Perhaps the
greatest honour that Louis Chalon held was as a member of King Louis
XIV's Privy State Council: *Conseiller du Roi*. He was a military man,
very largely at the service of his king.[9] He maintained and commanded
two regiments, of cavalry and of infantry, at the King's disposition. With
them he travelled so constantly that his biography is filled with little more
than dates and the places of battles and sieges, of captures and suppres-
sions of revolts.[10] The Marquis d'Uxelles seems rarely to have had the
leisure to enjoy his hearth, his family and a good meal at Cormatin.

---

de la reine Anne d'Autriche, ministre d'Etat, surintendant des finances" (Jeanton and
Martin, *op. cit.*, p. 227). Following the death of her husband in 1658 and that of
the first of her two sons at the age of 20 in 1668, the Marquise d'Uxelles became
an habituée of the Court in Paris and a close friend of Mme de Sévigné (1626–96).
Like De Sévigné she is highly respected for her correspondence. She died 1712.

[8] The function of a *bailli* in France was complex and powerful. Cotgrave explains:
"*Bailli*. A Bailife (but of much more authoritie than ours) a Magistrat appointed
within a Province, or precinct certaine, to execute justice, maintaine the peace, and
preserve the people from oppression, vexation, and wrong: To which end he takes
notice of treasons committed, false money coyned; robberies, and murthers done;
rebellions, or seditions raised; unlawfull, or populer assemblies made; Armes borne,
or souldiours levied, without warrant; Protections, or Sanctuaries violated; Pardons,
and Charters abused; Faires, markets, freedomes, and other priviledges usurped, or
unjustly stood on: He makes proclamations in his owne name; he calls the Ban, and
Arriereban; leads those that he raised by it; and appoints th'ordinarie musters of his
Province: hee determines Appeales from the sentences of Provosts, and other inferior
judges, at Assises, whereof he is the principall Judge; and is thereby held the most
proper Judge for Gentlemen, who have ever pretended that their causes must bee
decided at Assises; and yet for all this, (and though hee may have a Lieutenant) he
is but a Deputie, either unto the king, or unto some lord; every one whereof (unto
the Chastellain) hath, or may have, a Bailli within his territories."

[9] Louis XIV (1638–1715) was five years old at the death of his father in 1643. During
his minority the queen mother, Anne of Austria, was regent but actual power was
exercised by her minister, Cardinal Mazarin. Before, as well as during, the period
of Louis's personal reign, the military might of France was a primary concern of the
state.

[10] For instance: 1638, Landrecies and La Capelle; 1639, in Lorraine; 1640, Turin;
1641, Sedan, Bapaume, Catalonia, Perpignan; 1642, Tarragona, Tortosa; 1643,
Rosas; 1645, Lillers, Armentières and nine other battles in Picardy; 1646, Orbitello
in Tuscany, Piombino, Porto Longone; 1647, Cremona; 1648, Tortosa in Catalo-

To work for such a personage of outstanding authority, power and dignity, who had the intimate confidence of the monarch and his governing council, to enjoy in turn the intimate confidence of that personnage by being assigned responsibility for his personal food service, must surely for François Pierre have represented the summit of all possible honour and glory. His master may not have been in continuous residence either at Cormatin or at the family's *hôtel* in Paris, but the Marquis could afford to ensure that the kitchens in both places had everything that La Varenne could wish for in terms of furnishings, personnel and victuals. Undoubtedly the nature of his master's life and the fact that he was away on campaign so often meant that La Varenne himself must occasionally have accompanied him, spending a good deal of time away from his home kitchens in Paris and in the new castle of Cormatin and having to make do with provisional arrangements and camp kitchens.[11] Working for such a socially and militarily prominent family as of the Marquis and Marquise d'Uxelles gave La Varenne a professional experience that was immeasurably broader than that of a cook who satisfied a more modest or reclusive master.

(ii) Historical circumstances: his daily professional work

François Pierre was almost certainly not of aristocratic birth. He would have been of a respectable bourgeois or middle-class family. As a young man he would have entered into the service of his lord, having perhaps been taken on even at the lowest level as scullery help in the Marquis's kitchen. There, while putting in very long hours scrubbing pots, hauling carcasses, replenishing coal bins, stoking fires and turning spits, he would have had plenty of opportunity to see the various phases of food preparation in a noble kitchen. In particular the work of the specialists, the baker

---

nia, Ypres in Flanders, Lens, Furnes; 1649, Paris and Charenton; Valenciennes in Flanders, Cambrai; 1650, Seurre; 1652, Italy and Flanders, Etampes, Paris; 1653, Seurre, Rethel, Mouzon, Sainte-Menehould; 1654, Belfort, Arras, Quesnoy; 1655, Landrecies; 1656, Clermont, Valenciennes, La Capelle, Montmédy, Mardick; 1658, Trèves, Dunes, Gravelines. Louis Chalon du Blé received a mortal wound at this last siege; on his deathbed, on Mazarin's recommendation he was invested with the highest military rank, Marshal of France.

[11] In this regard see the rubric to the Table of Contents of Chapter V in the *Cuisinier françois*: *Table des entrées qui se peuvent faire dans les armées ou en la campagne.*

cum pastry chef, the confectioner, and the cook himself — who, in the Uxelles' establishment, would likely have functioned as the kitchen's butcher as well — would have attracted the young lad's attention. He would have begun his professional apprenticeship by the age of fourteen or sixteen as an assistant to one of those specialists, being promoted over the years as his seniors retired and as he acquired demonstrable understanding and expertise in the various areas.

The summit of the skilled, professional activities in such a kitchen as that of the Marquis d'Uxelles — the "technical" side of food preparation — was represented, as it had been since the late Middle Ages, by the Cook. In the largest households, that of a count, a duke, a queen[12] or a king, a chief cook might perhaps direct the work of several other cooks of lesser standing, as well as the specialized work of the butcher, roaster, sauce-maker, pottage-maker, fruiter and perhaps salad-maker. More modest households, both bourgeois and noble, managed with the services of a single cook. Through long years of hands-on work he had acquired sufficient professional experience to oversee effectively the whole broad range of activities in the kitchen. He ensured that all the kitchen's work progressed efficiently and with deliberate, careful co-ordination. Writing a generation after La Varenne, Audiger indicates that the annual remuneration of a cook in an affluent household should, depending on the cook's abilities and the master's means, by roughly 300 pounds. That amount is the same as should be paid to the master's secretary but is considerably less than the 500 pounds of the chief functionary in the household, the *maistre d'hostel*, although more than the 200 of the almoner or the *sommelier*.[13]

---

[12] Some very large houses had separate households, separate staffs, facilities and accounting, for the lord and his lady. Most also distinguished in the kitchen between food for the lord, his family and guests, and food for the staff: a different cook and kitchen staff might be responsible for each. So in 1570 Bartolomeo Scappi was able to boast that he was the personal cook (*cuoco secreto*) of Pope Pius V.

[13] N. Audiger, *La maison reglée* (Amsterdam: Paul Marret, 1697 and 1700; originally published Paris: M. Brunet, 1692 and Paris: Nicolas le Gros, also 1692). See the modern French version of the work in *L'art de la cuisine française au XVIIe siècle* (Paris: Payot, 1995), 451. Interestingly the *Dictionnaire de biographie française* (Paris: Letouzey & Ané), Vol. 4 (1948), Col. 400, notes that Audiger was in Paris about 1660 and *contribua à vulgariser l'emploi des liqueurs, du thé, du café et du chocolat*.

What happened to an old cook? Did the chief merely expire one day, stooped from stirring endless cauldrons, labour-weary, eyes chronically inflamed, coughing from lungs impaired by decades in the fumes of wood and coal fires? In a more affluent French establishment a chief cook had one further rung on to which he might exceptionally be elevated: he could be appointed kitchen steward, *écuyer de cuisine*. At that point in the household hierarchy the kitchen steward had over him only the *maître d'hôtel*, the person responsible to the lord (or to the bourgeois wealthy enough to emulate the estate of a lord) for all the living arrangements of his house.[14] This last august retainer was remunerated at the top of the scale of all a household's employees, at a rate that normally ran about twice the salary of a master cook; the kitchen steward in turn would receive a pay packet somewhere between the other two rates. The dependable provision of good food was very important in a noble French house.

The person exercising the duties of kitchen steward had ultimate responsibility for the good operation of what today we might call the food services in a household. He was in part a book-keeper, maintaining records of the inventory in the larder, knowing in which foodstuffs the estate itself was or was not self-sufficient at every period in the year, knowing which of the various local suppliers were reliable, submitting budgets, seeking approval for expenses for both foodstuffs and kitchen equipment, keeping accounts of all expenditures within his domain, and justifying and rendering those accounts to the steward and the lord's accountant. He recommended new appointments in any of the offices under his jurisdiction. He was in part, too, a food professional, proposing interesting but feasible menus, proposing long-term victualling contracts, verifying the quality of what arrived at the kitchen door, demanding redress from provisioners whenever their goods were inadequate. He worked closely with the household's butler (*bouteiller*), or wine steward, ensuring that good supplies of potables and cooking liquors were on hand. In conjunction with the household's steward he ensured that service of meals to his lord's dining table was proper. In conjunction with both the steward and chief

---

[14] The *Maître d'hôtel*, almost invariably an aristocrat, was normally in charge of all his master's employed and appointed staff whether they worked with food, minded the stable, maintained living accommodations, watched accounts or kept game on the estate's reserves.

cook he determined any special grand *entremets* that a formal banquet might require.[15]

In short, an *écuyer de cuisine* occupied a middle-executive position. The person appointed to it furnished a vital connection between the lord, his palate, his purse and his kitchen.

Such a position of responsibility was normally reserved for individuals with some claim to gentry. That François Pierre, *dit de la Varenne*, should have been exalted to the rank of Kitchen Clerk to the Marquis d'Uxelles speaks to the high esteem in which both his technical and intellectual abilities were held by his lord. It also says a great deal for the Marquis' respect for La Varenne's personal integrity, to say nothing of his gastronomic taste. At the very least, La Varenne must have been a competent and trustworthy person.

The fifteenth and sixteenth centuries, respectively the end of the Middle Ages and the Renaissance in France, saw the aristocracy and nobility growing markedly in personal wealth — at least relative to the continuing indigence of the peasants who worked their land. In turn this increase in affluence encouraged an expansion in the opulence of lifestyle. In former feudal times an aristocrat earned and retained his position by his martial prowess and his ability to place armed troops at the service of his liege lord. Much of his life was spent away from his estates and the comfort of his hearth and home. With the end of the Hundred Years' War, though, and the sporadic engagements of the Wars of Religion, the aristocrat's domestic arrangements and mode of daily living reflected an increasing affluence. Furthermore French military incursions into Italy had revealed the truly amazing possibilities of craftsmanship and art at the service of wealth. French nobles began to be ashamed that Italians held them to be merely Frankish barbarians.

By the opening of the seventeenth century the aristocracy of France were conceiving ideas of luxury in architecture, furniture, tapestries and artistic accoutrements generally, dress and foods that their forefathers might have thought thoroughly decadent — if not beyond the realm of possibility. To be wealthy no longer meant merely possessing the means

---

[15] See Appendix 2 for a contemporary definition of an *entremets*.

to raise and equip companies of knights and foot soldiers but rather being able to give oneself a magnificent style of life, to afford to immerse
oneself in the material pleasures of modern life.

In this pursuit of grand pleasure, emulation played then as always
an important role. As Kings Louis XIII and Louis XIV secured absolute
authority in their kingdom and the role of arbiters of taste in all matters, so
their court became the ultimate model for nobles who wished to assume,
in small measure, at least the trappings of that authority. In the same way
the parading of munificence in the grand style was more important than
ever. If the definition of nobilty was manifest wealth, then it was largely
through ostentation that each member of the aristocracy could affirm his
membership in the class, and by vying to outdo his peers in magnificence
that he could claim superior standing within that class.

From the earliest times the dining table has always been a means of
demonstrating an exceptional refinement of taste that is directly related
to an exceptional social position. Food is one of the basic tributes that a
person can pay to his ego. The gift of food is also a highly effective way
to impress and flatter a guest; hospitality, the sharing of hearth and board,
is remarkably many-dimensioned in its benefits to donor and recipient.

From the end of the Middle Ages onward, the complexity of work
in aristocratic kitchens continued to grow. The responsibilities of kitchen
personnel multiplied as mounting demands were put on it to create dishes
suitable for the ever-swelling grandeur of the master's name. Within the
kitchen of an aristocratic household perfection in traditional work was
not the only requirement; the grandeur of the master's name could also
be enhanced by exceptional creations. The preparation of food for daily
meals and banquets in such kitchens became more onerous.

Traditionally the cook's craft was learned orally, by observation and
by practice. Apart from what was copied in a few manuscripts, that craft
was transmitted by apprenticeship and retained over the generations only
in the memories of a succession of cooks. The craft tended to be highly
traditional and limited to each individual's personal experience.

The printed book gradually changed that, of course. The printed
recipe book might threaten the exclusivity of access the professional master
cook enjoyed to an accumulated body of culinary knowledge, oral and
idiosyncratic though it might tend to be. But it allowed a professional

cook (and others) to broaden his repertoire and to improve his skills. With a printed recipe book a professional cook had a solid means to be a conventionally good cook.

Such practical talents as culinary skill honed by experience and imagination were not enough, though. In order to succeed at his craft a cook had to possess other qualities than strictly culinary competence. Of those, trustworthiness was perhaps uppermost. The trust that his master might eventually have in him had to be earned, and earned with an incessant effort to allay the suspicions under which eternally cooks have laboured. A household cook had in a real way to identify himself with the fortunes of the house itself. He could, of course, never let the kitchen for which he was responsible imperil the health or well-being of his master or his master's family or guests — even though the risks inherent in food preparation were certainly no less common four centuries ago than today.

He had to cook well, and safely, for his master, but he had an obligation also to do it in a way that was said to be "honourable". By that term was meant that what he did confirmed the lustre of his master's reputation and, if at all possible, exalted it. The good cook had to understand gastronomic taste, not only that of his master but that of his time as well, and of his master's social circle. He had to understand the obligation that bore upon his master to show himself worthy of the social rank he occupied. In providing "honourable" food and meals, the good cook was in a real sense an instrument, often an indispensible instrument, to ensure the enduring grandeur and glory of his master's very name.

B. The Nature of the Three Works

Reflective, perhaps, of François Pierre's hubris, the name of his principal cookbook bears a play on his own name: *Le cuisinier François*
— that is, "François's (or Francis's) Cookery Manual" or even "François
the Cook". In the fifteenth and sixteenth centuries the word *cuisinier* had
primarily the meaning of "cookbook" or "cookery manual". The word
for "cook" remained still the very old term *queu* or *queux*,[16] although
it was gradually being replaced by another word, *cuisinier*, properly an
adjective: one would say, *un serviteur cuisinier* or, commonly, with the
adjective preceding the noun, *un cuisinier serviteur*. This word order of
adjective-noun was normal in French up until the seventeenth century, and
even then in ordinary speech remained common in roughly half the cases
of a noun qualfied by a single adjective.

By the middle of the sixteenth century, the earliest printed cookbooks,
bearing such titles as *Livre de cuysine, Livre fort excellent de cuysine, La
Fleur de toute cuysine*, and later *Le grand cuisinier* and *Le grand cuisinier
de toute cuisine*, all offered relatively slight variations on much the same
contents.[17] To a remarkable extent, all those early cookbooks derived
more or less directly from the *Viandier* which in manuscript copies had
established itself the French culinary authority and survived for a couple
of centuries at the end of the Middle Ages. The word *viandier* itself, a
common noun, was in fact the term for a cookbook, until displaced in
the Renaissance period by the word *cuisinier*. By the mid-seventeenth
century, the use of the word *cuisinier* in the sense of "cookbook" in fact

---

[16] This word has nothing to do with a "tail", a feminine word, but derived directly from
the Latin for "cook", *coquus*. As final *es* became mute in standard modern French,
the similarity between *queu* and *queue* may have contributed to the demise of the
first word.

[17] On the monopolistic reign of these manuals over noble French kitchens right up into
the seventeenth century see Philip Hyman and Mary Hyman, "Les livres de cuisine
et le commerce des recettes en France aux XVe et XVIe siècles," *Du manuscrit
à la table*, ed. Carole Lambert (Montréal and Paris: Université de Montréal and
Champion-Slatkine, 1992), 59–68.

was archaic.[18] Semantically it was coming to designate the "person who cooked" rather than a manual on cooking.

Because the qualification *françois* identifies the author and is in fact a proper noun, it should properly be capitalized. Early printers used capital letters throughout the first words of a title, so that the ambiguity between "Francis" and "French" remained entirely possible — as was the identification of adjective and noun in the phrase: "The Cook Francis" or "Francis the Cook," or "Francis's Cookbook". Universally, however, since the time of the book's earlier editions, French printers and bibliographers have used a minuscule on the name, thereby ensuring that *françois* be understood as an adjective. In the *Catalogue général des livres imprimés de la Bibliothèque nationale* every edition of our cookbook, from the very first of P. David, Paris, 1651, is unfortunately lettered *Le Cuisinier françois*.[19] Likewise translators have universally read, and translated, *françois* solely as "French": for instance, *The French Cook*,[20] *Il cuoco francese*,[21] and *Der frantzösische Koch*.[22]

When the *Pastissier françois* was translated the play on the author's name was similarly lost: *The Perfect Cook* and *Der frantzösische Becker*(?).[23]

In every case of the books known to be by François Pierre de La Varenne or attributed to him, we should properly understand: *Francis the Cook* (or, with a slight archaic flair, *Francis's Cookbook*), *Francis the Pastry Chef*, and *Francis the Confectioner*. The author's double pun on his own name is a fine instance of clever hubris.

---

[18] See A. Hatzfeld, A. Darmesteter and A. Thomas, *Dictionnaire général de la langue française*, 2 vols. (Paris, 1892–1900; 8th edn., Paris: Delagrave, 1926), 1: 607; and *Trésor de la langue française*, 16 vols. (Paris: Centre National de la Recherche Scientifique; Gallimard, 1971–94), 6: 587b.

[19] Volume 90, column 630. It is curious, however, that the *General Catalogue of Printed Books* of the British Museum (Volume 131, column 650) consistently and correctly shows *Le Cuisinier François*.

[20] London: Charles Adams, 1653; etc.

[21] And not *Francesco*: Bologna: Longhi, [1670?]. Other Italian editions using this name followed in 1695, 1728, etc.

[22] Hamburg, 1665.

[23] London, 1656 and Hamburg, 1665, respectively. Also bound with this latter translation were the German translations *Der frantzösischer Confitirer* and the *Koch* mentioned above. (See later the important *caveat* concerning the *Frantzösische Koch*).

For our titles in this translation we have chosen unboldly to do as everyone else has done.

Each of these three works aims to be exhaustive in the subject area it treats. The first, the largest, deals with general cookery, presenting some 800 recipes intended to guide a professional cook in a wealthy household on the preparation of dishes for various courses in meals served on days that were or were not designated by religious custom as days of so-called fasting. The second assembled all that La Varenne knew about pastry and batter and the wide assortment of dishes they entered into — or at least all that he thought it might be useful to set down for the guidance of a professional cook, such as himself, working in a relatively affluent household. Similarly the third book, the shortest and least attributable to La Varenne, presents a survey of ways in which a number of foodstuffs can be treated with sugar syrups, both to preserve them and to enhance their savour. Appended to this last work is a curious and apparently unrelated little treatise on the folding of table napkins.

(i) *The French Cook*

The dedication printed on the first page of the *Cuisinier françois* makes full use of the impressive list of titles to which La Varenne's master had a right. ·

> To the High and Mighty Lord, My Lord Louis Chaalon du Bled, Counsellor of the King in his Privy State Councils, Knight of his Orders, Baron of Tenar, Marquis of Uxelles and of Cormartin [*sic*], Field Master of a Regiment of Cavalry maintained in the Service of His Majesty, one of his Lieutenant Governors in Burgundy, Baillif of the Nobility of that Province, Governor of the City and Citadel of Chalon-sur-Saône, and Lieutenant General of his Armies, etc.[24] My Lord, although my condition does not endow me with the capacity for a heroic heart, it does nevertheless

---

[24] *A haut et puissant seigneur Messire Louis Chaalon du Bled, Conseiller du Roy en ses Conseils d'Estat & Privé, Chevalier de ses Ordres, Baron de Tenar, Marquis d'Uxelles & de Cormartin, Mestre de Camp d'un Regiment d'Infanterie entretenu pour le service de Sa Majesté, l'un de ses Lieutenans generaux en Bourgongne, Bailly de la Noblesse en ladite Province, Gouverneur des Ville & Citadelle de Chaalons sur Saone; & Lieutenant general de ses Armées, &c.* If he was involved in the proof-reading of his dedicatory epistle La Varenne seems not to have noticed the error of the second *r* of Cormatin. A later printer further misread the first syllable of

give me enough sensitivity not to forget my duty. During my em-
ployment over ten full years in your household I have found the
secret of preparing foods finely.[25] I dare say that I have exercised
my profession with the strong approval of Princes, Marshals of
France, and countless persons of quality who have highly esteemed your Table both in Paris and in the field,[26] where you
have compelled Fortune to accord to your virtue Offices worthy
of your Courage. It seems to me that the public ought to benefit
from my experience, so that it might owe to you all of the usefulness it will derive from it. I have, therefore, set out in writing
what I have for so long practised in the honour of your service,
and of this have made a little Book which bears the title of Clerk
of your Kitchen. But, given that what it contains is but a Lesson
which the desire to please you has taught me, it seemed to me
that it ought to be honoured by your Name; and that, without
sinning against my duty, I could seek for it no stronger support
that yours. This is but a token of the ardour that I have always
rendered, and shall all my life render, to your service.

For that reason, My Lord, I beg you to call upon your customary generosity: do not despise this book, though it may be
unworthy of you. Bear in mind that it is a depository of the
sauces whose flavours have pleased you from time to time; and
that, all told, it is the life's handiwork of him who will be, all
his life, My Lord, Your most humble, most obedient and most
grateful Servant, François Pierre, *called* La Varenne.

Both the author and the publisher affixed prefaces to the *Cuisinier
françois*. First La Varenne spoke to his reader, this person clearly being
conceived to be a member of the confrerie within the profession.

Dear Reader:[27]
I thought it proper in all modesty to provide you with some idea
of the purpose and use of this Book, whose author I am. My
purpose is neither to shock nor offend anyone, although I have
no doubt that certain malevolent or envious individuals will talk

---

the placename and thereafter *Caumartin* was typeset. See also I. D. G.'s translation
of this dedication which I have reproduced below in the Bibliography, D (ii) (a).

[25] Cotgrave: "*Délicatement*. Neatly and daintily"

[26] *& dans les Armées.*

[27] *Amy Lecteur.*

immoderately about it. Rather the book's purpose is to provide help and service to any who may need it, of whom some, lacking experience or a ready memory, are unwilling or too timid to become involved in learning what they do not know, partly out of pride and partly too for some other reason. Some of them think they demean themselves by getting advice in a matter that they ought perhaps to be knowledgeable; others, being unfamiliar with any persons who might instruct them, are ashamed to approach them empty-handed, their sometimes poorly-lined purse leaving them without the means to express their gratitude. That is why, holding as I do my fellows in the profession in particular affection, I have deemed that I owe it to them to set forth what little I know about it, and to deliver them from their embarrassment.

To facilitate the use of this material, I have arranged it for you in four courses;[28] at the head of each one you will find a Table of its contents and then the text afterwards.[29] I have divided them according to the various sorts of meals that are made for meat days and lean days, during Lent, and particularly on Good Friday.

I have added many other things of a general sort, whose Tables and texts you will see. Into it all I have stirred a Table on ways to make Pastries, depending on the time of year, and other little household hints, useful for anyone. Should you find some items in a Table that are not in the text, do not blame me: I have not forgotten them — rather they are simply too commonplace, and I have put them into the Table merely as a reminder.

Finally, dear Reader, in recompense all that I would ask of you is that my book be for you as pleasurable as it is useful.

Following this very modest preface a certain Guitonneau receives a page on which it is declared that Pierre David, *Marchand Libraire à Paris*, has been granted the royal privilege of printing *Le Cuisinier françois* of *le sieur de la Varenne, Escuyer de Cuisine de Monsieur le Marquis d'Uxelles*, along with what amounted to copyright on the book's

---

[28] *quatre services*: "four services". See below the comment on La Varenne's servings or courses.

[29] The various Tables that precede the recipes proper in each chapter have been done away with in this translation. The recipe names of all three books can be found in alphabetical arrangement in the Appendices, below.

publication for a period of ten years. That priviledge is dated 17 July 1651.

La Varenne's publisher, Pierre David, does not pass up the chance to insert preface of his own. This amounts to a relatively long screed, the modern equivalent of which, though much abbreviated because of space, would appear on the back of a book's dust jacket.

Dear Reader,

Though this book, whose subject and title may seem novel in Paris, nothing similar ever having yet been printed here, you will nevertheless, I think, not find it entirely fruitless. Many have been seen and well received that have dealt with remedies and cures for illnesses, cheaply had and without having to turn to pharmacists, such as *The Charitable Doctor*,[30] and the like. But this book, which aims only at keeping and maintaining a good, well-balanced state of health, to teaching how to correct the vicious nature of foodstuffs by means of various opposite seasonings; which tends, I say, only to give a man food that is solid and well prepared and answers his appetite — this latter being in many the determining factor of their life and fitness — should not, it seems to me, be considered any the less since it is much more pleasant to put out decent, reasonable funds according to one's means for ragouts and food delicacies in order to preserve life and health than to use up enormous sums on drugs, herbal remedies, medicines and other bothersome cures in order to recover them.

So I was resolved, after many appeals from my friends, to publish it, and to do so in this great city which accepts everything, rejects nothing and where what is unavailing to some is useful to others. In his Preface its author has set out the usefulness and benefit it can furnish you. I shall make bold to enlarge upon that by saying that not only is the book useful but, further, it is necessary, in that its author, not content with explaining

---

[30] Philibert Guybert, *Le Médecin charitable* was first published by Gui Patin in Paris, 1625 and remained in strong demand: its twelfth edition is dated 1627 and it was reprinted until 1680. Henri-Jean Martin (*Livre, pouvoirs et société à Paris au XVIIe siècle*, Geneva: Droz, 1969, p. 233) attributes the exceptional success of this book, and other ones similarly devoted to popular, do-it-yourself alternative medicine, to a widespread suspicion that professional pharmacists had "sacrified too much to the gods of chemistry."

the finest, most refined ways of preparing dishes, pastries and
other things that are served on the tables of the Great, gives
you instructions on the most common and ordinary things that
are handled in household food, that represent only a controlled,
moderate expense, and in whose preparation many people sin by
intemperance or by frugality. He teaches you how to handle a
thousand sorts of vegetables and other foodstuffs that are found
in abundance in the country, where most people are ignorant of
how to dress them decently and satisfyingly. Therefore it will
be seen that I was fully justified in rendering this service to the
public, for not only its refinement but its needfulness.

To that may be added that our France, among all the world's
nations, first in honour, in civility, in courtliness, in propriety
in all sorts of relations, is not any less esteemed for her decent,
refined style of living. And the City of Paris is eminently in first
place above all the provinces in the Kingdom, of which she is
the metropolitan centre, the capital and the seat of our Kings.
Undeniably her subordinates will form the same admiration as
she does for it. And that gives me hope that, offering her these
first-fruits, she will welcome them and the provinces likewise
after her. Following that, the other nations may well be bitten by
the desire to fall into line with that one which, excelling in every
one of life's events, must surely know how to keep it happy and
peaceful by the use of those things that maintain it and make it
endure.

I can assure you that for my part I have applied all imaginable
care to present it to its best advantage and to enhance a little its
subject, which may perhaps seem to a few critics quite unworthy
of serious treatment. But the more judicious readers may well
think otherwise, and consider that all books, both ancient and
modern, being primarily for the nourishing of the mind, it was
entirely reasonable that the human body, without whose good
condition the mind cannot function well, should be represented
among them, and principally concerning something so necessary
for its conservation.

Enjoy it then, Dear Reader, while I turn my attention to publishing for you something worthy of your more lofty and substantial study.

The *French Cook* presents a broad survey of its author's culinary repertoire. The heterogeneous nature of the body of recipes that such a seventeenth-century professional cook was master of demanded some system of organization if he were ever to take them from his memory and write them down. The principle that La Varenne chose for his life's masterwork derived from a major element in his work as kitchen clerk to the Marquis d'Uxelles, his regular responsibility to determining interesting and varied menus for his master's meals. As he tells his reader in his preface, the recipes have been arranged according to the courses of a meal and according to the succession of those courses.

Such an organization of culinary recipes is by no means novel in a cookbook. Late-medieval collections tended to prefer to group dishes according either to principal foodstuff being prepared or to the nature of the finished dish.[31] An alternative procedure was alphabetical.[32] By the fifteenth century, however, to provide the structural outline for his cookery manual Maître Chiquart made use of four archetypal meals: dinners and suppers for meat days and fast (lean) days.[33] In each section of his work the choice of dishes for which his recipes are given follows the accepted progress of the particular meal in question. To all those recipes he appended a standard subsidiary section of food recipes for the sick or invalid. In sixteenth-century Italy Bartolomeo Scappi divides the cookery portion of his *Opera*[34] into chapters on meats and fowl, fish and pastry; in Part Four of his work he indicates summarily the generic preparations that might appropriately compose a meal on various days throughout an ecclesiastical year.

---

[31] Such remains the basic organization in the various avatars and titles under which the *Viandier* was still read in the fifteenth and sixteenth centuries. See some of these works in Section D. (III), below.

[32] This arrangement might appeal to the reader, perhaps a more experienced member of the cookery profession, who might wish to consult a recipe collection in order to jog his memory about a particular dish. An instance of an alphabetical ordering of recipes can be seen in the so-called *Libro per cuoco*, the extant manuscript of which dates from the end of the fifteenth century although the material is older, ed. Ludovico Frati, *Libro di cucina del secolo XIV* (Livorno, 1899); and Emilio Faccioli, *Arte della cucina*, 2 vols. (Milan: Il Polifilo, 1966), I, 61–105.

[33] "*Du fait de cuisine* par Maistre Chiquart 1420," edited by Terence Scully and published in the periodical of the Archives du Valais, Switzerland, *Vallesia*, 40 (Sion, 1985), pp. 101–231.

[34] Bartolomeo Scappi, *Opera* (Venice: Michele Tramezino, 1570).

Several advantages of each variety of structure are evident: there is some sort of recognizable logic behind it which will assist in its composition and in the consultation of it; for the author there are fewer chances of overlooking a dish or procedure; for the reader seeking details of a specific recipe he has a better initial idea of where to find it. In the case specifically of the "meal" outline, used by Chiquart and chosen by La Varenne, a further advantage is offered to a reader. If he is uncertain about the name or (perhaps even) the fundamental nature of a dish, or (most importantly) if he wishes to survey the possible options for any given course in any given day's meal, a work organized in such a way is more immediately useful.

La Varenne's major subdivisions for his recipes are three in number: dishes for meat days, those for lean days and those for Lent. For each sort of meal he clearly conceives four courses, without actually naming them. Among *The French Cook*'s thirty-one divisions,[35] we can readily identify the four courses set out in three distinct series as follows:

– for serving on meat days: Pottages (Chapters III and IV), Entrées (Chapter V), the Second Course (roasts, Chapter VI), Entremets (Chapter VIII);

– for serving on lean days: Pottages (Chapter XV), Entrées (Chapters XVI and XVII), the Second Course (Chapter XVIII), Entremets (Chapter XIX);

– for serving during Lent: Pottages (Chapter XXV), Entrées (Chapter XXVI), the Second Course (Chapter XXVII), Entremets (Chapter XXVIII).

There are, furthermore, two chapters devoted to dishes appropriate for serving in two courses on Good Friday: Pottages (Chapter XXIX), Entrées (Chapter XXX). Missing from the dining table on Good Friday were the third and fourth servings — that is, a Second Course and an Entremets.

The organization of this collection of recipes and bits of culinary advice is clear and apparently complete. However, what curiously is

---

[35] I call them chapters although La Varenne does not designate them as such. The term he uses to refer to each section of recipes in his book is *discours*. He does not number them, either, which I have done (with Roman numerals) in order to make reference to each of them easier.

missing in *The French Cook* is any distinction between "dinner" and "supper".[36] Nowhere does La Varenne identify a meal or a dish that might be suitable for one or the other of these daily meals. In only one place does he refer to either.[37]

Clearly an important role was played in a cook's menus by the Christian identification of days on which the faithful should "fast" or abstain from certain sorts of food. These lean or fish days, as opposed to fat or meat days, were generally three in every week of the year: Wednesdays, Fridays and Saturdays. The whole period of Lent, the forty days preceding Easter, was likewise designated as a penitential time during which only lean foods could be eaten. A cook in a Christian house accepted the obligation — more or less strict depending on the devoutness of his master or mistress — always to have a gastronomically interesting assortment of dishes available for those many days of the year on which red meat and animal oils (along with fowl and eggs in some places) were taboo.[38] Frequently, as in the *French Cook*, the clever cook could have recourse to pairs of possible dishes in his repertoire: for a particular dish one version would consist of a set of ingredients for meat days while the other version would substitute a variation of the set suitable for lean days. Throughout medieval and modern times the competent cook preparing food in a Christian milieu had religious strictures as part of a range of restrictions governing what he might like to do.

---

[36] Furetière distinguishes clearly between the two meals: *"Disner. Repas qu'on prend vers le milieu du jour. Souper. Repas du soir."* Antoine Furetière, *Dictionaire universel* (La Haye and Rotterdam: Leers, 1690). His illustration of the latter gloss suggests that the late-seventeenth-century *souper* was relatively substantial: *"Ce n'est pas un souper par ordre, ce n'est qu'une collation."* Richelet comments: "Congregations, communities and religious houses sup at six o'clock, but Parisian bourgeois rarely sup before eight or nine; at court they sup even later." Pierre Richelet, *Dictionnaire françois* (Geneva: Widerhold, 1680; repr. Geneva: Slatkine, 1970).

[37] In Recipe V,69 of the *Cuisinier françois* he directs that a piglet be mounted on a spit for roasting *une heure & demye avant diner*. The word *diner* in this case may well be verbal: "an hour and a half before eating." In any case contemporary dictionaries state that in proper usage the verb *dîner* means *"manger du bouilli & autre viande sur le milieu du jour"* (Richelet).

[38] For instance *The French Pastry Chef* describes three types of Pastry Chef's Cream, normally made with milk and eggs; in the third variety — Recipe IV,3, for *Lenten Cream* — the eggs are replaced by butter and saffron.

Besides the recipes for courses in meals throughout the year, *The French Cook* incorporates a wide variety of subsidiary material organized in chapters that are inserted at places that must have seemed reasonable either to La Varenne or to his publisher, Pierre David. This latter, in his preface To the Reader, claims for himself some credit for having imposed a degree of order in the author's subject matter. Since La Varenne identifies the essential organizing principle of his recipes as being the four courses prepared for several types of day in the week and the year, we can classify the other material as ancillary or merely secondary.

Of the chapters devoted to such accessory preparations, two describe the making of bouillons, for meat-day pottages (Chapter II) and for Lenten pottages (Chapter XXIV) and several others deal with thickeners, stocks and garnishes (for meat-day preparations, Chapters X, XI, XII). A brief mention of meat stocks suitable for the sick or sickly (Chapter XIII) is a particular extension of the same general sort of material, and a pale survivor of the quite extensive assortment of dishes that could be prepared for the sick or convalescent according to medieval recipe collections. One further chapter is concerned exclusively with sauces (Chapter VII), although again there are surprisingly few of them here, the chapter's rubric confirming this by stating, "A Few Sauces." Two sections (Chapters XX and XXII) group listing of local produce and the use of roots, herbs and suchlike.

Three chapters deal with the practical concerns of the availability of foodstuffs, particularly meats: when various animals and fowl are "in season" (Chapter 1); how to preserve a few general-purpose foodstuffs (Chapter XXIII, on artichokes, beef palates, butter and so forth); and how to prepare one traditionally important foodstuff for keeping (Chapter IX, on ham).

La Varenne's assortment of subject matter for his *Cuisinier françois* is in a sense supplemented and completed by chapters of recipes falling into two significant areas: pastry preparations (for meat days, Chapter XIV; for lean days, Chapter XXI), and the appended chapter on Confections.[39]

---

[39] That chapter on confections appears originally in the second edition (1652) of the *Cuisinier*. The *Table Générale* which concludes the book is in three separately alphabetised segments: *Viandes grasses* (dishes, including pastries, for meat days), *Viandes maigres* (lean dishes, including pastries, egg and vegetable preparations), and *Confitures*.

Those are significant components in his work in part because of the amount of space given over to each (respectively seventy-seven and thirty-one recipes), and in even larger measure because entire books in French will be devoted to each subject a few years after the appearance of the *Cuisinier françois*. There is, furthermore, an extensive and close overlapping of those recipes in the three chapters with those in the *Pastissier françois* and the *Confiturier françois*. La Varenne is believed to be the author of the first of these subsequent books; given the parallels with material in the second, he is almost certainly either the author of or the inspiration for the second — or, alternatively, a plagiarist of it while it was as yet unpublished. Since we offer translations of the other two books as well as the three chapters in question in the *French Cook*, the reader may decide which is the most likely explanation.

In looking at such a question what should be borne in mind is that among the professional cooks of La Varenne's day — to say nothing of before or after his time — traditional and conventional practice had a lot to do with the forming of a useful repertoire. Among those professional cooks working for wealthy bourgeois households or the aristocracy right across France in 1650 a large number of pies and tarts, tourtes and flans, fruit conserves and marzipans were prepared in identical fashion, with or without reference to a written recipe. As La Varenne says in the preface to his "Dear Reader," he is writing in order to help colleagues whose memory may not be wholly dependable but who have no close professional mentors to whom they can turn without embarrassment for help. The book will serve as a "memory-jogger" — *pour en faire souvenir*, he says. He implies that there exists a large body of standard culinary processes and preparations, though often these have many possible variations and substitutions. Experience is the most dependable teacher, but there are times when those with more experience can offer to help others who run into the odd difficulty in their work. These others are "the fellow practitioners of my profession" whom he holds "in particular affection." Apparent in this work is not only the pride that La Varenne has in his own highly competent abilities as a professional cook but his deep devotion to the profession itself and respect for those colleagues of his who also want to do their best by their exacting profession.

The publisher's preface "To the Reader" is longer than the author's. It is also less modest and, understandably, much more hortative, an almost breathless spiel of a salesman who is set on laying out the irresistible benefits of his wares. His sales pitch for the *Cuisinier françois* invokes a number of themes: the scientific basis of the subject matter, national jingoism, Parisian hubris, above all a defence of cookery as a subject worth *his* attention (as a publisher) and therefore worthy in turn of the Dear Reader's attention. The arguments he presents are worthy of at least a little of our attention.

The publisher assimilates food to medicine. Since the earliest Greek treatises on medical theory down to early modern Europe such an assimilation had been customary. Because Greek, Arabic and medieval medicine considered an individual's good health to be a matter of not disturbing a natural physiological equilibrium, which "dis-ease" would lead to a state of bad health, a physician's primary concern, and usually greater success, lay with maintaining good health rather than with curing sickness. In medicine questions of regimen always included considerations of food and its preparation. Although La Varenne's publisher may initially apologize for the novelty of his handling such a mean thing as a lowly cookbook, he immediately argues that food, after all, is a sort of medicine, and a relatively cheap one at that. It should, therefore, be to everyone's interest to have such a book at hand for home consultation and to keep the money-grubbing druggists at bay.

It is further remarkable that the publisher is still familiar with the argument that was a foundation of much medieval cookery, that most foodstuffs were unsuitable for human consumption unless and until they were treated in ways — by cooking, by combining with other foodstuffs, or by skillful saucing — designed to correct their harmful humoral natures. As an argument to sell a cookbook to a home market, it is admirably clever. Furthermore it appeals to the seventeenth-century French affection for logic and utility.

The author, Pierre David goes on to say, can offer you more than just good, wholesome food. With his many recipes he can explain how to go about preparing the latest, most fashionable dishes. And he can show you how to do it economically, with neither parsimony nor waste. Again, the information in this book is *practical* and *useful*.

Then, having already mentioned the contemporary Paris book scene, the publisher launches into what he may have felt was his clinching argument. It appeals directly to the potential buyer's national pride. By any

measure, but particularly intellectual and civil, France is the admired centre of the world; Paris is the undisputed centre of France, in part because
it dares to examine new things; *ergo* this book is going to participate in
all that is boldly innovative and admired in Paris and in France. The alert
reader should not be hesitant: it may be assumed — "hoped" is the term
Pierre David uses — that any book published in Paris will inevitably make
its way and have influence not only out in the provinces but throughout
the civilised world as well.

His curious last sentence seems to undermine much of the solidity
Pierre David has just claimed for La Varenne's book. Pierre David may
have realized that he had a reputation to uphold. He was unwilling to put
it wholly at risk for the sake of a provincial cook who, when all was said
and done, wouldn't really be likely to persuade those Parisians with spare
cash to part with much of it.

Pierre David, and La Varenne himself too, may have been surprised
at the success of the *Cuisinier françois*. Like the *Viandier* some three
centuries before it, it became a best-seller of its age. Because of the numerous editions that various publishers produced of it over the succeeding
century — there were something like forty-eight French editions during
that time, an average of one every other year! — the name La Varenne became synonymous with proper cookery, a sort of Bible for French kitchen
clerks and cooks. Neither the author nor the original publisher could have
hoped for a better reception.

(ii) *The French Pastry Chef*

Pastry had been an integral part of French cookery since the earliest times.
In the late Middle Ages, though, when French cooks made up dough for
a pie or flan it was of a very heavy consistency, a plain, glutinous mixture
of flour and water similar to school-room glue-paste today. This pastry
dough was used as a container for the filling rather than as an edible part
of the preparation. Its primary function was to hold a foodstuff, whether
that was a large solid such as a fish or a moderately viscous mixture
of smaller particles, while that foodstuff was cooking in an oven; only
incidentally was some flavour of the pastry shell imparted to the filling.

The same thick dough is still occasionally called for in La Varenne's
day, one and two inches thick around a standing pie; but over the years

pastry-making had developed in the direction of refinement and delicacy, essentially toward edibility. The making of a so-called "fine" or "fat" pastry,[40] that usually depended upon butter for its characteristic nature, and thin "leaved" or flaky pastry that entailed the inter-layering of dough and butter, were by then, too, relatively common practices in the craft. The batter genres of the waffles and fritters, known and described in the Middle Ages, had also developed a little in the direction of lightness.

Traditionally, pastry- and bread-making were distinct trades. In 1420 the chief cook of the Duke of Savoy stipulated that, ideally, "fine, large" pastry quarters, containing two "fine, large" ovens, should be set up as close as possible to the kitchen. From this domain of the pastry chef would issue "meat and fish pies, tarts, flans and talmouses, ratons and everything else that cookery needs."[41] Whether a household engaged the services of a pastry specialist, though, and granted him space in which to produce his pies and flans depended largely upon the relative size, wealth and gastronomic interest of that household. The author of the *The French Cook* assumes that his reader may well occupy the same modest sort of situation as he himself apparently did, where the cook had to be his own pastry chef and was required to direct the making of any dish that involved a dough or a batter. Two of that work's chapters (XIV and XXI) deal expressly with varieties of pastry and batter preparations.

The book entitled *Le Pastissier françois* (Paris: J. Gaillard, 1653) is devoted primarily to the making of pastry dishes. In the preface to the reader printed by Jean Gaillard at the head of the book, much the same arguments are made for the *Pastissier* as for the *Cuisinier*: the book

---

[40] *Paste fine* or *paste grasse*. See the *Cuisinier françois*, Recipe XXI,0, where fine dough calls for a combination of flour and butter in a ratio of eight to three (with water), and Recipe XIV,37; and the *Pastissier françois*, Recipe I,2. In Recipe VII,4 of the latter work the reader is advised that with a half-bushel of flour two pounds of butter will produce a fine dough, and that for a very fine dough the amount of butter should be raised to between two and a half and three pounds. Dough for a frangipane pie is made with egg whites and is thin enough to be transparent.

[41] *... pastelz de chars et de poissons, tartres, flons et talmoses, ratons et toutes autres chouses que sunt necessaires pour le fait de la cuisine.* The most detailed cookery manual of the late Middle Ages is the *Du fait de cuisine* by Maître Chiquart (ed. cit.); the passage quoted is on p. 136. This work is translated as *Chiquart's "On Cookery." A Fifteenth-Century Savoyard Culinary Treatise* (New York: Peter Lang, 1986).

presents French usage (and should be therefore of consuming interest to foreigners), the book's contents are wholly novel, of easy, practical and inexpensive utility, and promote good health.[42] Of these arguments for the reader's attention the most significant one from an historical point of view is that which makes the claim of novelty for the subject matter. As we have seen, La Varcnne writes of pastry-making and pastry dishes, covering the topic to the extent that such coverage was required by his general outline of dishes for various sorts of meals. In essence *The French Cook* does little more or less than medieval French authors and their subsequent adaptors and printers had done with regard to pies and tourtes. He transmitted recipes for the normal, "everyday," useful pastry preparations that should be in every professional cook's repertoire. However, the writer of the preface to *The French Pastry Chef* laments the widespread ignorance of pastry-making in his society, blaming a determined effort on the part of what he calls court cooks in Paris to stifle knowledge about the art. *The French Pastry Chef* is an original undertaking in its aim to give a broad and detailed exposition solely of the craft of pastry-making. As with *The French Cook* much of the contemporary success of the book must also have been due to the clarity of its instructions.

Of further inherent interest is the author's plan to encompass as many genres of pasty as possible, including those that, in the daily work of an ordinary cook, might occupy only a very secondary place. The baked goods presented in the treatise range from the standard pies and tourtes to waffles, fritters and biscuits through to macaroon and marzipan. The traditional old preparations of flans, rattoons, darioles and talmouses, presented in fourteenth- and fifteenth-century texts, are examined but the contemporary cook (or pastry chef) can also find explanations of newer sorts of pasties: the feuillantine, the *flamiche*, the *poupelain*. Matters apparently of secondary importance but of just as great concern for a pastry

---

[42] The publisher's confidence in the usefulness of the book was not hyperbole. In "Imprimer la cuisine: les livres de cuisine en France entre le XVe et le XIXe siècle" (*Histoire de l'alimentation*, ed. Jean-Louis Flandrin and Massimo Montanari, Paris: Fayard, 1996, 650; in English, *Food. A Culinary History from Antiquity to the Present*, New York: Columbia, 1999, 307) Philip and Mary Hyman consider that *Le Pastissier françois* was the only book devoted solely to pastry published in France between the middle of the seventeenth century and the end of the eighteenth. See a contemporary English version of this preface "The French Epistle to the Reader, Translated," which we reproduce in the Bibliography, (ii)(a), below.

chef are treated as fundamentals preliminary to the main subject and with the same care as the survey of pastry genres: pastry chefs' spice mixtures (Chapter II), pastry chefs' gilding (Chapter III), pastry chef's cream (Chapter IV).

A *gasteau* is not really a modern cake. The *Pastry Chef*'s *gasteau* (Chapter XV) is, however, recognizable in the etymological, generic sense of the word "cake": something caked.[43] It is a traditional sort of bread which, prepared variously with fine flour, butter, eggs, cream and cheese, warrants the qualification found in several of the recipes, *mollet* or "soft".

The compilation of the comprehensive index at the book's end would also very likely have enhanced the book's appeal for a contemporary reader, whether he was professional or lay, from a noble or bourgeois house.

Two features of the work may be of interest to a modern reader. In a brief outline of weights and measures the author advises the contemporary reader about the values that are intended for particular units found in those pages (Chapter VI). Remarkably, too, the author appends to his work a final six chapters of recipes for egg dishes (Chapters XXIX–XXXIV).

(iii) *The French Confectioner*

While the *Pastissier françois* is unique in being the first book to be devoted wholly to the making of baked pastry goods, the *Confiturier françois* takes its place in a short line of works that had already presented the craft of using sugar and honey to candy and preserve foodstuffs. Any claims to originality that might be made for the book would be that it is among the first *French* works to deal exclusively and broadly with this subject.[44] In Italy, Magninus Mediolanensis (d. *c.* 1364) had composed a

---

[43] See the note at the beginning of Chapter XV in *The French Pastry Chef*.

[44] At the end of the Middle Ages a number of paragraphs here and there in the *Menagier de Paris* show that candying fruits and nuts was a relatively common practice. In the category of a monograph on confectionery, the *Confiturier françois* has only one known antecedent in French: as a relatively brief treatise on the same topic, called *Le Confiturier de la cour*, the work was incorporated by Pierre David into his *Le Maistre d'hostel* in 1659. This treatise underwent some revision before appearing independently from the press of Jean Gaillard the following year as our *Confiturier françois*. Abroad Michael Nostradamus had published his *Vray et parfaict embellissement de la face ... & la façon et maniere de faire toutes confitures* (Antwerp:

chapter for his *Regimen sanitatis* which was given over to the practice of candying: *De confectionibus*.[45] In the fifteenth century Platina still sang the praises of foods candied with honey or sugar: "Summer honey," he wrote, " does not allow bodies to decay, is considered best in preserving apples, gourds, citron, and nuts, and creates mouth-watering appeal in many foods" (II, 14); "No kind of food is made more tasteless by adding sugar. By melting it, we make almonds (softened and cleaned in water), pine nuts, hazelnuts, coriander, anise, cinnamon, and many other things into sweets. The quality of sugar then almost crosses over into the qualities of those things to which it clings in the preparation" (II, 15). In Spain, most immediately influenced by the Moorish use of sugar and long a home of candied fruits, nuts and vegetables, the fifteenth-century *Libre de totes maneres de confits* affords a fine survey of the possibilities developed by Catalan confectioners.[46] The craft of confectionery may not have lapsed wholly in France, but considering the production of printed texts that craft was no more vigorously alive than other branches of food preparation.

Of the three manuals translated here, whose origins all date within the same decade of the 1650s and which have at one time or another been attributed to La Varenne, the *Confiturier françois* is the one where serious doubts have been raised about its authorship. According to Vicaire,[47] however, the 1667 edition of this work bears a *privilege* which grants

---

Christophe Plantin, 1557; repr. Paris: Gutemberg-Reprint, 1979). In 1667 a *Parfaict confiturier* appeared (Paris: Jean Ribou) which Philip and Mary Hyman attribute to La Varenne : "Imprimer la cuisine: les livres de cuisine en France entre le XVe et le XIXe siècle," *Histoire de l'alimentation*, ed. Flandrin and Montanari, 655; in the English translation, 401.

[45] Part 2, Chapter 3, Paragraph 26. *Sciendum ... que meliores confectiones que sunt in usu, et magis delectabiles, sunt hec: zinziber conditum, zinzibriatum cum zuccara vel cum melle, et pineatum, et pisticatum, et avelane condite, et anisum conditum, et coriandrum conditum, et dragea grossa, et dragea in tabula, et zuccarum rosatum in tabula, et dyaciminum, et confectio que nominatur marcepen* [marzipan], *et nuces confecte cum zuccara vel cum melle, et avelane condite cum zuccara, et dactili.* The *Regimen* was one of the first medieval works to be printed, in Louvain by Johannes de Westfalia in 1482; it was reprinted at least three times even before the end of that century.

[46] Luis Farraudo de Saint-Germain, "Un tratado manual cuatrocentista de arte de dulcería," *Boletín de la Academia de Buenas Letras de Barcelona*, 19 (1946), 97–134.

[47] Georges Vicaire, *Bibliographie gastronomique* (Paris: Rougette, 1890; repr. Geneva: Slatkine, 1993).

permission to the Parisian printer Jean Ribou to publish *Le parfaict con-fiturier françois* composed by *le sieur de La Varenne*.[48] There are only very tenuous grounds for suggesting that the book ever had anything at all to do with La Varenne.

Several peculiarities mark the introductory matter of the *Confiturier françois*. The dedication at the head of the book is directed to a certain Monsieur de Maridat, Junior, a person for whose father the writer (the author? printer? publisher?) expresses a great deal of respect and devo-tion. Nowhere in any edition other than the 1667 one, on the title page or in a preface or dedication, does the name La Varenne appear, as it did several times in the *Cuisinier*. The dedication in the *Confiturier* is in fact modestly signed with the initials *I. G.*. Furthermore the prose style of this prefatory material is exceptionally elegant, rhythmical, Latinate and scholarly, quite unlike what either La Varenne or Pierre David had written in the *Cuisinier*. In its three paragraphs it contains textual quotations of no fewer than four Latin passages identified by the learned I. G. as from Virgil, Horace and Solomon.

> TO MONSIEUR DE MARIDAT, THE SON
> Sir,
> The person bearing confections is always welcome with children. But when I consider that you have never been a child, and that your bent as well as your merit have always outstripped your age, I have reason to fear that you may well blame me for daring to offer you so slight a thing. Nevertheless you know that in times past God promised His people a land of milk and honey (in those days confections weren't yet made with sugar). You know also that Virgil, pointing toward a happy age, used to say,
> > *Et duræ quercus laudabunt roseida mella.*
> So I could say that presenting you my *Confectioner* is not to deal with you as a child, and that the sweetness of your good nature invited me to give you the sweetest goods that could come

---

[48] This attribution may very well have been a publisher's ploy to capitalize on a name that had acquired a relative celebrity and that had proven its consistent ability to sell other books on cookery. Without hesitation, perhaps on the authority of Vicaire, the *National Union Catalog* (Volume 319, page 9 c) attributes this work to La Varenne, François Pierre de. Another edition of the *Confiturier*, printed by Jean Gaillard in Paris, is of disputable date: the title page clearly shows M.DC.L (1650), though some bibliographers believe that this must be in error for M.DC.LX (1660).

from my shop. I gladly admit that, having nothing better at the moment, I ought to put it off until I had something worthy of you, were it not that, unable to hope for anything becoming your worth, I thought I should hasten to achieve at least the advantage of being the first to dedicate a book to you. I have no doubt that the day your ability becomes known authors will seek you out to become their patron and you will be offered the finest things in this field, continuing to hold for your person the same respect and esteem as they bear for your Father. Then I shall be satisfied to see your virtue recognized as it ought to be, and I shall be content to echo them.

At tibi prima puer nullo munuscula cultu.

At least I shall have been the first to tender this sort of gift to you. Being unable to acknowledge the obligations I bear to your Father, I address you in order to give expression to my feelings, and to offer you a part of the service that I owe to your whole house, giving you a slight intimation as a token of my affection.

Quamius & voce paternæ
Fingeris ad rectum, & per te sapis, hoc tibi dictum
Tolle memor. *Horace*

Although you have a precocious wisdom, although you have been raised by a most worthy father, yet my *Confectioner* will be bold and remind you of a counsel which Solomon offered in his proverbs:

Comede me [sic] *fili mi, quia bonum est.*

Eat honey because it is good — that is, always keep that sweetness of nature that God gave you; He doesn't give that gift to everyone. And there is no better attitude to help you grow from virtue to virtue, and from understanding to understanding, which is the desire and the warmest wish

SIR,

of your very humble and very obedient servant,

I.G.

In any case it is likely that the initials by which the writer of the dedication signed his name are those not of the book's author but of its "original" Paris publisher: Jean Gaillard. The dedication and those initials I. G. appear even in the Troyes, 1690 edition by Febvre,[49] sold in Paris by

---

[49] "Febvre?": *Catalogue of the British Museum.*

Antoine de Raffle, printer and bookseller. We have seen in the *Cuisinier françois* how the publisher Pierre David was bold enough to insert a preface three times as extensive — and twice as polished — as the one that La Varenne himself provided with obligatory formal humility. That the *Confiturier*'s publisher should compose a flowery dedication to a patron, and probably protector, should not surprise us, particularly as immediately after it we find an *Avertissement au lecteur* that the anonymous author has certainly written. The contents of this foreword consist entirely of practical information and advice relating to the recipes in the book, and its style is concrete and unadorned.

The book itself was first published at Paris (probably in 1660) by the same publisher, Jean Gaillard, as was entrusted with the *editio princeps* of the *Pastissier françois* (1653). Another link, a textual one, also exists between those two works besides their sharing of the same publisher. In the latter book, in Recipe XVI,1 for Plain Marzipan, there is a reference to the *Pastissier françois*: "Marzipans and biscuits are described in the *French Pastry Chef*." Either the author assumes that the reader will already own a copy of the earlier book, and should have it at his elbow ready for consultation, or else the enterprising publisher, Jean Gaillard, saw no harm in publicizing this reference to his earlier book.

The intertextual references in the *Confiturier françois* that are most intriguing, however, are the implied ones. As with recipes in the *Pastissier françois* that closely echo certain material already printed in the *Cuisinier françois*, the *Confiturier* repeats a good deal of the material about preserves written and published nine years earlier by La Varenne in Chapter XXXI of his *Cuisinier*. The *Confiturier* amplifies upon it, of course. In the *Cuisinier* the subject of confections occupies an addendum: the second edition (1662) is not only *reveu* and *corrigé* (extremely important considerations for the potential purchaser of any cookbook) but is *augmenté d'un Traitté de Confitures seiches & liquides, & autres delicatesses de bouche*.

La Varenne may or may not have distilled the information in his Chapter XXXI from his own experience. He may simply have cribbed it from another — probably foreign[50] — book on the subject. The author

---

[50] As the fourteenth-century *Menagier de Paris* proves, questions of preserves and pre-

of the *Confiturier* may or may not have got his material directly from the *Cuisinier* — instead of drawing upon the printed source or sources that La Varenne had used eight years earlier.

What we may observe is that the *Confiturier* understandably enlarges to an important extent upon what the *Cuisinier françois* had made available in the way of confections. In technical details, such as the vessels and utensils to be used by a confectioner, and the various degrees to be recognized in the cooking of sugar, the later treatise aims to be an exhaustive treatment of the subject, rather than merely to furnish enough information to satisfy the requirements of a one-cook kitchen. As with the volume on *pâtisserie*, which was likely intended as a handbook for a professional *pâtissier* or pastry chef, the *Confiturier* presupposes a reader who is a specialist, nowadays a *confiseur* or confectioner. Each of the two works is simply more comprehensive in its special subject than the *Cuisinier*.

In glancing through such a work as the *French Confectioner* a modern reader may well think of candies and jams. These recipes for candied foods, syrups, stewed fruits, marzipans, sugary drinks and so forth seem to fall somewhere under a slightly archaic rubric of "sweetmeats", or perhaps just "treats". For the seventeenth century, each of these so-called confections were undoubtedly valued for the heightened pleasure that the sugar in them afforded the palate. We should be aware, though, that historically over many centuries across Europe this sort of confecting or confectioning functioned — in very extensive practice that was founded upon a thoroughly studied body of "scientific" theory — as a means to preserve foodstuffs. Throughout the millennia before electric refrigerators, or even efficient ice-boxes, ensured fresh foods long past the date on which

---

serving had had a place in general cookery books for a long time in France. However, Catalan and Spanish readers — with their more ready access to products, including sugar, imported from Moorish lands — had themselves been familiar with treatises devoted wholly to such matters. From Catalonia in the fourteenth century, for instance, we can read the *Libre de totes maneres de confits*, ed. by Luís Faraudo de Saint-Germain in "Un tratado manual cuatrocentista de arte de dulcería," *Boletín de la Real Academia de Buenas Letras de Barcelona*, XIX (1946), 97–134. Furthermore, a recent English book, Hugh Platt's *Delights for Ladies* (London, 1600), dealt extensively with sugar confections and garnered a certain popularity on the market. Of the three French books presently translated, the *Confiturier* alone did not seem marketable to contemporary English printers.

they were harvested, the grocer, householder and cook depended on a very limited group of treatments to extend the life of a foodstuff. At least the treatments pushed back the food's "best before" date for a valuable length of time, and held actual putrefaction at bay. Honey or sugar, vinegar, salt, desiccation and smoke offered the primary means. Foodstuffs so treated became, literally, conserves. The last three procedures, salting, drying and smoking, had been practised and relied upon since time immemorial and involved relatively simple techniques.

The first means of preserving, by the use of a sweetener in the form of honey, was known and so employed for as far back in Mediterranean civilisations as records exist.[51] Honey played a necessarily minor role as a preservative, however, because of the relatively small quantities of it available to the average household. In Europe sweet-preserving really came into its own only from the time, from the later Crusades of the thirteenth century onward, that raw cane sugar was imported from Islamic lands into Europe. At first its novelty and limited availability restricted sugar to strictly medicinal use; it was dispensed from the stores of the apothecary along with myriad other esoteric simples and compound drugs. Over time a vigorously expanding Mediterranean commerce ensured ever larger amounts of sugar in local markets, at affordable prices, most of it refined for culinary use. By the end of the Middle Ages its common use in preserving fruits and some vegetables is evident in "noble" recipe collections across Europe.

Although salt was produced just about everywhere in Europe, either from evaporated sea-water or from mined salt beds, its price remained relatively high. In large part this pricing was determined by a stable, strong, broadly based demand for salt; this demand in turn encouraged authorities to tax its sale correspondingly — but never enough to hurt either the salt trade or to diminish state revenues from it. Salting was the universal, popular means of preserving. Sugar, on the other hand, was the

---

[51] Some of the earliest printed books are devoted to the techniques of confectioning. In France, for example, the *Petit traicté contenant la maniere pour faire toutes confitures, compostes, vins saulces, muscadetz & autres breuvages, parfunctz savons, muscadz pouldres, moutardes, & plusieurs autres bonnes recettes* ... (Paris: Jehan Longis, 1545) was reprinted as *Manière de faire toutes confitures* (Paris: Jean Bonfons, n.d.) and as *Pratique de faire toutes confitures* (Paris: B. Rigaud, 1558 and 1590). Initially such books seem intended as apothecaries' manuals.

precious aristocrat of rather unique foodstuffs, forever an exotic product whose mystical qualities quickly ignited in the upper classes a delectation that refused to accept a use limited to medically prescribed lozenges and theriacs.

Sugar swept through aristocratic kitchens across fifteenth-century Europe. While salt remained a "common" substance, used everywhere by everyone, sugar could never be anything but fundamentally exotic, its full enjoyment known best by the well-to-do in society. Yet despite a constantly growing demand, supply kept pace. As a culinary ingredient sugar came to displace most other spices in late-medieval cookery. As a preservative in the fifteenth and sixteenth centuries it was a tool that was experimented with in the kitchens of wealthy bourgeois and aristocrats — and more and more enjoyed even if the foodstuffs so candied or conserved never had much of a stay in the larder or the cellar. By the seventeenth century, candies, jams, sweet marzipans and fruit pastes had ready and enthusiastic consumers among the populace at large. Printers clearly believed that such sugar confections were well within the reach of a good segment of the reading public.

What clearly had happened between the late Middle Ages and the seventeenth century was that in the use of sugar the vital need to preserve foods bulked less large, became less important a consideration than the creation of sugar-coated and sugar-permeated foods themselves, for their own sake, for the pleasure they could offer the palate. To such an extent is this so that in the *French Confectioner* (Chapter XIII b) so-called "counterfeit" recipes instruct how to replace fruits that are seasonally unavailable. When cherries, raspberries and red currants are not in season, apples can be mashed, coloured red and sweetened; the person eating them can experience the same pleasure. The same process can be followed but a colourant introduced to create ersatz, but just as delectable, apricots or plums. In such a way the confectioner can continue throughout the year to produce a full range of sweetmeats to indulge his clients' cravings.

The final chapter in the *French Confectioner* is of particular interest. At first sight this chapter of 23 "recipes" seems inexplicably foreign to the content of the book as a whole. As the book's title page makes clear, this chapter is indeed an addendum: "*The French Confectioner* ... Along with / the Way of Folding Table Linen, and of Making all Sorts of Shapes with It." A mini-treatise on napkin folding seems quite irrelevant to sugar boiling and confection making. We might even think of these pages as a sort of publisher's gimmick, bold and singularly mercantile, thrown in as an unexpected, "free" supplement and intended to appeal to the frugality of the casual book buyer.

Historically, though, there was a relationship between sugar, preserves and linens. The link was, indirectly, in bread. Since the Middle Ages, in a household large enough to have defined narrowly specialized responsibilities, the pantler had one essential function, the provision of bread. His work, along with that of the butler or wine steward, reflected the age-old fundamentals of any meal whether the table on which it was set out was a peasant's board or an aristocrat's dining table: bread and wine. In early times the office of pantler came to include among the duties allocated to it the care of all table linens — perhaps because fine bread for the master's table was wrapped and presented in fine white linen.

The responsibilities of each function changed over time. The provision of bread became a specialized trade, carried on outside most households; the kitchen clerk could assume the responsibility of ensuring that quantities of the proper sorts of bread were delivered fresh as needed. This traditional part of the pantler's job declined in importance.

Contrarily, with the growth of varieties of wine, beer, ale, and a burgeoning new array of distilled and flavoured liquors, the office of the wine steward (*sommelier*) or butler (*bouteillier*) took on a much increased importance. To the extent that sugar and spices were deemed integral to the making of variously flavoured liquors, the wine steward's responsibilities covered the making and keeping of tasty confections as well. Furthermore, spiced candies were traditionally associated with spiced wines, particularly as digestives at the conclusion of a meal. To the office of wine steward was normally also passed the responsibility for maintaining the stores of table linens.

In 1659 the same Pierre David who printed the earliest editions of the *Cuisinier françois* also published a volume whose full title reads: *Le Maistre d'hostel. Qui apprend l'ordre de bien servir sur table et d'y ranger les services. Ensemble le Sommelier qui enseigne la manière de bien plier le linge en plusieurs figures. Et à faire toutes sortes de Confitures, tant seiches que liquides. ...* Combined in this volume are two works, in the second of which, *Le Sommelier*, the anonymous author sets out expressly that person's responsibility for folding table linen. Subsequent to instruction in that matter is a body of information about the making of "all sorts of confections, dry as well as moist."

When the outline on napkin folding appeared in the *Confiturier françois*, the subject matter of the supplement was not novel. In particular wealthy Italian households, of which in the sixteenth century there were many, had paid particular attention to the proprieties and decencies of formal dining. The regular use of the dainty dining fork (as distinct from the larger implement long known in the kitchen) originated in dignified aristocratic Italy. The conventionally correct way of laying a dining table and arranging individual place settings was studied and published there. Specifically there was the dainty and whimsical matter of using table linen to delight the master and mistress, along with his or her guest, at mealtime. By the seventeenth century in noble and wealthy circles across Europe, linen folding had become a more or less standard discipline in which stewards and housekeepers had to have at least some skill.

The Parisian printer of the *Confiturier françois*, Jean Gaillard, may have been publishing the original work of some anonymous author who submitted it to him, or he may have been copying or adapting a version of the material already circulating in printed form in one language or another. A remarkable treatment of the subject had been published at about the time that La Varenne assumed his duties as chief cook in the Uxelles' kitchens. This had been compiled by a German named Giegher, was in Italian, and bore the seriously formal title of *Treatise on Linen Folding*.[52]

Eventually in France following the marriage in 1533 of Catherine de' Medici (1519–89) with Henry of Valois, Duke of Orléans and future Henry II — and even more, with the marriage in 1600 of Marie de' Medici (1573–1642) to Henry IV and with her later regency (1610–1617) in the midst of her Italian favourites — a marked Italian influence came to determine much of the French court's taste and manners. Proper, elegant dining required that a high degree of attention be paid not only to prepared

---

[52] Messer Mattia Giegher, *Trattato delle piegature*. The work was probably first written in the 1620s, but was made most readily available to the public when it was published with two other "treatises" of the same author, on meat carving and on a steward's duties: *Li tre trattati* (Padua: P. Frambotto, 1639).

dishes but also to the table and its setting. The art of linen folding played a significant role in laying out a table that would delight a seventeenth-century diner. With it the art of the confectioner offered a further valued contribution to the pleasures of refined society in La Varenne's France.

C. French Cookery of the Seventeenth Century

(i) Major works of the time[53]

When La Varenne's *Cuisinier françois* was printed in 1651 it appeared in a category of French publication where a quasi void had existed for more than a century. The enormous and durable popularity it would enjoy was due in large measure to its virtually unique place in that category when the book first appeared.

Sixteenth-century France experienced a surprising dearth of new manuals on cookery. Printing presses flourished in both number and output throughout the period we now call the French Renaissance, publishing a large number of volumes on a wide range of topics. However, when it came to disseminating advice about food preparation the French presses of Paris, Lyon, Troyes, Rouen, Arras, Geneva, Antwerp and Amsterdam almost unanimously declined to contribute to the body of public knowledge. Available to the person who, apparently quite exceptionally, was inclined to purchase a cookery book were publications derivative of two traditional families. There were on the one hand reprints of reprints of the *Viandier*, attributed in the second half of the fourteenth century to the royal cook Taillevent and possessing what seemed like an immortal celebrity as the *only* French cookbook;[54] and on the other hand, reprints

---

[53] An initial brief survey of the topic can be read in the article of A. Girard, "L'Edition de livres de cuisine 1485–1620," in Jean-Claude Margolin and Robert Sauzet, eds., *Pratiques et discours alimentaires à la Renaissance* (Paris: Maisonneuve et Larose, 1982), pp. 107–117.

[54] For a listing of some 24 distinct editions of the *Viandier* between 1486 (?) and 1615, see Philip Hyman and Mary Hyman, "Les livres de cuisine et le commerce des recettes en France aux XVe et XVIe siècles," in Carole Lambert, ed., *Du manuscrit à la table* (Montréal: Université de Montréal and Paris: Champion-Slatkine, 1992), pp. 59–68. As many adaptations of this work appeared at the same time under a variety of titles such as *Livre fort excellent de cuysine, La Fleur de tout cuysine, Le grand cuisinier* and *Le grand cuisinier de toute cuysine*. Generally, on the influence of printers in the choice of cooking material that was published, see Henry Notaker, "Comments on the Interpretation of Plagiarism," *Petits Propos Culinaires*, 70 (July 2002), 58–66.

of translations of adaptations of a slightly later anonymous Italian work —
by the mid-fifteenth century claimed by Martino, then modified by Platina
and only a generation afterwards rendered into French.[55]

In Italy readers had a much broader choice of manual to which to
turn for guidance of food, cooking and dining. There were revisions and
reprintings of the work taken up in turn by Martino and Platina. But
there were other works as well, new and imaginative presentations of the
practice of cookery. Italian cooks and household stewards in the sixteenth
century seem not to have been shy about sharing their knowledge and
advice.[56]

Michel de Montaigne, that inquisitive, open-minded representative
of the French Renaissance, is astounded when an Italian, the household
steward to Cardinal Caraffa (nephew of Pope Paul IV), speaks to him
about food as if it were a matter worthy of being treated on the same
exalted plane as the abstract sciences.

> I made him give an account of his office. He gave me an oration
> on the science of the gullet with magisterial gravity and compo-
> sure, as if he had been handling some profound point of divinity.

---

[55] *Neapolitan Recipe Collection. Cuoco napoletano*, ed. Terence Scully (Ann Arbor:
University of Michigan Press, 2000); Maestro Martino, *Libro de arte coquinaria*
(*c.*1450; published in Emilio Faccioli, *Arte della cucina*, 2 vols. (Milan: Il Polifilo,
1966), I, 115–204); (Bartolomeo Sacchi, *alias*) Platina, *De honesta voluptate et
valetudine* (*c.*1465), ed. and trans. Mary Ella Milham, *Platina. On Right Pleasure
and Good Health* (Tempe, Arizona: Medieval & Renaissance Texts & Studies, 1998);
Platine en françois tresutile & necessaire pour le corps humain (trans. *c.*1475 by
Desdier Christol, prior of Saint-Maurice, near Montpellier; printed Lyon: Françoys
Fradin, 1505 with nine editions in the sixteenth century).

[56] The *Opera* (Venice: Michele Tramezino, 1570) of Bartolomeo Scappi, identified as
the *cuoco secreto* or personal cook of Pope Pius V, was a grand, landmark document
on the evolution of refined cooking in that period. Its full title provides a broad
synopsis of its contents: *Opera ... divisa in sei libri. Nel primo si contiene il
ragionamento che fa l'Autore con Gio. suo discepolo. Nel secondo si tratta di
diverse vivande di carne, sì di quadrupedi, come di volatili. Nel terzo si parla
della statura, e stagione de pesci. Nel quarto si mostrano le liste del presentar le
vivande in tavola, cosi di grasso come de magro. Nel quinto si contiene l'ordine
di far diverse sorti di paste, & altri lavori. Nel sesto, & ultimo libro si ragiona
de'convalescenti, & molte altre sorti di vivande per gli infermi.* A series of plates
detailing the layout and activities of a contemporary kitchen, as well as a great many
illustrations of particular items of kitchen equipment, accompany this text. A modern
reproduction of Scappi's book was made in Milan: Stedar, 1959; and a facsimile in
Rome: Arnaldo Forni, 1981.

He distinguished for me the difference in appetites: that which a man has before he begins to eat, and that which he has after the second and third course; the means, first, of simply satisfying it, and then of rousing and provoking it; the principle of his sauces, first in general, and then particularizing the qualities of the ingredients and their effects; the differences of salads according to the seasons, those which ought to be heated and those which ought to be served up cold; the manner of their garnishing and decoration to make them agreeable to the eye also. After this he entered upon the order of service, full of beautiful and important considerations .... And all this swelled out with rich and magnificent words, the very same we make use of in discussing the government of an empire.[57]

Two factors may be important in the apparent interest in cookery in Italy at this time. In the first place is the healthy tradition of regional food habits in Italy.[58] Undoubtedly, too, the number of publications having to do with food is directly proportionate to the number of wealthy cities, courts, high dignities and potent families throughout the length of the Italian peninsula, and above all proportionate to the rivalries that existed among them. One consequence of this competing affluence and power was a demand for good cooking and good cooks. This in turn produced a good market for good cookbooks.

Italian cookbooks of the early period possess one peculiarity. They are not *merely* recipe collections of the traditional sort found right across fourteenth- and fifteenth-century Europe, but they show a distinct intent of facilitating an impressive *display* of magnificence and elegance.

The case of the banquet entremets can be taken in point. In fifteenth-century Savoy, in a ducal court strongly influenced by fashionable Burgundian life-styles, the master cook Chiquart describes a dining-hall diversion that he built in which a castle, made of meat paste, hung with banners and pennants, and mounted on a large rolling platform — with musicians hidden beneath — presents edible animals (a boar's head, a pike, a piglet

---

[57] *The Essays of Michel de Montaigne*, tr. and ed. by Jacob Zeitlin, 3 vols. (New York: Knopf, 1934); Vol. I, Ch. 51. The last edition of the *Essais*, thoroughly revised by Montaigne, dates from 1592.

[58] See especially Alberto Capatti and Massimo Montanari, *La cucina italiana. Storia di una cultura* (Rome: Laterza, 1999).

and a swan) in the castle's four corner towers; the courtyard of the castle contains a Fountain of Love gurgling with rose liqueur and mulled wine and surmounted by a pea- and bean-paste aviary. All in all, the elements of this culinary creation combine to make a wondrous, edible display. But it is a static one. Food is converted into representations of reality, and cooked animals are used to evoke the amazement and pleasure of the Duke's guests. It is only one step beyond the traditional French practice of designing a noble guest's armorial bearings in gold leaf upon a pie's upper crust, or in making a roast peacock, still wearing all of its glorious feathers, breathe flames like some terrific dragon!

In Italy by the second half of the fifteenth century such mid-banquet efforts to entertain would be considered feeble and old hat. A generation or two after Chiquart, the *Neapolitan Recipe Collection* has a series of recipes qualified with the Latin rubric *Incipiunt mirabilia gule*: "Here Begin Gastronomical Marvels." Furthermore the manuscript containing this recipe collection describes a particular historic *intermezzo* which amounts to a living, dramatic *divertimento*. Real people are costumed to represent mythological personages: Venus, Jove, Juno, Diana, Neptune, Arion, Pan, Pomona, along with sirens and a couple of nymphs. With song and text, they accompany foods which are integral parts of the meal. Real cooked animals — a whole ox, a whole stag — would be stood in a recreated field or woods to help form a pseudo-natural setting for these pieces of theatre. The aristocratic Italian banquet offered more than merely little marvels of artificially manipulated foodstuffs.[59]

Italian books on food of the sixteenth century seem to be as much concerned with arranging the experience of dining as with the making of prepared dishes. Cuisine and recipes certainly have their place in the Italian cookbooks, but there are regularly as well chapters outlining

---

[59] *Neapolitan Recipe Collection*, ed. cit., pp. 101–05. More than a century later the French tendency to extravagance in the matter of food preparation is noticed, even by a Scotsman. Travelling through France (1605–17) Moryson remarks: "Their Feasts are more sumptuous than ours, and consist for the most part of made fantasticall meates and sallets, and sumptuous compositions, rather than of flesh or birds. And the cooks are most esteemed, who have best invention in new made and compounded meats" (Fynes Moryson, *An Itinerary* (New York: Macmillan, 1908; quoted by Paula Marcoux in "The Thickening Plot," *Petits Propos Culinaires*, 60 (December 1998), 14.

proper table settings, exemplary menus, model manners. Entire volumes are devoted to defining the role of the household steward, *lo scalco*.[60] In Italy from the Renaissance onward food and dining were only partially the responsibility of the kitchen. Today we might say the Italians had an interest in the art of the food services.

For many centuries in France the craft of cookery was the property of the certified master, the individual who had trained under a recognized older authority and received from him all the accrued truths and techniques passed down over the years from generation to generation, from master to apprentice. Those bourgeois and aristocrats with the means to hire someone to cook for them engaged only those individuals whom members of the profession approved of and on whom they bestowed the cachet of "master". Cookery was a closed shop. Even when a senior member of a large food services staff died, or a vacancy occurred for some other reason, promotion was frequently from within; generally advancement followed a recognized formal progression from scullion to butcher to sauce-maker to roaster to cook to chief cook.

In France professional cookery had always been a rather recondite practice. For members of the general public who could not secure apprenticeship to a master cook, the only possible access to this cabalistic knowledge was through written or printed books. Between the fifteenth and seventeenth centuries, though, very few French cookbooks were in fact published. While the hoary, medieval *Viandier* continued for several decades to be printed and reprinted, with increasing numbers of egregious errors, professional cooks kept their professional secrets. Culinary practice in France was changing, must have been changing, but there was no effort to trace and record any changes. In Renaissance Italy on the other

---

[60] For instance Giovan Battista Rossetti, *Dello scalco* (Ferrara: Mammarello, 1584); Mattia Giegher, *Lo scalco* (Padua, 1623); Vittorio Lancellotti, *Lo scalco prattico* (Rome, 1627); Antonio Frugoli, *Pratica e scalcheria* (Rome: Francesco Cavalli, 1632). Some books were published with chapters on the steward's vital function incorporated into them: Cesare Pandini, *Il maestro di casa* published with the *Il trinciante* of Vincenzo Cervio (Rome: Gabbia, 1593). It is only well on in the seventeenth century that such books were written and published in France: for instance Pierre de Lune, *Le nouveau et parfait Maistre d'hostel royal* (Paris, 1662. See Françoise Sabban and Silvano Sirventi, *La Gastronomie au Grand Siècle* (Paris: Stock, 1998), p. 89.

hand a good number of cookery manuals help us follow the gradual introduction of novel foodstuffs as well as developments in gastronomic taste.
In Spain, too, books showed that "medieval" culinary practice and gastronomic taste were being superseded.[61] Germany had produced its cookery
writers[62] and, most significantly, a cookbook by a woman.[63] The phenomenon of a woman writing, publishing and actually being able to sell a
cookbook was evidently peculiar to Germany and England;[64] there seems
to have been much greater interest among members of the middle classes
in those countries not only to cook "well" but to accept that good cooking
might not be exclusively a preserve of knowledgeable professionals and its
enjoyment reserved for the wealthy. From 1500 onwards English readers
could purchase printed cookery books, both continally revised reprintings
of such late-medieval manuscript works as *This is the Boke of Cokery*[65]
and translations of Italian books such as the *Epulario* of Giovanni de'
Rosselli.[66]

---

[61] In particular the book of Francisco Martínez Montiño, *Arte de cocina, pastelería
vizcochería, y conservería* (Madrid: Juan de la Cuesta, 1617), presented a rich
panorama of contemporary food preparation.

[62] For instance Marx Rumpolt with his extensive *Ein new Kochbuch* (Frankfurt am
Main: Sigmundt Feyerabendts, 1581), with subsequent editions in 1587 and 1604.

[63] Anna Wecker, *Ein neu Kochbuch* (1597); *Ein köstlich neu Kochbuch von allerhand
Speisen, an Gemüsen, Obs, Fleisch, Geflügel, Fischen und Gebachens* (Basel, 1605);
Ein new, köstlich und nutzliches Kuchbuch (Basel: König, 1652). The work was
available for Danish readers as well, as *En artig oc meget nyttelig Kogebog* (Copen-
hagen, 1648); see Henry Notaker, "Danish Cookery Books 1616–1800," *Petits Propos Culinaires*, 65 (September 2000), 29–37 for the interest in printed cookbooks in
Denmark even before La Varenne.

[64] The enormous success of Hannah Glasse and her principal work, *The Art of Cookery
Made Plain and Easy* (London, 1747; facsimile London: Prospect Books, 1983), is
a case in point.

[65] London, 1500. One subsequent version bore the title *A proper newe booke of cokerye*
(London, 1545; ed. C.F. Frere, Cambridge, 1913).

[66] *Opera nuova chiamata Epulario* (Venice: Agustino da Portese, 1516). This book
continued to be popular enough to warrant reprintings up to 1683. Its English
translation was titled *Epulario, or, The Italian Banquet: wherein is showed the
maner how to dresse and prepare all kind of flesh, foules or fishes, as also how
to make sauces, tartes, pies, &c.* (London: W. Barley, 1598). An enterprising
Frenchman (according to the 1516 frontispiece), Rosselli chose to publish in Italy in
Italian, much of his *opera nuova* being a slavish reproduction of an earlier Italian,

In England at the very beginning of the sixteenth century the cook-book just mentioned that bore the straightforward, uncompromising title, *This is the Boke of Cokery* is reprinted continually throughout the century right up to 1620. Still in the sixteenth century, the public acceptance of printed cookbooks, and indeed the demand for them, led Thomas Dawson to publish his own original *Good Hus-wifes Jewell*.[67] Inspired by the success of this work another similar work appears to have traded upon its title: *The Good Huswifes Handmaide for the Kitchin*.[68] Having gained experience in French kitchens at the beginning of the seventeenth century Robert May (1588–1665?) returned to England and, significantly, what he seems to have turned his attention to was disseminating that experi-ence by publishing his *The Accomplisht Cook, or the Art & Mystery of Cookery*.[69] In England a long tradition of "household" cooking existed. English printers appreciated that a market for cookery manuals did exist, that it was broad and, remarkably, that it included the domestic kitchen governed by women, housewives. Nothing similar is anywhere in evidence in France.

Since the inception of the printing industry in France a firm concept existed, among publishers and readers alike, concerning the subject mat-ter worthy of being fixed and distributed in print. At the beginning of the seventeenth century French publishing activity was still almost uni-formly devoted to learned academic treatises;[70] theology (both Reformist

---

Maestro Martino. For an attempt to identify Rosselli, see Claudio Benporat, *Cucina italiana del quattrocento* (Florence: Olschki, 1996), p. 72.

[67] London, 1585. This was closely followed by *The Second Part of the Good Hus-Wifes Jewell* (London, 1585). Dawson's work was reprinted at least nine times up to 1610.

[68] London, 1594. This was reprinted only a few years later under the title *A Book of Cookerie otherwise called the Good Huswives Handmaid* (London, 1597). Before the end of the century a certain A. W. published yet another recipe collection similarly entitled *A Book of Cookrye* (London, 1591). In 1615 John Murrell released his *New Booke of Cookerie* (London: John Browne) whose title page ends, a little surprisingly, with the words: "Hereunto also is added the most exquisite London cookerye, all set forth according to the now, new, English and French fashion."

[69] London, 1660. The term "mystery" could still have its earlier meaning of "service" or "rite", but we may sense something of the way French cooks guarded the secrets of their profession.

[70] See in particular Henri-Jean Martin, *Livre, pouvoirs et société à Paris au XVIIe siècle (1598–1701)*, 2 vols. (Geneva: Droz, 1969).

and Counter-Reformist), humanistic science (both Christian and erudite, free-thinking), philosophy (Aristotelian and medical), law, history (especially political, and especially that which glorified the monarchy) and fine literature. In sum, substantial works dealing earnestly with sober subjects were alone liable to receive the *grace & Privilege du Roy* which, in theory, was essential for their publication.[71]

In France La Varenne led the way in convincing at least one member of the printing establishment that the subject of cookery was a legitimate one, or a not entirely frivolous or disreputable one, for his press. It should be noted, though, that La Varenne's book is by no means a generalist work. Far from including mere "housewives" among his audience, he writes expressly for and directly to fellow members of the profession.[72] There is no democratic, populist surge of goodwill evident in either his preface or his text. It is true that his treatise is well organized, the exposition is generally clear and the index (added in the second edition) helpful; but these features will, as he states, tend to make his work more useful to his junior and less experienced colleagues in the profession. As he commits his recipes and advice to print and to a wider distribution than a manuscript would have allowed, in all likelihood he has no altruistic vision of sharing his knowledge and skills with the public at large, the great culinarily unwashed.

However, following the public acceptance of such material — by no means assured, if we take his publisher's apology at face value — and the clear commercial success of La Varenne's bold new venture, competition was awakened. Other French publishers immediately scrambled to share in this brand-new market. The sudden flurry of publishing interest in cookery in France in the second half of the seventeenth century can undoubtedly be understood at least in part as a consequence of vigorous competitive salesmanship.

In the course of the following decades the printers' efforts to exploit this market to the fullest took three directions: the cookery books

---

[71] On p. 562 Martin (*op. cit.*) estimates that in 1644 of all Parisian presses then operating 150 were turning out approved material, 80 dealt primarily with religious or theological works, 15 published literary novelties, 10 handled official, political or juridical texts and the remaining dozen or so managed to survive on medical, scientific or academic textbooks.

[72] See the two prefaces to the *Cuisinier françois* translated above.

they published became increasing specialized, as we have seen with the *Pastissier françois* and the *Confiturier françois* themselves; more and more they claimed an exalted social source for their material; and there is in each successive publication an insistence upon "modernity" in taste and practice.

La Varenne was the kitchen clerk of the *Marquis* d'Uxelles; in 1656 the author Pierre de Lune proclaimed on his title page that he was the kitchen clerk of the *Duke* de Rohan; by 1660 a re-edition of this latter's *Le Maistre d'hostel* was now entitled *Le nouveau et parfait Maistre d'hostel royal*: the bidding, upped from marquis to duke, could only go up to royalty itself. Not to be outdone in this claim of supremely exalted (if implicit) patronage and approval, in 1662 a volume called *L'Escole parfaicte des officiers de bouche* contained, as its title page set out, *Le Sommelier royal, le Confiturier royal, le Cusinier royal, et le Patissier royal*. Such a parade of royalty was counted upon to catch the buyer's eye. It was not until yet another decade later that the mysterious L. S. R. could publish his *Art de bien traiter*[73] and make no magnificent claims that royal, noble or even aristocratic taste informed his cookery or his taste. Quite the contrary, rather with almost a whiff of something like democracy his title page surprisingly proposes that his "new" work will be useful for "everyone". By the last quarter of the century French printers had decided that cookbooks could quite profitably be directed to the general public at large. For the sake of sales printers were led to insist that their authors tailor their recipes to the scope of more modest households and more modest budgets.

By the end of the century a composite volume published in Amsterdam by Pierre Mortier combines *Le Vray cuisinier françois*, a *Nouveau Confiturier*, a *Maistre d'Hostel*, and a *Grand Ecuyer-Tranchant*, all purportedly by *le Sieur de La Varenne*, in a "*nouvelle édition*". The name La Varenne could still be counted upon to sell books, even if his authorship of particular works was often only implicit. What became more important was to offer volumes that contained as wide a range of subject matter as

---

[73] *L'Art de bien traiter. Divisé en trois parties. Ouvrage nouveau, curieux, et fort Galant, utile a toutes personnes, et conditions. Exactement recherché, & mis en lumiere, par L. S. R.* (Paris: Jean du Puis, 1674).

possible — and, as was frequently the case, to associate that material with La Varenne.

The final promotional ploy is one that, far from riding on La Varenne's coat-tails in a positive sense, a later author used vigorously in the campaign to publicize his own work at the expense of La Varenne and his reputation. The anonymous L. S. R. devotes much of his preface to denigrating the cookery of the *Cuisinier françois* as being antiquated if not simply "disgusting" (*dégoûtant*, "out-of-favour" gastronomically), its author wholly ignorant of far better modern practice.[74] To some extent the slander flung on the *Cuisinier françois* stuck as far as many of L. S. R.'s contemporaries were concerned. More of a shame is the extent to which modern food writers continue to repeat L. S. R.'s accusation that La Varenne's work can properly be discounted, even disregarded, because it represents the old ways of doing things.

For the French cookbook reader of the end of the second half of the seventeenth century the competition among publishers resulted generally in substantial improvements over what had previously been available: a more readable style in the text, clearer explanations, more rigorous organization (including indices), and a growing breadth of kitchen and household subjects treated between the covers of a single volume. At the middle of the century publishers may have felt a need for a defensive apology when they handled works dealing with such mundane, earthy topics as food and food preparation. By the century's end there could be little doubt that French publishing had moved a great distance toward accepting such profane subject matter as entirely legitimate fodder for the printing press. François Pierre was the person who did the most to bring about that shift in French intellectual history.

La Varenne's initial publisher, Pierre David, played a primary role in disseminating works on cookery. It was a role that must have involved a good deal of risk for him at first. For La Varenne's *Cuisinier* (1651) he had written a long and earnest justification. Then in 1656 he took on and printed Pierre de Lune's own *Le Cuisinier*, still carefully qualifying the author as (formerly) kitchen clerk to nobility. The *Pastissier françois* having been published by a competitor in 1653, Pierre David made sure

---

[74] See also Notes 77 and 80, below.

that Pierre de Lune's title page proclaims that this new cookery book includes a full treatise on pastry-making as well: ... *Ensemble la manière de
faire toutes sortes de patisseries, tant froides que chaudes, en perfection.*
Then, by 1659, he is ready to present a French version of the material
that Mattia Giegher had earlier given to Italian readers,[75] and at the same
time to compete with the *Confiturier françois* by publishing *Le Maistre
d'hostel* which combined instruction on serving at table, on linen-folding
and on the making of various confections.

The Paris printer Jean Gaillard presented an anonymous *Pastissier
françois* (1653) to the public; an anonymous *Cuisinier methodique* (1660);
and the (anonymous) *Confiturier françois* (1660 or before). The bid to
secure a share of the cookbook market was upped by a work published
by Estienne Loyson who made sure that the author, Pierre de Lune, was
clearly qualified as cook to a duke (and no mere marquis), and that the title contained the word royalty: *Nouveau & parfait Maistre d'hostel royal*
(1662). To help sweep the market this book was set in the bookstalls
simultaneously by three Parisian publishers. By its title this work clearly
declared a competition with Pierre David's 1659 publication. It was answered the very same year by the heir of La Varenne's publisher, the
Veuve Pierre David. At this point her re-entry into the competition was
the *Ecole parfaicte des officiers de bouche*, which work, the title page
declares, consists of the *Vray maistre d'hostel* augmented by *Le grand Escuyer tranchant, Le Sommelier royal, Le Confiturier royal, Le Cuisinier
royal, Le Patissier royal* (1662). The insistence upon *royal* manners and
taste should have overwhelmed the potential buyer.

As Pierre David had predicted back in 1661, what Parisians took
to would inevitably spread to the provinces. The burgeoning interest in
cookbooks did. In Lyon, Jacques Canier and Fleury Martin published the
anonymous *L'escole des ragousts* (1668). By this time it was clear that
to succeed such a work had to included chapters on general cookery, on
pastry making and on confections, which their book did. Back in Paris
again, Jean du Puis published the *Art de bien traiter* (1674) written by
an individual who was not certain whether he wanted to join the ranks
of contemporary anonymous cookbook authors, L. S. R. That publication

---

[75] See the work of Mattia Giegher described in the section of *The French Confectioner*,
above.

marked the end of the flurry of enthusiasm for cookbooks. The market must have been saturated by this time. Reprints of the old and well-known works, especially of the *Cuisinier françois*, continue unabated, but we must wait a surprising seventeen years for the next appearance of a new work on the subject of cookery. Still brought out by a Parisian, Charles de Sercy, *Le Cuisinier royal et bourgeois* (1691) was still anonymous. What is novel now, and remarkable, is the qualification *bourgeois*; the publishing fraternity must have guessed that snobbery could sell only so many cookbooks.

La Varenne's *Cuisinier françois*, with its appended *Traitté de Confitures seiches & liquides*, was undoubtedly at the origin of the great "popular" surge of interest in cooking — or at least in reading recipes — in France in the second half of the seventeenth century. At the outset La Varenne may have intended merely to be of practical help to less competent members of his profession, rather like some benevolent master extending assistance to an apprentice who had gaps in his training or was not so well versed in the hoary traditions of his craft. In doing so he inadvertently recreated the genre of the cookbook, a genre that had virtually lain dormant in France for more than a century. It was the Parisian printing trade that very rapidly changed the nature of the "new" genre. Printers saw a market and scrambled to profit from it. While the "popularization" of fine and sophisticated cookery may never in France have been pursued to the degree that it was in England, printers right across Europe were responsible for nourishing the idea that anybody who could afford to buy a book could hope to learn how to eat as the gentry ate. It was just one of the democratic ideas that became current in the eighteenth century.

La Varenne quickly knew celebrity. His name became the cynosure of culinary art, his *Cuisinier françois* the definition and guide to great French cooking. Almost as quickly his name faded from the focus of popular respect.

Historians speak of jealous rivalries among La Varenne's contemporaries, and particularly of disparagement on the part of his younger, perhaps more inventive or aggressive colleagues in the profession. Printers had the most at stake in the struggle and, if they didn't actually design it, were certainly wholehearted parties to this self-aggrandisement. According to the mysterious L. S. R., La Varenne was just no longer "with it."[76] "Modernity" became a notion that hadn't had much currency in the realm of the French kitchen before La Varenne's rivals began to swarm. Not for the last time, France, the home of *mode*, got to see a wave of *nouvelle cuisine*. As is so often the case when something is touted as "new," it was a *cuisine* that was "new" mostly in the way that it denigrated the old and traditional taste.

Modern critics have been willing to repeat the claims of La Varenne's rivals, that La Varenne was old-fashioned, not to say archaic, in his practice. But this attitude is neither fair to La Varenne nor historically accurate. In La Varenne are to be found a good many novelties if we look back to the most recent French culinary texts before his time. In all probability, however, La Varenne's practice is that of his contemporaries: he says so himself. His book is intended to help his colleagues keep up to date with things that they and every self-respecting professional cook of the day should know. This is the solid professional repertoire of 1650. Far from "archaic" La Varenne's cookery is the good contemporary French practice of his day.

Furthermore we can find traces in La Varenne of most of the foodstuffs, combinations and procedures that writers of the following generation will preen themselves on having incorporated into their own cookery.[77] La Varenne presented the broadest spectrum of respectable French practice current in his day, both his own personal practice and what was current among the best professional cooks who were working in the 1650s throughout France for the class for which he had been engaged to cook. It was not popular cookery. It was fine cookery, approved and valued by his employer.

---

[76] His *Art de bien traiter* was printed in Paris by Jean du Puis in 1674. The first paragraph of his Preface reads: "I realize that in the matter of novelties it is not easy to please everyone and that, like humours, tastes are different; but if in this regard the reader will take the trouble to reflect about the subject that I deal with today along lines that are totally contrary to those followed by a few old authors [read: La Varenne] in their fashion, he cannot but agree with me, and admit that I have been right in reforming that ancient and tasteless manner of preparing and serving food, whose inconvenience and rusticity produce only useless, uncontrolled expense, only excessive, disordered profusion and, lastly, only troublesome, unprofitable, dishonourable excesses." Most of what follows in this Preface has the same tenor.

[77] See subsection (ii), La Varenne's cookery, below.

Printers made La Varenne. In very large measure the lowered esteem
in which La Varenne's work came to be held can also be blamed upon
two sorts of printers. There were those who jumped on the cookbook
bandwagon by publishing rival works and promoted them by encouraging a
denigration of La Varenne's successful enterprise. But there were also the
various printers who continued to reprint La Varenne's *Cuisinier françois*
through to the end of the seventeenth century, long after his death in 1678,
and on into the eighteenth. Unfortunately they had much more faith in the
celebrity of his name, and in the proven ability of his book to sell, than
respect for his text.

On the whole printers at that time did not seem to have been exceptionally knowledgeable about food or cooking. When they were faced
with unfamiliar words and phrases that had to be set in type, strange things
were apt to happen. In the case of La Varenne's texts, when he was no
longer around to proof-read a new edition, very strange things indeed often
did happen. What the successive generations of readers, who in good will
purchased the various later editions, began to think about the renowned
master chef from the 1650s and 1660s is only too clear: La Varenne's
reputation suffered; it waned. It was not merely that his books had increasingly vigorous competition from numerous works of other, younger
cookbook writers — who insisted that they alone represented the *nouvelle
cuisine* of the day. Over the years the texts of the *Cuisinier françois* began
to suffer irreparable vandalism at the hands of a succession of careless
printers in Paris, Lyon, Troyes and Rouen.

The invention of printing in the mid-fifteenth century promised a
new era in which texts would no longer be subject to the vagaries of
many scribes' bleary eyes and weary hands. Many, many readers could
thenceforth have absolute faith that the text they had before them in neat,
legible, printed form was correct and dependable, error-free. It turned
out not to be so. In the infancy of printing in Europe typesetters had to
depend upon manuscripts for their source material. Any results of scribal
lapsus in those manuscripts were generally reproduced in books that were
typeset from them. And, even worse, the typesetters themselves turned
out to be just as prone to making mistakes in their own work as scribes
had been. The results of the mistakes the printers made were immensely
more consequential than those made by scribes copying from a single

manuscript to a single manuscript. Many people could read copies of one edition. Many people bought and read La Varenne's *Cuisinier françois*. By the end of the seventeenth century and into the eighteenth, many people were reading such a collection of errors that in many cases La Varenne's name must have become synonymous with worthless nonsense.

Some examples of typesetters' errors current in the *Cuisinier françois* by the beginning of the eighteenth century may illustrate the egregious injustice done to La Varenne's work.

A few types of error may indeed result from a good-hearted desire to do justice to a text that is not clear, to a passage that the printer thinks he can improve in some way or that he finds incomprehensible and perhaps assumes can be attributed to the carelessness of some bygone colleague.[78]

– typical changes

> XVI,25–27: *soies* [dace] > *soles* [sole]
> Confections,16: *leur donnerés tout doucement un bouillon ou deux* [gently bring to a boil] > *les ferez bouillir tout doucement un bon quart-d'heure* [boil gently a good quarter hour]

No matter how much some printers may have wanted to deliver a comprehensible text to their public, incompetent typesetting and careless proof-reading are the only explanation of the number of letters that were set upside-down or backwards in some posthumous editions of La Varenne. That that sort of error was never noticed or corrected during a print run is proof of lackadaisical publishing. In the realm of the accidental error:

– omissions

> VI,51 (a word is omitted): *faites la mitonner avec la sauce, pour laquelle lier vous vous servirez de peu de farine* > *faites la mittonner avec la sauce, pour laquelle vous vous servirés de peu de farine*
> XXI,38 (a word is omitted): *servés la chaude & sucrée* > *servez la chaude*

---

[78] In the quotations that follow, the sign ">" marks the change in a word or passage between the second edition, Paris: Pierre David, 1652 of the *Cuisinier françois* and that of Troyes: Veuve Pierre Garnier, 1728, as this latter is reproduced by Jean-Louis Flandrin, Philip Hyman and Mary Hyman in their *Le Cuisinier françois* (Paris: Montalba, 1983). The number identifies the text as it is presented in our translation.

XVI,82 (several words are omitted): *Hure, ou entre-deux de saumon > Hure entre deux Saumons*

VIII,64 (a line or lines is omitted): *faites en six abbaisses fort deliées, & les beurrés l'une apres l'autre, estendés vostre cresme dessus vos six abbaisses, & faites en encore six autres > faites-en six abaisses fort deliées, & en faites encore six autres*

XV,33a (a line or lines is omitted): *de la purée* [of peas] *ou de l'eau, sel, persil, siboules, une poignée d'amandes pilées > de la purée d'amandes pilées*

– a change in punctuation

XIV,6: *cette chair est fort seiche quand elle est cuite … > cette chair est fort séche; quand elle est faite …*

– insertion or omission of a single letter

Confections,10: *fueille de papier laquelle vous replirés* [fold back] *de deux doits de hauteur > feuille de papier que vous remplirés* [fill] *à deux doigts de hauteur*

VI,53: *une pointe* [a drop] *de vinaigre > une pinte* [a pint] *de vinaigre*

XIV,31: *roignons* [kidneys] *> oignons* [onions]

XXI,21 (burbot liver, a masculine word) *estant fort peu blanchy dans l'eau chaude, bien net & essuyé* [with the liver lightly blanched in hot water, very clean and dry] *> étant fort peu blanchi dans l'eau chaude bien nette & essuyée* [with the liver lightly blanched in very clean, dry, hot water]

– confusion arising from the ambiguous shape of the long "s" used by printers

Confections,19: *verjus sec > verjus fée*

– misread letters, making nonsense

III,35: *moviettes* [thrush] *> moulettes* [rowel of a spur]

XIV,2: *une gousse d'ail > une dosse d'ail*

XV,33: *en cerises* [cherries: manner of preparing frogs' legs] *> en cotises* [pork spareribs]

XVI,81: *Hure de saumon à la sauce rousse > Hure de Saumon à la sauce douce*

– misreading of a word

III,23: *dans le pot* [into the pot (that already contains other ingredients)] *> dans un pot* [into a pot]

V,28: *lorsqu'il vous paroistra bien roux* [russet-coloured] > *lorsqu'il vous paroîtra bien doux* [sweet]

V,31: *levez ce qui aura esté sallé, comme les peaux: si vous voulez, resallez la* [salt it again] > *levez ce qui aura été salé comme les peaux si vous voulez, rasez-la* [scrape it]

V,77 *y meslés sucre* [sugar], *jaunes d'œufs* > *y mêlés sauce* [sauce], *jaunes d'œufs*

VIII,64 *Prenés un chaudeau de laict* [Get a caudle (a warmed liquid) of milk] > *Prenez un chaudron de lait* [Get a cauldron of milk]

XIV,25: *deux chevreaux* > *des chevreaux; qui rendra* [which will make] > *qui tiendra* [which will keep]

XIV,36: *pignons* [pine nuts] > *champignons* [mushrooms]

XVII,17: *Œufs faits dans des verres* > *Œufs frais dans des verres*

XXI,0 of dough: *maniez* [work] > *marinés* [marinate]

XXI,31: *autant de beurre que de pistaches* [as much butter as pistachios] > *autant de beurre ou de pistaches* [as much butter or pistachios]

XXI,37: *la douziesme partie de vostre paste* [one-twelfth of your dough] > *la deuxième partie de votre pâte* [half of your dough]

XXI,40: *le feu vif, & deu* [hot, as necessary] > *le feu vif & peu* [hot, cool]

XXIV,1 of a bouillon: *puis dresserés* [you set it out] > *puis presserez* [you press it]

XXIX,8: *roussir* [to brown] > *rôtir* [to roast]

XXXI,31: *un morceau de gomme* > *un morceau de pommes*

XVi, 90 of a pie: *puis le couvrez & dorer* > *puis l'ouvrir & dorer*

XVII,8: *une sauce rousse ou verte* > *une sauce rousse couverte*

– gross misreading of a word

VI,49 *Ce qu'estant fait, brochetez la ou cousez, & la faites blanchir* > *Ce qu'étant fait couses* [sic] *le trou, & la faites blanchir*

XIV,6: *l'assaisonnez, & farcissez* > *l'assaisonnés & fricassés*

XIV,6: *cette farce est propre* > *cette sorte est propre*

XV,36: *delayez des œufs avec des framboises* [mix eggs with raspberries] > *délayés du lait avec framboises* [mix milk with raspberries]

XV,68 regarding cod: *il la faut beurrer* [you must butter it] > *il la faut pétrir* [you must grind it]

XVIII,17: *autrement* > *vîtement*

XIX,2: *ayant bouilly trois ou quatre tours* [three or four stirrings] > *ayant bouilli trois ou quatre heures* [three or four hours]

XXI,21: *mousserons, morilles, troufles* [agaric, morels, truffles] > *mousserons, moulles, trufles* [agaric, mussels, truffles: the nature of the dish would change radically]

– misreading of several words

XIV,13: *vous prendrez en suite un liévre ou deux, ou deux membres de mouton* [a hare or two, or two mutton legs] > *vous prendrez ensuite une livre ou deux de membre de mouton* [one or two pounds of mutton leg]

XVIII,24: *un oignon escartelé* [quartered], *beurre frais* > *un oignon, étant ébeurré de* [buttered with] *beurre frais*

– plain carelessness

V,4: *farine nette, delayée dans du bouillon, & garnirés vostre plat de champignons, palets de bœuf . . .* > *farine nette délayée dans du pigeon, palets de bœuf . . .* [*champignons* misread for *pigeons* and some text omitted]

XVI,85: *avec de la moutarde, ou* [or] *avec des poix* > *avec de la moutarde &* [and] *des pois*

XVIII,1: *garny de fleurs & persil* > *garni de fleurs de persil*

XIX,1: *mettez y de la cresme, ou un jaune d'œuf, ou un peu de chapelure de pain* > *mettés-y de la crême, un jaune d'œuf, un peu de chapelûres de pain*

XIX,12: *que la sauce se reduise à peu* [the sauce should reduce to little] > *que la sauce se reduise peu à peu* [the sauce should reduce gradually]

XXV,14 and 15: the two recipes become jumbled together

XVI,55–59: several recipes become jumbled together, confused: the beginning of XVI,56 is appended to 55; the title of 56 is kept but the text of 57 is printed under it; Recipe 57 instructs "for Lobster do the same as for Lobster"; Recipe 59 is omitted altogether

XVI,71 serve the fish with parsley: *dessus & autour* [above and around] > *dessus & dessous* [above and below]

– simply garbled text

> XIV,11: "ribs of greens, squab or beef palates; and make
> the bottom layer out of your minced veal" > "a layer of
> ribs of greens and squab, beef palates, so that the upper
> layer is of ribs of greens or squab, beef palates, and do
> it so that the lower layer is of your minced veal"
> XXV,25: *vous n'y mettés point d'œufs* > *vous y pouvez
> mettre des œufs*

– trying to make sense where a passage is not understood

> XX,1: *meslez y du fromage à petits choux* [cheese like
> little cabbages: *i.e.* fresh curds] > *mêlez-y du fromage,
> petits choux* [cheese and little cabbages]

Such errors as these abound in later editions of La Varenne. In innumerable places they made La Varenne's text incomprehensible or else effectively destroyed the nature and value of his recipes. They must have made the use of the *French Cook* a bewildering experience, not to say a frustrating and even dangerous one. In many cases, his book having produced quite unpalatable results, eighteenth century cooks must have decided that La Varenne had the most remarkably bizarre taste.

There is some justification for the arrogant contempt that L. S. R. expresses for La Varenne in the preface of his *Art de bien traiter* of 1674:[79] "I am certain that you will find here none of the absurdities and disgusting lessons that *le sieur de Varenne* is bold enough to propose and teach, lessons by which he has for so long mislead and beguiled the foolish,

---

[79] This work is most easily read, in modern French, in Gilles and Laurence Laurendon, *L'art de la cuisine française au xviie siècle* (Paris: Payot & Rivages, 1995). However, it was undoubtedly La Varenne's very success, broad and "popular", that provoked a disparagement of his work; the belittling of a person who had so rapidly become iconic seems often intended primarily to enhance the prestige of the individual voicing the criticism. In his *Historiettes* Gédéon Tallemant des Réaux (1619–1692) wrote of Mme de Sablé, an ostentatiously epicurean contemporary: *"Depuis qu'elle est devote, c'est la plus grande friande qui soit au monde; elle pretend qu'il n'y a personne qui ayt le goust si fin qu'elle, et ne fait nul cas des gens qui ne goustent point les bonnes choses. Elle invente tousjours quelque nouvelle friponnerie* [pastry]. *On l'a veûe pester contre* [rail against] *le livre intitulé* le Cuisinier françois, *qu'a fait le cuisinier de M. d'Uxelles. 'Il ne fait rien qui vaille,' disoit-elle; 'il le faudroit punir d'abuser ainsy le monde.'"* The text was originally in manuscript, *c.* 1657 but with many later additions); ed. Antoine Adam, 2 vols. (Paris: Gallimard, 1960), I, 516 (and note 3).

naive populace, feeding them his productions as if they were so many
infallible truths and, as far as cookery goes, the most accredited dogma in
the world. ... But if we take a close look at his work, we see so many
contemptible things and so many absurd ideas and instructions in matters
he claims to be thoroughly unquestionable that we can find few chapters
consisting of anything more than repugnant abominations, confusion and
intolerable blunders." L. S. R.'s condemnation of La Varenne's work becomes detailed and even more acerbic, railing at the stupidity and lack of
sensible good taste that would propound such egregious nonsense.

The continual degradation of La Varenne's text over the several decades
after his death goes a long way to explain not only the decline in interest in his work but also the rapid deterioration of La Varenne's exalted
reputation as the age's preeminent cook.

(ii) La Varenne's cookery

In the "Epistle to the Reader" found in the *Pastissier françois* — and that
"Mounsieur" Marnette kindly translated for his version of *The French
Pastery-Cooke* in 1656[80] — the author presents a justification for having compiled and published his cookbooks. By that date La Varenne
was almost certainly receiving criticism from culinary masters who perceived that they might have to establish grounds to challenge his acclaimed
sovereignty. The author of the *Pastissier françois* asserts that "the ill nature of our most famousest Pastry Cooks of the French Court, and of the
City of Paris" had "smothered" and "hoorded up" their art so effectively
that few people other than themselves, in Paris and at the French court,
had any understanding of this sort of cookery let alone expertise in it. His
book, the *Pastissier françois*, and its English translation were intended to
relieve some of this ignorance.

Where before, in the *Cuisinier* (1651), La Varenne had extended assistance to less experienced members of the brotherhood, now, five years
later, the "Epistle to the Reader" in the *Pastissier* insists that his cookery
is broadly, generally accessible by virtually anyone anywhere — even, as
he declares, by "good Houswives" and "ingenuous young Maidens"! Such
a shift in stance is remarkable. From the courtliest castle to the humblest

---

[80] See below, Bibliography, (ii)(a).

hamlet *The French Pastery-Cooke* will suddenly, almost miraculously, let *anyone* give "a most noble and delicious treatment" to food and, in doing so, "a great deal of ease and pleasure" to themselves.

Perhaps, knowing English custom well, Monsieur Marnette advised the author that a long tradition of unpretentious household cooking in England, in every social class, might make an appeal more effective that stressed universality and practicality. In any case the themes of this Epistle and the claims made there for the recipes in the *French Pastery-Cooke* accord surprisingly with the plain, exoteric manner of La Varenne's instruction and, to some extent, with the nature of his cookery, as that instruction and cookery are set out in the *Cuisinier françois*.

La Varenne's cookery must have been, if not cheap, at least reasonably affordable by the middle-to-upper classes for whom it was intended. It is difficult to judge by a master ingredients list, where not-overly-commonplace items such as truffles and veal sweetbreads abound, just what the cost of normal dinner at the Uxelles table might actually have cost. But La Varenne assures his reader that the *Cuisinier* will let him fulfill his professional obligations efficiently.[81] Furthermore, central to the *Cuisinier*, the Entrées of the long Chapter V can all be made far distant from any urban centre and in the most rustic of places.[82] Furthermore his is food for all seasons — that is, his recipes involve foodstuffs that are available at one time or another throughout the full year, whatever the season.[83] He provides recipes appropriate for any sick members of the household or visitors, as well as for the healthy.

Perhaps surprisingly the quantities that La Varenne prescribes are modest. Earlier recipe collections, specifically the French collections of

---

[81] The first recipe of the *Cuisinier*'s Chapter XXII opens with the frugal advice that, "When butter is cheap you can buy a good amount of it and melt it for use as needed."

[82] In very rare instances La Varenne will advise his reader that a particular ingredient may be picked up at a local retailer's: ox tongue, for example, can be had ready-cooked from the tripe dealer (Cook VI,53); a green colourant, from a spicer (Cook VIII,28). The *Confiturier françois* informs that tragacanth gum can be had from spicers and apothecaries (Conf II,3).

[83] His Chapter I, a sort of preliminary to his carefully ordered listing of dishes, servings and meals, provides the cook (or kitchen clerk) a "Table of the Meats that are Normally Found and Served during the Various Seasons of the Year."

the Middle Ages that relate to a particular time and place, suggest that the court and household for which a kitchen prepared food were often numerically large. La Varenne's experience with the Uxelles' dining hall may have led him to assume that his reader would normally have to satisfy the appetites of only a dozen diners at most — a number which is similar to what is generally found in household recipe books of the Italian Renaissance.[84] La Varenne is not cooking for a large household or a great number of family members and guests. In the *French Cook* there are no grand banquets for the cook to worry about; nor does La Varenne ever advise his reader what to do if faced with a demand from his master that he do his best to impress and flatter a guest. As far as his recipes are concerned, his sole interest is to provide interesting and varied fare, for the most part relatively unpretentious dishes, for relatively small numbers of people.

The expository style of his book, its organization and certain professional considerations indicate that La Varenne knew the audience he was addressing, as well as their peculiar circumstances and the difficulties they might be facing as craftsmen in their office. He is aware of the constraints under which all of his fellow professionals undoubtedly must work, not the least of which are such mundane considerations as the costs of foodstuffs and labour. He assumes that any cook worthy of the name should be able to find his way around in this *Cuisinier*, from

---

[84] Italian courts were likely somewhat smaller than those of the higher French aristocracy of the same time. In the collection edited by Domenico and Giacomo Zanichelli and Salome Morpurgo, *Cinquantasette ricette d'un libro di cucina del buon secolo della lingua* (Bologna, 1890) many recipes are prefaced with the phrase *per xii persone* and sometimes though rarely *per xx persone*. Again, a recipe's relatively small yield is specified with the phrases "for six bowls of ... " (*per sei scodelle di ...*) and "for six (ten) servings of ... " (*per sei (diece) minestre di ...*) in the Italian collections of the manuscripts Wellcome (London, Wellcome Institute, MS 211 (unpublished), Recipes 276, 288, 368 and 337) and Lucano (ed. Michael Süthold, *Manoscritto Lucano. Ein unveröffentlichtes Kochbuch aus Süditalien vom Beginn des 16. Jahrhunderts* (Genève: Droz, 1994), Recipe 5). Of course such quantities of six and ten may be useful units of measurement that the cook could easily multiply (or divide) as necessary, but quantities of two are also found in Italian recipes: "For two plates of Sicilian macaroni (*volendone fare doi piatelli*), Recipe 15 in the *Neapolitan Recipe Collection*; of game in a pepper sauce (*volendone fare duo piattelli*), Recipe 5, and of jelly (*per fare dui piattelli de gelatina*), Recipe 24, these last two recipes in Maestro Martino, *Libro de arte coquinaria.*

day to day (Lenten, lean and meat day) and from course to course. In Recipe XVIII,30 he gives a foretaste of the sort of abbreviation he will later indulge in, perhaps at the prompting of his publisher.

> You will find the recipe for plaice, along with all of the ones that follow in the Table,[85] in the section on Fish Entrées, which it would have been useless and superfluous to list by recipe number and page number, and all the more so as they can easily be found. However, I can advise you that what I indicate will not oblige you either to increase or reduce your proper expenditure of funds or labour, but I do it solely to remind you of what can be served, without forgetting to say that you can choose whatever you like, and insert a reasonable assortment of pies or tourtes among your dishes, always minding that a pie or tourte is served after six other dishes.

The *Cuisinier françois* is a clearly written book. Its earliest editions make understandable good sense. Undoubtedly in very large measure it was that comprehensibility that appealed to the public, a public that went far beyond the corps of master cooks in France in the 1650s and whose readership accounted for the renown that La Varenne's name was to enjoy.

Above all, La Varenne shows a constant preoccupation with the quality of the food he handles. His foodstuffs are frequently qualified as "fresh" or "very fresh".[86] The reader has an impression that he would frown on any sort of shortcut a colleague might be tempted to make. He would not hesitate to discard a fish that was past its prime or butter that showed the slightest sign of turning rancid. There is a sense of doing things right because the profession demanded that every one of its members respect an inherent code of professional honour.

---

[85] That is, in the listing of all the recipes contained in Chapter XVIII and printed at the beginning of the chapter. La Varenne's point is that some dishes for "Fish Entrées" ("Entrées for Lean Meals Outside of Lent": Chapter XVI) can also serve in this present "Second Course for Lean Meals". Their recipes need not be repeated. The same sort of abbreviating is incorporated into several of the later chapters: see the preamble to Chapter XXVI as well, for instance.

[86] This requirement of freshness is applied in particular to butter: *beurre frais, beurre bien frais*. La Varenne specifies that his cook use only fresh eggs (*œufs bien frais*), cream (*cresme fraische, cresme bien fraische*), milk (*laict frais, laict bien frais*), oysters (*huistres bien fraisches*), sole (*solles bien fraisches*), and so forth.

This is domestic cooking that La Varenne offers, good, at times very appealing, but never really grand or exceptional. There are no magnificent entremets here, the result of a week's labour by a gang of specially engaged assistants, designed to create a gasp of awe among the Marquis' honoured guests and leave them clapping their hands with delight: La Varenne satisfies any expectations raised by the designation "Entremets" (in Chapter VIII, for instance) by offering a choice among seven sorts of jelly, three recipes for veal sweetbreads, dishes of deer udder or cow's udder. This could all be the work of one professional cook in a well appointed kitchen. Occasionally there will be some attention to detail, such as the varied colouring of a particular dish, or the decorative finishing of an upper pie crust. But there are no prodigious creations here, such as are to be found in earlier and later French cuisine. La Varenne's work would honour his employer and the employer of any other member of his profession who was guided by the *Cuisinier françois*.

(a) His kitchen and its utensils

La Varenne's kitchen, and the one he supposed his reader to work in, had a ready supply of fresh water, a sink and a draining-board. It is handy to a cellar or, failing that, to some place in which prepared foods can be stored in a relatively cool and constant temperature.

Generally La Varenne makes use of three sorts of cooking: in a pot or pan, on a spit, or in a dish or mould. For this cooking he refers to three sources of heat: a pit or hearth fire, an oven or a fire basket.[87] While there is some reference to a grill or gridiron, particularly with regard to fish, its use is not very common. There are two sorts of oven in his kitchen, a large baker's one, with a stopper, suitable for baking the generously-sized pastries that he will assemble, and a smaller metal oven or "stove" in which foods can be dried. He rarely cooks a foodstuff by setting it directly on or among hot coals, a procedure common in earlier centuries.

Apart from those fixtures, among the heavier funishings in La Varenne's kitchen are a table, a chopping block, a pastry table, a pastry

---

[87] Many of the things mentioned in this subsection are listed in the Appendices, especially in Appendix 4. References to recipe numbers there will let the reader better see how La Varenne and his contemporaries might have used the particular item or article.

wheel and a press (used for extracting juice and for caking a mixture). A good-sized stone or marble mortar claimed inviolable, long-consecrated space on the kitchen floor (and smaller metal ones were forever ready at the back of a table); in them sat wooden or iron pestles of suitable sizes. A salting-tub was available seasonally for the treatment of certain foodstuffs. Tripods, fire shovels, oven peels, spits and skewers (some of wood) were indispensable, as was the whole ratcheted apparatus, the trammel (never expressly mentioned in La Varenne but standard and always assumed) for suspending receptacles and swinging them more or less over a fire.

Among the receptacles for which La Varenne could reach for various purposes were basins of several metals[88] and bowls, wooden and earthenware. For boiling he had a cauldron and a bronze kettle or stew-pot, and a metal mortar, in which something had just been ground and mixed, could also be used for the same purpose. For stewing he had lidded pots of various sizes, a double boiler and a braising bell; frying pans and skillets extended the choice of receptacles for cooking over the fire. A dripping pan could collect juices from a meat and also serve for mixing them with other ingredients and reheating. For baking he had casseroles, terrines and tourtières, and a range of moulds including a variety used for biscuits; a wafer or waffle iron was available; and La Varenne had fish pans. For various general purposes he had crocks (glazed and unglazed) and earthenware and metal (iron, bronze) pots; he had convex dishes and flat plates, trencher plates and platters, these last items being either of earthenware or various metals. Pitchers (of silver) and flasks (of glass) carried liquids to the dining table.

Always needed were various sizes of hooks; brass grills, marble slabs, slate slabs, tin sheets, wicker mats of different dimensions; graters and rasps. Sieves, of coarse fabric or fine hair, a straining bag, a colander all hung within reach, as did funnels of different sizes, shapes and materials. A round pastry board or two were in regular use, as were rolling pins. A squasher could be used with cheese; a sausage filler was available; a syringe or piping bag had its particular use.

Utensils included large forks (to manage meat, for instance, in cauldrons); spoons, some holed, some designed for skimming, of various sizes

---

[88] Although *The French Pastry Chef* (XXXIII,25) does warn the cook that it is not advisable to set pewter directly on the coals in case it melts.

and materials; a broad assortment of knives, of course, from the largest down to a humble pen knife (normally for trimming a writing quill), and for every specific purpose; spatulas and fish turners; a larding needle or two; metal rings held a foodstuff off the bottom of a pot.

Among the miscellaneous items at hand in La Varenne's kitchen were pine boxes, wicker baskets and trays, small leather bags (to contain spices; alternatively for that purpose, a "box" with many drawers), glasses, glass bottles, pins, sticks, fine skewers, rods, brushes, a whisk (of birch twigs), feathers (singly for beating egg whites, in bunches for applying glazes), straw, string, thread, cardboard, paper, an assortment of fabrics, from coarse sackcloth to fine linens, for wiping, filtering and protecting the food that was in the process of being prepared or was dished out and ready to be carried into the hall for serving.

In sum, it is in a well-equipped kitchen that La Varenne prepares his various dishes. It is only rarely that he suggests that his reader can "make do" by substituting for some incidental appliance or utensil.

It is a clean kitchen, too. The author will insist on the words "clean" and "new": tables, mortars, basins, bottles, crocks, terrines, frying pans, straining bags.[89] The scullions in those kitchens had little time to spend sampling the chef's latest creations.

(b) Preferred ingredients

Among the recipes of the *Cuisinier françois* certain edibles appear more frequently than others. They seem to have been preferred ingredients, favoured particularly either by La Varenne, by his employer or by the taste of the time. We can take note of these foodstuffs and condiments, whatever any significance of such preferences may be.

Beatilles are a curious component in seventeenth-century cookery. They do not represent any particular ingredient or ingredients, yet under that vague generic name *beatilles* (nowadays *béatilles*) enjoy a remarkably frequent use in certain types of dishes that La Varenne makes. The name

---

[89] For instance: *dans un pot de terre neuf, dans un coquemar de terre neuf, sur une table bien nette, dans un mortier de marbre bien net, dans une terrine bien nette, dans une poësle à frire bien nette, dans quelque vaisseau bien net & qui ne puisse pas donner de mauvais goust, tenés vostre chausse preste & bien nette, tenez bien nets vos bassins, prenez garde que les bouteilles ... soient bien nettes.*

itself is not especially helpful in identifying the specifically culinary nature of that group of ingredients. Back in the fifteenth century the word *beatille* originally applied to certain little articles made by nuns (*beates*); then by the beginning of the sixteenth, the word had come to designate an ornament worn on a coiffure; by the end of that century that sense had shifted into a more general one of any "trinket".[90] By the beginning of La Varenne's century Cotgrave's gloss of the word, now usually in the plural, still gives no hint of a culinary sense: "Trinkets, or vaine toyes, wherewith finicall people decke themselves; trifles."[91] Huguet did, however, find a figurative use that for the first time related the word to food: *Objets de parure; fig., friandises*: "Adornment; figuratively, tidbits."[92] And by the end of La Varenne's seventeenth century the semantic shift of the word is complete: the word designated "delicate bits with which pasties are garnished or which are served separately."[93]

La Varenne's *beatilles* have a varied composition that can include varying combinations of cockscombs, veal sweetbreads, beef palates, truffles, artichoke bottoms, pistachios. The items are both animal and vegetable, the determining factor apparently being distinctness of flavour. Capers and anchovies can constitute *beatilles* and are freely thrown into a sauce or stuffing. It is as if the cook had at his disposal bins of such ingredients stacked along his work table. Any list of what goes into these "tidbits" would have to end with an "etc."; La Varenne frequently writes *beatilles telles que* ... "such tidbits as ... ." In all likelihood what was used to satisfy any call for undesignated *beatilles* would depend entirely upon what happened to be available at that moment in any given cook's kitchen. It may surprise those who are not experienced cooks themselves, but this cookery occasionally allows a good deal of latitude in the choice

---

[90] *Le Robert Dictionnaire historique de la langue française* (Paris: Dictionnaires Le Robert, 1992).

[91] *Dictionarie of the French and English Tongues* (London, 1611).

[92] Edmond Huguet, *Dictionnaire de la langue française du seizième siècle* (Paris, 1925).

[93] *Morceaux délicats dont on garnit les pâtés ou que l'on sert à part* (1680). *Le Robert Dictionnaire historique de la langue française*. The reader of La Varenne can see that neither this definition nor that given by at least one late-seventeenth-century dictionary (see Richelet in the Appendix) is entirely accurate. *Beatilles* did have a broader use.

of minor or secondary ingredients; a particular direction has several forms but will amount to something like, "throw in whatever you have on hand." Enrichment of flavour, the sense of the very common term *ragoust* (which will be looked at below), is one of the cook's fundamental aims. If it is not precisely the ingredients of the *beatilles* that help to identify them, it is their function: "tidbits" are rare bits or delicacies that act as condiments by adding an interesting flavour.

The usual source of La Varenne's grease and oil is animal fat, specifically pork lard. On lean days either olive oil or melted butter may serve for frying or be consumed in dishes. On meat days either lard or butter may be eaten, as well as olive oil.

– Meats and fish

The meat of domestic animals is much more common than that of game animals. Goat is not eaten, only kid, and in general it seems that tougher meats are not cooked, probably because there was no need to use them. Lard — fat bacon or bacon fat — moves in very large quantities through the kitchen in one form or another and onto the dining table. There is still, as in earlier periods, a considerable use of giblets and offal — lungs, organs, brain, feet; marrow as well enters into several preparations; several sorts of sausage are stuffed for immediate or future use. Meat "juices" are common, probably for flavour;[94] the ubiquity of mutton juice suggests also that there was a lot of roast mutton on the aristocratic French table at the time.[95] In any case meat stocks were always on hand.

There was a fair representation of game fowl on those tables, of which a broad variety is listed in Chapter I of the *French Cook*, particularly of waterfowl. For the most part these are taken up in the roast course; few (except for scoter ducks) enter into prepared dishes. Domestic fowl are very well represented by chickens (along with other members of that

---

[94] The alchemists' notion of obtaining and consuming the quintessence of some substance may go some way to explain the favour that such "distillates" enjoyed. See particularly the recipe at Cook XIII,2 for a sick dish that uses the quintessence of meat.

[95] On the displacement of pork by mutton by La Varenne's time, see Massimo Montanari, *The Culture of Food*, trans. Carl Ipsen (Oxford & Cambridge, MA: Blackwell, 1994), 76–77.

family), turkeys, ducks and geese. Doves were raised in domestic dovecots to satisfy a strong gastronomic demand, especially for squab.[96]

Very few meats, domestic or game, had been unknown in French kitchens during the century or two before La Varenne's day. The most remarkable novelty in seventeenth-century France was the so-called "turkey": confusion in the use of the qualification of *d'Inde* (*poules d'Inde, coqs d'Inde, dindons*) to identify both Guinea fowl and turkey points to the way in which both species of fowl, though known, raised, cooked and eaten over some decades, retained a little of the mystery of their exotic origins.

Similarly, compared with earlier French cuisine, there are relatively few varieties of fish handled in the kitchen that La Varenne knew. Those fish, however, are for the most part fresh, perhaps delivered live from the estate's fish ponds to the kitchen door.[97] Novel in La Varenne is the incorporation of anchovies into his sauces or dishes.

Milk will be mentioned among liquids, below. Besides milk the remarkable dairy ingredient in this cooking is butter. In the three works studied here butter is referred to close to an amazing 600 times. It is used in pastry, in sauces and garnishes, as a basting and as a frying medium. There is even a Butter Tourte. Its use is so pervasive that La Varenne feels he must insert a paragraph advising his reader how to treat oil in order to remove its odour and so let it be used just like butter. He even offers a dish called Herb Pottage *Without* Butter.[98] Some recipes call for "a lot of butter" and "a great deal of butter," or that the pie be "much enriched with butter"[99] Whereas in earlier French cookery lard had provided almost all of the fat in culinary preparations, La Varenne, now with Italian chefs, turned

---

[96] Interestingly, in view of La Varenne's apparent predilection for squabs, Escoffier wrote that they "are not very highly esteemed by gourmets, and that is more particularly to be regretted, since when the birds are of excellent quality, they are worthy of the best tables" (§1775).

[97] For instance live carp (Cook XVIII,27), pike (XVIII,20) and perch (XVIII,24). La Varenne's use of fresh fish is part of his insistence on fresh ingredients in general.

[98] Cook XV,25.

[99] *du beurre à force* (Cook XV,16), *force beurre* (XXV,15), *bien nourry de beurre* (XIV,8).

to butter, particularly in his sauces.[100] Generally speaking La Varenne's
cookery is remarkably rich.

Cheese seems not to have been an exceptionally interesting foodstuff
for the author of the *Cuisinier*, at least if we were to look at the frequency
of its use in the cookery of previous generations. On the other hand
the *Pastissier* does compensate for La Varenne's relative indifference by
recognizing several types of cheese and the appropriate use of each.

Eggs are very much in demand here, playing an important role not
only by the frequency of their use in recipes but also in the number of
dishes that are essentially egg dishes. In his *Dictionaire universel* of 1690,
Antoine Furetière adds a note to his article on "eggs":

> En termes de Cuisine on dit, Faire des œufs farcis, frits, fricassez,
> au miroir, à l'oseille, au verjus, au lait, à la coque ou mollets, des
> œufs durs, ou œufs rouges, œufs filez, pochez, à la Huguenotte
> quand on y met du jus de mouton. Un bon Cuisinier doit sçavoir
> faire cinquante sortes d'œufs.

To make sure *his* cook has an opportunity to verse himself in a good many
of these standard egg dishes, and others, La Varenne devotes the whole
of Chapter XVII in the *Cuisinier* to them.

– Vegetable matter

Thanks to the contemporary predilection for *ragoust*,[101] members of the
onion family are very commonly handled by La Varenne. He slices, chops,
grinds and sautés onions themselves in large quantities, but chives (scallions) are a close runner-up in popularity. However, the leek, a great
favorite of cooks several generations before, seems on the point of passing out of culinary fashion, and with it garlic is virtually absent from La
Varenne's kitchen. The decline in interest in both of these latter plants
may have something to do with aristocratic perceptions of the social class
for which perhaps they seemed appropriate foods.

Artichokes are one of La Varenne's surprises. Although they are
found in Italian recipe books of the Renaissance, and cannot really be

---

[100] See Massimo Montanari, *The Culture of Food*, (Oxford & Cambridge, MA: Blackwell, 1994), 117.

[101] See further on, in the subsection "Cookery techniques".

called a recent discovery for French cuisine, in La Varenne's cookery they are used much more often than at any time in the past. Their use amounts to something like a vogue in the *Cuisinier françois*. Similarly asparagus had been grown in kitchen gardens since the late Middle Ages but seems only recently to be coming into its own as a valued ingredient. The roots such as the carrots, parsnips and turnips that we find thinly scattered in these recipes had become quite well known over the centuries but had received only a modicum of favour on French tables; La Varenne neither increases nor decreases their presence in his master's meals. The Jerusalem artichoke, a new-world find, is an exceptional tuber in that its popularity is both new and assured. Along with it, both the skirret and salsify had rarely been seen before La Varenne's day. The relatively frequent use of chicory marks it as much more than experimental.[102] Beet greens and chard (the ubiquitous *poirée*, perhaps a successor in aristocratic taste to the medieval leek *poireau*) had been commonly consumed in stewed salads of a century and more before, and beet greens occasionally as a colourant; however, beetroots — called "red parsnips" by I. D. G., the English translator of the *Cuisinier françois* — now turn up in La Varenne's kitchen.

Cabbage retains some slight recognition as a dependable staple worthy of use in eight or nine recipes. Broccoli — called cabbage broccoli so that readers might more easily identify what was meant — though certainly not a novelty, is still not cooked very often, but cook and patron seem willing to experiment. Unlike the modern variety with tightly formed heads, which in Italy in the previous century Scappi was using, La Varenne's broccoli, as he describes it, was the "sprouting" sort with flowerlets. Cauliflower on the other hand has clearly established an enthusiastic following in both kitchen and dining hall. La Varenne's use of lettuce is much more extensive than in earlier French recipe collections.

Among the gourds, which are otherwise not represented, pumpkins are very much a novelty on the French dining table, being used for several sorts of pottage and a tourte.

---

[102] Before La Varenne chicory appears in only Italian recipe collections, the earliest being the one edited by Ingemar Boström in *Anonimo Meridionale, Due libri di cucina* (Stockholm, 1985); Book "A," pp. 5-31, Recipe 103: *Cicoree*; and Platina, ed. cit., Recipe IV,9: *De conditura intybi*, and then in the *Platine en françois* (Lyon: Françoys Fradin, 1505), Recipe IV,8: *De la cycoree & comment s'apreste*, f. xxxix.

Pinenuts have all but lost the favour they enjoyed in earlier times. Similarly walnuts and filberts (hazel-nuts) are little more than mentioned, the latter only in the *Pastissier*. Pistachios seem to have been the nut to invest in when the *Cuisinier françois* was popular. Thanks in part to the requirements of lean-day cooking and the demands of easy garnishing, almonds — whole, slivered, ground, puréed, reduced to oil, "milk" or "cream" — are almost as popular as in the past. Aniseed is used occasionally for its flavour.

Remarkably missing among La Varenne's foodstuffs is any mention of beans, whether of genera that had long been common in Europe such as the *Vicia faba* or *Faba vulgaris*, the broad bean; or of the genus *Phaseolus*, the haricot bean (including both the shelled flageolet bean and the unshelled, immature french or snap bean). The former genus, the *fève*, was as much a staple in earlier French cookery as cabbage; on the other hand the haricot was native to Central America but had been introduced into Europe and was widely known by the second half of the seventeenth century.

Peas remain in common use in La Varenne.[103] In his lean cookery, particularly for sauces and garnishes of one sort or another, we can say in constant use. The exigencies of lean-day and Lenten menus account in large measure for the continuing dependence of seventeeth-century cooks on peas and pea purée. As in older cooking, pea purée — called merely *purée* without any qualification by La Varenne — was habitually substituted for a meat broth as the base of a cooking bouillon or sauce for lean dishes.[104]

Capers likewise had secured an important role for themselves by the mid-seventeenth century. Rice is present in La Varenne's kitchen though it is not used quite so much as in earlier times in France.

---

[103] An age-old traditional French dish was "peas with lard", a counterpart to the modern pork and beans, or beans and bacon: see Cook III,29, *Potage de salé aux poix*. The *Menagier de Paris* has this dish (in §29) back at the end of the fourteenth century, as does Chiquart a generation later (Recipe 62). The version in the *Neapolitan Recipe Collection* (Recipe 21) is called *Piselli cum carne salada*; it is reproduced by Martino, by Platina and by a series of Italian recipe books that echo these earlier works.

[104] In the second half of the seventeenth century peas, particularly the immature, green *petits pois*, will become the rage of upper-class French gastronomy, but this chic fad is not yet apparent in the Marquis d'Uxelles' house. See Sabban and Sirventi, *op. cit.*, p. 23.

La Varenne's dependence upon several varieties of fungi is a novelty, and perhaps a surprise. Mushrooms were far from unknown to medieval French cooks,[105] but now mushrooms, morels and agaric must have become quite familiar in the hands of the modern French cook. Truffles might head the list of "new foodstuffs" in La Varenne, at least as far as the relatively high frequency of their use goes.

Herbs are broadly represented, although individually they are not frequently used. Borage, buglose, chervil, fennel, juniper, purslane, rosemary, sage, sorrel, turn up once or twice, here and there, serving a specific purpose in a specific dish. Remarkably a number of other herbs which medieval and (presumably) Renaissance French cooks had known and on which they had depended extensively are entirely absent — or at least not explicitly named — in La Varenne: basil, clary, hyssop, mint, pennyroyal, savory, tansy and tarragon. Of all of the herbs, parsley is by far the most common here, often as a green colourant, being incorporated in a preparation or sprinkled as a garnish. The collective "bouquet" is the means by which La Varenne usually introduces herbal flavour into his preparations, and he does it quite frequently for his pottages. A standard composition of the bunch of herbs is, unfortunately, never defined, although the *Cuisinier françois* does in a few rare instances mention components specific to a recipe: "a bouquet of parsley, chives and thyme" (Recipe II,0), "a bouquet of parsley and chives" (V,2) and "a bouquet of sage" (V,14).[106] Less commonly La Varenne will merely indicate that a dish needs *bonnes herbes*, without specifying which "good herbs". The *bouquet garni* is by no means original to the seventeenth century, being quite a common ingredient in late-medieval French cookery. It should be noted in passing that the advantage of such a bag of herbs is that only the

---

[105] See, for instance, the brief disquisition on *champignons* and recipes for their preparation in the *Menagier de Paris* (§160). Even a century before, at the end of the thirteenth, itinerant merchants in the streets of Paris were peddling two varieties of mushroom to bourgeois housewives: *borgons* and *veilles*. See Guillaume de la Villeneuve, *Les Crieries de Paris* in Etienne Barbazan, *Fabliaux et contes des poètes françois*, 2 vols. (Paris, 1808; repr. Geneva: Slatkine, 1976), I, 276–86; l. 153.

[106] We may compare this *ad hoc* practice to the general-purpose preparation of a "seasoning bundle" explicitly laid out by Pierre de Lune in his *Le cuisinier* (reprinted in Laurendon, *L'art de la cuisine français au XVIIe siècle*, p. 242): "a bard of bacon, a chive, a little thyme, two cloves, chervil and parsley, bound with a string."

flavour and not the herbs themselves with their often irreducible texture will enter the dish.[107]

The taste for spices in general had waned greatly by La Varenne's day: where ginger, for instance, used to be grated or ground into a great many preparations, we find it on a mere one occasion in the *Cuisinier*, twice in the *Pastissier* and twice in the *Confiturier*. (By this phenomenon alone we may declare that the Middle Ages has clearly closed for French cookery.) Similarly mustard, always associated with Germanic taste, has suffered a decline in its approval rating; and likewise saffron. On the other hand cinnamon is the flavour of the decade(s), seasoning more than three dozen preparations. And strangely, the flavour nutmeg has achieved a sort of revered respect if we are to judge by its presence in a large number of garnishes; mace on the other hand is all but ignored. Cloves retain a marked favour. The traditional practice of premixing four or five of the most commonly used ground spices survives in La Varenne's kitchen as *espice, espice douce, espice preparé*. Salt and pepper remain constantly within the cook's reach.

Sugar has not only retained the following of addicts it acquired over the previous three centuries or so, it may even have built upon its past success. Certainly the mini-treatise on confections with which the *Cuisinier* ends, and whose material reappears later in the *Confiturier françois* itself, are ample proof of popular enthusiasm for sugar and all its works.

Among the fruits there is a very good sampling in La Varenne: apples, cherries, plums, apricots, peaches, pears, quince, currants, strawberries, raspberries, grapes. Several of the tree fruits in particular, apples, plums, peaches and pears, are remarkably differentiated by variety. French orchard growers have developed different varieties, and French cooks can now distinguish the various merits of each variety clearly enough to specify the use of one or the other for their dishes.

As far as frequency of use goes, the exceptional fruits are those of the citrus family, oranges and lemons. The liking for *ragoust* again goes far to explain how often recipes call for the peel, candied or not, of these two fruits; for La Varenne the word "zest" says it all. Orange and lemon

---

[107] The use that the *Confiturier françois* makes of herb bouquets is different: its bunches of fennel (in Recipes VIII,1 and XIV,3) are literally just that, several sprigs of fennel for blanching and tied by their stem for candying.

juice further flavoured many dishes, and the fruit itself was prepared in a broad variety of ways.

Missing among the fruits are the "exotic" figs and dates (except for a single instance in the *Pastissier françois*) that medieval cooks seems to have been happy to incorporate into a good number of their common dishes — and seem to have been able to obtain. A similar gastonomic disinterest seems to have banished peaches, apricots and pears from La Varenne's prepared dishes, though a wide variety of fruits is quite naturally found in *The French Confectioner*. The relatively brief season of many fruits greatly restricts their usefulness. Unless they are preserved by drying (as raisins) or candying (as nuts), they will not be available in a kitchen most of the year.

A word has to to be said about flowers. Although flowers constitute much of the substance of the *Confiturier* and of the appended material in the *Cuisinier*, roses, violets, jasmine, lilies, marigolds, pinks, to say nothing of orange blossoms, enter by one means or another into these dishes. We may be tempted to think that such an extensive use of flowers makes this a natural cookery. It would be safer to say that La Varenne and other professional cooks of the day took their flavours and colours where they could find them both cheaply and in the most profusion.

And finally, the two "other" flavouring agents, amber and musk, linked together here as so often in La Varenne's text itself. An imported Italian influence, they are new to French cooking, and both seem quickly to have assumed a status as refined, even noble ingredients.[108] In a good number of his recipes it seems that the cook may choose one or the other indifferently; either will satisfy the notion of a satisfactory flavouring. There are in fact other flavours in La Varenne, but these two alone are common enough to have verbs made just for them: *ambrer* and *musquer*.

– Liquids

Wine, vinegar and verjuice remain as greatly in use in the mid-seventeenth-century French kitchen as in the past. There is now, however, little

---

[108] Sabban and Serventi term amber and musk the *aromates exotiques de luxe* of seventeenth-century Italian and French gastronomy: *La Gastronomie au Grand Siècle*, p. 55. The Manoscritto Lucano makes use of one or the other in ten recipes; see Recipes 60 and 68 where they flavour a dish in combination. Both are current in Scappi's work in the previous century.

interest in must — that is, fresh grape juice. Of the wines we find a somewhat more specific designation regarding their origins: besides red and white, the normal kitchen of La Varenne's day should have on hand a sweet wine (of some sort), a full-bodied wine, claret wine, blanquette, malmsey wine, Scipion wine and Spanish wine (again presumably, of some sort). On rare occasions it should also have access to distilled wine, known as wine spirits, as a cooking ingredient.

Fresh milk is much used. The only sort explicitly named by La Varenne is cow's milk. Shunned by earlier French cooks because it was apt to sour quickly, animal milk seems to be available from farms close enough to the kitchens of the well-to-do not to present that problem. On a large estate a cook was not obliged to accept yesterday's milk, or the watered variety too often peddled by itinerant milk sellers. It was, of course, a whole milk, rich in butterfat and suitable (in *The French Pastry Chef*) for making the "cream" (*cresme de pastissier*) that with the addition of eggs entered into quite a few of the tourtes and other pasties of the time. Almond milk, the liquid staple in French cookery up to only a century before, is now relegated to quite incidental use in La Varenne. The particular taste with which almond milk imbued a very great proportion of earlier cookery has definitely been lost.

Fruit juices and the so-called "savoury waters" lend this newer cookery their own flavours. Primary among them is orange juice and orange-blossom water; the kitchen must have stocked large quantities of both. The cook could draw freely on these and other juices and waters as ingredients in his broths or in garnishes.

Though a number of fruits and flowers are used for these taste delights, rosewater is perhaps noteworthy. In the *French Pastry Chef* it is used an impressive fifty times. A potent distillate, rosewater was able to give a dish a highly appreciated flavour with merely a drop or two: *une goutte d'eau rose, quelques gouttes d'eau rose, plein une cuillier d'argent d'eau rose*. Rosewater was not a new taste sensation in the seventeenth century; it had been produced by the alembics of Arabic physicians and medieval European alchemists along with a great array of other "spirits" that distilled the essence of common substances. La Varenne's patron and the class for which La Varenne's colleagues worked much enjoyed the gastronomic pleasures that rosewater brought to their tables, and particularly to the meat pies that were served up there in profusion. A few, very few, other foodstuffs were more recent "discoveries" and were only just being acclaimed in seventeenth-century France as contributing to delectable dishes.

Three beverages — chocolate (sweetened), coffee and tea — became known and consumed in France in the latter half of the seventeenth century, but none of them appears in La Varenne. That does not indicate that they were not drunk in the Uxelles household, but merely that they were not handled in La Varenne's kitchen as ingredients in prepared dishes.

(c) Other observations

As with the utensils of which La Varenne makes use in his kitchen, he never ceases to harp upon the need to ensure that all of the foodstuffs entering into a dish be properly prepared and, especially, clean. He never takes it for granted that a cook will remove all traces of dirt from rice, parsley, flour, carrots, sorrel and other greens, spinach, beetroot, prunes, mushrooms, cockscombs, oysters, even the most commonplace "tidbits"; or that a mutton bone or a chunk of musk be throughly clean.[109] He is quite explicit in his directions in this regard. The verb *nettoyer* is one of the most frequently used in the *French Cook*.

– Cookery techniques

Randle Cotgrave compiled his *Dictionarie of the French and English Tongues* in 1611. Because of Cotgrave's thoroughly competent study of the two vocabularies and bodies of locutions, his work remains one of the most useful guides to the development of French that we have today. Significantly a good number of terms used by La Varenne and his colleagues in the 1650s were not in common enough use at the beginning of the century to have been picked up by Cotgrave. Such terms include, for example: *abbatis, passer* (in either the sense "to sauté" or "to strain": see below)

---

[109] For instance: ... *du persil bien net & bien sec, estant le riz bien lavé & bien net, farine nette, estant bien nette & egoutée l'oseille, oseille, buglose, bouroche, chicorée ou laictues, poirée estant bien nettes, bettes-raves estant bien nettes, lavez bien les pruneaux, des champignons bien nets, vous aurés bien nettoyé vos huistres, vos beatilles bien nettes, que le bout du manche soit net, soignés à bien nettoyer le musc.*

caramelle, ragoust, barder, biscuit de gamby, prasline, sorbet, abaisse.
La Varenne worked at a time when the French members of his profession
were experimenting and inventing, introducing new techniques and refining or changing others as they developed new dishes. Such inventiveness
or creativity is of course always to be found to some degree in a field like
professional cookery, although in the medieval and Renaissance periods
it was to be found more in Italian kitchens than in French ones. In the
seventeenth century, however, the rate of creation, the instances of novelty
in French cuisine, seem suddenly to increase. Given the Italian influence
at court it is not surprising that a number of the new methods and new
dishes seem to have come directly from Italy or to have been inspired by
Italian practice: *bisque, daube* (an *adobbo* is an Italian braising sauce that
functioned much in the way of La Varenne's *ragoût*),[110] *sorbet, caramel*
and *caramelle, macaron, macaroni, massepain* [marzipan], *populo, rosoli*
and *syrop.*[111] La Varenne's *soupresse* (Recipe XVI,72) is nothing more
or less than the product of a process that was very common in Scappi's
kitchen. La Varenne's *fricassée* (as in Recipe V,46) can be traced back to
Scappi's *fricassea*, but is unknown in early French cooking.

Of the French recipe books from just before Scappi's time perhaps
the most original and most interesting is that of Lancelot de Casteau, a

---

[110] The word *daube* is, in fact, a neologism in French, based upon the Italian preparation
which was very common in Bartolomeo Scappi's practice three or four generations
before La Varenne.

[111] Among La Varenne's recipes the number of dish names that are related geograph-
icallly to Italy is noteworthy as well: Italian Platter Pie, Milanese Eggs, Milanese
Dragées, Milanese Cake, Genoese Paste, Savoy Biscuit, Piedmontese Biscuit, along
with the whole category of "Italian Waters" (Conf IV). Although the fragrance of
frangipane was not originally in culinary use in Italy, it was certainly an Italian "invention" and made its way out of Italy to become celebrated throughout Europe. In
earlier French cookery a number of French dish names incorporated an attribution to
Lombard, Parmesan and Pisan sources: see Jean-Louis Flandrin, "Internationalisme,
nationalisme et régionalisme dans la cuisine des XIVe et XVe siècles," *Manger et
boire au moyen âge*, 2 vols. (Paris: Les Belles Lettres, 1984); II, 89–90. Claudio
Benporat attributes a Italian culinary influence upon French habits not only to the
Italian queens (and attendant aristocrats) at the French royal court in the second
half of the sixteenth century, but to French tourists, military expeditions, merchants,
importers, artists and pilgrims, all of whom experienced Italian food and courtly
elegance in Italy during that century. See his "Evoluzione della cucina italiana alla
fine del '500," *Appunti di Gastronomia*, 33 (2001), 35–43.

professional cook writing in Liège in about 1585. In a preamble he declares a quite un-French concern: his book, *Ouverture de cuisine* (Liège: Leonard Streel, 1604),[112] was designed to help "Ladies" who, in the matter of cookery, are more needful of such professional help than cooks. The *cuisinier* was certainly a *cuisinière* in only moderately wealthy houses.[113] He may, of course, have been hoping to be read by the mistresses of affluent households, the "Ladies" who would direct the steward of their house on the foods to be prepared. Like Bartolomeo Scappi, however, Lancelot de Casteau worked for various high-ranking prelates — several bishops, an archbishop, a cardinal; undoubtedly he was on occasion directly exposed to an Italian culinary influence and, with his *capilotade, cervelade, maquaron, marsepain, mortadelle, neige* and *saulsisse de Bologne*, and his braising and stewing, he introduced Italian cookery to French-speaking cooks and "Ladies".

These three works, the *French Cook, Pastry Chef* and *Confectioner*, embodied the repertoire of professional chefs and kitchen stewards, both of whom were vitally concerned with proper, efficient procedures with regard to the activities that fell within their purview. For us moderns some interest may lie in observing on the one hand to what degree the recipes are didactic — that is, how much they appear to wish to expand the abilities of a competent cook with novel preparations, techniques or procedures — or on the other to what degree these recipes are assumed already to be more or less within the basic experience of the reader. What hints do the books offer to the cook, the pastry chef and the confectioner to help them do good and honourable work?

No help or advice that one professional cook could offer another at this time could overcome the difficulty of specifying a correct degree of cooking heat or the time necessary for an operation.[114] Contemporaries must have been resigned to writing, and reading, "hotter than ... ," "only moderately warm, the same as for cooking [some common foodstuff or

---

[112] Ed. Herman Liebaers, Léo Moulin and Jacques Kother, in facsimile and modern French translation, Antwerp/Brussels (De Schutter), 1983.

[113] In 1692 for a *manoir* a list of the "standard" servants whose duties and stipends Audiger outlines (*La maison reglée*, 1692) includes only a female cook and not a male.

[114] See Appendix 5 e) and f).

preparation]." Instructions about heat could only be descriptive. The trammel and the fire basket, placing a food in front of the fire, on the live coals or in a warming oven certainly helped determine how rapidly the food cooked. The chafing dish in particular answered a need for finer control over heat. In the same way the length of cooking time could be only approximate: a cook could depend upon an hour glass to measure half an hour or a quarter of an hour but for anything less, such as half of a quarter of an hour (eight minutes in this translation), he would have to resort either to estimating the proportion of sand that had flowed or (as in olden days) the time required to say a certain number of *Pater noster*s or to walk around a field of a given size. Until the advent of accurate timepieces and a source of heat that could be regulated objectively the cook could, after all was written and read, depend only upon his own expertise.

One feature of these operations is the reliance upon pre-prepared ingredients. There are, of course, the spices, pre-ground and neatly available in their little leather bags or in a set of tiny drawers. Certain staples, too, that will be in high demand when the various dishes of a meal are being hastily put together, such common ingredients as the *gaudivaux*, the *andouillettes* and the *beatilles*, are ready-made and perhaps sitting in one of the pine boxes in the kitchen's cellar. Also in that cellar are all the preserved vegetables and fruits that had come fresh from the kitchen garden or orchard several months before and been preserved for future use. The salting vat had likewise been put to use, normally in the fall, so that choice cuts from freshly slaughtered animals could be available on the master's table throughout the year. Several of the chapters in *The French Cook* are devoted to aspects of just that sort of planning for the future: putting down a Mayence Ham, thickeners to keep on hand, various stocks to make up ahead of time, roots and herbs and how to put them away, things to salt for keeping, clarifying butter, prepared colourants, prepared bouillons in Lent.

When the cook is actually at work on a dish, a certain culinary sagacity, garnered from long years of practical experience and now shared, can be of help to him. For instance, before larding a meat for roasting, La Varenne advises, it should be blanched very carefully: just the right amount will be enough to hold the lardoons; too much will toughen the surface of the meat and make insertion of the lardoons too difficult.

Incidental advice of a general nature is occasionally inserted between chapters: saffron is useless for gilding pastry in Lent — instead use ground pike eggs or melted butter. When the advice applies to work on a particular genre of dish, the author groups this generic instruction in paragraphs at the head of a chapter, preambles, as it were, that should make the elaboration of the individual recipes of that chapter a little easier and more masterly. His aim throughout continues to be what we might call culinary efficiency through systematic organization in the kitchen.

Certain processes or sequences of procedures are regular in this cookery. Very often an ingredient, particularly meats and fish, is either roasted (briefly) or fried or sautéed preliminary to being further cooked in a distinctly flavoured sauce. La Varenne's intention is, as it has been for every professional cook since time immemorial, to retain as much of the natural flavour and "juice" of the foodstuff as possible.

The whole matter of such initial, preparatory treatment given a foodstuff is interesting. Very often this preparing involves what La Varenne calls, literally, a "blanching". His word for the operation is *blanchir* — unfortunately, because this verb has several senses not only in contemporary French but in La Varenne's own usage of it. There is in the first instance the action of literally making a foodstuff clean or "white": you can blanch meats, fish, or vegetables, for example. It can be done in hot or cold water; it can be done dry, over the fire, particularly where meats are being prepared for a meal's second or roast course.[115] In a few instances La Varenne states that this blanching works to plump a foodstuff.[116] In others, the blanching being carried out attentively, it has to do with creating an appropriate surface consistency.[117] Such a prelim-

---

[115] This last sort of blanching is seen specifically in Chapter VI of *The French Cook*. See Appendix 3 for an index to the various methods of blanching.

[116] Again, see Appendix 3, to plump.

[117] In Recipe VI,46, for instance, La Varenne advises that a doe fawn should be blanched over a flame *pour le picquer, en sorte qu'il ne soit trop blanchi, d'autant que cela vous causeroit trop de peine à larder.*

The word *blanchir* has other meanings, as well, ones that seem somewhat removed from the usual sense, "to blanch," "to plump" or "to toughen". See *The French Cook*, Confections,5–9, where sugar syrup is stirred with a wooden spatula; *ibidem*,14, 16, where chestnuts and a variety of flowers are "blanched" or confected (*cf.* Chapter VIII of the *Confiturier françois: La maniere de blanchir les fruicts & les fleurs*); as well as Appendix 3, to glaze.

inary treatment of a great many foodstuffs points, if nowhere else, to his concern that a cook's basic ingredients be in the best possible condition before undergoing the subsequent steps in the preparation of a dish.

A second, relatively common verb in these texts whose sense on rare occasions is ambiguous is *passer*. In the field of cookery the traditional, limited sense of the word had to do with the *passeoire* or sieve: for cooks *passer* meant to put a food through a sieve, strainer or filter: "to strain." That sense is still a possibility for La Varenne. However, the verb also became usual in the phrase *passer par la poësle*, "to put in and out of the (frying) pan," in other words to fry briefly or sauté. Because so many of La Varenne's recipes involve this sautéing of at least some of their ingredients at some stage in the elaboration of a dish, *passer* often stands alone, merely implying *par la poësle* by the context.[118] From the way written recipes can in many cases leave the sense of these verbs *blanchir* and *passer* as only implicit we may infer a couple of conclusions: the actions denoted by each verb are quite common, even habitual, in the mid-seventeenth-century French kitchen; the actions depend upon a context that would be most clearly appreciated by an experienced cook, for La Varenne a fellow member of the professional fraternity. Blanching, plumping, searing and glazing, straining and sautéing were fundamental steps in the preparation of a good number of common dishes at this time.

Steeping and marinating are frequent intermediate actions in the preparation of a dish.[119] Very often, too, the final step in a preparation before the actual dishing out is to set a foodstuff to simmer in a savoury liquid. We may assume that the intention behind this cooking sequence is first to conserve and then to heighten the foodstuff's taste while it is being cooked. Such a multi-phased preparation is common with meats whatever the genre of dish that is being prepared.

Cooking *à l'estouffée* or between two dishes fulfilled the same function, retaining the natural flavourful juices of the foodstuff and in effect making them do the actual cooking.

---

[118] For occurences of these two uses of the verb *passer*, see Appendices 3 ("to fry," "to strain") and 4 ("colander," "filter," "napkin"). Furthermore La Varenne will also rather nonchalantly write *passer* in directing that an ingredient merely be put *into* a container or a mixture.

[119] See Appendix 3 for these verbs and others having to do with actions involved in preparing food in the three texts.

Closely related to that procedure is that of "stewing" in a "stove" or *estuve*. Although in 1611 Cotgrave defined the process of cooking a food *à l'estuvée* or *en estuvée* as "soaked, bathed, stued, washed in warme liquor." By La Varenne's day, in culinary use the sense of the phrase or the verb *estuver* was that understood by cooks today: to simmer in a closed vessel. For this sort of cooking a respectable kitchen had to have a so-called stove, an *estuve*, a metallic container that sat on hot coals or adjacent to a baking oven.[120] In the same way it was further customary for La Varenne to cook pears, and presumably other relatively hard fruits, under the convex metal or earthenware utensil — known as a cooking bell — which, heaped judiciously with coals, served to stew a small quantity of food in its own juices.

Whenever a foodstuff is boiled in water the water becomes bouillon. As had been the case in cookery as far back into the Middle Ages as documents exist, much of this bouillon is not discarded; kept on hand in the kitchen it is subsequently put to an important use. In the Middle Ages the bouillon is almost without exception specified to be beef bouillon — in large measure because beef, being deemed by physicians to be a "dry" meat, was uniformly boiled and rarely if ever roasted. That is not the case for La Varenne. In *The French Cook* the varieties of bouillon that are used in pottages, sauces and other compositions where some amount of a tasty liquid is required are numerous. There are, of course, the bouillons produced by whatever meat is being boiled — the bouillon in which goslings have been boiled, for example.[121] As a basic ingredient in conscientiously prepared dishes Chapter II of *The French Cook* thoughtfully provides a recipe for a Bouillon to Enrich any Pot whether for Pottages, Entrées or Entremets; this bouillon is itself much enriched with various condiments. In the present three books an "ordinary" bouillon whose source is basically a meat broth is called simply *bouillon*.

---

[120] In Cook XVI,50 for *Anguille à l'estuvée* see the phrase *la mettés en façon d'estuvée*; and "stewed foods," "to stew" and "stove" in Appendices 2, 3 and 4 respectively.

[121] *The French Cook*, III,23. Interestingly this particular recipe begins with "goslings or anything else you may like"; presumably the bouillon of whatever meat or fowl was being cooked would be usable later in the recipe. In La Varenne's day possible meat bouillons included a relative novelty in French cookery, pork bouillon. Conversely to the treatment for beef, pork was generally roasted in medieval and Renaissance France. The cheaper if less healthy procedure was to boil pork.

Among bouillons of other, specified origins, we find that most favoured of medieval cooking liquids, formerly called almond milk but now
termed almond bouillon and sometimes white broth.[122] It commonly afforded an alternative to a meat broth on lean days. For lean-day duty in La
Varenne we can now also use a fish bouillon. A so-called herb bouillon is
apparently assumed to be available to any cook as well.[123] A bouillon of
some sort was considered important if not vital in this cookery. A major
function of it was to enhance a dish's flavour, and for this a cook had a
good range of choice.

The use of meat juices is also common. The moisture that is exuded
by any cooking substance is analogous to the liquid that distills at the
output of an alembic. Both have been purified or refined, both contain
the very essence of the original substance. Great nutritional and culinary
value is attached to these juices and many dishes benefit from them as
ingredients.

In former days to mix two or more ingredients together was conceived
in a real sense to be a mystical undertaking. The cook was practising
chemistry by altering the physical properties of each ingredient and, consequently, the effect of the final dish upon the person who digested it.
The verb "to temper" is still found in these seventeenth-century recipes,
but only very rarely. It has been replaced by verbs such as *allayer* whose
original sense was much the same as *temperer* and *tremper*, "to allay the
strength of" but which now has come to mean merely "to mix together".
This modern cookery is concerned with food less for its physical, humoral
properties than for its gastronomic effect.

La Varenne makes use of several means to thicken his liquid and
semi-liquid preparations, whether sauces or pottages. He will keep a pot
on the fire until the heat alone or the boiling has reduced the fluidity of the
contents; a reduced sauce or seasoned bouillon is then said to be "short".[124]
Otherwise he can make use of any one of a number of possible thickeners,
preparing them in advance and adding them judiciously to a preparation

---

[122] *Bouillon blanc.* See a recipe for Lenten Almond Bouillon in *The French Cook*,
XXIV,4.

[123] This sort of bouillon would come from the boiling of greens or one sort or another:
see *The French Cook*, XV,46 and XV,2, for instance.

[124] See, for instance, Recipe Cook V,36: *faites le cuire jusqu'à la sauce courte.*

at the point when it should begin to thicken: his Chapter X provides direction for making four standard *liaisons* of almonds, mushrooms, flour and truffles.[125] The third variety of these thickeners, that which depends on flour, is one of the most commonly used among the recipes in *The French Cook*. It is also a preference that, in its importance there, is novel in seventeenth-century French cookery. Furthermore, La Varenne's dependence on that particular thickener distinguishes his practice from that of his English contemporaries and relates it to earlier Italian practice. He often refers to the liaison merely as "fried flour".[126] This is by no means a novel thickener in the seventeenth century; from Antiquity flour had been treated to produce a dry starch which was added to a liquid mixture in order to bind it. What is unusual now is the "sautéing" of flour in lard, which procedure makes a russet-coloured thickener. While La Varenne never uses the noun *roux* to identify this sort of thickener generically, he does identify the proper colour to which the flour should be "fried" as *rousse*;[127] and by the verb *roussir* he directs the cook on the degree of frying necessary to make the flour an effective thickener.[128] Flour, alone and apparently uncooked, can be added to a liquid mixture to thicken it.[129] Though less frequently than flour, the common medieval thickener

---

[125] Chapter X, *Maniere de faire les liaisons à conserver, pour n'avoir la peine de les faire à tous momens que vous en aurez affaire.*

[126] *farine frite* or *farine cuite*, for instance in Cook VIII,102; XXI,28; XXV,4, 20; V,42. Later, Pierre de Lune's variety of what he too calls *farine frite* differs somewhat from La Varenne's: "Put melted, browned lard into a terrine; when it is very hot put in some flour and stir it with a silver spoon. When the flour is browned and cooked, add bouillon to it and season it with a bundle of seasoning, a bit of lemon . . . , salt and a part-slice of roast beef. You can use this mixture for brown pottages, *ragoûts*, entrées, entremets, sauces and other things"*Le Cuisinier*, ed. cit., 242). See note 107, above, for the contents of the "seasoning bundle" introduced into Pierre de Lune's starch. Very useful in establishing distinctive procedures in this regard between English cookery and La Varenne's is Paula Marcoux's "The Thickening Plot: Notable Liaisons between French and English Cookbooks," *Petits Propos Culinaires*, 60 (December 1998), 8–20.

[127] As for instance in Cook XXV,40. Properly this is not "red" (*rouge*, a carmine colour to which La Varenne refers elsewhere, but "russet", a brownish red.

[128] As for instance in Cook V,1. Today we would say "to brown". In Cook III,16, *Alloüettes au roux* the word *roux* describes the procedure followed in sautéing the fowl and not any sauce prepared for them.

[129] Cook III,45.

of grated breadcrust or breadcrumbs is still seen in these recipes.[130]

Apart from these four standard thickeners several other sorts are serviceable. A mixture of eggs (sometimes specifically egg yolks) and verjuice recurs in many recipes.[131] Eggs are mixed with flour;[132] sometimes eggs or egg yolks are used alone to bind a preparation.[133] A "turnip thickener" is mentioned.[134] A short sauce made of pork bouillon will thicken to the point of jelling as it cools and can be used later in this state with the cold left-over meat.[135]

In former days a cook would deal with a wide range of colours in his dishes and know all the ways to produce blues and greens, yellows, reds and browns. Many dishes were actually named by the colours that the finished dish had to have. The Green Sauce still exists in the seventeenth century, as does a White Sauce (of varied composition); a sort of custard called a *nulle* can be prepared in either a green or an amber version; there are recipes for a White Fennel, a Red Fennel and a Blue Fennel; the cook can choose between a Red Jelly, a Yellow Jelly, a Green Jelly, a Violet Jelly and a Blue Jelly. He can make either a *Brochet au bleu* or a *Carpe au bleu*. The *French Confectioner* offers a chapter on "Prepared Colours" which turn out to be only two in number: green and cochineal. Colourants are still used by La Varenne, though in an largely inconsequential way. Appearance does indeed matter, but primarily in the decorative garnish: pastry is glazed or gilded; touches of colour are appended to a dish in the form of flower petals or bits of fruit or candied peel.

Flavour is perhaps *the* predominant preoccupation of La Varenne and his colleagues. Now in the mid-seventeenth century the operative French verbs are *parfumer* and, especially, *assaisonner*. Virtually every single dish must receive its "seasoning" before it is worthy to be served.

This is the primordial function of La Varenne's *ragoust*. A whole genre of preparation is qualified as having been dealt with in a *ragoust*

---

[130] For instance in Cook III,4, V,40 and VI,52.

[131] For instance in Cook V,70, 31 and 42.

[132] Cook XXIII,4.

[133] Cook V,45 and V,34 respectively.

[134] *liaison de navets*: Cook VI,51.

[135] Cook V,32: *la sauce courte y demeure en gelée pour servir froid.*

fashion. The phrases *mettre en ragoust, passer en ragoust, servir en ragoust, faire un ragoust* and *donner un ragoust à* direct the cook to do a dish in which a striking flavour is of foremost importance. Chapters V, VIII and XVI of *The French Cook* contain remarkably large numbers of recipes which depend upon that procedure: *Canards en ragoust, Langue de bœuf en ragoust, Queue de mouton en ragoust, Troufles en ragoust, Lamproye en ragoust.* Such dishes are peculiar in their sharp or pungent taste. The heightened flavour is not necessarily that of the principal foodstuff itself in any dish, but rather of the complex of secondary ingredients with which, combined in a liquid,[136] the foodstuff is either cooked or steeped, and occasionally also garnished. It is during this hot, moist contact with the *ragoust* that the flavour of the foodstuff is enhanced or modified and a new, gastronomically interesting flavour is created for a dish.

Etymologically the term *ragoust* derives from a capacity to enliven a food's taste. As Furetière defines the noun, of postverbal etymology, its verbal sense is never entirely lost: "Ragout. What is done to stir the appetite of those who have lost it, whether through ill health or satiety."[137] *Ragoust* is, simply, a culinary treatment. Looking at the recipes in *The French Cook* (among the three texts the procedure occurs only there) the reader should remember that the word "ragout" does not refer to a single treatment or even a specific preparation, but merely to any means of making a dish's flavour more appealing by the use of savoury minor ingredients. La Varenne has recourse to this sort of treatment very frequently.

The condiments that accomplish this sharpening of a dish's flavour are termed *ragousts* or *petits ragousts*.[138] They vary considerably, according

---

[136] Chapter XI of *The French Cook* helpfully offers "Mushroom, Beef and Mutton Stocks which can be used in many sauces and ragoust preparations."

[137] *Ragoust. Ce qui est fait pour donner de l'appetit à ceux qui l'ont perdu, soit par quelque indisposition, soit par la satieté. Op. cit.* A little more specifically I. D. G. glosses the word in 1653: "Ragoust. It is any sauce, or meat prepared with a haut goust, or quicke or sharp taste."

[138] In *The French Cook* see, for instance, Recipe VI,34: *faites un ragoust avec verjus, peu d'eau, peu de vinaigre, écorce d'orange, & chapelure de pain*; Recipe VIII,89: *mettez en ragoust avec vinaigre, verjus, sel, poivre, jus d'orange, & capres achees*; and Recipe XXIX,8: *petits ragousts, comme trouffles, artichaux, asperges, & champignons frits.* In Recipe XI,1 mushroom stock or juice is recommended as being useful in *toutes sortes de ragousts.*

to the foodstuff the *ragoust* is intended to enhance, although capers or citrus juices seem generally to be preferred.

Occasionally no specific ingredients are identified for a particular *ragoust*. For instance, in Recipe V,17, for Beef Tongue in Ragout, when the tongue is boiled, the cook is instructed, *l'assaisonnés de haut goust*, without any indication at all of the composition of this seasoning; later in the same recipe, when the tongue is roasted, the same mixture is used as a basting compound: *arrosés de son ragoust*; and, finally, the same tongue is simmered in the same mixture which is by then termed a *sauce*. Clearly, wherever La Varenne does not prescribe the condiments that will constitute a *ragoust*, he relies on the professional experience and judgement of the cook, specifying only that the resultant combination be suitable to tweak the taste buds of the diner and presumably to arouse his appetite.[139]

The prime consideration in doing a food *en ragoust* is that, when served to the table, the dish have some sort of strikingly distinct and gastronomically interesting flavour.

A further means that La Varenne uses to ensure that a dish has a remarkable flavour is in its serving garnish. Often the sharp tang of citrus fruits, their juice or flesh or even their zest, surrounds a preparation, accompanying it to the table. One of the most common serving garnishes for both pottages and pasties is a dash of the distillate called rosewater, perhaps along with a sprinkle of ground sugar, the cook's final tribute to the flavour of what he has created.

In La Varenne's day the repertoire of the professional cook was, of course, determined by his employer, often, we may suppose, through a kitchen clerk where there is one. A factor that has faded into the background — but that can still be glimpsed here and there in the *Cuisinier françois* — is the influence of the household or court physician. A modern reader no longer has the sense that all of the cook's inclinations and decisions are being vetted by a physician, forever leaning over his shoulder as he did in the late Middle Ages. Health concerns are rarely raised by La Varenne. He cooks to please.

---

[139] For the *Loustre de mer sur le gril* (which later printers change to *Loutre de mer rôtie en ragoust*), the cook is directed, *Faites-y une sauce telle que vous voudrez, pourveu qu'elle soit de haut goust*: "For it make whatever sauce you like provided [only] that it be highly flavourful." (Recipe XVIII,13).

– Dishes and meals

What does La Varenne make in his kitchen? Much, we have to assume, what his competent colleagues were cooking in their own kitchens. The *Cuisinier françois* is not presented as a revolutionary or innovative book; rather its expressed purpose is that it serve as a corrective, a manual to guide those who for one reason or another don't quite come up to the mark of what contemporary gastronomy or their employers could expect of them. Culinary tradition, assuming that contemporary practice in the kitchen represents a cumulative composite, is never questioned. While many dishes and a few genres of dish may have been only recently introduced in aristocratic France, we never have the feeling that La Varenne is *teaching* something that is novel. He is, as he graciously claims in his preface and elsewhere in his book, merely providing a memorandum of how to go about doing a good job on a repertoire that is fairly standard. For instance, the Sauce Robert prescribed several times by La Varenne was known back in the fourteenth century and remained unchanged in his kitchen.

Despite that — maybe the exception proves the rule here as with other matters — a few preparations do seem to have been original with La Varenne. There is (we suggest[140]) first of all the sauce dubbed "Dux-elles" or "d'Uxelles", not by La Varenne himself in his book but by later generations. Then there are his "Eggs La Varenne".[141] With those few preparations we seem to have exhausted the list of La Varenne's obvious culinary novelties.

The genres of dish that La Varenne uses are very much tied to the contemporary notion of the proper progression of a meal.[142] As we saw

---

[140] See the note to Recipe VIII,75.

[141] Recipe VIII,82.

[142] For an overview of the historical development of a French meal, and in particular the proper sequence of courses at the time of La Varenne, see Jean Louis Flandrin, *L'Ordre des mets* (Paris: Odile Jacob, 2002). Flandrin recognizes that, despite the existence of a conventional scheme, there were in practice at any time many variations in both the sequence and the understanding of the nature of each course. See also, by the same author, "Les heures des repas en France avant le XIXe siècle," in Maurice Aymard, Claude Gagnon, Françoise Sabban (eds.), *Le temps de manger: alimentation, emploi du temps et rythmes sociaux* (Paris: Editions de la Maison des Sciences de l'Homme; Institut National de la Recherche Agronomique, 1993), 197–226.

above (and will mention again in the next section), the respectable French diner could expect to sit to a regular succession of a pottage, an entrée, a second course and an entremets. In his *Cuisinier* La Varenne provides instruction on a broad choice of recipes falling into each of those courses.

For the seventeenth century the original sense of the word *potage* has shifted somewhat. Etymologically the genre of preparation was, broadly, anything cooked in a pot by boiling. It was essentially a sort of stew and was eaten out of a bowl either with a spoon or by sopping up with a piece of bread or toast. In La Varenne's time the pottage was still in part semi-liquid, was generally prepared at some stage in a pot, but was served in quite a different way. The cook used thick slices of bread, plain or toasted, usually steeped in a savoury fluid, as a base for the main boiled foodstuff. The bread held the sauce by which the foodstuff was flavoured. Secondary ingredients such as pea purée or rice or cheese might be used to lend interest. A garnish of some sort, rich and tangy, sweet or fairly plain, occasionally even a glazing over the top of the whole dish, usually completed the presentation.

The entrée was normally a boiled preparation of a meat, although the meat could be sautéed or fried. A number of additional, secondary ingredients always produced a savoury sauce of some sort which could serve either as a medium for cooking or simmering in a pot or pan, as well possibly as a serving sauce. Here the piquancy that was rather imprecisely known as *ragoust* (discussed above) was much used and lent a distinct character to the cookery of La Varenne's period. The number of recipes for entrée courses (for meat days, lean days, in Lent and on Good Friday) in the *Cuisinier françois* indicates that it was the course that was the most seriously dealt with by professional cooks. The name of this serving of boiled meat, the *entrée*, suggests a sort of prelude to a meal, or an appetizer. Literally it was that, back in the days when the solid substance of a good meal in a noble's great hall consisted primarily of good big joints of meat freshly removed from a massive spit or grill and brought dripping in their grease to the trencher's station at high table. As meals in the higher levels of society developed in complexity, boiled meats of various sorts functioned as initial servings. An open roasting fire is an inefficient way to cook meat; boiling is easier and simpler, and boiled meats lend themselves readily to further culinary treatments which will enhance both their palatability and their digestibility. By the middle of the seventeenth century, the *entrée* had come simply to designate the boiled-meat course. Thereafter the culinary sense of the word *entrée* drifted in French usage, and even more so and more erratically in the usage of English-speaking countries where the French word was used.

Traditionally the second course continued to call for roast meats in French and Italian meals. In the past cooks spoke merely of preparing "the roast".[143] In La Varenne we rarely find "a large joint of meat" among the recipes for this second course. More often than not the meat to be roasted is much smaller and more delicate: game birds, small game animals, select cuts from larger game animals and from domestic animals. A roast was omitted from the sequence of courses on Good Friday.

It was to accompany roast meats, fowl and fish that French cooks from the thirteenth to the sixteenth centuries most commonly used a range of standard prepared sauces. In La Varenne, however, those staples, spice-based for the most part,[144] have virtually disappeared. About all that remain are a pepper sauce (*poivrade*), a green sauce and the durable Sauce Robert. What instead we find is that the modern cook looks not for a spicy garnish but for a tangy one. He depends upon citrus juices, vinegar and verjuice, and in the case of pasties, upon rosewater. Chapter VII in *The French Cook* provides instructions for such garnishings, referring expressly to specific roast meats of the preceding chapter. Only two of the sauce preparations are "generic": the pepper sauce and the green sauce — but these, too, now contain additional ingredients that give them a modern tang. With regard to the relative paucity of garnishing sauces in this cookery, we should keep in mind that for La Varenne a garnish was usually only a final stage in instilling or enhancing a preparation's flavour. The so-called white sauce of egg yolks and verjuice is a case in

---

[143] In this regard Antoine Furetière's gloss on the word *rost* is instructive. He writes: "*Roast*. Meat roasted on a spit. People call it good ordinary fare (*un bon ordinaire*) when they are served roast meat at dinner and at supper. The roast is served in the middle of the meal. A 'big roast' is a large joint of meat, roasted. A 'little roast' is fowl, game, small [animals'] feet." (*Dictionaire universel*)

[144] The ginger *jance* and the cinnamon *cameline*, and a multitude of varieties of them, helped determine the gastronomic flavour of the Middle Ages. One herb-based sauce was common, the *sauce verte*, which used parsley rather than the wheat sprouts preferred by La Varenne.

point. It can be both a cooking sauce and a serving sauce.[145] But the
ubiquitous "tidbits" and the quenelles and all the means used to produce a
ragout for a dish involve a rich array of secondary ingredients ranging from
cockcombs to capers, from fungi to anchovies. La Varenne's "saucing"
was a continuous business.

The course that concluded most formal meals — except, again, on
Good Friday — was the so-called entremets.[146] Historically the entremets
was a preparation that was served *between* courses and intended to provide
a sort of break, with amusement. It could be a checkerboard of two-
coloured jelly, it could be a boar's head; some demand was put on the
cook's imagination. In Italy over time this *intermezzo* grew into live
entertainment, an actual dramatic representation with actors, a setting, a
script and music. By the seventeenth century in France the entremets was
in effect a grand finale to a meal, a sort of dish that would both impress
a diner and leave a pleasurable impression after the meal's end. It was in
a sense a precursor to modern dessert.[147]

The recipes that La Varenne provides for this course are the most
numerous of any chapter in the *Cuisinier françois*. Generally speaking,
the dishes of his entremets consist of delicacies or dainty preparations,
gourmet foods appealing to the epicure: delectable morsels of animal
organs or glands, truffles, cauliflower, jellies, egg dishes, and especially
deep-fried pasties, pies.

Two sorts of baked dishes dominate this cookery and enjoy an em-
inent position among the entremets: pies (*pastés* and *tartes*) and tourtes
(*tourtes*). Few of them were especially dainty or delicate as far as their
shells normally went. Generally the pie could be open-faced; the tourte
had a domed or conical upper crust, through a hole in which additional

---

[145] In fifteenth-century Italy sauces were identified as either *sapori* or *salse*, primarily
for cooking or for garnishing: see *The Neapolitan Recipe Collection*, ed. Scully
(Ann Arbor: University of Michigan Press, 2000), Recipes 100–111 and 112–120,
respectively.

[146] In earlier days the English had a roughly equivalent term for this culinary creation,
the *subtlety*; in Italian a literal translation gave *intermezzo*. The words in all three
languages help explain what the dish used to be long before La Varenne's day. For
want of an accurate word we have followed the usual English practice nowadays in
matters of cuisine and kept the French word.

[147] See below.

flavouring agents could be poured toward the end of the baking process and which at the table could either be left on or removed before the tourte itself was sliced; either could have a latticework upper crust. La Varenne lists several sorts of dough among which a cook can make a choice appropriate for any particular one of his baked goods,[148] but any pastry dough, whatever its mix, was intended basically only to *contain* a delicious preparation of some sort while it is baking. When, as was normal, the dough functioned in place of a pie plate, with the encasing shells between one-half and two inches thick on a normal "standing" pie or around a fish *en croûte*, it was not expected that the diner consume both crust and filling. Thinner pastry required banding with greased paper and string in order that a fluid filling not burst burst a shell in the oven. La Varenne's puff pastry alone might have interested a really hungry gourmand. Other pasties, such as the *tartelettes* and *feuillantines*, the *darioles* and *rattoons*, are wholly edible, both filling and shell. As a broad genre, pastry- and batter-enclosed dishes are not a novelty; their presence on the French dining table is merely an instance of modern survival of a long established traditional dish. The novelty they presented in La Varenne's day was threefold: a slightly broadened variety of such pasties, the possibility of a richer, thinner pastry, and the proposition that fillings need not be exclusively meat, fowl or fish. The bakery oven in La Varenne's kitchen must have been in constant use from long before dawn to after dusk. On the dining tables the opening of hot (and cold) pies and tourtes, flans, fritters, rissoles, talmouses, feuillantines and so forth must have been one of the joys of any meal prepared by his contemporaries.

Jellies have now largely replaced the older *galantine*. Where the medieval and Renaissance galantine set off pieces of meat or fish, acting both as a preservative of them and as a sort of serving embellishment, La Varenne's jelly tends to be related to fruits which give it a flavour and make it a dish in its own right.

Two remaining elements in a meal should be mentioned and they are a salad and a dessert. Neither had a firmly established existence. In two chapters (interestingly located between chapters on lean dishes and on

---

[148] At the end of Chapter XIV; a much more extensive survey of doughs is found in *The French Pastry Chef*, Chapters I and VI.

Lenten dishes) the matter of salads comes up, almost incidentally; Chapter XXII in particular deals with various possibilities using cucumbers, lettuce, asparagus, chicory or cabbage. Elsewhere La Varenne writes of doing a salmon in, as or with a salad;[149] and he describes a lemon salad and a pomegranate salad.[150] According to contemporary dictionaries the salade does have some role in a meal. Furetière glosses the word *salade* as "a sort of entremets served to the table to accompany the roast [*i.e.* the second course]. Normally it is composed of raw greens [*herbes cruës*], seasoned with salt, oil and vinegar. Occasionally eggs and sugar are put in. [There is] a salad of greens, lettuce, celery, chicory, tarragon and other minor greens, which is called a garnishing salad [*de la fourniture*]. Salads are also made with fruit, or greens pickled in vinegar, such as cucumbers, ribs of purslane, saxifrage, sometimes with anchovies, etc."[151] It may be that salads are not very prominent in *The French Cook* in part because of the very fact that generally they were indeed "raw" and did not need to concern a professional cook very much. Some salads that are "cooked" in one way or another do turn up in Chapter XXII. In any case a paragraph in the preface to *The French Confectioner* (see a note just above) suggests that the preparation of salads fell to some extent within the purview of the confectioner's office where that office existed in a large or wealthy household.

The term *dessert* does not appear in any of the three texts presented here. It is fairly clear, however, that the traditional entremets (examined above) had something of the role we now associate with the concluding course in most meals. The various pasties and sweets, the jellies, wafers

---

[149]   *Hure, ou entre-deux de saumon à la sallade*, XVI,82 (and perhaps XXVI,70).

[150]   Recipes Cook, VIII,34 and 92 respectively. These are to be served as entremets. Salades are not mentioned in *The French Pastry Chef*; in *The French Confectioner* they receive only a passing — and curiously obscure — reference in the preliminary *Advertissement au lecteur*: *Les Salades ausquelles je ne mets point d'assaisonnement, se servent avec le vinaigre & le sucre*: "Salads, on which I put no seasoning, are served with vinegar and sugar."

[151]   *Dictionnaire universel.* Richelet confirms Furetière's list of ingredients in a standard seventeenth-century salad: *Salade. Ce sont ordinairement de certaines herbes comme chicorée, laituë, pourpié* [purslane] *et quelques autres qu'on assaisonne dans un saladier avec du sel, du vinaigre & de l'huile d'olive & qu'on mange l'été pour se rafraichir.*

and (even) prunes of Chapters VIII, XIX, XXVIII in *The French Cook*, along with the apparently somewhat extraneous final chapter on Sundry Sorts of Dry and Moist Confections,[152] were likewise intended to create pleasure and a last sigh of satisfaction along a formal dining table. These confections were known as *préparations d'office*, meaning that they might be prepared by a master confectioner, who could be an independent artisan and tradesman supplying the public with candies, candied fruits, jams and sorbets along with a variety of so-called flavoured waters,[153] or a trained specialist who exercised the charge or "office" of confectioner within a wealthy household. That in La Varenne's day such dishes could be alternatives to delicatessen produce like cow's udders, flavoured pork tongue, eel saveloy, fried mushrooms or cream omelet may merely show that we have lost a few succulent means to bring a meal to a delightful conclusion.

The dining table was by that time a "permanent" piece of furniture, dismantled only on infrequent occasions. The newest fashion, Italian in origin, preferred a circular or oval table rather than the old rectangular board-and-trestle arrangement. Guests could interact socially with greater ease; what was ostentatiously set out in the centre space of the table, gold and silver plate as well as prepared food, could be displayed most effectively. For a meal the butler or wine steward (*sommelier*), whose responsibility besides all beverages included linens, covered the table with a fine white cloth which might be pleated lengthwise or crosswise. On it at every place setting he set out napkins, each a square metre or more in size; these he had pleated and then formed into a variety of delightful shapes such as are described at the end of *The French Confectioner*. After the requisite hand washing each diner opened the napkin to use as a towel; then it or a second napkin was spread out to protect clothing from inadvertent stains. Those folded napkins also covered the loaves of table bread that were set out in baskets. The dining cutlery was graciously provided by the house: at every place setting were now laid out a metal fork — which Louis XIV was known to despise — as well as the traditional knife and spoon. A personal drinking goblet was now also of metal, either pewter or silver; it was no longer customary to share it with a neighbour.

---

[152] Medieval meals typically ended with a serving of spiced candies known as *dragées*.

[153] See Chapter IV of *The French Confectioner*.

Prepared dishes were served to the table on silver or pewter platters or in bowls of the same material. All of the dishes of any course were set out simultaneously, and then cleared away all together. Quantities could be sufficient for several guests, who, in the absence of a servant appointed to slice a roast fowl or open a tourte and serve up a portion of it, would help themselves to whatever they wanted. In offering a formal meal a generous French host in the seventeenth century must have been concerned primarily that his guests be able to converse at ease, that they have ample choice among the appetizing foods set out for their enjoyment, and that the meal progress in a regular fashion. La Varenne and his contemporary colleagues working skillfully in the great kitchens of France had much of the responsibility for ensuring their masters' success at the dining table.

D. Bibliography

This Bibliography is concerned with works on food of three sorts: in part (i), seventeenth-century editions of works attributed to François Pierre de La Varenne; in part (ii), early translations of those works; in part (iii), French cookbooks published before the *Cuisinier françois*. For works bearing upon La Varenne, cookery or culinary language, see the various footnotes throughout, and the reference works listed at the beginning of the Appendices.

(i) Works attributed to La Varenne: early editions[154]

The arrangement of the following publications is chronological and extends only to the end of La Varenne's own century.

La Varenne, François Pierre de. *Le cuisinier françois ... par le sieur de La Varenne* .... Paris: Chez P. David, 1651. In-8°, 8+309 pp.

— *Le Cuisinier françois, enseignant la maniere de bien apprester, & assaisonner toutes sortes de viandes, grasses & maigres, legumes, Pastisseries, &c. Reveu, corrigé, & augmenté d'un Traitté de Confitures seiches & liquides, & autres delicatesses de bouche. Ensemble d'une Table Alphabetique des matieres qui sont traittées dans tout le Livre. Par le sieur de La Varenne, Escuyer de Cuisine de Monsieur le Marquis d'Uxelles.* Seconde edition. Paris: Chez Pierre David, au Palais, à l'entrée de la Gallerie des Prisonniers. 1652. In-8°, 14+370+29 pp.

— 3rd edn. Paris: Chez P. David, 1652. 8+354 pp.

— 2nd edn. Amsterdam: Chez R. Smith, 1653. 5+328 pp.

---

[154] As listed primarily in Georges Vicaire, *Bibliographie gastronomique* (Paris: Rougette, 1890; repr. Geneva: Slatkine, 1993); and in the *National Union Catalog*, the *Catalogue* of the British Museum (British Library), and the catalogues of various other libraries. As well, in their *Cuisinier françois* Jean-Louis Flandrin, Philip Hyman and Mary Hyman provide a very useful "Inventaire des livres de cuisine édités pour la 1re fois au XVIIe siècle" (pp. 100–105).

Le Pastissier françois, Où est enseigné la maniere de faire toute sorte de Pastisserie, tres-utile à toutes personnes. Ensemble Le Moyen d'aprester les œufs pour les jours maigres, & autres, en plus de soixante façons. A Paris: Chez Jean Gaillard, 1653.

Le Cuisinier françois. La Haye: Chez A. Vlacq, 1654. 12+297 pp.

— 5th edn. Paris: Chez Pierre David, 1654. In-8°, 8+354 pp., index.

Le Pastissier françois. Amsterdam: Louis & Daniel Elzevir, 1655.

Le Cuisinier françois. Derniere edition, augmentée et corrigée. La Haye: A. Vlacq, 1656. In-12°, 6+426 pp., index.

Le Pastissier françois. Paris: Jean Gaillard, 1657.

Le Cuisinier françois. Paris: P. David, 1658.

— Amsterdam: R. Smith, 1658.

— 8th edn. Paris: P. David, 1658.

— Paris: P. David, 1659.

— Paris: Veuve David, 1660.

Le Confiturier françois, où est enseigné la maniere de faire toute sorte de confitures, dragées, liqueurs, & breuvages agréables. Ensemble la maniere de plier le linge de table, & en faire toute sorte de figures. Paris: Chez I. Gaillard, 1650.[155]

Le Cuisinier françois. Troyes: N. Oudot, 1661.

Le Pastissier françois. Paris: Promé, 1662.

Le Cuisinier françois. Troyes: N. Oudot, 1662.

— Lyon: J. Canier, 1663.

Le Pastissier françois. Lyon: J. Canier, 1663.

Le Cuisinier françois. La Haye: A. Vlacq, 1664.

Le Confiturier françois. Troyes: Nicolas Oudot, 1664. [With a dedication signed by I.G.]

La Varenne, François Pierre de.[156] *Le Parfait confiturier, qui enseigne à bien faire toutes sortes de confitures tant seiches que liquides, de*

---

[155] The date, printed on the title page as M.DC.L, is considered suspicious by some bibliographers who believe that a final X was omitted. The work was published in a single volume together with *Le Cuisinier methodique où est enseigné la maniere d'apprester toute sorte de viandes, poissons, legumes, gelées, cresmes, salades, et autres curiositez.* Paris: Chez Iean Gaillard, 1660. The *National Union Catalog*, Volume 319, page 9 c., attributes both works to La Varenne.

[156] The licence to print, granted to the publisher on December 6, 1664, names *le sieur de La Varenne* as the author of this book. Printing was finished April 4, 1667.

compostes, de fruicts, de sallades, de Dragées, Breuvages delicieux et autres delicatesses de bouche. Paris: Jean Ribou, 1667. In-12°, 132 pp., table.

Le Cuisinier françois. Troyes: N. Oudot, 1668.

— Paris: Cie des imprimeurs et marchands libraires associés, 1670. In-12°, pièces limin., 358 pp.

— Rouen: P. Amiot, 1670.

— Lyon: J. Canier, 1675.

— Rouen: L. Machuel, 1676.

— Rouen: F. Vaultier, 1676.

— Lyon: J. Canier, 1680.[157]

La Varenne, François Pierre de. *Le Vray cuisinier françois ... Par le sieur de La Varenne .... Nouveau confiturier ....* Paris: J. Ribou, 1682. 2 parts in 1 vol. in-12°

— Rouen: R. L'Allement, 1683.

— Lyon: A. Molin, 1685.

— Troyes: [Febvre?], 1687; sold Paris: Raffle.

— Rouen: J. Dumesnil, 1689.

Le Pastissier françois, Où est enseigné la maniere de faire toute sorte de Pastisserie, tres-utile à toute sortes de personnes. Ensemble Le moyen d'apprester toute sorte d'œufs pour les jours maigres, & autres en plus de soixante façons. 4th edn. Troyes: [J. Febvre, 1690?]; vendu à Paris chez Antoine de Raffle.

Le Confiturier[158] *françois, Où est enseigné la maniere de faire toutes sortes de confitures, dragées, liqueurs, & breuvages agreables. Ensemble La Maniere de plier le Linge de Table, & en faire toutes sortes de figures.* Troyes: [J. Febvre, 1690?]; vendu à Paris chez Antoine de Raffle.

Le Cuisinier françois. Rouen: J.-B. Besongne, 1692.

---

[157] Though the title page of this work states expressly that this *Cuisinier* is ... *par le Sieur de la Varenne, Ecuyer de Cuisine de Monsieur le Marquis d'Uxelles* and *Unziéme* (*sic*) *Edition*, it has, in fact, only an incidental relationship here and there with La Varenne's text. The *Patissier françois* and *Confiturier françois* are reprints of those earlier books, the only variations being accidental errors in the type setting.

[158] The *General Catalogue of Printed Books* of the British Museum (now the British Library) shows this as *Confeturier*.

*Le Vray cuisinier françois … par le Sieur de La Varenne … augmenté
d'un nouveau Confiturier … du Maistre d'Hostel et du Grand Ecu-
yer-Tranchant.* Nouvelle édition. Amsterdam: Pierre Mortier, [*c.*
1696]. In-12°.[159]
Le Cuisinier françois. Bruxelles: G. de Bacher, 1697.
— Bruxelles: G. de Bacher, 1698.
— Troyes: J. Oudot, 1699.
— Lyon: F. Sarrazin, 1699.
— Rouen: J.-B. Besongne, 1700. In-12°, 408 pp.
— Rouen: Veuve J. Oursel, 1700.
— Amsterdam: P. Mortier, 1700.

(ii) Early translations

No sooner had the *Cuisinier françois* appeared from the press of the
Parisian printer Pierre David in 1651 than a printer in London set about
arranging for an English translation that he would publish. That translation, based on the original French edition, came out in the course of the
second year following, 1653. Given that a substantial volume could in
those days take as long as a whole year to set in type, and that every single
impression of each page was a separate operation by a muscular pressman
operating the large screw-and-lever mechanism, such a rapid appearance
of Charles Adams' *The French Cook* is surely significant. I. D. G. himself,
the translator, must have launched into the extensive labour of translating
the technically recondite text almost the very day that La Varenne's book
appeared in Pierre David's shop window.

It may not seem difficult today to understand why the English —
perhaps more properly, Londoners — were so interested in French gastronomy and culinary practice as to hurry to acquire a foreign publication
in that field. England had a solid tradition of interest in its own printed
cookbooks — an interest quite unknown in France. Why import such a
bizarre blip among foreign publications as the *Cuisinier françois*? In its
home market in Paris and in much of France it was only as the years passed
that the book was to prove itself not only a significant ground-breaker but
a best-seller.

---

[159] Listed in the 1995 catalogue of Daniel Morcrette, Luzarches.

The reasons for the book's English translation are probably at least threefold. Firstly, current French practice in virtually every field was of more than passing interest to the English, even still in the seventeenth century. The magnificent efforts of Louis XIV to spread the glory of France and confirm it as the arbiter of absolutely all questions of taste throughout that part of the world that was then worth influencing had a good and easy start across the Channel. The prefaces of La Varenne's book in both French and English make it clear already in the 1650s that a vast admiration of things French (and Parisian) was expected and due. Abroad it may well have been in part a matter of snobbery, much as publishers on both sides of the Channel insisted on dedications that tied their books as flatteringly as possible to the high and mighty of their land. The high and mighty were still very broadly related internationally and a little flattery could carry a book over several borders. But for a publisher of a cookbook one consideration remained primary: to call a cuisine "French" seems to have been enough to catch a potential buyer's attention.

Secondly, a negative observation, in the middle of the seventeenth century, roughly from 1640 to 1660, a momentary lapse in the persistent hostility that traditionally marked relations between France and England appears to have settled in. During the regency of Louis XIV[160] the prime minister, Cardinal Mazarin (Giulio Mazarini, 1602–1661), governed France sternly, only distracted by endemic civil rebellion and engaging in foreign conflicts with only Spain. Only in the 1660s, as Louis himself (and his war minister Louvois and generals Turenne and Condé) developed the French army into a formidable force, was England reminded that the other state, with five times its population and ten times its wealth, demanded more than admiration. In the 1650s there was no political reason for an English reader not to be curious about what was said to be the best in French cooking.

Thirdly, perhaps, we may speculate that an English translation of La Varenne was the first to appear from a foreign press simply because the English reader, unlike his counterparts in France and elsewhere, did have a relatively long tradition of browsing through cookery manuals. In England

---

[160] Louis was thirteen years old in 1651, the year in which the *Cuisinier françois* appeared.

the cookbook occupied a valued place on booksellers' shelves. Furthermore, the literate English were not only more open to such books as a legitimate genre among much more scientific and philosophical literature, but the nature of the readership itself was proportionately broader.[161] English "housewives" were used to being considered potential clients whom a cookbook writer, his printer and publisher could properly and profitably target. English ladies, gentle or bourgeois, might well be interested enough in such a work — if it were sufficiently novel, well patronized in its dedication and, of course, French — as to procure their own copy of it.

Moreover and in general, by the nature of its organization and its treatment the subject matter of the *Cuisinier françois* was accessible. No matter what the language into which the text may have been translated, its substance spoke clearly for itself. In London as in Paris a visitor to a bookshop or bookstall could see at a glance that La Varenne's work promised a rich fund of easily accessible, practical usefulness.

(a) English translations

– Of *Le Cuisinier françois*

> THE FRENCH COOK. Prescribing the way of making ready of all sorts of Meats, Fish and Flesh, with the proper Sauces, either to procure Appetite, or to advance the power of Digestion. Also the Preparation of all Herbs and Fruits, so as their naturall Crudities are by art opposed; with the whole skil of Pastry-work. Together with a Treatise of Conserves both dry and liquid, a la mode de France. With an Alphabeticall Table explaining the hard words, and other usefull Tables. Written in French by Monsieur De La Varenne, Clerk of the Kitchin to the Lord Marquesse of Uxelles, and now Englished by I. D. G. London, Printed for Charls [*sic*] Adams, 1653. 276 pp.[162]

---

[161] See above, section C.(i).

[162] The Cataloguer of this work for the *General Catalogue of Printed Books* of the British Museum (Volume 131, column 650) interprets the initials of the otherwise anonymous translator as J.D.G.

This publication was reprinted in 1654 (the publisher presumably being gratified by a strong and continuing demand), and again in 1673. On the title page of the first English edition its publisher is identified: "Printed for Charles Adams, and are to be sold at his shop, at the Sign of the Talbot neere St. Dunstans Church in Fleetstreet."

The translator of this particular version of the *Cuisinier*, the mysterious I.D.G., writes a little too fluently in English to have been a recent immigrant from France; his evident dependence upon the *Dictionarie* of Randle Cotgrave suggests that a number of French terms in La Varenne's text gave him a bit of difficulty. He is, though, fairly knowledgeable about current practices in cookery and has a good idea of what might be a reasonable translation of technical terms, even if, on occasion, he is quite wrong in his interpretation. In a three-page dedication of the book, a "most humble servant" of the patron, signing himself only Du Fresne, commends the author, La Varenne, and his culinary skills to his lord. With quaint pleasantry Du Fresne claims that he "taught him [the author] to speak English" — that is, that Du Fresne was himself the translator who put La Varenne's work into English.[163] He may indeed have been La Varenne's English translator, although it is difficult to reconcile the name Du Fresne with the initials I.D.G. on the title page.

Most of the basis for Du Fresne's commendation is, interestingly, nationalistic in substance. (The italics below are reproduced from the text.)

TO THE RIGHT HONOURABLE JOHN Earl of TANNET &c.
My very good Lord. Of all Cookes in the World, the French are esteem'd the best, and of all Cookes that ever *France* bred up, this may very well challenge the first place, as the neatest and compleatest that ever did attend the French Court and Armies. I have taught him to speak English, to the end that he may be able to wait in your Lordships Kitchin; and furnish your Table with severall Sauces of *haut goust*, & with dainty *ragousts*, and sweet meats, as yet hardly known in this Land. I hope your Honour

---

[163] At the least Du Fresne may be taking credit for arranging for or promoting the English translation. The identity of this Du Fresne cannot be certain. The most important Du Fresne of the seventeenth century was Charles Dufresne, better known as Sieur Du Cange, a classical scholar and historian, responsible for the most significant dictionary of late Latin before the end of the twentieth century.

wil forgive my boldnesse of begging your Lordships Patronage, in his behalf, entreating your Honour to consider, that having first set out his skill in *French*, under the protection of a *French* Marquess, he now as a stranger doth humbly crave to be sheltred under the lustre of your honourable name, that so with the more credit and confidence, he may impart his skill for the publique good, in teaching every body how to continue and prolong comfortably by a well relished diet, the sweet marriage of Soul and Body. Besides, my Lord, your former commands are indeed the first and chief cause of my presuming thus far, esteeming it to be a part of my duty, which will never be satisfied untill some better occasion doe furnish me with a more serious subject, whereby I may let all the world know, that all my ambition is to deserve the glorious title of - Your Lordships most humble Servant - Du Fresne.

At this point there follows a brief passage which is headed, "To the Reader," unsigned but presumably coming from the translator, I.D.G. The "noble Knight" mentioned at the beginning may well be the Du Fresne who had just inserted the dedication; "the master" is perhaps the publisher.

Courteous Reader,
I was desired by a noble Knight to English this Book; besides being solicited and intreated about the same, by many of my Friends, and persons of good quality, I have taken the pains to doe it, as punctually and exactly as the master could give me leave, endeavouring to make it intelligible for every body. As concerning some few words which are not Englished, they are words of things which are not in England, or some words of art, which you will finde explained in a Table set before the Book. I have had all the care possible to make it compleat and easie, to the end that it may be usefull, not onely for Noblemen and Gentlemen, but also for every private family, even to the Husband man or Labouring man, wheresoever the English tongue is, or may be used. If you doe accept of it for your own use, as kindly, as I doe give it heartily to the publick, I am fully satisfied for all my labours, wishing that you and I may long enjoy the comfortable refreshments prescribed therein. Farewell.

Three further bits of prefatory material precede the book's text proper. The first two of these were actually written by La Varenne himself and are found at the head of the French work: the "Epistle Dedicatory" (as the English version calls it) addressed to Louis Chaalon du Bled and signed "Francis Peter, (*alias*) La Varenne";[164] and the author's original *Avis au Lecteur*, which now begins with the salutation, "Friendly Reader". The final piece is the longest. It has the rubric "The French Stationer to the Reader" and is a faithful rendition of Pierre David's sales pitch to his potential French customer. Curiously it remains a paean not only to the practical utility of La Varenne's book but to all things French at that time.

> Courteous Reader;
> This Booke, the matter and the title whereof doe seeme new, be-cause the like was not as yet printed, will not be, as I thinck, unfruitfull for you. There hath been many Bookes, and which have been well accepted of, as the charitable Physician and oth-ers, for remedies and the healing of sicknesses with little cost, and without the use of Apothecaries. But this book which tends only to the preserving and the keeping of health in a true and constant course, in teaching how to correct the vitious qualities of

---

[164] The gracious style of this translation is worth reproducing: "For the High and Mighty Lord, Lewis Chaalon Du Bled, Counsellor of the King in both his Counsels of State and Privy Counsell, Knight of his Orders, Baron of Tenar, Marquesse of Uxelles, and of Cormartin, &c. My Lord, Although my condition doth not afford me a Heroick heart, it gives me nevertheless such a one, as not to be forgetfull of my duty. During a whole tenne years imployment in your house, I have found the secret how to make meates ready neatly and daintily. I dare say that I have exercised this profession with a great approbation of the Princes, of the Marshals of France, and of an infinite number of persons of quality, who did cherish your Table in Paris, and in the Armies, where you have forced Fortune to grant to your Virtue some Offices worthy of your courage. I think, that the publique ought to receive the profit of this experience of mine, to the end that it may owe unto you all the utilitie, which it will receive thereby. I have therefore set down in writing what I have so long practised in the honour of your service, and have made a small Book of it, bearing the title of the Clerk of your Kitchin. But, as all what it doth contain, is but a lesson, which the desire of pleasing you hath caused me to learne, I have thought that it ought to be honoured with your name, and that without sinning against my duty, I could not seek for it a mightier prop than yours: It is a token of the passion which I have alwaies had, and which I shall have all my life time for your service. Therefore, my Lord, use your accustomed generosity, doe not despise it, though it be unworthy of you. Consider that it is a treasure of the Sauces, the taste whereof did once please you; and, to conclude, that it is the Master-peece comming from the hands of him, who will bee all his life time, My Lord, Your most humble, most obedient, and most obliged Servant, Francis Peter, (*alias*) La Varenne."

meates by contrary and severall seasonings; the scope whereof, I
say, is only to afford unto man a solid nourishment, well dressed,
and conformable to his appetites, which are in many the rule of
their life, and of their (*en bon point*) looking well, ought, as I
think, to be of no lesse consideration, since that it is sweeter by
farre to make according to one's abilitie an honest and reasonable expense in sauces, and other delicacies of meates, for to
cause the life and health to subsist, then to spend vast summes
of money in drugs, medicinall hearbs, potions, and other troublesome remedies for the recovering of health. This hath perswaded
me, after many sollicitations of my friends, to let it see the light,
and to set it forth in this great City, which makes profit of all,
rejects nothing, and where what is not fit for one, is usefull for
another. It's [*sic*] author hath told you in his word of advise what
use and profit it may bring; And I dare boldly enhanse it, and
say, that it is not only usefull, but also necessarie, because that
he doth not onely set out the finest and the daintiest fashions of
making ready meates, pastrie works, and other things which are
served upon great mens tables, but he gives you also the precepts
of the most common and most ordinarie things, which are used
in the food of households, which doe onely make a regulated
and moderate expense, and in the making ready of which, many
doe amisse in the too much or too little; He doth teach you the
fashions of a thousand kinds of hearbs (and legumes) and other
victuals, which are found plentifully in the country, where the
most part are ignorant of the meanes of making them ready with
credit and contentment: and thus it is cleere, that with great reason I have done this good service to the publicke, not only for
daintinesse, but also for necessities sake: Considered also, that
France carrying it above all other Nations in the world in point of
civility, courtesie, and comeliness in every kind of conversation,
is not lesse esteemed, because of it's [*sic*] comely and daintie
fashion of feeding. And the City of *Paris* carrying it farre above
all the other Provinces, as the Metropolitan head City, and the
seat of our Kings, doubtless her inferiours will in this follow the
esteeme that she will make of it. And I hope, that since that I
doe give her the first fruits of it, she will accept of them kindly,
and others will imitate her: After which other Nations may very
well be stirred forward to conforme themselves to her, who as
she doth excell in all what belongeth to life, cannot be ignorant

of the meanes how to preserve it contented and peaceable, by the use of the things which doe maintaine it, and cause it to subsist. I may assure you that for my part I have had a most speciall care to set it in its luster, and to enrich a little its matter, which perhaps will seeme to some Criticks, to be less worthy of precepts; but the most judicious will judge otherwise, and will consider, that all the books both ancient and moderne, being for the most part for the nourishment of the spirit: There was a good reason, that the body, without the good disposition of which it cannot act, should have a share in it, & specially in a thing so necessary for its conservation. Enjoy it, Courteous Reader, whilest I will study how to put forth to sale something which will deserve your more elevated and more solid occupations.

So Pierre David's expectation that fine French gastronomy would eventually — almost inevitably — make its way abroad was indeed realized. *Le Cuisinier françois* became *The French Cook*.

– Of *Le Pastissier françois*

[The FRENCH Pastery-Cooke.[165]] The Perfect Cook,[166] being the most exact directions for the making all kind of Pastes, with the perfect way teaching how to Raise, Season, and make all sorts of Pies, Pasties, Tarts, and Florentines, &c. now practised by the most famous and expert Cooks, both French and English ... With fifty five ways of dressing of Eggs. By Mounsieur Marnettè. Printed at London for Nath. Brooks at the Angel in Cornhil [Sold at the Angell in Cornhill by N. Brooke], 1656.

This book appears not to have been reprinted.

The English text of the *Pastissier françois* is in places carelessly typeset and either inattentively or ignorantly proof-read. Mounsieur Marnette is not content merely to translate his source but is often inclined, even apparently eager, to insert his own recipes, experience and explanations.

---

[165] This title is printed on the left-hand page opposite the title page proper. It appears over the top of a full-page woodcut of a contemporary kitchen in which three men are working.

[166] The volume combines the French work with a much shorter one entitled *The Perfect English Cook*. The title chosen for the joint publication, *The Perfect Cook*, is a sort of claim to universality. The volume is catalogued as Vet A3 f.1782 in the Bodleian Library of Oxford University.

The dedication reads:

To the Right Honourable the Lady *Dethick*, Lady Mayoress of
the Noble, Ancient, and most Renowned City of *London*, and
the Right Worshipful Ladies, the Ladies *Tomson*, and *Frederick*,
the Wives of the Right Worshipful Sheriffs of the aforesaid City,
&c.

Honoured Ladies:

Having had the happiness to draw my first breath in this renowned City, though of Forreign Parents, and being turned young into
the wild and Military World, to become a Son of *Mars*, I was
forced to relye on *Esau*'s Blessing, and to content my self with
Alexanders Portion; but being of late returned again to this the
place of my Nativity, and permitted to endeavour an honourable
and honest subsistence, I have resigned my self to *Minerva*'s
milder tuition and protection.

In prosecution whereof, meeting with the ensuing Treatise,
originally written in my Predecessors Language, I have adven-
tured to make it speak English, and presumed to publish it under your Ladiships Patronage, the better to shelter it from such
Criticks of the Times, who savour no Viands but of their own
fancying and Cookery.

And although this work in itself may seem very improper to
be communicated to this Nation, where every *Matron*, and young
Damsel are so well vers'd in the Pastry Art, as that they may
out-vie the best Forreign Pastry Cooks in all the World besides,
yet this said Treatise containing nothing save *Out-landish* Cates
and Junkets (farre inferiour I must confess to ours) I doubt not
but will give that satisfaction unto your Ladiships, and unto all
other worthy Matrons, and ingenuous Damsels, as may encourage
my self, the Translator, to proceed to the Englishing of other
Treatises of the like nature, proper for the knowledge, and use of
so judicious personages as your selves.

A Second Motive which made me to adventure upon this peece
of Pastry, was, to testifie my gratitude to this my Mother City, by
preparing (for her Sons and Daughters pleasures and divertise-
ments at their spare hours) some Forreign Cates and Delicacies,
happily never as yet tasted within her walls.

Nor could I omit to dedicate them unto your selves (most
Honoured Ladies) who all three of you, may be justly termed to
bee the Mirrours of Knowledge and Excellency in these laudable

Professions, that thereby I might give a testimony to the whole World of my submission and obedience unto my Political Parents, your selves being such, in reference to those Honourable places of trust so deservingly conferred, and so worthily supplied by your Honoured second Selves, who as they are the Supporters of this flourishing Cities admirable Government, so will their renown, and yours (honoured Ladies) live to all eternity by theirs and yours Patronizing, and cherishing of Vertue and Learning.

In confidence that this my presumption may meet with a favourable construction, and a kind acceptation, I crave your pardon for this importunity, only requesting an additional Boon, That I may have leave to stile my self, Honoured Ladies,

Your most devoted humble observator:

This 17 of May, 1656 M. M.

As was the case with I. D. G.'s translation of the *French Cook*, the translator's dedication in the *French Pastery-Cook* is followed immediately by a translation of the author's or publisher's preface in the source edition: "The French Epistle to the Reader, Translated."

Courteous Reader:

Being informed that Forreigners and Strangers do give a favourable construction, and a kind admission unto several new Books, when they finde the Names of *French* Authours annexed unto their Titles, or Inscriptions, as the *French Gardner*, the *French Cooke*, and divers others, although they have several such like Editions extant in their own Languages, treating on the self same subjects; yet I was easily induced to beleeve they would the rather countenance and cherish such as should denote unto them some new Faculty, Art, or Science, which happily may not as yet have been made publick; wherefore I do presume to present unto them our *Pastissier Francois*, or French Pastry Cook, which may be said to bee one of the first (if not the only first) of the number of those which as yet have been extant.

Nor have I met with any Author as yet (in this our French Dominions) who hath penned the least instructions concerning this Art, or who hath deigned to offer them to the Publick; and the ill nature of our most famousest Pastry Cooks of the French Court, and of the City of *Paris* hath been hitherto so predominant, that notwithstanding this said Art is known to bee very profitable unto all such persons as are in health, and most requisite for such as are sick; yet they have endeavoured to smother it at least have hoorded it up in such a manner amongth themselves, as that there are many famous Cities and Provinces in France, may I dare say whole Countries in Europe, where hardly one sole person is to be found, who is learned in this Art, and who hath a capacity to put it in practise.

To remedy and prevent which default, the perusing and practising of this ensuing Treatise may in some measure be assisting unto you; and bee an effectual means, that hence forwards there will not be any City, Town, Burrough, Village, Hamlet, Castle, nor the least Gentlemans Country-house, or habitation, where the good Maidens may not on a sudden be able to give a most noble and delicious treatment unto their Kindred, Allies, and Friends, upon all occasions, and in all the several seasons of the year, as well to the sick, as to those which are in health, with a great deal of ease and pleasure to themselves, and a very inconsiderable charge or expence; all which they may perform in their several particular, and private habitations, though never so remote from any Cities, Towns, or Villages whatsoever.

Assuring you besides, that this Book doth not contain any composition or mixture which is not very easie to bee prepared, farre more pleasing to the palate, and not at all chargeable to the purse, since you are at liberty to imploy as much, or as little in the making & imbellishing of these Cates, and Junkets, as your means, the times, and your own occasions will permit you to bestow thereon. Thus promising my self your favourable acceptance of these my puny endeavours on so mean a subject, I shall commend you to the Almighties protection:

Farewell.

That preface is unsigned.

(b) Translations into other languages

As well as by English publishers, books attributed to La Varenne were taken up by printers in Germany and Italy. Presumably the works were considered to have a good enough potential for sales to warrant the expense of both a translation and a printing. Although the German version seems not to have been reprinted, the Italian *Cuoco francese* enjoyed a respectably long existence.

– Purportedly of *Le Cuisinier françois*

Il Cuoco francese ove è insegnato la maniera di condire ogni sorte di vivande e di fare ogni sorte di pasticcieri e di confette ... , Bologna: Longhi, [1670]; and subsequent editions in 1695, 1728, 1802, 1815.[167]

Il Cuoco Francese ove è insegnata La maniera di condire ogni sorte di Vivande, E fare ogni sorte di Pasticcierie, e di Confetti, Conforme le quattro Stagioni dell'anno. Per il Signor De La Varenne Cuoco Maggiore del Sig. Marchese d'Uxelles, Trasportato nuovamente dal Francese all'Italiana favella. All'Illustrissimo Signore Sig. e Padron Collendiss. Il Sig. Antonio Tiarini. Bologna: Giuseppe Antonio Davico Turrini, 1682; Bologna: Longhi, 1693; Venetia: Giuseppi Tramontin, M.DC.IVC [1596?]; Bologna: Longhi, after 1695; Venetia: Lorenzo Baseggio, 1703; Venezia: Giovanni de Paoli, 1715; etc.[168]

Der Frantzösische Koch. (Bound also with *Der Frantzösische Becker* and *Der Frantzösische Confitirer*). Tr. G. Greflinger, [Hamburg], 1665.[169]

Der Frantzösische Koch. (Bound also with *Der Frantzösische Becker* and *Der Frantzösische Küchen-Gärtner*). Hanover: T. H. Hauenstein, 1677.

– Of *Le Pastissier françois*

Der Frantzösische Becker. (Bound also with *Der Frantzösische Koch* and *Der Frantzösische Confitirer*). Tr. G. Greflinger, [Hamburg], 1665.

---

[167] In actual fact this is not La Varenne's work but the translation of a book whose compiler, Jacques Canier, in 1680 renamed it *Le Cuisinier françois ... par le Sieur de La Varenne* in order to profit by the master's name. See Philip and Mary Hyman, *The French Cook*, xii, n. 4.

[168] From Lord Westbury, *Handlist of Italian Cookery Books* (Florence: Olschki, 1963), 130–31. These are probably the same as the previous book, and its various editions, examined by P. and M. Hyman.

[169] This, too, in the context of La Varenne's great success in the 1650s and 1660s, is deceptive, as is the next "translation". The *Koch* is based on Nicolas de Bonnefons, *Les délices de la campagne* (Paris and Amsterdam: Jean Blaev, 1654).

Der Frantzösische Becker. (Bound also with *Der Frantzösische Koch* and *Der Frantzösische Küchen-Gärtner*). Hanover: T. H. Hauenstein, 1677.

– Of *Le Confiturier françois*

Der Frantzösische Confitirer, welcher handelt von der Manier, die Früchte in ihrer natürlichen Art zu erhalten. (Bound also with *Der Frantzösische Koch* and *Der Frantzösische Becker*). Tr. G. Greflinger, [Hamburg], 1665.

(iii) Earlier French cookbooks[170]

Works ultimately derived from the *Viandier* "of Taillevent", whether so called or not but whose titles generally attribute their origins to the celebrated fourteenth-century cook, are printed in at least twenty-three editions between roughly 1486 and 1615. Other books owe some part of their content to the *Viandier*, as well as to one another, and include the following:

Petit traicté. Paris: Pierre Sergent, n.d. [1536–38].

Livre de cuysine tres utille & prouffitable contenant en soy la maniere dhabiller toutes viandes. Avec la maniere de servir es bancquetz & festins. Paris: Pierre Sergent, [1539]; repr. [1540].

Livre fort excellent de Cuysine tres-utille & proffitable contenant en soy la maniere d'habiller toutes viandes. Avec la maniere de servir es Bancquetz & festins. Lyon: Olivier Arnoullet, 1542; repr. 1555. Small in-8°, 8 f.l., 72 f. Repr. Paris: Veuve Jehan Bonfons, n.d. [1566–1574].

La fleur de toute cuysine, contenant la maniere d'habiller toutes viandes tant chair que poisson ... . Paris: Pierre Sergent, n.d. [1543–47]. Paris: Alain Lotrian, 1543.

Le Grand Cuisinier de toute cuisine tres utille et prouffitable, contenant la maniere dhabiller toutes viandes tant chair que poisson, et de servir es banquetz et festes, avec un memoire pour faire un escriteau pour

---

[170] See in particular Philip Hymen & Mary Hyman, "Les livres de cusine et le commerce des recettes en France aux XVe et XVIe siècles," *Du manuscrit à la table*, ed. Carole Lambert (Montréal: Presses de l'Université de Montréal & Paris: Champion-Slatkine, 1992), pp. 59–68.

un banquet. Paris: Jehan Bonfons, n.d. [1543–68]; Rouen: Thomas Daré, [1620].

The same book, attributed to Pierre Pidoux and under the name *Fleur de toute cuysine, contenant la maniere d'habiller toutes viandes tant chair que poisson, et de servir es bancquetz et festes, aussi la maniere de faire un escripteau pour un bancquet.* Paris: N. Chrestien, 1548.

Michael Nostradamus [Michel de Nostre-Dame], *Le vray et parfaict embellissement de la face & conservation du corps en son entier ... & la seconde partie, contenant La façon et maniere de faire toutes confitures liquides, tant en succre, miel, qu'en vin cuit.* Anvers: Christophe Plantin, 1557.

Le bon cuysinier [ou] Fleur de toute cuysine. Paris: Guillaume de Nyverd, n.d. [1562–73].

Le livre de honneste volupté. Contenant la maniere d'habiller toutes sortes de viandes, tant Chair que Poisson & de servir en Bancquets & Fests. Avec un memoire pour faire Escripteau pour un Bancquet [ou] Fleur de toute cuysine. Lyon: Benoist Rigaud, 1567; Lyon: F. Durelle, 1571; n.p., 1575; Lyon: Benoist Rigaud, 1588, 1602, 1604.

Lancelot de Casteau, *Ouverture de cuisine* [written about 1585], Liège: Leonard Streel, 1604; ed. Herman Liebaers, Léo Moulin and Jacques Kother, in facsimile and modern French translation, Antwerp/Brussels (De Schutter), 1983.

Le grand cuysinier. Paris: Veuve Jehan Bonfons, [1568–73]; Paris: Nicolas Bonfons, 1576; Paris: Bonfons [?], 1580–1620; Douay: J. Bogard, 1583, 1600, 1606–26.

Nouveau et parfait Cuisinier françois. Rouen, 1692.

E. Principles of this Translation

A ny translation is necessarily a sort of adaptation. Though a translator may wish to remain wholly faithful to his original text, for which he develops a profound respect, inevitably his translated text becomes something other than the original text. This modification is only partly a matter of different languages and different ways of expressing the same thing. In some cases, such as this present translation, it is also a matter of different times, different conventions, different norms. If a text from an older time is to recover as much of its meaning as possible for a modern reader, then the translator must make it speak more or less directly to the experience of that reader, using an idiom and referring to circumstances that will have meaning for the reader and yet still remain true to the intent of the long-dead writer. Moreover, when the text bears upon the relatively narrow preserve of a particular historical trade or profession, then the translator who wishes his source text to continue to remain vital in its contribution to "civilisation" is obliged further to adapt the text to fit within the professional domain of the modern practitioner — to the extent that he, the translator, understands it.

The present translation does reproduce the content of the original texts as faithfully as possible. For the *Cuisinier*, of the many editions to choose from I have taken the second, assuming that La Varenne himself would have made emendations to the original publication, but wishing to avoid editions in which as the years passed it was increasingly probable that the author had no voice.

The ingredients and the kitchen hardware that the seventeenth-century chef made use of, his procedures, and above all the finished product that he served up, will be found reproduced here in modern English, with explanatory commentary where appropriate. Where as translator I have exercised some freedom is in the style in which the directions of the recipes are couched. Punctuation, for instance, in the original is often far from helpful; a modern scheme will often replace it here for the sole purpose of making the original idea as clear as possible. Square brackets — [ ]

— enclose words that have been inserted into the text, again solely to the end of clarifying its sense. For a similar reason certain French terms have been kept in the English text.[171]

A major problem is posed by the measurements used in the books. Before the French Revolution and its universal metric system, the units measuring weights and volumes varied widely across the kingdom, each province having inherited and evolved often quite different local usage. For some units of weight or volume there were even differences in value depending upon whether what was being measured was one thing or another.[172] The odd contradiction that survived even in the *Cuisinier*'s second edition may be due to the fact that La Varenne practised and wrote in lower Burgundy — where Savoyard influence was strong — but that his book was printed in Paris and was intended, in the first instance, primarily for the Parisian market. (That is one reason why I tend to prefer the Parisian measurements wherever a choice is to be made among various values for a given unit.) In any case translating measurements from

---

[171] For instance I retain the word "ragout" (*ragoût*, originally *ragoust*): an advantage in this particular case is that something of the vagueness of the original sense is kept. The 1653 English translator I. D. G. did the same, not attempting to find an English equivalent for the word but contenting himself with inserting a line apropos of it into his little glossary of "hard and strange words". Likewise the French word *tourtière* has been kept here. Normally one might safely translate this term as a "pie dish"; but in the history of French cuisine a *tarte* is not a *tourte*, and is never to be confused with the modern German *torte*, even though etymologies may overlap. The very shallow dish in which a *tourte* is baked may usefully be distinguished by keeping the original word.

[172] The "pound", for instance, could weigh 12 oz. or 16 oz. depending upon what was in the weigh scale. Cotgrave ties up the confusion neatly with his gloss on *chopine*: "A Chopine, or the Parisian half pint, almost as big as our whole one; at Saint Denis, and in divers other places around Paris, three of them make up only one pint." He does little better with the *livre*: The *livre* of Spicers, Grocers, and so forth contains only 12 ounces — whereas our grocers' pound contains 16. The merchants' *livre* contains in some places 14 ounces, in others 18 ounces, but in most places 16 ounces. Furetière, a late contemporary of La Varenne, handles the unit of weight this way (we translate): "*Livre*. A measure of the weight of bodies being weighed which varies according to the locale. The Avignon, Provence and Languedoc pound weighs 13 ounces; the Paris pound weighs 16 ounces; the medical pound weighs 12 ounces." Modern systems are of course themselves far from uniform: the North-American "cup" normally contains 8 oz. while the British version has 10 oz. It is the 8-oz. unit, a *demi septier*, that is common in these three books and that we translate as "cup".

one system to another is always a bit approximate unless carried out by a mathematician. In La Varenne's own day readers likely did a fair amount of guessing as they measured out weights and amounts.

As translator I have endeavoured, as consistently as possible, to bring the original style a little closer to that with which a modern cook or chef is familiar. Awkward passages still remain. In a very few instances this is because the sense of the original is not entirely clear, whether the fault is La Varenne's or his printer's; we suspect that contemporary seventeenth-century readers may have been equally baffled or, worse, badly mislead. For those passages a brief footnote will usually point out the nature of the difficulty that the original text presents.

In a few obscure passages, some help is afforded by the text of the contemporary English translator who is identified as I. D. G. on the title pages of *The French Cook* (London, 1653). In many more cases I. D. G. has clearly misconstrued La Varenne's intention, or is straining unsuccess-fully to interpret his meaning. Marnette's English version of the *Pastissier françois* is even less useful because slightly less successful in getting at the original author's intentions.

The first five Appendices at the end of this translation constitute an index to the material of the three books. They offer as well a guide to the specific French terminology used by their authors; the original French dish names can likewise be found there (particularly in Appendices 1 and 2). Throughout, references to specific contents of the three works take the general form of an abbreviated mention of the book in question (Cook, Past, Conf), the Chapter (by Roman numeral) and the particular recipe: *e.g.* Cook IV,3. References to preambles in a chapter, before the first recipe, use a zero in place of a recipe number: *e.g.* Cook XXVI,0.

Footnotes are numbered according to the number of the recipe in which they occur; a numbered sequence (3.1, 3.2) is used if more than a single note is needed in any given recipe. For chapter titles, for introduc-tory material in chapters, and for those chapters that have no individually numbered recipes, the Roman numeral of the chapter is in lower case, with the same sort of sequence if necessary: *e.g.* iv.1, iv.2. It should be mentioned that the many footnotes referring to textual variants are merely representative of a vast number of similar instances. The reader may find them somewhat tedious but the few I include serve a little to substantiate a thesis I have already proposed: La Varenne's reputation suffered incalculable damage at the hands of the printers who profited from reprinting his work. Textual variants repeatedly point up an attitude verging on indifference that marks the work of many of those working in seventeenth-century printing houses.

Finally, I should identify two editorial interventions in my translation of the *Cuisinier* text, Second Edition. For the sake of consistency and functionality, I have supplied chapter titles in a few places where these seem called for but are lacking. In all such cases I enclose my supplied title in brackets. Additionally, many chapters in the *Cuisinier françois* are preceded by a listing of the contents of the chapter; both the *Pastissier françois* and the *Confiturier françois* are followed by an alphabetical index, which the printers compiled, to the contents of the whole book. I have suppressed all of these Tables, incorporating the material into Appendices 1 and 2 at the end of the present work.

For the rich contributions made from a modern professional perspective, I am very grateful for the observations that Eleanor Kane and Deborah Reid — respectively Co-Founder and Director, and Cookery Instructor, of the Stratford Chefs School (Stratford, Canada) — offered in reviewing my typescript of the *French Cook*. They identified modern counterparts to La Varenne's recipes; marginal notes refer to those modern survivals of, or at least adaptations of, dishes in La Varenne's collection.[173] I am equally and warmly grateful for the keen editorial eye that Pat Phillips brought to my text, saving it from a number of flaws and blunders.

In summary, in both this modern translation and commentary I have wished to present to a modern reader — one who is familiar with the workings of an ordinary kitchen and with the procedures for making standard culinary preparations — a rich set of recipes from another time and place. These recipes are broadly representative of the best of what was eaten and enjoyed by a particular class of people in the society of that time

---

[173] Those marginal notes refer to the following works: Auguste Escoffier (1846–1935), *The Escoffier Cook Book. A Guide to the Fine Art of Cookery* (New York: Crown Publishers, 1969 and 1989); Paul Bocuse, *Paul Bocuse's French Cooking* (New York: Pantheon, 1977); Albert Roux and Michel Roux, *The Roux Brothers French Country Cooking* (London: Sidgwick & Jackson, 1989); Jean-Georges Vongerichten, *Simple Cuisine* (New York: Prentice Hall, 1990). Esteemed cooks in modern France continue to make use of traditions to which La Varenne contributed.

and place. We may hesitate to applaud too warmly the "French Stationer" (La Varenne's publisher?) who wrote in a prefatory Epistle to the Reader of the English translation of 1653: "Considered also, that France carrying it above all other Nations in the world in point of civility, courtesie, and comeliness in every kind of conversation, is not lesse esteemed, because of it's comely and daintie fashion of feeding. ... Other nations may very well be stirred forward to conforme themselves to her, who as she doth excell in all what belongeth to life, cannot be ignorant of the meanes how to preserve it contented and peaceable, by the use of things which doe maintaine it, and cause it to subsist." But we have to recognize that the cookery that La Varenne helped codify stirred a great admiration not only within France but beyond its borders. His various publishers certainly hoped so.

I in turn hope that this modern translation will make both that cookery and the enjoyment it provided accessible to the modern diner. My intention has been to present these texts as comprehensibly as possible, and so to encourage an appreciation of culinary practices and gastronomic tastes of a time that was, after all, only a dozen generations ago.

Frontispiece in *The French Cook ... Englished by I. D. G.*
London, printed for Charles Adams neere St. Dunstans Church in Fleetstreet, 1653.

THE FRENCH COOK

Instructing on the Manner of Preparing and Seasoning
All Sorts of Lean- and Meat-Day Foods, Legumes, Pastries, etc.

Revised, corrected & augmented with a
Treatise on dry and moist Confections
& other tasty delicacies.

Together with an Alphabetical Table
of the subjects dealt with throughout the Book.

by Mr. *LA VARENNE*, Kitchen Clerk*
of the Marquis of Uxelles[†]

SECOND EDITION

AT PARIS
By PIERRE DAVID, at the Palais,
at the entrance to the Prisoners' Gallery.

M.DC.LII

WITH ROYAL PRIVILEGE

---

* *Par le sieur de LA VARENNE, Escuyer de Cuisine.*

[†] The incidental material that heads La Varenne's book — the dedicatory epistle from
La Varenne to the Marquis d'Uxelles, the author's preface addressed to "Dear Reader"
in which he explains the purpose of his book, the Extract of the King's *Privilege*,
dated 17 July 1651 and signed Guitonneau, and the publisher's letter to the reader
— can be seen in the Introduction: B. (i) *The French Cook*.

Chapter I

Table of the Meats
that are normally found and served during the various Seasons of the Year[i.1]

Between Easter and Saint John's Day

Grain-fed chickens[i.2]
Year-old turkeys
Goslings
Lambs
Dovecot squab or young wood-pigeons
Young hares
Young wild boar
Partridge
Pheasant
Ortolans (buntings)
Rabbits, young rabbits

Between Saint John's Day and Saint Remy's Day

Young partridge
Young stockdoves
Turtledoves
Young pheasant
Young quail

[i.1] This section has been inserted before the recipes proper, which, along with a formal statement of the book's title, will begin after it. This listing of seasonal foods underscores just how dependent cooks used to be, up until relatively recent times, upon nature for the fresh provision of foodstuffs. The age-old methods of preservation, by salting and dessication, smoking and candying, were of only limited help in extending the useful life of foodstuffs.

La Varenne did not number his chapters, and in some chapters not even the recipes. All such numbering has been added here in order to facilitate indexing and references.

[i.2] Though sometimes translated as "spring chickens" these *poulets de grain* are listed as available foodstuffs within each of La Varenne's three seasons. In his *Delices de la campagne* (Amsterdam, 1654) Nicolas de Bonnefons writes that the term *poulets de grain* is applied to the smallest chickens.

Young hare
Young wild boar
Young turkeys[i.3]
Young capons
Dovecot doves
Grain-fed chickens
Pullets
Fat goslings
Rails
Buntings
Young ducks
Fawns
Goat kids
Snipe

Between Saint Remy's Day and Lent

Fat capon
Fat pullet
Norman castrated poulard
Barnyard and chicken-run capons
Fat hens for boiling
Turkey hens
Turkey cocks
Lambs
Young hares
Partridge
Young woodcock
Wood-pigeon
Plovers
Teal
Red partridge
Wood pheasant
River birds
Woodhens

[i.3] *poulets d'Inde*: see also the more mature *poules d'Inde* and *cocqs d'Inde* available later in the year, below. As for the designation *d'Inde*, see the note in Recipe IV,13.

Snipe
Large Thrush (Throstle)
Small thrush
Grain-fed chickens
Young January hares
Curlew
Dovecot doves
Fat quail
Cockscombs
Foie gras
Dotterel
Magpies
Fat goose for salting,[i.4] with peas
Larks
Barnyard ducks
Suckling piglet
Young waterhen
Heron
Sea-swallow

[i.4] Nicolas de Bonnefons relates that *On sale des Oyes grasses coupées par quartiers, que l'on met dans des pots de grez* [stoneware] *ou dans des Saloirs pour la provision de la maison, les cuisant dans le pot au lieu de Cochon; quand elles sont sallées de nouveau, c'est un tres-excellent manger, & de bon profit* (op. cit., 216).

The French Cook

Instructing on the Proper Manner
of Preparing and Seasoning Meats
that are served in the four seasons of the year
at great and private tables.

Chapter II

Bouillon to enrich any Pot
whether for Pottages, Entrées or Entremets[ii.1]

Escoffier, *Fonds brun*, §7

Get hind leg and rump of beef,[ii.2] a little mutton and a few fowl — depending upon the amount of the bouillon you want, use that amount of meat; then cook it well with a bouquet of parsley, chives and thyme bundled together, and some cloves. Keep hot water on hand to add in. When it is done, strain the bouillon through a cloth for [later] use.[ii.3]

For roast meat, after having extracted its juice,[ii.4] set it to boil with a bouquet as above. Cook it well, then strain the bouillon for use in your entrées,[ii.5] or for brown pottages.[ii.6]

[ii.1]   Though La Varenne is not explicit here, these bouillons, and the dishes in which they may be used, are all suitable for meat days only. Recipes for such pottages follow in Chapters III and IV; instances of meat-day entrées are in Chapter V, and of meat-day entremets in Chapter VIII. The counterpart to this chapter, showing bouillons for lean (and Lenten) days, is found in Chapter XXIV.

   Comparisons with Auguste Escoffier's recipes refer to sections in *The Escoffier Cook Book* (New York: Crown Publishers, 1969).

[ii.2]   Somewhat ambiguously, the text has *trumeaux derriere de simier*. The word *trumeaux* (in the plural) is the upper leg or round (of beef); the *simier* or *cimier* (in the singular) is a rump (of beef). The *simier* seems to include the whole hind of beef. The 1653 translation has "Take knuckles of beef, the hinder part of the rump, ..."

[ii.3]   *pour vous en servir*: "for to make use of it at your first courses, or for brown potages." The 1653 translator's eye has skipped to the end of the next paragraph.

[ii.4]   See Recipe XI,2 on the making of meat stocks.

[ii.5]   That is, as part of the first course of a meal, as for instance in Chapters V, XVI, XXVI.

[ii.6]   In the next chapter, for instance, Recipe III,22 for a Pottage of Roast Squab makes

Chapter III

All sorts of Pottages
that can be served on Meat Days[iii]

1. Squab Bisque[1.1]

Get squab,[1.2] after they have been cleaned and trussed up — which

---

use of a "good bouillon" and is of a reddish-brown or russet colour.

iii We might be tempted to understand the term "pottage" as "stew", a sense the French word *potage* had in days long before La Varenne's. In many instances the basic substance, cooking method and consistency may approximate the modern stew. In its presentation, however, the seventeeth-century pottage, with its base of bread or toast and burden of a simple or complex, semi-liquid garnish, is well on its way to becoming the modern canapé. At La Varenne's table the proper place of the *potage* in a meal was at its beginning. Richelet defines the word very usefully as: "Bouillon du pot, soit gras, ou maigre, qu'on verse sur des soupes de pain coupées fort proprement & qu'on sert ensuite au commencement du dîner." (For some bibliographic references, here and elsewhere, please see the Appendices, below.)

Theodora FitzGibbon offers a somewhat anachronistic picture of a *potage*: "A familiar culinary term which in 17th-century France denoted a large meal of meat or fish, slowly cooked with vegetables in an enormous pot. The pot was made of glazed earthenware, with a lid, and might contain several chickens, ham, meats, etc., as well as a variety of vegetables. When cooked, the meats were drained and then often arranged in elaborate and picturesque structures." *The Food of the Western World*, New York (Quadrangle-New York Times Book Co.), 1976, p. 358. At refined French tables the "pot" of itself yielded no "large meals" but mainly two sorts of dishes: the *potage*, a sort of appetizer, and the *ragoût*.

These recipes in Chapter III are all for meat days of the week and of the calendar. Corresponding groupings of recipes for lean pottages outside of and during Lent are placed in Chapters XV and XXV respectively. A few of La Varenne's *potages* still remain among Escoffier's appetizers and snacks, §§280–394 and 2298–2337.

[1.1] The modern bisque is a thick soup made from puréed shellfish. In La Varenne's day poultry and game birds could be prepared in a bisque, that being a merely a dish of boiled fowl on sops. Another dish of the same sort is seen at Recipe 48 in this chapter. (*Cf.* Escoffier, §241.) Interestingly, in view of La Varenne's great use of squabs, Escoffier wrote that they "are not very highly esteemed by gourmets, and that is more particularly to be regretted, since when the birds are of excellent quality, they are worthy of the best tables" (§1775).

[1.2] These *pigeonneaux* are undoubtedly the domestically-raised fowl that are qualified as *pigeonneaux de voliere*, "dovecot squab," that are listed in the earlier Table of Meats. Likewise whenever *pigeons* are called for, they are almost certainly the *pigeons de voliere* of that same Table. Dovecots were, and are, a commonplace on European

you do by making a hole in the bottom of their belly with a knife and sticking their legs into it. Blanch them — that is, put them into a pot with boiling water or bouillon from the pot, covering them well; then pot them with a sprig of fine herbs and fill your pot with your best bouillon. Be very careful not to let it darken.[1.3] Dry your bread[1.4] and simmer It[1.5] in the dove bouillon; then set it out after it is well seasoned with salt, pepper and cloves. Garnish it with the doves, and with cockscombs, veal sweetbreads, mushrooms, mutton stock,[1.6] then pistachios. Serve. Garnish the rim of the platter with slices of lemon.

2. Healthy Pottage[2.1]

Healthy Pottage is made from capons. After they have been cleaned well, truss them up and put them into a pot with bouillon, and cover it to keep it from darkening. It should be well seasoned with salt and cooked well. Put in many good herbs, and in winter white chicory.[2.2] Then set it

---

farms and estates.

[1.3] In Recipe 2 that eventuality is prevented by covering the pot.

[1.4] The loaf of bread in La Varenne's day was still a round, somewhat flattened mound of bread. Its consistency was rather compact. In the "pottages" of the present series of recipes, that loaf, previously soaked in some appropriate sort of savoury liquid, regularly serves as a presentation base for the meat that constitutes the main element of a dish. Later references to "crusts" of bread (as in Recipe 22) suggest that the loaf is cut in half, much as two medieval bread trenchers were occasionally sliced from a single flat, round or square loaf.

[1.5] *le faites mittonner*: "stove it," according to the English translator. The anonymous I. D. G. provides a brief glossary of "hard and strange words" in which he defines the verb *mittonner* as "To stove or soak. It is to cause to boile very softly before, or over the fire, that so the juice or liquor may be imbibed, or drunk in by degrees, to the end that the potage, or sauce, may be well allayed, or a good consistence, or well thickned." That work was reprinted in 2001 by Southover Press of Lewes, East Sussex.

[1.6] For this ingredient see Recipe XI,2, below.

[2.1] See also the variety of this dish found at Recipe XXIX,1.

[2.2] This *chicorée*, used in several recipes, may be understood as the modern endive. Charles Estienne has a couple of pertinent paragraphs in his scholarly *Agriculture et maison rustique* (Paris: Jaques du Puis, 1564). In Ch. 12 (f. 45 r): *L'endive autrement nommee scariole ou laictue aigre sert plus en medecine, qu'autrement*; and in Ch. 13 (f. 40 v): *La cichoree [sic] est de la nature de l'endive, & sans la culture & bon traittement retient toujours son amertume* . . . .

out and garnish it with your herbs — that is, with the stems[2.3] and roots of parsley or chicory. Serve it.

3. Pottage of Partridge with Cabbage

Escoffier, *Perdreau aux choux*, §1869

When the partridges are well cleaned, lard them with plain lard then truss them up, blanch them and put them into a pot with good bouillon. Get cabbages and put them into the pot with the partridges. After they have cooked, you add in a little melted lard and season them with cloves and pepper. Then simmer your crusts [of bread] and garnish them with veal sweetbreads, or with sausages if you have any. Then serve.

4. Pottage of Duck with Turnip

Duck-and-turnip is a classic French combination: *e.g.* Escoffier, *Caneton braisé aux navets*, §1748; Bocuse, *Caneton aux navets*, p. 264

After the ducks have been cleaned, lard them with plain lard, then sauté them[4.1] in a pan in clarified or melted lard, or else roast them for three or four turns of the spit and then put them into a pot. Then get your turnips, cut them up however you wish, blanch them, flour them, sauté[4.2] them in clarified or ordinary lard until they are a good russet colour. Put them with your ducks and cook everything well. Simmer your bread so that everything is thick.[4.3] If you have any capers, you can put some in, or a drop of vinegar. Set out the sops and garnish them with turnips. Serve.

5. Pottage of Chicken Garnished with Asparagus

After the chickens have been properly trussed up, blanch them well and put them into a pot with a bard[5.1] on top. Fill your pot with your best bouillon and season the chickens with salt and a very little pepper.[5.2]

[2.3] *cordes*: likely a misprint for *cardes*, "the tender, succulent part of a leaf"?

[4.1] *les passez*: "pass them." The translator's glossary defines the phrase *passer dans la poële* as "To Passe in the panne. It is to frie a little, or to parboile in the frying panne."

[4.2] See the previous note. The author consistly uses the phrase *passer par le poële* to indicate a rapid or limited frying. "To sauté" or "to brown" might be reasonable translations. In recipes 60 and 70 of the entrée section, it seems that as food is fried in this way it may normally be *rotated* or rolled around a frying pan.

[4.3] The text, *afin que votre pain soit lié* is clearly in error. I. D. G., the English translator, corrects this by writing, "to the end that your potage be thickned."

[5.1] *une barde*. This bard is a relatively thin slice of salt pork or bacon. I. D. G. translates "a sheet of lard." In Recipe 31 La Varenne writes, *une barde, c'est un morceau de lard*.

[5.2] *un grain de poivre*: literally, "a peppercorn".

Do not let them cook too much. Dry your [slices of] bread, simmer them and garnish them with your chickens, with asparagus that has been broken and fricasseed, mushrooms, cockscombs or tidbits[5.3] from your chickens, a few pistachios and mutton stock. Garnish the rim of your platter with lemon. Then serve.

6. Pottage of Marbled Partridge

After your partridges have been properly trussed up, lard them with plain lard and blanch them, then put them into a pot. Cook them well and season them with salt.[6.1] Then put your bread into that bouillon and let it simmer. Garnish your pottage with mushrooms[6.2] and boil them a little on the fire, adding in white almond broth and mutton stock, pistachios and lemon. Then serve it.

7. Pottage of *Fricandeaux*[7.1]

Get a round of veal,[7.2] slice it very thin, lard the slices carefully and brown them in a pie plate or between two dishes;[7.3] slice them into a

---

[5.3] The term *beatilles* — which Randle Cotgrave (*A Dictionarie of the French and English Tongues*, London, 1611), a generation or two before La Varenne, glossed merely as "trinkets, or vaine toyes, wherewith finicall people decke themselves; trifles, nifles, odde attires, also, women of low stature" — refers to relatively minor but tasty offal, such as poultry giblets and sweetbreads, or to virtually any toothsome ingredient that could itself be used in a garnish. Though La Varenne rarely says so expressly, it is likely intended that the *beatilles* undergo some sort of partial precooking before being used: see Recipe 19, below.

[6.1] The text erroneously has *& les assaisonnez d'eau.*

[6.2] The 1653 translation has "with it [*i.e.* the bouillon] and with mushrooms."

[7.1] Cotgrave offers the following gloss for this dish: "*fricandeaulx*: m. Short, skinlesse, and daintie puddings, or Quelkchoses, made of good flesh and hearbes chopped together, then rolled up into the forme of Liverings, &c, and so boyled." I. D. G. seems to be guided by Cotrave's gloss, here and elsewhere in his English translation, because he renders the title of this recipe as "Potage of Quelckchoses, or Liverings." In modern cookery Theodora FitzGibbon still defines *fricandeau* as "a long thick piece from the top rump of veal. It is also used to describe a dish made from *noix de veau*, larded and braised or roasted." *Food of the Western World*, 163. These *fricandeaux* will be seen in their more usual treatment in Recipe V,45, below.

[7.2] The term *rouelle de veau* is glossed by Cotgrave as, "The broad end of a leg of Veale, cut round, and divided from the knuckle." The word means literally a "little wheel". The translator writes merely "fillet of Veale."

[7.3] This alternative procedure is relatively common. The *plats* referred to were metal

6. Potage de perdrix marbrées.

little pot with your best bouillon and season them. Simmer your bread and garnish it with your *fricandeaux*, along with mushrooms, truffles, asparagus, mutton stock, and pistachios if you wish, or lemon. Then serve.

8. Pottage of Marbled[8] Quail

After your quail have been trussed and blanched, flour them and sauté them in plain or clarified lard; then set them into a pot. Cook them well and season them with salt. Simmer your bread and garnish it with your quails, and with truffles, mushrooms, cockscombs, lemons and pistachios. Then serve.

9. Garnished Pottage of Wood-Pigeon

Get wood-pigeons or large doves, blanch them and lard them with lard of a moderate size;[9] then put them into a pot and cook them with a seasoning of salt and a sprig of thyme. Simmer your bread, then garnish it with your wood-pigeons, artichokes and asparagus. Serve.

10. Profiterole[10.1] Pottage

It is made thus: you have to get four or six large buns and dig out all

Escoffier still uses profite-roles made of bread as a garnish, §493

---

and resembled modern soup plates with a relatively broad rim and a considerable dish in their middle. When one was inverted over the other, their flat rims let them seal a foodstuff for cooking as in a miniature oven. They are set in or on the coals of a fire. Early pictures even show such pairs of dishes, or a stack of them, being brought to the table.

[8] The sense of this qualification is not immediately obvious in this recipe. It recurs in Recipe III,26, where the cook is instructed to pour mutton stock over a garnish of pea purée "in order to marble it." There seems to be no similar explanation of any marbling in this present recipe.

[9] In the brief glossary which he places ahead of his translation of *The French Cook*, I. D. G. defines *meane lard*: "They are slices of lard, of a middle sise." For the *moyen lard* in this recipe he writes "middle sised lard."

[10.1] "*Pourfiterolle*: f. A cake baked under hot imbers" (Cotgrave). A modern definition of a profiterole is choux pastry filled with whipped cream — a very distant descendant of La Varenne's dish. A lean version of the dish is found at Recipe XV,23; a Lenten version at XXV,23; and a Good Friday version at XXIX,8. The preparation seems to have been a reliable standby. For the English of *profiteolles* (*sic*), I. D. G. put "small vayles," undoubtedly getting this from Cotgrave: "in the plural (*profiterolles*) be the small vayles, as drinking money, points, pinnes, &c., gotten by a valet or groome in his maisters service." As we might say: "pin money" or "tip" or, generally, in an archaic sense of the word *perquisite*, any cast-off article no longer of value to its owner and given to an employee. See the *Oxford English Dictionary*, 2nd edn., 19, 398: *vail* II.4 and II.5. In a culinary context a *profiterolle* would seem orginally to have been an insubstantial, "no-account" creation.

the soft part through a little hole on top.[10.2] Take the cover [lid] and dry it with the bread, and sauté it with plain or clarified lard. Then simmer your breadcrumb in your best bouillon and sprinkle it with almond broth. Then you set out your buns to be garnished with your pottage, and fill them with cockscombs and sweetbreads, tidbits,[10.3] truffles and mushrooms, and put on their cover; add bouillon until the bread is soaked. Before serving, pour juice[10.4] over the top, and with it whatever you have on hand. Then serve.

11. Queen's Pottage[11.1]

Get almonds, grind them and set them to boil with good bouillon, along with a bouquet of herbs, a bit of lemon pulp, and a little bread-crumb; then season that with salt. Take care they don't burn, stirring them frequently, and strain them. Then get your bread and simmer it in the best bouillon you have.[11.2] After you have deboned some roast par-

---

[10.2] These *petits pains* could well be small loaves of bread.

[10.3] *béatilles*: "gibblets." I. D. G.'s glossary says of *beatilles of pullets*, "They are the gibblets." Yet La Varenne's list of garnishes here has word *beatilles* without any qualification; I. D. G.'s glossary of this word alone, *béatilles*, is much broader: "They are all kinds of ingredients, that may be fancied, for to be put together into a pie, or other wise, viz. Cock's combes, stones or kidnies, sweet breads of veale, mushrums, bottoms of hartichocks, &c." The early-eighteenth-century *Dictionnaire universel françois et latin . . . vulgairement appellé Dictionnaire de Trévoux* still glosses the word in the same way: "Petites viandes délicates, dont on compose des pâtés, des tourtes, des potages, des ragoûts, comme ris de veau, palais de bœuf, crêtes de coq, truffes, artichaux, pistaches, etc." The *etc.* in both cases is very significant: the composition of the *beatilles* seems to depend in large measure upon what "delicacies" the cook happens to have on hand. During the rest of his translation of *The French Cook*, I. D. G. will merely keep the word *beatilles* in English. Uniformly we shall translate *béatilles* as "tidbits".

[10.4] This *jus* may be some undefined stock or bouillon. For two varieties of stock — presumably for La Varenne the most common —available in a seventeenth-century kitchen, see Chapter XI, below.

[11.1] The essence of this particular pottage is the bouillon that is produced by boiling the bones of fowl. See a lean version of the dish at Recipe XV,7.

[11.2] At this point, following a comma, the text continues with *Puis après que vous aurez désossé quelque perdrix . . . .* The passage presents directions for preparing that "best bouillon" just mentioned. Between the two passages I. D. G. has a helpful "which you shal make thus." The beginning of the next recipe refers back to this preparation.

tridge or capon,[11.3] get some good bouillon, cook all of the bones with a few mushrooms, and strain everything through a cloth. Simmer your bread in the bouillon [so prepared] and, as it is simmering, sprinkle it with [the] almond milk[11.4] and with meat stock;[11.5] then add in a little finely chopped partridge flesh or capon, until it is full. Then get the fire shovel, heat it to red hot and pass it over the top.[11.6] Garnish your pottage with cockscombs, pistachios, pomegranate seeds and meat stock. Then serve.

12. Princess Pottage[12]

Get the same Queen's Bouillon or Potage, drawn off from the roasted bones. Simmer a loaf of bread, still with its crust, and then a little chopped partridge meat which you sprinkle on your bread — so thinly that it is barely visible. Simmer it and build it up little by little, garnishing it with the smallest mushrooms, cockscombs, kidneys, pistachios, lemon and a lot of meat stock. Then serve.

13. Jacobin Pottage[13.1]

Get capons or partridges, roast them, remove their bones, and chop up the white meat very finely. Take the bones, break them up and put them to boil with the bouillon, along with a bouquet of herbs, in a crock;

Potage à la Princeffe.

_12._

[11.3] I. D. G. has an additional direction here: grind up the bones in a mortar.

[11.4] This is likely the mixture that has been prepared at the beginning of the recipe. In earlier periods, ground almonds, moistened with a little liquid, made a staple that was called _lait d'amandes_. Here La Varenne calls it _bouillon d'amandes_. Its use here and in Recipe 13, below, suggests that Queen's Pottage and Jacobin Pottage may be relatively old dishes.

[11.5] See Recipe XXI,2.

[11.6] This procedure is a common means to colour a dish, to set a glazing, and perhaps also to seal the surface of a composition.

[12] See a lean version of this dish at Recipe XV,8.

[13.1] This dish has a venerable history in French cookery. During the late Middle Ages _Jacobin Sops_ were prepared with layers of chicken, cheese and herbs on bread. The Savoyard chef Master Chiquart has a delightful version of these sops in his _On Cookery_, Recipe 18 (_Chiquart's 'On Cookery'. A Fifteenth-Century Savoyard Culinary Treatise_, New York: Lang, 1986). A recipe for a Jacobin Cheese Pottage is written at Recipe 49, below. The qualification in the name of the preparation likely derives from a long-standing recognition that the brothers of the urban order of Dominicans, under the sway of its most celebrated convent, Saint-Jacques in Paris, appreciated a rich gastronomic fare. See also Recipe 49, below.

then strain them through a cloth. Simmer your bread, set on it a layer of meat or of cheese if you wish, a layer of almond milk,[13.2] boil it well and build it up little by little; then garnish it at one end with little deboned wing-ends. Get three eggs with a little almond milk, or some other nut paste, beat them together and pour it over your pottage. Pass the fire shovel over it. Then serve it.

14. Cockerel Pottage

Get cockerels, dress them and blanch them — that is, let them steep for a while in cool water or in bouillon; then put them into a pot with some other bouillon which is well seasoned with salt. Set them out and garnish them on a loaf of simmered bread along with whatever remaining garnishing you have on hand. Then serve.

15. Hippocratic Pottage of Teal[15]

Get teals, clean them thoroughly and blanch them as above. When they are larded on the inside with a lardoon, coat them with plain or clarified lard; then put them into a pot. When they are almost cooked, you throw in brignol plums along with a bit of sugar. You garnish your pottage with the teal and the brignols.

16. Pottage of Browned Lark[16.1]

Get your larks, eviscerate them, blanch them, flour them and sauté them in a frying pan in butter or in plain or clarified lard until they are a good russet colour. Then put them into a pot with good bouillon and a bouquet of herbs; cook them well. Simmer a loaf of bread well, which

---

13.2 The phrase *bouillon d'amandes* in the text here should not make us think of a watery consistency. The ground almonds, moistened with a little bouillon, resemble a paste.

15 *Potage de sarcelle à l'hypocras*. The name of the dish raises questions: hypocras is a traditional spiced wine (see *The French Confectioner*, Recipe IV,1), yet there is nei-ther wine nor spices, let alone spiced wine, among the ingredients here. On the other hand there is no indication that the dish is meant to be served or eaten *with* the usual hypocras. The title may derive from a belief that this was a healthful preparation, commended by the most respected of ancient medical authority, Hippocrates.

16.1 The name of the dish anticipates the initial cooking which the fowl will undergo: *Potage d'Allouettes au roux*. The phrase *au roux* appears again in Recipe XV,51 (*limandes au roux*) but neither here nor there does it designate a sauce. The phrase refers to a manner of cooking in which the foodstuff (larks here, turnip in Recipe 4, teal in Recipe 18, for instance) is dredged in flour and fried in fat. La Varenne's antecedent of the modern "roux" is regularly called a *sauce rousse* or *beurre roux*.

you garnish with your larks, beef palates,[16.2] mutton stock and lemon.
Then serve.

17. Squab Pottage

Get young doves, scald them well, then put them into a pot with
good bouillon and a bouquet of herbs; cook them well with a trimming
of lard.[17.1] Then set them out on a simmered loaf and garnish them
with artichokes and fricasseed asparagus stalks, green peas[17.2] or lettuce.
Serve.

18. Pottage of Teal with Turnip Juice

To make it, get teal and roast them; then put them into a pot with good
bouillon. Get turnips and blanch them, flour them and sauté them in the
frying pan so that they take on a good russet colour; put them with your
teal and cook them together. When you are about to set everything out,
strain the turnips through a linen cloth so as to draw off their juice, with
which you will garnish your pottage, along with your teal and pomegranate
seeds. Then serve.

19. Tidbit Pottage

Get tidbits,[19.1] scald them thoroughly, and sauté them in a frying pan
like a chicken fricassee; then put them into a pot with good bouillon
and cook them down thoroughly.[19.2] Simmer a loaf of bread, which you
garnish with your tidbits along with a lot of mutton stock and ram kidneys.
Then serve it.

[16.2] These *palets de bœuf* were a delicacy of the day. The term represents the long piece
of meat attached to the palate bone and stretching between the animal's snout and
cheek. The cut is called for on close to two dozen occasions in the *Cuisinier françois*.

[17.1] La Varenne's phrase, *avec une parade de lard*, suggests a preliminary treatment to
bedeck or dress the fowl. I. D. G. writes merely "with a sheete of Lard."

[17.2] Peas are used fairly frequently in La Varenne's dishes. For the most part these are
white peas (see Furetière's gloss, *s.v.* "peas," in Appendix 1 a), but occasionally they
are specifically to be *poix verts*. That appears to be commonly the case when La
Varenne is preparing a garnish as here. See La Varenne's method for colouring his
"common" pea green in Recipe XV,46.

[19.1] See the note in Recipe 10, above.

[19.2] In his text La Varenne wrote *faites-les bien consommer*: his intention is that, whatever those bits of meat collectively called *beatilles* may be, whether sweetbreads,
cockscombs, truffles, pistachios, and so forth, an extensive boiling will cause them
largely to decompose into a chunky homogenous paste.

20. Pottage of Chicken with Cauliflower

Put your chickens into a pot with good bouillon; cook them, seasoned with salt and a bouquet of herbs, cloves and pepper, and grate in a little nutmeg or bread crust. When you are ready to serve, garnish your simmered bread with cauliflower[20] and mutton stock. Then serve it.

21. Pottage of Chicken in Ragout[21.1]

When the chickens are roasted, quarter them,[21.2] then put them between two platters as for a ragout with some bouillon from the pot. Simmer your bread, still with its crust on, and garnish it with your chickens, setting a few mushrooms and aparagus stalks around them. Then serve.

22. Pottage of Roast Squab

Put young doves into a pot with good bouillon that is well seasoned with salt and cloves, and cook them. Simmer your crusts; garnish them with your doves and with whatever you have on hand to put on them. Make your pottage reddish-brown. Then serve.

23. Pottage of Gosling in Pea Purée

Get goslings, or anything else you may like, put them into a pot and cook them well. Then get your peas,[23] boil them thoroughly and put them through a very fine strainer; put that purée into a pot with a bouquet of herbs. Put a little lard in a frying pan and, when it has melted, throw it into the pot. When you are about to serve, simmer your bread in the bouillon of your goslings, then pour your purée over top. To make the purée green you should not cook your peas completely but, after they are half cooked, grind them in a mortar and strain them with a good bouillon. Alternatively, if it is winter, you get chard or sorrel, ground and pressed, and pour the juice around your pottage when you are ready to serve.

---

[20] The original text has a plural here, as does the recipe's title. We should perhaps understand "bits of cauliflower".

[21.1] The phrase *en ragoust* identifies an extremely common procedure by which the flavour of a foodstuff is heightened by its being exposed to a variety of secondary ingredients, properly condiments, usually incorporated in a cooking or steeping sauce. The composition of the sauce is never precisely defined but its function is always to add zest to the foodstuff. See the Introduction, C, (c).

[21.2] The text has *escartelez les*; later typesetters misread that as *écrasez-les*, "crush them."

[23] It should be remembered that the pea which was cooked and eaten up to La Varenne's time is a white pea. This recipe goes on to explain how the purée from these peas can be made green.

21. Potage de poulets en ragoust.

24. Pottage of Gosling Giblets

Blanch them well and put them into a pot with bouillon, a bouquet of herbs and a piece of lard. Cook them well, so that when they are cooked they will look white. Simmer your bread; garnish it with your giblets, which you may blanch if you wish, and add on a few chopped capers. Then serve.

25. Pottage of Goslings with Peas

Put your goslings[25.1] into a pot with bouillon, after having prepared and blanched them carefully; cook and season them well. Sauté your peas in a frying pan, then put them into a small pot with a little bouillon. After they are well cooked, simmer your bread and garnish it with the goose and its giblets[25.2] and your peas, whole or strained. Then serve, garnished with lettuce.

26. Pottage of Salted Goose in Pea Purée

With your goose being well salted and quartered, if it is too salty, desalt it,[26.1] then lard it with plain lard and cook it thoroughly. When your peas have cooked, purée them through a strainer and season them according to your taste; bring your goose to a boil in that purée. Simmer your bread, in more bouillon if you have another pot of it, and over the pea purée pour a little mutton stock in order to marble it.[26.2] Then serve.

27. Pottage of Chicken with Green Peas

When your chickens are scalded well and trussed up, put them into a pot with good bouillon; skim them carefully. Then sauté your peas in the frying pan in butter or lard, and simmer them with some lettuce which you

---

[25.1] The text here and in the title reads *oysons*: "goslings"; later in the recipe the text has *l'oye*: "the goose." I. D. G. has "geese" throughout.

[25.2] *ses abbatis, s'entend la petite oye.*

[26.1] This procedure had been very common in kitchens, undoubtedly since the distant age when salt was first used as a preservative. The salted meat had to be soaked a length of time sufficient to dissolve excess salt out of it.

[26.2] That is, in order to give the purée (which may be green or white, depending on the colour of the peas used) a streaked effect evocative of marble. Recipes 8 (above, for quail) and 47 (below, for roast woodcock) mention the possibility of making use of that marbling effect. The latter recipe refers also to a dish called Marbled Partridge — which may well be the *Pottage of Fricaseed Partridge* of Recipe 6 — in which white almond broth and mutton stock are mixed in a garnish.

have blanched — that is, having put the lettuce into cool water. Likewise simmer your bread, and then garnish it with your chickens and lettuce. Serve.

28. Pottage of Dove with Green Peas

This is made in the same way as the Pottage of Chickens with Green Peas, except that, if you like, you can omit puréeing your peas.[28]

29. Pottage of Salt Meat with Peas[29]

Cook your salt meat fully, whether it is pork or goose or whatever. Set it out and pour your purée over it. Then serve.

This combination of salt meat and peas, a variety of *garbure*, survives in Québecois pea soup.

30. Pottage of Young Rabbit

When they have been carefully dressed, blanch them and sauté them in the frying pan in butter or lard; them put them into a pot with good bouillon and a bouquet of herbs and cook them appropriately. Simmer your bread well and garnish it with your young rabbits, mushrooms and truffles, and with whatever else you have on hand. Then serve.

31. Pottage of Lamb Offal

After your offal[31.1] have been blanched, put them into a pot with good bouillon, a bouquet of herbs and a bard — that is, a piece of fat bacon; cook them well. Simmer your bread. When you are ready to serve, pour over the bread a white bouillon — that is, of egg yolks and verjuice.[31.2]

---

[28] *... vous pouvés ne point passer vos poix en purée*: in Recipe 27 the peas are to be reduced to a "purée" in the frying pan.

[29] This dish is a version of the traditional combination of *pois au lard*, pork and peas, found in European cookery since the fourteenth century: *Menagier de Paris*, ed. cit., §29; Chiquart, *Du fait de cuisine*, (ed. Scully, *Vallesia*, XL (Sion, 1985), pp. 101–231), Recipe 62; *Neapolitan Recipe Collection*, Recipe 21; Platina, *De honesta voluptate et valetudine*, (ed. and trans. Mary Ella Milham, *Platina. On Right Pleasure and Good Health*, Tempe, Arizona: Medieval & Renaissance Texts & Studies, 1998), Recipe VII,33; and so forth.

[31.1] In his translation I. D. G. merely leaves the original French term, *abatis*. His preliminary *Table for the explaining of the hard and strange words contained in this Book* states that *abatis* are "the purtenances of any beast *viz.* the feet, the eares, the tongue, &c. They are also the gibblets of any foule *viz.* the neck, wings, feet, gisard, liver, &c."

[31.2] This tangy juice from early forming but unripe grapes has not quite been abandoned in modern cookery. See, for instance, Maggie Beer, *Cooking with Verjuice* (London: Grub Street, 2001). As Theodora FitzGibbon says (*Food of the Western World*, 502), its use has generally been supplanted in modern recipes by a "squeeze of lemon juice."

Then serve.

32. Pottage of Lark with a Sweet Sauce[32.1]

Pluck them, remove the gizzards, then flour them and sauté them in a pan in clarified or plain lard and put them into a pot with good bouillon, a cup[32.2] of white wine and a half pound of sugar; then cook everything well. Simmer your bread, garnish it with your larks. Serve.

33. Pottage of Knuckle of Veal

Put your knuckle of veal into a pot with good bouillon, cook it well and skim it; add in some white chicory. Simmer your bread, garnish it with the knuckle, chicory and mushrooms. Then serve.

34. Pottage of Breast of Veal

Blanch it in cool water, then put it into a pot with good bouillon, cook it; add in good herbs with a few capers, and season everything. Set it out on your simmered bread. Then serve.

35. Pottage of Small Thrush[35]

Truss them up, remove their gizzards, then flour them and sauté them in a pan in butter or lard; then put them into a pot with good bouillon and cook them well with a bouquet of herbs. Simmer your bread, and garnish it with your larks, with beef palates and mushrooms. Then serve.

36. Pottage of Tortoise

Get your tortoises, cut off their heads and feet, cook them in water and, when they are almost done, add in a little white wine, fine herbs and lard. When they are done, take them out of their shell and remove the gall bladder. Cut them up and sauté them in a frying pan in good butter. Then simmer them in your bouillon in a platter, along with your bread. And, finally, garnish that bread with your tortoises, seasoned with cut aparagus stalks, juice and lemon.[36] Then serve.

Potage de mouiettes.

35.

[32.1] The so-called sweet sauce is used with a variety of foods. See Appendix 2 under "sauce".

[32.2] *demi-septier.* I. D. G. shows "half a pint".

[35] The text has *Moulettes*, likely a type-setting error for *Moviettes*, the small bird whose name is normally spelled *mauviette*. Recipes for *mauviettes* are also found in VI,20, VII,5 and VIII,22. For the present recipe I. D. G. safeguards himself by putting "Mavis, or Thrushes."

[36] The text is explicit here: *d'asperges coupés, de jus, & de citron.*

37. Pottage of Piglet

After you have dressed the piglet properly, cut it into five pieces; blanch them in bouillon or in cool water, and put them into a pot along with good bouillon and fine herbs and a piece of lard — but take care that they do not boil dry. Simmer your bread and garnish it with your piglet, with its head in the middle of its quarters and with the offal set out around the platter. Then serve.

38. Pottage of Chopped Mutton

Get a leg of mutton, chop it up with beef fat or beef marrow and simmer it in a pot. Also simmer your bread in a platter with your best bouillon. After that, garnish it with your minced meat along with meat stock,[38.1] with cockscombs and with tidbits filled with a dry loaf of bread.[38.2] Alternatively, heap it up with fingers of bread[38.3] — that is, with pieces of bread the length and thickness of a finger — in the shape of lardoons, that you sauté in a pan in good butter until they take on a russet colour and look roasted; simmer them well, too. Then serve.

39. Pottage of a Leg of Beef

Braise it thoroughly in a pot, seasoned with a bouquet of herbs, cloves, capers, mushrooms and truffles, until it is almost disintegrating. Simmer your bread, and garnish it with your leg of beef and with its garnishing salad.[39]

40. Pottage of Capon with Rice

Get a capon, dress it carefully and put it into a pot with good, well seasoned bouillon. Get your rice which has been carefully picked, wash it, dry it by the fire, then cook it slowly with good bouillon. Simmer your bread, put your capon on it and garnish it with your rice. If you like, add in some saffron. Serve.

[38.1] For the probable nature of this *jus*, see Chapter XI, below, Recipe 2: Beef or Mutton Stock.

[38.2] I. D. G. handles the phrase, *beatilles emplies d'un pain sec*, literally: "Beatilles filled with dry Bread."

[38.3] These fingers are a standard preparation called *tailladins*.

[39] *& de sa fourniture*. A *fourniture* is mentioned only here in the *French Cook* and seems to consist of an assortment of relatively minor herbs. I. D. G. writes "Garnish it with your Knuckle and it's implements." See Furetière's gloss of the word *fourniture*, Appendix 2, *s.v.* salad (garnishing salad).

41. Pottage of Chicken with Rice

A Chicken-with-Rice Pottage is done in the same way as with the capon: dress the chickens, truss them up, put them into a pot and season it in the same way. Prepare your rice in the same way, too. When your bread has simmered, it is garnished in the same way. Serve.

42. Pottage of a Leg of Beef with Bread Fingers

Blanch your leg of beef, cook it thoroughly and season it well. With the bouillon, cook your fingers of bread[42.1] — you can also drop in an onion stuck with cloves[42.2] and a little thyme. Then simmer your bread. Garnish it with the leg of beef, with the fingers — which are bits of bread the length and thickness of a finger — roasted in a pan with butter or lard as was said above in Recipe 38. If you like you can add in some saffron. Then serve.

Capon (and any other meat) with Bread Fingers is made in the same way: prepared thus, it is called Such-and-Such Meat with Bread Fingers.

43. Stewkettle Pottage[43.1]

Simmer some crusts of coarse bread with some good bouillon from your stewing kettle, seasoned with pepper, salt and a little chopped parsley. Then serve. The outer slices of bouillon bread can be used the same way,[43.2] with neither parsley nor pepper, if you wish.

[42.1] See La Varenne's description of these *tailladins* in Recipe 38, above.

[42.2] This procedure is quite common. The reason for pricking an onion with cloves is explained in Recipe XVI,17, below: the cloves are felt to dull the pungency of the onion.

[43.1] I. D. G. translates the qualification in this rubric, *de marmite*, as "of the Boyler, or great Pot." Further on for the same word *marmite* he writes "boyler, great pot or beefe pot."

[43.2] The text reads: *L'entameure de pain boüillon se sert de même.* I. D. G., who writes "The first cuttings of loafes are served in the like manner," seems not to understand that *pain boüillon* designates a variety of coarse bread. *Brod* is an old word meaning the broth of boiled meats (Godefroy); at the same time, *brode* designated a mixed-grain bread, half-wheat, half-rye (Godefroy). Cotgrave glosses *pain de brode* as "browne bread, course houshold bread, a loafe whereof is to weigh 96 ounces, or six pound." A coarse bread, the name *pain bouillon* or *pain de brode* presumably indicates either that its most common use was as a sop or else that its very toughness required it to be softened in bouillon.

44. Pottage of Fried Calf's Head

When a calf's head is cooked, remove its bones and cut it up into as many pieces as you wish, then flour it and fry it with butter or lard. Simmer your bread and garnish it with what you have fried. Serve the platter very heaped up, and garnished with such garnishes as mushrooms, sliced pomegranates or lemons, and lemon juice.

45. Pottage of Mutton Fried with Turnip

Get the upper ends of breast of mutton, fry them and boil them well until they can take the turnips, which, cut up and fried well, you will put with your mutton — this latter well cooked and seasoned with cloves, salt and a bouquet of herbs. Simmer your bread, and set it out. If your pottage is not thick enough, sift[45] a little flour into the bouillon to thicken it; and add in white pepper and vinegar. Then serve.

46. Pottage of Shoulder Knuckle[46] in Ragout

With your knuckles blanched in cool water, flour them and sauté them in a pan in butter or lard. Cook them in a terrine along with all garnishes that can take such cooking, such as asparagus, mushrooms or truffles. Simmer your bread or crusts in good bouillon and garnish it with your knuckles, asparagus stalks, mushrooms and with whatever you happen to have. Then serve.

47. Pottage of Roast Woodcock

When woodcocks have been roasted, put them into a pot with good bouillon and a bouquet of herbs, and cook them well. Afterwards, simmer your bread, and garnish it with your woodcocks and with whatever you happen to have. Then serve.

You could also do it in the same way as for Marbled Partridge.[47]

---

[45] *passez un peu de farine dans le bouillon*: either "sift" or merely "pass" or "put" is possible here for *passez*.

[46] The original phrase is *manche d'épaule*. For that, I. D. G. hesitates a little with his "handles or knuckles of shoulders." See also Recipe XIV,27.

[47] The author has not identified any of his recipes expressly as Marbled Partridge. However, in the Pottage of Marbled Quail at Recipe 8 of this chapter, the dish's name seems to point to the same procedure. An explanation of the marbling effect can be found in Recipe 26, above; and Recipe 6 for *Pottage of Fricaseed Partridge* has a garnish which mixes white almond broth and mutton stock, which combination is almost certainly intended to produce a marbled appearance.

45. *Potage de mouton frit aux navets.*

48. Half Bisque [of Large Dove]

Get rather large doves, open them and cook them in the same way as for the Bisque — which method you can easily find by looking at the Table.[48] Garnish and season them in the same way, too, so that, if you can, it will be as good as the Bisque. Then serve.

49. Jacobin Cheese Pottage[49.1]

Get a capon — still with all its proper members[49.2], such as wings and legs — and some cheese with which you make as many layers as of the meat[49.3] if you can.[49.4] If it is not thick enough, mix in two or three eggs. With the fire shovel you can give it colour. To strengthen your bouillon and improve it, grind up the capon bones and boil them with your best bouillon, well seasoned. Simmer your bread, which you can garnish with pistachios, lemons or pomegranate seeds. Then serve.

---

[48] We can save our reader the bother: see the first recipe in this chapter. Since this present version of the preparation insists that the cooking and garnishing in both recipes are identical, it remains unclear in just what way they are intended to differ. Normally a "half-bisque" would designate a partial treatment. Because the smaller doves (of Recipe 1) are trussed and the larger doves (here) are cut open, their cooking time may be less than in the previous case, and so perhaps the bisque is merely a half bisque.

[49.1] See also Nicolas de Bonnefons, *Delices de la campagne*, III, Ch. 1: . . . *Pottage fait au Formage, qu'aucuns appellent à la Iacobine* (p. 202 in the Amsterdam, 1661 edition).

[49.2] The text reads, *chapon garni de ses os appropriés*, which I. D. G. renders as, "a Capon garnished with his bones fitted" — that is, properly arranged.

[49.3] The recipe is not explicit — is even a little confusing: it assumes that the reader recalls the details of Recipe 13, above, for "standard" Jacobin Pottage, and realizes that the capon has to be cooked, perhaps with herbs, and its meat chopped very finely and strained. It is then the resultant meat paste (optionally thickened with eggs) that is layered alternatively with the cheese. Previously the minced capon was layered with almond paste; here cheese replaces the almond paste.

[49.4] In I. D. G. this last phrase concludes an instruction not found in the 1651 French text: " . . . and you shall besprinkle all with almond broth, if you can; If it be not thick enough, allay two or three egs, ..." The question of suitable thickness would seem to arise with regard to a finishing garnish of almond milk rather than with the cheese.

49. Potage à la Iacobine au fromage.

Chapter IV
Stuffed Pottages

1. Pottage of Stuffed Capon

After having dressed them, remove their bones through the neck[1] and fill them with all sorts of tidbits — such as squab and the meat of the capon itself chopped up with beef fat or mutton fat; when they are seasoned and trussed up, put them into a pot with bouillon and cook them. Simmer your bread, which you garnish with your capons and with all sorts of tidbits. Then serve.

2. Pottage of Stuffed Deboned Cockerel

After your cockerels have been dressed, remove their stomach bone; fill them with minced veal[2.1] which you make of chopped veal, raw egg yolks, chives, parsley, pepper or spice[2.2] according to your taste, the whole seasoned with salt. After you have trussed them up and blanched them, put them into a pot and garnish them with good seasoning; simmer them well. Set them out, garnishing them with whatever you have on hand. Serve.

3. Pottage of Stuffed Chicken

After they have been carefully dressed, blanch them in cool water. Remove their skin with your finger and fill them with a stuffing made of veal and white capon meat, together with fat and egg yolks, everything chopped up and mixed together. Truss the chickens and put them into a

---

[1] This procedure avoids having to cut the fowl open.

[2.1] This *gaudivaux* or *godiveau*, which La Varenne goes on immediately to describe, is a sort of "sub-preparation", either on hand in the kitchen or made up as needed, as is the case here. I.D.G. keeps the term *godiveaux*, though in the plural. In his preliminary glossary he defines *gaudiveaux* as "forced meat of veale, that is, meat of veale minced, seasoned, and wrought into small long peeces like chitterlings." This minced, spiced, veal mixture, though not necessarily shaped as I.D.G. writes, is again called for as a stuffing in Recipes V,10, V,69, V,78 and V,82.

[2.2] La Varenne frequently specifies an ingredient which he calls simply *épice*, "spice" in a sort of collective singular. This should likely be understood to be a ground mixture of the more common spices: cinnamon, ginger and perhaps nutmeg, to the taste of the cook.

pot with bouillon and a bouquet of herbs. Simmer your bread, garnish it with your chickens, artichoke hearts and asparagus stalks. Then serve.

4. Pottage of Stuffed Squab

When they are thoroughly scalded and dressed, with their skin off, and they are stuffed like the chickens, blanch them in cool water; put them into a pot, cook them suitably and season them with a strip of lard. Then simmer your bread and garnish it with your young doves, along with their liver and wings, and the drippings from a spit-roasted shoulder of mutton. Serve.

5. Pottage of Stuffed Duck

Get your ducks, debone them through the neck, fill them up with whatever good things you have — such as squab, mushrooms, truffles, veal sweetbreads and other similar things; make your stuffing with a lean piece of fresh[5] pork, chopped up with raw egg yolks, parsley, chives, pepper or spices according to your taste. Sew up your ducks, blanch them in cool water and put them into a pot with bouillon. Cook them and season them; moisten a little flour with the bouillon in order to thicken your pottage. Then simmer your bread and garnish it with your ducks and with whatever you have on hand for serving.

6. Pottage of Stuffed Knuckle of Veal[6.1]

Cut the veal knuckles up to the loin,[6.2] remove the skin from them cleanly and bind up the end of the knuckle;[6.3] then soak them in cool water. Remove the meat from them and take out the ligaments; chop the meat up with beef or mutton fat, bacon, egg yolks and fine herbs. When everything is chopped up and seasoned, fill them,[6.4] and put them into a

---

[5] Fresh as distinct from preserved, salted pork, normally used for such purposes.

[6.1] In modern meat-cutting the *jarret* is the hind shin and knee of an animal. La Varenne wants his *jarret de veau* to include a little higher than the calf's knee. I.D.G. translates the phrase more generally as "legs of veal".

[6.2] *jusques contre la longe.*

[6.3] The skin, removed in a single piece from around each hock, is to be bound around the joint ready to receive the chopped meat mixture. See a similar procedure in Recipe 10, below.

[6.4] The skin still surrounds the shank; it is this skin which is now stuffed, so that the knuckle is restored to a semblance of its original form.

pot with some bouillon. Cook them, adding in herbs, depending on the season, or a little white chicory. Simmer your bread and garnish it with the knuckles, which you can glaze with egg yolks or verjuice if you like. Then serve.

7. Pottage of Stuffed Breast of Veal

Get a breast of veal and make an opening in its end. Make a stuffing with a little meat and grease, the soft inner part of a loaf of bread and all sorts of good herbs; chop everything up and season it. Then blanch the breast and put it into a pot with bouillon; cook it well with capers, chicory and chopped herbs. Simmer your bread. Garnish if you wish. Then serve.

8. Pottage of Deboned, Stuffed Calf's Head

When the calf's head is thoroughly scalded, remove its skin and cook it thoroughly. When it is done, debone it; remove the brain and eyes so as to set them back later in their places. Chop up the meat with beef fat or marrow, and with raw egg yolks to bind the stuffing. Then put the brain and eyes back where they belong. When the calf's head is stuffed, sew it up neatly again, blanch it in cool water and put it into a pot with bouillon; cook it well. Then get calf's feet and give them a piquant treatment[8] by half cooking them in water, splitting them in half and sautéing them in a frying pan in butter and lard; then put them into your pot with capers. Then simmer your bread, garnish it with the head and feet, along with the capers. Serve.

9. Pottage of Deboned, Stuffed Lamb's Head

Do this the same as the Calf's Head. After it is well scalded, remove its skin and cook it. When cooked, remove the meat, dress it with grease or lard, seasoned according to your taste; stuff it with a piece of liver and lamb's lungs, beef fat or marrow, raw egg yolks, parsley and fine herbs, everything chopped up together. Blanch it and put it[9.1] into a pot with

---

[8] The text has *les passez en ragoust*. I. D. G. translates this as "frie them into Ragoust." The phrase, however, merely summarizes what will follow.

[9.1] *Puis les empotez . . . faites-les cuire & les assaisonnez . . .* : the lamb's head, which has been singular up to this point in the recipe, suddenly becomes plural as soon as the stuffing has been inserted.

7. Potage de poitrine de veau farcie.

some bouillon; cook it and season it with fine herbs. Simmer your bread, and garnish it with your heads and giblets — which you can blanch if you want, with[9.2] egg yolks diluted in verjuice. Serve.

10. Pottage of Stuffed Leg of Mutton[10]

Get a leg of mutton, debone it and chop the meat up very finely with grease and lard, then stuff the skin with that and sew it up again neatly so that the end of the knuckle is clean; everything is seasoned with salt and spice according to your taste. Put it into a pot and cook it well with a bouquet of herbs, capers and turnips. Simmer your bread, set it out and garnish it with your turnips. Then serve.

11. Pottage of Stuffed Gosling

When they have been dressed, draw the breastbone[11] out of them and stuff them with whatever stuffing you like. Then flour them and put them into a pot with bouillon. Simmer your bread and garnish it with your goslings, along with peas, with pea purée or with whatever you like. Then serve.

12. Pottage of Deboned, Stuffed Partridge

Draw out the partridges' brisket. Get veal and[12] capon meat, chop it up and season it as you like with salt, spice and fine herbs, and stuff your partridges neatly with it. Put them into a pot with bouillon and cook them well with a bouquet of herbs. Simmer your bread; garnish it around the platter with asparagus stalks and artichoke hearts. Then serve.

13. Pottage of Stuffed Young Turkey[13.1]

After having dressed a young turkey and drawn out its brisket, get

12. Potage de perdrix defoſſées farcies.

[9.2] In the original there is no punctuation before "with": . . . *blanchir si vous voulez avec jaunes d'oeufs . . . .*

[10] The French phrase which appears in this recipe, *membre de mouton*, is glossed by Cotgrave: "Un membre de veau, de mouton, &c. A joynt of Veale, Mutton, &c."

[11] *brechet*, translated by I. D. G. as "brisket".

[12] I. D. G. has "or" here.

[13.1] The *poulet d'Inde* here and elsewhere may possibly be understood to refer to a Guinea chicken as well. Throughout his *French Cook* I. D. G. translates *poulet d'Inde* as "turkie"; La Varenne mentions *dindons* and *dindonneaux* elsewhere. Even back in the sixteenth century, when this was a novel creature, newly arrived in Europe, there was already some confusion about the origin and proper name of the fowl. Even as

veal and fat, chop it up as finely as if it were minced; thicken your stuffing with eggs, mix in tidbits or squab, and raw egg yolks. Put the young turkey into a pot with bouillon and cook it, putting in chestnuts and truffles. Simmer your bread, and garnish it with what is in your pot. Then serve.

To make the bouquet,[13.2] get chives, parsley and thyme and bind them up together.

---

late as the beginning of the nineteenth century the *Théâtre d'agriculture et ménage des champs* (original edition Paris, 1600) of Olivier de Serres, Seigneur de Pradel (1539-1619), 4 vols. (Paris, 1802; Vol. 2, Ch. III, p. 274) still calls the bird *la volaille d'Inde*.

[13.2] This bouquet must be intended to be used in a way similar to that mentioned in the preceding recipe: it is to go into the cooking pot along with the chestnuts and truffles.

Chapter V

Entrées
that can be made in Military Kitchens or in the Field[v]

1. Young Turkey[1.1] with Raspberries

After a young turkey is dressed, remove its brisket and its meat, which you chop up with fat and a little veal; mix that with egg yolks and squab, all of it well seasoned with salt, pepper, capers and ground cloves. Stuff your young turkey with that. Then mount it on a spit and turn it gently. When it is almost done, take it down and put it in a terrine with bouillon, mushrooms and a bouquet of herbs.[1.2] To thicken the sauce, get a little cut-up lard and put it into a frying pan; when it has melted, draw it off and mix it with a little flour and let it brown, and dilute it with a little bouillon and vinegar; then put it into your terrine with lemon juice. Serve.

---

[v] This chapter of entrées presents possible dishes for the initial (and main) course in meals on meat days during most of the year; it will be one of the longest and gastronomically most interesting of the entire book. The contemporary English translator, I. D. G., usually renders the word *entrée* as "first course".

The qualification that La Varenne places in the title, *qui se peuvent faire dans les armées ou en la campagne*, is not a limitation. Rather it claims a much broader usefulness for these recipes: they are suitable not only for normal meat-day use at home but all 86 of these dishes can be made also when the cook and his master are away from home. Such "portability" was presumably of great interest to the class for which La Varenne's readers were apt to be working professionally. It may be recalled that La Varenne's master was himself a military man. As the chief cook of the Marquis of Uxelles, La Varenne was very aware of the particular difficulties inherent in providing proper meals for a noble household which was not only itinerant but from time to time had to put up temporarily in entirely makeshift accommodations — in places and conditions that, as far as the kitchen staff were concerned, were apt not to be conducive to their best work. That aspect of La Varenne's responsibilities bulked so large in his own professional consciousness that he included a relatively extensive reference to his master's military qualifications in the sub-title of *The French Cook*.

[1.1] *poulet d'Inde*. Later editions more helpfully show this rubric as "Young Turkey *Stuffed* with Raspberries".

[1.2] To this I. D. G. adds, " ... which you shall make with Parsley, thime and Chibols tied together."

If it is in raspberry season, put a handful of them on top.[1.3]

2. Cardinal's Leg of Mutton[2.1]

Get a leg of mutton, beat it[2.2] and lard it with coarse pieces of lard[2.3], then skin it.[2.4] Flour the mutton and sauté it in a frying pan in lard. Cook it with some bouillon and a bouquet of parsley, thyme and chives bound with mushrooms, truffles and tidbits. The sauce should be thick. Then serve.

3. Veal Hocks *à l'épigramme*[3.1]

When veal hocks are blanched in cool water, flour them and sauté them in a frying pan in melted or clarified lard. Then break them apart and put them into a pot seasoned with salt, pepper, cloves and a bouquet of herbs; add in an onion, a little bouillon and capers. Then coat them in batter[3.2] and braise them with the pot's lid on; cook them gradually covered like that for three hours. After that you uncover them; reduce your sauce until everything is the better for it; add in some mushrooms if you have any. Then serve.

[1.3] This final option hardly seems significant enough to determine the title of the dish, particularly given that I. D. G. appends here: " . . . if not, some Pomgranate."

[2.1] The sense of the qualification in this dishname is not clear. I. D. G. translates the phrase *à la Cardinale* as "after the Cardinal's way", which implies a particular historic tradition, perhaps exclusive to the household of the Marquis of Uxelles. In Chapter V there is also a *Pasté à la Cardinale* (Recipe 85). Escoffier offers a recipe for a *Sauce Cardinal* (§69), used with lobster, which seems quite unrelated to anything to which La Varenne attaches the qualification *cardinal*.

[2.2] This "beating" of raw meat is an initial step in the preparation of the meat in many dishes.

[2.3] Just as I. D. G. glosses *meane lard* as "slices of lard, of a middle sise", he likewise says of *great lard* — the expression by which he translates La Varenne's *gros lard* — that "They are big slices of lard."

[2.4] The sequence here of larding the mutton and *then* skinning it seems strange.

[3.1] There seems to be only a slight similarity between this dish and a modern *épigramme*. A common element is perhaps that the meat is cooked coated. In Pierre de Lune's *jarrets de veau à l'épigramme*, however, no such coating is apparent: see *Le cuisinier*, in *L'art de la cuisine française au XVIIe siècle* (Paris: Payot & Rivages, 1995), p. 336. See also Escoffier, §1871.

[3.2] The text reads *les farinés avec de la paste*: "flour them with some batter." This procedure may account for La Varenne's qualification, *à l'epigramme*.

4. Loin of Veal in a Marinade[4.1]

Beat loin of veal and lard it with coarse lard; marinate it in vinegar, salt, pepper, spice,[4.2] cloves, lemon, orange, onion and rosemary or sage. Then mount it on a spit and roast it, basting it with the sauce until it is cooked. When it is done, simmer it in the sauce, which you thicken with grated bread or with clean flour moistened with some broth. Garnish your dish with mushrooms, beef palates or asparagus stalks. Then serve.

5. Canards en ragoust.

5. Ducks in Ragout

Lard ducks with coarse lard and sauté them in a pan; then put them into a terrine or a pot and add in good seasoning of salt, ground spice, chives and parsley, depending on your taste; let them cook well. Garnish with whatever you find that goes best with their colour. Then serve.

6. Squab in Ragout

Pluck them dry, clean them out and sauté them in a pan in plain or clarified lard. Put them into a pot with good bouillon and cook them with a bouquet of herbs. When they are cooked, garnish them with their livers and veal sweetbreads, with everything seasoned with salt and spice. Then serve.

7. Pullets in Ragout

Get pullets[7] after they have hung properly and lard them with coarse lard; then cut them in half and sauté them in a pan. Put them into a pot with bouillon and a bouquet of herbs; let them cook at length with several truffles, mushrooms or a few little bits of roast meat — that is, mutton or unsalted pork — in order to flavour them. Garnish them with their livers, with pistachios or lemon. Then serve.

4.1 *à la marinade*: this is a sort of pickling, in which apparently, the vinegar and acidic citrus flavours predominate rather than the salt.

4.2 See IV,2, note 2.2, concerning the powdered spices that La Varenne calls simply *épice*.

7 The term La Varenne uses here is *poulardes*. These seem not to be the modern neutered, fattened hen chicken. Chapter I lists both *poulardes* and *poularde grasse* (for this latter, see also Recipe VI,56), but then, expressly, further lists *poularde châtrée de Normandie*: the neutering of a pullet is a particular practice. The term *poularde* is not in Cotgrave; perhaps because of that, uncertain, I. D. G. translates merely "henne".

8. White Pudding[8.1]

Cf. Escoffier's *Boudin blanc or dinaire*, §1405.

Get sheep's intestines and scrape them very clean. Then get four pounds of solid fresh pork fat and cut it up very small; also get the white meat of two capons and chop it up as finely as powder and mix that with your fat; then mix in fifteen raw eggs, a quart of milk, and the soft part of half a loaf of bread, everything being seasoned with sausage spices, which you will find ready made at the pork butcher's, and a little anise. If you cannot get those prepared spices, take pepper, cloves, salt and ginger, mix them together. Then feed all of that mixture into the intestines by means of a copper or white-metal instrument made for the purpose, which is called a sausage stuffer.[8.2] Roast them on the grill with a piece of greased paper under them. Serve.

9. Sausages of Partridge White-Meat

Your partridges having been roasted, take off their white meat and chop it up very small. Get some solid fresh pork fat, four times as much as the minced meat, and mix everything together, with it well seasoned as for the White Pudding;[9.1] add in milk as well in an appropriate quantity. Feed[9.2] everything into sheep's intestines as for the White Pudding. Those also you blanch in milk, and tie up their ends. Roast them [on a grill] on some greased paper. If you like, you can stuff the mixture into an intestine of a suckling piglet or into a young turkey.[9.3] Then serve.

[8.1] The French word *boudin*, designating a sort of sausage, was early adopted by the English with the (mis-)pronunciation *budding* and, eventually, *pudding*. There were, and are, two main varieties: *boudin noir*, black (or blood) pudding, and the present *boudin blanc*, white pudding. The black variety is not represented in La Varenne, but see a reference to a *boudin gris* in Recipe 64, below.

[8.2] At this point, rather than the phrase *que l'on nomme Boudiniere*, I. D. G. has a vital direction not found in the original French edition: " . . . and whiten them in milk, & rost them . . . ." The next recipe refers back to this missing direction.

[9.1] That is, in the immediately preceding recipe. The seasoning there is a commercially available "sausage spice" or, if home-made, pepper, cloves, salt and ginger. To that spice mixture for the White Pudding is added a little anise.

[9.2] What is implied here is the use of the sausage stuffer mentioned in the previous recipe and in Recipe 11, below. The verb here is *entonnez*, as if the device were funnel-shaped.

[9.3] The text reads " . . . into an intestine of a suckling piglet or *of* a young turkey."

10. Large Sausages[10.1]

Get calves' entrails, cut them up with solid pork fat and pork meat, and simmer everything together in a pot. When it is cooked and cool, mix in a little milk and raw eggs, then feed it into a pig intestine with the same seasoning as for the White Pudding.[10.2] Make some with half milk, half water. When that is done, set it to roast on the grill with greased paper beneath. Serve.

11. Saveloy

Get an ox intestine and scrape it thoroughly. Get lard, pork or mutton or any other meat you like, chop it up and grind it with pepper, salt, white wine, cloves, fine herbs, onion and solid fresh pork fat. Then feed that mixture into pieces of the intestine cut to the length of a Saveloy. Tie their ends and hang them in the chimney.[11.1] When you wish to use them, cook them with a little wine and fine herbs.[11.2] After they are cooked, you can keep them a month. Then serve.

12. Marinated Chicken[12]

Get your chickens, split them in half and beat them, then steep them in vinegar which is well seasoned with salt and spice. When you wish to use them, flour them — or else make a little batter of raw eggs and a little flour moistened with the eggs; fry them in melted plain or clarified lard. When they are done, set them to simmer a little in their marinade. Then serve them.

[10.1] I.D.G. provides a gloss for the French *andoüilles* which is found here: "They are the great guts of porke, or beef, filled up with thinne slices of tender meat, or small guts of porke well seasoned with peper, salt, fine hearbs, &c. Some doe call them Chitterlings."

[10.2] See Recipes 8 and 9, above.

[11.1] The throat of large kitchen fireplaces was furnished with hooks for the purpose of smoking or merely drying such meats.

[11.2] Perhaps more abstemious, or just frugal, I.D.G. has, "When you shall use them, seeth them in water, and about the latter end, put into it a little wine, and some fine herbs."

[12] See also Recipe VIII,23. The procedure in Recipe XXIII,4 is intended to preserve the chicken for future use.

13. Shoulder Knuckles *à l'Olivier*[13]

Beat your knuckles, blanch them in cool water and dry them. Then, when they are floured, sauté them in a pan in plain or clarified lard. When they are fully fried, put them into a pot with extremely little bouillon, and put in a bouquet of herbs, a little sautéed onion, along with mushrooms, capers, kidneys and beef palates, everything seasoned well with salt, spice or pepper. Cover the pot with a lid; make up a bit of soft pastry to seal the lid to keep it from letting air in. Then set the pot on some coals and cook the knuckles slowly. Then serve.

14. Piece of Beef in the English or Chalon[14.1] Fashion

Get a piece of breast of beef and boil it well. When it is almost cooked, take it out and lard it with coarse lard, then mount it on the spit with a marinade, and the dripping pan below. That marinade is made up as for the Loin of Veal,[14.2] and you baste it on with a bouquet of sage. If the beef doesn't stay on the spit, get sticks and tie it on at each end.[14.3] After it is roasted, take it down and put it into a terrine and simmer it in its marinade until you are ready to serve. Garnish it with whatever you like, with capers or with turnips, or with both together, or with beef palates or parsley, or with the marinade itself, provided it is thick enough.[14.4] Then serve.

15. Braised Breast of Veal[15]

Get a good fat breast of veal, put it into a terrine in the oven with

14. Piece de bœuf à l'Angloise ou Chalonnoise.

---

[13] The phrase *à l'olivier* (the noun is without a capital in the printed text) may mean either "as a olive tree" or else "Oliver-style". I. D. G. seems to choose the second sense: "Knuckles, or Handles of Shoulders, Oliveir (*sic*) way." Neither interpretation helps much here. However, in Recipes VIII,75 and XXVIII,21 the term is applied to a mushroom dish and that may provide a clue as to the sense of the phrase.

[14.1] The town of Chalon was the seat of La Varenne's employer, the Marquis d'Uxelles. Later editions of the *Cuisinier françois* drop this latter alternative and clearly provincial qualification, *ou Chalonnoise*.

[14.2] See Recipe 4, above. There the basting sauce is composed of vinegar, salt, pepper, spice, cloves, lemon, orange, onion and rosemary or sage.

[14.3] The sticks are placed parallel with the spit and around the meat.

[14.4] Recipe 4 has already explained how to thicken the marinade for this purpose.

[15] *Poitrine de veau à l'estoffade.* In seventeenth-century France the culinary term *estouffade*, its origins in early Italian cookery, continues to exist but has lost a little of its original sense. For La Varenne it describes something "smothered" while sealed

bards of lard under it. Then season it and cover it until it becomes coloured and is half cooked. Then add mushrooms, beef palates, capers and sweetbreads in such a way that they get mixed in and finish cooking. Then serve.

16. Partridge in Ragout

Get your partridges, dress them and lard them with three or four lardoons of coarse lard; then flour them and sauté them in a pan in plain or clarified lard. Then cook them in a terrine until they disintegrate;[16] season them with salt and spice. When you are ready to serve, get lard, beat it in a mortar and mix it into your ragout. Serve.

17. Ox Tongue in Ragout

Escoffier, *Langue de bœuf*, §1153

Bard an ox tongue with coarse lard, put it into a pot, cook it and season it highly.[17] When it is almost done, let it cool, lard it, mount it on a spit and baste it with its ragout until it is roasted. After you have taken it down, simmer it in the sauce with a little ground onion, a little lard and a little vinegar. Then serve.

18. Pork Tongue in Ragout

Get it fresh and sauté it in a pan in lard; then cook it well in a pot, seasoning it highly. When it is almost done, mix in a ground onion, truffles, and dry flour with a little white wine; simmer it in that same bouillon. When cooked, serve.

19. Mutton Tongue in Ragout

Get a number of mutton tongues and, when they are cooked, marinate[19] them and sauté them in a pan. Simmer them in some bouillon, then

17. Langue de bœuf en ragoust.

---

in a covered terrine. La Varenne uses the expression *à l'estoffade* only rarely. A similar cooking method is found elsewhere (for instance in Recipes 13, above, and 20, below; in no place, however, is an oven specified), but the exact term *estouffade* is found again only in Recipes 54 and 57, below. See also the cognate expression *à l'estuvée* in Recipe 62.

[16] *bien consommer*: as in Recipe III,19, La Varenne uses the verb to indicate a cooking which is so thorough that the meat begins to fall apart.

[17] In this and the following recipe the phrase *de haut goût*, which qualifies the basic seasoning to be used, actually defines the sense of the dishes' name: *Langue de Bœuf en ragoust* and, below, *Langue de Porc en ragoust*. See the note to the term *ragoust* in Recipe III,21.

[19] The type-setter has printed *matinez* rather than *marinez*. La Varenne does not give

mix in onion, mushrooms, truffles and parsley, the whole being seasoned with salt and pepper according to your taste, with a dash of verjuice and vinegar. Then serve.

20. Mutton Tail in Ragout[20.1]

Get a sheep's tail still attached to the leg. Lard all of it with coarse lard, set it to cook with a piece of beef. When it is half done, take it out[20.2] and sauté it. Then put it into a terrine with bouillon; season it well with mushrooms, capers and beef palates. Cover it and let it cook well. Then serve it.

21. A Daube of a Leg of Mutton[21]

It should be larded with coarse lard, then put [to cook] in a pot with water, and seasoned. When it is almost done, add in a suitable amount of white wine, and finish cooking it with fine herbs and lemon rind or orange rind — but very little so that it won't be bitter. When you wish to serve it, garnish the rim of the platter with parsley and flowers.

Escoffier, Daube à l'Avignonnaise, §1346

22. A Daube of Young Turkey

This is done in the same way as the Leg of Mutton,[22] except that they should be bound up before being set to cook; they should be amply garnished with salt and all spices — the same seasoning as above. Serve with parsley.

Escoffier, Dindonneau en daube, §1719

23. Hare Civet

Get a hare, cut it into pieces and put it into a pot with bouillon; then cook it, seasoning it with a bouquet of herbs. When it is half done, add

Escoffier, Civet de lièvre, §1821

---

the composition of the marinade, although a complex one is described in Recipe 4, above.

[20.1] Cf. Recipe 30, below.

[20.2] I. D. G. suggests "flowre it" here.

[21] *Membre de Mouton à la daube*: the daube remains today a standard way to braise a meat in a wine stock with herbs. See Recipe 33, below, where the nature of La Varenne's *daube* seems to be determined largely by the ingredients that are added to the bouillon, in particular the white wine. The word is an early borrowing from an Italian verb, "to garnish, daub."

[22] This dish is described in the preceding recipe, *Membre de mouton à la daube*.

24. Poiĉtrine de mouton en aricot.

in a little wine, and sauté a little flour with an onion[23.1] and extremely little vinegar. Serve it properly with Green Sauce.[23.2]

24. Haricot of Breast of Mutton[24.1]

Sauté it in a pan in butter or melted lard, then put it into a pot with bouillon and season it with salt. When it is half cooked, likewise sauté turnips in a pan, sliced in half or any other way; mix them in, not forgetting [when sautéing them] a little lard with a little flour, a finely chopped onion, a dash of vinegar and a bouquet of herbs. Serve it with the sauce short.[24.2]

25. Lamb in Ragout

Roast it, then put it into a terrine with a little bouillon, vinegar, salt, pepper, cloves and a bouquet of herbs, a little sautéed flour[25] with ground onion, along with capers, mushrooms, lemon or orange rind — everything simmered well together. Serve.

26. Sirloin[26] of Veal in Ragout

Cut the meat up into ribs, flour them and sauté them in the pan in

---

[23.1] The frying medium, normally lard, is not specified; it is possible there is none. Generically a *civet* is a preparation based upon a *cæpa*, onion; it has a very long tradition in early French cooking. The onion here is probably chopped, as the following recipe, and mixed with the flour.

[23.2] See Recipe VII,2.

[24.1] The French text has *Poictrine de mouton en aricot.* The *Hericoc de mouton* had been in French recipe collections since the *Viandier* of Taillevent in the early fourteenth century. Traditionally this was a dish of chunks of mutton first sautéed in lard with chopped onions and then boiled in beef bouillon with herbs and verjuice. The modern dish called *Haricot de mouton* is glossed by the *Nouveau Larousse Gastronomique* merely as "mutton stew."

[24.2] *à sauce courte.* In Recipes 36 and 66 in this chapter of entrées, and elsewhere, the term *sauce courte* designates a seasoned bouillon that has been reduced by boiling; it may also be thickened by adding ingredients such as flour, as in Recipe 66, but that manner of thickening is of course not essential for the designation "short".

[25] This *farine passée* or "fried flour" is a fairly common thickener, an alternative to starch where the colour of the finished sauce need not be clear or white. See Recipe 42, below.

[26] This may be slightly misleading a translation for La Varenne's *haut costé*, even though Cotgrave glosses this phrase as "a surloine" and I. D. G. writes *Syrloine* here. The first direction in the recipe indicates that the cook is likely dealing with rib cutlets.

lard. Then put them into a pot and cook them with a little bouillon, capers, asparagus and tuffles — everything simmered well. Serve.

27. A Daube of a Piece of Beef

When it is half cooked, lard it with coarse lard and put it back again to cook in the same bouillon, if you like. Then, when it is well cooked and seasoned — not forgetting the wine — serve it like a leg of mutton.[27]

28. Leg of Mutton *à la logate*[28.1]

After choosing a leg of mutton, beat it well, remove its skin and the flesh of the knuckle, of which you cut off the end. Lard it with medium-sized pieces of lard, flour it and sauté it in a pan in plain or clarified lard. When it looks quite russet-coloured,[28.2] put it into a pot with a spoonful of bouillon, seasoned well with salt, pepper, cloves and a bouquet of herbs; you can add capers, mushrooms and truffles. Stop up the pot with a lid sealed with flour moistened with water, neither too soft nor too hard. Cook it on a few coals for three hours. When it is done, remove the lid and garnish it with whatever you have, such as kidneys, artichoke hearts, sweetbreads and a short sauce.[28.3] Serve; around the platter put sliced lemon or pomegranate.

29. Piece of Beef as a Fool's Bauble[29.1]

When a piece of beef is almost cooked, lard it with coarse lard. Then

This *daube* remains standard in modern French cooking: Escoffier, *Daube chaude à la provençale*, §1172.

---

[27] ... *Servés comme l'éclanche.* An *éclanche*, the term appearing here, is the same as a *gigot de mouton*. The comparison in treatment may be with reference to the manner of serving the Leg of Mutton in the next recipe, or perhaps in Recipe 2, above.

[28.1] I. D. G. reads this qualification as "after the Legate's way." A century later, Diderot's *Encyclopédie ou Dictionnaire raisonné des sciences, des arts et des métiers* (Paris, 1751 ff.) seems to have had at hand a later version of La Varenne's recipe which it reproduces, with its errors, for its definition of the phrase: "Gigot de mouton à la *logate*, est un gigot qu'on a bien battu, qu'on a lardé avec moyen lard, fariné & passé par la poële, avec du lard ou du sain doux, après avoir ôté la peau & la chair du manche, & l'avoir coupé. Lorsqu'il paroît assez doux, on l'empote, avec une cueillerée de bouillon, assaisonné de sel, poivre, clou, & un bouquet. On l'étoupe ensuite avec un couvercle bien fermé, on le garnit de farine délayée, & on le fait cuir ainsi à petit feu."

[28.2] *roux* in this second edition. In later editions typesetters perpetuate an error: *doux*, "sweet," "soft."

[28.3] Though La Varenne is not explicit, this short sauce is probably meant to be same bouillon from which the mutton has just been removed, but quite a bit boiled down.

[29.1] *Piéce de bœuf à la marotte.* See also the preparation called Bauble Pie at Recipe

Queuë de mouton roſtie.

make up a pastry of dark dough[29.2] of about the size of the piece of beef; that is seasoned with whatever you like, garnished likewise, along with capers. When it has cooked at length in bouillon, add in[29.3] crushed onion and garlic. Then serve.

30. Roast Mutton Tail[30]

When it has cooked, remove its skin, cover it with salt, breadcrumbs and chopped parsley; then sauté it in a pan in front of, and not over, the fire. Then serve it with verjuice and parsley around the platter.

31. A Piece of Beef; Plain Mutton Tail[31.1]

30.

Get a piece of beef as it comes from the butcher's, sprinkle it with a little salt, but not too much in case you wish to use its bouillon later. Cook it thoroughly [in water], and remove whatever may have been salted, such as the skin. If you like, salt it again, sprinkling it with fine salt. Serve it with parsley or fried bread around the platter, and occasionally with little pasties, or some piquant thickener.[31.2]

Plain Mutton Tail is made the same as the piece of beef: when it is

---

83, below. In both recipes we may suppose that the finished pasty had the elongated shape of a mock sceptre.

29.2 *un paste de paste bise*: see Recipe XXI,0, as well as the *French Pastry Chef*, Chapter I, Recipe 1, where the principal ingredient of this dark dough is rye flour: see also Recipes VIII,3 and XIV,1 and 37. The adjective *bis* describes a generally dark shade — "browne, duskie, swart, blackish," as Cotgrave glosses it. Cotgrave also has an entry for *pain bis*, which he defines as "rye bread, course bread, browne bread." The shell of this beef pasty is tough, able to hold any shape (as of a fool's bauble?) when wrapped around its meat; it is not intended to be a normal fine pastry. Generally this coarse, even rustic, *pâte bise* is associated with venison pies, as in Recipes VIII,5, XIV,6 and 9; see also the Venison Pie in VIII,3.

29.3 *passés-y oignon & ail battus*: The verb *passer* often has the sense of "to sauté" (as in *passez par la poële* in the following recipe), although the presence of *-y* seems to rule out that sense here. The onion and garlic are likely raw here.

30 *Queuë de mouton rostie*. Cf. Recipe 20, above. Both there, here and twice in the following recipe, I. D. G. interestingly persists in translating the meat as "loyne of mutton".

31.1 *Queuë de mouton au naturel*. The conjunction of these two, separate recipes is justified by similar procedures to be followed for each: preparation (salting), cooking, skinning and garnishing (with salt).

31.2 *liaison de ragoust*: La Varenne is suggesting a sauce garnish that will be both thick and flavourful.

well cooked, remove its skin and sprinkle it with salt. Garnish around the platter with parsley. Serve it hot.

32. A Daube of Piglet

When a piglet is dressed, cut it into five parts.[32] Then apply a little coarse lard to it and set it [to cook] in some bouillon, white wine, fine herbs and onions. When it is well seasoned with salt and other ingredients, serve it with parsley around the platter.

The short sauce stays with it in jelly form for serving [the dish] cold. Add saffron to it if you like.

33. A Daube of Goose

Lard a goose with coarse lard, and cook it well. Then put in a quart of white wine and season it with all that a daube calls for.[33.1]

If you wish to sauté it on a grill and serve it, quartered, with a Sauce Robert[33.2] on top, you can.

34. Goose in Ragout

Get a goose and quarter it. When it is beaten well, flour it, sauté it in a pan. Then cook it with bouillon; season it with all sorts of spices and a bouquet of herbs. Garnish it with all of the giblets[34] — that is, liver, gizzards, wings and neck. The sauce should be short and thickened with egg yolks mixed with verjuice. Then serve.

35. Teal in Ragout

When they are dressed, lard them with medium lard. Sauté them in a pan, simmer them in bouillon,[35] then put them with a little lard and flour,

---

[32] That is, cut off its legs?

[33.1] In the preceding recipe, the additional ingredients in the daube are fine herbs, onions, salt and "other ingredients". In Recipes 21 and 27, white wine is mentioned explicitly; it seems to be an essential ingredient.

[33.2] This Sauce Robert will again be called for in VI,44 in *The French Cook* and in Recipes XXXI,2 and XXXIII,24 of the *French Pastry Chef*. Recipe 56 of this present chapter identifies a thin sauce of pork drippings, vinegar, verjuice, sage and onion as *Sauce Robert*. Its essential ingredients, however, in the twentieth century as in the fifteenth, normally include mustard.

[34] *tous les abatis*. Earlier, in Recipe III,25, these goose giblets were rather tentatively given their traditional French designation of *la petite oie*. It seems that La Varenne is not confident that this older term will be understood.

[35] I.D.G. has "with well seasoned broth."

onion, capers, mushrooms, truffles, pistachios, lemon rind — everything together. Then serve.

36. Young Turkey in Ragout

Split a young turkey and beat it; then lard it[36] with coarse lard, flour it and sauté it in a pan. Then set it to simmer in a terrine with bouillon seasoned and garnished with whatever you like. Cook it until the sauce is short. Then serve.

37. Piglet in Ragout

After dressing it, remove its skin if you like, then quarter it; flour it and sauté it in a pan, well seasoned, according to your taste. It should be garnished with capers, truffles and mushrooms.

38. Loin of Veal in Ragout

When it is beaten, lard it with coarse lard and mount it on a spit. Then, when it is half cooked, set it to simmer in bouillon. Make a thick sauce,[38] with sautéed onion. The dish is garnished with mushrooms, artichokes, asparagus stalks and truffles; the calf's kidney is also cut up. Serve.

39. Lark in Ragout

When larks are dressed, remove their gizzard; crush their stomach a little; flour them and sauté them in lard. When they are a russet colour, simmer them and season them with capers and mushrooms; you can add in lemon peel, or the stock of a leg of mutton or orange juice[39.1] or a bouquet of herbs; remove their fat. Serve them with whatever you have served.[39.2]

---

[36] I. D. G.: "if you will."

[38] The bouillon is to be thickened into this sauce. No thickening agent is mentioned, although flour may be either implied, or else accidentally omitted by the type-setter. At this point I. D. G.'s English version is, "Make a sauce of flowre and onion fryed." The procedure is common enough in La Varenne: see Recipe 23, above, for instance.

[39.1] The use of citrus pulp and peel is frequent in La Varenne's cookery. We should remember that the bitter orange is still more common in the seventeenth century than the sweet orange, and that citrus fruits are generally relied upon to provide a tangy savour to a preparation.

[39.2] *... avec ce que vous aurez servi.* I. D. G. puts this into a simple tense: "... with what you have to serve."

40. Fricasseed Veal Liver

Cut veal liver into thin slices, then sauté the slices in a pan in lard or butter, well seasoned with salt, pepper, finely chopped onion, a drop of bouillon, vinegar or verjuice mash.[40.1] To bind the sauce, add grated and finely sieved breadcrumbs.[40.2] You can serve it without simmering it — so it doesn't harden[40.3] — with capers and mushrooms.[40.4] And garnish around the platter with whatever you have on hand.

41. Calf's or Sheep's Feet in Ragout

When the calf's feet have been boiled well, flour them and sauté them in a pan in plain or clarified lard. Then set them to simmer with little bouillon, little verjuice, a bouquet of herbs, a bit of lemon and sautéed flour,[41.1] everything being well seasoned and the sauce short. Mix in capers. Serve.

Sheep's Feet are done up in the same way: when cooked and the bone removed,[41.2] flour them and sauté them in clarified lard and set them to simmer in little bouillon and verjuice, a bouquet of herbs a bit of lemon and sautéed flour; everything seasoned and the sauce short. Mix in capers. Serve.

42. Fat Tripe[42.1] in Ragout

When blanched and cooked, cut the tripe up small; fricassee it in lard, with parsley and chives, and season it with capers, vinegar, sautéed

Modern descendents are Bocuse, *Foie de veau sauté à la lyonnaise*, p. 225; and Escoffier, §1251.

41. Pieds de veau & de mouton en ragoust.

[40.1] The *verjus de grain* is a very old ingredient in the history of European cookery. As well as the sharp flavour, it lends an interesting texture to the serving sauce.

[40.2] *chapelûres de pain bien passez.* I.D.G.: "chippings of bread well fried."

[40.3] *crainte qu'il ne durcisse*: that is, either "over-thicken, solidify" in the pan, or "set, congeal" when the sauce is used as a garnish.

[40.4] These capers and mushrooms are presumably to go into the liquid mixture in which the slices of liver have sautéed but not simmered. In the next recipe, capers are added to a sauce that has been used to simmer the meat and has been thickened.

[41.1] *farine passée.* The next recipe has *farine fritte*. In Recipe XXV,40 directions are explicit: *passez un peu de farine par la poesle, jusqu'à ce qu'elle soit rousse*: "fry (or sauté) a little flour in a pan until it is a russet colour."

[41.2] *le ver osté* : I.D.G. has quite literally " . . . and the worm taken away," but *le ver* refers to the woody process within the hoof proper. It is appears again in Recipe 70.

[42.1] The phrase *gras double* is so glossed by Cotgrave.

flour[42.2] and an onion. Simmer it. Then serve it.

Alternatively, you can also mix in egg yolks and verjuice as a thickener.

Otherwise

Get very fat tripe, cut it up, and sprinkle it with salt and breadcrumbs. Roast it on a grill, seasoning it with verjuice mash or vinegar, orange juice or lemon juice. Then serve it.

Escoffier, Fricassée de poulet à l'ancienne, §1667

43. Fricasseed Chicken[43.1]

When dressed, cut chickens into pieces, wash the pieces well and boil them with good bouillon. When they are almost cooked, set them to drain; then fricassee them; after five or six turns,[43.2] season them with salt and good herbs such as parsley, chives, etc. Mix in some egg yolks to thicken the sauce. Serve them.

44. Fricasseed Squab

After scalding young doves, cut them up and sauté them in a pan in lard and butter, half and half. When they are fricasseed, throw in chives, parsley and asparagus stalks, pepper, salt and ground cloves, and sprinkle that with seasoned bouillon. Then serve them or not.[44]

[42.2] *farine fritte*, literally "fried flour," in the text. The same thickener appears in Recipes VIII,102; XXI,28; XXV,4 and 20. Pierre de Lune's variety of what he, too, calls *farine frite* but, compared with what La Varenne wrote in the preceding recipe, is quite different: "Put melted, browned lard into a terrine; when it is very hot put in some flour and stir it with a silver spoon. When the flour is browned and cooked, add bouillon to it and season it with a bundle of seasoning, a bit of lemon ... , salt and a part-slice of roast beef. You can use this mixture for brown pottages, *ragoûts*, entrées, entremets, sauces and other things." *Le Cuisinier*, ed. Laurendon (Paris: Payot & Rivages, 1995), p. 242). In the Introduction above, C(ii)(b), I have reproduced Pierre de Lune's description of the "bundle of seasoning" that he introduces into his thickener. See also *farine passée* in Recipe 25, above, and the brief note on starch in Recipe XXI,28.

[43.1] Bonnefons writes: *La fricassée de Poulets se fait ordinairement à la haste* ... (p. 204).

[43.2] So I. D. G. has this passage. The printed text reads, *les fricassez, après cinq ou six jours, assaisonnez* ....

[44] Presumably the sense of the last phrase is: ... or else keep them for another meal, cold. I. D. G. has, " ... and serve them whitened, or not."

45. *Fricandeaux*[45.1]

To make them, get veal, slice it thinly and beat it with a knife handle. Chop up all sorts of herbs, beef or mutton fat and a little lard; when that is well seasoned and thickened with raw eggs, roll the bits of meat in it, then cook them in a terrine or tourtière.[45.2] When they are cooked, serve them with sauce.

A variant survives in Escoffier's *Fricadelles*, §1277.

46. Fricassee of Veal

Get veal and slice it very thin, flour the slices very lightly and sauté them in a pan, seasoned with salt with an onion stuck with cloves. Then set them to simmer with a little bouillon. The sauce is thickened. Serve.

Escoffier, §1276

47. Round of Veal[47] in Ragout

Lard a round of veal with coarse lard, mount it on a spit and roast it until it is a little over half done. Set it to simmer with a little bouillon and a bouquet of herbs, covering it carefully. When it is cooked, serve it with a sauce thickened with grated bread or flour and an onion, and garnished with truffles and mushrooms.

48. Shoulder of Veal in Ragout

Blanch a shoulder of veal and flour it, then sauté it in a pan. When it is a good russet colour, set it to simmer in a terrine.[48.1] When it it almost cooked, season it with a bouquet of herbs, along with all sorts of tidbits, mushrooms, a little sautéed flour[48.2] and a little chopped onion, with a dash of vinegar. Then serve.

49. Shoulder of Mutton in Ragout

Beat a shoulder of mutton well and remove its skin, then flour it and sauté it in a pan in butter or melted lard. Then set it to simmer

---

[45.1] The seventeenth-century *Dictionnaire universel* of Furetière defines the term *fricandeau* as "a very thin slice of veal, beaten, seasoned with several herbs, cooked with beef or mutton fat in a terrine or *tourtière*, and which is thickened with raw eggs, and served in the first course." One might justifiably suspect that Furetière had a copy of this recipe of La Varenne right at his elbow.

[45.2] Recipe 36, above, specifies a bouillon for simmering in a terrine.

[47] See the note about *Ruelle de veau* in Recipe III,7.

[48.1] Recipes 36 and 54 specify a bouillon for this simmering.

[48.2] The text, *passez y un peu de farine, un peu d'oignon haché* , should likely be understood in the sense of "sauté *for it* flour and onion."

46. *Fricassee de Veau.*

with bouillon, a bouquet of herbs and a good seasoning. Garnish it with whatever you have, including capers. Then serve it.

50. Fried Breast of Veal

When a breast of veal is blanched, cook it in a large stew-pot or in some other pot — it does not matter whether it cooks along with some other meat. When it is done, split it open. Make a runny batter with a little flour, eggs, salt and a little parsley, then moisten the meat[50] with that preparation and fry it in clarified or melted lard. When you take it out of the pan, throw a handful of very green, very dry parsley over it — that is to say, [parsley that has been] sautéed in a pan in hot butter and browned on the fire. Then serve it.

51. Loin of Roe-Buck in Ragout

When the loin is larded, mount it on a spit. When it is half roasted, baste it with pepper, vinegar and little bouillon. Thicken the sauce with grated bread or moistened flour. Then serve.

52. Mutton Cutlets[52] in Ragout

Cut mutton cutlets up into pieces, then beat them, flour them and sauté them in a pan. When they have been sautéed, put them with bouillon and capers, everything well seasoned. Serve.

53. Stylish Beef[53]

Beat it, lard it with lard, then put it to cook in a pot with bouillon, a bouquet of herbs and all sorts of spices. When everything is boiled down, serve it with the sauce.

54. Braised Beef[54.1]

Slice it very thin; when the slices are beaten, flour them and sauté them in a pan in lard. Then put them into a terrine or pot with bouillon,

---

[50] The text has a plural pronoun, *les*, referring to the two halves of the breast of veal which are now separate.

[52] *côtelettes*: literally, as I. D. G. translates, "small ribs." In American usage, "chops."

[53] It is not immediately apparent just why *Bœuf à la Mode* should turn out to be a very plain and simple stewed beef.

[54.1] *Bœuf à l'estouffade*. Compare this dish with the *Poitrine de Veau à l'estouffade* in Recipe 15, above, and the *Perdrix à l'estoufade* in Recipe 57, below.

everything being seasoned.[54.2] Serve them with short sauce.

55. Young Rabbit in Ragout

You can fricassee young rabbits like chickens, or sauté them in a pan in a little flour mixed with butter. Then set them to simmer in bouillon seasoned with capers, orange or lemon juice, and a bouquet of chives. Serve.

Another way

When the young rabbits have roasted, cut them up, sauté them in a pan and set them to simmer in a platter with orange juice, capers and a little grated bread. The sauce piquant[55] and short. Serve.

56. Loin of Pork with Sauce Robert

Lard loin of pork with coarse lard, then roast it, basting it with ver-juice and vinegar, and with a bouquet of sage. When the grease has dripped, take it to fricassee an onion, which, when done, you put under the loin together with the sauce with which you basted it, everything being simmered together for [only] a short time so that it doesn't become [too] thick. Then serve. That sauce is called Sauce Robert.

Escoffier, *Côtes de porc sauce Robert*, §1396; *Sauce Robert*, §52

57. Braised Partridge

Get your partridges and bard them with coarse lard, and sauté them in a pan in butter or melted lard. When they are russet coloured, put them into a pot with bouillon and cook them, seasoned well.[57] For their garnish, you get truffles, mushrooms and fricasseed asparagus stalks with which you simmer them. They are served with lemon and pistachios. If the sauce is not thick enough, get a little flour or [whatever] liaison [you use], [but] do not bind it too much for fear of it being too thick.

Escoffier, *Per-dreau en estouf-fade*, §1866

58. Capon with Oysters

When your capon is dressed and barded with lard and has buttered paper over the top of it, roast it; as it is roasting, put a dripping pan

---

[54.2] It is likely that this terrine is to be sealed with a lid and put into the oven, as in Recipe 15.

[55] *sauce de haut goust*: the phrase defines a *ragoust*.

[57] Because the name of this dish indicates that it is to be prepared *à l'estouffade* (as in Recipes 15 and 54, above), we should expect the meat and its seasoning to be sealed in its pot and baked in an oven.

beneath it. After you have cleaned your oysters well, blanch them if they are old. When they are clean and blanched, sauté them in a pan of what has dripped from your capon; season them with mushrooms, onions stuck [with cloves][58] and a bouquet of herbs. When they have fricasseed, remove the bouquet and put everything else into the body of the capon, which you simmer with a few capers. Serve.

59. Young Wild Duck in Ragout

When the young wild ducks are dressed, sauté them in a pan in butter or lard; then simmer them in a terrine with bouillon and a bouquet of herbs, everything well seasoned. When they have cooked and the sauce has thickened, put in capers, mushrooms and truffles. Serve.

60. Fried Mutton Tongue in Ragout with Fritters

Escoffier, *Langues d'agneau*, §1323

Get your mutton tongues and split them in half; then sauté them in a pan in butter or melted lard, and season them well. Then put them onto a plate with verjuice and nutmeg. Then get a little flour and moisten it with an egg yolk and with the sauce which is under your tongues, then you put that into the mixture. Fry it in melted or clarified lard; when done, throw a handful of parsley into the pan, being careful to keep it green.[60] Serve them dry, or with a marinade, and with the rest of your sauce.

61. Calf's Liver in Ragout

Lard it with coarse lard and put it into a pot well seasoned with a bouquet of herbs, orange peel and capers. When it is well cooked and the sauce thickened, slice it and serve.

62. Stewed Chicken[62]

Cut chickens up very small and set them to cook with a little bouillon,

---

[58] *oygnons picqués*: "with cloves" is understood though frequently not expressed by La Varenne. The practice is widespread; see for instance Recipe 46, above, and the note to Recipe III,42.

[60] Frequently, as in Recipe 50, above, or 63, below, parsley will be described as dry or browned, sautéed in fat. Here it is meant to look fresh.

[62] *Poulets à l'estuvée*: the *estuve* or *étuve*, a "stove", was a sealed oven whose distance from the coals could be regulated; see Recipe Confections,3. The cooking method called *à l'estuvée* (cognate with the phrase *à l'estoffade*: see Recipe V,15, for instance) stewed the meat by "smothering" or "stifling" it in a sauce or its own juices. It was commonly used, appearing in some two dozen prepared dishes in *The French Cook*.

white wine and fresh butter; season them with chives and parsley chopped together. When they have cooked, mix egg yolks with some verjuice to thicken the sauce. Serve.

63. Fried Calf's Head

When a calf's head is dressed and cooked, you remove its bone. Then you make a batter with seasoned eggs; dip the head into it and set it to fry in clarified lard. When it has fried, sprinkle it with salt, lemon juice or verjuice. Then serve it with fried parsley.

64. Larded Calf's Liver

Lard calf's liver thickly with lardoons, then mount it on the spit; beneath it make a marinade[64.1] with which you baste it while it is roasting, so that the marinade becomes a sauce. When it is done, simmer it [in that sauce] with capers. Serve it.

Escoffier, Foie de veau braisé à la bourgeoise, §1247

You can use calf's liver instead of a sauce, and at other times in order to make Grey Pudding.[64.2]

65. Giblets of Young Turkey

Blanch young turkey giblets in cool water and cook them in bouillon. When they are almost done, sauté them in a pan in lard and seasoning. The sauce should be short.

66. Shoulder of Boar in Ragout

Lard a boar's shoulder with coarse lard, then put it into a cauldron full of water seasoned with salt, pepper and a bouquet of herbs; be careful not to over-season it because the bouillon must be reduced into a short sauce. When it is more than half done, add in a quart of white wine, cloves, a bay leaf or a sprig of rosemary. Then, when it is done and the sauce short, you thicken it: to do that, melt lard and sift a little flour into it, then add in a finely chopped onion; take it around a pan once or twice, then pour it into your sauce, which you simmer with capers and mushrooms. With everything seasoned, serve it.

[64.1] See Recipe 4, above, for a possible composition of this marinade.

[64.2] This *boudin gris* is a companion preparation to *boudin blanc* (Recipe 8, above) and *boudin noir*.

Escoffier, *Selle de chevreuil et cuissot*, §1791

67. Haunch of Roe-Buck

The haunch of roc-buck can be done the same way as the Shoulder of Boar, and likewise the loin and shoulder. Or else, after having larded them with coarse lard, you can sauté them similarly in a pan in lard and flour, after which you cook them in bouillon. Bind the sauce the same way.

68. Leg of Mutton *à la logate*

See Article 28.[68]

Escoffier, *Cochon de lait farci et rôti à l'anglaise*, §1398

69. Stuffed Piglet

The piglet should be taken from under its mother. Bleed it in water that is about to boil, scald it, cut it up between its legs, remove its skin, its tail, its feet and its head;[69.1] then set them to soak until you need them. Leave the carcass [as is][69.2] — you will find it all right afterwards. To stuff the skin, get some veal and some beef fat, fry them as for a minced-veal mixture,[69.3] then fill the skin [with that and] with mushrooms, squab, sweetbreads, a sprig of fine herbs and with whatever you happen to have on hand; sauté everything in a pan.[69.4] When it has the shape of a piglet, sew up what is open, truss it up and blanch it in water ready to be mounted on the spit.

An hour and a half before dinner, mount it with a spit through its head; wrap it in buttered paper and bind it at each end with wooden splints. As it cooks, baste it with butter. When it is done, unwrap it and remove the cords, so that it will not look as if it has been stuffed. Then serve.

Then the carcass of the piglet: when it has been prepared, blanch it

69. Cochon farcy.

---

[68] This Recipe 28 is for *Membre de mouton à la logate*. The titles of the two recipes are identical. The reason for the second occurence of the recipe is mysterious. I. D. G. skips any mention of the recipe here, proceding immediately to *Pigge farced* which recipe he numbers 68. His numbering of the recipes in this chapter is one less from this point on.

[69.1] All of the appendages remain attached to the skin, so that when the skin is stuffed the pig will appear whole and "natural".

[69.2] That is, without being immersed in anything.

[69.3] See the notes concerning this *gaudiveau* in Recipes IV,2 and XIV,7.

[69.4] The mixture is sautéed before being stuffed into the pig's skin.

— but very slightly — prick it well,[69.5] and roast it as if it were whole, or like a lamb.[69.6] When it has cooked, you can serve it with a Green Sauce.[69.7]

70. Fricasseed Calf's Feet[70.1]

When they have been well cooked, cut them up very small and sauté them in a pan in lard or butter; when they have gone round three or four times, add in chives and parsley chopped together; immediately add in a very little bouillon and season it all well. When it is ready to serve, mix some eggs[70.2] with ordinary verjuice mash proportionate to the amount of your meat — in the ratio of three eggs for four hooves; you can use red currants[70.3] rather than verjuice mash. Then, when your sauce is short,[70.4] mix in your thickener. Serve.

Sheep's feet are done in the same way: get them very blanched and well cooked; cut them up very small, remove the woody process that is inside, fricassee them and season them with parsley and chives chopped together. Make your thickener as above, mix it in, and serve.

71. Roast Mutton Tongues

Dress sheep's tongues and cut them in half, then baste them so that breadcrumbs and fine salt stay on their surface, and set them on the grill. Make a sauce with a little bouillon, fresh butter, chives and whole parsley, a little grated bread, salt, pepper and nutmeg, all of which has been sautéed together in a pan. Then simmer the tongues in the sauce. When ready to serve, garnish your plate or platter, in winter with capers, lemon juice or mushrooms. Then serve.

Escoffier, *Langues d'agneau*, §1323

[69.5] The carcass is probably to be stuck with cloves for the roasting.

[69.6] See Recipe 25, above, or VI,15, below.

[69.7] Recipe VII,2.

[70.1] The title here reads, *Pieds de Mouton fricassez*. I. D. G. is clearly correct in putting "Calfes feet fried" here. See the same sequence of treatment, calf-sheep, in Recipe 41.

[70.2] The text reads *les œufs*.

[70.3] *groseilles*, normally "gooseberries" and probably red, although many varieties were known in Europe since the earliest of times.

[70.4] It seems that this sauce is to boil.

Otherwise

When they are cooked, season them and cut them in half; then fry them in a runny batter. Serve them with lemon juice, fried parsley; and garnish.

Otherwise, in Ragout

Clean them well, wash the palates, split them, then put breadcrumbs and fine salt on top and roast them. When they have roasted, put them in the dripping pan under the roast. Make a sauce with finely chopped parsley, chives or onion,[71.1] fresh butter and verjuice mash. When you are ready to serve, mix egg yolks into your sauce and pour it onto[71.2] your tongues. Then serve them immediately.

Otherwise

Get your tongues when they are half cooked, dress them, then simmer them in a pot with bouillon. Sauté them in a pan in melted lard, a little flour and chopped onion, everything seasoned. Serve them garnished with whatever you have on hand, including chopped capers; with short sauce.

Otherwise

When your tongues are roasted and pricked, serve them simmered in your short sauce, thickened as above.[71.3] Or you can simmer them with a sweet sauce.

72. Minced Roast Meat

Roast Minced Meat, whether it is [for] hash or something else, is made thus: when the skin is off, you cut the shoulder close to the knuckle, remove the bone from the knuckle and set the skin before the fire; then you likewise remove the shoulder blade [from the flesh] and chop up the meat very finely with capers and parsley. When that is done, simmer the minced meat with a scallion or an onion stuck [with cloves], everything seasoned well.

[71.1] *avec persil, siboule ou oignon aché menu.* The "chives" here may rather be the bulb of a scallion, as seems to be the case in the next recipe, 72. See the comment in the Appendix.

[71.2] The text has *dans.*

[71.3] The reference may be to the thickening agent described in the first version of Recipe 70: eggs and a mash of verjuice grapes. Another thickener has been described in Recipe 66.

To make your Minced Meat more dainty, add in some breadcrumbs and fresh butter. If you wish, put it in a platter or on a plate, and sprinkle it with its stock or with some other juice, with its skin on top. Then serve. You can garnish it with pomegranate seeds, with lemon or with toast.

Minced Meat of Partridge is made the same way except that you can enrich it with meat stock.[72] Garnish it with whatever you think appropriate.

73. Haslets

Get a round of veal and slice it very thinly in places where there are no ligaments. Lard your slices with lardoons and set them to cook in a covered tourtière; then simmer them with a little bouillon. Thicken your sauce and serve garnished.

74. Minced Raw Meat

Get whatever meat you like, remove the ligaments and chop it up, whether blanched or not. Then mix in twice as much again of beef suet from around the kidney, with the ligament removed. Then, when everything is chopped up and seasoned, moisten it with bouillon and simmer it. You can garnish that with chestnuts or with whatever appropriate garnishing you happen to have. When it is cooked, serve it.

75. Pupton[75.1]

Get veal, along with beef or mutton fat, chop them up together and season that, mixing in eggs to bind the mixture. Then cut three or four strips of lard upon which you spread out your chopped meat, covering that with young doves, tidbits:[75.2] sweetbreads, aparagus stalks, mushrooms, egg yolks, kidneys, cockscombs and artichokes. On top of all that you again put the meat. Everything being seasoned, cook it. Then serve.

76. Lard Tourte

Get lard, cut it up and melt it between two platters. Season it in the same way as for the Marrow Tourte you will find in the following article. When it has cooked, serve it.

74. Achis de viande cruë.

---

[72] *vous le pourrez nourrir de jus*; I. D. G. has "you may feed it with juice."

[75.1] *Poupeton*, in the singular, a sort of tourte. See Pupton in Appendix 2.

[75.2] In the original text there is only a comma after the word *beatilles*.

77. Marrow Tourte

Get marrow and melt it. When it has melted, sauté it and mix in sugar, egg yolks, pistachios or ground almonds. Then make a very thin shell of fine pastry,[77.1] on which you put your mixture; band it[77.2] if you wish. Cook it. Serve it sugared.

Cf. Escoffier, *Tourte de poussins à la paysanne,* §1650

78. Squab Tourte

Make your fine pastry and let it sit. Then get your young doves, clean them and blanch them; if they are too big, cut them up. Get *gaudiveaux*,[78.1] aparagus stalks, mushrooms, artichoke hearts, beef marrow, egg yolks, chard ribs,[78.2] beef palates, truffles, verjuice or currant mash. Garnish your tourte with whatever you have on hand, not forgetting the seasoning. Then serve it.

79. Veal Tourte

Get a piece of veal, blanch it and chop it up with twice the amount of beef fat, well seasoned. Make a shell of fine pastry dough, put the meat on it, in the middle of which put whatever you have on hand, such as tidbits and whatever; sugar if you wish. Then, when it is cooked, serve it.

80. Pie of Deboned Capon

When your capon is deboned, stuff its inside[80.1] with all sorts of tidbits, veal quenelles,[80.2] mushrooms, truffles, marrow, capers, chard ribs,

---

[77.1] This "fine pastry" is defined in *The French Pastry Chef*, Chapter I, Recipe 3. It will be called for in the next recipe as well.

[77.2] Elsewhere this verb *bander* refers to the making of an upper crust from strips of pastry.

[78.1] This is the minced, spiced veal that La Varenne expects his reader to have on hand as a staple in his kitchen. The plural is likely determined by the meat's normally being kept in the shape of sausages. See the note in Recipe IV,2.

[78.2] I.D.G. glosses this word *cardes*, "They are the ribs of beets, of hartichocks, and such like." In Chapter XX La Varenne deals expressly with only *cardes de poirée*, chard midribs (Recipe 17) and *cardes d'artichaux*, artichoke midribs (Recipe 18). Throughout this translation wherever the word *cardes* is not qualified, we translate simply "chard ribs".

[80.1] *fricassés au dedans de toutes sortes de* ... : clearly a type-setter's error, probably for *farcissés*.

[80.2] These *andouillettes* are basically a compound of minced veal and egg yolks and sweetbreads and minced veal *gaudiveaux*. When the capon is stuffed, set it out on fine pastry, wrap it in buttered paper[80.3] that is tied on with a cord, and cover it; well seasoned. When cooked, serve it.

81. A Minced Veal (*Gaudiveau*) Pie[81.1]

Set out your pastry dough in an oval, garnish it with your minced veal,[81.2] in the middle of which you put all sorts of garnishings, such as mushrooms, fat capon liver, chard ribs, hard egg yolks and sweetbreads; and season everything. Cover[81.3] it with pastry on top. When it is cooked, serve it with a sauce of verjuice, egg yolks[81.4] and nutmeg.

82. Platter Pie[82.1]

Get veal along with beef or mutton fat, and make a sort of minced veal paste.[82.2] Then set out your pastry very neatly [with a rim] half a foot high, and spread a layer of the meat in it; on that place a layer of mushrooms, another layer of ribs of greens, large or small,[82.3] and squab,

---

shaped like small balls or sausages. They are prepared in advance, kept on hand in the kitchen and generally used as a garnish. For a lean dish in Recipe XV,14, the cook is instructed to put a mash of carp flesh in pieces of the fish's skin and "roll them in the shape of *andouillettes*."

[80.3] That is, wrap the pastry-encased capon. The paper will reinforce the pastry shell while it is baking.

[81.1] Furetière writes that "un pasté de godiveau ou de beatilles se mange à desjeuner." Such a substantial preparation as this must still have been served primarily at dinner.

[81.2] The minced, spiced veal mixture called *gaudiveau* is a sort of culinary pre-preparation normally kept on hand in the kitchen in the shape of small sausages — hence the usual French plural *gaudivaux*. Here the oval shape of the pie's pastry blanket is appropriate. This same recipe is repeated in XIV,7; see also *The French Pastry Chef*, Recipe VII,9.

[81.3] The verb *barder* is glossed by Cotgrave in one sense as "to bind, or tye acrosse, overcrosse, or overthwart." La Varenne's intention may be that the upper pastry is in latticework.

[81.4] A sauce of verjuice mash and egg yolks is described in Recipe 70, above; in Recipe XIV,10 a mixture of verjuice and egg yolks is called a *sauce blanche*.

[82.1] *Pasté d'assiette*: apparently a small pie intended to serve as an appetizer or hors d'œuvre. See Recipe VII,8 in *The French Pastry Chef*.

[82.2] This is again the *gaudiveau*, ground veal (and no other meat) in a thick mixture with a variety of condiments.

[82.3] The French text has *de cardes ou de cardeaux*, this latter a word which I. D. G.

beef palates, kidneys and egg yolks, all that in such a way that the top layer is of the minced veal. Cover it and season it. Then serve it.

83. Bauble Pie[83.1]

Get rye flour, to which you add salt. Make your dough and roll it out in a pie shape. Then get a hare or two, or two legs of mutton, along with a little beef fat, which you chop up finely all together; season it. Make up your pie; on top of it leave a vent hole.[83.2] When it has baked for three hours, take it out and fill it with good bouillon and put it back into the oven. When it has baked fully, serve it.

84. English Pie[84.1]

Get a hare, young or mature, chop it up well with beef or mutton fat, or even with the white meat of capon; mix everything well together and season it, putting in some capers and some sugar if you like. Make your dough thus: when it is floured, spread it out and fold it in three or four layers, like a napkin,[84.2] spreading some fresh butter on each layer of dough, so that proportionately for one pound of dough there is half a pound of butter. When the pastry has been done in that way, let it sit a while; then make up your pie, whose outside you cover with buttered paper.[84.3] Then bake it well, and glaze it with an egg yolk. Then serve it.

Pasté à l'Angloise. 84.

---

reproduces without translating but which he glosses as having exactly the same sense as the first word: "*Cardes, Cardons, Cardeaux.* They are the ribs of beets, of hartichocks, and such like."

[83.1] The dish is called *Pasté à la marotte*: the *marotte* was, as Cotgrave glosses it, "a (Princes) Scepter; also, a fooles bable (because made commonly like a Scepter)." See also Recipe 29, above: *Piéce de bœuf à la marotte.*

[83.2] This hole through the upper crust is a common detail in the pies of the late-Middle Ages and Renaissance. It serves not only as a vent for steam but as an access by which last-minute ingredients, such as the bouillon here and rosewater elsewhere, can be added toward the end of a pie's preparation. See also Recipes VIII,3 and XIV,1 and 13, below, as well as the general instructions at the beginning of Chapter XXI.

[84.1] The same *Pasté à l'Angloise* is reproduced *verbatim* at XIV,3; see also *The French Pastry Chef*, Recipe VII,14. Properly the name is "in the English style." The reason for that attribute in the name seems to have to do with the dough being, exceptionally, a sort of puff pastry. For anything having to do with types of pastry see *The French Pastry Chef*, Chapter I.

[84.2] *The French Confectioner* offers extensive directions on the folding of table linen.

[84.3] The nature of the dough makes the pie's walls relatively fragile; the paper serves to

85. Cardinal's Pie[85.1]

Make your pies very high and very slender, fill them with minced veal *gaudiveaux* and cover them over, with the upper crust also very tall. Then serve them as garnishing for a piece of beef[85.2] or on a platter.

86. Chicken in Ragout in a Bottle

Wholly debone a chicken. Put its skin into a bottle which has no wicker around it; outside the bottle leave the opening of the chicken's neck, which you tie to the bottle's neck. Then make up whatever stuffing you wish, with mushrooms, truffles, sweetbreads, squab, aparagus stalks and egg yolks; with that stuffing you fill the chicken's or capon's skin. Tie up the fowl's neck and let it go into the bottle, which you stop up with pastry. Cook your ragout, well seasoned, in a kettle, from which you take it just before serving, and set it to simmer in front of the fire. When you are ready to serve, cut the bottle with a diamond, so that the bottom stays full and whole. Then serve.[86]

All sorts of other meats can be put into ragout, such as beef, mutton, lamb, pork of any cut you wish, roebuck, doe and young wild boar. Be careful, though, to do them properly and so they taste good.

reinforce the pastry as it bakes. The same procedure will be suggested in Recipe XIV,30 as well.

[85.1] This recipe is repeated at XIV,12 and XXI,13 (as well as in *The French Pastry Chef*, Recipe VII,13.) The primary feature of this variety of pie seems to be that it is shaped like a very small but relatively tall cylinder, as La Varenne's first line indicates here. A so-called Leg of Mutton *à la Cardinale* has been seen in V,2. As before, I. D. G. translates the phrase not too helpfully as "after the Cardinal's way."

[85.2] *les servez mettant pour garniture une piéce de bœuf*: the version of the recipe at XIV,12 clarifies this textual obscurity by reading *le servez principalement pour garniture à une piéce de bœuf*.

[86] The table at the beginning of this chapter on meat-day entrées ends with the listing of yet another ragout recipe, numbered 87: Thin Slice of Beef in Ragout. This recipe does not appear in the text, nor is it translated by I. D. G., even though the entry for it in I. D. G.'s Table does. Following this listing in the original text is the paragraph that follows.

86. Poulet en ragoust dans vne bouteille.

Chapter VI

Meats that can be served in the Second Course[vi.1]

Before discoursing on the way to prepare the meats, I advise you to trim your platters with flowers, depending on the season and their availability. At the end of this section you will find how to make the sauces mentioned in some of the following directions.[vi.2]

1. Pheasant

Sear pheasant over the flames,[1.1] that is to say, sear it on the grill,[1.2] and leave on one wing, the neck and the tail. Prick it with lardoons and wrap the feathered parts with buttered paper; cook[1.3] it. Serve it and unwrap it.

[vi.1] This is the course that is commonly termed "the roast course" or simply "the roast". In La Varenne the meats of this second course tend generally to be relatively small in size: fowl, game fowl and either small game animals or small cuts of game animals.

[vi.2] This paragraph was added in the second edition of the *Cuisinier françois*. The next division of the author's work, Chapter VII, is in fact devoted to the sauces called for in the present Chapter VI, as well as others. Where a specific sauce is mentioned in the following chapter, we shall indicate under what recipe number that sauce is to be found.

[1.1] *Faites le blanchir sur le feu.* The procedure will be repeated in most of this chapter's directions for preparing fowl and smaller animals, but does not seem primarily to serve the purpose for which it is used when larger animals are "blanched" in water, that of "plumping" the meat. Here it seems to be a method of sealing the surface of the meat, in part so that this may better receive and hold any lardoons inserted into it. For this latter function, see Recipe 46. An open fire may also, of course, clean away any remaining fine feathers or hairs on a carcass. A later recipe in this chapter, VI,58, for Roast Shoulder of Veal, will allow a choice between the two "blanching" methods, by water or by flame.

[1.2] *refaire sur le gril.* Cotgrave glosses one very old culinary sense of the verb *refaire*, found here, as "to parboyle, or make plumpe by parboyling." Though I. D. G. chooses "plump it on the Gridiron" for this passage, we repeat that such does not appear entirely to be La Varenne's intention. The *re-* of *refaire* seems to have retained its original value of intensifying the action of the verb: "to perfect [the preparation of the meat]."

[1.3] Although La Varenne may occasionally use the verb *cuire* in this chapter, its sense is usually "to roast".

2. Woodhen

Woodhen is dressed in the same way.

3. Red Partridge[3]

This is dressed in the same way.

4. Turtledove

When a turtledove is dressed, lard it and mount it on the spit.

5. Young Hare

When a young hare is dressed, sear[5.1] it over the fire, coat it with its blood, lard it and mount it on the spit. When it is done, serve it with a Pepper Sauce[5.2] or a Sweet Sauce[5.3].

6. Quail

When dressed, sear quail on the fire and bard it with a strip of lard which you cover with vine leaves, in season. When roasted, serve.

7. Partridge

When dressed and seared on the fire, you must lard partridge well and roast it. When done, serve it.

8. Capon

After you have dressed a capon, if it is excessively fat, bard it with a greased piece of paper and put into it an onion stuck [with cloves],[8] salt and a little pepper. When roasted, serve.

---

[3] *Le rouge*: Ricard describes this *perdrix rouge* as being larger than the common grey partridge.

[5.1] Throughout this Chapter VI the verb *blanchir* will uniformly be translated "sear" whether the phrase "on/over/by the fire" is expressed or not. Recipes 35, 40 and 49 contain obvious exceptions. In Recipe 58 for Roast Shoulder of Veal La Varenne writes that searing on the fire rather than blanching in water is both better and "more appropriate."

[5.2] Recipe VII,1.

[5.3] At Recipe 53, below, when a mixture of wine, sugar and cloves is heated, it is said to produce a "sweet sauce". Otherwise, no sauce recipe is explicitly so identified.

[8] In Recipe 40, below, and elsewhere, an onion is "pricked" by being stuck with whole cloves. See also the note in Recipe III,42, as well as La Varenne's explanation of the practice in Recipe XVI,17.

II.   Poulet d'Inde.

9. Roasted Squab

As the young doves come from the dovecot, bleed them in water, then scald and dress them; you can bard them if you wish laying vine leaves over the top, or lard them. When they are roasted, put a Pepper Sauce under them and serve them.

10. Grain-Fed Chicken[10]

Those chickens are plucked dry, dressed and seared on the fire. When that is done, lard or bard them; roast them. Then serve them.

11. Young Turkey

A young turkey is plucked dry likewise; it must be seared on the fire. After roasting, serve.

12. Young Wild Duck

Dress young wild ducks and sear them on the fire. If you wish, make four rosettes of lardoons for them, one for each of their four members. When roasted, serve them with Pepper Sauce[12.1] or a Sweet Sauce[12.2].

13. Rock Dove

When the rock dove is dressed, lard it and mount it on the spit. Then serve it.

14. Cockerel

Get your cockerels, dress them and sear them on the fire; then lard them and roast them. Then serve them.

You can serve them dry or with a sauce made of water, salt, pepper and chopped chives. You can also put them in ragout in the same way as pullet.[14]

15. Lamb

If the lamb is plump, when it is roasted spread some breadcrumbs on it along with a little salt and parsley if you like. Then serve.

---

[10] I. D. G. interprets the phrase *poulets de grain* as "Pullets fed with corn, or cram'd Pullets." His second phrase suggests that the chickens may deliberately have been fattened on grain.

[12.1] Recipe VII,1.

[12.2] See Recipe 53, below.

[14] See the recipe for this below at 56.

16. Teal

When dressed, mount teal on a spit. When they have roasted, serve them with orange.[16]

17. Gosling

As the gosling is taken from the mother, scald it and dress it, cutting off its neck close to the body and its legs; then, seared on the fire and trussed up, set it to roast. To put under it, make a stuffing from its liver and a quantity of good herbs chopped up together, which you then sauté in a pan in lard or butter with a few egg yolks; everything seasoned. Serve.

18. Young Wild Boar

Skin the young boar up to its head, dress it and sear it on the fire; cut off its four feet; lard it with lardoons, and into its body put a bay leaf or fine herbs. When roasted, serve.

19. Young Rabbit

Dress the young rabbit, sear it on the fire, lard it and roast it. With verjuice beneath.[19] Serve it. When it is roasted, you can put salt, a little pepper and orange juice into its body — stirring those things together well. Serve it.

20. Small Thrush

When plucked, truss up the small thrush and sear it;[20.1] lard it and mount it on the spit. Then [when roasted], under it set a piece of toast,[20.2] and [over it] a sauce made with verjuice, a little vinegar, onion and orange peel. Then serve.

---

[16] The text reads merely *orange*: we may understand either the fruit or, more likely, just the bitter juice.

[19] The punctuation in the text suggests that the verjuice is a presentation sauce: *le faites rostir; du verjus dessous, & servés.* (See roast meat served with its sauce *under* it in Recipes VI,9, 44 and VII,1, 2.) However, the verjuice may well be intended for a dripping pan. Later editions reduce the semi-colon to a comma and change the adverb *dessous* to *dessus*, "on top," assuming the verjuice to be a basting sauce.

[20.1] The bird is not eviscerated. See the following recipe.

[20.2] In the manner of a pottage (where, in conformity with the nature of the dish, the bread is plain and not itself "roasted"), this toast (*rostie*) forms a serving platform for the meat; it may, as in this case, be soaked in a sauce with which the roasted bird is dressed. The same serving procedure is followed in Recipes 25 and 31, below. For the saucing see also Recipe VII,5.

21. Rail

Rail is done up the same way as a thrush, without cleaning it out.[21]

22. Young Partridge

Dress young partridge, sear them on the fire, lard them with lardoons, and roast them with verjuice beneath.[22] Then serve them.

23. Young Quail

Young quail have to be barded with vine leaves in season.[23]

24. Turkey Chicks

After being plucked warm, let the turkey chicks cool and dress them; then sear them on the fire, lard them and roast them. Then serve them.

25. Plover

When plovers have been plucked, truss them up and sear them; then they have to be larded and roasted. Serve them with a sauce, and a piece of toast under them.[25]

26. Loin of Stag

Remove all of the skin from a loin of stag, lard it and mount it on a spit. Serve it with a Pepper Sauce.[26]

27. Fillet of Stag

A fillet of stag is done the same as the loin. [It is garnished] with Pepper Sauce.

28. Loin of Roe-Deer

A loin of roe-deer is done the same, too, as the loin of stag. [It is garnished] with Pepper Sauce.

---

[21] The appropriate saucing is mentioned in Recipe VII,5, below.

[22] The wording here, *rostir avec verjuis dessous*, suggests that the verjuice is added into the dripping pan and that it may be intended for basting or serving, or both: see also Recipe 19, above. A possible serving sauce for young partridge is said in VII,4 to be a mash of verjuice grapes.

[23] Given the procedure already described in Recipe 6, the text here may allow some ambiguity; see, however, the first option in the recipe for Squab (9, above) as well as for Snipe (Recipe 32, below).

[25] The undifferentiated "sauce" for plover should likely be that in Recipe VII,7.

[26] Recipe VII,1

29. Bunting

When the buntings have been dressed, truss them and bard them with lard, placing vine leaves on top in season; in spring they should be eviscerated. When they have roasted, serve them.

30. Large Thrush (Throstle)

Dress large thrush like the small;[30] and the rest of the preparation likewise.

31. Woodcock

When a snipe has been plucked, truss it with its beak being used as a skewer; sear it on the fire and lard it; set it to roast. [Set it out] with a piece of toast under it, in the manner of a Pepper Sauce, [garnished] with orange juice.[31]

32. Snipe

Snipe is done up the same as woodcock.

Another way of doing snipe

Do up snipe in the same way as the bunting above, except that some people eviscerate them: I consider that to be quite appropriate in every season but winter, all the more so since during the three seasons of spring, summer and fall those birds live only on caterpillers, ants, lice, herbs and tree leaves. In any case, cleaned out or not, bard the snipe with vine leaves in season, put it on a spit and roast it in such a way that it doesn't dry out. And serve.

33. Wood-Pigeon

When dressed, sear the wood-pigeon on the fire, lard it and roast it, with a Pepper Sauce beneath.[33] Then serve.

34. Loin of Veal

When a loin of veal has been hung[34] and seared, lard it densely, and

Autre façon de Beccaſsine.

---

[30] Recipe 20, above, and VII,6, below.

[31] A specific sauce for snipe is the same as for plover: see Recipe VII,8.

[33] *une poivrade dessus*: see Recipe VII,9. A basting sauce, this Pepper Sauce may be intended as a serving sauce as well; however, see Recipe 41, below.

[34] *mortifiée*. Cotgrave glosses this verb as "to mortifie, or make tender, flesh thats to be eaten," but without explaining how this is done. The verb *amortir* is used for the tenderizing of a capon in a sauce (Recipe 39, below). See also Recipe XIV,2.

roast it. Make a ragout of verjuice, a little water, little vinegar, orange peel and breadcrumbs. Then serve it well seasoned.

35. Larded Piglet

Skin a piglet, cut off its head and the four legs, blanch it in hot water and lard it, or if you wish, bard over half of it.[35] When roasted, serve it with breadcrumbs and salt on top.

36. Wild Goose

When the wild goose is dressed, sear it on the fire and lard it only on its quarters in the shape of a rosette.[36] Roast it; serve it.

37. Domestic Goose

A domestic goose is done in the same way as the wild goose.

38. Young Water-Hen

When the young water-hen has been plucked, clean it out, sear it on the fire, lard it and roast it. [Set out] with a Pepper Sauce beneath. Then serve it.

39. Capon with Cress

Bard your capon with lard, roast it. Season your cress with salt and vinegar. Otherwise, tenderize it in capon sauce with a little vinegar. Then serve it.

40. Whole Suckling Piglet[40]

Take a suckling piglet from under the sow, scald it, dress it and roast it with a bouquet of herbs, salt and pepper in its body. Then serve it.

Another way

Take the piglet also from under the sow, bleed it in water that is close to boiling; then, when it is scalded, eviscerate it through its side, truss up its forelegs toward its neck and its hindlegs with a skewer; blanch it

38. Poulette d'eau.

Escoffier, *Cochon de lait,* §1397

---

[35] *bardez le par la moitié.* I. D. G. has "barde it half."

[36] This is the same decorative treatment specified for the Young Wild Duck of Recipe 12 and the White-Tails of Recipe 41.

[40] *Cochon de lait au naturel.* I. D. G. has "Sucking Pig to the natural"; in the table to the chapter he put "Sucking Pig after the natural". The piglet is to be served unskinned, whole and "lifelike". The second version is a little more explicit about the intended pose.

in hot water. For cooking, slit it along its body. Put into its stomach an onion stuck with cloves, fine herbs, a little butter, salt and a little pepper; then sew up the opening again and roast it. So as not to have the trouble of basting it, rub it with olive oil: that gives it a good colour and a very tender hide. When it is well roasted, serve it trimmed with flowers. You can baste it with salt and water, or rub it with some lard.

41. White-Tails, or *Thiastias*[41]

Pluck the white-tails, leaving their head; clean them out, truss their legs as with a woodcock, then sear them on the fire, larding them with the shape of a rosette on their thighs if you like. When roasted, serve them with a Pepper Sauce beneath.

42. Heron

Pluck a heron and clean it out; then you look for six bitter substances that are on its body, one other one making the seventh which is inside it.[42] Truss up its legs along its thighs, sear it on the fire, lard it, wrap its neck in buttered paper, then roast it. When it is done, serve it.

43. Saddle of Hare[43.1]

When you have skinned a hare and cleaned it out, cut it in a saddle — that is, as far as its shoulders. Then remove three skins that are on it;[43.2] then truss up its hindquarters, lard it and roast it. Then serve it with a Pepper Sauce.

Escoffier, *Râble de lièvre*, §1812

44. Shoulder or Loin of Wild Boar

After having beaten a boar's shoulder[44.1] well, remove its meat,[44.2]

---

[41] An unidentified wildfowl, this bird seems to have been named onomatopoetically after its call: *tia-tia*.

[42] La Varenne is not otherwise explicit. A heron's bones contain an unpalatable fluid which should not be left to taint the meat.

[43.1] *rable de liévre*. Escoffier, with La Varenne, defines the saddle as "the whole of the back of the hare, from the root of the neck to the tail, with the ribs cut very short." Following Cotgrave, I. D. G. translates this title as "Chine of Hare".

[43.2] The "skins" of the body and the two hind legs.

[44.1] The text identifies the shoulder to be dealt with in this part of the recipe only as "it". The next paragraph will specify *la longe de sanglier*.

[44.2] *ostez en la venaison.*

which is commonly called *le lard*; lard it, then roast it. Serve it with Sauce Robert[44.3] or a Pepper Sauce.

For the Loin of Wild Boar, bard it with coarse lard and sauté it in a pan in clarified lard and flour, then cook it in bouillon and water in a large terrine or a kettle; season it well. When it is almost done, add in a quart of white wine. When everything has reduced to the consistency of a sauce, you can serve it under the shoulder. Alternatively, if you wish to serve it dry, it has to be of a sharper taste.

45. Domestic Pork

You can present ordinary pork in somewhat the same way as wild boar — that is, after having pounded it you coat it with blood; right after that, you lard it and mount it on a spit, not forgetting to coat its legs with blood before it is roasted. Serve it in the same way as wild boar, with or without sauce.

46. Doe Fawn

Before it has hung too much, dress it quite neatly; truss it up and remove that [layer of] skin on top that looks like egg white;[46.1] then sear it on the fire in order to lard it — taking care not to sear it too much since that will give you much trouble in larding it.[46.2] Be careful, too, not to burn its head, or to let its hair blacken. Mount it on a spit and wrap its head in buttered paper. When it has roasted, serve it with a Pepper Sauce.

47. Roe-Deer Fawn

Dress it in the same way as doe fawn; truss it up and lard it. Likewise wrap its head in buttered paper. And when it has roasted, serve it with a Pepper Sauce, with orange [juice] or with a Sweet Sauce.[47]

Faon de chevreuil. 47.

[44.3] This Sauce Robert is described in Recipe V,56.

[46.1] *glaire*: Cotgrave glosses this word as "a whitish, and slimie soyle" (from which I. D. G. likely took his translation of "slime"), but also adds the phrase *la glaire d'un oeuf*.

[46.2] This sort of "blanching" procedure is intended, at least in part, to seal the underskin sufficiently to hold the pieces of larding that will be pushed into it. The danger that La Varenne recognizes is that the skin might be toughened too much for that latter operation.

[47] See Recipe 53, below.

48. Fillet of Roe-Deer

After having larded a fillet of roe-deer, roast it, wrapped in buttered paper. When it has roasted, serve it with Pepper Sauce.

Another way

You can lard it with medium lard and lard it on top with smaller lardoons. When it is on the spit, make a marinade beneath it. When it has roasted, set it to simmer [in the marinade]. Serve.

49. Stuffed Breast of Veal

Select a breast of veal that is white and fat; steep it in water until your stuffing is made. That you do thus: get the meat of a round of veal, beef fat, boiled crustless bread, capers, mushrooms, a few fine herbs, egg yolks — everything chopped up together and seasoned; fill the breast with it. When that is done, use skewers or sew it up, and blanch it in hot water. The preceding is if you are serving it boiled.[49]

If you are going to roast it, put beef palates and other things into your stuffing, and do not fill it as full as for boiling. When it is larded and mounted on a spit, for beneath it make whatever ragout you wish. When it has roasted and the sauce is well seasoned, simmer it in it. Then serve it.

Escoffier, *Poitrine de veau farcie*, §1208

50. Sirloin of Mutton

To serve a sirloin of mutton in a ragout, whether in cutlets or whole, it has to be sautéed, floured, in a pan in butter or melted lard. Then simmer it in bouillon with a bouquet of herbs and capers. To bind the sauce, sauté a little flour with lard and, when the flour is russet coloured, put in a chopped onion and a dash of vinegar;[50] then simmer everything together. Serve it garnished with whatever you have on hand.

You can roast it stuck with parsley. When it is done, serve it quite dry or with verjuice mash.

51. Loin of Mutton

When a loin of mutton has fully hung, lard it with coarse lard and mount it on a spit. Make a marinade with onion, salt, pepper, very little

49. *Poictrine de veau farcie.*

---

[49] Such a boiled meat would appear to be exceptional in this second course of a meal.

[50] This is the *Liaison de farine* for which the recipe is given in X,3.

orange or lemon peel, bouillon and vinegar. When the loin has roasted, simmer it in that sauce, to bind which you use a little flour sautéed in lard in a pan as in the previous recipe. Garnish it with whatever you have: capers are good on top and a few anchovies. For thickening you can give it sautéed turnips. Serve it.[51]

52. Short Ribs

Select the best cut of short ribs,[52.1] well interlarded with very white fat; mount it on a spit. When it is almost roasted, cut away the fillet and baste it with a little bouillon.

To make your ragout, cut it into very thin slices with two or three scallions, whole or otherwise, salt, pepper, a few breadcrumbs or whatever thickening you have on hand; then mix everything together and simmer that without a lid. Serve the ragout with a little vinegar or the stock of a leg of mutton;[52.2] into that you can mix whatever you have on hand. Take care that the sirloin does not darken from over-cooking.

53. Fresh Ox Tongue

Cook ox tongue — or else get it ready-cooked at the tripe-dealer's.[53.1] Dress it, lard it and roast it on a spit. When roasted, split it in half and serve it with whatever ragout you like.

Another way

Simmer the tongue in a little wine with sugar and cloves until a Sweet Sauce is made. If it is not strong enough, add in a drop of vinegar.[53.2] Then serve.

---

[51] *Vous pouvez luy donner la liaison de navets passez, servez.* The reference here is likely to the sort of procedure touched upon in Recipes III,4 and 18, and XV,48, in which sliced turnips are floured, fried and perhaps strained. The word *passez* found here is omitted in later editions.

[52.1] *un Alloyau de la premiere piéce.*

[52.2] For this ingredient, see Recipe XI,2, below.

[53.1] This is one of the rare occasions that La Varenne mentions the possibility of having recourse to a commercial supplier. Interestingly in editions that are contemporary with La Varenne we read *chez la Tripiere*, whereas later in the seventeenth century that is changed to the masculine: *chez le Tripier*. Salted ox tongue will be dealt with in Recipe VIII,57.

[53.2] Interestingly, for *une pointe de vinaigre* later printers show here *une pinte* [one quart] *de vinaigre*. That would indeed have added to the sauce's "strength."

54. Royal Leg of Mutton[54]

Select a good leg of mutton which is large and short. Pound it and remove its skin, then remove the knuckle bones; flour it and sauté it in a pan in plain or clarified lard. Then cook it with a little bouillon, seasoning that well with mushrooms, truffles and tidbits. When it is almost cooked, sauté a little flour with an onion, a dash of vinegar and a little lard; simmer everything. Serve it with Short Sauce, and garnish it with pomegranate seeds or lemon.

55. Stuffed Leg of Mutton

You will find the way to stuff a leg of mutton in the directions for pottages.[55.1] When it is stuffed, simmer it in bouillon and a bouquet of herbs; put flour into that, with mushrooms and cutlets to be garnished.[55.2] Cook everything well together, and thicken the sauce giving it whatever sharpness of flavour you wish — of lemon, orange or verjuice. Serve it, with whatever you have, on top of your cutlets.

56. Fat Pullet

When you have selected a pullet, dress it, cut off its extremities and lard it with medium lard. When it is floured, sauté it in a pan in plain or clarified lard; then simmer it in bouillon, seasoning it. When it is almost cooked, sauté for it mushrooms, fat liver, a little flour and an onion stuck with whole cloves. When all of that is cooked and the sauce thickened, you can serve it garnished with pomegrantes.

Another way

You can stuff a pullet with oysters or with squab and with all other sorts of tidbits. Cook it in the same way [as above]. Garnish it with whatever you have on hand; then serve it.

Another way

Cut it in half, sauté it in a pan; season and garnish it as before, then serve it.

---

[54] This *Membre de mouton à la Royalle* has nothing to do with the modern *royale*, as in Escoffier's §206f.

[55.1] The reference seems to be to Recipe IV,10.

[55.2] Both here and at the end of the recipe I. D. G. translates these *costelettes* as "stakes" — that is, steaks.

54.

Membre de mouton à la Royalle.

Another way

When it is larded or barded, with paper over the barding, cook it. When it is well cooked, spread breadcrumbs and fine salt over it. Then serve it with the Poor Man's Sauce: verjuice or orange juice;[56] and in winter with cress.

57. "Vagrants"[57]

To put vagrants into a ragout, cut off their head and feet; when they are dressed, lard them with medium lard, flour them and sauté them in a pan in butter or melted lard. Then simmer them in well-seasoned bouillon, with a bouquet of herbs and mushrooms; sauté a little flour and onion. When everything has simmered well, serve them with a sauce thickened with whatever liaison you like.

58. Roast Shoulder of Veal

When a shoulder of veal has been well blanched in water or seared on the fire — this latter procedure being more appropriate and better — lard it or bard it; or if you prefer, while cooking[58] it, baste it with butter. When it is done, put breadcrumbs and fine salt on top. Serve it.

You can serve it roasted with a Pepper Sauce.

59. Veal Liver

Bard veal liver with a moderately thin sheet of fat bacon, then lard

58. Espaule de veau roſtie.

---

[56] The name of this *sauce au pauvre homme* is likely ironic. There is no other instance of it.

[57] *batteurs de pavé*: a descriptive name for a domestic fowl, likely a web-footed duck; see Recipe 61, below, where the culinary treatment for wild duck is identical. Chapter I lists *canards de pallier*, "barnyard ducks," though they are not dealt with by that name in any recipe. I. D. G. does not translate La Varenne's name for the fowl.

Literally, the expression means "pavement slappers" and figuratively "vagrants". In his *Dictionnaire*, Furetière writes, "On appelle proverbialement des filous & des faineants, *batteurs de chemin, batteurs de pavé*." Cotgrave gives extensive glosses of the same expression, in the singular, twice: *s.v. bateur* — "An idle, or continuall walke-street; a ietter abroad in the streets; one that sees the towne served when honest men are in bed; a lascivious, or unthrifty, night-walker; generally, any loose or mad youth, dissolute or disorderly yonker"; and *s.v. pavé* — "A pavement-beater; a rakehell, unthrift, loose youth, dissolute or deboched fellow; one that walkes much abroad, and riots it wheresoever he walkes."

[58] Understand, "roasting".

it.[59.1] Heat up the spit at the spot where the liver will sit,[59.2] and as it roasts baste it with a Pepper Sauce composed of scallions, salt, an onion stuck [with cloves], pepper and a little bouillon.[59.3] When it has roasted, simmer it in the basting sauce; then serve it whole or sliced, garnished with the sauce which has been much thickened with whatever liaison you wish.

60. Larks

Roast larks larded or barded with lard. When they are done, if they are barded sprinkle them with breadcrumbs and fine salt. Then serve them.

61. Wild Duck

You can set out a wild duck in the same way as the vagrant,[61] and with whatever garnishing you wish. You can also do it roasted, serving it with a Pepper Sauce.

[59.1] *Lardez le de moyen lard, puis le picquez.*

[59.2] *faites chauffer la broche à l'endroit où il doit demeurer.* I. D. G. may be unsure: "warm the spit about the place where it ought to remaine."

[59.3] This is different from the standard Pepper Sauce described in Recipe VII,1, and already called for in several previous recipes, in that the latter is somewhat more piquant with vinegar rather than the bouillon used here and has either onion *or* scallion along with a citrus peel.

[61] See Recipe 57, above.

Chapter VII

A few Sauces,
of which mention has been made
in the Recipes for the Second Course[vii]

1. The sauce called Pepper Sauce is made with vinegar, salt, onion or scallion, orange or lemon peel, and pepper. Cook it, and serve it under those of your meats for which it is appropriate.

Escoffier, §130; this sauce is perhaps better known now by the Italian, *Salsa verde.*

2. Green Sauce is made in this way: get green wheat, make some toast, add vinegar, a little pepper and salt; grind everything together in a mortar and strain it in through a linen cloth. Then serve your sauce under your meats.[2]

3. Sauce for young rabbit or wild rabbit is such that, when the rabbit is roasted, you put salt and pepper into its body together with orange juice, mixing everything up well together.[3]

4. For young partridge: orange [juice] or verjuice mash.[4]

5. Another appropriate sauce for small thrush and for rail is for you to put pieces of toast under your spit. When your birds are almost done, you remove your toast and set it aside; get vinegar, verjuice, salt, pepper and orange peel, and boil everything together, along with your toast. Serve it.

[vii] The recipes that are referred to are the subject of the preceding Chapter. This present Chapter presents only a disappointingly few particular sauces; the first two were staples across Europe throughout the Middle Ages and Renaissance. In a slightly disconcerting way, exceptional in La Varenne, the recipes switch from directions for making up particular *sauces* to comments on the *saucing* of particular game fowl and animals.

[2] Interestingly, the *Encyclopédie* (1751) of Diderot distinguishes between two sorts of *sauce verte*. Older — it is, in fact, standard in medieval cooking — but still in use is a variety made with ginger, verjuice, parsley juice or green wheat, and thickened with bread crumb. The "new" Green Sauce is identical with what we read in La Varenne.

[3] This procedure and recipe has previously been mentioned only for young rabbit: Recipe VI,19.

[4] In Recipe VI,22 for young partridge liquid verjuice is mentioned as either a basting or a serving sauce.

6. Large thrush (throstle) and woodcock are served with toast and a Pepper Sauce beneath.

7. Plover is served with a sauce made of verjuice, orange or lemon peel, a dash of vinegar, pepper, salt and chives — without overlooking the toast.

8. Snipe, the same.

9. Wood-Pigeon, with a Pepper Sauce.

10. Piglet and lamb, with Green Sauce.

Chapter VIII
Entremets for Meat Days

In serving the Entremets you should remember to trim the platters with seasonal flowers. Take note as well that after the following recipes you will find directions for making liaisons[viii.1] and mushroom stock[viii.2] and other useful little oddities, even ones necessary for those who desire to serve the Great with honour and favour.

1. Feet and Ears of Pork

When those have been well cooked, sauté them in a pan in butter or melted lard and a little onion, and season them well; mix in bouillon. When the sauce is quite thick, add in a dash of vinegar with mustard, if it is the season for it.[1] Then serve them.

2. Delicacies[2.1] of Stag

When they are well dressed, set them to cook in a pot. When they are well cooked, simmer them in wine; then sauté them in a pan in lard, all of it well seasoned; then put them back to simmer between two plates[2.2] with a little onion and some good bouillon. When the sauce is much reduced and thick, serve them.

3. Venison Pie

If the venison flesh is tough, pound it. Remove the upper skin and lard the meat with coarse lard, season it with salt, pepper, vinegar and ground cloves. If the pie is for keeping, make your dough with rye flour,

2. Menus droits de cerf.

[viii.1] These thickeners are dealt with in Chapter X.

[viii.2] Concerning this ingredient, see Recipe XI,1, below.

[1] *la moutarde s'il est en saison*: *il* does not refer to *la moutarde*. Traditional medical lore held that one should avoid eating particularly warm foodstuffs, such as mustard, in the warm season.

[2.1] Cotgrave offers the following gloss for the term *menus droicts*: " ... Particularly, the head, feet, skin, and intralls of a slaughtered beast, or all such parts as a Cooke, or yeoman of the slaughter-house, reserves for himselfe." A long-established hunting designation, these *droits* could translate as "special reserved bits".

[2.2] See this procedure in Recipe III,7.

without butter, [but with?] salt and pepper.[3] Bake your pie for three and a half hours. When it is done, use dough to stop up the hole you left in it to let it breathe. Serve it in slices.

4. Slicing a Pie[4]

The way to slice a pie is to look for the side where the lard appears the most; then, with it cut very thin, serve it.

5. Ham Pie

Steep the ham well[5.1] and, when it is desalted enough, boil it briefly. From around it remove its skin, which is called its hide. Then put it into a dark dough as for venison,[5.2] and season it with pepper, cloves and parsley. To my way of thinking you can also lard it, the same as you'd do venison. Cook the pie according to its size: if it is big, for five hours; if smaller, for less time — all depending on whether it is big or small. When it is cool, serve it in slices.

6. Truffles in Ragout

Peel truffles very neatly, so that any dirt is removed; cut them up very thin and sauté them in a little lard — on lean days, in butter — with a little chopped parsley and a little bouillon. When they are well seasoned, simmer them, so that the sauce is thickened. Serve them on a platter garnished with pomegranate seeds, lemon if you have any, and with flowers and leaves.

7. Dry Truffles

Wash them well in wine; cook them in rough wine[7.1] and a little vinegar, with salt and a good deal of pepper.[7.2] When they are well cooked, let them sit in their bouillon so as to absorb salt. Then serve them in a napkin, folded or not.

Escoffier, Truffes à la serviette,§2278

---

[3] In Recipe V,83 the rye dough is salted. According to the preamble of Chapter XXI, salt and pepper are optional in such a dough.

[4] *Tranche de pasté.*

[5.1] This *jambon,* almost by definition, a preserved, salted meat.

[5.2] This dark pastry is the rye dough of Recipe 3, above, and is described in *The French Pastry Chef,* Recipe VIII,3. The preamble of Chapter XXI, below, states that a pie meant to be eaten cold, as this ham pasty is, should be prepared with dark dough.

[7.1] *gros vin:* perhaps what we might call a "cooking wine".

[7.2] The phrase *à quantité* may apply to both the salt and the pepper.

8. Plain Truffles[8]

When truffles have been well washed in wine, cook them with salt and pepper. Then, when they are well cooked, serve them in a folded napkin or on a plate trimmed with flowers.

9. Tidbit Omelet[9]

Get tidbits — that is, cockscombs, kidneys, squab wings — and cook them well. When they are cooked and seasoned, drain them. Get some eggs, remove more than half the whites, beat the eggs and, when beaten, combine them with your clean tidbits. Then get lard cut up into pieces, sauté it in a pan; in that melted lard — even with [unmelted] pieces of lard, if you wish — make your omelet very thick and not too cooked. Then serve it.

10. Fried Veal Sweetbreads

The veal sweetbreads shouldn't be too old. Steep them in water and blanch them well, then dry them. Slice them up and season them with salt, flour them and fry them in clarified or melted lard, so that they are quite yellow and dry; put in orange juice or lemon juice. Serve them neatly.

11. Larded Veal Sweetbreads

Select the finest and best-formed veal sweetbreads you can; blanch them in cold water, lard them, mount them on a spit and roast them neatly. When they have roasted, serve them with lemon juice over the top.

12. Veal Sweetbreads in Ragout

After blanching them, cut them up and sauté them in a pan, or do them whole if you like, in lard, seasoning them well with parsley, a whole scallion, mushrooms and truffles. After simmering them well in good bouillon, and the sauce being reduced and thick, serve them.

Omclettes de beatilles.

9.

Bocuse, *Escalope de ris de veau sautées,* p. 233.

---

[8] *Troufles au naturel.*

[9] Only a few omelets will be represented in *The French Cook*, here and in Recipes 14 and 15, later in the chapter on Egg Dishes, XVII, and in Chapter XIX. However, *The French Pastry Chef* devotes an entire chapter, XXXIII, to no fewer than twenty-five varieties of omelet.

13. Deer Liver

As the liver comes warm from the deer's body, cut it into small slices and sauté them in a pan in lard — remove the cracklings[13.1] — fricassee the slices well with a little parsley and a whole scallion. Let them simmer in a little bouillon.[13.2] Then serve them with the sauce quite thickened.

14. Deer-Liver Omelet

You can also make an omelet with deer-liver in this way: when its liver has been removed from the animal, chop it up small and make your omelet of it with lard. Do the omelet so that it is neither overcooked nor undercooked, but just right. Serve it.

15. Deer Udder[15.1]

After blanching it well in water, cut it into round slices and fry those with lemon juice. Otherwise, set it to cook in some sort of ragout; when done, chop it up small, and make an omelet with lard, as with the Tidbit Omelet.[15.2] Then serve it with lemon juice.

16. Cow's Udder

Cook a cow's udder well. When it is cooked, cut it up into slices and garnish your entrée courses with them.[16]

Otherwise, sauté them in a pan with fine herbs and a whole scallion, all of that well seasoned; then simmer it in your best bouillon so that it will be highly flavoured, and the sauce made thick. Then serve it.

17. Cauliflower

When cauliflowers have been well cleaned, cook them with salt and a bit of grease or butter. When cooked, peel them and set them out with fresh butter and a dash of vinegar, and a little nutmeg as a garnishing

---

[13.1] With Cotgrave, I. D. G. translates these *crêtons* as "mammocks".

[13.2] This bouillon is likely to be added to the lard, parsley and scallion; all together, they form the ingredients of the sauce.

[15.1] Early editions of *Le Cuisinier François* show the same title, *Tetine de vache*, for this recipe as for the next one. By the end of the century, though, the title had been changed to *Tetine de chevreuil*.

[15.2] Recipe 9, above.

[16] On lean days, the normal meat-and-sauce entrée course (recipes for which appear in Chapter V, above) would be replaced by dishes for fish or eggs (Chapters XV and XVI, below) — for which cow's udder would not be appropriate.

around the platter. If you want to serve them by themselves, do them the same way and, when you are ready to serve, make a sauce with good, very fresh butter, a scallion, salt, vinegar and nutmeg; that sauce should be very thick.

If it is for a meat day, put in a few egg yolks — which, however, you can do without if the sauce is well stirred by several people. Then garnish your platter on top, and serve.

Escoffier, *Pâte de pistaches pour infusions*, §2388

18. Cream of Pistachios

Get a handful of ground pistachio nuts and three cups of milk,[18.1] mix in some flour and boil the whole mixture. When that is almost cooked, mix six egg yolks and a little very fresh fresh butter in with your pistachios; put all of that into a large pan with a good amount of sugar and a little salt; if you wish, add in musk or amber,[18.2] which are appropriate, too, with a lot of sugar, but extremely little musk; beat everything well together. Serve it trimmed with flowers.

19. Ham in Ragout

Whether the ham is cooked or not, cut it into very thin slices, then put them into a pan [to sauté] in a very little wine. Then simmer them with a little pepper, a small amount of fine breadcrumbs, and lemon juice. Then serve them.

20. Roast Ham

Slice it and set it to steep in a little bouillon and a dash of vinegar; warm it. Then take it out and put breadcrumbs over and under it, and roast it well. After the sauce has begun to boil, pour it over the ham; then serve it trimmed with flowers.

21. Sliced Ham

When ham is well cooked, cut it lengthwise and very thinly. Then serve it.

[18.1] Generally the seventeenth-century French *chopine* held 16 oz (two cups, one pint) of a liquid (water, wine, etc.) but 24 oz (three cups, one and one-half pints) of milk. Dairy measure was traditionally more generous.

[18.2] In Recipe 79, below, the author will instruct that *ambre gris* is to be used to produce an amber colour.

22. Small Thrush

Dress small thrush neatly; cut off their wings, legs and neck, remove their gizzard, and flatten them a little; then flour them and fricassee them in lard. Then set them to simmer in well-seasoned bouillon with a small bouquet of herbs. When they are well cooked and the sauce thickened, serve them with lemon juice over the top, and garnish round about them with pieces of whole lemon.

23. Marinated Chicken[23]

When chickens are well dressed, split them in half; if they are small, break their bones. Set them to marinate in vinegar, salt, pepper, scallion and lemon peel; let them steep in that until you need them, and then set them to drain. Flour them and fry them in clarified or plain lard. When they have fried, simmer them very briefly in their marinade. Serve them with thick sauce.

Escoffier, *Fritôt ou marinade de volaille*, §1669

24. Lamb Offal in Ragout

Take a lamb's feet, ears and tongue, and sauté them in a pan in butter or lard, a scallion and parsley. Then set them to simmer in good bouillon; when they have almost cooked, add in chopped capers, broken asparagus stalks, mushroom or truffle stock,[24.1] and season it all well. Serve them neatly with the sauce quite thickened with whatever thickener you like.[24.2] Trim with flowers, especially if your giblets are very white.

25. Lark in Ragout

When larks have been well plucked, remove their gizzards, flatten them, flour them and sauté them in a pan in butter or lard. Then set them to simmer in bouillon, with a bouquet of herbs and a few chopped capers, all of it seasoned. When they are well cooked and the sauce is well thickened with whatever thickener you like, serve them with pistachios or pomegranate seeds and lemon slices.

24. Abbatis d'Agneaux en ragoust.

---

[23] Compare this recipe with the version in V,12.

[24.1] See Chapter XI, below.

[24.2] See Chapter X, below.

26. Jelly

To make Jelly, get a cock and remove its skin; also get a hock and four calf's feet. Break them[26.1] and blanch them, then put them into a new crock and cook them for two and a half hours. When everything is almost cooked, get very clear white wine and put it into the pot. When it is completely cooked, strain the meat out and squeeze it in a napkin. Take your bouillon and put it into a big pan on the fire; when it is on the point of boiling, add in one-and-a-quarter pounds of sugar; when it boils, pour in the juice of six lemons and the whites of a dozen very fresh eggs. When everything has boiled, put it through a linen filter until it is good and clear. Mix in whatever colour you like; flavour it with musk.[26.2] Serve it.

27. Jelly of Stag's Antler[27.1]

At a spicer's or a cutler's,[27.2] get grated stag antler in a suitable amount: to make three dishes [of jelly], you need two pounds [of grated antler]. Set it to cook in white wine for two hours, so that, having boiled, there is enough left to make up your three dishes [of jelly]; strain it carefully through a napkin. [Put it in a pot along with] sugar and the juice of six lemons; when that is on the point of boiling, mix in the whites of twelve very fresh eggs and, as soon as they are in, you put everything through the linen filter. Put it away in a cool place [in order to jell]. Serve it as is,[27.3] garnished with pomegranate seeds and slices of lemon.

28. Green Jelly

You take your ordinary jelly, such as we have described above; at a spicer's you get the green colour[28] which you mix with your jelly. Serve it.

26.1 In later editions this *les cassez* has bizarrely become *les fricassez*.

26.2 See the note in Recipe 18, above.

27.1 Or "Gelee of Harts horn," as I. D. G. translates.

27.2 This source for stag's horn is understandable if we realize that much of the elegant cutlery of the time had this material for its handles.

27.3 *Servez la naturelle*: that is, plain.

28 This green colourant would likely be had from either new wheat sprouts or from chard or sorrel leaves. For such a use of the first, see Recipe VII,2; the second, Recipe III,23; the third, Recipe XV,25. Cooks traditionally resorted also to ground parsley for green dishes. And in Recipe XXI,40 ground pistachio nuts yield a green colour for a Marzipan Tourte. I. D. G. omits the phrase "at a spicer's."

27. Gelée de corne de Cerf.

29. Red Jelly

As your jelly comes out of the filter, set it to simmer with very red beetroots that have been well cooked and grated; strain everything through a linen cloth and set it to cool. Then serve it and garnish it with another colour

30. Yellow Jelly

The same way, adding [yellow] colour.[30]

31. Violet Jelly

The same way, making it a violet colour.[31]

32. Blue Jelly

The same, too.[32]

33. White Dish

Get the most opaque part of your jelly and warm it along with well ground almonds; strain them together through a napkin and, if it is not white enough, mix a drop of milk in with it. When it has cooled, serve it; garnish it with another colour.

34. Lemon Salad

Get whatever quantity of lemons you like, peel them and slice them up very thinly; set them out with sugar and orange blossoms and pomegranate seeds.[34] Then serve them.

35. Partridge Hash

When your partridges are roasted, cut off the white meat, chop it up very finely, moisten it with bouillon and season it. Then simmer it with a scallion. When you wish to serve it, add in an egg yolk and some lemon

---

[30] This yellow hue would have been the prime choice of earlier cooks. To produce it saffron was always on hand in medieval and Renaissance kitchens.

[31] A violet food colourant was know to be available from the orchil lichen *Gozophora tinctoria*. If the food mixture was acidic, this litmus colourant would be predominantly reddish; if alkali, bluish.

[32] Finely ground lapis lazuli provided an ultramarine pigment for foods in the late Middle Ages. With perhaps fewer serious after effects in his patrons the later cook could resort to crushed, unopened columbine blossoms.

[34] *fleurs d'orange & de grenade*. I. D. G. takes this literally as "orange and pomegranat flowers."

juice. Garnish it with whatever you like, such as pistachios, pomegranates and cut-up lemon. Then serve it.

36. Fried Rissoles

Get the white meat of partridge or some other meat, chop it up very small and season it. Then make an extremely thin sheet of dough, and with it do up your rissoles. Then cook them in clarified or melted lard.

37. Puff Pastry Rissoles[37.1]

They are made the same way as the others, except that the meat has to be rather fat. When they are seasoned well, cook them neatly, and serve. You can also make rissoles of any other meat in the same way as above. Serve them sugared, with a savoury water over the top.[37.2]

38. Marrow Fritters[38.1]

Before detailing the different sorts of fritters, the general procedure should be described to you first. Get cheese, pound it well in a mortar or in a dish, and if the cheese is quite settled, that is, hard, put a little milk into it, then some flour and a number of eggs proportionate to the amount of cheese; season all of that with salt. Then sauté the mixture in clarified lard or, on lean days, in refined butter. Then serve it with a good deal of sugar and a little orange-blossom water or rosewater over the top.

If you want to make beef-marrow fritters, get the largest chunks of marrow you have. When that marrow is steeped,[38.2] slice the chunks and set them out in your batter.[38.3] Then fry them and serve them in the same way.

[37.1] *Rissoles feuilletées*: I. D. G. shows "Rissoles puffed." La Varenne's instructions for regular feuilletée dough can be read in in Recipe XXI,0 or in *The French Pastry Chef* in Recipe I,4. La Varenne calls puff pastry dough appropriate for "English-style pies": *le pasté à l'Angloise* (Recipe XIV,37).

[37.2] *avec eaux de senteur pardessus* (in the plural): that is, with orange-blossom water or rosewater (see the next recipe) or some variety of the syrupy "waters" described in *The French Confectioner*, Chapter IV.

[38.1] In sixteenth- and seventeenth-century France, *baignets, beignets* or *bignets* were, as Cotgrave says, a sort of "flat fritter made like a pancake". The lean version of these fritters can be seen at Recipe XIX,9.

[38.2] Presumably in water or a beef bouillon.

[38.3] *ajustez-les dans votre paste*: I. D. G. has "fit them in your paste." We may wonder whether the sense is rather "coat them with."

39. Apple Fritters

Apple Fritters are done the same as the marrow ones.

40. Artichoke Fritters

Prepare your artichoke hearts, half-cook them and, with the choke removed, slice them up. Make up a batter of flour, eggs, salt and a little milk, then put your artichokes in it. When your clarified lard is hot, set them in it slice by slice and fry them. Then serve them.

41. Whore's Farts[41]

Make up your fritter batter stiffer than ordinarily by increasing the flour and eggs, then set them out very small. When the fritters are cooked, serve them hot with sugar and a savoury water.

42. Spun Pastry Dough[42.1]

Get cheese and grind it up well; also get the same amount of flour with a small amount of egg, the whole seasoned. Cook it in a pan [until it is] like a well-cooked gruel[42.2] — that is, somewhat firm — and put it through a strainer onto greased paper. When it is cooked, draw out[42.3] the dough any way you like, then fry it. Serve it in a pyramid with sugar and savoury water.

43. Lemon Dough

Lemon Dough is made in the same way as that which we have called "Spun Dough", except that you mix in lemon. It should be served like the other, well trimmed with flowers.

44. Almond Dough

The same as Spun Dough.

45. Pistachio Dough

The same, too.

Escoffier, *Beignets de pommes*, §2588; cf. *Beignets de pomme à la Normande* in *The Roux Brothers French Country Cooking*, p. 34.

41. *Pets de putain.*

---

[41] Delicately, I.D.G. does not translate the dish's name, *Pets de putain*. The lean version of this preparation is at Recipe XIX,10. The *Cuisinier* of Pierre de Lune (1656) also contains a version of this recipe.

[42.1] *Paste filée.*

[42.2] In later editions this *une boulie* becomes printed as *une siboule*, a well-cooked scallion!

[42.3] *filez*: literally "spin out."

46. Ramequin de roignon.

46. Kidney Ramekin[46.1]

Remove the kidney from a cooked[46.2] loin of veal, chop it up with parsley or garlic and an egg yolk. Then, with that well seasoned, spread your mixture out on bread and toast that in a pan or on the grill. Serve it dry. You can put on sugar if you like.

You can make veal kidney toast[46.3] almost the same way, except that you shouldn't put in either parsley or onion; rather, when the kidney is well seasoned, spread it out on your toast which you brown in a pan in front of the fire. To serve it, you can sugar it; you can even add sugar into the mixture, if you like.

47. Meat Ramekin

Get whatever meat you like and chop it up very finely. When it is chopped up, mix an egg into it and season it as necessary. [Spread that on toast and] roast it in a pan. Serve it with lemon juice.

48. Cheese Ramekin

Get some cheese and melt it along with some butter, whole or crushed onion, salt and a lot of pepper. Spread all that on bread, then pass a red-hot fire shovel over it.[48] Serve it warm.

49. Chimney-Soot Ramekin

When your bread is a little over half-sautéed in a pan in butter or oil, sprinkle soot on it, along with salt and a lot of pepper. Serve it hot.

50. Onion Ramekin

Get onions and grind them in a mortar with salt and a lot of pepper; then [optionally] you can add in anchovies decomposed into a small

---

[46.1] The series of dishes called *ramequins* take their generic name from a north-German practice of spreading cream (*Rahm*), and a variety of edibles, on toast. They might perhaps be thought of as a sort of "dry" version of a sop or pottage. I. D. G. does not translate the term *ramequin* but merely glosses that "It is a kind of toste." At the beginning of the second paragraph see the phrase *rosties de roignon de veau*, which seems to be synonymous for this dish name, *ramequin de roignon*.

[46.2] *cuite.* Generally this verb implies cooking by boiling. For no apparent reason I. D. G. translates *cuite* as "rosted" here.

[46.3] *rosties de roignon de veau.*

[48] This is the same procedure for browning the surface of a prepared dish that the author uses in Recipe III,11 and elsewhere.

quantity of melted butter.[50] When your onions are spread on the bread [which has been] sautéed in oil or butter, pass the red-hot fire shovel over the top. Serve.

51. Garlic Ramekin

This must be done the same way as the Ramekin of Onions.

52. Bunting in Ragout

Dress buntings and sauté them in butter or melted lard. When done, set them to simmer in a small pot with some bouillon, and season them well. To thicken the sauce, mix in veal sweetbreads, meat stock and mushrooms. When it is all well cooked, serve it garnished with pistachios and pomegranate seeds.

53. Ox Tongue in Ragout

You will find directions for preparing this dish among the entrées, at Recipe 17.

54. Pork Tongue in Ragout

When a pork tongue has been salted and boiled, cut it up very thinly and set it to simmer in a little bouillon; then sauté it in a pan in melted lard, ground onion and a dash of vinegar. When you have done that, serve it with lemon juice, and garnish it with capers and whatever you happen to have, mixing in verjuice [grapes] or red currants in season.

55. Flavoured[55] Pork Tongue

When pork tongue is cooked, serve it dry and garnish it with whatever you like, whether flowers or anything else. You can slice it open lengthwise.

56. Grilled Pork Tongue in Ragout

Half cook it slit open, then grill it. Make any sauce you like for it, provided it is thick and well seasoned; and serve. [Alternatively] you can lard it and roast it on a spit, basting it with a marinade that you make

---

[50] The text reads *anchois bien fondus avec peu de buerre*: if not a misprint, as it stands the sense of "melted" must be that the anchovies themselves are disintegrating: one might be reminded of the *garum* of Roman cookery.

[55] The word *parfumé* refers to the procedure, apparently common, outlined in the paragraph on making Mayence Hams in Chapter IX. The flavouring used there is juniper, *geniévre*.

under it with seasoning and an amount of salt you think proper. Then serve it.

Escoffier, *Lan-
gue de bœuf*,
§1153

57. [Salted] Ox Tongue[57]

Cook a salted ox tongue in water; as it finishes cooking, put in some wine. When it is done, skin it. When you are ready to serve, slice it in rounds, or else split it; then serve it.

58. Squab

To put squab in a ragout, get them as they come from under their mother, kill them and scald them immediately. When they have been dressed, blanched and floured, sauté them in a pan. Then set them to simmer in a pot in good, well-seasoned bouillon with a bouquet of herbs, until they are well cooked and the sauce thickened. Serve them with chopped capers, mushrooms, sweetbreads and whatever you have that is suitable for squab.

59. *Foie gras*[59] in Ragout

Pick out the fattest and whitest livers, clean them and throw them into hot water in order to remove their bitter taste; immediately take them out again, though. When they have dried, sauté them in a pan in butter or clarified lard. Then simmer them in a little bouillon with parsley and a whole scallion. When they are cooked, remove the scallion and serve the sauce quite thick. Into that you can you can put truffles, mushrooms and asparagus stalks.

60. Grilled *foie gras*

Put fat liver on the grill and sprinkle it with breadcrumbs and salt. When it has roasted, splash lemon juice over it. Serve.

61. *Foie gras* Cooked in Coals

You should bard fat liver with lard, and season it well with salt, pepper, ground cloves and a very small bouquet of herbs; then wrap it in

---

[57] A recipe for Fresh (*i.e.* unsalted) Ox Tongue appears at VI,53.

[59] The *Foie gras* in this series of recipes is not exclusively goose liver. It could be the fat liver of any domestic fowl.

four or five sheets of paper and set it to roast in the coals like a quince.[61]
When it has cooked, be careful not to lose its sauce by turning it. Remove
the upper paper and serve it with the lower if you like, or on a platter.

62. Fried *foie gras* in Fritters

You can see how liver should be prepared for serving in this way
by the previous directions for preparing with a ragout, by frying and in
fritters.

63. Tidbits

Get wings, livers, cockscombs. When all those things have been
blanched in water, cook the cockscombs on their own; when cooked,
skin them. Then simmer everything together in a good, well-seasoned
bouillon. When you are almost ready to serve, fricassee the combs and
your tidbits in good lard, with a little chopped parsley and chives.[63] Then
set everything to simmer in the bouillon until it is time to serve; you can
mix in egg yolks. Then serve.

64. Frangipane Tourte

Get a caudle of milk[64.1] — that is, boiled milk — and make up your
mixture for the cream in this way: get a little flour which you cook in your
milk; when it is cooked, get five egg yolks and mix everything together
with ground pistachios, almonds, a little salt and a good deal of sugar.[64.2]
Then make up your dough, mixing into it egg whites[64.3] and salt, and let
it sit. Out of that dough make six very thin sheets of pastry and butter
them one after the other, then spread out your cream over the six; again

---

[61] The fifteenth-century Italian *Libro de arte coquinaria* of Maestro Martino contains
a recipe for a Quince Pie for which the fruit undergoes a preliminary baking in live
coals. See Emilio Faccioli, *Arte della cucina*, 2 vols., Milan (Il Polifilo), 1966; Vol.
1, p. 160: *Altre torte*.

[63] These *siboules* may be "scallions".

[64.1] Later editions change *chaudeau* to *chaudron*, "kettle, caldron." La Varenne's inserted
explanation of his word shows that it was already becoming archaic.

[64.2] Compare this recipe for frangipane cream in *The French Cook* with the recipe for
it in *The French Pastry Chef*, IX,15. See also the directions for the varieties of
so-called Pastry Chef's Cream in the same book, Chapter IV.

[64.3] See Recipe XIV,37 where the essential ingredient in the dough for the Frangipane
Tourte is said to be the egg whites.

make six others,[64.4] and set them out, one after the other, well buttered, especially the upper one to give it a good colour. When each one has baked in a tourtière or on a plate, exchange it with another one and sugar it. Then serve them with flowers.

You can make the Frangipane Tourte with any other sort of cream, and serve it in the same way as here.

65. Nulle[65.1]

Get a dozen egg yolks and two or three whites, add in a little cream, a little salt and a lot of sugar; beat it all well together, then put it through a strainer and pour it on a platter or in a plate. When you are ready to serve, cook it on the chafing dish or in the oven. When it is cooked, serve it with sugar and savoury waters,[65.2] and trim with flowers.

66. Ambered Nulle

Get fresh cream or milk, mix in egg yolks, very little salt, sugar, and musk or amber.[66] When you are ready to serve, make a layer of your mixture and a layer of orange juice, and successively up to five or six. Then pass a red-hot fire shovel over the top; garnish it with sugar and musk, or with orange-blossom water.

[64.4] This second set of six buttered layers of pastry is to form the upper, gilded crust. Unfortunately for La Varenne's reputation, a line or two at this crucial point in his directions was omitted from later reprintings.

As for the name of the cream that goes into this delightful creation, contemporary dictionaries explain that a certain Italian, Signor Frangipani, achieved international fame with a perfume with which fine leathers were scented, particularly those from which gloves of the time were made. As Furetière writes: *Frangipane est un parfum fort exquis qu'on donne à des peaux pour faire des gands* [sic], *des poches, des sachets, &c. Il a pris son nom d'un seigneur Romain de la maison fort ancienne des Frangipani, ou Fricapane, qui en a esté l'inventeur. Les peaux du Frangipane sont fort estimées par toute l'Europe. On fait aussi des liqueurs parfumées, à qui les Limonadiers ont donné ce nom pour les mettre en vogue.* Frangipani's fragrance must have suggested the delicate aroma of the cream.

[65.1] The *Larousse gastronomique* quotes this recipe of La Varenne as an example in its article on this preparation. The book defines *nulles* as "amber and musk-flavoured dessert creams that used to be very popular in France."

[65.2] For these *eaux de senteur*, see *The French Confectioner*, Chapter IV.

[66] See the note in Recipe 18, above. For this flavouring Recipe 79 specifies the use of *ambre gris*.

67. Green Nulle

It is no different from the previous ones except for the colour, which you can make as for the jelly whose directions were given earlier.[67]

68. Fricasseed Artichokes

Cut artichokes almost down to their hearts,[68.1] remove the choke[68.2] and put them into boiling water to blanch them. Dry them and flour them, then sauté them in clarified lard or refined butter. Serve them hot, garnished with fried parsley. (To fry parsley, it has to be very fresh[68.3] and not at all damp.)

69. Fried Artichokes

Cut artichokes into quarters, clean them, remove the choke, then blanch them in hot water and dry them; coat them with flour and fine salt. Heat up clarified lard or refined butter or melted lard; when it is very hot, put your artichokes into it and fry them well; then let them drain. Put into your frying oil a handful of green parsley which, when dry, you put on your artichokes. Serve them.

70. Artichokes in a Pepper Sauce

Quarter your artichokes, remove the choke and blanch them in cool water. When you wish to serve, put them on a platter with pepper and salt. Then serve them.

71 Artichaux en cus.

71. Artichoke Hearts

Peel away all the leaves from your artichokes and cut them down to the choke; then cook them in bouillon or water, with butter and salt. When they have cooked, take them out of the bouillon; pick them clean and remove the choke. Then put them with butter and salt. When you wish to serve them, make a sauce out of fresh butter, a dash of vinegar and nutmeg, with an egg yolk to thicken it. Then serve them in such a way that they are very white.

Escoffier, *Artichauts aux sauces diverses*, §2030

---

[67] The reference is to Recipe 28, above, although at that place the reader is told merely to go pick up a green colourant at the spicer's.

[68.1] The *cus*, "bottoms," or stem of the thistle's head, without its choke or its leaves.

[68.2] This is the hairy seed cap on the top of the heart.

[68.3] *bien verd*. The word *verd* (modern French *vert*) regularly identifies a new, ripe fruit or vegetable. See, for instance, the definition of broccoli in Recipe XXIX,9 as *des rejettons de choux verds*, "sprouts of new cabbage."

Escoffier, *Champignons sautés*, §2073

72. Mushrooms in Ragout

When mushrooms are thoroughly cleaned, sauté them in a pan in very fresh butter, with chopped parsley and chives; season them. Simmer them. When you are ready to serve, put in lemon juice and peel and a little White Dish.[72] Then serve.

73. Stuffed Mushrooms

Select the best shaped mushrooms to hold the stuffing — which you make of a few meats or good herbs, so that it is delicate; it is thickened with egg yolks. Then, when your mushrooms are stuffed and seasoned, put them in a plate on a bard of lard or on a little butter, and cook them. Serve them garnished with lemon juice.

74. Fried Mushrooms

Blanch mushrooms in cool water and dry them; then marinate them in a little vinegar, salt, pepper and onion. When you are almost ready to serve, make up a batter[74] thinned with egg yolks; fry your mushrooms. Serve up and garnish.

Escoffier, *Duxelle sèche*, §223

75. Mushrooms *à l'Olivier*[75.1]

When the mushrooms are cleaned well, quarter them and wash them in several changes of water to remove the dirt from them. When they are very clean, put them between two dishes[75.2] with an onion and some salt, then on the chafing dish so they will give off their moisture. After they have been pressed between two platters, get very fresh butter with parsley and chives, and fricassee them. Then set them to simmer. When they are

73. Champignons farcis.

---

[72] The *blanc manger* is a genre of preparation of long and venerable history. With Cotgrave, I. D. G. translates this *manger* a little misleadingly as "meat": white meat. La Varenne's version of the dish is found at Recipe XIX,17.

[74] *une paste liquide*: literally, a "runny dough". The mushrooms are apparently to be coated with this.

[75.1] The sense of the qualification of this dish's name, *à l'Olivier*, is not immediately obvious. As in Recipes V,13, *Manches d'espaules à l'olivier*, and XXVIII,21, where this present recipe is referred to, the word *olivier* is not capitalized. The similarity between this preparation and the modern sauce known as Duxelles — chopped mushrooms browned in butter with chopped onions, shallots and parsley — with whose creation La Varenne is traditionally credited, suggests that Olivier may have been the name of someone in the Uxelles household.

[75.2] See this procedure in Recipe III,7 and in Recipe 2, above.

well cooked, you can put in some cream or some White Dish.[75.3] Serve
them.

76. Ham Omelet

Get a dozen eggs, break them, remove the whites from half of them
and beat them. Then get as much of your ham as you think suitable, chop
it up and mix it in with your eggs. Get some lard, cut it up and melt it,
pour your omelet onto it; and make sure that it doesn't cook too much.
Serve it.

77. Tortoises

Cut off their feet, tail and head, put the body to cook in a pot and
season it well with fine herbs. When they are almost done, put in wine
and boil them. When they are cooked, take them out and cut them into
pieces — and be particularly careful to remove the gall. Then fricassee
them in butter or lard, with parsley and chives. Then set them to simmer
in a little bouillon. When you are ready to serve, mix an egg yolk with
some verjuice and mix that in together. Serve it well seasoned.

78. Pistachio Tourte

Melt some butter and put six egg yolks into it, with some sugar; grind
a handful of pistachio nuts and stir them in, along with a grain of salt.
Then make your pastry, form it into a shell and put your mixture into
it; close[78] your tourte and wrap it around with bands of buttered paper.
When it is baked, serve it sugared, and garnish it with candied lemon
peel.

79. Portuguese Eggs

Get a quantity of egg yolks; get a pound or half a pound of sugar
with which you make a syrup and, when that is made, mix your eggs into
it along with a drop of orange-blossom water; cook it all. When it has
cooked, make a cone of layers of buttered paper[79.1] and pour your mixture

---

[75.3] See Recipe 72, above.

[78] The text of the second edition reads *formez*, "shape," though later editions show
fermez.

[79.1] The cone is formed, pointed end downwards, by shaping several sheets of paper,
overlapped for strength. These are buttered on their inner surface and constitute a
mould as the eggs-and-syrup mixture sets.

into it. When that has cooled, remove the paper and put the preparation pointed end up on a platter. Sugar it and garnish it with nonpareille,[79.2] cinnamon, candied lemon peel and flowers. Then serve it.

Another way

Make a syrup similar to that of the previous recipe; then break a dozen or more eggs and beat them well; heat up your syrup and, when it is quite hot, mix in your eggs. Strain everything together and cook it. When it has cooked, serve it with biscuit, cut up and set up in a pyramid, with savoury water, musk or ambergris.[79.3]

80. Darling Eggs[80]

Make your syrup as above; then get egg yolks and mix them well into that syrup. When they are cooked, put them on a platter along with a drop of orange-blossom water and of musk. Then serve them.

Escoffier, *Œufs
filés*, §217

81. Threaded Eggs

Get two cups of white wine with a chunk of sugar, and boil them well together. Then break some eggs, beat them well, strain them and then put them into your skillet where your white wine and sugar are boiling: in that way they are cooked in a moment and are spun out.[81] Remove them from the syrup and set them to drain. Then serve them heaped in a pyramid with savoury water.

82. Eggs La Varenne[82]

Make a well-made syrup; fry some egg whites in a pan in butter and put them into your syrup. When they are cooked, serve them with orange-blossom water.

[79.2] Still today, a small sugar-almond. Following Cotgrave, I. D. G. translates the word as "the peare called nompareill (or non such)."

[79.3] According to the *New Larousse Gastronomique*, Brillat-Savarin (1755–1826) still hailed the use of ambergris with chocolate.

[80] In modern culinary practice, Eggs Mignon generally use potatoes for the substance of an egg-shaped casing which is coated with egg, deep-fried and filled with something. La Varenne's *œufs mignons* are presumably to be shaped as in his previous recipe.

[81] More properly, perhaps, "strung out": *se trouvent enfilez*. As the beaten egg dribbles from the strainer's holes into the hot liquid, the threads are cooked quickly: the dish becomes multiple strings of egg.

[82] *Œufs à la Varenne*: otherwise, more literally, "Game-Preserve Eggs." Not quite convincingly I. D. G. shows "Egs after the Varenne."

Another way

Make your syrup; with your fresh eggs, mix in a little very fresh milk. When they are cooked, serve them very white on a platter, garnished with savoury waters.

83. Snowy Eggs

Boil some milk with a little flour dissolved in it, then put in more than the half of a dozen egg whites,[83.1] stirring everything together, and sugar it. When you are ready to serve, put it back on the fire and ice them[83.2] — that is, get the rest of your egg whites, beat them with a feather and mix everything together. Alternatively, fry[83.3] the rest of your egg whites well and pour them over your egg-white-and-milk mixture. Lightly pass an oven stopper[83.4] or the red-hot fire shovel [over that]. Serve it sugared, with a few savoury waters.

Instead of egg whites, you can put in the yolks of your eggs in a suitable amount, with the whites fried on top.

Mazarin Cream is made the same way, except that you don't put in any egg whites.[83.5]

Escoffier, *Œufs à la neige*, §2735

83. Oeufs à la neige.

84. Huguenot Eggs

Get the stock of a leg of mutton[84.1] and put it on a platter or in a dish;[84.2] get very fresh eggs and break them into that stock; cook them with a little salt. When they are cooked, put in some more stock and some nutmeg. Then serve them.

85. Spanish Cardoons[85]

When blanched, remove their skin very cleanly and set them to steep in cool water. Then serve them with pepper and salt.

[83.1] The entire recipe will take twelve egg whites; only seven or so of them are used now, the balance later.

[83.2] *les glacez*: "glaze them."

[83.3] Later editions change this "fry" to merely "cook well": *faites bien cuire.*

[83.4] This item is omitted in later editions.

[83.5] *vous n'y mettez point de blancs d'œufs*: for "in it" I.D.G. shows "on it".

[84.1] See Recipe XI,2, below. The designation "Huguenot-style" may stem from the use of meat broth on lean days.

[84.2] *sur une assiette, ou dans un plat*: clearly both receptacles have some concavity or rim.

[85] The cardoon is an edible thistle, a rudimentary form of artichoke, whose stem seems to be eaten here.

Escoffier, *Crème*
d'asperges, dit
Argenteuil, §697

86. Asparagus in a Sweet Sauce

Select the largest asparagus stalks, scrape their lower ends, wash them, then cook them in water, salting them well — and do not let them cook too much. When they have cooked, set them to drain. Make a sauce with very fresh butter, a little vinegar, salt, nutmeg, and an egg yolk to thicken the sauce, being careful that that doesn't turn. Serve them well garnished with whatever you like.

87. Asparagus in Ragout

Get your asparagus stalks and break them up very small, then sauté them in a pan in butter or lard, mixing in parsley and chives, with everything well seasoned. Set them to simmer until you are ready to serve. You can put in cream or egg yolks or the stock of a leg of mutton. And you can use them to garnish something else.

88. Creamed Asparagus

Cut asparagus stalks very small, leaving nothing but the green; fricassee them in fresh butter or melted lard, parsley, chives or a bouquet of herbs. After that, simmer them very briefly with some fresh cream. If you like, serve them with a little nutmeg.

89. Mutton Tongue in Ragout

When well cleaned, split a mutton tongue in two, then flour it; sauté it in a pan and put it into a ragout composed of vinegar, verjuice, salt, pepper, orange juice and chopped capers. When it has simmered well and the sauce is quite thick, serve it.

90. Larded Mutton Tongue

Get the tongue when it has cooked, and clean it carefully. Prick it with little lardoons and roast it. Then serve it with lemon verjuice or some orange.

91. Grilled Mutton Tongue

Split the tongue in half and set it on the grill with salt and breadcrumbs on top. Then make a sauce[91] with verjuice mash or red currants, a few breadcrumbs, finely chopped parsley and chives. Then, when it has cooked well, serve it.

90. Langue de mouton picquée.

---

[91] We do not later read that the tongue is to be simmered in this sauce. La Varenne probably intends it as both a cooking and serving sauce.

92. Pomegranate Salad

Peel your pomegranates and put [the seeds] on a platter. Sugar them, garnish them with lemons; then serve them.

93. Boar's Head

Cut it off close to the shoulders to make it more attractive and better looking, and to keep the neck,[93] which is the best part, provided it is well seasoned. Having cut it off, singe it, or scald it if you want it to be white. Then cut the skin three fingers away from the snout right around the head in order to prevent it from shrinking and falling elsewhere. Cook it and season it well. When it has half-cooked, put white or red wine in with it; finish off its cooking, with it well seasoned with pepper, onion, cloves, orange peel and fine herbs. You can cook it, and wrap hay closely around it to keep it from falling apart. When it is well cooked, serve it cold, whole, trimmed with flowers; if you have wrapped it up, you can serve it in slices, which you can present in several sorts of ragout.

94. Slice of Boar's Head

Cut it on its neck, or alongside, or under its ear. Then serve it.

95. Slice of Boar's Head in Ragout

Having been cut that way, boil the slice in wine along with a few breadcrumbs. When it has cooked and the sauce has thickened, serve it.

Another way

When sliced as has been said, sprinkle the slice with breadcrumbs and put it on the grill. When it has grilled, serve it with lemon juice; in vine-leaf season, wrap your slice in them. Serve it promptly with verjuice mash.

96. Green Peas

If you want, sauté green peas in a pan in butter, and cook them with closed lettuce[96] or purslane. When they are well cooked, with a bouquet of herbs, and well seasoned, serve them garnished with lettuce. You can do them and season them with cream, just like asparagus, as is mentioned above in Recipe 88: Creamed Asparagus.

---

[93] That is, to keep it for preparing and serving separately.

[96] The expression *laituës pommées* describes heads of iceberg lettuce, as opposed to leafy romaine lettuce.

Escoffier,
§§1329 & 1331

97. Ram Kidneys

Blanch ram kidneys well in cool water, skin them and slice them very thinly. Sauté them in a pan with melted butter or melted lard, seasoned with whatever you have. Then simmer them with mushrooms and the stock of a leg of mutton. Serve them.

Another way

Cut them in the same way in slices, and steep them in only a little vinegar and salt. Some time before serving, when they have dried, dip them in fritter batter and fry them. Splash lemon juice or orange juice over them; then serve them.

98. Beef Palates

Get beef palates that are well cooked and soft — and be certain to boil them briefly to remove the taste of the tripe-shop. When that is done, cut them up very thin and sauté them, well seasoned, in a pan. Simmer them. Your sauce should be thickened with lemon juice. Then serve them.

When they are used to garnish a dish, beef palates are fricasseed in the same way, except that you cut them up individually.[98]

99. Herb Omelet[99.1]

Melt a little butter; get some cream, egg yolks, pear juice and very little salt, and cook all that together. When it is done, sweeten it with flower waters.[99.2] Serve it good and fresh.

Escoffier, *Pi-
geonneaux en
compôte*, §1780

100. Squab

When squab have been well blanched in water, floured a little and sautéed in lard, simmer them in good bouillon, with mushrooms, truffles and a bouquet of herbs, the whole seasoned well. Serve with the sauce thickened. Garnish with cut lemon.

The same ragout can be made for roast squab.

---

[98] *vous les coupés en détail*: I. D. G. has "you cut them peecemealing."

[99.1] This is a simpler version of the *Herbolade* described in *The French Pastry Chef,* Recipe XXIX,11.

[99.2] Some of these *eaux de fleurs* are to be found in *The French Confectioner*, Chapter IV.

101. Large Thrush (Throstle)

Remove the gizzards of large thrushes, sauté them in the same way as the squab, and cook them longer because they are tougher. When they are done and seasoned — in the same way, too — serve them garnished with pomegranate seeds or cut lemon.

102. Young Partridge

Get a couple of pieces of sliced beef, and beat[102.1] them well with lard seasoned with salt and pepper; sauté them in a pan until the lard is a good russet colour. Then simmer the mixture in a little bouillon with a ground onion; then strain everything through a linen cloth, and you will extract a very red juice which you mix with a tang of verjuice mash, a little cooked flour[102.2] or breadcrumbs. Then get your young partridges, remove their legs and wings, and simmer them in your sauce, adding in mushrooms and truffles, until the sauce is very thick; cook them. Serve them promptly to keep them from becoming tough.

[Fully mature] partridge are done in the same way.

102.

Perdreaux.

[102.1] Later editions show *bardés* here, rather than *battez*.

[102.2] *farine cuite*, normally *farine frite*. For the latter, see Recipes V,42 and XXV,4 and 20; the phrase *farine cuitte* is used again in Recipe XXI,28. Compare the present recipe's compound of beef, lard, bouillon and "cooked flour" with the mixture that Pierre de Lune describes in his *Le Cuisinier* (1656) and which he calls *farine frite*: see the note in Recipe V,42, above.

Chapter IX
Mayence Hams[ix.1]

When your pig is dressed, remove its hams;[ix.2] stretch them out to set them, and put them in the cellar for four days during which time they will exude moisture which you must wipe off quite often; if the weather is humid, leave them there only twice twenty-four hours. Then put them in the press between two boards and leave them there for the same length of time as the pig has been dead. After that, salt them with salt, pepper, cloves and ground aniseed; let them absorb that salt for nine days. At the end of this time you take them out and put them in the lees of wine for another nine days. Then wrap them in straw and bury them in the cellar in a spot that is not too damp. When you take them up again, hang them by the chimney on the side with the least smoke; do not forget to scent them twice a day with juniper. When they are dry and slightly smoked, until you need them hang them from the ceiling in a room that is not at all humid; check on them often to see that they are not rotting.

To cook them, get whichever one you want, clean it and set it to desalt in a big kettle full of water, seasoned with fine herbs, and do not put in any wine. When it is cooked, remove its hide, sprinkle it with pepper and chopped parsley, stick it with cloves, then replace the skin on it and put it in a cool place until you want to use it, which you do trimmed with flowers if you have any.

[ix.1] See Appendix 3 for a contemporary definition of this treatment of ham. I. D. G. calls these *jambons de Mayence* "gammons of Westphalia-bacon".

[ix.2] *levés en les jambons*, the word being here just an augmentative form of *jambes*, "legs".

Chapter X

Thickeners to keep on Hand
to save you the trouble of making them whenever you need them[x]

1. Almond Thickener

Skin your almonds carefully and grind them in a mortar, then put them into good bouillon with breadcrumbs, egg yolks, lemon juice, an onion, salt, cloves and three or four mushrooms. Bring all that to a boil;[1] put it through a strainer and put it into a pot for use when you need it.

2. Mushroom Thickener

Get mushroom stems with a small amount of ground almonds, onion, parsley, breadcrumbs, egg yolks and capers. Boil all of that in good bouillon, season it well; mix in a slice of lemon. Put it through a strainer and put it into a pot for use when you need it.

3. Flour Thickener

Melt your lard, remove the cracklings; throw your flour into your melted lard and fry it well — being careful, though, that it doesn't stick to the pan; mix in a suitable amount of onion. When it is done, put all of it with good bouillon, mushrooms and a dash of vinegar. Then, that having boiled, along with its seasoning, put all of it through the strainer and put it into a pot. When you want to use it, you hold it over the hot coals to thicken your sauces.

4. Truffle Thickener

Get dry flour, which you mix with good bouillon. [Get] truffles, onions, mushrooms and a sprig of thyme, grind everything together and boil it with your moistened flour. Put everything through a strainer and put it into a pot. You can use that to thicken your entrée dishes or ragouts.

You can use these thickeners in Lent provided you put no eggs into them. You can also use them everywhere, as in entrée dishes, second course dishes, entremets dishes.

Liaiſon de trouffles.

---

[x] The recipe numbers have been added for this translation.

[1] Later editions misread this line as "Boil all of that in good bouillon."

Chapter XI

Mushroom, Beef or Mutton Stocks
which can be used in many sauces and ragout preparations[x]

Cf. the Mush-
room Broth in
Jean-Georges
Vongerichten,
*Simple Cui-
sine*, p. 74.

1. Mushroom Stock

Get the worst of your mushrooms, wash them carefully with their skins and stems on, without removing anything. Boil them in a pot with good bouillon; as they boil, put in a bouquet of herbs, an onion stuck with whole cloves and a few bits of roast meat, everything well seasoned with salt. After it has all boiled well, put it through the strainer; put it into a pot to use it as you need it.

That can be used in all sorts of ragouts, even in pottages, and often it can be used in place of mutton stock.

2. Beef or Mutton Stock

Cook your meat,[2] whether beef or mutton, a little less than half. Prick it with a knife and press it in a press if you have one because that will be much more effective. When the meat is pressed and the juice is extracted, get a spoonful of good bouillon and baste your meat with it, and again extract as much juice as you can to make up what you need. Put it into a pot with a little salt. Mix the juice of a lemon into it when you are ready to use it.

---

[x] The recipe numbers have been added for this translation.

[2] *Faites cuire vostre viande*: I.D.G. interprets that instruction as "Roast your meat ... ." Generally the verb *cuire* implies a boiling. In Recipe XIII,2, however, La Varenne writes explicitly of using the "juice" of *roast* meat — both its drippings and whatever can be squeezed out of it — and states that such juice is preferable to what is expressed from boiled meats.

Chapter XII

Garnishes[xii]

1. Pistachio Garnish

Skin your pistachios in hot water and put them in cold water. To use them, chop them however small you like, to set around your dishes.

2. Lemon Garnish

You have to remove its seeds, slit it lengthwise and cut it into slices; then put it into water ready to be used on top of and around your dishes.

3. Pomegranate Garnish

Pick the reddest pomegranate and trim it — that is, remove its peel — and extract the seeds to garnish on top of and around your dishes.

Chapter XIII

Meat Juices and Stocks
suitable for serving to the Sick[xiii]

1. Mutton, Veal or Capon Stocks

When roasted and pressed, extract the juice. Because mutton stock is warmer than the others,[1] you have to correct it by mixing it with that of veal. And, the one sort or the other thus prepared, give one spoonful of it to your patient every two hours.

[xii] The printer forgot to insert a rule separating this chapter from the preceding one. The title for the first of the following recipes is set in the larger italic of chapter rubrics as if it applied to all three recipes: *Maniere de faire la garniture de pistaches.*

[xiii] This rubric, *Methode pour tirer les jus* ... becomes *Méthode pour tenir les jus* ... in later editions. In the present chapter recipe numbers have been added for ease of reference.

[1] According to classical humoral theory, mutton is warm in the second degree, whereas veal and chicken are only moderately warm in the first degree.

Autre façon de la mesme eau.

2. Another way for the same stock[2.1]

For those who need a great deal of cooling,[2.2] get a bottle without wicker around it and with a very large mouth; cut up your meat, veal and fowl, quite small, so that it will go into that bottle. When you have done that, stop it up carefully with a bit of tough dough, with a piece of parchment tied tightly on top; put it into a kettle of hot water up to its neck and boil it for three hours. When it has cooked, unstop your bottle and remove the juice in it, which you will administer to your patients, or even to those who, although healthy, need a cooling refreshment, along with other juice from roast meat or with a bouillon, all according to the various [relative] needs and the strengths of each.

Note, in passing, that the juice of roast meat is much stronger and more nourishing than that of boiled meat, even though there is much more of the latter.

If you lack a bottle, you can use a large-bellied pot[2.3] in the same way, stopping it tightly up with dough and with parchment over that.

3. Chicken Stock[3]

Dress your chicken and, when it is very clean, fill it with barley.

[2.1] This particular preparation for the sick has a long history in the aristocratic cookery of Europe. It is known among fourteenth-century French recipes, and in the fifteenth century it becomes known as a "distillate": in the procedure described here the juice of the meat is produced without any liquid having been added to the meat during its cooking. The analogy between this procedure and the so-called quintessence produced by the alchemist's alembic heightened the physicians' belief in its efficacy.

[2.2] *rafraischissement*, nowadays "refreshment". Here the "cooling" is intended in a humoral sense: someone whose healthy complexion has been unbalanced by an abnormal influence of bilious or sanguine humours will likely run a fever; his normal temperament needs to be restored by the effect of foods possessing a relatively cool nature.

[2.3] *coquemare*: Cotgrave indicates that a *coquemart* is of brass and has its own lid.

[3] It may be observed that both chicken and barley had enjoyed a very long reputation, going back to medieval times and before, as reliable foods to offer the sick, the convalescent and those of generally finicky digestions. In 1654 Nicolas de Bonnefons wrote, "By poultry we mean ordinary roosters, hens, capons and chickens, in whose production Nature seems so fecund that one cannot adequately appreciate the liberality of its Author, who so abundantly dispenses to us food so exquisite both for its excellent flavour as for its natural delicacy and goodness; food not only fit for the healthy but necessary for the sick as well, for it seems that without poultry broths the sick cannot recover and strengthen themselves." *Les delices de la campagne*, Book 3, Chapter 1; in the Amsterdam: Jean Blaev, 1661 edition, p. 197.

Cook it in a pot with a quart of water so that it reduces to two cups. When it has cooked until the barley has burst, put everything through a strainer and let it cool. It must be used cold; and that same water can be given to nursing babies.

4. Panada[4]

Get bouillon and fine breadcrumbs, and boil them well together. Towards the end, put in egg yolks, very little salt and lemon juice.

5. Another panada

Get well-chopped-up capon or partridge meat, beat it well in a mortar, then moisten it with healthy bouillon — that is, bouillon from the cooking pot — and a little breadcrumbs and salt. When it has simmered, mix in a few egg yolks to thicken it, and lemon juice.

Cf. Escoffier, *Farce de volaille à la panade et au beurre*, §193

---

[4] *panasde*: one modern sense of the French *panade* is a kind of thick soup of bread boiled with butter to a pulp.

Chapter XIV

Pasties that can be served throughout the Year[xiv]

1. Venison Pie

If the flesh is tough, pound it; remove its upper skin and lard it with coarse lard, then season it with salt, pepper, vinegar and ground cloves. If it is for keeping, make your dough from rye flour,[1.1] without butter, [but with] salt and pepper.[1.2] Bake your pie for three and a half hours. When it has cooked, stop up the hole you left to let it breathe. Serve it sliced.

2. Pie of a Leg of Mutton

When the mutton has properly hung,[2.1] it has to be pounded well; remove its skin and its bone and, if you wish, lard it with coarse lard and season it with salt, pepper and a little vinegar. You can leave it in sauce, tightly covered, for three or four days until you wish to put it in pastry. You do that using fine dough or dark dough,[2.2] and season it well with salt, pepper, ground cloves, nutmeg and a bay leaf — even with a crushed garlic clove if you like. When the pie is closed and glazed with an egg yolk, bake it for three and a half hours; do not forget to prick it — that is, to give it an opening on top a little while after it has been in the oven.

[xiv] See the paragraphs on the common varieties of pastry dough and their respective uses that La Varenne has appended at the end of this chapter and that for ease of reference I have numbered Recipe 37.

[1.1] This is the tougher pastry that we have seen used in Recipes V,29 and 83, VIII,3 and 5 and whose making will be described in the preamble to Chapter XXI. There La Varenne writes: *Faites en pastez de venaison.*

[1.2] See the previous, textually identical version of this pie in VIII,3. The structure of the sentence does not make it clear whether salt and pepper are meant to be included or excluded. In the preamble to Chapter XXI the cook is told that such *paste bise* made from rye flour has little butter but may optionally have salt and pepper.

[2.1] *mortifié.* This is the first step in a tenderizing process. See the same preliminary treatment for loin of veal in Recipe VI,34.

[2.2] For the distinction, see the preamble to Chapter XXI.

3. English Pie[3.1]

Get a young hare or a mature one, chop it up well with beef or mutton fat, or even with the white meat of capon; mix everything well together and season it, putting in some capers and some sugar if you like. Make your dough thus: when it is floured, spread it out and fold it in three or four layers, like a napkin,[3.2] spreading some fresh butter on each layer of dough, so that proportionately for one pound of dough there is half a pound of butter. When the pastry has been done in that way, let it sit a while; then make up your pie, whose outside you wrap around with buttered paper. Then bake it well, and glaze it with an egg yolk. Then serve it.

4. Wild Boar Pie

Wild Boar Pie is made and seasoned in the same way as the Pie of a Leg of Mutton.

5. Capon Pie

When a capon is well dressed, lard it with medium lard and put it into fine dough and build up your pie. If you want to serve it hot, you shouldn't season it as much as for serving it cold.[5.1] Therefore, for serving it hot, make it up and garnish it with whatever you have, and you can even stuff it. It should be baked for two and a half hours; and if it dries out — that is, if the sauce is insufficient — make up a white sauce[5.2] for it or put in some sort of juice.[5.3] Serve it hot and open.

6. Young Turkey Pie

When dressed, pound it down and truss it; lard it with coarse lard and season it, then put it into a fine or dark dough enriched with butter

---

[3.1] With slightly different punctuation, this recipe is identical to what was already printed at V,84. See also Recipe 37, below.

[3.2] *The French Confectioner* offers extensive directions on the folding of table linen.

[5.1] The author rephrases that principle as a general rule in his preamble to Chapter XXI: "Pies that are to be kept [that is, eaten cold] have to be of a stronger taste than those made to be eaten hot."

[5.2] This *sauce blanche*, which is called for in several of the following recipes as well, is made from egg yolks and verjuice according to Recipe 10, below. Given the presence of yolks, the name is surprising. It functions as a sort of glazing.

[5.3] This *jus* may be either a citrus juice or a meat stock.

or lard because that flesh is very dry when it is cooked. Season it as a Venison Pie.[6.1] Bake it for a length of time that will depend on the meat's toughness and size. Then serve it.

Another way

Dress your young turkey, remove its skin and its breastbone,[6.2] then season it and stuff it with squab, beef palates, mushrooms, truffles, artichoke hearts, cockscombs, ram kidneys and veal sweetbreads. That stuffing is proper where you remove the brisket alone.

If you remove the skin whole, take the flesh of your young turkey, chop it up very finely with beef fat, season it with whatever you have on hand, and with one or two egg yolks; stuff the skin [with that] and sew it up again. Put it into fine dough; garnish that pie with small tidbits, mushrooms and whatever stuffing you have left over. Cook it and serve it hot with whatever sauce you like.

Escoffier, *Farce de veau à la graisse, ou godivaux*, §198

7. Minced Veal (*Gaudiveau*) Pie[7]

Set out your pastry dough in an oval, garnish it with your minced veal, in the middle of which you put all sorts of garnishings, such as mushrooms, fat capon liver, chard ribs, hard egg yolks and sweetbreads; and season everything. Bind it with pastry on top. When it is cooked, serve it with Verjuice Sauce, egg yolks and nutmeg.

8. Partridge Pie

When the partridges are dressed, lard them with medium lard and season them; then put them into a crust of fine dough. Make up your pie, much enriched with lard or butter, and bake it for three hours. Serve it hot.

Paſté de perdrix.

8.

9. Ham Pie[9]

Steep the ham well and, when it is desalted enough, boil it briefly. From around it remove its skin. Then put it in a dark dough as for venison,

---

[6.1] Above, Recipe 1 and Recipe XIV,1; in the *French Pastry Cook*, Recipe VIII,3.

[6.2] As in Recipe IV,11, *brichet*; again I. D. G. translates "brisket".

[7] This same recipe is found in V,81. See the notes there. See also *The French Pastry Chef* at Recipe VII,9.

[9] This recipe repeats what has been given in the Chapter on Entremets, Recipe VIII,5. See the notes at that place.

and season it with pepper, cloves and parsley. In my opinion you can also lard it, the same as venison. Cook the pie according to its size: if it is big, for five hours; if smaller, for less time — all depending on whether it is big or small. When cool, serve it in slices.

10. Pie of Breast of Veal

When veal is well blanched, you can stuff it with whatever you like.[10] You can also put it, well-seasoned, into fine dough; or, if you wish, cut it up into small pieces. Make up your pie; bake it. Serve it with a white sauce made of egg yolks mixed with verjuice.

11. Platter Pie

Get veal, along with beef fat or mutton fat, and make a sort of *gau-diveau* of it. Then make up your pie shell very neatly to half a foot in height, and fill it with a layer of meat, then over that a layer of mush-rooms, another layer of ribs of greens,[11] or squab, beef palates, kidneys and egg yolks, so that the top layer is of your minced veal *gaudiveaux*. Cover it and season it. [Bake it.] Then serve it.

12. Cardinal's Pie[12]

Make your pies very high and very slender, fill them with minced veal *gaudiveaux* and cover them over, with the upper crust also very tall. Then serve them, mainly as garnishing for a piece of beef or on a platter.

13. Bauble Pie[13.1]

Get rye flour and salt it, and make your dough of it, shaping it into a pie. Then get a hare or two, or two mutton legs,[13.2] with a little beef fat chopped up together finely with that, and seasoned. Then make up your pie, on the top of which you leave a breathing hole. When it has baked for three hours, take it out, fill it with good bouillon and put it back into the oven. When it has baked fully, serve it.

---

[10] For a possible stuffing, see Recipe VI,49.

[11] *de cardes ou de cardeaux*: in his glossary, I. D. G. makes no distinction between these two words. The difference may have to do with relative size.

[12] See this pie also at Recipe V,85, above; Recipe XXI,13 has a lean version of it.

[13.1] See this dish at Recipe V,83 also.

[13.2] In later reprintings *un liévre ou deux, ou deux membres de mouton* becomes *une livre ou deux de membre de mouton*: "a pound or two of mutton leg".

14. Pie of Young Rabbits

When the rabbits are dressed, lard them with coarse lard and make your pie as that for venison.[14.1] If you are serving it hot, make it a little milder.[14.2] Then serve it.

15. Chicken Pie

Dress chickens, and flour them if you wish; garnish them and season them, then put them into very fine pastry. Serve them hot with a white sauce of thinned egg yolks.[15] If your chickens are large, you can prick them with medium lard, season them, garnish them and put them into pastry the same way.

16. Lark Pie

Dress larks, remove their gizzards and crush them, then sauté them in a pan with mushrooms, truffles, tidbits and kidneys, everything well seasoned. Then put them into fine dough, bake them for two and a half hours, with the sauce very thick and rich.[16.1] You can add in some sugar, as for hypocras,[16.2] and, if done that way, serve it cold; if it is done with a ragout,[16.3] serve it hot.

17. Veal Pie

Get a round of veal and do it up in the same way as boar — that is, well larded, and seasoned in the same way. Put it into fine or dark pastry, whichever you like. Serve it sliced, cold or hot.

[14.1] This Venison Pie is common enough to serve as the model of a particular variety of preparation. See it in at the beginning of this Chapter, and in *The French Pastry Chef*, Recipe VIII,3.

[14.2] The cook is repeatedly advised (in Recipes 5, above, and 25, below, as well as in the preamble to Chapter XXI) that a pie that is to be served cold should be somewhat more spicy than one served directly from the oven.

[15] These egg yolks are said to be *délayés*, "with verjuice" being understood: see, for example, Recipe 10, above and 17, below.

[16.1] This last term here, *nourrie*, designates in Recipe 6 and 8, above, a pastry dough which is "enriched" with an admixture of butter or lard. Though the present text is inexplicit, the thickened, creamy sauce is likely intended to be a serving garnish.

[16.2] For this spiced cordial, see *The French Confectioner*, Recipe IV,1.

[16.3] *si en ragoust.*

Another way

Chop up whatever veal you like, along with beef fat, and season it. Make up your crust and make the bottom [layer] of your pie, or the whole of it, of that meat chopped up that way and seasoned; furthermore, you garnish the chopped meat with mushrooms or artichokes, the chard ribs, kidneys, veal sweetbreads and hard-boiled egg yolks. After that, you cover the pie over and bake it. When it has baked, serve it opened with a sauce of egg yolks thinned with verjuice.

18. Quail Pie

For eating cold, Quail Pie is made like that of partridge. For eating hot, like that of larks, it is made of fine pastry; and serve it hot with a ragout.

19. Woodcock Pie

Dress your woodcocks, remove their gizzards, lard them with medium lard, and season them in the same way as the Partridge Pie, whether for eating hot or for eating cold. If you serve it hot, garnish it with whatever you have, and season with whatever you think suitable. Bake it for two and a half hours. Serve it hot or cold.

20. Blackbird Pie

Dress your blackbirds, remove their gizzards and put them into pastry. Season and bake them the same way as the larks, for eating hot or cold.

21. Duck Pie

When the duck is dressed, lard it with coarse lard and season it well; put it into fine pastry, or dark pastry if it is for keeping. Bake it for three hours. Serve it garnished, if eating it hot.

22. Pie of Scoter Duck in Lard

It is made and served in the same way as the Duck Pie, immediately above.

23. Lamb Pie

Get the fore-quarters of lamb and cut them up very small; blanch them in cool water, then put them into carefully formed, fine pastry with a little

19.

Pasté de beccasses.

parsley and chopped fine herbs. When well baked and well seasoned, serve with a white sauce.[23]

Another way

You can get your lamb whole or quartered, and, without cutting it up, lard it with coarse lard; put it into pastry seasoned with chopped parsley, salt, pepper and ground cloves, and garnished with mushrooms, morels and capers. When it has baked, serve it with a white sauce of egg yolks thinned with verjuice.

24. Mutton-Tongue Pie

Wash mutton tongues in warm water and clean them, then put them into pastry. Get mushrooms, small, cut up beef palates, tidbits, a little parsley and chives; sauté all of that in a pan, throwing on top of it egg yolks and artichoke hearts, with beaten lard or fresh butter; put it into your pie. Bake the pie for two hours. Serve it with a sauce of egg yolks thinned with verjuice.

25. Hot Goat-Kid Pie

Dress a goat kid and remove its head, lard the kid with medium lard and season it; put it into fine pastry, whether raised or not.[25.1] Garnish it with tidbits, mushrooms, morels, truffles and agaric. Serve. If you wish to serve it cold, make its seasoning stronger.[25.2]

Another way

If you have two kids just born of the hind,[25.3] lard them, season them and put in a good amount of sugar which will make your meat and your sauce sweet. If your kids are small, put them, dressed, into a pie shell separately, with one in sugar and the other in a ragout. Serve them hot.

---

[23] This so-called white sauce is used frequently on La Varenne's pies. Despite its name, it is merely a mixture of egg yolks and verjuice. See the following version of this recipe.

[25.1] *dressée ou non*: that is, set up in the form of a dressed or standing pie rather than lying for a turnover. See Recipe XXI,18.

[25.2] This principle will be stated in the preamble to Chapter XXI: "Pies that are to be kept [that is, eaten cold] have to be of a stronger taste than those made to be eaten hot." See also Recipe 5, above.

[25.3] *deux chevreaux tirés du corps du chevreuil ou de la biche*. I. D. G. translates this as "kids, or roebucks, taken out of the body of the wild goate, or of the hinde."

26. Gosling Pie

When dressed, lard the gosling with very coarse lard and set it into pastry seasoned as in the Venison Pie. Serve it similarly, hot or sliced.

27. Shoulder-Knuckle Pie[27]

Dress the bones of your knuckles, blanch them, break them and lard them with coarse or pounded lard; then put them into fine pastry. Garnish and season your pie with everything you have on hand, then bake it for two and a half hours. When it is done, serve it with whatever sauce you like.

28. Squab Tourte[28.1]

Make your dough fine and let it sit. Then get your squab, clean and blanch them; if they are too big, cut them up. Also get minced veal *gaudiveaux*, asparagus stalks, mushrooms, artichoke hearts, beef marrow, egg yolks, chard ribs, beef palates, truffles and verjuice mash or red currants. Garnish your tourte with whatever you have, not forgetting the seasoning. Serve it.

Another way

When your squab are well dressed and blanched, make a shell of fine or puff pastry dough.[28.2] On its bottom put a few minced veal *gaudiveaux*[28.3] with your squab on top — whole, if they are small; if they are big, cut them in half. Garnish your tourte with cockscombs, [beef] palates, mushrooms, truffles, chard ribs, morels, agaric, egg yolks, veal sweetbreads, artichoke hearts and chopped parsley, the whole well seasoned with salt, pepper, cloves and nutmeg. Cover your tourte and bake it for two and a half hours. When it is done, serve it opened, with a sauce of egg yolks mixed with verjuice mash.

29. Lard Tourte

Get lard, cut it up and melt it between two dishes. Season it the same

Cf. Escoffier, *Tourte de poussins à la paysanne,* §1650

28. *Tourte de pigeonneaux.*

---

[27] *Pasté de manches d'espaules.*

[28.1] See also Recipe V,78.

[28.2] La Varenne provides directions on the making of puff pastry in Recipe XXI,0; see also *The French Pastry Chef*, Recipe I,4. I. D. G. regularly translates this *paste fueilletée* as "puft paste."

[28.3] The plural *quelques gaudiveaux* indicates that the spiced, minced veal has been pre-formed into a sausage shape.

as the Marrow Tourte you will find in the next recipe. When it has baked, serve it.

30. Marrow Tourte

Get marrow and melt it; when melted, strain it and add in sugar, egg yolks, and ground pistachios or almonds. Then make a very thin shell from very fine dough on which you set your mixture; wrap it with a band[30] if you like. Bake it. Serve it sugared.

31. Veal Tourte

Get a piece of veal, blanch it, then chop it up with twice as much beef fat. When it is well seasoned, make a shell of your fine pastry dough and set your meat on it; in the centre of the meat, put whatever you have on hand, such as tidbits, etc.; sugar it if you like. Then, when it has baked, serve it.

Another way

Garnish a shell of fine or puff-pastry dough, and half-fill it with your chopped meat; on top of the meat put mushrooms, kidneys, cockscombs, artichoke hearts, chard ribs and egg yolks, the whole well seasoned; finish filling your tourte with that same meat. Cover it over and glaze it with a thinned raw egg.[31] Bake it for an hour and a half. Serve it opened, with a sauce.

32. Tidbit Tourte

Blanch your tidbits, then put them into a pastry shell, seasoned and garnished the same as for the Squab Tourte.[32.1] Bake it in the same way. Serve it with a white sauce,[32.2] or juice,[32.3] or with some sort of toast ragout.[32.4] You can use pistachios, cleaned — that is, skinned — and chopped.

32. Tourte de beatilles.

---

[30] The procedure consists of wrapping one or several sheets of greased paper around the outside of a pie shell — particularly one with a relatively mobile filling or a thin crust — in order to reinforce its walls while it is baking. See Recipe XVI,89.

[31] "Thinned" with verjuice, presumably.

[32.1] Recipe 28, above.

[32.2] That is, a mixture of egg yolks and verjuice.

[32.3] As in Recipe 5, either a citrus juice or a meat stock.

[32.4] *quelque ragoust de rosties.* See three varieties of this preparation in the *ramequins* of Recipes VIII,46, 47 and 48.

33. Sparrow Tourte

Sparrow Tourte is made in the same way as that of squab.[33] [It is served] with a white sauce.

34. Lark Tourte

You can do up a Lark Tourte also the same as for squab. But here is yet another way: dress them, remove their gizzards, crush them and sauté them in a pan with lard, parsley and mushrooms. Then put them into your pastry shell, seasoning them with egg yolks, capers and with whatever you have on hand. Cover your tourte and bake it for two hours. When it is done, serve it with a good sauce or some sort of juice.[34]

35. Veal Sweetbread Tourte

You can put veal sweetbreads, larded and roasted, well seasoned and garnished, into fine or puff pastry. Otherwise sauté them with mushrooms, cockscombs, truffles, morels, egg yolks, artichoke hearts or a few broken asparagus stalks. With that make up your tourte. Serve it with a mushroom thickener[35] on top.

36. Tourte of Capon White Meat

Get any amount of capon white meat; chop it up very small and moisten it with two egg yolks, fresh butter, a little salt, pistachios, a lot of sugar, a little stock or good bouillon. Make up your tourte with fine or puff-pastry dough, sugar it well and if you like, in addition to the above ingredients, add in pinenuts and currants.

37. Note [on pastry dough][37.1]

You can make your pies for keeping, if you want to carry them far, with rye flour.

Those you want to eat immediately should be made with a dough that is quite fine.[37.2]

---

[33] Recipe 28, above.

[34] As before, probably a meat stock.

[35] See Recipe X,2.

[37.1] These paragraphs do not have a recipe number. Appearing on a separate page (p. 157 in the second edition) at the end of this Chapter XIV, they are headed with a rubric in capitals: *ADVIS*. They might as usefully have been printed as a general preamble to the chapter.

[37.2] *faites les de paste plus de moitié fine.*

The English Pie is made with puff-pastry dough.

The Frangipane Tourte is made with a dough thinned with egg whites.

All varieties of tourtes are made with fine dough or puff-pastry dough.

If you do not find all the different sorts of pasties here, do not be surprised: I did not undertake to make a whole book of them, but only in passing, in order to give elementary directions on the most essential things, and on what is most commonly served so as to mix and vary the courses.

Chapter XV

Lean Pottages outside of Lent[xv]

1. Herb Pottage

Heat up water with butter and salt, then get sorrel, bugloss, borage, chicory, or lettuce, and chard;[1] when these have been thoroughly cleaned, cut them up and put them into a crock with a crust of bread; boil everything for a while until it is quite boiled down. When that has been done, steep your bread. Set out and serve.

2. Crayfish Pottage

Clean your crayfish and cook them in wine and vinegar, with salt and pepper. When they have cooked, shell their feet and tail, and sauté them in very fresh butter and a little parsley; then take the bodies of your crayfish and pound them in a mortar with an onion, some hard-boiled eggs and a crustless loaf of bread. Set them to simmer in some good herb bouillon or in some other sort — if you have purée[2.1] and you'd like to use it, it must be very thin. When boiled, strain everything together; when that is done, set it in front of the fire. Then get some butter with a

2. Potage d'escrevisses.

[xv] This Chapter XV forms a counterpart to both Chapters III and IV, on meat-day pottages (normal and "stuffed"), as well as to Chapter XXV, on lean pottages specifically during Lent.

The reader should be reminded that a *potage* in La Varenne's usage is similar to a medieval *soppe*: the principal foodstuff is prepared, served and garnished *on* or *with* a sop of bread. A *potage* is a complex liquid preparation, which may also contain solid elements, and which is eaten *by means of* bread.

Note: Among La Varenne's recipes in this chapter, there seem to be two types of *potage*: one in which a cooked meat is served upon bread which has been steeped in a relatively plain bouillon; and another in which the bread is steeped in a complex broth and is served (alone) much in the manner of the older sop. Both types of pottage require a serving garnish.

[1] The punctuation here — *chicorée, ou laictuës, & poirée* — is not particularly helpful.

[2.1] Though La Varenne does not explicitly indicate the nature of this purée, he undoubtedly intends what is a traditional staple ingredient in lean dishes: pea purée. That is made by boiling, mashing and straining peas, common white peas. I. D. G. translates that *purée* as "pease porridge."

little chopped parsley and fricassee it and put it to simmer in your well-seasoned bouillon with your dry crusts, covered with a dish or a plate. Also put some small amount of mashed carp and mushroom stock[2.2] on top of your bread. Build up your dish;[2.3] garnish it with your crayfish feet and tails, with pomegranate seeds and lemon juice. Serve.

3. Carp Pottage

Debone a carp and set the bones to boil in pea purée along with some onion or hard-boiled eggs and breadcrumbs. When they have boiled, strain them, fricassee them with a little parsley, and put them back into your bouillon. When they have boiled, dry and steep your bread. Make a hash of your carp's flesh. When that has cooked, put it on your bread and build it up. Garnish it with quenelles,[3] everything well seasoned. Serve with lemon juice and mushrooms on top.

4. Pottage of Stuffed Tench[4.1]

Get your tench, debone and fillet them,[4.2] then stuff them with their flesh which you have chopped up very finely. After that you neatly close the opening through which you inserted your stuffing. Everything is well seasoned. For the bouillon, make it up from pea purée if you like, or from turnips or herbs or tench or almonds or carp or crayfish — it doesn't matter what, provided it is good. Steep your bread; garnish it with stuffed or roasted tench, [and] with whatever garnishing you like. Then serve.

5. Pottage of Stuffed Carp

Debone and fillet your carp,[5.1] then stuff them with their flesh, neatly sewing up the opening through which you stuffed them, the same as with

4. Potage de tanches.

[2.2] For the making of this *jus de champignons*, see Recipe XI,1.

[2.3] This direction, *emplissez votre plat*, "fill your dish," is found repeatedly in these recipes. The serving dish is to be heaped up generously with the various ingredients and garnishes, with the steeped bread providing a base beneath everything.

[3] These "quenelles" are what La Varenne calls *andoüillettes*. I. D. G. does not translate the French; he does, however, provide a gloss for the word: "These are balls, or roundish small peeces of minced flesh well seasoned." For that lean dish the "flesh" would be understood to be that of fish, probably minced, seasoned carp, mixed with eggs: see Recipe 14, below.

[4.1] Though the name of the dish is merely *Potage de tanches*, it should probably indicate, as in the next recipe, that the fish are actually to be stuffed.

[4.2] The fishes' skins are to remain more or less intact.

[5.1] The fishes' skins are to remain whole, as with the tench of the previous recipe.

the tench. Cook them in a dish[5.2] with bouillon, butter, verjuice, chives and pepper. Boil the carps' bones; remove them from the pot and strain the bouillon, which you have seasoned with salt, pepper and breadcrumbs. Steep your bread [in that bouillon] and garnish it with your stuffed carp, capers and mushrooms Then serve.

6. Pottage of Roast Carp

When dressed, slice the carp along their top; melt some butter and glaze your carp with it; then set them on the grill and cook them, without their scales. Make a sauce with butter, parsley, chives, a dash of verjuice and vinegar, the whole being well seasoned and simmered in bouillon drawn from another pot, or with pea purée. Then get some turnips, cut them in half and, when they have been blanched, flour and fry them. When that has been done, put them into a pot in water or pea purée. When they have cooked and are seasoned, steep your bread and garnish it with your carp, your turnips and capers. Then serve.

If you don't put in any turnips, you can garnish your bread with mushrooms or cut asparagus stalks and carp milt.

7. Queen's Pottage[7.1]

Get carp or tench and cook them in water along with some salt, an onion, parsley, hard-boiled eggs and a crustless loaf of bread. When they have cooked, strain your bouillon, and put it into another pot with the amount of butter you would put into any other pottage.[7.2] Get some almonds, grind them up, then mix them with half of your bouillon; after you have boiled them together a while, strain them, add in an onion stuck with whole cloves and let that sit on a few hot coals. Steep your bread in a little of your first broth and fill your dish with white broth,[7.3] an egg

---

[5.2] This stuffed fish is cooked in a dish perhaps because it would be difficult to transfer from a pot or pan onto a proper serving dish.

[7.1] La Varenne gives a "meat-day" version of this preparation at Recipe III,11.

[7.2] Unfortunately La Varenne never gives an indication anywhere just what he considers to be a normal amount of butter for a pottage.

[7.3] The term *bouillon blanc* refers to the almond mixture. In the Middle Ages, the preparation would have been called a sort of almond milk. The so-called White Dish of almonds, or *blanc manger* (Recipes VIII,33 and XIX,17), shared the same qualification.

yolk mixed with verjuice and mushroom stock,[7.4] without it becoming too thick, though. Then serve, garnished with pomegranate seeds and lemon slices.

8. Princess Pottage[8.1]

Get very thin pea purée in which you cook carp bones along with a few egg yolks and a bouquet of herbs, everything well seasoned. Then dry a loaf of bread and, after steeping it, add in a very little carp hash and mushroom stock. Build up your dish gradually while it is simmering, and garnish it with mushrooms, truffles, milt,[8.2] burbot liver, all sorts of herbs, pomegranate seeds and lemon slices. Then serve.

9. Tortoise Pottage[9.1]

Get your tortoises, dress them, cut them up into bits and sauté them in a pan with butter, parsley and chives. When they are well done and seasoned, set them to simmer in a little bouillon in a dish on the hotplate. To make that bouillon,[9.2] you clean your tortoises well, you cook them in well-seasoned water, and you make use of it. Be careful not to burst the gall-bladder as you cut them up. Steep your bread, then garnish it with your tortoises and their sauce, with broken asparagus stalks around the dish, mushrooms, truffles, lemon slices and mushroom stock. Then serve.

10. Pottage of Stuffed Mushrooms

Take mushroom parings, wash them well, and set them to cook in water or some other bouillon with a [clove-]stuck onion and a sprig of thyme, everything well seasoned; strain that bouillon and put it into a pot. Then sauté your mushrooms in butter in a pan, along with parsley and capers, and put them, too, into that same pot. You can make the stock of your pottage with some carp bones which you boil with your mushrooms.

[7.4] For this mushroom juice, see Recipe XI,1, above.

[8.1] *Potage de Princesse*. See a similar *Potage à la Princesse* for meat days at Recipe III,12.

[8.2] Elsewhere among these recipes the milt is specifically from carp.

[9.1] *Tortuës*. It may be noted that the semi-aquatic habitat of the creature apparently qualified it for consumption on a lean day.

[9.2] La Varenne has overlooked a previous step in the preparation of the tortoises, which step will yield the bouillon necessary here.

Steep your bread; when it is well done, set out on it a layer of carp hash and then build it up with your mixture while it is simmering. When it is built up, garnish your pottage with your mushrooms stuffed with the same stuffing of which you have made your hash, cooked between two dishs, and with milt. When you are ready to serve, set out pomegranate seeds or lemon all around. Then serve.

11. Pottage of Deboned, Stuffed Sole

Fry them almost completely, then open them along the backbone, which you extract. Get milt, oysters, capers, mushrooms and truffles, and sauté everything in a pan with whole parsley and chives; stuff your sole with that mixture. When they have been stuffed, set them to simmer in a little bouillon, fresh butter, and lemon or orange juice or verjuice. Steep your bread in whatever fish bouillon you have and like. Garnish it with your sole, with mushrooms, truffles, milt and mushroom stock, and set lemon slices around the dish. Serve.

12. Smelt Pottage

Make a bouillon with almonds or fish or mushrooms or pea purée, the whole well seasoned. Steep your bread, and on it put a little white broth,[12.1] thinned egg yolks[12.2] and mushroom stock. Get your smelt, fry them and garnish your pottage with them. Alternatively, if you like, before that garnishing, put the smelt into a ragout — for the making of which you get parsley, chives, butter and verjuice; fricassee these all together, then strain the mixture; when it is strained, you put it with your smelt. Serve that garnished with pomegranate seeds and lemon.

13. Asparagus Pottage

Get a quantity of herbs and put them into a pot with breadcrumbs; season them well; strain them.[13.1] then, when they have been been strained put them back into the pot. Steep your bread. Garnish it with asparagus

---

[12.1] This *bouillon blanc* is the common white almond bouillon first mentioned in Recipe III,6, otherwise called simply almond broth in Recipe 7, above. See the recipe for it at XXIV,4.

[12.2] No liquid is named here for the "thinning.". Normally (as in Recipe XIV,10) verjuice is used to dilute egg yolks.

[13.1] Although no liquid is mentioned here, and is presumably water, the first variant recipe refers to this as a bouillon.

stalks which you have cooked in salted water and which, when drained, you have put with fresh butter, salt and nutmeg. On top of your pottage you use broken, fricasseed asparagus stalks. Then serve.

Another way

Make use of the same bouillon as above. Add a little carp hash on top, garnished with fricasseed asparagus stalks and some other mushrooms and milt. Serve.

Another way

After your bread has been steeped well, garnish it with herbs, asparagus stalks, capers and egg yolks. Serve. You can glaze your pottage[13.2] if you like.

14. Pottage of Fish Haslets[14]

Get carp, debone them and make a well-seasoned hash of them with butter and good herbs. Take the carp bones and boil them in pea purée or some other bouillon, with a bouquet of herbs, some butter and salt. Then, with your carp skins, make some haslets — that is, by taking bits of carp skin, stretching them out and putting your seasoned hash on them, with eggs to thicken it, then rolling them up in the shape of quenelles. When they are rolled up, cook them in a dish with butter, a little verjuice and a scallion. When they are done, garnish your bread with the hash and the haslets; put mushrooms and broken asparagus stalks on top. Then serve.

14. Potage d'Attereaux de poiſſon.

13.2 *Vous pouvez blanchir vostre potage.* Throughout this chapter of Lean pottages a recurrent serving garnish makes use of a mixture of eggs (sometimes just egg yolks) and verjuice which is poured over the top of whatever is heaped on the bread sop. The verb that refers to the application of this final, decorative coating is *blanchir*; clearly it derives from the name of the *sauce blanche* which usually has the same composition.

14 The word *attereaux* derives from the word *haste*, meaning a roasting spit. By the end of the Middle Ages the diminutive, *hastelettes* and *menue haste* came to designate a collection of small bits of meat or of giblets which were roasted on a small spit or skewer, somewhat in the manner of a shish kebab. Here, by the time of La Varenne, these seasoned, grilled or sautéed bits of meat or fish could be used as an ingredient in a dish.

The Lenten *Potage d'attereaux* of XXV,12 is probably this present recipe.

offier, *Lai-
farcies*,
62

15. Pottage of Stuffed Lettuce

Get your lettuce[15] and blanch them in cool water. Make a stuffing of fish hash or of herbs; after having stuffed them with that, set them to simmer in a pot of pea purée or some other bouillon, seasoned with butter, salt and an onion stuck with cloves. Steep your bread, garnish it with your lettuce, which you split in half; you can set out a layer of fish hash on it. Serve.

16. Cabbage Pottage with Milk

Quarter your cabbages, blanch them, then put them into a pot in water, with a lot of butter, some salt, some pepper and an onion stuck with cloves. When well cooked, put in milk. Steep your bread. Serve it garnished with your cabbages.

17. Cabbage Pottage with Fried Bread

Blanch your cabbages and put them into a pot in the same way as in the previous recipe. Serve garnished with fried bread.

18. Cabbage Pottage with Pea Purée

This is done in the same way as in the preceeding recipes, except that instead of water you cook your cabbages in a pot of pea purée. Garnish and serve the same way.

19. Pumpkin Pottage with Butter

Get your pumpkin, cut it up into pieces and cook it in water with salt. When it is done, strain it and put it into a pot with an onion stuck with cloves, and fresh butter and pepper. Steep your bread. If you like, thin three or four egg yolks putting them, with some bouillon,[19] on top. Then serve.

20. Pumpkin Pottage with Milk

Cut up a pumpkin, cook it as above, then put it through a strainer with some milk and boil it with some butter, seasoned with salt, pepper and an onion stuck [with cloves]. Serve it with egg yolks thinned as above.

---

[15] It is not clear whether *vos laictuës* (in the plural) means heads of lettuce, to be hollowed and stuffed, or (perhaps more likely) leaves of lettuce, to be wrapped around the stuffing as the carp skins were in the previous recipe.

[19] *Sic.* The next recipe implies that the egg yolks are to be thinned with the bouillon, then used as a serving garnish.

21. Pottage of Fried Turnip

Scrape your turnips well and quarter them or split them in half; blanch them. Flour them and sauté them in a pan in clarified butter, taking them out when they are a good russet colour. Then put your turnips into a pot of water or pea purée; cook them well and season them. Steep your bread and garnish it with your turnips and capers. Then serve.

Another way

With your turnips scraped, quartered and blanched, set them to cook in water with butter, salt and an onion stuck with cloves. When they are well cooked, steep your bread. After having put fresh butter in with your turnips, stir the pot often until the butter is melted. Then make up your pottage with it. Serve.

22. Milk Pottage with Egg Yolks

Get very fresh milk and boil it; season it with salt and sugar. When it is on the point of boiling, mix in several egg yolks for a large dish, and for a small one proportionately fewer; put them into your milk stirring carefully as it is making its bouillon. Get biscuit[22] or bread and make your pottage, which you serve sugared.

Another way

Prepare your milk and garnish it with eggs poached in water — the eggs carefully selected and very fresh so that they poach better. Then serve.

23. Profiterole Pottage[23.1]

Steep your bread in your best lean bouillon. Then get six small loaves,[23.2] made for the purpose; dry them thoroughly and make an opening in their top the width of a testoon[23.3] through which you remove the soft bread within. When they are quite dry, sauté them with clarified butter. When they have thoroughly drained, set them to steep on your bread.

---

[22] This use of biscuit is rare. See also Recipe VIII,79.

[23.1] A meat version of this dish is found at Recipe III,10. See also Recipe XXV,23 among the Lenten Pottages.

[23.2] Presumably these are somewhat like what we might call buns.

[23.3] The *teston* was a silver coin of slightly more than an inch in diameter. I. D. G. renders the size of this hole as "the bignes of one shilling."

When you are ready to serve, fill them with all sorts of things, such as milt, mushrooms, broken asparagus stalks, truffles, artichokes and capers; stop up your small loaves again with their plugs. Garnish them with milt, mushrooms, pomegranate seeds and lemon slices. Then serve them.

24. Pottage of Green Peas[24.1]

Sauté green peas — the smallest and freshest you can get — in a pan in butter or melted lard.[24.2] Put them to simmer in a small pot, well seasoned, with a little parsley and chives. Then steep a loaf of bread in some herb bouillon or in purée of old peas.[24.3] When done, garnish it with the green peas and serve.

Another way

Get the largest peas and set them to cook, then reduce them to purée, putting in some butter[24.4] with a little chopped parsley and chives; season it well. Steep your pottage,[24.5] add capers, and garnish it with fried bread.

25. Herb Pottage without Butter

Get a good quantity of new fresh herbs, pick them apart and put them into boiling water along with a crust of bread; season them well, so that they are slightly bitter with sorrel. Steep your bread and make up your pottage, adding capers if you like. Then serve.

To make your pottage tart, take half of the herbs when they are half-cooked and strain them. To make it green, you have to grind sorrel.

Escoffier, Petits pois à la française, §2193

25. Potage d'herbes sans beurre.

[24.1] The pottage made with this less common variety of pea, the green pea, stands as a counterpart to the Pottage of Purée of Green Peas in Recipe 46, below. Compare also Recipe XXIX,20.

[24.2] The inclusion of lard as an alternative in this "lean" recipe is surprising and surely an oversight. Where other dishes in this chapter are intented for meat-day use (for instance, Recipe 28 alt.) they are so titled.

[24.3] It was customary, then as today, to keep peas throughout the year by drying them.

[24.4] *puis en tirés la purée, y passés du beuree.* I. D. G. translates this *tirés* literally: "then take out the broath of them, and frie some butter into it . . . ."

[24.5] It is possible that *potage* may be a lapsus for *pain* on the part of the typesetter, but in the recipes of this chapter the word *potage* occasionally implies the bread which is the basis of the pottage. In Recipe 31, below, the earliest editions read *faites mitonner vostre pain*, whereas that has become, as here, *faites mittonner votre potage* in later versions.

26. Onion Pottage

Slice your onions very thinly and fricassee them in butter; when done, put them into a pot with water or pea purée. When they are well cooked, add in a crust of bread and let it boil very little; you can put in some capers. Dry your bread, then steep it, set it out. Serve with a dash of vinegar.

27. Pottage of Stuffed Cucumbers

Get your cucumbers, peel them, clean them out neatly, blanch them in cool water and then drain them. Make a stuffing with sorrel, egg yolks and whole eggs, everything well seasoned; pour it into your cucumbers. After that, put them into a pot with water or pea purée, and cook them well; season with capers if you like. Then steep your bread and garnish it with your cucumbers, which you cut in quarters. Then serve.

28. Snow Pottage

It is made with milk well-seasoned with salt and sugar. When you are ready to serve,[28.1] take the egg whites of the yolks[28.2] that you will have thinned[28.3] to mix them into your milk; fry [the whites] well and put them with your milk.[28.4] Serve sugared.

Another way for meat days

Steep your bread in some almond bouillon, a little chopped meat and mutton stock all together. When you are ready to serve, have some egg whites fried and put them on your pottage. Heat up the fire shovel to red hot and pass it over the pottage to finish cooking them. Then serve.

29. Mussel Pottage

Escoffier,
*Moules Pou-
lette*, §2980

Get your mussels, scrape them, wash them well, then put them to boil in some water in a skillet, with some salt and an onion. When they have cooked, take them out and open them, removing the shell from some

---

[28.1] La Varenne's cook will understand this to mean that the base of steeped bread has been prepared and set out.

[28.2] Rather confusingly La Varenne uses this sentence to catch up on a forgotten instruction.

[28.3] Again, presumably, with verjuice.

[28.4] *& les jettez avec vostre laict*: as with the alternative version that follows, the fried egg whites are a garnish on top of the pottage.

of them, leaving it on others that will be used as a garnish. When they
are thus cleaned, sauté them in a pan with chopped parsley. As for your
bouillon, when it has settled, don't disturb the bottom in case there is any
sand there, and boil it. When it is boiling, add in[29.1] a little parsley with
very fresh butter. Steep your bread, when it is well steeped, make up your
pottage and garnish it with your mussels. If you like, glaze it[29.2] with egg
yolks thinned with verjuice. Then serve.

30. Oyster Pottage

With your oysters well blanched and floured, sauté them with a little
parsley; then set them to simmer in a pot. Steep your bread in another
bouillon, such as White Dish.[30.1]   When it is well steeped, garnish it
with your oysters, some of which you fry as fritters;[30.2] garnish with
pomegranate seeds, lemon slices and crayfish juice.[30.3] Then serve.

31. Gurnard Pottage

Dress gurnards and cook them as if stewing them,[31] seasoned with
all sorts of good herbs, butter and a dash of white wine. Steep your bread
and garnish it with your gurnard, capers, mushrooms, and carp milt if you
have any. Then serve.

32. Salmon Pottage

Slice up a salmon, fry the slices, then set them to simmer in a little
white wine with some sugar. Also steep your bread in any other bouillon

---

[29.1] *passez y*: I. D. G. renders that as "frie into it."

[29.2] *le blanchissez*. This sort of embellishment by means of diluted egg yolks will be
repeated below: see Recipes 34, 35 and 38. Egg yolks and verjuice are the ingredients
which produce the so-called white sauce (*sauce blanche*) that is called for in Recipes
XIV,5, 10, 15, 23 and 24; see also Recipe 34, below.

[30.1] This *blanc manger* is found at Recipes VIII,33 and XIX,17. What La Varenne
probably intends here, though, is not the prepared dish but merely almond milk, the
bouillon blanc of Recipe 7, above.

[30.2] The procedure for making such oyster fritters is found in Recipe XVI,20.

[30.3] This *jus d'escrevisses* turns up again as *bouillon d'escrevisses* in Recipe 49, below.

[31] *les faites cuire en façon d'estuvée*. This manner of cooking fish will be used frequently in Chapters XVI and XXVI.

30.

Potage d'Huiſtre.

you have, provided it is well seasoned. Garnish it with your salmon, with the sauce over the top; let it boil like that briefly.[32] Then serve.

Escoffier, *Nymphes à l'aurore*, §351

33. Potage de Grenouilles au saffran.

33. Pottage of Saffran Frogs' Legs[33.1]

Truss up your frogs' legs and put them to boil in bouillon or pea purée; season them with parsley, a clove-stuck onion and a sprig of thyme. Steep your bread and garnish it with your frogs' legs, glazed with[33.2] saffron or egg yolks. Then serve.

Another way

Truss up your frogs' legs done like cherries;[33.3] fry them and set them to simmer between two dishes with a little fresh butter, a dash of verjuice, and orange or lemon juice; season them well with a bouquet of herbs. Then, to make up your bouillon, boil some of it with some pea purée or water, salt, parsley, chives, a handful of ground almonds and egg yolks; then strain everything together. Steep your bread, on which you can put a little hash of carp or of some other fish. Build up your dish and garnish it with your frogs' legs, lemons and pomegranates. Then serve.

34. Bran Pottage

Get some of the largest wheat bran you can find, boil it well in water with a handful of almonds and a bouquet of herbs; season it well. Strain it, then put it back to boil. Steep your bread. Build up your dish with that bouillon which you can glaze, if you like, with eggs thinned with verjuice.[34.1] Garnish it with rosettes[34.2] if you have any. Then serve.

---

[32] *le laissez ainsi bouillir un bouillon*: the *ainsi*, "thus," seems to indicate that the "sauce" of fried-salmon bouillon, wine and sugar is to be brought to a boil *after*, rather than just before, being poured over the dish. If so, the serving dish is kept close to the heat for that purpose.

[33.1] The name of this dish is *Potage de Grenouilles au saffran.* Here and in the various other recipes for *grenouilles* we should understand that what La Varenne is handling is "frogs' *legs*". See Recipe XXI,26. Being aquatic creatures, frogs qualified as "lean" food.

[33.2] *vos grenouilles blanchies, avec . . . .*

[33.3] The term *en cerises* will be explained in Recipe XXVIII,35. One end of the leg bone is bared for holding like the stem of a cherry.

[34.1] The verb here which is translated "glaze" is again *blanchir.* We may suspect that *des œufs delayez* is an error for the usual *jaunes d'œufs delayez* as, for instance, in Recipe 29, above.

[34.2] For the inexperienced cook La Varenne offers an explanation of these decorative

35. Hops Pottage

Get a good amount of herbs which you season as for a pottage, with a crustless loaf of bread; strain everything[35] and set it all to boil in a pot. Also sauté fresh butter in a pan with a little parsley and a bouquet of herbs; put that into your pot. Steep your bread in your bouillon. After that, cook your hops in some water with some salt; when it is done and drained, put it with some butter and garnish your bread with it. Then serve your pottage — glazed, if you like, with egg yolks mixed into some verjuice.

36. Raspberry Pottage

Mix eggs with raspberries and strain both together. Boil some milk that is well seasoned with salt and, when it boils, pour your mixture into it, stirring it well. Set it out;[36] garnish it with raspberries. Serve.

37. Parsnip Pottage[37]

Clean the parsnips well, choosing the medium-sized ones. Cook them with some butter and a bouquet of herbs, seasoning them with salt and sticking them with cloves. Then take them out, and peel them if you like. Then put them with butter and a drop of bouillon and simmer them, and your sauce will turn out to have thickened. With your bread well steeped and your pottage built up, garnish it with your parsnips. Then serve.

38. Leek Pottage

Get the white of your leeks, cut it up very small — reserving some of them which you cut lengthwise for garnishing — and tie them together; blanch them and set them to cook in pea purée or water. When they are done, steep your bread. Garnish your pottage with the leeks you have cut lengthwise. Serve.

You can glaze them with egg yolks thinned with a little verjuice. You can also put in some milk and pepper, and serve straight away.

---

fleurons in Recipe XXIX,13: "These are small lumps of puff-pastry dough." I. D. G. adds that they are fried.

[35] *passez le tout*: I. D. G. translates this as "fry all." See the following recipe.

[36] A bread base for this pottage is merely implied.

[37] In later editions this *Potage de panets* becomes *Potage de navets*, "Turnip Pottage."

If you want to serve them without glazing them, they must be cooked in pea purée; put capers into it, season it well, simmer it and serve it garnished in the same way as the other.

39. Pottage of Stuffed Scoter Duck

When a scoter has been well dressed, remove its flesh,[39] chop it up with butter, mushrooms, egg yolks, salt, pepper, fine herbs — such as parsley, chives and thyme — and a raw egg to bind the meat. Then stuff your scoter and close it up with a skewer or a thread; put it into a pot with the thinnest pea purée you can get get, and cook it well. As it boils, it will thicken quite enough. Steep your bread. Set out your scoter with whatever garnishing you have. Then serve it.

40. Burbot Pottage

Flour burbots, fry them, and garnish your pottage with them after your bread has been well steeped in your best bouillon. When fully built up, garnish it with whatever you have, such as mushrooms, truffles, asparagus stalks, milt. Glaze them[40] with some almond bouillon or, alternatively, with some crayfish bouillon.

41. Pottage of Broken Aparagus Stalks

Dry some bread crusts and steep them in your best bouillon. Garnish them with your [broken] asparagus stalks and mushrooms. The asparagus can be laid full length, if you like. Serve.

If you want them to taste really fresh,[41] glaze them with the bouillon in which you steeped your bread.

42. Cauliflower Pottage

Prepare your cauliflowers as if for putting into butter.[42] Blanch them extremely little, then finish cooking them; season them well. Steep your bread in any sort of bouillon you have. Garnish it with your cauliflowers sautéed in butter, salt and nutmeg. Sprinkle them with almond bouillon. Then serve them.

41. Potage d'asperges rompuës.

---

[39] The text does not explicitly direct that the skin be saved. That must be the case, however, because "the duck" is later to be be stuffed and carefully sealed up.

[40] *les blanchissez.*

[41] *qu'elles sentent le verd.*

[42] The reference is probably to Recipe VIII,17.

43. Vermicelli Pottage[43] Peel five or six onions, chop them up and boil them in water with butter. When they have cooked, strain them through a linen filter; in that bouillon cook your vermicelli, seasoning them with salt and pepper. When they are done, steep your bread and garnish it with them. Then serve.

44. Rice Pottage

Blanch your rice. When it is very clean, make it burst[44.1] in water or milk; cook it. When it is done, take a suitable amount of it and strain it to make your bouillon. When seasoned as the vermicelli,[44.2] steep your bread; put a little rice on top of it and garnish it with fingers of puff pastry[44.3] and rosettes. Then serve it.

You can make a milk pottage the same way. And, if you like, serve it garnished with sugar and macaroons.[44.4]

45. Pottage of Pastry Fingers

Make a dough seasoned only with salt, roll it out and cut it out as finely as you can into the shape of fingers.[45.1] Sauté these and simmer them in an extremely small amount of good bouillon. When they have simmered well, get a very small amount of bread and garnish it with the rest of your pastry fingers, season like the vermicelli,[45.2] then serve.

---

[43] See also the Lenten version of this pottage at Recipe XXV,36. Concerning vermicelli (*fidelles* in La Varenne, *fidâwsh* in Arabic, *fideos* in Spanish and *fidiaux* in Provençal) see Jean-Louis Flandrin, "Les pâtes dans la cuisine provençale," *Médiévales* 16–17 (1989), 66; as well as Flandrin and Massimo Montanari, eds., *Histoire de l'alimentation* (Paris: Fayard, 1996), 358; in the English translation, *op. cit.*, 218.

[44.1] That is, "boil it until it bursts out of its hull." See Recipe XXX,35.

[44.2] With salt and pepper, according to the previous recipe.

[44.3] In Recipe III,38 these "fingers" (*tailladins fueilletés*) are expressly of bread (*tailladins, c'est à dire des morceaux de pain*), "in the shape of lardoons." Directions for making them of pastry are given in the following recipe.

[44.4] For these *macarons* Recipe Confections,47. La Varenne's macaroons have a base of almond paste and not coconut, of course.

[45.1] These are the *tailladins fueilletés* already called for in the previous recipe. In Recipes III,38 and 42, the "fingers" are of bread.

[45.2] Of Recipe 43, above. There the seasoning is, a little surprisingly, only salt and pepper.

Another way

If you have a little fine pastry dough or puff-pastry dough, roll it out and cut it into fingers. Sauté these in clarified butter. Garnish your pottage with them. Then serve.

46. Pottage of Purée of Green Peas[46]

Cook your peas only very little, pound them in a mortar and strain them with a well-seasoned herb bouillon. Then get chives, parsley and butter, and, with everything sautéed together, put it all into your pottage; boil it. For the garnish, clean some lettuce, chicory, cucumbers, along with small peas that have been sautéed and cooked with butter, salt and a little pepper. When you are ready to serve, steep your bread in your pea purée. Garnish with whatever you have, or even with artichoke hearts if you like. Then serve it.

47. Pottage of Green Purée of Common Peas[47.1]

Cook old peas[47.2] with water to do it most quickly; draw out your purée very thin. When you are ready to use it, put into it parsley, chervil, fresh sorrel, butter and capers; then boil it with all these seasonings. Steep your bread in your purée. If you have nothing to garnish this with, garnish it with fried bread or rosettes. Serve.

To serve it[47.3] green, beat leaf greens or sorrel. Sprinkle some of these around your dish.

---

[46] Compare this dish with the Pottage of Green Peas in Recipe 24 and the Pea Purée Pottage in XXV,21.

[47.1] *Potage de purée de poix communs, servie verte*: the last phrase is necessary in order to make it clear that the adjective *vert* applies to the colour of the purée and not to the greenness or freshness of the peas. Later typesetters, unable to understand the sense of the phrase, change the title to *Potage de pois vieux servis verds*. La Varenne's original syntactical agreement makes his sense clear.

[47.2] These old — that is to say, dried — peas are still the white pea, the so-called "common" pea. They are reconstituted by boiling in water. According to Furetière peas were sown in March and harvested in May and June. In any case it seems that only the common white pea was dried and kept for use out of season. Directions for colouring the purée of these peas green are given in the subsidiary paragraph of this recipe.

[47.3] This "it" is feminine in the text, and refers to the purée. The greens and sorrel are squeezed to express a green juice: see Recipes XVI,49 and XVII,8, for instance. The sop itself will also be given that green colour.

48. Pottage of Scoter Duck with Turnip

When your scoter is dressed, lard it with eel or carp. Then sauté it, and cook it in a mixture of half water, half pea purée, well seasoned with butter and a bouquet of herbs. When it is almost done, cut up your turnips, flour them and sauté them in butter in a pan; when they are a russet colour, put them in to cook with your scoter. When they are done, steep the bread and garnish it with the duck along with your turnips. If your pottage is not thick enough, add into it a little flour, capers or a drop of vinegar. Then serve.

49. Pottage of Garnished Scoter Duck

This is done in the same way as the other, except that, if you want your turnips to stand out,[49] you can sauté them seasoned with a bouquet of herbs, onion and good butter. When your pottage is well cooked, serve it garnished well with mushrooms and artichokes; not too thick.

Escoffier, *Caneton braisé aux navets*, §1748

50. Pottage of Leeks in Pea Purée

Blanch them very little, and cook them in a pea purée which is well seasoned with butter and salt. Steep your bread; garnish it with your leeks. To glaze them,[50] moisten egg yolks with some bouillon, and throw that over the top.

Another way

With your leeks cooked and little liquid left, add in well-seasoned milk. Serve.

51. Dab[51.1] Pottage

Get your dab, remove their tail and head, and half fry them. Then brown them or put them into a casserole pan,[51.2] without reducing the

50. Potage de poireaux à la purée.

---

[49] That is, to be noticeable in flavour: *que vos navets paroissent, . . .* : I.D.G., "to make a shew, ..."

[50] *pour lesquels blanchir*: bouillon replaces the usual verjuice in this serving sauce.

[51.1] I.D.G. shows "flounder" here for *limandes*. The two fish are similar.

[51.2] *les mettez au roux, ou en castrolle.* This is the second of only two instances in La Varenne in which the word *roux* is used as a substantive. As in Recipe III,16 it refers to a relatively common manner of preparation where a foodstuff is dredged in flour and sautéed in fat (oil, lard or butter).
For La Varenne's description of the cooking receptacle called a *castrolle*, see Recipe XVIII,28. For its use in another recipe, see XVI,34. Recipe XVIII,11, for Fried Dab in Ragout, refers to this present recipe.

sauce but thickening it very much.[51.3] Steep your bread in your best bouillon; garnish it with your dab on top, along with mushrooms and capers. Then serve.

If you don't have any fish bouillon, pea purée is good.

52. Herb Pottage Garnished with Cucumber

Get all sorts of herbs; clean them well, simmer them in butter in a bouquet[52] on a low fire, then gradually cover them with hot water. When they have boiled well and been seasoned, put in bread crusts with an onion stuck [with cloves], and capers if you like. You can garnish it with cooked lettuce; you can also cook some peas among the herbs. Serve promptly, and garnish with cucumbers.

53. Onion Pottage with Milk

With your onion cut up very small and sautéed in butter so that it is browned, cook it in a little water well seasoned with salt and pepper. When it is done, add milk in with it and boil it. Then, steeping your crusts, serve it promptly.

54. Loach[54.1] Pottage

Stuff the loach whole with a little sorrel, egg yolks and milk, and season them well with melted butter; mix everything together without flouring them except individually.[54.2] Cook them in butter with parsley, salt and pepper. Steep your crusts in your best bouillon; garnish them with your loach, which you glaze with egg yolks.

You can serve them in an entrée, or fry them; you can also garnish a pottage with them, or use them to make it brown: garnish [the pottage with them] just as soon as they are fried.

[51.3] *la sauce fort longue & bien liée*: I. D. G., "with a very long sauce, and well thickned." In Recipe XVI,2 we read the usual phrase *la sauce courte et bien liée*.

[52] La Varenne's typesetter has put *avec du beurre & un bouquet sur . . .* : surely this is an error, persisting into the second edition and reproduced in I. D. G.'s English translation: "with butter and a bundle of herbs, over . . . ."

[54.1] *losches*; later typesetters change the fish of this recipe to *lothes*, "burbot." La Varenne has already described a *Potage de lottes* in Recipe 40, above.

[54.2] *meslez le tout ensemble sans les fariner que d'elles-mesmes.*

55. Weever-Fish Pottage

When weevers have been cleaned well, boil them in little pea purée, white wine, a stuck onion or a bouquet of herbs, the whole well seasoned. Then take your weevers out and put them into a ragout, getting some sort of good thickener or truffles; let them simmer, well seasoned with salt, fresh butter, chopped capers and an anchovy; cover them. For the bouillon, sieve it through a cloth and boil it with fresh butter,[55] parsley and chopped capers. Steep the crust of a loaf of bread; on top of it put a few chopped mushrooms, and some weever flesh. When it has steeped, garnish it with your weevers, and the ragout on top. Serve it.

56. Red-Mullet Pottage

This is done the same way as for weever-fish. Serve it the same way, garnishing it with whatever you have.

57. Pottage of Stuffed Mushrooms

This is done the same way as the Princess Pottage.[57.1] Garnish it with your stuffed mushrooms and with milt. Build it up[57.2] with your best bouillon, using whatever garnish you like. Serve.

58. Almond-Milk Pottage

When your almonds are ground, set them to simmer in some milk with a crustless loaf of bread; then strain them and season them with salt and sugar. When you are ready to serve, put in some more sugar. Serve.

---

[55] Next in this list is the word *paste*, which normally means either paste, batter or dough. It may well be an error. Later printers read the word as *peu de* before *persil*.

[57.1] Recipe 8, above. Recipe 10 has the same title as this, but apparently this present version presents a variation on the other.

[57.2] *remplissez*: The recipe is a bit sketchy because the important ingredient is, of course, the stuffed mushrooms. Presumably the bread is to have been steeped also in the "best bouillon".

Chapter XVI

Entrées for Lean Days outside of Lent[xvi]

1. Sole in Ragout

Get your sole, scrape and gut them, set them to drain and dry them; flour them and put them into a pan to half-cook by frying. Then open them up and remove their backbone. After that you stuff them with capers, mushrooms, truffles, milt,[1] a little bread crust, a scallion, only a little verjuice and bouillon; simmer everything together. Serve with the juice of a little lemon on top.

2. Pike in Ragout

Cut it up and put it [to cook] with white wine, a bouquet of herbs and very fresh butter; season that well with capers and mushrooms. Then, with the sauce much reduced and thickened, serve with slices of lemon and pomegranate seeds.

3. Tench in Ragout

Scald and dress them, cut them into rounds and wash them carefully; then set them to boil in a skillet with salt, pepper and onion; add in a cup of white wine and a little chopped parsley. When the sauce is very reduced, thicken it with egg yolks. Serve.

4. Stuffed Tench in Ragout

Scald and debone them; then with their flesh and hard-boiled egg yolks make a stuffing which you season and with which you stuff your

---

[xvi] This section-title appears at the head of a listing of the dishes in this Chapter. Immediately before the recipes themselves the rubric which appears is: "How to Prepare the Fish Course." Chapter XVIII, consisting also of fish (*i.e.* lean) preparations, provides only a third as many recipes; there the dishes are expressly for the second course of a lean meal.

A common sequence of steps in the preparation of a fish is seen, simplified, in Recipe 15: cook (seasoned), steep in a (seasoned) sauce, serve (garnished).

[1] Although the source of this milt is not specified here, elsewhere the author directs that the cook use the milt of carp (Recipes XV,6 and 31; XVI,61, 88 and 93). Milt is quite a common secondary ingredient for La Varenne; Recipe XIX,13 is for a dish whose principal ingredient is carp milt.

tench.[4.1] Then set them to simmer in a dish in a little bouillon and white wine, with a few bread crust crumbs,[4.2] mushrooms if you have any, asparagus, milt and truffles. Serve.

5. Fried and Marinated Tench

When the tench have been dressed, split them in half; then set them to marinate in salt, pepper, onion and lemon peel. When they have marinated, take them out, dry them and flour them; alternatively, mix a little flour into two or three eggs and salt; fry them in clarified butter. When done, set them to come to a boil in their marinade. Serve, garnishing them with whatever you have.

6. Stewed Carp[6]

Dress your carp, scale them and cut them up according to their size. Set them to cook in a pot, cauldron or skillet, in white or claret wine, and season them well with salt, cloves, pepper, chopped onion, scallions, capers and a few crusts of bread; cook everything together. When they are done and the sauce is quite thick and reduced, serve them.

7. Stuffed Carp in Ragout

With your carp carefully scaled, gut them and split them along the backbone; remove their skin,[7] and their flesh which you chop up very small and season with parsley, fresh butter, salt, pepper, egg yolks, milk and milt. Then make a ragout of bouillon, verjuice, fresh butter, mushrooms, asparagus and scallions. When the stuffed fish are well cooked, and the sauce quite thickened with crust crumbs and capers, serve.

8. Fried Carp in Ragout

The carp has to be scaled and gutted; then split it and remove its

---

[4.1] La Varenne has forgotten to mention earlier that the tench skin is to be removed in order to be stuffed. See Recipe 7, below.

[4.2] As La Varenne writes in Recipe 52, "to thicken the sauce."

[6] This recipe will constitute a model for this procedure of "stewing" a fish. The defining feature of the procedure is that the fish does not undergo any preliminary, or subsequent, cooking: it is, simply, only boiled. The seasoned bouillon is then reduced to make a serving sauce.

[7] It is this skin that is to be stuffed. *Cf.* Recipes XV,4 and 5, as well as Recipe 4, above.

5. Tanches frittes & marinées.

backbone. Sprinkle it with salt, flour it and fry it in clarified butter.
When it is done, serve it dry,[8] with orange juice on top.

9. Roast Carp in Ragout

Gut it as it comes out of the water;[9.1] cut it open on top, butter
it and set it on the grill. When it has roasted, make a sauce of fresh
butter browned in a pan, parsley and chives, both finely chopped, verjuice,
vinegar and a little bouillon;[9.2] season all that; cook it with capers. If you
like, serve it with Green Sauce as soon as you have set it out.[9.3]

10. Carp in a Half Court-Bouillon

Get your carp straight out of the water, gut it and cut it up according
to its size; then put it with vinegar, very little salt, pepper and chopped
onion, then put with it capers and very fresh butter. Then cook it in a
cauldron with your mixture. As soon as the sauce has thickened, put it
into a dish for fear that your cauldron may give a brass taste.[10] Serve.

11. Carp Hash

Get carp, scale and gut them; remove their skin by cutting it by the
gills and pulling it downwards. When they are skinned, remove their flesh
and chop it up with parsley; then mix in a little bouillon and very fresh
butter; season it well; cook it with a bouquet of herbs. When it is done,
add in some cream or milk, with egg yolks if you like. Serve them well
garnished with asparagus stalks and carp milt.

12. Bream in Ragout

Gut a bream and put a bouquet of herbs inside it. Melt butter, rub
that on its top and put it on the grill. When it has roasted, make a sauce

Achis de carpes.

11.

---

[8] The title of this recipe is a little strange: other than the serving sauce of orange juice,
which is rather bitter, there is no piquant treatment (*en ragoust*) here. Compare the
seasonings for fried carp with those for roast carp in the following recipe.

[9.1] The implantation of carp and eel ponds on noble estates meant that noble kitchens
could always depend upon an immediate source of very fresh fish.

[9.2] This is the *ragoust* in which the cooked fish will be simmered to enhance its flavour.
See the note in Recipe III,21 about this method of preparation known as *en ragoust*.

[9.3] For Green Sauce, see Recipe VII,2.

[10] La Varenne is uneasy that brass vessels may impart an undesirable flavour to foods
cooked in them. For the same reason in Recipes 75, below, and XVIII,1 he likewise
warns his reader not to leave a rayfish or a turbot for too long in a brass fish kettle.

with fresh butter, capers, chopped parsley and chives; simmer it well with vinegar and a little bouillon. With the sauce well thickened, serve.

13. Salmon in Ragout[13]

Roast a salmon stuck with cloves. When it has roasted, put it with a little very fresh butter, wine, salt, pepper and sugar; simmer everything together until the sauce is reduced almost to a syrup. Then serve.

14. Stewed Salmon

Cut a salmon into slices two or three fingers thick. Then put it, stuck with cloves, into a kettle — as if for stewing[14] — with white or red wine, well seasoned with butter, salt and chopped onion. Cook it well with capers, if you have any. With the sauce reduced and thickened, serve, garnished with whatever you like.

15. Salmon Trout

You cook salmon trout and marinate them and serve them the same way as ordinary ones, the directions for which you have below.[15]

16. Burbot in Ragout

Scrape burbots in hot water until they are white, and gut them. Put them into white wine, fresh butter, salt, pepper, onion and capers; simmer, and keep your sauce from turning — that is, from becoming oily. Garnish them with mushrooms and milt, then serve them.

17. Fried Burbot in Ragout

When burbots have been dressed, if they are big score them on top; flour them, then half-cook them by frying them in clarified butter. Put them into a ragout and put in fresh butter, capers, mushroom stock,[17.1]

---

[13] Because of the syrupy consistency of the sauce here, this dish is probably what is called Salmon in a Sweet Sauce in Recipes XVIII,35 and XXVI,69.

[14] *en façon d'estuvée*: the name of the dish is *Saumon à l'estuvée*. The kettle here must have a tight fitting lid. This manner of cooking fish will be common in Chapters XVI and XXVI, although an *estuve* or "stove" will be the usual appliance for the operation.

[15] The reference is to Recipe 87, for *Truites communes*. The present recipe is for *Truites saumonnées*.

[17.1] For this sub-preparation, see Recipe XI,1. La Varenne writes there that mushroom stock is appropriate for ragout treatment, particularly in place of mutton stock on lean days.

parsley, chives, salt and pepper. With the sauce quite reduced and thickened, serve.

Another sort of Burbot that is Stewed

When scalded (some people then skin them), either cut them up or leave them whole. Put them to stew in white wine with a small amount of onion — and if you don't want it to to be too strong, stick it with cloves[17.2] — salt, pepper, butter and a sprig of fine herbs. When they have cooked, and the sauce is very reduced and thickened, serve. You can also put in capers or anchovies.

18. Oysters in a Half Court-Bouillon and Salted

Blanch them in water, then sauté them in a pan in some butter with parsley and chives; season them well. Simmer them in a little white wine. When they are cooked and the sauce is thickened, serve.

Another way

As oysters come out of their shell, put them in a chafing dish[18.1] with fresh butter, nutmeg, scallions stuck with cloves,[18.2] thyme, a little crust crumbs and orange or lemon juice. When they have cooked, serve them.

Another way

Get oysters either dead or alive, clean and blanch them well; then sauté them in a pan with a very finely chopped onion, good fresh butter and capers; and season them well. When they are cooked, serve them. You can fricassee them in some lard, and use the same seasoning.

19. Oysters in Ragout

Get them very fresh and open them — to make sure they are not spoiled,[19] knock on them and knock them together: those that sound

---

[17.2] The reason for the common insertion of cloves into onions is to be noted.

[18.1] The *rechaut* mentioned here is not the dish itself but the apparatus for holding a relatively gentle source source of heat, such as live coals, over which a plate of food is warmed.

[18.2] Presumably the reason for sticking cloves into scallions is the same as for sticking them into onions: cloves are felt to moderate or counter the pungency of these bulbs. See the same in Recipe V,72.

[19] *alterées*: "changed" — that is, no longer with the same flavour as the freshest oysters.

hollow and are spoiled are good only for salting. Then, when they have been taken out of their shells, clean away any sand. Put them in a dish with their water and fricassee them with fresh butter, onion, well chopped parsley, capers and a little crust crumbs. When they are well cooked, serve them.

20. Oyster Fritters[20]

Again get very fresh oysters, blanch them, drain them well and dry them. Make a batter by moistening your flour with verjuice or milk, seasoned with salt, and with one or more eggs depending on the quantity. Put your oysters into that mixture. Get clarified butter and heat it up hot, then put your oysters into it one after the other. When they are done, drain them and sprinkle a little fine salt and fried parsley over them. Then serve.

21. Roast Oysters

Open the oysters, select the best ones and leave them in their shell if they are to be eaten fresh. On the ones that are a little off put a very little fresh butter along with a little sieved bread[21.1] and a little nutmeg; then put them on the grill. When they have cooked, heat the fire shovel red hot and pass it over them until they take on colour,[21.2] and do it in such a way that they don't get too dry. Then serve.

22. Chub in Ragout

When a chub is dressed, roast it on the grill with a bouquet of herbs, well seasoned, inside it. When it has roasted, sauté a chopped onion in fresh butter with crust crumbs, capers and anchovies, the whole seasoned to your taste. Simmer everything together. Serve.

23. Chub in a Court-Bouillon

Having taken the chub out of its bouillon,[23.1] roast it. Make up a

20. Huiſtres en baignets.

---

[20] These *baignets* are, as elsewhere in La Varenne, merely a fried (perhaps deep- fried) battered foodstuff.

[21.1] This *pain passé* may well be "fried bread," as I. D. G. translates.

[21.2] This procedure is common. It is called for usually for the purpose mentioned here and occasionally to finish off the cooking of a dish.

[23.1] In later editions *bouillon* is changed to *court-bouillon*.

Sauce Robert[23.2] and simmer the fish in it.   Serve it garnished with parsley.

24. Stewed Chub

It can be prepared stewed in the same way as a carp.[24] Season it well with capers, chives, parsley and good fresh butter. With the sauce very reduced, serve.

25. Roasted Stuffed Dace[25]

Dress them just as they come out of the water, and coat them with butter and set them on the grill with a little stuffing or with some salt and a small sprig of sage or fine herbs.

To make your stuffing get sorrel, parsley and raw egg yolks, chop and season it all together with a sprig of thyme; then put it into your dace. Make a sauce with fresh butter, salt, vinegar, pepper, chives and parsley, all of that sautéed in a pan. When the sauce is greatly reduced, serve, with a little nutmeg on top.

26. Roast Dace without Stuffing

Roast dace without putting any stuffing in them. Then make a sauce of the same sort [as previously], to which you add capers. Then serve.

27. Stewed Dace

Do them the same as a carp.[27] Thicken the sauce well; garnish your dace in it and serve.

[23.2] In Recipe 80, below, the Sauce Robert seems to consist of butter, verjuice and mustard, with optional capers and chives. See also the version of this standard sauce that is found in Recipe V,56: there it is composed of verjuice, vinegar, a bouquet of sage, onion and drippings from a pork roast!

[24] As in Recipe 6, above.

[25] The dace resembles a small chub, for which three recipes have just preceded. Later printers are baffled by the word *soies* found in this and the next two recipes. They assume that an error had been made and they print *soles*, "sole," even though La Varenne has already given a treatment for this fish in Recipe 1, above. In the singular the fish shows up again as a *la soif* in Recipe XXVI,20; incredibly, later printers render that later occurrence as *le foye*, "liver"!

[27] See Recipe 6, above. The dace are, in fact, of the same family, *Cyprinidæ*, as carp.

25. Soies rosties & farcies.

28. Barbels in Ragout

If the barbels are small, do them stewed; cook them well and serve. That is the most their taste can be heightened.[28]

29. Roast Barbels

If the barbels are moderately large, dress them and roast them on the grill. Serve them with a very tasty sauce.[29]

30. Barbel in a Half Court-Bouillon

Get quite large barbels. Put them into a half court-bouillon with white wine, fresh butter, salt, pepper, chives, parsley and capers. When they are well cooked, and the sauce thickened, serve them.

31. Barbels in a Court-Bouillon

Cook barbels well in their court-bouillon. When they are done, skin them and put them on a dish. Then thicken your sauce and pour it over them. To do the sauce well, get half a pound of fresh butter with a dash of vinegar or a little half court-bouillon; melt it and, while doing so, put in one or two egg yolks as needed, thicken it well and be careful it doesn't turn to oil.

To make it of vinegar alone, get nutmeg, salt, red currants or verjuice; cook all of that in butter. When it is done, take it out of your butter and put it with your sauce. Then serve, because the sauce shouldn't be reheated.

32. Stewed Barbels

Stewed barbels are done the same as carp,[32] whether whole or cut up. [Served] with verjuice mash.

33. Brill in a Casserole

Dress brill and gut them on their side beneath their gill, clean them and set them to drain. When they have drained, put them into a basin or a skillet with butter and chives beneath, ground cloves, salt, pepper, capers, a little white wine or vinegar, and mushrooms. Cook everything together gently so the flesh doesn't fall apart. When they are done, and the sauce

---

[28] *C'est tout le ragoust que l'on leur peut donner*: La Varenne seems to admit that the recipe's name is rather misleading.

[29] *avec sauce de haut goust.* La Varenne offers no suggestions for the composition of this ragout.

[32] The reference to the Stewed Carp of Recipe 6, above.

has been thickened, serve them with their white side down, garnished with your mushrooms.

34. Dab in a Casserole
Dress dab and do them up the same as the brill.

35. Fried Dab
Fry dab and put them into a ragout made with orange juice, fresh butter, a whole scallion and chopped capers.

36. Roast Dab
Roast dab on the grill. Make a sauce of butter, onion, parsley, pepper and vinegar. With all that fricasseed together, put your dab in it to simmer. Make the sauce very thick, and serve.

37. Plaice in a Casserole
Plaice must be dressed on the other side from the brill.[37] Cook them, and for the rest do the same. Serve.

38. Roast Plaice
Roast plaice is done the same as dab.

39. Scoter Duck[39.1] in Ragout
Pluck it carefully and dress it the same way as a duck,[39.2] then lard it with big lardoons of eel or carp. Mount it on a spit and, while it is turning, baste it with butter, vinegar, salt, pepper, chives and lemon peel. When it is half-roasted, put it into a pot with some water and the sauce with which you basted it. When it is well cooked and seasoned, add[39.3] mushrooms with capers and serve.

40. Scoter Duck in a Court-Bouillon
Dress it and lard it the same as before, and cook it in water and season it well. When it is half done, put in a quart of white wine; cook it well. Then serve it with parsley on top.

---

[37] *Habillés les d'autre costé que les barbuës.* Recipe 33 tells the reader to gut the brill from beneath its gill on its side.

[39.1] Note that for La Varenne and his milieu this variety of waterfowl qualifies as a "lean" foodstuff.

[39.2] There is a recipe for *Canards en ragoust* at V,5.

[39.3] *mettés y:* I. D. G., "put to it." These ingredients may be intended as a serving garnish.

41. Roast Scoter Duck in Ragout

Roast the scoter on the spit. When it is well done, put it on the grill. For it make a Sauce Robert[41] or any other sauce you like. Then serve.

42. Scoter Duck Deboned and Stuffed

Stuff a scoter with whatever you have on hand, mixed and chopped up with its flesh; then do it in a ragout. When it has cooked, garnish it with whatever you can, such as mushrooms, truffles, asparagus stalks, quenelles, milt or rissoles or rosettes; season all of it well. Serve.

43. Roast Shad in Ragout

Gut the shad through its gill. Into it put a little salt, fine herbs and an onion; roast it. When it has roasted, make a sauce of fresh butter, chopped chives and parsley, capers and red currants or verjuice mash, everything sautéed in a pan and well seasoned; afterwards, simmer it with your shad in it. Mix its liver into the sauce if it isn't thick enough, or garnish with it. Then serve it.

44. Shad in a Court-Bouillon

Cook the shad in a court-bouillon. When it is half done, take it out and set it on the grill. Then simmer it in a russet sauce.[44] Serve.

45. Stewed Shad

Scald shad well, cut it up and cook it in the manner of a stew.[45] When it is well cooked and the sauce thickened in such a way that it doesn't turn oily, serve.

46. Lamprey in Ragout

Do it up and serve it the same as the Stewed Shad.

---

[41] For this Sauce Robert see either Recipe V,56 or Recipe 80, below.

[44] *avec une sauce rousse*: this is La Varenne's first explicit reference to the sauce that becomes known as a "roux". The verb *roussir*, "to brown," is used when a foodstuff, including butter, is sautéed in a pan. In Recipe XXV,40 flour will likewise be fried until it is a russet colour preparatory to its being used as a thickener. La Varenne uses the *sauce rousse* fairly often in his fish dishes. Later recipes suggest that the browned butter of this sauce can be accompanied by a variety of ingredients, although an onion or scallion and some vinegar seem to be standard: see Recipe 64, below.

[45] *en façon d'estuvée*. The reader may be expected to refer back to Recipe 6, above, for Stewed Carp.

47. Grilled Lamprey in Ragout

When the lamprey is dressed, it must be cut up according to its size. Put it on the grill. When it has roasted, make whatever sauce you like for it, provided it is very tangy. Then serve.

48. Lamprey in a Sweet Sauce

Dress the lamprey and cut it up the same.[48] Make a sauce of vinegar, sugar, two or three cloves, little butter and little salt; simmer it. Serve.

Another way

Cut the lamprey up into small pieces and set them to cook in some wine with some sugar. Season that very little because of the sugar; add in little butter and few capers. Then serve.

49. Anguille roſtie à la ſauce verte.

49. Roast Eel in Green Sauce

Cut an eel lengthwise and roast it on the grill. Then get sorrel or chard and extract their juice. Sauté a very small onion[49] and season that with salt, pepper, a dash of vinegar, chopped capers and orange peel; simmer your eel in that sauce. When you are ready to serve, with your sauce well thickened, pour your juice over the top. Then serve.

50. Stewed Eel

Cut the eel into pieces and do them up in the manner of a stew with parsley, capers, white wine and fresh butter, all of it seasoned well. Then serve.

51. Eel Saveloy[51]

Dress your eel and skin it: to do that you take it and cut it close to its head and then, with a wad of straw so it doesn't slip, you pull the end of the skin downwards. With the eel skinned, slit it in half and take out its backbone. Pound the eel well and slice it in two; lay out your two slices and put salt, pepper, butter and parsley on them; roll them up, tie them tightly and put them in a pot in white wine, well seasoned, and cook

---

[48] There is no explicit direction here on how the lamprey is to be cooked.

[49] *Passés un oygnon bien menu*: La Varenne uses the word *menu* to describe the small size of things (for instance, small barbels in Recipe 28), but also for finely chopped particles (for instance *achez la bien menue* in Recipe 60). It is conceivable that in this case he intended that a finely chopped onion be sautéed.

[51] *Anguille en servelast*, that is, eel prepared in the form of saveloy.

them well. When they are well done, take them out; cut them in slices and garnish a dish with them. Then serve them.

52. Eel in Ragout

Cut up the eel into pieces and put them into a skillet with white wine, butter, chopped chives and parsley, capers, salt, pepper and a few crust crumbs to thicken the sauce. When they are well cooked, serve them. Also, if you like, glaze them with egg yolks thinned with verjus.[52.1]

Another way

You can fry an eel in clarified butter or oil. When it has been dressed, cut its sides and remove the bone. Marinate the flesh a little. If you want to use the eel as a garnish,[52.2] fry it as soon as you like; if it is for serving hot, fry it only when you will be needing it — which you do after having dried it well, cut it very thin and floured it or dredged it in a fine batter. Serve it with orange or lemon juice.

Another way

Roast the eel like a lamprey. Season it strongly; [serve it] with whatever garnishing you like.

53. Sea Eel

Do up a sea eel the same as in the first version of the common Eel in Ragout, above.

54. Stewed Sea Eel

When it is dressed, slice a sea eel crosswise and season it in the same way as the other stewed dishes.[54]

55. Fried Sea Eel in Ragout

This is done as with the second version of the common Eel in Ragout.[55] Then serve.

[52.1] This mixture of egg yolks and verjuice is called a white sauce elsewhere, particularly in Chapter XIV. In Recipe 90, below, it is called a thickener.

[52.2] As a garnishing for another prepared dish, an eel done this way can be used cold.

[54] For this seasoning, see in particular the recipe for Stewed Carp in Recipe 6, above.

[55] Recipe 52, above.

Escoffier, *Ho-mard à la hol-landaise*, §941

56. Lobster in a Court-Bouillon

Cook lobster in a court-bouillon that is well seasoned with whatever it needs. When it is done, split it in half and serve it with vinegar and parsley.

Escoffier, *Ho-mard à la New-burg*, §949

57. Lobster in a White Sauce

When the lobster is cooked, debone it and cut up its flesh into pieces which you fricassee in some butter with chopped parsley and a dash of verjuice. When that has been done, get three or four egg yolks along with a little nutmeg, and put that into the pan. Serve immediately, garnishing with the feet of your lobster.

58. Langouste au court bouillon.

58. Crawfish in a Court-Bouillon

Cook it, season it and fricassee it the same as for the Lobster.[58] Garnish it with the feet of your crawfish. Then serve.

59. Crawfish in a White Sauce[59.1]

This is also done the same way as the lobster.[59.2] Serve it dry, [garnished] with parsley.

60. Stuffed Pike

Split the pike along its back and remove its skin from its head right to its tail; remove the flesh and the small bones, but leave the backbone to stiffen the fish when it is stuffed. For that stuffing get equal quantities of pike flesh and the flesh of either carp or eel, chop it up very finely along with parsley, raw egg yolks, salt, pepper, fine herbs, butter and milk all mixed together, and mushrooms. Stuff your pike and sew it up again, then set it to cook in a dripping pan. Make up your sauce with a fish bouillon or pea purée, a dash of verjuice and a little vinegar, which you sauté with parsley, capers and mushrooms; season. Cook it well. When it is well cooked, serve, and garnish with whatever you like.

---

[58] Recipe 56.

[59.1] In the second edition the printer blundered in setting *Langue*, "tongue," for *Lan-gouste*, "crawfish." Both the title and the text of this recipe were simply dropped by later printers, even though the same numbering was kept.

[59.2] Recipe 57, above.

61. [Stuffed] Pike Roasted on a Spit

Do up the pike in the same way, and mount it on a spit; to hold it on, wrap it around with buttered paper. When it is cooked, take it down off the spit and simmer it in the same sauce as for the other pike, and garnish it with mushrooms, carp milt, pistachios, truffles and broken asparagus stalks; and be careful that the sauce is not too rich. Then serve it with pomegranate seeds or lemon peel.

62. Roast Fresh Mackerel

Roast them with some fennel.[62] When they are done, open them and remove the bone. Then make up a good sauce with butter, parsley and red currants, all of it well seasoned; simmer your mackerels in it briefly. Then serve.

Escoffier, *Filets de maquereau au persil*, §1012

63. Roast Fresh Herrings

Clean the herrings out through their gill and roast them buttered on a grill. When they have roasted, make up a sauce with some fresh butter, a dash of vinegar, salt, pepper and nutmeg; mix some mustard into it and serve.

64. Herrings in a Russet Sauce[64]

When your herrings have been roasted, make a russet sauce by browning your butter in a pan with some chopped chopped parsley and scallions which you put into your butter along with a dash of vinegar. If you like, add in capers. Serve.

65. Royan Sardines[65.1]

After you have scaled the sardines, do them up in the same way as the roast herrings. Serve them with white sauce or russet sauce, with mustard.[65.2]

---

[62] Diderot's *Encyclopédie* (VI, 491 b) attests to the longevity of La Varenne's practice of wrapping a roasting fish in fennel leaves: "Quelques Apicius de nos jours ordonnent d'envelopper le poisson dans les feuilles de fenouil, pour le rendre plus ferme & plus savoureux, soit qu'on veuille l'apprêter frais, ou le garder dans de la saumure."

[64] *à la sauce rousse*: I.D.G. translates this as "with brown sauce." See above in Recipe 44.

[65.1] These *Sardines de Royant*, named after a fishing town on the Atlantic coast at the mouth of the Gironde River, become *Sardines de Rouen* in later editions. Rouen is on the Seine River some 80 km from salt water.

[65.2] The mustard can accompany either the *sauce blanche* or the *sauce rousse*.

Cf. Escoffier,
*Rougets au sa
fran à l'orien-
tale*, §379

66. Red Mullet in Ragout

After dressing a mullet well, put it into a dish; season it well with butter, salt, pepper, a bouquet of herbs, mushrooms, chopped parsley, verjuice and bouillon; cook it between two dishes. When it is done, serve it with the sauce thickened.[66] For its garnishing use anything you happen to have; otherwise just do without.

You can also do it up like the gurnard that follows just below.

67. Gurnard in Ragout

Dress a gurnard and cut it, then butter it well on top and set it to roast on the grill. When it is done, make a russet sauce in which to simmer it in order to make it absorb seasoning[67] and the flavour of whatever you have been able to put in. Serve.

Escoffier, *Ca-
billaud grillé*,
§991

68. Fresh Roast Cod in Ragout

When it has been dressed, it has to be buttered and roasted on the grill, seasoned with salt and cloves stuck into it.[68.1] While it is roasting, baste it with butter. When it is done, make up a sauce of very fresh butter; when that has half browned, throw chopped parsley into it and, if you like, onion or scallions — which you can take out for hard-to-please individuals.[68.2] Mix in a little bouillon, a dash of vinegar and chopped capers; simmer your cod in its sauce. When it is ready to serve, add in some mustard if you like. Then serve.

69. Cod in Half Court-Bouillon

Cook a cod in some white wine, salt, pepper and a bouquet of herbs. When it is done, set it to drain. Make a sauce of butter, a dash of the court-bouillon, a little nutmeg and salt; set it on the fire and stir it well. While stirring it, mix in two egg yolks. Pour that over your cod. Then serve.

69. Morüe au demy court bouillon.

---

[66] The text has an indefinite article: *avec une sauce liée.*

[67] If the word *sel* is meant literally, the source of this "salt" is not mentioned. If its sense is figurative, it would be broader: "seasoning." The same use of *sel* is seen in Recipe 75.

[68.1] *assaisonnée de sel & clou picqué*: the construction is not usual, but the sense is clear.

[68.2] *pour les fantasques*; perhaps, "those with a strange taste" or "fussy people". Furetière glosses the word *fantasque* as "capricieux, bouru ("churlish"), qui a des manieres ou des humeurs extraordinaires."

70. Fresh Cod in Ragout

When the cod has been scaled, gut it, cutting it from above. Then put it into a dripping pan or a flat basin with good butter, salt, pepper and ground cloves, along with scallions and some bouillon or pea purée on top. Boil everything putting in some parsley, a dash of vinegar and a small amount of crust crumbs on top. Cook it in front of the fire[70] or even better in an oven. When it is done, serve it.

Escoffier, *Cabillaud à la flamande*, §994

71. Newfoundland Cod[71.1]

Get that cod after it has been desalted;[71.2] scrape it and cook it in a cauldron with cool water; bring it to a boil and remove the scum. When the pot has been skimmed, take it off the fire and cover it with some sort of folded cloth. When you are ready to serve, set the cod to drain. Make a sauce of butter alone — watch that it doesn't turn — pour it over your cod, and serve it with parsley on top and around it.

72. Fish Cake[72.1]

Get flesh of carp, eel and tench, chop it all up together and season that with a little very fresh butter, capers and fine herbs. Bundle it all in a linen cloth and tie it up, then cook it in white wine as a court-bouillon. When it is done, let it drain, then untie it and slice it. Serve the slices on a plate like ham.[72.2]

73. Fish Ham[73.1]

Fish Ham is made the same way as the Fish Cake, except that you wrap your mixture in carp skin, with a wrapping of buttered paper over

---

[70] That is, with a low or indirect heat.

[71.1] Perhaps not recognizing the geographical reference, I. D. G. renders this *Morue de terre neufve* as, literally, "Green fish"!

[71.2] *Prenez-la dessalée.* Naturally enough, that fish was available in French markets only in a dried or salted-and-dried state. To remove the preserving salt from a foodstuff, a cook generally soaked it in water: see Recipes XVII,13 or XXII,13, for instance, and most recipes in Chapter XXIII.

[72.1] The history of the preparation that La Varenne calls a *soupresse* involved placing a forcemeat "under pressure" and so causing all the ingredients to meld intimately together. The procedure is common in Scappi's cookery in the preceding century.

[72.2] See Recipes VIII,20 and 21. There the ham is garnished with flowers, and the slices are very thin. See also the following recipe.

[73.1] This recipe begins in much the same way as Recipe XIX,24.

that and a linen cloth over that again. Cook it the same way. Serve it cold just the same as a ham.[73.2]

74. Fish Mussels

Clean the mussels and bring them to a boil with a bouquet of herbs. As soon as they open, take them out of their shell. Then fricassee them in fresh butter with well chopped parsley and chopped chives, seasoned with pepper and nutmeg. Then dilute egg yolks with a little verjuice and mix them together. Serve them, garnished with their shells.

75. Fried Rayfish[75.1] in Ragout

Rayfish has to be dressed, well washed and the slime on it removed; then gut it and remove the liver very neatly and the gall[75.2] skillfully. If your rayfish is big, remove its two wings and leave its body. Cook them[75.3] in white wine or verjuice with salt, pepper, onion and fine herbs. When they are done, let them soak up the seasoning a little,[75.4] being careful about the brass taste;[75.5] then take it out and remove its skin. Make up a russet sauce with some butter and finely minced parsley and chives, sautéed in browned butter, adding in a dash of vinegar and a bit of liver; simmer the fish in that. Then serve, with red currants or verjuice mash in season, and garnished on top with the rest of the liver which you put into the kettle when your rayfish is half-cooked. Cut it into slices.

76. Smelt in Ragout

String smelt through the eye row by row onto a small rod; flour and fry them. When they are well done, put a little fine salt on them and, pulling out the rod, place them on the dish. Then serve them with an orange or a lemon.

76. Esperlans en ragoust.

[73.2] No mention is made of slicing this lump of cooked fish paste. With imagination its appearance is that of a small, whole ham.

[75.1] The ray is otherwise known as skate.

[75.2] This latter is called mere *l'amer*, "the bitter matter". The liver will be put to several uses subsequently.

[75.3] That is, the body and wings. Later printers are confused and write, in the singular, *Faites-le cuire.*

[75.4] *laissez la un peu prendre sel.* As in Recipe 67, La Varenne can still use the word *sel* in the slightly archaic sense of "piquancy."

[75.5] La Varenne has mentioned the need for this precaution in Recipe 10, above.

77. Fricasseed Cod Tripe[77]

Cook cod tripe. When they are done, fricassee them in some butter with chopped onion or chives, parsley, salt, pepper and, towards the end, vinegar and a little nutmeg. You can glaze them with egg yolks and verjuice. Serve.

78. Fricasseed Cuttlefish

Boil cuttlefish. When they have cooked, cut them up into pieces and fricassee them like cod tripe. Serve.

79. Fried Hake

When hake has been desalted, cut it up and cook it. When done, put it to drain. Fricassee it in butter with onion, pepper and vinegar.

80. Hake in Sauce Robert

You can put hake with butter, a dash of verjuice and mustard, [and fricassee it]. You can also mix in some capers and some chives.[80.1]

Another way

Hake can also be served with oil, vinegar and onion.[80.2]

81. Salmon Jowl in a Russet Sauce[81]

Desalt a salmon jowl well, scale it and put it to boil in water; let it

---

[77] Probably, as the *Delices de la campagne* states (p. 338), the qualification "cod" is incorrect. Fish tripe is not unknown as a foodstuff in late medieval cookery. In the French domain, see Chiquart *Du fait de cuisine* (or *On Cookery*), eds. cit., Recipes 24, 36, 38 and 78: *Un gravé de trippes de poissons*; in English, the second book published by Austin (Oxford, Harleian MS 4016, ed. Thomas Austin, *Two Fifteenth-Century Cookery-Books*, Early English Text Society, Original Series, 91, London: Oxford University Press, 1888; repr. 1964): Recipe 179 for *Tripe de Turbot* [and of *haddok or codlynge*]; and in Italian by Martino (Maestro Martino, *Libre de arte coquinaria*, ed. Emilio Faccioli, *Arte della cuccina*, 2 vols., Milan: Il Polifilo, 1966; II, pp. 117- 204): Recipe 61, *Menestra de trippe de trute*. This last recipe uses pepper, parsley, mint and sage; it turns up again in Platina, *De honesta voluptate*, ed. cit., Recipe VII,36, *Cibarium ex intestinis trutæ*, and is so perpetuated into more modern Italian cooking.

[80.1] This seems to be a more "modern" idea of Sauce Robert than the one described in Recipe V,56; see the variant recipe that follows below.

[80.2] These ingredients correspond more closely to the Sauce Robert for a roast loin of pork in V,56; there it is constituted of verjuice, vinegar, a bouquet of sage, onion and pork drippings.

[81] This *Hure de saumon*, properly a salmon "head", corresponds among lean dishes to the *Hure de sanglier* (of Recipe IX,93) — as a dish if not in its actual preparation.

cook a length of time that will depend on its size; then let it sit. When you are ready to use it, make up a russet sauce with some butter, onion, pepper and vinegar; put it over the top. Serve it.

Another way

When the salmon jowl is cooked, set it to drain and cool. Serve it up with some chopped onion, olive oil and vinegar.

82. Jowl, or Sandwich, of Salmon in a Salad[82]

When the jowl is cooked, put it with oil and vinegar, along with garden cress or whatever other salad greens you like, and capers if you have any. Then serve.

83. Marinated Tuna

Dress the tuna and cut them into slices or rounds three fingers thick. Stick them with cloves and put them into a pot with salt, pepper, vinegar and a few bay leaves; cover it well. When you wish to use them, desalt[83] your slices, then cook them in some wine. Serve them dry or with a russet sauce seasoned with whatever you care to put into it.

84. Salted Mackerel

Split mackerel along their belly and salt them. To use them, they have to be desalted and cooked in water. When done, they are served with some parsley, vinegar and pepper; you can also add in some oil if you wish.

Another way

When similarly cooked, make a sauce for the mackerel of butter, onion, vinegar, pepper and mustard; simmer [them in that]. Serve.

It is interesting to note that La Varenne assumes that the salmon will come to the kitchen in salted form: the salmon is not caught locally. In later versions *à la sauce rousse* in the title inexplicably becomes *à la sauce douce*.

[82] *Hure, ou entre-deux de saumon à la sallade.* The term *entre-deux* is applied to any interleaved arrangement. Furetière glosses the word as "Partie qui est au milieu de deux choses, avec lesquelles elle a relation ou contiguité"; he provides an illustration drawn from gastronomy contemporary with La Varenne, *un entredeux de moruë* ("cod"). In La Varenne's recipe the salmon jowl is apparently to be sandwiched quite simply between clumps of salad greens. I. D. G. translates this title as "Joale or chine peece of salmon into salat." With no more understanding of the term, later printers put *Hure entre deux Saumons en salade.*

[83] *faites dessaller:* that is, drain the marinating liquid from the slices of tuna, perhaps steeping them in water.

85. Salted Herrings

Herrings are salted as they come out of the sea; they are gutted through the gill, then straight away packed in casks.[85] When you want to use them, desalt them, drain and dry them; after that you roast them. Serve them with mustard or with peas.

Another way

You can serve herrings stewed, cutting them up into pieces and cooking them with some onion and butter.

86. Smoked Herrings[86]

Being half salted, string them and put them to smoke in the chimney. When you need them, open them up and soak them in some milk. To serve them, take them out and roast them very briefly on the grill; then serve them with some mustard if you like.

87. Common Trout[87.1]

Clean trout out through their gills and marinate them. Then make slits in them according to their size and cook them gently in a court-bouillon, seasoned with whatever is appropriate and for which you'll find directions in many places dealing with fish courses. Be careful, though, that they don't fall apart. When they are cooked, serve them whole, garnished with parsley, in a pleated napkin.[87.2]

88. Burbot Pie[88]

With your burbots dressed and blanched, cut them up and put them into a shell of fine or puff pastry, together with some sort of garnishing

86. Harans sorets.

Escoffier,
Truites au bleu,
§817

---

[85] The gutted herrings are salted by being packed in casks of salt, that is.

[86] *Harans sorets*: "Kippers" or properly, as I. D. G. translates, "Red Herrings". The words *saur, sor* and *soret* (*cf.* also *surmullet* for the red mullet) describe the russet or reddish-yellow colour of a salted and smoked, or kippered, herring. The verb *saurer* still exists in modern French: "to cure, kipper (a herring)." The word kipper is cognate with the word copper, again describing the colour of the fish after that treatment.

[87.1] That is, "common" as distinct from the "salmon" variety that have been treated in Recipe 15, above.

[87.2] *& une serviete ployée.* This manner of presenting fish within a folded serviette was common in La Varenne's day and is referred to in Recipe XVIII,6.

[88] This Chapter concludes with a series of fish pies. Fish pies are dealt with in *The French Pastry Chef* (VII,20), but only those that are to be served cold.

such as carp milt, broken asparagus stalks, mushrooms and egg yolks;
season everything. Then serve.

89. Eel Pie

Slice an eel in rounds and put it into your pastry shell. Season it well
with egg yolks, parsley, mushrooms, asparagus, milt, verjuice mash or red
currants in season, sparing neither butter nor salt nor pepper. Cover your
pie and gild it.[89.1] To strengthen your pie, get small bands of paper, butter
them and put them round about, tying them gently with a cord.[89.2] When
the pie is baked, dilute three or four egg yolks with a dash of verjuice, and
a little nutmeg. When you are ready to serve, put your thickener in and
mix it around well. Then open the pie and serve it garnished all around
and the crust cut into four.[89.3]

90. Gurnard Pie

Your gurnard, or several if you have them, must be dressed and cut
from above. Make a shell of fine dough any way you like; make up your
pie and, when it is formed, put your fish into it garnished with whatever you have on hand — such as mushrooms, capers, chopped parsley,
hard-boiled egg yolks, artichoke hearts and broken asparagus stalks — everything well seasoned with butter, salt, pepper and nutmeg. Then cover
it over and gild it. If the pie is tall, it should be banded around with
buttered paper. Bake it. Do not forget to give it an air-hole as soon as a
crust has formed,[90] for it would make its own hole by itself, and possibly
down below, and through that its sauce would be lost that you couldn't
put back in again. When it is baked, make a thickener of raw egg yolks
and a dash of verjuice, and put it into the top of your pie by means of
a funnel, and mix it around stirring thoroughly. Serve this pie hot, open,
and garnished all around with the upper crust cut however you like.

[89.1] Egg yolks and verjuice are normally used to effect this glazing.

[89.2] This procedure is customary, and prescribed in a number of La Varenne's pie recipes.

[89.3] This manner of presentation is fairly common: the upper crust is lifted off, cut into
quarters, and these quarters are set out against the perimeter of the pie.

[90] As soon, that is, as the outer surface of the pastry — which is normally quite thick
— has become relatively hard.

91. Little Fish Pies

Debone a carp and an eel, chop up their flesh with parsley, a small sprig of thyme and some butter. When these are well chopped and seasoned with nutmeg, make a fine dough and build your shells up as high as you like. Fill, cover and glaze them. On tall ones you can put a cap.[91] When they are baked, serve them.

92. Plaice Pie

When the plaice have been dressed, you should build up your pastry shell the size of your plaice, and put them into it cut only on top[92] and garnished with mushrooms, asparagus, artichokes, capers and hard-boiled egg yolks, everything well seasoned with very fresh butter, salt, pepper, chopped parsley and a slice of lemon or orange. Cover the pie over and bake it. When it is done, mix in egg yolks thinned with a little vinegar. Then serve it.

93. Milt Tourte

Blanch the carp milt and drain it. Then make up your pastry shell and garnish it with your milt, mushrooms, truffles, capers, hard-boiled egg yolks, broken asparagus stalks, artichoke hearts, salt, pepper, parsley and fresh butter. Cover it over and bake it in an oven or in a tourtière, gilded with eggs if it is for a meat day. When a crust has formed, make an air-hole in it. When the pie has baked, take off its upper crust neatly, cut it into four and set out the quarters all around. Serve.

93. Tourte de laittances.

---

[91] La Varenne defines this *chapiteau* as a *petite couronne de paste faite en façon d'un entonnoir, si le pasté est dressé*: "a little funnel-shaped crown of pastry, [added on top] if the pie is tall."

[92] That is, cut only to gut and debone them, and not reduced to smaller pieces.

Chapter XVII

Egg Dishes Served those Days as Entrées

1. Stuffed Eggs

Get sorrel, alone, if you like, or along with other herbs; wash them and shake them, then chop them very finely and put them between two dishes with some fresh butter[1.1] or else sauté them in a pan. When that is done, set them to simmer[1.2] and season them. When your sauce is cooked, get hard-boiled eggs, cut them in half crosswise or lengthwise, remove the yolks and chop them up with your herbs. When everything is mixed together, simmer it on the fire adding in a little nutmeg. Then serve it, garnished with your egg whites which you can brown in a pan in some browned butter.

Escoffier, *Œufs brouillés grand-mère*, §468

2. Eggs with Bread

Get some bread, crumble it and put it through a colander if you like. Melt some butter and, when melted, put it with your bread, along with some sugar. Then choose whatever number you need of very fresh eggs and beat them with your bread, sugar, butter, salt and a little milk. To cook them, melt a bit of butter, heat it very hot, put your mixture into it and cook it. To give your eggs colour, heat a fire shovel red hot and pass it over the top.[2] Serve your eggs sugared. They can be done in a dish or in a tourtière.

3. Mirror Eggs[3]

Choose very fresh eggs. Melt a bit of butter that is likewise very fresh, and put your eggs into it with a little salt. When they are cooked,

---

[1.1] This method of cooking is common: see also Recipe 6, below.

[1.2] No mention is made of any liquid for this simmering in addition to the butter and any remaining moisture from the herbs themselves.

[2] A standard procedure, used to colour various foods: see Recipe XVI,21, for example, as well several other recipes in this present Chapter. The fire shovel is always heated red hot.

[3] *Oeufs au miroir*. The name of this preparation evokes the image of a round (yellow) face in a (shiny, white) mirror. The imaginative reader might further see the nutmeg garnish arranged as the face's features. *Cf.* Recipe 16, below.

sprinkle a little nutmeg on them. Be careful that the yolks are neither broken nor overcooked. Then serve.

4. Eggs in Brown Butter

Break your very fresh eggs into a dish — and be careful the yolks don't break; put in some salt. Brown some butter in a pan and cook the eggs. When they are done,[4] pour a dash of vinegar into the pan, pass it over the fire, and pour it over your eggs. Serve.

Escoffier, *Œufs au beurre noir,* §397

5. Eggs in Milk

Break your eggs, salt them, and sugar them if you like; beat them well and put in your milk. To cook them, melt a little fresh butter in a dish and, when melted, put your egg mixture into it. Cook it, and give it colour with the fire shovel. When they are cooked, serve them, sprinkled with sugar.

6. Sorrel Eggs

Choose very young sorrel that is well washed and drained, put it [to cook] between two dishes with some butter, salt and pepper. When they are well cooked down,[6] mix in an egg yolk. Garnish that with quartered [hard-boiled] eggs, or however you like. Serve.

To keep your eggs always fresh, put them into cool water.

7. Sliced Fricasseed Eggs

Hard-boil eggs. Shell them, slice them, then fricassee them in good butter with chopped parsley and chives, pepper, red currant [mash] or verjuice mash. When they are well done and seasoned, put them in a dish with a dash of vinegar heated in a pan. If the sauce is too reduced, add in a drop of bouillon, then serve with nutmeg. If you like, mix in capers, mushrooms, broken asparagus stalks — fricasseeing these as well as the mushrooms beforehand because, otherwise, the other cooking would not be enough.[7]

7. Oeufs fricaßez en tranches.

---

[4] La Varenne does not say explicitly whether the eggs are then to be removed from the pan. In Recipe 7 the vinegar is heated *with* the eggs.

[6] *bien consommée*: the leaves are "reduced" or stewed.

[7] That is, merely frying these additional ingredients with the egg slices. La Varenne's words are stronger: ... *car la cuisson n'en vaudroit rien.*

8. Poached Eggs[8]

Choose the freshest eggs you can. Boil some water and, when it is boiling, break your eggs into it; let them cook a little, knocking the skillet handle to keep them from sticking to the bottom and burning. Then take them out gently and set them to drain. To serve them, make a russet sauce; or else make a green sauce by drawing the juice from a handful of sorrel; then melt a little butter, with salt, nutmeg and an egg yolk, everything well seasoned and mixed together; after that you put in your [sorrel] juice and stir. Serve immediately.

9. Creamed Eggs[9.1]

Break a suitable number of eggs; remove half of their yolks and beat them well with some sugar and a little salt; mix in your cream. Then cook everything[9.2] in a skillet. When it is well done, serve it on a plate, sprinkled with sugar. If you want to give it colour, you can do so with the fire shovel. If you would like some sort of flavour, you can add some in.[9.3]

10. Omelette de cresme.

10. Cream Omelet

Break some eggs, remove half of their whites; season them[10] with salt and cream, then beat everything well together. Heat a little more butter than ordinarily. When the omelet has cooked, serve it in squares or triangles or just as it is; then sprinkle it well with sugar if you like.

11. Parsley Omelet

Escoffier, *Omelette à la lyonnaise*, §507

Break your eggs and season them with salt, finely chopped parsley, and chives if you like; beat them well with butter and make your omelet. When it is done, you can roll it up if you like and cut it in rounds; garnish a plate with them, sprinkled with sugar. Then serve them as quickly as you can.

---

[8] La Varenne's title is explicit: *Oeufs pochez à l'eau.*

[9.1] See also Recipe XIX,8.

[9.2] That is, the egg whites and the remaining half of the yolks, still whole, will be cooked in the cream-and-yolk mixture.

[9.3] *vous y en pouvés mettre.* La Varenne leaves the option completely open. Later printers put *vous y pouvés mettre un peu de musc:* "you can put in a little musk."

[10] That is, seemingly, the remainder of the whites along with all of the yolks.

12. Eggs with Verjuice Mash

After breaking your eggs, season them with salt, beat them well and remove their chalazas. Draw out some hot coals, on which you stir the eggs [in a pan], adding in butter and beaten verjuice mash sautéed in a pan When they are cooked, serve, but take care they are not too thick.[12]

13. Eggs with Anchovies

Clean your anchovies well and desalt them, changing the water or wine often; remove their backbone and set them to disintegrate[13] with some very fresh butter in a dish. When they have disintegrated, break in a number of eggs that depends on the amount of sauce you have. When all that is cooked and scrambled, serve it with a little nutmeg.

14. Eggs with Cheese

Get butter and cheese and melt them together — which you can do easily by cutting up your cheese very small. When they have melted, break as many eggs as you think can cook in what is melted; when they have been beaten well, put them on the fire; as they cook, stir them around. When they have cooked, without being too thick,[14] you serve them with a little nutmeg.

15. Scrambled Eggs

Melt some butter with some eggs in a dish; season them with salt and nutmeg. When they are on the fire, stir them with a spoon until they are cooked. Serve.

16. Eggs with a Cream Mirror[16]

Make a layer of butter in your dish and break your eggs on it. When they are broken, season them with salt, then put in some cream until the eggs are covered — or else some milk, provided it is good. Cook them. Give them colour with a red-hot shovel. Then serve.

---

[12] *trop liez*: "too thick" in the sense of "set," "hardened," "overcooked."

[13] The text reads "to melt" (*fondre*). Butter is heated, melts and cooks the anchovies as they, in turn, "melt".

[14] That is, as in Recipe 12, "too hard, overcooked."

[16] *Oeufs au miroir de cresme*. I. D. G. offers a picturesque translation: "Egs in the moon shine with creame."

17. Oeufs faits dans des verres.

17. Eggs Made in Glasses

Make up a mixture similar to the Eggs with Bread,[17.1] add in some cream that is quite fresh[17.2] and, in addition, sugar and breadcrumbs. Then get fern glasses and set them on a plate close to the fire with a very little butter in them. When the butter has melted, put your mixture, too, into these glasses to cook while they are in front of the fire. While it is cooking, turn the glasses. When it is done, tip it out onto another plate — it will come out of the glasses pointing upwards. Serve the eggs like that, garnished with cinnamon sticks and candied lemon peel.

18. Stuffed Omelet

Break your eggs, putting in more yolks than whites; add in some left-over stuffing[18] if you have any, or make up some specially with all sorts of herbs depending on your taste; cook that stuffing before adding it into your eggs. Season everything with salt; and if you like sugar, beat it well. Cook that with some butter or lard. Then serve your omelet sprinkled with sugar if you like, folding it into a square or triangle, or rolling it up to slice it.

Escoffier, *Œufs*
à la neige, §2735

19. Snowy Eggs[19]

Break some eggs, separating the whites and yolks and putting the yolks in a dish on some butter; season them with salt. Set the dish on hot coals. Beat and whip the whites well; a little before serving, pour them over the yolks along with a drop of rosewater. Pass the fire shovel over top; then sprinkle with sugar and serve.

Another way

You can set the yolks into the middle of the snow that is made from your whipped whites, then cook them in front of the fire with a dish behind.

[17.1] Recipe 2, above. La Varenne calls the dish *Œufs de pain* here and *Œufs au pain* back at Recipe 2.

[17.2] The phrase in the text is "not at all sour" *qui ne soit point aigre* — that is, cream that has not begun to turn.

[18] *quelque reste de farce*: any appropriate additional ingredient. Parsley, chives, pepper, capers, mushrooms and broken asparagus stalks have entered into previous egg dishes in this Chapter.

[19] Or, "Eggs in Snow."

Chapter XVIII
Second Course for Lean Meals[xviii]

1. Turbot in a Casserole[1.1]

Dress a turbot, gutting it either through the underbelly by means of a very neat slit you make there, or else through the gill. Put it to steep in white wine in a pan seasoning it well with salt, pepper, cloves and fine herbs such as rosemary, thyme and onion; let it cook slowly so it doesn't disintegrate. When it has cooked, let it sit very briefly so that it doesn't take on the taste of the brass.[1.2] Serve it garnished with blossoms[1.3] and parsley.

You can cut the turbot up before going on to cook it the same way.

2. Brill in a Court-Bouillon

Brill is prepared in the same way as the turbot, except that the court-bouillon shouldn't be so strong-tasting because brill takes seasoning more readily, and all the more so because it is softer. When it is cooked, serve it garnished with parsley on top.

3. Weever Roasted on the Grill

Weevers are dangerous because of certain stingers they have near their

---

[xviii] The *Second de Poisson* is made up of seafood dishes any of which could constitute the second course in a lean meal. While La Varenne has already presented a number of the recipes in this Chapter previously, particularly in Chapter XVI among the Entrées for Lean Days, some are unique to it: see, for example, Recipes 6 and 7. In principle this Second Course in a meal should be the "roast course", as clearly it is in Chapter VI. Here, however, the main ingredient is either roasted, grilled or boiled.

The Table at the head of the Chapter lists 57 dishes; the actual recipes, though, end with the thirtieth. At that point La Varenne inserts a note to the effect that recipes for the remainder of the dishes appropriate for this particular course can easily be read elsewhere.

[1.1] In Recipe 28, below, a *castrolle* is defined as "a vessel shaped like a large tourtière, like a sort of dripping pan." This pan gave its name to a method of preparation, particularly of fish. In the present case, the cooking vessel will be referred to merely as a pan, *une poële*.

[1.2] See this same concern about a possible contamination from a brass pot expressed in Recipe XVI,10.

[1.3] The *fleurs* that are intended here are not specified.

head;[3] that is why when you dress them you must remember to scrape them, cutting off their three stingers as well as their head near their gills, by which, too, you gut them. When they have been dressed like that, slit them on top, melt some butter and pour it into the slits along with salt and cloves; then put them on the grill. When they have roasted, make a russet sauce with fresh butter, salt, pepper, chopped parsley, red currants or verjuice mash, and a dash of vinegar; simmer them in your sauce. Serve.

4. Fried Sole

When sole have been dressed, dry them. If they are big, split them along their back, flour them and fry them in olive oil or clarified butter. When they have fried, sprinkle them with salt on top. Serve them with orange.

Cf. Escoffier, *Cuisson des poissons à l'eau salée,* §776

5. Salmon in a Court-Bouillon

Salmon has to be gutted through its gill. Make slits along its back and put it into your well-seasoned court-bouillon. When it is cooked, serve it.

6. Sturgeon in a Court-Bouillon

Sturgeon can be served roasted on the grill, but in the second course it must be put into court-bouillon and served the same as the salmon — except that, when it is cooked, you get two or three pleated napkins[6] and place them on top sprinkled with parsley and serve it like that. Then serve.

7. Gurnard in a Casserole

Although it is normally served in a court-bouillon, nevertheless in the second course it can be served in a casserole; for that, it must be put in a

---

[3] The weever fish, of the family of *Trachinidæ*, is known also as a sting-fish. The base of the spiny rays in their first dorsal fin contains venom glands; the same glands are found also at the base of a strong spine on their gill cover. Nicolas de Bonnefons writes: "*On doit bien prendre garde avant que de les vuider par l'oreille, de couper les Arestes qui sont aux coings des Oreilles, & deux ou trois sur le dos; desquelles la picqueure est si veneneuse, qu'elle fait venir la grangrene* [sic] *si l'on n'y remedie promptement, par les remedes ordinaires que la Medecine enseigne, ou simplement en faisant un cataplasme avec du Foye de Vive, que l'on mettra sur la picqueure*" (*Les delices de la campagne,* 322).

[6] It is customary to serve fish in a folded or pleated napkin. See, for example, Recipe XVI,87. Despite the text, the parsley goes on the fish and not on the napkin: see Recipes 12 and 16.

skillet, seasoned as necessary and garnished with mushrooms and truffles. Above all be careful when it is cooked that the flesh doesn't disintegrate. Serve.

8. Old Salmon in a Court-Bouillon[8]

Dress an old salmon and serve it in the same way as the sturgeon, in Recipe 6, with three napkins sprinkled with parsley.

9. Porpoise in a Court-Bouillon

Porpoise is served and done up in the same way as the sturgeon and the old salmon, except that it is cooked longer. When it is cooked, serve.

10. Porpoise in Ragout

Cut the porpoise up into pieces. Roast it on a spit, basting it with butter, salt, vinegar and pepper. When it is well done, coat it with a sauce made of butter and chopped onion; then mix everything together and simmer it; mix in a little flour and serve.

11. Fried Dab in Ragout

Dab are done up the same as in the section of Fish Entrées, above.[11]

12. Sea-Otter in a Court-Bouillon

Dress a sea-otter and prepare it for putting into court-bouillon, which you make up in the same way as for the brill. When it has cooked, serve it dry, with parsley in a napkin on top.

13. Sea-Otter on the Grill[13.1]

Dress the sea-otter and roast it. When it is done, make whatever sauce you like for it, provided it tastes strong and, because those large chunks[13.2] don't readily take on a flavouring, split it or slice it on top.[13.3] Simmer it in its sauce until it has soaked up almost all of it. Then serve it, garnished with whatever you have on hand.

10. *Marsouin en ragoust.*

---

[8] According to contemporary dictionaries, La Varenne's word for this fish, variously spelled *bescard, beccard* and *becare*, apparently identifies a variety of salmon with a long, hooked jaw. In none of the four instances where the term occurs does I. D. G. know of an English equivalent; he merely keeps the French word.

[11] Directions for making Roast Dab, served with a sauce, are found in Recipe XVI,36.

[13.1] Later printers title this dish *Loutre de mer rôtie en ragoust.*

[13.2] *ces grosses masses*: the sea-otter is apparently not to be cut up small.

[13.3] *fendés-le ou le découpés par dessus*: the incision is apparently to be deep. *Cf.* the *cizelés* in Recipe 25, below.

14. Fried Rayfish

When a ray has been well dressed and cleaned, set it to marinate in well-seasoned vinegar. A little before serving, fry it in clarified butter or in olive oil. When it has cooked well and browned,[14.1] set it to drain; sprinkle it with fine salt. Then serve it whole, or with the two wings[14.2] set together again,[14.3] with orange.

15. Tench in a Court-Bouillon

After scalding tench well, you can put them into a court-bouillon as above, then serve them with parsley.

16. Shad in a Court-Bouillon

You can also put shad in a court-bouillon, serving it with its scales still on, well seasoned with parsley, with a napkin over it.

17. Roast Shad

As shad comes out of the court-bouillon, set it on the grill. When it has roasted, make a sauce of the Sauce Robert sort and simmer everything together — but only briefly. Then serve. And if you like, put in capers.

Another way

When the shad is scaled and dressed very cleanly through its gills, and dried, sauté it in fresh butter. Then roast it. Then split it all along its back and remove all the bones there are, and close it up again. Take the milt, along with a quantity of good herbs, and make a sauce that is a bit piquant, particularly as this fish is by its nature bland: into that sauce put capers, anchovies and mushrooms, and thicken it with a little pan-fried bread crust.

Alternatively, make a well-seasoned mixture with sorrel. When it[17] comes to a boil, serve it.

18. Fresh Cod

Put the cod into some sort of court-bouillon: let it boil only very briefly, then take it off the fire and let it sit,[18] covered with a cloth or

17. Alloze rostie.

[14.1] *rissollée.*

[14.2] *les deux testez,* an apparent error. I. D. G., along with later French printers interpret this as "the two sides," *les deux costez.*

[14.3] In Recipe XVI,75 the rayfish's two wings are removed.

[17] That is, the sauce with the fish in it.

[18] The fish is to continue steeping in the warm water.

napkin. When you wish to serve, set it to drain. Make a thick sauce, then serve with parsley.

19. Roast Bream

When the bream has been dressed, roast it on the grill, buttered on top. When it is done, make a sauce of fresh butter, parsley, chives, vinegar, salt and pepper; simmer everything together. Then serve.

Another way

You can put the bream in a court-bouillon and then roast it. Afterwards make a sauce with fresh butter, chopped parsley and chives, sautéing everything together. When you wish to serve, mix in some sorrel juice. Serve.

20. Pike *au bleu*[20.1]

Dress pike as it comes out of the water;[20.2] cut it or leave it whole; and in that water, slit it along its back, then put it into a basin. Get salt, vinegar, onion, pepper and a good amount of lemon or orange peel, bring all that together only to a boil, then pour it over your pike and immediately it becomes blue.[20.3] To cook it, boil your white wine, well seasoned with salt, put your pike into it and let it cook. Taste your court-bouillon to see whether it is strong enough, and let your pike sit in it until it takes on its flavour, being careful not to leave it there too long; in that case, take it out until it is to be served. That is done with it warm, with parsley, in a napkin.

Escoffier, *Brochet*, §756

21. Pike in a Sauce

With the pike cooked the same as before,[21.1] remove its skin. Take a drop of your court-bouillon, put it in a dish with half an egg yolk, well diluted,[21.2] along with some fresh butter and nutmeg; thicken the sauce,

---

[20.1] Cf. the *Carpe au bleu* in Recipe 27, below.

[20.2] Fishmongers offered fish live from vats of water.

[20.3] The acid vinegar reacts with the protein film on the pike's skin. For that the fish must be very fresh. The same procedure is prescribed for carp (Recipe 27); there La Varenne's recipe insists that the fish be procured live. Trout *au bleu* is similarly prepared today.

[21.1] That is, in white wine and salt.

[21.2] *bien delayé*, presumably with a little vinegar, the usual liquid for thinning egg yolks.

seasoning it well with salt, chives and peel; if you like, add in some
anchovies — but be careful that it doesn't turn.[21.3] Serve your pike hot.

Escoffier, *Truites au bleu,* §817

23. Truites saumonnées.

22. Trout in a Court-Bouillon

Depending on the size of the trout, make a number of slits in them and
make your court-bouillon strong. Before cooking them, gut them through
their gill and marinate them; after that they have to cook gently so they
don't fall apart. When they are done, serve them with parsley in a pleated
napkin, which you cover with flowers if any are in season.

23. Salmon Trout

Do up salmon trout and serve them the same as the ordinary ones,
just above.

24. Perch in a Court-Bouillon

Dress perch through their gill as they come out of the water,[24] and
put them into a court-bouillon of wine and all sorts of seasonings such
as salt, pepper, cloves, lemon or orange peel, scallions and onions. When
they have cooked, take them out and remove their skin. Make a sauce
with a drop of your court-bouillon mixed with vinegar, an egg yolk, a
quartered onion, fresh butter, salt and very little white pepper — with
everything mixed together quickly over the fire — and pour it over your
perch. Serve.

25. Burbot

Warm up some water, put burbots into it and take them out after a
short while. Remove their slime[25.1] with a knife, and you make them
quite white. Then dress them, wash them, put between two cloths and
dry them. Set the big ones[25.2] aside and slit them on top for serving with
oil or clarified butter, with salt and orange. Serve.

[21.3] *qu'elle ne tourne*: I.D.G. shows, "Take heed it become not oilie."

[24] We see here again La Varenne's expectation that an aristocratic household will either
have immediate access to a fish pond or else that an itinerant fish merchant will
deliver live fish in a vat of water.

[25.1] This *limon* is the natural coating, rich in protein, carried on the skin of some fish.

[25.2] Recipe XVI,17 makes a similar distinction betwen large and small burbots. There,
as here, only the large ones are slit on their backs.

26. Burbot in a Casserole

Put your burbots into a casserole and season them with butter, salt, ground cloves, pepper, peel, a bouquet of herbs, verjuice, a dash of vinegar and a very little good bouillon. When they have cooked, serve them. If you wish, garnish them with anchovies, capers, mushrooms and any other sort of garnish you have.

27. Carp *au bleu*[27.1]

The best sort of carp is soft-roed;[27.2] get it live and season it for putting in a court-bouillon the same as the pike above, in Recipe 20. If it is big, you can quarter it or make slits along its back. Put it into a basin for bluing.[27.3] If you wish to cook it in a fish pan, get a leaf[27.4] to put on the bottom of the pan. Take your carp with a bit of cloth, season it well with onion, pepper, salt, cloves and peel — all of that carefully wrapped in your linen cloth — and set it to cook, with the leaf beneath to keep it from burning with all the boiling, or to keep the cloth from sticking to the fish pan. Mind that your court-bouillon stays unchanged in any way,[27.5] but that it is well seasoned with whatever is necessary. When the fish has finished slowly cooking, serve it with parsley in a napkin.

28. Stuffed Carp[28.1]

Remove the carp's skin from the back down to the belly; take out all the bones, guts and milt, and from the head remove the gills and tongue. Then make up a stuffing from a little well-chopped carp flesh seasoned with an equal amount of butter, little parsley, chives and a pinch of fine herbs, binding everything with an egg; or mix in mushrooms, milt or mussels, capers, chives, carp tongues and artichoke hearts. Put your stuffing into your carp throughout its full length, leaving space where you will put what you have sautéed; season everything well. Close it up. Cook

---

[27.1] Cf. the *Brochet au bleu* in Recipe 20, above.

[27.2] *la meilleure sorte de carpe est laitée*, that is, the one with milt.

[27.3] In the text: *la mettre dans un bassin & au bleu*. The process seems to have been relatively common; it is described in Recipe 20, above, where La Varenne's cook could find the specific composition of the vinegar mixture.

[27.4] This *fueille* may be some sort of very large leaf or a sheet of heavy paper.

[27.5] *ne soit alteré d'aucune chose*. I.D.G. puts "be altered with any thing."

[28.1] Later reprintings of the *Cuisinier françois* add the qualification *en ragoût*.

it in a basin or in a casserole — which is a vessel shaped like a large tourtière, like a sort of dripping pan — or in a dish, in front of the fire, with a dash of verjuice, a little bouillon, butter and whatever you have left over of your mushrooms, truffles or milt; simmer everything together slowly. And to keep it from sticking, put a few chives underneath with a little verjuice and a few egg yolks.[28.2] Thicken the sauce. Serve.

Stuffed Carp of this sort can be put into fine or puff pastry, and garnished with whatever you have on hand.

29. Smelt[29.1]

Get smelt very fresh. String them and dry them well. When you are ready to serve, flour them, fry them in oil or in butter; remove the rod,[29.2] sprinkle them with fine salt, and serve them with orange.

30. Plaice

You will find the recipe for plaice, along with all of the ones that follow in the Table, in the section on Fish Entrées,[30] which it would have been useless and superfluous to list by recipe number and page number, and all the more so as they can easily be found. However, I can advise you that what I indicate will not oblige you either to increase or reduce your proper expenditure of funds or labour, but I do it solely to remind you of what can be served, without forgetting to say that you can choose whatever you like, and insert a reasonable assortment of pies or tourtes among your dishes, always minding that a pie or tourte is served after six other dishes.

31. Scoter Duck [XVI,40 (?)]

32. Scoter Duck in Ragout [XVI,39]

33. Brill in a Casserole [XVI,33]

[28.2] La Varenne has put only his normal punctuation here, a comma: the sense of the passage may be different. However, there is no punctuation between "chives underneath" and "with a little verjuice."

[29.1] Later reprintings add *en ragoût*.

[29.2] *la verge*, that is to say, the skewer along which the smelt have been strung in order to be dried and cooked. See Recipe XVI,76.

[30] This is Chapter XVI with entrées for ordinary lean days. For the subsequent twenty-seven fish recipes listed in the Table of this present Chapter and which we reproduce below, we indicate the location of the recipe that La Varenne probably has in mind.

29. Eſperlans.

34. Pike Stuffed and Roasted [XVI,61]

35. Salmon in a Sweet Sauce [XVI,13 (?)]

36. Burbot in Ragout [XVI,16]

37. Carp in a Half Court-Douillon [XVI,10]

38. Fried Tench in Ragout [XVI,5]

39. Barbel in Ragout [XVI,28]

40. Barbel in a Casserole [XVI,33 (?)][40]

41. Sole in Ragout [XVI,1]

42. Chub in Ragout [XVI,22]

43. Chub in a Court-Bouillon [XVI,23]

44. Salmon Jowl [XVI,81]

45. Fish Ham [XVI,73; XIX,24]

46. Red Mullet [XVI,66]

47. Fresh Mackerel [XVI,62]

48. Roast Shad [XVI,43; XVIII,17]

49. Fresh Herrings [XVI,63 Roast Fresh Herrings]

50. Royan Sardines [XVI,65]

51. Lampreys of All Sorts [XVI,46–48]

52. Eels of All Sorts [XVI,49–55]

53. Lobsters of All Sorts [XVI,56–57]

54. Crayfish in a Court-Bouillon [XVI,58]

55. Roast Oysters [XVI,21]

56. Fried Carp [XVI,8]

57. Barbel in a Sauce [XVI,29]

58. Roast Plaice in Ragout [XVI,38]

59. Plaice in a Casserole [XVI,37]

---

[40] Here, *Barbeaux en castrolle*; at XVI,33, *Barbues en castrolle*.

Chapter XIX

Entremets for Lean Days outside of Lent

1. St. George's Agaric

Get agaric very fresh, remove any sand and wash it in some water or some white wine; then put it on a dish [to simmer] with some good fresh butter well seasoned with salt, white pepper and grated bread crust — being careful that it doesn't burn. When it is cooked, add in a little nutmeg, orange juice or lemon juice. Then serve.

Another way

Sauté it in some very fresh butter with parsley, a bouquet of herbs, pepper and salt; let it steep in another pan or in a pot. When you wish to serve it, add in some cream, or an egg yolk, or a little bread crust and a little nutmeg. Serve.

[Alternatively,] with that you can garnish whatever you like, using a suitable amount of it.

2. Creamed Mushrooms

Escoffier, *Champignons à la crème*, §2072

Get mushrooms very fresh, and get the smallest ones because they are the best. Skin them dry, wash them in some water, taking them out promptly and draining them. Cut up the largest ones, and with the smallest fricassee them in some fresh butter with finely chopped parsley and chives, salt and pepper. Then simmer them in a little pot until you are ready to serve; then you can add in some cream. When all that has boiled quite a short while[2] and the sauce has thickened, you can serve them.

3. Truffles

Cook truffles in a court-bouillon. When they have cooked, serve them in a pleated napkin.[3.1]

2. *Champignons à la crefme.*

---

[2] *trois ou quatre tours.* Interestingly, later printers misread this as "three or four hours."

[3.1] This fashion of serving a prepared food to the table is relatively common. It seems often used for presenting whole, cooked fish.

Another way

Serve the truffles done the same way as the agaric, adding in a little bouillon, cream and some sort of juice. When they have been sliced very finely and cooked, serve them.

Another way

Skin the truffles and slice them quite small and very thinly. Then sauté them in a pan, seasoning them with very little salt because they have to boil for a long time with some sort of bouillon that you consider good. When they have cooked, skim off their grease and thicken the sauce a little by means of some sort of thickener[3.2] or with bread crust crumbs. Then serve.

Another way

As they come out of the sand, wash the truffles in some white wine, cook them in some full-bodied wine, a lot of salt, and pepper. When they are done, serve them in a pleated napkin.

Escoffier, Truffes à la serviette, §2278

4. Threaded Eggs

You will find these in the Entremets for Meat Days, along with the way to serve them.[4]

5. Nulles

Get four or five egg yolks, some very fresh cream, a good amount of sugar and a grain of salt. Beat everything well together and cook it on a hollow platter or a dish. Pass a red-hot fire shovel over it and sprinkle it with a savoury water.[5.1] Serve it sprinkled with musk sugar.[5.2]

6. Darling Eggs

You will find the way to do them and serve them among the Entremets for Meat Days.[6]

[3.2] A few possible thickeners are described in Chapter X.

[4] The reference is to the *Oeufs filez* of Recipe VIII,81.

[5.1] *eau de senteurs*: see Chapter IV of *The French Confectioner* for some examples of possible savoury waters.

[5.2] This *sucre musqué* is one of many varieties of flavoured sugars available in the seventeenth-century kitchen. In this case ground musk has been absorbed into re-clarified sugar. Rose sugar was commonly produced in that way.

[6] These directions are at Recipe VIII,80.

7. Frangipane Tourte

You will find this Frangipane Tourte among the recipes and in the table for Pasties for Meat Days.[7]

8. Cream Omelet[8]

You need a quantity of egg yolks, few egg whites, a little cream and an appropriate amount of salt. Beat everything together and, a little before serving, make your omelet. If you like, garnish it with sugar. Serve.

9. Fritters[9.1]

Get four cheese curds[9.2] — I mean soft, white cheeses — six eggs, six ounces[9.3] of flour and a little salt. Beat everything together. Try it out,[9.4] because cheeses are sometimes too soft or too dry, etc.

10. Whore's Farts[10.1]

Do them the same way [as above], except that they need a little more flour. Draw them out[10.2] very small with the handle of a spoon. When they are cooked, serve them sugared and sprinkled with orange blossoms.

11. Spun Pastry

You will find the way to do Spun Pastry and to serve it in the Chapter on Meat Days.[11]

11. Paste filée.

---

[7] Recipe VIII,64. There is also at the end of the Chapter XIV (Pasties that can be Served Throughout the Year) a passing reference to the special dough required for this tourte.

[8] See also Recipe XVII,9.

[9.1] The generic meat-day treatment of these *baignets* is found at VIII,38.

[9.2] *fromages à petits choux*, "cheeses like little cabbages." Later printers, perhaps mystified by the word *choux* here, change the phrase to a more understandable *à petits trou* (*sic*), "with little hole(s)."

[9.3] *un demi litron*: roughly three-quarters of a cup or half a pint.

[9.4] This instruction, *l'essayez*, leaves the exact mixture a decision for the cook to make.

[10.1] This lean version of the dish can be compared with its meat-day counterpart at Recipe VIII,41.

[10.2] This preparation also being deep fried as the previous fritters, the "drawing out" is probably to be done in the cooking grease.

[11] This is the *Paste filée* in the Entremets for Meat Days, Recipe VIII,42.

12. Eel Saveloy[12.1]

Dress your eel and slit it in half; remove its bone, beat its flesh well and season it, roll it up and bind it. When it is bound, wrap it up in a small linen cloth and cook it in a pot with some wine, salt, pepper, cloves, onion, and fine herbs. Do it in such a way that the sauce reduces to very little.[12.2] When it is well cooked, unwrap it and cut it into very thin slices. Then serve it either dry or with some of the sauce.

13. Fried Carp Milt

Clean carp milt well, blanch it in water and dry it. When you want to serve, flour it and fry it. When it is done, serve it with salt and orange.

14. Milt in Ragout

Blanch the milt[14.1] in water and put it, well seasoned with butter, salt, a bouquet of herbs, some mushroom stock,[14.2] a few capers and anchovies, into a dish with a dash of white wine. When the sauce is thickened, serve with orange or lemon juice and nutmeg.

15. Burbot Liver

Take the liver out of a burbot and put it into a dish with some very fresh butter, a few fine herbs, finely chopped parsley, mushrooms likewise finely chopped, some of your best bouillon, chopped capers and an anchovy. When it is well cooked and the sauce thickened, serve.

Another way

Fry the liver if you like. Serve it with salt and orange or lemon juice.

15. Foye de lotte.

16. Fish Jelly

Get carp scales, half a dozen tench, and six cups[16.1] of white wine. Cook it well all together with a little salt, a little cinnamon and four cloves. Strain everything through a napkin — that is, press it to squeeze out the juice; into that put a pound of sugar. Get a dozen eggs and fry

Cf. Escoffier, Gelée de poisson au vin blanc, §161

[12.1] See also Recipe XVI,51.

[12.2] I. D. G. renders this direction, *que la sauce se reduise à peu*, by "let the sauce be reduced to a short one."

[14.1] This is probably carp milt, as in the previous recipe.

[14.2] See Recipe XI,1.

[16.1] *trois chopines*, that is 48 ounces, or three pints.

their whites. Keep your straining bag at hand and very clean. Heat up your jelly[16.2] and, when it is on the point of boiling, throw in the juice of five lemons and your egg whites. Then, just as that begins to boil, pour it into the straining bag, putting it through repeatedly until it is very clear. Then put it, plain,[16.3] on a plate or in a dish. Serve.

17. White Dish

Make it with your left-over jelly; put in ground almonds and a drop of milk. Strain it and turn it into White Dish.[17] Serve it when it has cooled.

18. Green Jelly

Green Jelly is made the same way, straining it with very little juice of chard, and serving it cold.

19. Fried Artichokes

Cut the artichokes as for Artichokes in a Pepper Sauce,[19] cutting off their pointed ends too, and blanch them in hot water; after that put them to dry. Flour them for frying when you need them. Serve them garnished with fried parsley.

20. Asparagus in a White Sauce

As the asparagus comes from the garden, scrape it and cut the stalks into equal lengths. Cook them in water with some salt. Remove them as little cooked as you can and set them to drain. Then make a sauce with some fresh butter, an egg yolk, salt, nutmeg and a small dash of vinegar, everything stirred well together. With the sauce thickened, serve your asparagus.

21. Creamed Asparagus[21]

Cut asparagus stalks in three and, having blanched them, fricassee them evenly, well seasoned. When they are done, put in your cream and

---

[16.2] That is, the filtered, sweetened wine rich in protein from the carp scales.

[16.3] *au naturel*: that is, without colouring or a garnish. I.D.G. writes,"Put it after the natural upon a plate . . . ."

[17] See also the directions for making a non-lean *blanc manger* jelly among the Entremets for Meat Days, at Recipe VIII,33.

[19] See this meat-day *Artichaux à la poivrade*, Recipe VIII,70.

[21] This dish has the same name, *Asperges à la cresme*, as in Recipe VIII,88.

simmer them with it; if the sauce is too thin, put in egg yolks to thicken it. Serve.

22. Celery

Celery is eaten with pepper and salt, or else with oil, pepper and salt.

23. Cauliflower

Dress cauliflower, blanch it and cook it with some butter, some water and some salt. When it is done, set it to drain. Make a sauce the same as for the asparagus. Then serve.

24. Fish Ham[24.1]

Get the flesh of several carp along with a small amount of eel; chop it all up together and season it with butter, and press it together in the shape of a ham. Fill your carp skins with that,[24.2] sew them up again and wrap them in a very greasy cloth. Cook them[24.3] in a pot with half wine and half water, well seasoned with salt, etc.; boil down your sauce. When they have cooked, take them out and unwrap them while they are hot. You can serve them either hot or cold, in either case garnished like a ham.

25. Tortoises in Ragout

Tortoises can be eaten at any time. A sort of thickener can be made of them, and they are served with pottages as a garnish, and for many other things.

26. Apple Fritters

You will find this recipe, and the four following ones, in the Chapter for Meat Days and in the one for making Egg Dishes: consult the Table.[26]

24. Iambon de poiſſon.

[24.1] This dish resembles what has been described in Recipe XVI,73. The French word, translated as "ham" throughout this recipe, is *jambon*, the upper leg of a pig.

[24.2] Because the fish ham will still retains the shape of a pseudo-ham, the carp skins are merely fastened snugly around it, with the cloth as added insurance that the skins will stay in place and not peel away or burst during the cooking.

[24.3] This plural is in the text though previously only one *jambon* has been mentioned.

[26] The meat-day version of Apple Fritters is at Recipe VIII,39. In what follows, the present translation indicates in square brackets where the reader may turn for full recipes of the dishes that La Varenne lists in the chapter's table but apparently did not feel it necessary to repeat fully here.

27. Artichoke Fritters [VIII,40]

28. Almond Pie [VIII,44 (?)]²⁸

29. Ramekins of All Sorts [VIII,48–51]

30. Creamed Eggs [XVII,9]

---

²⁸ In the present chapter the name of the dish is *Pasté d'amendes*, which I. D. G.
faithfully gives as "Almond Pie". This may well be a misprint for *Paste*, as in
Chapter VIII. In Chapter XXI we find a *Tourte d'amandes*.

Chapter XX

What is found in Kitchen Gardens
that can be used if necessary and served as an entrée and entremets
on lean days, on meat days or during Lent

1. Skirrets[1.1]

Boil skirrets very lightly, then peel them and fry them in browned butter. When they have fried, serve.

Another way

For meat days, make rather a runny batter of some eggs, very little salt and very little flour; to make that batter more delicate, mix in some cheese curds.[1.2] Dip your skirrets in that and fry them. Serve.

Another way

To fry skirrets in Lent, mix your flour with a little milk or verjuice, and more salt and moisten your skirrets in that mixture. The best thing to fry them in is clarified butter. If you wish, garnish them with fried parsley: to prepare that you throw it, very clean and very dry, into your frying medium when it is very hot; immediately take it out again and set it in front of the fire so that it is very green. Serve your skirrets with the parsley around them.

2. Wheat Flour Porridge

This is made the same way as Rice Flour Porridge[2.1] and both need to be cooked the same length of time. To make them, moisten the flour

---

[1.1] La Varenne acknowledges the contemporary popularity of *chervis* by providing several possibilities for its preparation. Furthermore, in Recipe 6, below, the author uses this present recipe as a model for preparing parsnips. Although native to east Asia this perennial root acquired great gastronomic favour in Europe from the middle of the sixteenth century. Because of its sweetish flavour the Dutch gave it the name *zuikerwortel*, "sugar root," which became skywort and skirret in English. Toward the end of the seventeenth century the esteem for it waned as the potato became better established.

[1.2] As in Recipe XIX,9 the ingredient *du fromage à petits choux* baffled later printers who assumed the text should read *du fromage, petits choux, ...* In the earlier recipe La Varenne explained his phrase: *j'entends fromage blanc & mol.*

[2.1] There is no recipe in La Varenne for a porridge of rice, though rice is used in a

with very little milk and salt; outside of Lent add in egg yolks, a little butter and some sugar. Let it cook slowly, so that it turns into a *gratin*.[2.2] Serve, sugared.

3. Hops

Clean them well, leaving only the green part. Bring that to a boil in some water, then drain it. Put it into a dish with a little butter, a dash of vinegar, a little of your best bouillon, salt and nutmeg; simmer it. You use it as a garnish or for anything else.

4. Lettuce Leaves

Lettuce leaves are for garnishing all sorts of pottage, whether of chickens or of doves, of pea purée, of herbs[4] or a Healthy Pottage. Blanch them well, wash them and set them to simmer in a pot with your best bouillon. On meat days season them with anything fat; on lean days add in some butter. As soon as they are cooked, split them in half and garnish your pottages with them. Serve.

5. Pumpkin

Cut up the pumpkin very thinly and fricassee it in some butter. When it has taken on a good colour, simmer it between two dishes with an onion or a scallion stuck with cloves, and salt, pepper and verjuice mash if you have any. When it has cooked, serve it.

Another way

You can put pumpkin with some cream.

Another way

Cut pumpkin into large chunks and boil it in a pot with some water. When it has cooked, pour off the water and strain the pumpkin. Fricassee that in some butter with a finely chopped onion; season it with a dash of verjuice and nutmeg. Serve.

---

pottage: see Recipe XV,44, for instance. This first line simply advises the cook that rice flour can be substituted here for wheat flour. Patches of wheat and of rice seem to be normal crops in La Varenne's kitchen garden.

[2.2] Cotgrave defines this *gratin* as "the remnant of childrens pap, left in, or sticking to, the bottome of the skellet wherein it was boyled." The modern culinary sense of gratin is the crust that forms on the upper surface of certain dishes when they are browned under a grill or in an oven.

[4] Later printers omit the comma: *de purée d'herbes*. The phrase that follows, *de santé*, still names a variety of pottage (see Recipe III,2).

Another way

When the pumpkin is well strained, as above, put it with some very fresh butter, melting that with your pumpkin, along with sugar and almonds. Put that mixture into a shell of fine pastry made like a tourte, and bake it. When it is done, sugar it and serve it

Many people like to add in pepper; put in very little salt. You can garnish it with candied lemon peel cut in slices.

6. Parsnips

Cut the stringy ends from the parsnips and wash them well. Cook them. When they are done, peel them and cut them up however you like. Put them into a dish with some very fresh butter, salt, nutmeg and a drop of bouillon or a dash of vinegar or verjuice; simmer everything together, stirring well. While doing that, you will find that your sauce thickens. Then serve.

Another way

Cook parsnips the same way as the skirrets, in Recipe 1, above. Serve them with orange juice or verjuice and a little salt.

7. Salsify

Cook salsify like parsnips. When they are done, make the same sauce. Serve. You can serve them fried.

8. Carrots[8]

Clean [white] carrots and cook them. When done, peel them and cut them in very thin rounds. Then fricassee them in some fresh butter with a chopped onion, salt, pepper and vinegar. Then serve.

9. Beetroots[9]

When beetroots are quite clean and well cooked, either in water or in the coals, peel them and slice them in rounds. Then fricassee them

---

[8] Later in this series of recipes, these carrots will be qualified as "white carrots" as distinct from "orange carrots", even though the preparation of the two varieties will be identical: see Recipe 14, below. A white, pale yellow or slightly purple variety of carrot was relatively common across sixteenth- and seventeenth-century Europe, the orange carrot just coming into favour at La Varenne's time. See Alan Davidson, *The Oxford Companion to Food* (Oxford: Oxford University Press), 1999, 140–41.

[9] I. D. G. isn't quite sure what to make of La Varenne's *bette-raves*. His title to this recipe reads: "Red beets (or Beete-radish, or red parsnips)".

in good fresh butter with a chopped onion, well seasoned with a dash of vinegar. When well done, serve.

Another way

When beetroots are cooked, cut them up the same way, and put them with some oil, vinegar and salt. Then serve.

10. Jerusalem Artichokes

Roast Jerusalem artichokes in the coals. When they are well done, peel them and cut them in rounds. Fricassee them in some very fresh butter with an onion, salt, pepper and vinegar. When done, serve them with a little nutmeg.

11. Cucumbers

Peel cucumbers, cut them in rounds and fricassee them in some very fresh butter. When they are done, add in an onion, salt and pepper, and let them simmer thoroughly in a chafing dish.[11.1] Then serve them with egg yolks if you like.

Another way

To pickle[11.2] cucumbers, get them very immature and very small; blanch them in cool water and drain them. Then put them into a pot with salt, pepper and vinegar; cover them over well. And do not forget some whole cloves.

Another way

To pickle cucumbers in a different way, cut them up very thinly, then put with onion, salt, pepper and vinegar. When they are well pickled, drain them. To serve them, put some oil on them and serve them in a salad.[11.3]

12. Turnips

Scrape turnips, blanch them and set them to cook in water with some butter and some salt. When they are done, you put them into a dish with

---

[11.1] This translation is not accurate: there is no change of dish. The *rechaut* is a basket that holds hot coals over which a dish is kept warm. Properly La Varenne writes, here and in Recipes 15, 16 and 19, *sur le rechaut.*

[11.2] *confire*: the basic idea of La Varenne's verb is "to preserve".

[11.3] The phrase *en salade* refers to a preparation of vegetables that are uncooked and (relatively) raw.

some very fresh butter; you can put in some mustard. Serve them with nutmeg.

13. Fricasseed Apples

Pare apples, cut them in rounds and fricassee them in some very fresh butter. When they are done, serve them, making a bouillon with a little nutmeg.

Another way

Cut apples in half, remove their seeds and what is around them; serve them in their peel. Put them in a dish with some butter, some sugar, water and a little cinnamon; cook them like that. When they are done, serve them sugared.

14. Orange Carrots

Orange carrots are prepared in the same way as the white ones.[14]

15. Fricasseed Asparagus

Break asparagus stalks, cut them into little pieces and wash them. When they have drained, fricassee them in some very fresh butter, seasoning them with salt, pepper and chopped parsley. When done, set them to simmer in a chafing dish with a drop of bouillon and an onion stuck with cloves. Then serve them with nutmeg. You can also put in some cream if you like.

16. White Chicory

Blanch white chicory well in water and set it to drain. Then bind it up and cook it in water in a pot with some butter and some salt. When it is done, take it out and drain it promptly. After that you set it to simmer in a chafing dish in some butter with salt, nutmeg and a dash of vinegar. When you are ready to serve, make a thick sauce for it. Serve.

16.

Chicorée blanche.

Escoffier, *Chicorée à la crème,* §2089

Another way

When it is blanched, prepare it for a salad[16] with salt, vinegar and sugar. Then serve.

---

[14] See Recipe 8, above. These *carrottes rouges* are the carrots with which we are more familiar today. *Rouge* is the colour by which the best oranges are described in Recipe Confections,24.

[16] See the note about *en salade* in Recipe 11, above.

17. Midribs of Chard

Remove the filaments[17] from the midribs of chard and blanch the ribs in cool water. Set them to cook in water in a pot or kettle along with some butter, a crust of bread and some salt. When they are done, take them out and set them to simmer in a dish with some butter until you need them. Then you warm them up and set them out properly on a plate. Then make a thick sauce with some very fresh butter, a dash of vinegar and some nutmeg. Serve.

18. Midribs of Artichoke

Select the whitest midribs of artichoke, remove their filaments and blanch them. When they are blanched, set them to cook in water with some salt, a little butter and a bread crust. When they are well done, make up your dish; make a white sauce for them. Serve.

19. Strained Peas

Steep your peas and wash them well. Cook them in hot water, filling them out with it.[19] When they are cooked, mash them and put them through a strainer. Take some of the thickest purée and simmer it in a chafing dish with some butter, some salt and a whole onion stuck with cloves. Then serve.

You can [also] serve whole peas that have been fricasseed in very fresh butter with salt, chopped onion, pepper and vinegar. In Lent, garnish them with herrings.

Escoffier, *Truffes*
à la crème,
§2277

20. Truffles as an Entrée[20]

Clean truffles carefully and peel them. Fricassee them in some very fresh butter with an onion stuck with whole cloves, a little chopped parsley and a drop of bouillon. Simmer them between two dishes and, the sauce being somewhat thickened, serve.

---

[17] *les filets*: I.D.G. calls these filaments "the strings."

[19] *& les en remplissez.* I.D.G. shows, "and fill them againe with it." La Varenne's sense seems to be that the peas, normally kept in a dried state, should be fully reconstituted.

[20] *Trouffles d'Entrée*: the rubric for this chapter has indicated that the dishes in it may appropriately serve as both entremets and entrées. I.D.G.'s title for this recipe is "Trouffles of Entree (or first course)." The presence of a recipe for truffles in a chapter entitled What is Found in Kitchen Gardens is a little surprising. The gardener of an estate may normally have been responsible for procuring this item.

Chapter XXI

Lean Pasties[xxi.1] for Eating Hot
including Pies and Tourtes

Before going on to explain how to prepare these dishes, especially as the different sorts of pastry will come up often, I have thought it sensible to give you a brief outline on doing them.[xxi.2]

To that end you should know that puff-pastry dough is made by getting four pounds of flour, moistened with some salt and water, though not too much salt.[xxi.3] When that has sat a little, you roll it out with an amount of two pounds of butter; fold it together,[xxi.4] leaving a third of your pastry plain, to fold it in three and, with your butter inside, you roll out your pastry again into a square shape to fold it in four. That done, you do it all three times more. After that you set it in a cool place until you need to make use of it. Then you roll out as much dough as you need for the pie or tourte you want to make. Note that that dough is harder to make up[xxi.5] than any other — just so you don't make any mistake with it.

Fine dough is made from four pounds of flour and a pound and a half of butter which you blend in fully together[xxi.6] along with some salt. After that you let it sit until you need to use it. Use it for pies and tourtes.

Warm-water dough is made the same way, except that you heat up the water and butter. When it is made, let it sit longer than the other sort,

---

[xxi.1] *La Pastisserie de poisson*: not necessarily "Fish Pasties" but those appropriate for a fish day or lean day. Despite this title the author deals here with both meat-day and lean-day pies. See the last sentence of his preamble.

[xxi.2] A similar preamble of general information is offered in *The French Pastry Chef*.

[xxi.3] *fort douce neantmoins*: literally, a "quite sweet" water.

[xxi.4] *ioignez les ensemble*: the rolled out dough, coated with butter, is folded on itself in thirds. The outer third is left *vuide*, "empty" or plain — that is, not coated with butter.

[xxi.5] *plus mal-aisée à nourrir*: literally, "more difficult to enrich." See the same verb in Recipe 6, below.

[xxi.6] The (cold) water is assumed here. See the next type of dough.

and handle it very little so it doesn't become too warm.[xxi.7] Use it for pies or tourtes.

Dark dough is made of rye flour, with water and a little butter; if you like you can add in some salt and pepper. When it is thick and has sat, use it for venison pies.

All sorts of meat- and lean-day pies for eating hot are seasoned the same way, depending on the sorts of meats in them. You can even put in garnishes from kitchen gardens,[xxi.8] such things as mushrooms, truffles, asparagus, egg yolks, artichoke hearts, capers, chard midribs, pistachios. In meat-day pies, as well as garnishings from the kitchen garden you can put in veal sweetbreads, onions, cockscombs and so forth.

Garnished meat pies, and those made with very tender meats, should be in the oven only two and a half hours. For fish pies, whether large or small, the baking time is the same as for the same size of meat pie.

It is different with a pie of young hare: although this is seasoned the same, it should be in the oven only two hours, whether the shell is of puff pastry or some other sort. It is served hot and opened.

Pies that you want to set aside to keep have to be of a stronger flavour than those made to be eaten hot. If they are to be conveyed any great distance, the dough should be on the dark side; and if it is fine, you must make a basket expressly to carry them.

You lard your lean-day pies with eel or carp, well seasoned with pepper, salt, vinegar and ground cloves. Make your dough fine or otherwise. Season your pie with cloves, salt, pepper, fine herbs and a shallot. When it is made up, glaze it — on meat-days with an egg yolk, in Lent with pike eggs moistened with some water. Put it in the oven, piercing it a little afterwards.[xxi.9]

[xxi.7] *de peur qu'elle ne se brusle.* I. D. G. writes "lest it burn." Furetière says that the verb *brusler* "se dit hyperboliquement pour signifier, Eschauffer beaucoup, ou estre eschauffé."

[xxi.8] The author may have in mind the previous chapter which deals with "What is Found in Kitchen Gardens."

[xxi.9] We have already seen (in Recipe V,83, for instance) how this vent hole has to be made in the upper crust after the pastry has hardened enough. That is done to avoid steam pressure building and, in some cases, to allow the last-minute addition of ingredients.

After that word of advice, which I believe is not useless, let us get to the details of making pastries that are served hot on meat days or lean days.

1. Salmon Pie

With your fish dressed, lard it with eel or carp seasoned with pepper, salt and ground cloves. Then put it onto the dough with a bay leaf on top, and either good fresh butter or beaten lard depending on the day you want to use it.[1.1] Sprinkle it with lard and a dash of vinegar. Close it up in the shape of the fish.[1.2] When it is baked, serve it hot or cold.

2. Trout Pie

Trout Pie is made and seasoned the same.

3. Pie of Old Salmon

A pie of old salmon is done the same way.

4. Carp Pie

Carp Pie is done the same.

5. Sturgeon Pie

Sturgeon Pie, also the same.

6. Brill Pie

Dress your brill and makes slits across its top; if you wish, lard it with well-seasoned eel. Then make up your pie shell to the size of your brill and put the brill into it well seasoned with salt, pepper, cloves, fine herbs, mushrooms, morels, a little parsley — sautéed in some fresh butter — agaric, artichoke hearts or broken asparagus stalks and good fresh butter. Cover it over with an open crust; if you like, decorate it in some sort of way. Bake it. When it is done and well enriched,[6] serve it with a sauce made of verjuice mash and egg yolks.

6. Pasté de barbuë.

[1.1] The determining factor would be whether the day was a usual lean day (generally a Wednesday, Friday or Saturday) or a meat day.

[1.2] Some of these pasties are not what La Varenne will elsewhere call standing pies or pie-plate pies (see, for instance, Recipe XIV,11): the fish remains whole and the dough is formed around the fish. If a baking form, such as a tourtière, is not used when a pie's filling is mobile, an alternative way to keep the pastry from bursting is to wrap it around with bands of greased paper: see Recipe 10, below.

[6] The phrase *bien nourry* describes a thorough blending and compounding of all the ingredients brought about by the cooking of the pie.

7. Turbot Pie

Turbot Pie is done in the same way.

8. Trout Pie

Trout Pie, the same.

9. Plaice Pie

Plaice Pie likewise, the same.

10. Eel Pie

Dress the eel, cut them crosswise into rounds and season them. Make up your pie shell[10.1] and fill it with eel, hard-boiled egg yolks, mushrooms, truffles if you have any, artichoke hearts and good fresh butter. Then serve it, opened, with a white sauce composed of egg yolks mixed into some verjuice.[10.2] To prevent your pie from collapsing, it has to be bound round with buttered paper and a cord;[10.3] then, when it is baked, remove the paper.

11. Fresh Cod Pie

Do a Cod Pie as with the brill[11] and serve it hot.

12. Pie of Deboned Carp

Stuff the [deboned] carp in the same way as for an entrée.[12] Make up your pastry, then put the carp in it garnished with whatever you like. Bake it covered. When it has baked for two hours, serve it opened, with a white sauce.

Another way

Cut your [deboned] carp into chunks and put into a standing pastry shell, seasoned with whatever you have. Bake your pie, and serve it opened, with a white sauce.

[10.1] The verb here, *dressez*, indicates that this pie is to be of the standing variety with a bottom and a continuous round wall. See also Recipe XXI,18.

[10.2] This so-called "white" sauce is perhaps the most common preparation in all of these recipes.

[10.3] Out of habit, after La Varenne's word *filet* the typesetter added the words *de vinaigre*: the paper is bound with a dash of vinegar!

[11] Recipe 6, above.

[12] La Varenne is likely referring to Recipe XVI,7 for Stuffed Carp in Ragout.

13. Cardinal's Pie[13]

Get the flesh of carp and eel, and chop it up with butter; season it with salt, pepper, fine herbs and a few mushrooms. Then make up your pastry shells as small as you can; fill them, cover and glaze them, and bake them. Then serve them.

14. Dab Pie[14.1]

When dab have been dressed, make slits on them and put them in your sheet of dough seasoned with salt, pepper, ground cloves, mushrooms sautéed in a pan in browned butter, fresh butter, along with whatever you have. Cover the pasty over and then bake it, banded with buttered paper. When it is done, serve it with a white sauce,[14.2] nutmeg, a shallot, lemon or orange juice and a slice of lemon or orange.

15. Gurnard Pie[15]

When a gurnard has been dressed, make slits on it and put it into your pastry dough seasoned with salt, pepper, fresh butter, mushrooms, truffles, agaric, morels, sautéed parsley and artichoke hearts. When the pie has been made up, covered and banded with buttered paper, bake it. When it is done, serve it, opened, with a white sauce or with any other thickener you have.

16. Sole Pie

Sole Pie is done the same as the one for brill,[16] particularly as it is of the same sort of flesh. It is eaten hot.

17. Pie of Half-Fried Sole

Half sauté sole in some butter; remove the back bone and stuff them with whatever you like, such as mushrooms, capers, truffles, agaric, artichoke hearts and fresh butter — all of that sautéed in a pan with finely

---

[13] A meat-day version of this very small but elongated *Pasté à la Cardinale* has already been seen at Recipes V,85 and XIV,12. As before, I.D.G. handles the mysterious name merely as "Pie after the Cardinal's way."

[14.1] I.D.G. translates *limandes* as "flounder."

[14.2] This white sauce has been described in Recipe 10, above, and elsewhere, as a mixture of egg yolks and verjuice. It serves as a variety of thickener — as is said in the next recipe.

[15] See also Recipe XVI,90.

[16] Recipe 6, above.

chopped parsley and chives. Put the stuffed sole into a raised pastry shell or onto a sheet of puff-pastry dough which you set into a tourtière; across its top spread the rest of your stuffing by way of a garnish, along with egg yolks and very fresh butter. Cover over your pie, and pierce it[17] after it has been in the oven a while. When baked, serve it with whatever sauce you like.

18. Raised Pie of Eel Hash

These pies are done the same as the ones for carp, except that — the eel flesh being fatter than the carp — it shouldn't be mixed with butter as is done with the carp; only mix them together and season them well with salt, pepper and a few fine herbs. Then [in the pie shell] make a layer of the hash; on top of that you put mushrooms, morels, truffles and a little chopped parsley sautéed[18] in a pan in some butter; on top of that throw the rest of your hash; then cover your pie and bake it. When it is done, serve it with a white sauce.

19. Dab Tourte

Dab Tourte is made the same as the Dab Pie, whose directions you have in Recipe 14, above.

20. Tourte of Fresh Oysters

Your oysters being cleaned and blanched in hot water, sauté them in a pan in very fresh butter, along with chopped parsley and chives, and mushrooms, everything well seasoned. Put that into a shell of whatever dough you like, and garnish it with hard-boiled egg yolks, artichoke hearts, morels and broken asparagus stalks, everything well sautéed. Cover over your tourte and bake it. When it is done, serve it with a good sauce which you make by sautéing two or three whole scallions in some butter in a pan, with salt, pepper and a dash of verjuice or of vinegar; when that is browned, add in two egg yolks well mixed with verjuice, and remove the scallions; then put your boiling sauce into your tourte along with a little nutmeg; stir it a very little. Serve it opened.

18. Paſté dreſſé d'achis d'Anguille.

---

[17] On the making of a vent hole in an upper crust, see the preamble to this chapter, above.

[18] Though *passé* is in the singular, La Varenne may well intend that the mushrooms, morels and truffles be sautéed along with the chopped parsley.

21. Tourte of Burbot Liver

With the burbot liver blanched very briefly in hot water, cleaned well and dried, put it into a sheet of dough. Then sauté agaric, morels, truffles, broken asparagus stalks, a little chopped parsley, artichoke hearts, cooked cardoons or cooked midribs of chard,[21] and egg yolks, all of that well seasoned — and in a quantity such that your tourte won't change its name and the garnish exceed the main ingredient. Bake it. Then, when it is done, serve it.

22. Tourte of Carp Milt

This is done the same as the one for burbot, in the next recipe below, with whatever garnish you have.

23. Burbot Tourte

Blanch a burbot well in water hot enough to remove its slime, until it is white; then cut it across in rounds half its head in size. Put these into a sheet of dough with salt, pepper, ground cloves, capers, mushrooms, hard-boiled egg yolks, artichoke hearts, well chopped parsley and chives, with very fresh butter spread on top. Cover it over with a sheet of puff-pastry dough if you have any. When it has baked, serve it, opened, with a white sauce and garnished with its upper crust cut into four.[23]

24. Carp Tourte

A Carp Tourte is made and seasoned the same as the one for burbot in the previous recipe, except that it must not be scalded,[24] but well scaled.

25. Crayfish Tourte

Cook crayfish with salt, pepper and very little vinegar; take off their feet and tail, then dress them. Sauté them in very fresh butter in a pan with mushrooms and anything you have for it, not omitting some chopped parsley. Then season it all well and put it into whatever sort of dough you like, whether fine or puff pastry. When the tourte has baked well,

23. Tourte de lotte.

---

[21] Both *cardons* and *cardes* are listed here, as alternatives. Both terms identify the tender, succulent part of an edible green that grows out from the plant's trunk. The difference in terminology refers to relative size.

[23] See the note in Recipe XVI,89.

[24] This is the "blanching" to which the burbot is first subjected for the purpose of removing the *limon* from its skin.

serve it with a russet sauce that you make by grinding up crayfish shells:[25]
when you have strained them through a cloth, mix them with some sort
of bouillon, a few egg yolks, a dash of verjuice and a little nutmeg; put
that sauce onto your tourte as it comes out of the oven and is ready to be
served. Serve it opened.

26. Frogs' Legs Tourte

Cut the big legs[26.1] off frogs and sauté then in very fresh butter in a
pan, together with mushrooms, parsley, cooked and cut up artichokes[26.2]
and capers, everything well seasoned. Put that into a sheet of fine or puff
pastry dough and bake it. When it is done, serve it, opened, with a white
sauce.

27. Tench Tourte

Scald tench, making them white, then dress them. Cut them across
in rounds and put them into your tourte or pie shell; do them up and
garnish them with whatever you have, such as very fresh butter, capers
and chopped parsley; bake them. When done, serve with white sauce and
a little nutmeg.

28. Butter Tourte

Melt a chunk of butter; when it is melted, add in sugar and ground almonds along with a little cream or milk, mixed with some cooked flour.[28.1]
Then lay down a sheet of fine or puff-pastry dough, put your mixture into
it, edge it[28.2] and bake it. Serve it sprinkled with sugar and with some

---

[25] Interestingly La Varenne terms these shells *ossemens*, "bones." In Recipe XXIV,1
the parts of the crayfish exoskeleton are (properly) called *les coquilles*.

[26.1] *les grosses cuisses*: literally "the big thighs".

[26.2] *artichaux cuits coupez*. For that phrase later printed versions show *culs d'artichaux
coupés*, "cut up artichoke hearts."

[28.1] That is, starch. La Varenne's text has ... *délayés avec de la farine cuite*. I. D. G.
understands this last ingredient as boiled flour: "flowre sod". Such flour is used as
a thickener; it appears also in Recipe VIII,102 as "cooked" flour — *cuite*, as here
— and in Recipes V,42, XXV,4 and 20, as "fried" or "sautéed" flour, *farine frite*.
The fried flour may, quite literally, be that which is described in Recipes V,41 and
XXV,40.

[28.2] *la bordez*: later versions have *bandés-la*, that is to say, wrap it around with a band
of greased paper which is held by a cord.

savoury water if you have any.[28.3]

29. Spinach Tourte

You get spinach leaves, and clean and blanch them; when blanched, they are drained and chopped up very small, then mixed with some melted butter, salt, sugar and a macaroon's weight of ground almonds. Put everything into your pastry shells and bake them. When they are done, serve them sugared. If you like you can garnish them with candied lemon peel around the dish.

30. Melon Tourte

Scrape your melon and pound it in a mortar. Melt some butter and put it with some sugar, a bit of pepper, salt and a macaroon,[30] mixing everything together. Fill your pastry shell with it and bake it. Serve it sugared.

31. Pistachio Tourte

With your pistachios cleaned, pound them, moistening them with orange-blossom water or some other savoury water so they don't turn to oil. Melt as much butter as there are pistachios and get the same amount of sugar, a little salt and sieved[31] white breadcrumbs, or a drop of milk. Then, with all of that mixed well together, put it into a shell of very fine pastry, the tourte and the shell being very thin. Bake it, sugar it, and serve it hot. Sprinkle it with whatever savoury water you like.

32. Almond Tourte

Almond Tourte is done in the same way, except that you sprinkle it with milk rather than savoury water.

33. Pumpkin Tourte

Boil pumpkin in some good milk and strain it through a strainer very thick;[33] then mix it with some sugar, butter, a little salt and, if you like,

---

[28.3] See Chapter IV of *The French Confectioner* for some examples of possible savoury waters.

[30] Recipe Confections, 47.

[31] The participle *passé* is found alone here, whose sense can be either "sieved" or "sautéed". I. D. G. has the breadcrumbs "fried".

[33] The end of this sentence indicates that the strainer is to hold out all but the most liquid element.

a few ground almonds; everything should be very thin. Put it into your shell and bake it. When it is done, it is sprinkled with sugar. Serve.

34. Pear Tourte

Pare your pears and cut them up very thinly, then cook them in water with sugar. When they are well done, add in a little very fresh butter, beat everything together and put it into a very thin sheet of dough, banding it around if you want; then bake it. When it is done, sprinkle it with blossom water,[34] sugar it, and serve.

35. Cream Tourte

Get some very fresh cream and into it mix a few ground almonds, some sugar and a little gruel made with milk and well cooked; boil it all together briefly. When that mixture has cooled, put it into your shell and bake it. When it is done, sugar it well; if you wish, give it a musk flavour. Serve.

36. Apple Tourte

Apple Tourte is made and served in the same way as the Pear Tourte of Recipe 34.

37. Frangipane Tourte[37.1]

Get the finest flour you can find and moisten it with egg whites. Immediately take one-twelfth of your dough[37.2] and spread it out until you can see light through it. Butter your plate or tourtière, put in that first layer and spread it out, and butter it on its upper surface. Repeat that up to six times. Then put in whatever cream you like.[37.3] Do the upper crust

---

[34] *eau de fleurs.* As in Recipe 37 La Varenne is indifferent about the flower whose "water" will flavour this garnish. In Recipe 31 he specified *fleur d'orange ou autres de senteur.*

[37.1] This lean recipe can be compared with its meat-day counterpart in VIII,64. The procedure here, setting out six thin layers of pastry, with butter between each and then within that multi-layered shell the cream filling of the tourte itself, resembles the Frangipane Tourte of *The French Pastry Chef,* Recipe IX,15.

[37.2] Presumably the recipe is intended for only one tourte, with a six-layered crust bottom and top.

[37.3] This nonchalance about the nature of the cream appropriate for a Frangipane Tourte is a little surprising to say the least. See Recipe IV,3 for Lenten Cream in *The French Pastry Chef.*

Tourte de poires.

34.

as you did for the lower one, up to six layers. Bake your tourte slowly. When it is done, sprinkle it with blossom water; sugar it well. Serve.

You have to be careful to use your dough as soon as it is made up because it dries out faster than you think: when it is dry, it is useless[37.4] — all the more so as your shells must be as thin as cobwebs. That is why you should choose a cool place to work in.

38. Egg-White Tourte

When your eggs have been well beaten, season them with a little salt and sugar. Melt some fresh butter with some milk and mix everything together. Then put your mixture into a shell of fine pastry and bake it. When it is done, serve it hot and sugared.

39. Egg-Yolk Tourte

Mix five egg yolks with some butter, some sugar, two macaroons, a little salt and milk. Shape up your tourte with that and bake it. When it is done, serve it sugared, with very thin lemon peel on top.

40. Marzipan Tourte[40.1]

To make it full, glazed and as big as a plate, get half a pound of almonds and a quarter-pound of sugar; grind up your almonds and add in some sugar. Roll out your dough, make up quite a low shell[40.2] and bake it on a shallow plate over a low fire. Make a cream with milk, the directions for which follow below; [with it] fill the pastry about half a finger high,[40.3] bake it, and pass the fire shovel over it. On top, over little more than half,[40.4] put either cherries, strawberries, raspberries, red currants, verjuice mash or candied apricots. When the tourte is filled, put it back into the oven. Make a glazing with half an egg white and six times as much sugar, beaten well together. When ready to serve, pour that over the top of your tourte and give it a suitably hot flame. Then serve on the plate.

Bocuse, Gâteau aux amandes dit Pithiviers, p. 384

[37.4] Curiously, later printers change this *hors de service* to *de bon service*.

[40.1] For the making of plain marzipan, see Recipe Confections,30.

[40.2] According to what we read next, this height would be about one finger's width.

[40.3] Interestingly, I. D. G. renders this *environ l'épaisseur d'un demy doigt* as "about the thickness of half an inche."

[40.4] This "half" may be half the surface of the tourte, although it is difficult to see why, or half the height of the tourte.

To make the cream that was mentioned above: moisten a little flour with three cups[40.5] of milk, and cook it well until it is very thin;[40.6] then add in a little butter, four egg yolks and two well-beaten egg whites, stirring it all on the fire, and mix in very little salt along with sugar, about half of the amount of the cream you have. To make it green, put in some ground pistachios, or some candied lemon peel scrapings.

You can serve your tourte glazed, without confections and with fruit as for an Entremets.[40.7]

[40.5] *une chopine*: of milk this would be 24 fluid ounces or one and a half pints.

[40.6] *fort claire.*

[40.7] This Marzipan Tourte is not represented among either the meat-day or lean Entremets, although a *Tourte de franchipane* and a *Tourte de pistaches* are described earlier (Recipes VIII,64 and 78, and XIX,7).

Chapter XXII

Several Sorts of Roots, Herbs and other Things
for preserving and keeping
in the stores of a private or public house[xxii]

1. Melted Butter

When butter is cheap you can buy a good amount of it and melt it for use as needed. To do that, put it in a pan[1.1] and melt it slowly until the cream goes to the bottom and it becomes clear on top. Put that[1.2] into a pot and when it has cooled put it away for future use.

2. Artichokes

Cut off their choke and the hard part around them — [leaving] what is called artichoke hearts.[2.1] Set them to soak in cool water to blanch them; drain and dry them. Then put them into a pot with salt, pepper, vinegar,[2.2] melted butter, cloves and the odd bay leaf; cover them well and keep them until you want to use them. At that time desalt them in warm water and, when they are desalted, cook them in some butter or

Escoffier, *Fonds d'artichauts sautés* §2036

[xxii] *pour garder dans le mesnage de maison ou de cabaret.* The significant word in this chapter title is *confire*, which has the literal sense of "to confect". Later, as a supplement following Chapter XXX, La Varenne will append a large group of recipes dealing with various sorts of confections in which sugar is the agent; in the present chapter salt or vinegar are the usual preservatives.

[1.1] Later editions change this *poësle* to a larger *chaudiere* or "boiler".

[1.2] The author says "it", meaning the clear liquid of which he has just spoken. The whole procedure is known as clarifying butter. Cf. the modern *ghee* in Hindi.

[2.1] *artichaux en cus* — properly "artichoke bottoms".

[2.2] Most of the "recipes" in this chapter involve either a pickling or a marination. For the former vinegar is present in most treatments. Soaking in a brine remains as well a very important means of preserving foodstuffs in the seventeenth century: the following Chapter XXIII will be devoted exclusively to this latter procedure.

In humoral terms, leafy vegetables generally were perceived as having a moist or cool temperament, or both. Salt, being extremely warm and dry in nature, afforded an ideal condiment or conditioner for such foodstuffs; vinegar, though moist, had likewise very warm properties, and pickling was deemed an appropriate treatment for those vegetables, such as roots, closely enough associated with the earth to share in its dry and cold nature.

with some piece of lard or grease. When they have cooked, serve them with a white sauce or garnished.[2.3]

3. Cucumbers

Get very small cucumbers and blanch them in cool water. Stick them with cloves, then put them into a pot with salt, pepper, vinegar and bay leaf; cover them over so tightly that no air can get at them. Serve them in a salad.[3]

4. Purslane

Purslane is done in the same way as the cucumber; you can serve them together.

5. Lettuce

Select the tightest heads of lettuce and remove their big leaves, blanch them in cool water and drain them. When have drained, stick them with cloves, season them with salt, pepper, vinegar and bay leaf, and cover them well. When you want to use them, desalt them.[5] Then, after cooking them, you serve them as a garnish or in a salad.

6. Truffles

Boil truffles in the best full-bodied wine[6] you can get, salt, pepper and cloves. Then take them out and put them into a pot with salt, pepper, vinegar, cloves and a few bay leaves, covering them well. When you want to use them, desalt them and cook them in some wine. Serve them in a pleated napkin.

7. Beetroots

Wash beetroots very clean and cook them. When done, peel them and put them into a pot with salt, pepper and vinegar for use whenever you want.

6. Trouffles.

[2.3] The so-called white sauce is the mixture of egg yolks and verjuice which is much used in La Varenne. He offers no suggestions for the alternative garnishing.

[3] That is, "as a salad preparation," uncooked, raw. Recipe 10 opposes *en salade* and "cooked".

[5] *faites les dessaller*: that is, remove the preservative seasoning from them. This direction is regularly given in these recipes, whatever the preserving agent is in each case. In Recipe 2 warm water is used for the "desalting".

[6] *du meilleur gros vin*: For his English readers I. D. G. puts "the best strong wine."

8. Asparagus

To keep asparagus, put the stalks into a pot with some melted butter, vinegar, salt, pepper and cloves, and cover them over well. To use them, desalt them; when that is done, cook them in hot water. When cooked, serve them with a white sauce, or else as a garnish on pottages, or in a salad or in pastry.

9. Green Peas

Take peas directly from their pod, sauté them in some butter and season them as if you were going to eat them directly, but do not fricassee them quite so much. Then put them in a crock, season them again, cover them over tightly and put the pot in a cool place. When you want to use them, desalt them and sauté them as before.

10. Chicory

Tie up chicory and blanch it in some sand.[10.1] When you think it can be kept, clean it carefully and put it into a pot with salt, pepper, a little vinegar and rosemary. When you need it, desalt it, for use in a salad, or for cooking as a garnish, or in a stuffing.[10.2]

11. Mushrooms

Select the firmest and most russet-coloured[11.1] mushrooms you can find; fricassee them whole in some butter as if for eating directly. When they have fricasseed and are well seasoned, put them into a pot with more seasoning, some butter and a dash of vinegar until they are steeped; cover them air-tight. To use them, steep them in several changes of warm water; then afterwards fricassee them as if they had come directly out of the ground.

[10.1] This procedure is curious and unique in La Varenne. Presumably the sand is seen to act as an efficient abrasive.

[10.2] Nicolas de Bonnefons has a little chapter dealing with chicory (*Delices de la campagne*, Paris, Anthoine Cellier, 1662, Book II, Ch. XXIV, p. 140; bound with the same author's *Jardinier françois*, 8th edn., Paris, A. Cellier, 1666): " ... Chicory is put in a pottage with other herbs; parboiled and drained, it is seasoned as other entremets; whole, it is used to cover pottages or it is served separately. With oil and vinegar it is used for cooked salads; in raw salads, with oil and viengar or else sugar."

[11.1] In La Varenne's terminology the word *rouges* denotes an orangy, rusty colour. Carrots, for instance, are white or *rouges*.

11.
Champignons.

Another way

Get the largest and broadest mushrooms and blanch them in their own moisture between two dishs, and drain them. Then marinate them in vinegar, salt, pepper and lemon or orange peel. When they have marinated for a while, take them out and fry them in some clarified butter with a little flour. When they are done, put them into another marinade if you want to keep them a long time. You can serve them as a garnish or in fritters or stuffed.[11.2]

12. Cabbage

Get the tightest heads of cabbage, slice an X into them[12] on the side where the stem is, then blanch them in cool water. Dry them and put them into a salting-vat or a pot with some salt, pepper, vinegar, and bay leaves or a little rosemary; you can stick them with cloves. When you want to use them, desalt them in warm water; put them into a pottage but not into a salad. When they have cooked, serve them.

13. Sole

Get very fresh sole and clean them; if they are big, makes slits on their back. After drying them, flour them, then half-fry them in some butter or oil. Put them neatly[13.1] into a pot with salt, pepper, ground cloves, orange or lemon peel, covering them over well. To use them, remove them from the pot and steep them in some water. When they are desalted, fry them in some butter — or in some oil, for those who like it — and do not forget to flour them well. Serve them with oranges or lemon[s]. Alternatively[13.2] if you like, after having sautéed them in a pan, open [and remove] their back bone, and put them into a ragout: for that, put in some capers, anchovies, mushrooms, truffles and whatever you can get, then simmer them. Serve with the sauce thickened, and orange or lemon juice.

14. Oysters

Take oysters out of their shell and blanch them; or else just as they come from the basket put them into a pot, seasoned with salt, pepper,

---

[11.2] See Recipe VIII,73 for Stuffed Mushrooms.

[12] *les incisez en quatre*: these cuts seem intended to improve both the blanching and the marinating of the heads of cabbage.

[13.1] That is, presumably, whole, without breaking them.

[13.2] This treatment resembles the *Solles en ragoût* of Recipe XVI,1.

ground cloves and the odd bay leaf; cover them well. Alternatively, if you like, you can dump oysters into a barrel.[14] When you want to use them, desalt them in warm water; when they are desalted, you can garnish with them or make fritters with them or fricassee them.

15. Salted Cockscombs

Their blood has to be drained from them; then they are put into a pot with dissolved salt, pepper, cloves, a dash of vinegar and the odd bay leaf. Cover them over well and put them in a place which is neither warm nor cold. When you want to use them, take out whatever amount you need and set them to desalt in some warm water, changing the water very often. When they are thoroughly desalted, boil some water and scald them. When they are very clean, cook them in some bouillon or water; when almost done, add in a bouquet of herbs, some butter or lard, and a slice of lemon. When they are well cooked, use them to garnish whatever you like.

15. Creſtes ſallées.

---

[14] This *baril* is likely the salting-vat, *un salloir*, spoken of in Recipe 12, above.

Chapter XXIII

Things to Salt for Keeping,
particularly for a Pastry Chef

1. Midribs of Artichoke

Select the whitest feet, cut them about half a foot long, remove their choke fully and set them to soak in cool water, changing it two or three times; blanch them, drain them and dry them. Put them into a pot and salt them. When they are salted, melt and clarify[1] a pound of butter, and pour it over them to put them away for keeping. Use them as you need them.

2. Beef Palates

Salt beef palates as they come out of the head, and put them away until you need them. Then have them desalted; when that is done, cook them and remove the skin on them and their barbs;[2] then cut them up into chunks or slices. Put them in a ragout, or use them to garnish whatever needs them, even in pastry, for which they can be very useful.

3. Mutton Tongues

As mutton tongues are taken out of the head, salt them. When you need them, desalt them and cook them. When they are done, dress them properly, split them and put them on the grill with breadcrumbs and salt. When they have been roasted, make up a sauce with verjuice, a dash of vinegar, chopped parsley, bread crust crumbs and a little bouillon; simmer them in that. Serve them.

4. Marinated Chicken

When chicken are dressed, split them in half. Dry them well, flour them and half-fry them. Then put them into a pot with salt, pepper, vinegar and fine herbs; keep them covered until you have a use for them.

2. Palets de bœuf.

---

[1] This procedure has been described in Recipe 1 of the preceding chapter.

[2] La Varenne's term, *barbillons*, refers to the rough processes along the palates. I. D. G. merely keeps the French term here, although he does gloss the word elsewhere: "*Barbillons*. They are the second skin of the pallats of beef."

Then desalt them in either cool or, preferably, warm water. When that is done, dry them, flour them, then fry them. When they are done, serve them. If you want to make an impression with them,[4] you need to make a thickener with eggs and flour; fry them and set them in the sauce with orange juice.

5. Ram's Kidneys

Remove the kidneys' outer membrane,[5] and slit their top to let them absorb salt. Put them in a pot [with a saline solution] and in a cool place. To use them, desalt and cook them, and then use them however you like.

6. Squab

After flattening squab, dry them, flour them and fry them. Then put them into a pot, with vinegar, pepper, cloves and fine herbs. When you want to use them, have them desalted[6] for use in a ragout or in a pottage or a pie, or else serve them marinated.

7. Salted Butter

Wash the butter well in cool water, drain it, then put it into a terrine; knead it with white salt, whole cloves, a few bay leaves, and with ground anise if you like. After that, put it into a pot and cover it tightly with a piece of paper or parchment. After removing its water,[7] put it into the cellar to be used as needed.

7. Beurre salé.

---

[4] *qu'ils paroissent* in the text. I. D. G. gives the sense of this with, "If you will have them to make a shew."

[5] Or "skin" as I. D. G. puts for *robbe*.

[6] No salt is included among the ingredients of the marinade. The term *dessaller* means generally to "remove the preserving agents."

[7] This water will tend to rise to the surface of the butter and is to be taken off.

Chapter XXIV

Lenten Bouillons[xxiv]
of Fish, Herbs and Almonds, and Pea Purée

1. Fish Bouillon

Your bouillon has to be made of water and purée[1.1] in equal amounts. Get the bones of carp or some other fish, with an onion stuck with cloves, a bouquet of herbs and some salt. Cook everything together well with breadcrumbs and some butter, then strain it. Use it for whatever bouillons you like, except for herb bouillons, pea purée and a number of bouillons that are made without fish.

You can use it in crayfish pottage,[1.2] bringing it to a boil with the shells of your crayfish, ground-up and strained through a cloth — whereby your bouillon will become russet coloured. After that you strain everything, seasoning it, then set it out and simmer it.

2. Pea Purée

To make a thin purée which is good,[2.1] steep your peas overnight after having cleaned them carefully. Then set them to cook in warm river water or fountain water.[2.2] When they are almost done, draw out your purée. Then use it for whatever purpose you like.

[xxiv] This chapter and the next four, XXV, XXVI, XXVII and XXVIII, are devoted to preparations proper for serving during Lent. The sequence of these chapters is that followed for meat days and ordinary lean days: bouillons, pottages, entrées, second course dishes, entremets. In some respects — the prohibition of eggs, for instance — the dishes in these chapters differ in a regular way from ordinary lean-day preparations.

[1.1] A recipe for pea purée follows.

[1.2] A recipe for this *Potage d'escrevisses* is the second in Chapter XV on Lean Pottages.

[2.1] Later printers enthusiastically change this *bonne* to *excellente*.

[2.2] Well water is excluded as a possibility. This specific concern about the proper cooking water for peas is found already back in the fourteenth century. *Potage de Pois Vielz. Couvient eslire, et savoir aux gens du lieu la nature des poiz d'icelluy lieu. (Car communement les pois ne cuisent pas d'eaue de puis* [well water]*; et en aucuns lieux ilz cuisent bien d'eaue de fontaine et de eaue de riviere* [fountain water, river water]*, comme a Paris; et en autres lieux ilz ne cuisent point de eaue de fontaine et d'eaue de* [riviere]*, comme a Besiers.) Et ce sceu, il les couvient*

3. Herb Bouillon

You will find the recipe for herb bouillon among the Lean-Day Pottages.[3] As it is a common preparation, there is no need to repeat the recipe here.

4. Almond Bouillon

Skin all your almonds in some very hot water, then grind them in a mortar. As you grind them, sprinkle them with cool water. When they are thoroughly ground up, put them with some fish bouillon and breadcrumbs, then boil all of that with salt, butter, an onion stuck [with cloves] and a lemon peel whose outer skin[4] is removed. When that is cooked, put it through a strainer and into a pot until you need it.

To make your almond bouillon with milk, skin your almonds; grind them, sprinkling them with milk from time to time. When they are ground, put them with some very fresh milk, some breadcrumbs, some salt, a few cloves and a little cinnamon; bring it all to a boil and then put it through a strainer. When you are ready to serve, set it to boil with some sugar. Serve.

Bouillon d'amandes.

---

laver en une paelle avec de l'eaue tiede, puis mectre en ung pot . . . . Menagier de Paris, ed. Georgine E. Brereton and Janet M. Ferrier (Oxford: Clarendon Press, 1981), §29.

[3] The first recipe of Chapter XV is for a *Potage aux herbes*.

[4] That *peau de dessus* would be the lemon's zest.

Chapter XXV
Lenten Pottages[xxv.1]

All Lenten pottages are made and seasoned like those for lean days, except that you do not put in any eggs. Rather, into some Lenten pottages you mix some pea purée; into others, those you wish to serve white or marbled, you put some almond bouillon. Simmer them the same way as the lean-day pottages, and garnish them the same. After the Table will be indicated which ones take almond bouillon and which pea purée.[xxv.2]

1. Crayfish Pottage[1]
Serve it with pea purée.

2. Pottage of Carp Hash[2.1]
Make it with pea purée and almond [bouillon].[2.2]

3. Herb Pottage[3]
With very little pea purée.

4. Pottage of Stuffed Tench with Turnips[4.1]
With starch[4.2] and little pea purée.

[xxv.1] Lent required special dishes or a special treatment of dishes. Most of the recipes in this chapter take up dishes described in Chapter XV for Lean Pottages, but require some minor variation in them. Only a few recipes here (for instance Recipe 24) expressly allow the cook to use pottages that might be prepared for ordinary lean days — that is, those that fall outside the forty days of Lent. A prime distinction between the two sorts of dishes is the Lenten prohibition against the consumption of eggs, permissible on lean days outside of Lent: see the general preamble here, as well as Recipe 29, for instance, and the rubric for the next chapter, XXVI: *Entrées qui se font en Caresme, & où il n'entre point d'œufs.*

[xxv.2] This paragraph precedes the Table at the head of this Chapter XXV.

[1] See the details of this dish in Recipe XV,2.

[2.1] See Recipes XV,3 and XVI,11.

[2.2] La Varenne has only *purée & amandes* here and in a couple of subsequent recipes, but has indicated "almond bouillon" in the above preamble.

[3] See Recipe XV,1.

[4.1] See Recipe XV,4. The turnips are not the stuffing but, as in Recipe 40, below, a garnish or flavouring agent.

[4.2] For this "fried flour", *fleur fritte*, see Recipe XXV,40. See also the *farine frite* of

5. Queen's Pottage[5]

With bouillon of carp or of some other fish, mixed with some pea purée and almond [bouillon].

6. Princess Pottage[6]

It is made with pea purée that you cook with carp bones.

7. Tortoise Pottage[7]

With pea purée.

8. Mushroom Pottage[8]

With pea purée.

9. Sole Pottage[9]

With pea purée.

10. Smelt Pottage[10]

With good bouillon mixed with almond [bouillon].

11. Asparagus Pottage[11]

With pea purée and herbs.

12. Pottage of Haslets[12]

Draw it from the best bouillon.

13. Lettuce Pottage[13]

With pea purée.

Recipe 20, below.

[5] See Recipe XV,7.

[6] See Recipe XV,8.

[7] See Recipe XV,9.

[8] See Recipe XV,10, *Potage de champignons farcis.*

[9] See Recipe XV,11, *Potage de Solle[s] desossées, farcies.*

[10] See Recipe XV,12.

[11] See Recipe XV,13.

[12] See Recipe XV,14.

[13] See Recipe XV,15, *Potage de laictuës farcies.*

14. Cabbage Pottage with Fried Bread[14]

[With] only a little pea purée.

15. Cabbage Pottage with Milk[15]

[With] only a little pea purée and a great deal of butter.

16. Cabbage Pottage with Pea Purée[16]

Into your pea purée put an onion stuck with cloves, and pepper and salt. When it has cooked, serve it well garnished with your cabbage and the odd piece of fried bread which you have cooked along with the rest.

17. Pumpkin Pottage[17.1]

Cook your pumpkin[17.2] well, so that it is a little thicker than normal. Then fricassee a scallion in some butter; put it in with the pumpkin, along with some salt. Then serve it sprinkled with pepper.

18. Pumpkin Pottage with Milk[18]

When the pumpkin has been cooked, put it through a strainer — and don't let as much bouillon go through as might, because of the milk that has to go in. When the pumpkin purée is well seasoned with milk and a little butter, steep your bread. Then serve it, sprinkled with pepper if you like.

19. Turnip Pottage with White Bouillon

Scrape your turnips and put them into a pot with some water [to cook]. When they are well cooked, season them with salt and a bouquet of herbs. When you wish to make up your dish, take them off the fire and add in some very fresh butter and stir it away from the fire without putting it back on. Then serve them with a little almond bouillon over the top.

Potage de citrouille au laiĉt.

17.

---

[14] See Recipe XV,17. There is no recipe number on this rubric and it is omitted from the Table that precedes the chapter. I. D. G. assigns it the number 14, as we do. From this point on, La Varenne's numbers are one less than are shown here.

[15] See Recipe XV,16.

[16] See Recipe XV,18.

[17.1] See Recipe XV,19 where the more descriptive title is *Potage de citrouille au beurre.*

[17.2] The author probably means the strained purée of the pumpkin flesh.

[18] See Recipe XV,20.

20. Pottage of Fried Turnips[20.1]

Scrape them and cut them in half or otherwise; blanch them and flour them; when they have dried, fry them. Set them to cook in some water with a little pepper and an onion stuck with cloves. When you wish to make up your dish, if your bouillon is not thick, you can put in a little starch[20.2] along with a dash of vinegar. Then serve.

21. Pea Purée Pottage[21.1]

Get the thinnest pea purée and put it into a pot. Then sauté some sorrel, some chervil and a little parsley in some butter; put everything into a pot and cook it well; season it well. Simmer your pottage and serve it [garnished] with parsley roots cooked with it.[21.2]

22. [Herb] Pottage without Butter[22]

Herb Pottage is made with a lot of well seasoned herbs, cooked with a bread crust. Simmer and serve.

23. Profiterole Pottage[23.1]

Draw it from several different bouillons.[23.2] Then open six loaves[23.3] that you have made expressly for this purpose; make a hole through their tops and remove their soft inside. Sauté them in butter and fill them with carp milt, mushrooms and broken asparagus stalks — note that these have to be cooked before being put in. When they are filled, set them to simmer gently on[23.4] your pottage, which you garnish with milt, mushrooms and broken asparagus stalks. Then serve.

22. Potage de profiteolles.

[20.1] See Chapter XV,21.

[20.2] This so-called "fried flour" is a staple that is on hand in La Varenne's kitchen; directions for making it are found in Recipe XXV,40. But see also Pierre de Lune's directions for his so-called *farine frite* quoted in a note to Recipe V,42.

[21.1] Compare this recipe with the *Potage de purée de poix verts* at Recipe XV,46.

[21.2] For some bizarre reason later typesetters put "parsley roots cooked with pistachios" here.

[22] See Recipe XV,25. The recipe's title there is *Potage d'herbes sans beurre.*

[23.1] See Recipe XV,23.

[23.2] *Tirez le de plusieurs bouillons*: I. D. G. has "Take it out of many broths."

[23.3] These will be similar in modern terms to large, crusty buns or rolls.

[23.4] The preposition "on" is to be noted: *Mettez les mittonner tout à loisir sur vôtre potage* .... The dish, or pottage, is "built up" by the addition of the stuffed buns and then garnished.

24. Onion Pottage

Onion Pottage is done the same way as outside of Lent: see among the Lean-Day Pottages.[24]

25. Mussel Pottage

Mussel Pottage is also done the same way as outside of Lent,[25] except that you put no eggs into it; you can put in some almond bouillon or some sort of ragout. Serve it garnished with mussels.

26. Frogs' Legs Pottage[26.1]

Break the [legs'] bones, truss them up, then blanch and drain them. Put them into a dish until you have made up a bouillon of pea purée putting into it[26.2] a little chopped parsley and butter. When it has boiled, put the frogs' legs into your bouillon and take them right out again. Moisten a little saffron and put it into your pot; steep your bread [in that]; garnish it with your frogs' legs and serve.

27. Gurnard Pottage[27]

Gurnard Pottage is done the same way as for lean days during meat-season: you will find it there.

28. Salmon Pottage with a Sweet Sauce[28]

Cut salmon into slices and set to marinate. Sauté your slices in a pan in some butter; stick them with cloves and then put them between two dishes with some butter, a bouquet of herbs, sugar, wine, a little salt and well-ground pepper; let that simmer. Then dry your bread and steep it too in some other bouillon; then garnish it with your salmon slices, with the sauce on top; and, if you like, garnish with figs or brignol plums.

29. Bran Pottage[29]

Bran Pottage is done in the same way as on lean days except that you put in no eggs.

---

[24] Recipe XV,26.

[25] See Recipe XV,29.

[26.1] See the first half of Recipe XV,33, *Potage de grenouilles au saffran*.

[26.2] The instruction *passez y* is ambiguous: the parsley should possibly be sautéed in butter before being added to the pea purée.

[27] See Recipe XV,31.

[28] See Recipe XV,32.

[29] See Recipe XV,34.

30. Frogs' Legs Pottage with Almonds[30]

You will find this among the Pottages for Lean Days: do it the same, but don't put in any eggs.

31. Hops Pottage[31]

Make a pea purée bouillon and set it to boil; sauté a few good, well chopped herbs and put them into the pot. Blanch your hops, then cook them in the pot. Just before serving up, take them out and put them in some butter, salt, nutmeg, vinegar and very little bouillon. When they are well seasoned, steep your bread; garnish it with your hops, making up your dish. Then serve.

32. Parsnip Pottage

This is done the same as on lean days, except that you do it with some pea purée and don't put in any eggs.[32]

33. Leek Pottage with Milk[33]

Cut up your leeks very small; blanch them and dry them, then cook them in thin pea purée. When they are done, add in some milk, pepper, salt and cloves. Steep your bread; garnish it with your leeks. Then serve.

34. Pottage of Broken Asparagus Stalks[34.1]

Break or cut your asparagus stalks and fricassee them in good butter, along with salt, pepper, chopped parsley and chives, simmering everything all together. Then make a bouillon of pea purée or of an herb pottage that you strain. Steep your bread, too, and garnish it with your asparagus. Then serve. You can add in mushroom stock[34.2] and mushrooms in a ragout.

---

[30] See Recipe XV,33, second version.

[31] See Recipe XV,35.

[32] The Chapter on Lean Pottages, XV, does not have a recipe for these *panets*. In XX,6 the alternative lean entrée for parsnips refers back to Recipe XX,1, for skirrets, into which eggs enter.

[33] See Recipe XV,38.

[34.1] See Recipe XV,41.

[34.2] For this sub-preparation, see Recipe XI,1.

35. Cauliflower Pottage[35]

Dress them, and blanch them in cool water. Then put them into a pot with good bouillon or some pea purée, well seasoned with butter, salt and an onion stuck with cloves. When they have cooked such that they have not broken apart, steep your bread, garnish it with your cauliflowers and serve. You can add in some milk and some pepper.

36. Vermicelli Pottage[36.1]

Cook vermicelli in some water or some milk. When they are done, and well seasoned, take out some of them for fricasseeing;[36.2] with the rest make a pottage with butter, salt, pepper and onion stuck [with cloves]. Serve.

37. Rice Pottage[37]

Rice Pottage is done in the same way as the one for vermicelli. Cook the rice until it has burst all open, then serve.

38. Pottage of Pastry Fingers[38.1]

This is done the same way, except that, when the fingers of pastry are cooked,[38.2] you can put in a very little saffron and some very fresh butter. You can also put in some milk to make them runny.[38.3] With everything well seasoned, serve.

39. Pottage of Scoter Duck in Ragout

You can find this pottage among the Lean Pottages,[39] and you make it the same way — but you don't put in any eggs.

---

[35] See Recipe XV,42.

[36.1] See Recipe XV,43.

[36.2] The fate of these fricasseed vermicelli (*fidelles*) is not explicitly followed.

[37] See Recipe XV,44.

[38.1] See the *Potage de tailladins* of Recipe XV,45.

[38.2] The participle used here is *cuits*, which I. D. G. renders as "sod", boiled. In the earlier, lean-day version, the pastry is sautéed before being simmered very briefly in bouillon.

[38.3] *liquides*. This adjective is used with pastry dough to describe a batter.

[39] A recipe for *Macreuse en ragoust* is among the lean entrées, XVI,39. However, no eggs are mentioned there.

40. Pottage of Scoter Duck with Turnip[40]

When the scoter is dressed, lard it with eel. Give it a turn on the spit, or sauté it in a pan in some butter. Then put it into a pot in some water, pea purée and a bouquet of herbs. When it has almost cooked, sauté some turnips in a pan, put these with your scoter, then season it all well. To thicken your pottage, sauté a little flour in a pan until it is brownish, moisten it with a dash of vinegar and put it in your pot. When that has come to a boil, steep your bread with your garnishing. Serve.

41. Pottage of Leeks in Pea Purée[41]

When they have been blanched in cool water, put the leeks into your pea purée along with capers; season them well. When they have cooked, steep your bread and garnish it with your leeks. Serve.

42. Dab Pottage[42]

Steep your bread with some of your best bouillon and garnish it with your dab which you have fried in a pan and put into a ragout with mushrooms, capers and asparagus. Then serve.

43. Red Mullet Pottage[43]

Dress red mullets and put them into a skillet with a bouquet of herbs and a little white wine; well seasoned. Steep your bread in some other bouillon and garnish it with your red mullets along with their sauce. Then serve.

44. Lentil Pottage

When lentils have been well cooked, and seasoned with butter, salt and a bouquet of herbs, dish them out and serve. You can put them, salted, on the pottage with some oil.

Escoffier, *Lentilles au beurre*, §2166

40. Potage de poireaux à la purée.

---

[40] See Recipe XV,48.

[41] See Recipe XV,50.

[42] See Recipe XV,51.

[43] See Recipe XV,56.

Chapter XXVI

Lenten Entrées
Containing no Eggs

Note

This Table[xxvi] did not seem very necessary, any more than the following ones, particularly as what is itemized here is prepared the same as at other times except that no eggs are put in, either for thickening or for any other purpose. Rather, as a thickener, instead of eggs you can get carp or eel flesh, with butter, which thickens much better than eggs. That is why I have left out all the directions except in the case of the last five dishes, about which I have not previously written; I thought it proper to insert their recipes here.

1. Sole [XVI,1 Sole in Ragout; XXII,13][1]

2. Pike [XVI,2 Pike in Ragout]

3. Stuffed Tench [XVI,4 Stuffed Tench in Ragout]

4. Fried Tench [XVI,5 Fried Marinated Tench]

5. Stewed Carp [XVI,6]

[xxvi] The listing of dishes suitable for serving as *entrées qui se font en Caresme* is much more ample than the recipes that are actually printed in this Chapter XXVI itself — 88 dishnames against five recipes. That will continue to be the case for Chapters XXVII and XXVIII. La Varenne assumed that his reader would be familiar enough with the contents of previous chapters in his book to be able to find all of the earlier recipes for dishes listed in the Tables of Chapters XXVI, XXVII and XXVIII but for which he doesn't reprint the recipe. We reproduce all of the items that appear in the three Tables, assigning numbers to the dishnames and recipes which they do not have in the original and indicating the location of the recipe that La Varenne probably intended his reader to turn to.

[1] As the author has just explained, the recipes for all but five of the dishes in the Table to this chapter have appeared earlier (generally in Chapter XVI on lean entrées) and so are not reproduced here. For this translation the number (or numbers) in brackets indicates the location of what is likely the recipe (or recipes) whose dish name is here; the name of the earlier recipe is also shown if it differs.

6. Stuffed Carp [XVI,7 Stuffed Carp in Ragout]

7. Roast Carp [XVI,9. Roast Carp in Ragout]

8. Fried Carp in Ragout [XVI,8]

9. Salmon [XVI,13 Salmon in Ragout; XVIII,5 (?)]

10. Carp Hash [XVI,11]

11. Stewed Salmon [XVI,14]

12. Burbot [XVI,16 Burbot in Ragout]

13. Stewed Burbot [XVI,17]

14. Carp in a Half Court-Bouillon [XVI,10]

15. Oysters [XVI,18 Oysters in a Half Court-Bouillon, Salted; XXII,14]

16. Oysters in Ragout [XVI,19]

17. Oysters in the Shell on the Grill [XVI,21 Roast Oysters]

18. Chub in Ragout [XVI,22]

19. Roast Chub in a Court-Bouillon and Roasted [XVI,23]

20. Dace [XVI,26 Roast Dace without Stuffing]

21. Barbel [XVI,28–32 (various preparations)]

22. Brill [XVI,33 Brill in a Casserole]

23. Dab in a Casserole [XVI,34]

24. Fried Dab [XVI,35]

25. Roast Dab [XVI,36]

26. Plaice in Ragout [XVI,37 (?) Plaice in a Casserole]

27. Fried Plaice [XVI,38 (?) Roast Plaice]

28. Scoter Duck [XVI,39 Scoter Duck in Ragout]

29. Scoter Duck in a Court-Bouillon [XVI,40]

30. Roast Scoter Duck [XVI,41]

31. Roast Shad [XVI,43 Roast Shad in Ragout; XVIII,17]

32. Shad in a Court-Bouillon, Roasted [XVI,44; XVIII,16]

33. Lamprey [XVI,46 Lamprey in Ragout]

34. Grilled Lamprey [XVI,47 Grilled Lamprey in Ragout]

35. Lamprey in a Sweet Sauce [XVI,48]

36. Stewed Lamprey

37. Eel Saveloy [XVI,51; XIX,12]

38. Stewed Eel [XVI,50]

39. Eel in a Half Court-Bouillon [XVI,52 Eel in Ragout (?)]

40. Stewed Sea Eel [XVI,54]

41. Sea Eel Fried and Stewed [XVI,55 Fried Sea Eel in Ragout]

42. Lobster in a Court-Bouillon [XVI,56]

43. Fricasseed Lobster in a White Sauce [XVI,57]

44. Crawfish in a Court-Bouillon [XVI,58]

45. Crawfish in a White Sauce [XVI,59]

46. Stuffed Pike [XVI,60]

47. Stuffed Pike Roasted on the Spit [XVI,61]

48. Roast Mackerel [XVI,62 Roast Fresh Mackerel]

49. Roast Fresh Herrings [XVI,63]

50. Fresh Herrings in a Russet Sauce [XVI,64]

51. Royan Sardines [XVI,65]

52. Red Mullet [XVI,66]

53. Gurnard [XVI,67 Gurnard in Ragout]

54. Roast Fresh Cod [XVI,68 Fresh Roast Cod in Ragout]

55. Fresh Cod in Half Court-Bouillon [XVI,69]

56. Newfoundland Cod [XVI,71]

57. Fish Cake [XVI,72]

58. Fish Ham [XVI,73; XIX,24]

59. Mussels [XVI,74]

60. Fried Rayfish [XVIII,14]

61. Rayfish in a Court-Bouillon

62. Fried Rayfish in Ragout [XVI,75]

63. Smelt [XVI,76]

64. Cod Tripe [XVI,77 Fricasseed Cod Tripe]

65. Cuttlefish [XVI,78 Fricasseed Cuttlefish]

66. Fried Hake [XVI,79]

67. Hake in Oil [XVI,80]

68. Fricasseed Hake [XVI,80. Hake in Sauce Robert]

69. Salmon in a Russet Sauce[69] [XVI,13 (?); XVI,81 (?)]

70. Salmon in Oil, Onion and Vinegar; or in a Salad, if you like[70] [XVI,82 Jowl, or Sandwich, of Salmon in a Salad (?)]

71. Salted Mackerel [XVI,84]

72. Stewed Herrings [XVI,85]

73. Smoked Herrings [XVI,86]

74. Salted Herrings [XVI,85]

75. Peas. Pea Purée [XX,19; XXIV,2]

76. Beetroots [XX,9; XXII,7]

---

[69] The printed text reads *Saumon à la sauce rousse*. A similar sequence of recipes in Chapter XVI contains a *Hure de saumon à la sauce rousse* (Recipe 81). However, a sweet preparation of salmon is relatively common: *cf.* Recipes XVIII,35, XXV,28 and XXVII,8. Later printers change the name of this dish to *Saumon à la sauce douce*. Inexplicably, the name of the next recipe is changed with the addition of the word *rousse* to qualify "oil".

[70] Later versions of the book show *Saumon à l'huile rousse* here. The next titles immediately after that are *Saumon en salade* and *Saumon à l'étuvée*, and then the Salted Mackerel.

77. Turnips [XX,12]

78. Carrots [XX,8, 14]

79. Parsnips [XX,6]

80. Jerusalem Artichokes [XX,10]

81. Salsify [XX,7]

82. Skirrets [XX,1]

83. Midribs of Chard [XX,17]

Lentilles.

84. Lentils[84]

When lentils have been well cooked, sauté them in a pan in fresh butter with salt, pepper, a few fine herbs and chives. When they are well fricasseed, serve them.

Escoffier, *Purée de lentilles*, §2167

They can be served in a purée in the manner of pea purée. If you have trouble straining them, pound them in a mortar.

They can also be served with olive oil, sautéed in a pan.

Escoffier, *Epinards à la crème*, §2134

85. Spinach

Get the blondest leaves of spinach, and do not use the greener ones except for want of the others. Clean them well and wash them several times; draw off their moisture by placing them between two dishes. Season them with half the amount of butter as of spinach, along with salt, pepper, and a scallion or an onion stuck with cloves. Sauté all of that in a pan and let it simmer it in a covered dish. When ready to serve, you can add in nutmeg and cream — otherwise serve them as they are.

Some people boil them in some water, but they are not so good, even though afterwards you do them up the same way.

86. Fricasseed Apples

Pare your apples and cut them in rounds up to the core. Brown some butter and fricassee them with a little salt and pepper. If you have any cream you can add some in. Serve them after they have just come to a boil.

---

[84] A *Potage de lentilles* is found also in Recipe XXV,44.

87. Apples in Sugar

Get some apples, split them in half, core them and prick them on top with a knife point. Half-fill your dish with them, along with a little water, cinnamon, butter and a good amount of sugar. Cook them slowly with an oven lid or [of] a tourtière [on top].[87] When they have cooked, serve them sprinkled with sugar.

88. Prunes

Get Tours prunes, or ordinary ones, and wash and clean them well. When they are very clean, cook them slowly in a pot. When they are half done, add in some sugar; when the bouillon is about to become syrup, serve them.

If you do not want to put sugar in while they are cooking, when the syrup[88] is quite thickened, sprinkle them with sugar and serve.

Pruneaux.

Note

Many people will eat nothing but [olive] oil, and they have to be served as they wish. So, to keep oil from smelling, boil it with a crust of burnt toast. After that you can serve it freely, like butter.

---

[87] The alternative La Varenne is suggesting may be that the apples be transferred to a tourtière for baking.

[88] We may wonder whether the word *syrop* here is in error, perhaps for *bouillon*.

Chapter XXVII
The Second Course in Lent[xxvii.1]

1. Turbot [XVIII,1]

2. Brill [XVIII,2]

3. Brill in a Casserole [XVI,33]

4. Weever [XVIII,3]

5. Sole [XXII,13 (?)]

6. Sole in Ragout [XVI,1]

7. Salmon [XVI,13 Salmon in Ragout (?); XVIII,5 Salmon in a Court-Bouillon (?)]

8. Salmon in a Sweet Sauce [XVI,13 (?)]

9. Gurnard [XVIII,7]

10. Porpoise [XVIII,9 & 10]

11. Old Salmon [XVIII,8]

12. Sea-Otter [XVIII,12 & 13]

13. Salmon Trout [XVIII,23]

14. Rayfish [XVIII,14]

15. Smelt [XVIII,29]

16. Mackerels [XVIII,45]

17. Sardine[17] [XVI,65]

[xxvii.1] *Table du Second de Caresme*; in later editions this rubric is erroneously typeset as *Table du second Poisson*. There are no actual recipes in this chapter, only a list of suitable dishes. Here, as in Chapter XXVI, the numbering of the dishes is supplied for convenience. Likewise, too, the numbers in square brackets give the location of the recipes to which La Varenne is probably referring; for the most part these are listed in Chapter XVIII, which deals with the Second Course on ordinary lean days, though the actual recipe may appear elsewhere.

[17] In later editions this *Sardine* is typeset as *Sarrazines*.

18. Red Mullet [XVI,66]

19. Pike [XVI,2 (?); XVIII,20 Pike *au bleu* (?)]

20. Pike in a Sauce [XVIII,21]

21. Stuffed Pike [XVI,60]

22. Carp [XVI,6–11]

23. Carp Stuffed with Milt [XVIII,28]

24. Burbot [XVIII,25]

25. Burbot in Ragout [XVI,16]

26. Perch [XVIII,24 Perch in a Court-Bouillon]

27. Tench [XVIII,15 Tench in a Court-Bouillon]

28. Shad [XVI,43–45; XVIII,16 & 17 (?)]

29. Fresh Cod [XVIII,18]

30. Roast Bream [XVIII,19]

31. Plaice [XVIII,30]

32. Scoter Duck [XVI,39–42]

33. Carp in Half Court-Bouillon [XVI,10]

34. Fried Tench in Ragout [XVI,5]

35. Barbel in Ragout [XVI,28]

36. Chub in Ragout [XVI,22]

37. Gilthead in a Court-Bouillon

38. Roast Gilthead

39. Fresh Herrings [XVI,63 Roast Fresh Herrings]

Note

All these dishes of the Second Course in Lent are served the same way and with the same seasoning as on lean days during the rest of the year.

As for Lenten pastry, you will find that in the chapter for lean days.[xxvii.2] You do it up the same way and with the same seasoning, except that you do not put in any egg yolks. And you gild your pastry with ground pike eggs or with melted butter, because saffron is quite useless [for the purpose].

[xxvii.2] That is, specifically, in Chapter XXI.

Chapter XXVIII

Entremets in Lent[xxviii.1]

In the section for Lean Days you will find the way of doing up everything for Lenten *entremets*,[xxviii.2] with the exception of the following recipes that I have added.[xxviii.3]

1. Mushrooms [XIX,2 Creamed Mushrooms]

2. Cardoons

3. Midribs of Chard [XX,17]

4. Skirrets [XX,1]

5. Truffles in Ragout [XIX,3]

6. Whitedish [XIX,17]

7. Fried Artichokes [XIX,19]

8. Fried Mushrooms [XXII,11]

9. Tortoises [XIX,25 Tortoises in Ragout]

10. Spun Pastry [XIX,11]

11. Asparagus [XIX,20, 21]

12. Frangipane Tourte [XIX,7]

13. Eel Saveloy [XVI,51; XIX,12]

14. Fish Ham [XIX,24]

[xxviii.1] The numbering of the recipes in this chapter is supplied.

[xxviii.2] The text has *tout le Second du Caresme*, an apparent error as the chapter's rubric is *Entre-mets*[sic] *de Caresme*. This paragraph, in which La Varenne refers his reader to the location of most of the recipes listed in the table for this chapter, is placed after the table and before the first actual, "added" recipe, number 29 here.

[xxviii.3] La Varenne provides the text of only two recipes (Recipes 29 and 35), contenting himself with referring his reader to other parts of his book for the majority of the recipes he lists here. These other locations are indicated below in square brackets.

15. Fried Milt [XIX,13]

16. Milt in Ragout [XIX,14]

17. Burbot Liver [XIX,15]

18. Jelly of all Sorts of Fish [XIX,16]

19. Celery [XIX,22]

20. Ramekins of All Sorts [XIX,29; VIII,48–51]

21. Mushrooms à l'Olivier [VIII,75]

22. Morels

23. Prunes [XXVI,88]

24. Brignol Plums

25. Salsify [XX,7]

26. Skirrets [XX,1]

27. Little Musk Cream Tourte [XXI,35]

28. Spinach Tourte [XXI,29]

29. Rissoles

Escoffier, *Rissoles*, §2518

Get left-over carp hash, mushrooms and milt, and chop everything together, enriching it with butter and with cream if you have any; season it with a bouquet of herbs. Bring it all to a boil to thicken it better. Use that to make your rissoles. To do them up well, get puff-pastry dough, roll it out and on it put an amount of your mixture proportionate to the size [of rissoles] you want. Moisten them around their edges, cover them and gild them with butter, for want of pike eggs, because saffron is useless for that. When they have been gilded, put them in the oven. When they have baked, serve them.

Small rissoles are made with fine dough, and there should be less of it than for a small pie. When your shells are rolled out, fill them with a suitable amount, moisten their edges and close them. Then drop them into very hot clarified butter until they are cooked and yellow; take them out promptly. Then serve them.

If you put sugar in them, you should also sprinkle them with sugar on top when serving.

30. Fried Burbot [XVI,17]

31. Asparagus in Green Peas[31]

32. Fried Burbot Liver [XIX,15]

33. Fricasseed Crayfish [XVI,58 (?)]

34. Crayfish in Ragout

35. Frogs' Leg Fritters

    Pick out the finest and the biggest frogs' legs; do them as cherries[35.1] — that is, scrape your frogs' legs so that the bone at one end is bare. Blanch them extremely little and dry them. Make up a batter with flour, salt, milk and white cheese — very little of everything; beat it all in a mortar and liquify it until it is like a fritter batter. Take your frogs' legs by their bone end,[35.2] dip them into your mixture and drop them into some very hot butter; fry them like fritters. Serve them garnished with fried parsley.

Bocuse, *Grenouilles frites*, p. 147

Baignets de grenouilles.

36. Frogs' Legs in Ragout [XXV,26 (?)]

37. Crayfish in Ragout[37]

38. Milt Nulle[38]

---

[31] No recipe in the *Cuisinier françois* seems to correspond to this dish name of *Asperges en pois verds*. However, the Lenten Pottage of Recipe XXV,11 has asparagus served with pea purée.

[35.1] See this term, *en cerises*, also in Recipe XV,33.

[35.2] *par la queuë*: the "tail" of the leg is the bared bone, the so-called "cherry" stem.

[37] This entry repeats the listing at 34, above.

[38] This is likely to be be made along the line of the nulle in Recipe XIX,5 but with milt substituted for the egg yolks.

Chapter XXIX

Outline of what can be served on Good Friday[xxix]

1. Healthy Pottage[1]

You make this of sorrel, lettuce, chard, purslane and a bouquet of herbs. Cook it all with salt, butter and a bread crust. Simmer. Serve.

2. Pottage of Very Thin Pea Purée

You make this by putting into it a few herbs, some capers, a bouquet of herbs and an onion stuck with cloves. When it is well cooked, serve it garnished with fried bread.

3. Almond-Milk Pottage

For this you will find the directions among the Lenten Pottages.[3]

4. Turnip Pottage [XXV,19 & 20]

5. Parsnip Pottage [XXV,32]

6. Asparagus Pottage [XXV,11]

7. Pumpkin Pottage [XXV,17 & 18]

8. Profiterole Pottage[8.1]

To make Profiterole Pottage get five or six buns, open them on top and remove their inside; then dry them by the fire or brown them in some fresh butter in a pan. Simmer them in a bouillon made for the purpose

---

[xxix] Though not expressly stated, this chapter presents options for the Pottage course alone; Chapter XXX will list possibilities for the entrée course. Only the two courses seem to have been normal fare on Good Friday. As before, the recipes here have been numbered for this translation. Where only the dish name is given, bracketted numbers refer to corresponding recipes that La Varenne has printed previously.

[1] Compare this with the *Potage de santé* that is found in Recipe III,2.

[3] There is, in fact, no similar recipe in Chapter XXV; see Recipe XV,58 for an ordinary lean-day pottage of this name. However, this and the preceding recipe do deal with the two fundamental ingredients used in Lenten Pottages and mentioned in the preamble to that Chapter XXV.

[8.1] See Recipe XXV,23 (a Lenten pottage). The process is echoed in Recipes XV,23 (a regular lean pottage) and III,10 (a meat-day pottage).

with mushrooms, pea purée and onion stuck with cloves, everything well seasoned and previously sautéed. Use that bouillon to make your pottage. Garnish your dish with your dried buns and fill them up with little seasonings,[8.2] such as truffles, artichokes, asparagus and fried mushrooms; garnish around the dish with lemon and pomegranate seeds and, if you like, sprinkle your pottage with mushroom stock.[8.3] Then serve.

9. Broccoli Pottage

Broccoli is the sprouts of new cabbage.[9] Cook them in some water with some salt, pea purée, butter, onion stuck with cloves and a little pepper. Simmer your crust, garnish it with your broccoli and make up your dish with it; then serve.

The same pottage can be made with milk and garnished the same way.

10. Hops Pottage[10]

This is made the same as the Broccoli Pottage and is garnished the same way.

11. Queen's Pottage

Queen's Pottage is made the same way as the Lenten one,[11] with the exception that you make a hash of mushrooms to garnish your bread with. When it is made up and sautéed several times in a pan, garnish the top with pistachios, pomegranate seeds and sliced lemons.

[8.2] *de petits ragousts*: little taste enhancers or flavour heighteners.

[8.3] For this, see Recipe XI,1.

[9] *des reiettons de choux verds*. This is a helpful definition because La Varenne seems to be using Italian broccoli (*Brassica oleracea italica* Plenck). Otherwise known as sprouting broccoli, it does not form solid heads as does today's commonly known variety but rather flowerlets on a stalk. See William Woys Weaver, *Heirloom Vegetable Gardening* (New York: Henry Holt, 1997); and Alan Davidson's *Oxford Companion to Food*, s.v. "broccoli", p. 108.

[10] Directions for this *Potage d'oublon* have already been given in Recipes XV,35 (a lean pottage) and XXV,31 (a Lenten pottage).

[11] See Recipes XXV,5 (the Lenten version referred to) and XV,7 (the ordinary lean version).

12. Pottage of Herb Juice without Butter

You will find how to make this in the Tables for Lent and for Lean Days.[12] You can use it if you like.

13. Princess Pottage[13.1]

Garnished with rosettes: rosettes are small lumps of puff-pastry dough.[13.2]

14. Milk Pottage[14]

15. Browned Onion Pottage [XV,26 & 53]

16. Pea Purée Pottage [XXV,21]

This is garnished with lettuce and broken asparagus stalks.

17. Vermicelli Pottage or Finger Pottage [XV,43 & XXV,36; XV,45 & XXV,38]

Garnished with fried pastry.

18. Cauliflower Pottage [XV,42 & XXV,35]

19. Rice Pottage [XV,44 & XXV,37]

Garnished with a dried loaf of bread.

20. Pottage of Green Peas[20]

To serve this, cook them very little, then pound them in a mortar, strain them and season them like the other ones. Then serve.

---

[12] As a Lenten pottage, see Recipe XXV,22; this derives from the lean pottage at Recipe XV,25.

[13.1] See Recipes XXV,6 (for Lent) and XV,8 (for ordinary lean days).

[13.2] *Ce sont des petits pastons feuilletez.*

[14] Among the lean pottages, Recipe XV,22 is a *Potage de lait aux jaunes d'œufs.* Perhaps for the present version La Varenne intends merely that the yolks be left out.

[20] Compare this dish with the *Potage de pois verts* of Recipe XV,24.

Chapter XXX

Entrée for Good Friday[xxx]

I have not inserted directions here on making these dishes, particularly as they are easy to find among the recipes for lean days and for Lent if you have recourse to the Alphabetical Table appended to this printing for greater convenience and to allow you to find whatever you need on any occasion. The listing for this present chapter is only to advise you what can be served on that day [Good Friday], on which very little fish is ordinarily served, mainly on the tables of the Great.

1. Beetroot cubed, in browned butter with salt[1] [XX,9 (?)]

2. Beetroot in white butter

3. Sautéed beetroot

4. Orange carrots, fried, with a russet sauce over

5. Orange carrots, ground, then sautéed with onion, breadcrumbs, almonds, mushrooms and fresh butter; all of that well thickened and seasoned.

6. Orange carrots, fricasseed in browned butter, with onion

7. Orange carrots, sliced in rounds, with a white sauce, with butter, salt, nutmeg, chives and a little vinegar

8. White carrots, fricasseed

9. Carrots in pastry, fried

10. Chopped carrots in a ragout, with mushrooms

[xxx] *Entrée* is in the singular. The recipes in this chapter have been numbered for the translation. The initial paragraph here is printed at the end of this list of possible dishes for the Good Friday entrée. La Varenne added it, along with the alphabetical index he mentions and the whole chapter on Confections, for the Second Edition of his work.

[1] I. D. G. glosses this dish as "Red beets, or red parsnips, cut like dice, with brown butter and salt."

11. Pistachio Tourte [XXI,31]

12. Herb Tourte

13. Butter Tourte [XXI,28]

14. Almond Tourte [XXI,32]

15. Parsnips, in a white sauce, with butter

16. Fried parsnips [XX,6 alternative]

17. Salsify, in white sauce, with butter

18. Fried salsify in pastry

19. Spinach [XXVI,85]

20. Apples in butter [XX,13 alternative]

21. Fricasseed Apples [XXVI,86]

22. Wheat Porridge [XX,2]

23. Porridge of rice and strained [ground] almonds[23] [XX,2]

24. Prunes [XXVI,88]

25. Asparagus stalks, broken and fricasseed [XX,15]

26. Rissoles of a hash of mushrooms, carrots and pistachios, enriched with butter, served hot, sugared and with orange blossom

27. Fried skirrets, in pastry [XX,1 alternative]

28. Skirrets, in a white sauce with butter [XX,1 alternative (?)]

29. Midribs of chard [XX,17]

30. Cardoons

31. Fricasseed pumpkins [XX,5]

32. Jerusalem artichokes [XX,10]

33. Whole artichokes [XXII,2]

34. Vermicelli [XV,43; XXV,36]

---

[23] These *amendes passées* could be sautéed almonds.

35. Rice in milk, highly sweetened

Some people make it break open or burst[35.1] in water when it is thoroughly cleaned, then put the milk in with it. Others cook it in a double boiler.[35.2] As far as I am concerned, having tried out every procedure, I think the most advisable way to go about it is, when it is thoroughly washed and clean, for you to dry it by the fire; when it is quite dry, you let it simmer in very fresh milk — being careful not to drown it. You cook it over a low fire, stirring it often so it doesn't burn. Add in milk gradually.[35.3]

36. Mushrooms in Ragout [XXII,11 alternative (?)]

37. Creamed Mushrooms [XIX,2]

38. Agaric in Ragout, garnished with pistachios [XIX,1 (?)]

39. Truffles cut up in a ragout and garnished with pomegranate seeds [XXII,6 (?)]

40. Asparagus in a white sauce [XXII,8]

41. Truffles in a court-bouillon [XX,20]

42. Lemon salad [VIII,34]

43. Boiled salad — whether chicory or lettuce [XX,16; XX,4]

44. Morels in Ragout

45. Stuffed morels

46. Creamed morels

47. Cream of pistachios

48. Almond Cream Tourte [XXI,35]

49. Almond Cakes [Confections,31]

[35.1] *percer ou crever*: the grains of rice still have their sheath or skin and bran layer; boiling is a means to shuck this hull.

[35.2] *un pot double.*

[35.3] No mention is made of the sweetening agent that the recipe's name seems to call for.

Riz au laict bien fucré.

50. Puff Cakes[50]

51. Fried Artichokes [XIX,19][51]

---

[50] *Gasteaux fueilletez.*

[51] The word *FIN*, "END," appears at the end of this chapter, marking the conclusion of the book as it had originally been published in 1651.

Directions on How to Make
Sundry Sorts of Dry and Moist Confections
along with a few other little oddities and tasty delicacies*

1. Moist Apricots

Into boiling water mix some pearl-ash,[1.1] about a handful of it for a hundred apricots, which you then put in stirring them with a spoon until you see their skin peeling off under your thumb. Then take them out and put them into cool water and peel them very neatly. Boil water again, put your apricots into it and leave them there only a short while. Let them plump[1.2] in the water, and prick them by the stem.[1.3] Get an appropriate amount of sugar and dip[1.4] your apricots in it; then cook them as long as is necessary.

2. Another way for Ripe, Moist Apricots

Get whatever number of apricots you like and peel them as good and clean as you can. Boil water and throw your apricots into it for a short moment; then transfer them into cool water. Cook your sugar as for

---

* *petites curiositez & delicatesses de bouche.* To some extent this supplementary chapter on *Confitures*, "Confections," summarizes, or at least anticipates, the material of the book called *Le Confiturier françois*, particularly Chapters VII, XI and XII of that work. The chapter first appeared in 1652 appended to the second edition of the *Cuisinier françois*. The terms "moist" and "dry" (*liquide* and *sec*) refer to the relative consistency of the finished confection.

[1.1] Pearl-ash is a variety of refined potash obtained by evaporation from a solution of wood ash or ash from wine lees. What is produced is a mono-potassium salt of tartaric acid. When dissolved in water the resultant alkaline solution would help soften the apricot skins. See a similar use for this substance in *The French Confectioner*, Recipe XI,2.

[1.2] *faites les raverdir*: literally, "make them fresh again." The procedure is common with fruits as well as with certain vegetables and meats. The term originally referred to restoring the foodstuff to its freshest state.

[1.3] *sur la queuë*: probably at the end of the fruit from which the stem grows. I. D. G. writes "on the stalk." Later printers change the preposition to *sous la queuë*.

[1.4] *trempés*: this sugar will be "cooking" — that is, melted and boiled into a syrup, as is explicitly the case in the alternative recipe that follows.

making a preserve,[2] put your apricots into it and boil them briefly. Leave them there until the next morning, keeping a low fire beneath them.

3. Dry Apricots

[Peel, wash and boil apricots.] Set them to drain and do them as ears or in rounds.[3.1] Then sprinkle powdered sugar[3.2] on them and set them to dry in a stove.[3.3]

4. Another way for Dry Apricots

Get the firmest apricots; [peel, wash and boil them, then] set them to drain. Then cook your sugar as for a conserve,[4] put your apricots into that, increasing the boiling rate a little over the fire. Take them out, then glaze them and put them on some straw. If they aren't completely dry, sprinkle powdered sugar on them and dry them by the fire.

5. Rose Preserve

Get the reddest Provins roses that can be had. Dry them out as much as you can in a silver vessel over a low fire, stirring them often with your hand. When they are very dry, pound them in a mortar and put them through a very fine filter. Then moisten them with some lemon juice, on top of which you put half an ounce of powdered roses; for want of lemon

---

[2] *en façon de Conserve*; in Recipes 4, 15 and 19 the phrase will be simply *en conserve*, literally "as for a conserve." This cooking stage is used primarily to produce dry confections. I. D. G. translates "as for to preserve with it."

[3.1] The first option is seen in *The French Confectioner*, Recipe XII,7, as a treatment for whole cherries: syrup is repeatedly poured over whole cherries; as it runs off and dries, it forms small flat puddles which have the appearance of ears. The phrase "in rounds" suggests slices of pitted apricots.

[3.2] In the text, here and in a number of recipes below, this is *sucre en poudre*. Sugar was available on the market in the form of solid cones into which it had been poured following its primary refining. Ordinary "granulated" sugar resulted when those cones were crushed, probably by the purchaser. In the recipes for confections in this chapter, La Varenne occasionally specifies a more finely ground sugar, one that approaches our modern powdered, confectioner's sugar.

[3.3] *les mettez seicher à l'estuve*: this operation calls for the use of an *estuve*, a metal box which can be kept warm over an extended period, occasionally of several days, for the purpose of thoroughly drying a foodstuff or preparation.

[4] *en conserve.*

juice, use verjuice. Get some sugar and cook it to the feather stage.[5.1] When it has cooked, take it off the fire and blanch it with the spatula.[5.2] Then put your roses into it until your syrup takes on colour. If your sugar happens to be overcooked, mix into it the juice of a lemon or of half a lemon, depending on what you think necessary. Then let your confection cool a little and take it out.

6. Lemon Preserve

Get a lemon, grate it and put the gratings in some water. A little while later, take them out and more or less dry them by the fire. Get some sugar and cook it, and as it begins to steam take it off the fire and put your lemon gratings into it; blanch it with the spatula, adding in whatever little amount of lemon juice is necessary. Then you set out your conserve.

7. Pomegranate Preserve

Get a pomegranate and squeeze it to express its juice which you put upon a silver plate and dry out over a low fire or on a few hot coals. Cook your sugar to the feather stage, and heavier than in other cases. When it is well cooked, take it off the fire and blanch it.[7] Afterwards, put in your juice and take out your conserve.

8. Pistachio Preserve

Get some pistachios and grind them. Cook some sugar to the feather stage and then blanch it. While you are doing that, put your pistachios

---

[5.1] *jusqu'à la plume.* I.D.G. expands this to an extensive, if not altogether accurate, gloss: "to the first plume, that is, till the first skin, or crust is seene on the sugar, when it is boiled enough." *The French Confectioner* begins with a useful description of the various stages in "cooking" sugar, and how to recognize them. This "feather stage" is defined there, in Recipe III,4, as having been reached "by putting a spatula [into it] and then shaking the sugar in the air and it flies off like dry feathers without birdlime." Alternatively, the author directs, "dip a skimmer into the sugar and blow through it until the sugar flies off in leaves." A century later the *Encyclopédie* of Diderot and D'Alembert (XV, 617b) contains a very detailed exposition of the process of cooking sugar to this stage.

[5.2] *espature.* I.D.G. has "the wooden slice" here; according to the *Oxford English Dictionary* the obsolete word "slice" is identified "a spatula used for stirring and mixing compounds." A spatula is used in several of these recipes for "blanching", that is, whitening the molten sugar by stirring and aerating it. Another sort of blanching can be accomplished by means of egg whites, as in Recipe 14, for instance.

[7] For this "blanching" the *espature* is very likely to be used as in the previous two recipes.

into it and stir them around. After that, lift out your conserve onto some paper.

9. Fruit Preserve

Get some lemon peel, pistachios, apricots and cherries. Cut them up into small pieces, sprinkle them with powdered sugar[9.1] and dry them by a low fire. Get some sugar and cook it to a rather heavy feather stage. Then, without taking it off the fire, put your fruit into it; when you see it reach the same feather stage again, take it off and blanch it. After that, when you see a little skin[9.2] forming on it, you lift out your conserve with a spoon.

10. Ham Slices[10.1]

On the one hand you get ground pistachios, on another powdered Provins roses moistened with the juice of a lemon, and on yet another a paste of ground almonds. When you have those things, separately like that, cook about a pound and a half of sugar to a syrup. When that is done, you divide it into three parts, holding two of them aside on hot coals and pouring your roses into the other. After moistening them in that sugar, you pour it all together[10.2] onto a double sheet of paper whose four sides you have folded two fingers high and fastened the corners with pins. As soon as the first sugar you poured in is half cooled, coloured like that, you get your almonds, mix them into another third of the sugar left on the coals, and pour it over the preparation. And you also do the same with the pistachios. Then when the whole can be cut with a knife, fold down the edges of the sheet of paper and cut the sugar into slices the thickness of a quarter écu.[10.3]

11. White Fennel

Get some fennel stems,[11] clean them well and dry them. When they have dried, take an egg white and some orange blossom water; beat these

---

[9.1] See the note in Recipe 3.

[9.2] The French term, *la petite glace*, "ice," describes a clear, hard film on the surface of the cooling syrup.

[10.1] See more of these pseudo *Tranches de jambon* in *The French Confectioner*, Recipe VII,18.

[10.2] That is, powdered roses and syrup.

[10.3] We may picture relatively thin slivers, evocative of the ham slices of the dish's name. I. D. G. translates the last phrase as "the thicknesse of halfe a crown."

[11] La Varenne's *fenoüil en branche* is perhaps the stem or stalk of the young plant.

together. Steep your fennel in that mixture, then put powdered sugar over it and dry it by the fire on sheets of paper.

12. Red Fennel

Get some pomegranate juice with an egg white; beat these together and steep your fennel in it. Put on powdered sugar, as with the other one, and dry it in the sun.[12]

13. Blue Fennel

Get some orchil dye[13.1] and rasp it into some water; into that add some orris powder[13.2] and an egg white, and beat it all together. Steep your fennel in that liquid. After that you put powdered sugar on it, and dry it like the other one.

14. To Blanch Pinks, Roses and Violets

Get an ̔egg white with a small drop of orange blossom water, beat them together and set your flowers to soak in that. Then take them out and as you do, shake them. Put powdered sugar over them and dry them by the fire.

You can proceed the same way to blanch red currants, cherries, raspberries and strawberries,[14] without any need for a separate recipe for each of these things — there being no difference among them and since they can be dried likewise either by the fire or in the sun.

15. Moist Cherries

Get the finest cherries you can and remove their pits. Get an amount of sugar suitable for your cherries and cook them together until the syrup

---

[12] Drying something in the sun offers a slower, gentler process than drying by the fire. See, for instance, Recipes 14 and 51.

[13.1] *du tourne sol*, which I. D. G. does not translate. The violet colorant, orchil or archil, extracted from several species of lichens, generally *Roccella tinctoria*, was available commercially in pastilles. Like modern litmus, the substance had the remarkable and useful virtue — familar to cooks since the Middle Ages — of giving a red colour in the presence of an acid or a blue when mixed with an alkali.

[13.2] This ingredient, the dried and powdered root of the orris, a variety of iris, is not primarily a colorant but might ensure that the orchil dye produced a distinct blue colour.

[14] Cf. the recipe in *The French Confectioner* for blanching "fennel, cherries, red currants, etc."

is well made and cooked as much as you think right. If you want to make up some dry ones[15.1] immediately, drain a portion of these same cherries; then get some sugar which you cook as for a conserve,[15.2] put your cherries into that and cook them well. Take them out again.

16. Moist Plums of all Sorts

Get some plums and prick them, then throw them into a basin of boiling water and boil them very gently and briefly.[16.1] Plump them, put them into cool water and drain them. Then cook your sugar very briefly, throw in your plums and boil them shortly.[16.2] Then put them in a warming oven if you like; alternatively, if you do not think they are cooked enough, reboil your syrup for a short while, put your plums back into it and give them another boiling.[16.3]

17. Green Almonds

Green almonds should be done the same way as the apricots.

18. Moist Verjuice Grapes

Get the finest verjuice grape mash you can and remove all the seeds. Boil some water and plump your verjuice mash a little in it, then put it[18.1] into some slightly cooked sugar. Give it a good round boiling,[18.2] and take it out.

19. Dry Verjuice Grapes[19]

Drain the verjuice mash well. Cook some sugar as for a conserve and put your verjuice mash into it, then set it on the fire and bring it back to

---

[15.1] That is, some cherries that will be served dry and not in the syrup conserve.

[15.2] *en conserve.*

[16.1] *un bouillon ou deux,* which later printers greatly extend to *un bon quart-d'heure.* A *bouillon* is merely a single wave of bubbles rising off a boiling liquid. This measurement of the time that something boils is common. In Recipe 1 the peeled apricots are boiled in water for "four or five *bouillons.*"

[16.2] The moderately short length of time is expressed here as *cinq ou six bouillons.*

[16.3] The sugar is reboiled for another *cinq ou six bouillons,* while the plums are reboiled in it for *un bouillon ou deux.*

[18.1] Throughout this recipe *le verjus,* always in the singular, refers to the grape mash; the name of the dish is *Verjus liquide,* the adjective still referring to the variety of confection being made here.

[18.2] *sept ou huict gros bouillons.*

[19] A "dry confection": see *The French Confectioner,* Chapter XII, Recipe 17.

the same boil as it had when you added in the verjuice, so that its feather is quite heavy.

20. Artichoke Hearts

Get whatever number of artichoke hearts you like, peel them fully, and carefully remove their choke. Then boil some water, throw your artichokes into it and leave them until they have cooked thoroughly. After that, you put them into sugar and let boil in it a short while, too. Let them sit there, then set them to drain and take them out.[20]

21. Dry Rose Hips

Get some rose hips, prick them with a knife six or seven times and boil them in water for a moderate length of time.[21.1] Then get some sugar, melt it, put your rose hips in it and let them boil for another short while.[21.2] To dry them,[21.3] prepare them like oranges, directions for which you will find a little further on.[21.4]

22. Citron

Get good citron, cut it into slices and put them into cool water with a handful of clean salt; let them steep five or six hours. Then boil them in water until they are cooked; take them out and drain them. Then get some sugar, boil it and throw in your citron slices. Cook them again in the sugar as much as is necessary, and take them out.

23. Whole Lemons

Peel some lemons down to the white and cut them through their pointed end. Boil some water and put them into it until they are half-cooked. Pour off that water and put them into some more rapidly boiling water to finish off their cooking. Take them out and put them into cool water. Melt some sugar and steep your lemons in it.

---

[20] *sic.*

[21.1] "Ten or twelve *bouillons*," which later printers simplify to "a quarter of an hour."

[21.2] "Eight or ten *bouillons*." For some reason in place of this phrase later printers show "and let them again take on flavour while cooking."

[21.3] That is, to prepare them as a dry variety of conserve.

[21.4] Recipe 24, below.

24. Oranges

Get those that are the most orange in colour and the smoothest,[24.1] or the yellowest. Peel them, split them into sections[24.2] and steep them two whole days in cool water which you change twice a day. Boil some water in a basin, put your oranges into it and let them half-cook; pour off the water and finish off cooking them in more boiling water; after that set them to drain. Get an amount of sugar suitable for your oranges, along with the same amount of water, and boil the whole lot rapidly with your oranges. Then take them out and drain them.

25. To Make White Walnuts[25.1]

Get some walnuts, peel them down to the white and put them to steep in water for six days — but don't fail to change the water twice a day. Afterwards cook them in water, too. When they are cooked, stick them with a whole clove, cinnamon and a lardoon of candied lemon. After that get some sugar, cook it, put your walnuts into it and leave them in it for a short length of time.[25.2] Then take them out, set them to drain and dry them.

Escoffier, *Confiture d'abricots*, §2956

26. Apricot Paste[26.1]

Get very ripe apricots and peel them. Then put them into a skillet without water, stirring them often with a skimming spoon until they are quite dry.[26.2] Take them off the fire and mix them with as much sugar syrup as you have paste.

27. Cherry Paste[27]

Get some cherries and, after boiling them in water, put them through a strainer. Onto a quart of cherry mash put four ounces of apple mash,

---

[24.1] *Prenés les plus rouges & les plus unies.*

[24.2] *les fendez par la pointe.*

[25.1] In *The French Confectioner*, Recipe XI,19, this preparation is classified as a "moist confection".

[25.2] " . . . for ten or twelve *bouillons*."

[26.1] Cf. *The French Confectioner*, Recipe XIII,2.

[26.2] This "drying" and stirring must begin a mashing of the apricots. In the next sentence, the syrup will be mixed with *paste* of the apricots.

[27] Cf. *The French Confectioner*, Recipe XIII,3.

which you cook and strain the same way; mix everything together. Dry it and prepare it as above.

28. Currant Paste and Verjuice Paste[28]

These are prepared and made up the same way as the Cherry Paste just above.

29. Quince Paste[29.1]

Get quince, cook them whole in water and put them through a coarse filter. Then dry that paste in a skillet on the fire as in the previous recipes.[29.2] You mix it with sugar and give the mixture five or six turns on the fire, being careful that it doesn't boil. Set them out half-cooled — and the other ones likewise.

30. Marzipan[30]

Get some almonds, peel them and set them to steep in water, changing it until at last the water looks quite clear. Grind them up with an egg white and orange blossom water, then dry them on the fire with a little sugar. After that you pound them four or five times in a mortar and work them as you like.

31. Cakes[31.1] of Cherries, Apricots, Pistachios and Almonds

Get however many cherries or apricots you want, pound them in a mortar with powdered sugar until the paste is thick enough to be usable. Cook them before glazing them; then glaze them top and bottom.[31.2] Pis-

---

[28] Cf. *The French Confectioner*, Recipes XIII,4 and 7.

[29.1] Cf. *The French Confectioner*, Recipe XIII,8 as well as the *Cottignac d'Orleans* at Recipe 48, below.

[29.2] See Recipe 26, where apricots undergo the same treatment in a skillet.

[30] For different varieties of this confection see Chapter XVI in *The French Confectioner*. Michael Nostradamus discusses the making of marzipan in his *Vray et parfaict embellissement de la face . . . & la façon et maniere de faire toutes confitures* (Antwerp: Christophe Plantin, 1557; repr. Paris: Gutemberg-Reprint, 1979).

[31.1] The so-called *gasteaux* that this recipe makes are flattened squares of thickened fruit purée, baked and then glazed or coated with a thin batter on both sides. They are a "cake" in the sense of a "shaped or moulded mass."

[31.2] The term used by La Varenne is *glacer*. This icing is described as a thin pastry batter, applied in both versions of this recipe *after* the fruit or nut mixture has been baked. The reader is left wondering how this coating, on both sides, is dried.

tachios and almonds are handled more easily and are easier to make cakes of.

To make the shells of these, set some gum[31.3] to soak in orange blossom water. Grind your almonds or your pistachios in the mortar with a bit of gum; mix all that with powdered sugar, then make up a paste however you like.

With that same paste you can make a very thin glazing, mixing in a little musk. Be careful to clean it well on top. Then cut it lengthwise or in rounds or some other way.

Baking it takes great care and great circumspection; put it into the oven or in a tourtière with heat above and below, but a little less above.[31.4]

32. Other Easy Pastes

Get an egg white, beat it well with a little orange blossom water and mix it with a little pistachio or almond, whatever you like. Work that fully with some powdered sugar and put in a little musk. Cook your mixture in a tourtière with a few hot coals both above and below.

33. A Combalet Tourte[33]

You must get three egg yolks clear of any whites, half a pound of lemon peel, with orange blossom water and some musk. Grind a lemon peel, mix everything together and dry it out with a handful of sugar while beating it. Then put everything also into a skillet and give it three or four turns over the fire. Form up a tourte and put it in a tourtière with some powdered sugar on its top and bottom. Close up the tourtière and surround it with fire. When it is half cooked, take it up and set it to dry in the oven.

34. Little Glazed Pastry Shells

Get all sorts of dry fruits and grind them with orange blossom water. Fill your pastry shells with that fruit; it will form a certain thickness which can glaze the shells. Leave a little of it on top and cook it in a tourtière until the glazing has risen. To do that put some fire over but none under [the tourtière].

[31.3] *gomme*: this is likely gum arabic.

[31.4] A tourtière has a lid on which hot coals can be placed.

[33] The name of this variety of tourte suggests an Italian origin for the preparation, the Italian word *comballo* designating a sort of boat. Here in La Varenne we would perhaps have a tourte in the form of a "small boat".

35. Cherry Syrup

Get some cherries, press them and extract their juice, strain it and put it on the fire briefly.[35] Then add in some sugar in the ratio of twelve ounces for a quart of juice.

Raspberry Syrup is made the same way.

36. Lemonade[36.1]

It is made in various ways depending on the different ingredients. To make it with jasmine,[36.2] you need about two handfuls of it and to set it to infuse in two or three quarts of water for eight or ten hours. Then for a quart of water you put in six ounces of sugar. Lemonades of orange blossoms, musk roses and pinks are made the same way. To do a lemon one, get some lemons, cut them and squeeze out their juice and put it into the water as above; peel another lemon, slice it and put it into that juice with an appropriate amount of sugar. The orange one is done the same way.

37. Dry Quince Confection

Get quince, peel them and boil them in water. Take them out and put them into some boiling sugar. When they are cooked, take them out again and dump them into cooked sugar; then take them out of that and dry them the same as the oranges and other fruits as described above.[37]

38. White Hypocras

Get three quarts[38] of the best white wine, a pound and a half of sugar, more or less, an ounce of cinnamon, two or three marjoram leaves and two unground pepper corns; put everything through a straining bag with a small bit of musk and two or three pieces of lemon. Then let everything infuse together for three or four hours.

Claret is made with claret wine and the same mix of ingredients.

---

[35] "two or three *bouillons*"

[36.1] The word *limonade* is a generic term for a range of sweetened drinks. A slightly more accurate translation might be "fruit drink".

[36.2] See particularly the Jasmine Water (and variants on it) in the *French Confectioner*, Recipe IV,13.

[37] Recipe 24 has dealt with oranges and has already been referred to in Recipe 21 as a model procedure.

[38] *trois pintes.*

39. Whipped Cream

Get six cups[39.1] of milk and put it in a terrine with about four ounces of sugar. Get three cups[39.2] of sweet cream, too, which you pour into your milk as you whip it with a whisk. As you do so, skim off the top and put it in a dish in the shape of a pyramid.

40. Cooked Cream

Get some sweet cream along with a quart or two of well beaten almonds, then mix them together in a skillet, stirring, and cook them over a low fire. When it looks to be getting thick, get two egg yolks, mixed with a little powdered sugar, put them into your cream and stir it around four or five more times.

41. English Cream

Get some sweet cream and warm it a little in the vessel in which you are going to serve it. Then get an amount of rennet the size of a grain of wheat and mix it with a little milk.[41]

Escoffier, *Gelée de groseilles*, §2966

42. Red Currant Jelly

Get some red currants, press them and strain them through a napkin. Measure out your juice and put about twelve ounces of sugar into a quart of juice. Cook it before mixing it, then cook it again after. When mixed, try it on a plate: you can tell it is cooked when it lifts up.[42]

Raspberry Jelly is made the same way.

43. Verjuice Jelly

Get some verjuice mash and bring it to a boil in water; strain it through a coarse linen filter. Cook some apples, then mix the decoction into the other and continue as above.

Cherry Jelly is made the same way.

Escoffier, *Gelée de pommes*, §2971

44. Apple Jelly

Make a decoction of your apples and strain it through a napkin. Mix in twelve ounces of sugar or so for a quart of the decoction.

[39.1] Being of milk this *pinte* would measure some 47 or 48 ounces, one and a half quarts.

[39.2] *une chopine*, some 24 ounces when measuring a dairy product.

[41] Presumably the rennet paste is added to the warm cream in order to curdle it.

[42] La Varenne writes *se leve* to describe the forming of a cohesive glob. See also the same test in Recipe 48.

45. Quince Jelly

Likewise make a decoction of your quince. Give it a reddish colour, too, strain it through a napkin and put it into sugar like the others.

Escoffier, *Gelée de coings*, §2964

46. Biscuit

Get eight eggs, a pound of powdered sugar and twelve ounces of flour. Mix it all well together: that way it will be neither too soft nor too hard.

47. Macaroon

Get a pound of shelled almonds, set them to soak in some cool water and wash them [replacing the water] until the water is clear; drain them. Grind them in a mortar, moistening them with three egg whites instead of orange blossom water, and adding in four ounces of powdered sugar. Make your paste which on paper you cut in the shape of a macaroon,[47] then cook it, but be careful not to give it too hot a fire. When cooked, take it out of the oven and put it away in a warm, dry place.

48. Orleans Cotignac

Get fifteen pounds of quince, three pounds of sugar and two quarts of water; boil everything together. When it is well cooked, strain it gradually through a napkin and draw out whatever you can. Then put your decoction into a basin with four pounds of sugar, and cook it; to tell whether it is cooked, try it on a plate and if it lifts up [in a globule] take it quickly off the fire. Put it away in boxes or otherwise.

49. Strawberries

Get marzipan paste, roll it in your hands into the shape of strawberries, then dip into some barberry juice or red-currant juice and stir them around in it vigorously. When that is done, set them out in a dish and dry them by the fire. When they are dry, dip them again three or four times in the same juice.

50. Caramel

Melt some sugar and a little water so that its cooking is stronger than for a conserve. Put in some syrup of lady's bedstraw[50] and put everything

---

[47] Cotgrave describes macaroons' shape as of "thicke Losenges."

[50] I. D. G. keeps the same term for *syrop de Capilaire*, "sirrup of Capilaire," without glossing the phrase. It is the flowers of the *Galium verum* plant that will yield a rich yellow hue.

into cool water.

51. Musk Pastilles

Get some powdered sugar, a little tragacanth gum[51.1] which you have soaked in orange blossom water, and musk. Grind everything together, make it up into pastilles[51.2] and dry it out far from the fire or in the sun.

52. Snow Paste

Get some powdered sugar and a suitable amount of tragacanth gum. Grind them together and add in some good sort of water.[52] Then make up your pastry shell.

53. Pistachio Cake

Get half a pound of powdered sugar, a quarter pound of pistachios, a pennyworth of tragacanth gum and a drop of savoury water; grind it all together. With the paste made, make your cakes the thickness of a testoon and bake them in the oven.

54. Candied Raspberries

Make your syrup with apple decoction. When it is well cooked, throw your raspberries into it, giving only a very brief boiling, and take them out again. Put them wherever you like for keeping.

55. Moist Quince

Get quince that are very yellow and without any dark spots. Quarter them and cook them in water until they are well cooked and quite soft. Then set them to drain and into that same water throw your sugar which you cook a little more than syrup. Put your quince back into it, throwing in as well their seeds which you have picked out and put into a bit of linen, to give them colour. When they are done, take them out.

[51.1] This gum functions as a stabilizer in the mixture.

[51.2] In the title and here La Varenne's word *muscadin* is in the singular: the recipe is for the paste from which the pastilles are made. See the *Muscadins* in *The French Confectioner*, Recipe XVI,23.

[52] There is no indication in the text whether *quelque bonne eau* refers to the source and quality of the water or whether, as in the next recipe, it might indicate a choice from among the savoury "waters" of *The French Confectioner*, Chapter IV.

56. Apple Compote[56.1]

Get some rennet apples which have no spots, and peel them evenly. If they are large, quarter them; if small, cut them in half. In either case remove their seeds and other inedible bits.[56.2]

As you peel them put them in some water. When they are all done put the water and the apples into a skillet with a suitable amount of sugar — six ounces of sugar for eight large apples — and a little cinnamon, instead of which in winter when the apples are drier you can put a glassful of white wine. Boil everything until your apples are soft to the touch; then take them piece by piece, squeeze them between two spoons and arrange them on a plate. Then strain your syrup through a doubled napkin; when strained put it into the skillet to make a jelly of it; you can tell it is cooked when you can take it in a small spoon and see that drops from it fall like little icicles; then take it off the fire. When it is half cooled, put it over your apples set out on the plate.

57. Calville-Apple Compote

It is done the same way, except that their peel is not taken off.

58. Apple Marmalade

Get ten or twelve apples, peel them, cut them carefully down to the core and put them into clean water. Next take the apples and the water they are soaking in, along with half a pound of sugar, or less if you like, and put them into a skillet and cook them; while they are cooking, mash them to keep them from burning. When there's almost no water left, put everything through a strainer; take up what has strained and put it back into the same skillet with the scrapings from half a lemon or orange previously steeped for half an hour in a little hot water and put through a cloth filter. To avoid and remove any bitterness while cooking, stir it constantly so your marmalade doesn't burn. You can tell it is cooked when it is like a jelly and gives off less moisture.[58] When it is properly done, take it off the fire and spread it out with a knife to a thickness of two testoons.

[56.1] This particular *Composte de pommes* and the next are hardly what we might call Apple Sauce.

[56.2] *& autres superfluités.*

[58] *moins d'humidité,* presumably steam.

59. Pear Compote

Get whatever varieties of pear you like provided they are good, peel them, and remove their seeds, the hard part that is in the top of the pear,[59] and the other inedible bits as you do with apples. If they are large, cut them in half or in quarters; if small, in thirds. Put them into a skillet with some water, sugar and cinnamon. When they are half cooked, pour in a glassful of full-bodied red wine. Keep them covered constantly, especially as that gives them a red colour. Give them as long a cooking as for the syrup of other confections.

60. Another way

Cook some pears in hot coals. When they are done, peel them, cut them in half or in quarters depending on their size and remove the insides. Make a syrup with some sugar and the juice of a lemon or some orange blossom water; pour your pears into that syrup and bring them to a boil. Then set them out on a plate.

61. Limousin Chestnuts

Cook chestnuts normally. When they are done, peel them and as you do flatten them a little between your hands; set them out on a plate. Get some water, some sugar and the juice of a lemon or some orange blossom water and make a syrup of them. When it is made, pour it boiling on your chestnuts. You can serve them hot or cold.

62. Another way

If you wish to blanch them, get an egg white and some orange blossom water and beat them together; soak your chestnuts in that. Then put them in a dish with some powdered sugar and roll them in it so they get covered with it; then dry them by the fire.

63. Lemon Compote

Make an Apple Jelly[63.1] and cook it. When it is cooked, get a large lemon and peel it very deep, down close to the fruit;[63.2] cut it across and lengthwise and divide each two parts into several slices; remove the pips.

---

[59] *la dureté qui est à l'œil de la poire*: the woody process above the core.

[63.1] Recipe 44, above.

[63.2] *pelez-le bien espais, & proche du jus.*

Throw the slices into your jelly, boil it a short while more[63.3] until your jelly has reached its first cooking stage again. Take it off the fire and let it half cool. Load up a plate with lemon slices and cover them with your jelly.

64. Lemon Paste

Get some powdered sugar and some egg whites with a few gratings of lemon flesh;[64] grind it all together in the mortar. It there happens to be too much egg, add in some finely powdered sugar so that as you pound you make what is in your mortar into a workable paste. Work it as you ordinarily do, making your cakes as you like, about half a finger thick or less if you like. Cook them on some paper in the oven or in a tourtière with a moderate heat above and below. Be careful they don't yellow; as soon as you see them yellowing, take them out because they'll be cooked then.

65. Savoy Biscuit

Get six egg yolks and eight egg whites, with a pound of powdered sugar, twelve ounces of good flour made from good wheat, and some aniseed. Beat everything together and put it to boil. Make a dough that is neither too soft nor too hard; if it is too soft you can mix in some finely powdered sugar to thicken it. When it is the right consistency put it into white metal moulds made for that purpose.[65] Then half bake them in the oven; when they are half done, take them out and moisten their top again with egg yolks. Then put them back in the over to finish baking. When they are done just right, neither too burnt nor too soft, take them out and put them away in some place that is neither too cool nor too dry.

The End*

[63.3] *encore dix ou douze bouillons.*

[64] *un peu de rapeure de chair de citron.*

[65] The moulds are probably semicircular. In his recipe for this biscuit (*Delices de la campagne*, 23) Nicolas de Bonnefons spreads the dough into an optional variety of shapes on paper and bakes it; when removed from the oven and a little cooled, it is lifted from the paper and set lengthwise on rolling pins so that the biscuit will be *creux par dessus en forme de gouttiere* — concave on top like a trough. That top is then glazed.

* The text of the Second Edition of the *Cuisinier françois* is followed by three Tables: for meat-day recipes, for lean-day recipes, and for the supplementary confections.

Frontispiece to *The Perfect Cook* by Mounsieur Marnettè.
Printed in London for Nath. Brooke at the Angel in Cornhill, 1656.
Reproduced by kind permission of the Bodleian Library, University of Oxford.

374

The French Pastry Chef

in which is taught the way of making every sort of Pastry, very useful for every sort of person

together with

the way to prepare every sort of egg dish for lean & other days in more than sixty ways

Chapter I

Pastry

1. Dark Pastry Dough

Get, for example, a bushel of rye flour, from which the coarse bran has been removed; knead that flour with warm water and make it firm. This sort of dough is useful mainly to make the shell of pies of ham and of gross venison that are to be carried any distance, and those whose crust should be strong and one or two thumbs thick[1.1] at the most. You can add half a pound of butter into this dough.[1.2]

2. White Pastry Dough to make a Large Pie

Put onto a pastry table,[2.1] — that is, on a very clean table — for instance half a bushel of wheat flour; make a hole or pit into its centre (pastry chefs call that hollow a well,[2.2]) put two pounds of butter — and

---

[1.1] The author's measurements of small distances tend to make use of the width of fingers and thumbs. The term for "thumb" is *pouce*, which we might give (though not too accurately) as "inch". The reader should understand a thickness of about two centimetres or three-quarters of an inch — as a rule of thumb. Marnette is more generous, showing this *un ou deux pouces au plus* as "at least two or three inches"!

[1.2] Marnette: " . . . which will make it the better."

[2.1] The *tour à paste* in this particular context is glossed by Richelet as a *terme de patissier: c'est une sorte de table grande & épaisse sur quoi on travaille en patisserie*. A century later Diderot's *Encyclopédie* still defines, and illustrates, this *tour* as a heavy rectangular table, but with high edges along its back and two ends. An alternative fixture is the *rondeau*, a large round pastry board, called for in Chapter VIII.

[2.2] The word *fontaine*, here and in the chapter on bread-making, evokes the appearance of a well-spring.

if the butter is hard, it should be handled so as to soften it before being set on the table. When the butter is blended into the flour, add in about three ounces of salt that has been ground and powdered;[2.3] also straight away add in about a cup of water. Then begin immediately kneading the dough and work it in your hands; and as you are making the dough, moisten it from time to time with a little water. When the dough is quite smooth, spread it out with a wooden rolling pin; throw a little flour under the dough, and on top, too, so that it doesn't stick either to the table or to the rolling pin.

Note that generally it is proper to make dough richer[2.4] in winter in order to make it more manageable; contrariwise, the dough should be a little less rich, consequently have a little less butter in it, when the weather is warm, so as to make it firmer, because warmth softens the dough too much and makes it so that it doesn't stand up when it is very rich; even so, the dough should be enriched[2.5] to the extent you wish to make it fine.[2.6]

Note, too, that if the weather is cold when dough is made, it is highly advisable to cover it with a warm cloth when it is half kneaded so as to take the chill off it.[2.7] Then finish working and kneading it until it is quite smooth and you don't feel any lumps when you work it.

[2.3] The author frequently specifies that salt be so prepared. In its natural, lumpy state salt would not blend smoothly as an ingredient.

[2.4] *plus grasse*: literally, "fatter". As the author explains, that is accomplished by increasing the amount of butter that is used. The different composition of the dough depends upon the variable ambient temperature in the chef's kitchen.

[2.5] *estoffer*: the term measures the relative amount of grease or fat in the dough.

[2.6] The feminine adjective *fine* is regularly applied to *la paste* in order to distinguish between a coarse dough and a more delicate dough. The first, usually composed of just flour and water, is intended to function primarily as a container for a pie filling; it is not normally intended to be eaten and, having served its purpose of containing a foodstuff in the oven, is cut away from its contents on the dining table. The author writes about that sort of dough in Recipe 1 (above), even though butter is optional in its composition. The second, and finer, type of dough is that which we see in the present recipe: a variable amount of butterfat — for half a bushel of flour normally two pounds of butter; for the "fine" pastry dough of the next recipe, three pounds — is incorporated into the flour and water, and the dough can therefore be rolled thinner. That sort of pastry shell may be eaten with the contents of the pie. To make it a little more palatable, a dash of salt is added to the dough.

[2.7] *afin de la degourdir*. Marnette shows "to the end that it may bee the better mollified."

3. How to make fine white dough to make crusts and other pastry that is to be eaten warm; and for the shells of pies, tourtes, talmouses, and other pasties.

Make white dough [as above] and, instead of putting in only two pounds of butter for half a bushel of flour, you put in three pounds. This dough is quite suitable for making crusts for breast of veal, for squab, tidbits and other things that are to be eaten warm.

When you set out a pie shell to make one of those crusts, make it about three or four quarter-crowns thick;[3.1] and make it so that the centre of the bottom of the pie is a little thicker so as to give more support to the pie.

If you use this dough to make tourtes or cheesecakes or other such pasties,[3.2] they should be given a thickness of one quarter crown or of a coin of thirty *sous*, more or less depending on the size of your pasty.

4. Puff Pastry

On a pastry table set out, for example, half a quart of wheat flour; make a well in it and pour in one glass of water, adding about half an ounce of ground salt. Work everything together to make the dough, moistening it from time to time with a little water as needed. When this dough is quite smooth, though rather soft, make it into a mound or heap, and let it stand for about half an hour, or a little more, so it consolidates;[4.1] then spread it out with a rolling pin until it is the thickness of a thumb, sprinkling it from time to time with a little flour.

Then get a pound of good firm butter — it mustn't be salted; spread that butter the full width of your dough and flatten it onto the dough with

---

[3.1] *trois ou quatre quarts d'escu.* Marnette: "three or four half Crowns." The author's measurements frequently make use of well known gold and silver French coins, the *écu, Louis, piastre, teston*, and others. It is probably good enough to imagine the thickness of a large modern coin, perhaps a dollar. For the pie described here, a rough equivalent is probably less than a centimetre or half an inch. Other, smaller pasties (in the next paragraph, for instance) have even thinner shells.

[3.2] Marnette expands the list of possibilities to include "Tarts, Custards, Cheese-Cakes, white-pots, Lambs-stones and sweet-breads, and the like." The original author likely intended to refer to pasties that are contained in dishes, so that their contents, even if relatively runny or "mobile", do not need quite so thick a pastry shell while in the oven.

[4.1] *afin qu'elle se restuie.* Marnette: "to the end that it may become drye and firm."

your hands; then fold the four corners of the dough inwards — or else fold the dough over twice so that the butter is enclosed inside. When that is done, roll out the dough again and make it very thin with the rolling pin, then again fold the four corners inwards to the centre, and again roll it out; and refold it the same way up to four or five times, reducing the dough to the proper thickness. And do not forget to sprinkle the dough from time to time with a bit of flour so that it doesn't stick to the table, the rolling pin or your fingers.

If you want to use this puff pastry to make a squab tourte,[4.2] or for some other pastry dish, take as much of it as you need, make a ball of it, then roll it out with the rolling pin, powdering it with a little flour, and reduce it to about the thickness of a silver Louis or of an *escu*.[4.3]

When that piece of dough is rolled out for the last time, flour it a little; then fold it in half, and on one half of the tourtière lay the half of the lower shell or sheet of dough; then you can fashion and make up the various baked-dishes whose recipes you will find below.

Note that if you put in less butter when making this dough, it will be dough that is only semi-flaky.[4.4]

5. Oil Dough, and How to Remove its Smell

You have to heat the oil on the fire, that is, boil it until it no longer makes any sound:[5.1] that way it will lose whatever is disagreeable about it. Some people add in a crust of bread.[5.2]

When your oil is ready, onto the table you put, for example, a little more than a pint[5.3] of wheat flour; add in three or four egg yolks, a pinch of salt, as much oil as you wish, and a quarter cup[5.4] or so of water;

[4.2] Because puff pastry does not make a strong pie crust, the pie is commonly contained in a baking dish such as a tourtière. See, for instance, Recipe VII,11 and the alternative offered at the end of Recipes VII,6 and 9.

[4.3] Marnette: " . . . the thickness of about a shilling peece in silver."

[4.4] In the text, *paste demy feuilletée*.

[5.1] Marnette: " . . . cause it to boyl till it bubbles no more."

[5.2] This alternative operation resembles that which is used for clarifying butter in Chapter XVIII, below.

[5.3] *un litron*.

[5.4] In the text, a quarter of a half-*septier*.

mix all that together well and work the dough well, making it a little stiff because it doesn't have the consistency of butter.[5.5] Then you can use it wherever you need to.

6. Sweet Dough

Get, for example, a quarter pound of sugar, powdered[6.1] and sieved, and put it into a very clean marble mortar; add in a quarter of an egg white and about half a spoonful of lemon juice. Stir everything together gently until the sugar begins to thicken; and if it is slow in thickening, add in a few drops of rosewater.[6.2] When the sugar begins to thicken, beat it with the pestle to reduce it to quite a thick, stiff paste. When it is done, make pastry shells or crusts of it.

Note that sometimes a semi-sweet dough is made by mixing together equal parts of sugar and wheat flour, which have to be blended as is directed above.

Chapter II
Pastry Chefs' Spices

1. How to Make the Mild Spice Mixture of Pastry Chefs

Get two parts of ginger (for example, two ounces), and one part (that is to say, one ounce) of ground pepper, and mix them together; add in ground cloves, very finely grated nutmeg, ground cinnamon — of each of those an ounce or thereabouts for a pound of spice mixture,[1.1] more or less, as you wish. Keep all those things mixed together in a box.

Note that each sort of spice can be kept separately in its own little leather bag, or in a box divided into several drawers.

Note, too, that some people use only pepper alone instead of the other spices, although the spice mixture is milder[1.2] than pepper alone.

[5.5] Marnette: " ... because the Oyl hath not so firm and solid a body as the Butter."

[6.1] This *sucre en poudre*, which is used fairly often in the recipes of *The French Pastry Chef*, seems to be finer than merely a granulated sugar that would come from crumbling a piece of sugar cone. It is likely close in texture to a modern confectioner's sugar.

[6.2] This rosewater is a distillate.

[1.1] The text has *pour une livre de poivre*, "pepper".

[1.2] Marnette expands the author's *plus douce* to "more pleasing and Aromatick."

2. Salty Spice

Dry some salt, then powder it and put some into the Mild Spice Mixture — four or five times as much by weight as there is of the spice mixture. Keep it in a place that is not damp.

Chapter III

Pastry Chefs' Gilding

How to Make Pastry Chefs' Gilding to give colour to pastry
Beat egg yolks and egg whites together as if you were going to make an omelet. If you wish the gilding to be strong and very good, it is enough to combine one egg white with two or three yolks; if you wish the gilding to be pale, use only egg yolks that are thinned with a little water.

To apply the gilding, moisten a feather with it, or a small brush or a whisk[iii.1] of feathers or hog's bristles; the brush should be soft. Then you gild your pastry.

If you do not like to use eggs to make gilding,[iii.2] you can moisten a little saffron or marigold blossoms with milk; or in Lent you can use pike eggs to make your gilding, because that gilding is lean. You will notice that pastry cooks put honey into their gilding in order to cut down on eggs.

Chapter IV

Pastry Chef's Cream[iv]

1. How to Make Pastry Chef's Cream
Get, for example, three cups of good milk, cow's milk, by dairymaid's

---

[iii.1] This *ballet* is called for in the *Confiturier* (see the Preface) as well, although there it must be more substantial and is made of slender birch or elm shoots.

[iii.2] Interestingly, Marnette interprets here, "Now in case you will not go to the charge [expense] of eggs to make your wash or varnish . . . ." See also the last sentence of this recipe. The alternatives were necessary also to satisfy the requirements of lean days when hen's eggs could not be eaten.

[iv] In this title and in Recipe 1, below, *Pastissier*, "Chef," is in the singular; in the titles to Chapters II and III the plural is used. For a number of tourtes in this book the *cresme de pastissier* is drawn upon to provide a particular consistency.

measure — that is, about a pound and a half by weight.[1] Put the milk into a small pan on the fire. You also need four eggs. While the milk is heating on the fire, break two eggs and mix the white and the yolk with a little more than a quarter pound of wheat flour, as if it was for making porridge, adding in a little milk. When the flour is thoroughly mixed in, so that there are no lumps, add in the other two eggs, one after the other into the mixture so as to incorporate them better.

As the milk begins to boil, pour into it the mixture we described of eggs, flour and milk, and boil it over a low flame which is clear and smokeless. Stir the mixture with a spoon as if it were porridge. It should be salted carefully while it is cooking. And add in a quarter-pound of good fresh butter.

That cream should be cooked in a time between a quarter of an hour and half an hour or so. Then it is poured into a bowl and you keep the mixture, which pastry chefs call Cream and which is used to make baked dishes.

2. A Finer Cream[2.1]

Get, for example, a quarter-pound of skinless sweet almonds and grind them in a mortar, gradually adding in a good quarter-pound or almost half a pound of sugar; incorporate those together, now and then adding a little rosewater. When the almonds are prepared in that way, you need three cups of milk by dairymaid's measure,[2.2] and four fresh eggs. Break your eggs and put only the yolks into a bowl, thinning them with a little milk. Then pour them into the almond paste and mix everything together.

Then you get an amount of wheat flour that can fit four times in a silver spoon,[2.3] moisten it with a part of your milk as if it were for making

---

[1] The *chopine* of milk is one-half of a *pinte* (which, of milk, weighed 47 ounces) and would amount to 24 fluid ounces or three cups by volume. The phrase *selon la mesure des laitieres* draws attention here and in the next recipe to an anomaly in volume measurement that the author will explain in Chapter VI. There we learn that milk was conventionally measured with a larger-than-normal *chopine*.

[2.1] Marnette: "Another kind of Cream which is farre delightfuller."

[2.2] Again, this so-called *chopine* or "half-*pinte*" of milk measures a quantity that is somewhat more than the normal *chopine*, or about twenty-four ounces.

[2.3] The specification that the spoon used here is silver probably implies a larger size of spoon that was standard in the kitchens of noble households of the time. Silver

a porridge. When that flour is thoroughly moistened, the rest of the three cups of milk is poured into it, then it is cooked like porridge. Hold back a little milk in order to put some into the porridge if it becomes too thick while it is cooking. When the porridge is half-cooked, pour your almond preparation into it, and stir the whole carefully as it cooks, and salt it, too. When that mixture is cooked and thickened to a proper consistency, it must be poured into a bowl. Let that cream sit until the next day, or at least until it sets like a jelly, so that you can cut it with a knife like dough or jelly.

3. Lenten Cream

Get three cups of good cow's milk[3.1] and boil it. Get as well a little more than three-eighths of a pound of wheat flour moistened or combined with milk, and pour it into the boiling milk. Then add in a good quarter-pound, by weight, of skinned sweet almonds that have been pounded in the mortar with a little milk — and they should be pounded a little less than would be to make macaroon.[3.2] You salt that cream while it is cooking, adding in as well a quarter-pound of fresh butter, and stir the mixture constantly while it cooks. Towards the end you can add in a little saffron moistened with a little milk in order to give the cream a yellow colour. When it is cooked to a proper consistency, it is poured out into a bowl to let it set and stand until you need it.

could be beaten more thinly than iron and consequently a larger spoon of it would be more manageable. As well, of course, silver was somewhat more sanitary. The author regularly directs that this silver spoon, or a chef's spatula, be used to stir large compounds of ingredients.

[3.1] The reader is expected to remember that that this *chopine* of milk will be about twenty-four ounces.

[3.2] To clarify, Marnette adds the phrase, "or little sweet Fritter-like buns." Directions for the making of this macaroon are given in Chapter XXVII, below. The preparation is a fairly common ingredient in this book. See also Recipes IX,15 and X.

Chapter V

Sugar Glazing

Into a glazed bowl put, for example, a quarter-pound of sugar which is finely powdered. To it add half an egg white, and a silver-spoon-full of rosewater, or more if necessary. Beat those things together until everything is reduced to the consistency of a very thick syrup or a very runny porridge. Pastry chefs call that mixture Sugar Glazing[v.1] because it is used to glaze baked dishes such as marzipan and English Pies,[v.2] upon which it must be spread properly, as will be directed below, with the back of a small spoon or with a knife or spatula, as you would do gilding.

Chapter VI

General Advice about Pastry

Note that if you have only a little pastry to cook in a large oven there is no need to heat the whole oven but only a part of it in which to cook your pastry.

People who are fussy[vi.1] have small private ovens in their house, and some fussy people [even] have portable ones.[vi.2]

Cooks ordinarily use covered tourtières to cook their tourtes and other dainty pasties.

[v.1] *de la glace de sucre*. Two verbs are commonly used when coating the surface of a prepared dish: *glacer* and *dorer*. In most cases they should be distinguished. Generally the first seems to refer to the use of a clear sugar syrup, "to glaze"; the second seems generally to impart a colour, and for this I consistently — though perhaps archaically and not entirely accurately — prefer the English "to gild". For the latter sort of coating see Chapter III, above, for Pastry Chefs' Gilding. I have avoided the words "icing" or "to ice".

[v.2] See specifically its use on the *Pasté a l'Angloise* of Recipe VII,14. There is covers an upper shell which has already been gilded as well.

[vi.1] The word *curieuses* evokes a personality that is seriously careful, earnest, painstaking, either exceedingly or excessively. It is interesting, and revealing, to note that the English translation interprets *les personnes curieuses* as "curious house-wives and Lovers of this Art".

[vi.2] Recipe VII,13 mentions the use of a small copper oven that can be used to bake pies of a smaller size.

Note that when we use the word "pound" as in "a pound of butter," we mean the pound that weighs thirteen ounces, or two goldsmith's marks, and other weights proportionately.

Note, too, that when we speak of a *pinte*, that it the pint used in the Paris wine measure, which holds the weight of two pounds, less an ounce or so, of water, and about the same weight of wine. The *chopine* is half a pint. Those measures have different names in different places, but you cannot make a mistake in holding to the measure of weights I have laid out.

Note that when we speak of a *pinte* of milk, the pint should weigh three pounds less an ounce or so, and the other measures proportionately.[vi.3] Consequently the *poinçon* of milk — that is, the eighth part of a *pinte* of milk in dairymaid's measure — should weigh five and a half ounces and three drams, or thereabouts.

Note, too, that when we speak of a bushel of flour we mean flour that still has its bran, and that the bushel of that flour should weigh twelve to thirteen pounds or so; and the other measures proportionately — that is to say, the half-bushel should weigh six pounds or a little more; the quarter-bushel should weight three pounds by good measure; the *litron* or sixteenth part of a bushel of fine flour should weigh three *quarterons*, that is, twelve ounces.

Chapter VII
Meat and Fish Pies[vii]

1. How to Put a Ham into Pastry

Soak a ham in water[1.1] depending upon it size, its thickness and its dryness. If a ham is very large and very dry or smoked, as Mayence or

---

[vi.3] These measures of milk were, therefore, roughly 50% larger than that of other liquids.

[vii] Some of these so-called *pastés* we would today qualify by means of the phrase *en crouste*: the meat to be baked, along with any sauce, is encased in relatively thick, and relatively inedible, pastry. See particularly the procedure called *en venaison* in Recipe 2, below.

[1.1] The assumption is that any "ham" will be pork that has been cured — that is, preserved — by salting. Before it is used in any preparation this meat must first be desalted, as is to be done here.

Bayonne hams are, it will have to be left to soak in water for at least 24 hours or more; then you can check whether the ham is sufficiently desalted. To do that, you take it out of the water and make a deep hole or cut into the middle of the meat and draw out a small bit of it which you put in your mouth to tell whether the ham is desalted enough. If you judge that it is, you go ahead and prepare it properly for putting into pastry.

First, you have to pare the underside of the ham down to the bare flesh so as to remove its outer layer and whatever is too dry and salty. Then you cut away the hide and skin from on top, and also cut the end of the knuckle.

When your ham is thus prepared, you roll out[1.2] on the pastry wheel as much dough as will be needed. You should make it about two inches thick. In the middle of that dough you make a layer of lard slices; the layer of lard should be the size of the ham. Onto that layer of lard you put a good handful of coarsely chopped parsley, then sprinkle the ham with mild spices and place it on the bed of lard and parsley. Then prick the top of the ham with some whole cloves and little bits of cinnamon, and put on the ham another layer of parsley, a layer of slices of lard and five or six bay leaves over the lard, then[1.3] a good half-pound of fresh butter which is flattened and spread out so that it covers all the lard slices that are on the ham.

Then on the wheel roll out as much dough as will be needed to make the upper crust to cover the pasty.[1.4] Moisten the dough a little with a little brush and cover the pasty. When the pasty is made up, put it into the oven right away. The oven should be as hot as to bake coarse bread. If the ham is very big it will take a good three hours to cook; if it is a moderate size, two and a half hours in the oven will be enough, or two hours depending on its size.

[1.2] La Varenne consistently writes only *estendre*, "to spread out," for that operation. In Recipes I,2 and 4, however, he indicates that a wooden rolling pin, *un rouleau de bois*, is used for that "spreading out".

[1.3] Despite this *puis*, it is clear from what follows and from the next recipe that the bay leaves are laid over the slices of lard and the butter. The bay leaves provide a final, protective covering.

[1.4] The author calls his preparation *le pasté*. It is clearly, though, not a "pie" in the usual modern sense, rather it is an extremely large pasty in the English sense: "ham *en croûte*".

When the pasty has been in the oven about half an hour, you need to make two or three holes in its covering to let it breathe; if you don't, it will burst. That should be done for any sort of large pasty.

If the pastry crust browns quickly and darkens, that means that the oven is too hot and that it is burning the pastry. In that case some of the coals will have to be removed.[1.4] If, on the other hand, the pastry crust doesn't brown, that means that the oven is not hot enough, in which case you will have to increase the amount of coals so that the pasty can cook thoroughly.

When it is cooked, you take it out of the oven. A day after the pasty is cooked, the holes in its lid have to be stopped up with dough so that it can't breathe, or air get in, through those holes: that would preclude its being kept any length of time.[1.5]

2. How to Make a Basque Pasty

Have a Bayonne[2.1] or Mayence ham, or an ordinary ham, desalted in water. When the ham has soaked enough, remove it from the water, wipe its underside, cut away whatever yellow there is[2.2] down to the bare flesh, and cut away the end of the knuckle, too; then the hide has to be removed. If the lard is more than a finger's thickness, cut away the surplus and that lard can be used for slicing and for enriching this pasty.

When the ham is thus prepared, you half-cook it in water with some bay leaves and other seasoning herbs. When it is about half-cooked, take

---

[1.4] *il faudra oster de la braise.* In the next recipe the author speaks of putting coals *into* the oven. (See also Recipe XXV,1.) The usual pastry oven in La Varenne's day is, therefore, a fairly large one, probably an architectural element rather than a relatively small portable oven, as is mentioned as a possibility at the beginning of Chapter VI. Adding or removing a judicious quantity of live coals will adjust the baking heat within the oven. Occasionally live coals will be placed under a baking dish in an oven, as for instance in Recipe IX,15.

[1.5] Marnette amplifies this warning a little: " . . . You must stop up the holes which you made in the Lidde, with some dough, lest your Pastie might be spoyled by the letting in of Air at those holes, which would be the cause that your Pasty would bee subject to grow mouldy, and would not keep at all" (p. 28).

[2.1] Marnette's title to this recipe has already explained to his English reader: " . . . according to the fashion of the Baskes, or the inhabitants neer Bayonne upon the Fronteers of Spain."

[2.2] Marnette writes "all the yellow rindes."

it out of the bouillon and put it on a wicker tray to dry. You can also debone the ham when it is half-cooked, especially if you want to use it in a raised pie.[2.3]

When the ham is dry, lay out a crust of dark or grey or white pastry,[2.4] made without butter. You can make this pasty in the venison way,[2.5] but it is better to make a raised pie or a platter pie[2.6] because of the thickness of this meat. That is why, in order to make a raised pie of this ham, you need to lay out the crust in a ring of sufficient size and make it about half a foot high; and it should be about a good inch thick. Then fill the inside of the pasty with a layer of big slices of lard similar to those used to bard capons; then put a little coarsely chopped parsley on the lard, then sprinkle the ham with two or three pinches of mild spice and two pinches of ground white pepper and two pinches of ground cinnamon. Then set the ham on the bed of lard, and stick it with about a dozen whole cloves and with as many little bits of cinnamon; as well, you put on it a couple of crushed scallions, a little sprig of parsley and of thyme, half a pound of pork fat, half a pound of beef marrow, and half a pound of good fresh butter which has been flattened out so that it covers the whole top of the

---

[2.3] *pasté dressé*: The term designates a pie whose shell is made up, filled and baked without the benefit of a container or tourtière. For such a pie the dough is normally thicker and coarser, and often bound round with one or more strips of buttered paper and a cord: see Recipe VII,8.

[2.4] The typesetter has put *paste bise ou gru ou blanc*; if adjectives, *gru* and *blanc* are inexplicably in the masculine. The usual sense of the word *gru* is a gruel, or a coarsely ground grain meal, usually but not necessarily oatmeal. Between *bise* and *blanc*, *gris*, "grey," would seem most logical; this might describe a dough composed of a mixture of rye ("dark") and wheat ("white") flours. See Chapter I, above. In his English translation Marnette fudges, writing, "Prepare a Rye-paste, *or dough*, or a paste of white meal, without any butter at all" (my italics).

[2.5] *en venaison*: five paragraphs later we shall be told that this expression means "length-wise": *en long*. The term is also used in Recipes 17, 20 and 21. In this present recipe the qualification likely refers to a traditional procedure of wrapping a foodstuff in pastry — putting it *en croûte*. Recipe 21 instructs the reader that for a venison-type pasty enough pastry must be rolled that a single piece can form a shell to enclose a large piece of flesh. This sort of pasty, its pastry being a relatively coarse dough made without butter, dispenses with a pie plate or tourtière in the oven.

[2.6] For the variety of pie called a *pasté d'assiette*, relatively small, round and with a conical lid, see Recipes VII,8 in particular, and 9 and 22. It seems to have functioned as an appetizer at the beginning of a meal. Its fine pastry shell is likely intended to be eaten.

ham. On the butter you again put a good pinch of white pepper and the same amount of ground cinnamon; then again on the butter you put a few slices of lard and a couple of bay leaves.

When the pasty is seasoned in that way, you have to cover it with an upper pastry crust, and that cover should be a good inch thick. The cover is then gilded, and you pierce it in its centre and set a peak[2.7] there or a little crown of dough made like a funnel if the pie is a raised sort. Then you put the pasty on a sheet of paper in order to put it in the oven.

It takes twenty-four or thirty hours to bake that pasty, and you give it a slightly less hot hearth than is used for baking coarse bread.

When the pasty has been in the oven for five or six hours, take it out of the oven and set it on a pastry board. You cut around the lid which has to be lifted in order to see whether the pie is really full of sauce or not; for if the sauce looks depleted, the pie has to be topped up with good meat bouillon in which there are no herbs or salt; and if you have mutton stock, you can mix that with the bouillon. Then the pie is covered again and put back in the oven right away. Every five hours or so it has to be taken out to see that it isn't dry and to put bouillon in it again. Carry on like that until the meat is cooked to the point of disintegrating[2.8] in the pie.

Three or four hours before the pie has finished baking, it can be garnished with tidbits, blanched[2.9] and properly prepared, and with mush-rooms and other garnishings. While that pie is baking, the oven's heat has to be maintained, and for that you put live coals into the oven, set some distance away from the pie, and sometimes bundles of very dry firewood.

If you made the pie in the venison way — that is, lengthwise[2.10] — it is filled in the same manner; furthermore, a bed of parsley has to be laid under the meat and another layer of parsley on top. And you shouldn't

---

[2.7] *un chapiteau*: A "capital" in the sense of an architectural element. See also the description of the pie's lid in Recipes 8 and 9, below, where the shape of an inverted cone is suggested. For the gilding of the top surface, see Chapter III.

[2.8] *la viande soit pourrie de cuire*: the idea of meat decomposing in cooking, literally "rotting", is at the origin of the *pot pourri*.

[2.9] In Recipe VII,13 the author provides a gloss for *chair blanche*: "blanched — that is, flesh that has been more than half-cooked."

[2.10] Marnette: " . . . that is to say, in a long form."

forget to put three or four holes in the pastry lid to let it breathe. And there is no need to put a crown on top.

3. Turkish Ham Pie

A ham should be prepared as in the previous recipe. When it is half cooked in water, and deboned, it is larded on the lean side with lardoons sprinkled with mild spices; those lardoons should be the thickness of a feather's quill. Then sprinkle the meat with a little mild spice and ground white pepper.

Then set up a pastry crust for use in a platter pie as in the previous recipe. Those who are really serious can use a semi-flaky pastry dough[3.1] to make the shell, especially in winter because that dough is stronger[3.2] during that season — but that pie is very difficult to handle when its dough is of regular puff pastry.

When the crust is set up, you coat it on the inside with slices of lard with the odd sprig of parsley and thyme. Then the meat is put in, into which you stick five or six whole cloves, a dozen little bits of cinnamon and two good pinches of ground cinnamon; add on a sprig of parsley, a ground scallion, two ounces of pinenuts, two ounces of currants,[3.3] four ounces of skinned pistachios, a side of candied lemon peel sliced small, a good six ounces of ground sugar, half a pound of fresh butter, half a pound of clarified lard, half a pound of beef marrow, and, on top, a big slice of lard, a bay leaf or two, and a sprig of thyme. Cover the pie, make a hole and a crown on the lid, and cook it as in the previous recipe. Check on the sauce from time to time and refill it in the same way.

Three or four hours before that pie is done you can add in mushrooms and blanched tidbits. Two hours before taking it from the oven you can pour into it a sweet sauce that is composed of a glassful of white wine,

---

[3.1] *paste demy fueilletée*: see Recipe I,4.

[3.2] *a plus de soustenance*: literally, "has greater holding power." The dough will give more support, will sustain the pie's contents better.

[3.3] The quantities of both the pinenuts and the currants are measured as *un demy quarteron*: "half a quarter pound." *Raisins de Corinthe* are defined by Cotgrave as "currans, or small Raisins." A *Raisin* is defined, in turn, as "a Grape; also, a Raisin": the French term could designate either the fresh or the dried fruit. Throughout my translation of these three works I assume an author refers to the dried raisin (or dried currant) unless he explicitly specifies the *fresh* fruit.

three ounces of sugar, a little ground cinnamon and, if you like, a little vinegar.

Note that if one of those pies is not wholly eaten at a meal, it can be reheated several times. And if it should want sauce, you can add in a little bouillon and meat stock.

4. How to Put *en croûte* the Flesh of Stag, Boar or Buck, or of any other coarse meat such as a round of veal, a slice of beef or a leg of mutton. And, too, How to Make a Pasty of Hare, Rabbit, Goose, Turkey Fowl, Ducks, Partridge, Old Doves and other coarse birds.

Note that no sort of flesh should be put into a pasty unless it is first hung. Therefore, let the flesh you wish to put into a pasty hang sufficiently;[4.1] then, with a wooden rolling pin or a bat, pound it more or less depending on whether it is more or less thick or tough.[4.2] And note that beef and mutton have to be pounded more than any other sort of meat.

Note, too, that it is proper to remove any superfluous bones from the meat you wish to put into a pasty — for example the knuckle of a leg of mutton. As for any bones that are left in the meat, they have to be broken if you don't prefer to remove them entirely from the meat; thus the bones that guinea fowl and other birds have in the breast are sometimes removed.

Note, too, that if the meat has coarse ligaments or hard bones,[4.3] they should be removed — for example, the skin of a leg of mutton should be removed. Likewise, if you have a hare to put into a pasty and it seems tough to you, the coarse skin that adheres to the flesh should be removed before larding it.

You should also note that, if there is any cavity in the flesh you want to put into a pasty — as there is in a hare and in fowl — the bones that make the cavity have to be broken so as to flatten out the meat — for

---

[4.1] Marnette amplifies this instruction by adding, "or by burying of it under ground for the space of twenty and four houres."

[4.2] Marnette adds: "which is a third way to mortifie it."

[4.3] This phrase here, *des os durs*, seems unlikely, particularly as the author has just dealt with unwanted bones in the previous paragraph. His manuscript may have mentioned something like "tough sinews" or "tough cartilege" here.

example, the belly of a guinea fowl. It should also be slashed every four finger-widths so as to lard it more easily.

If the venison or coarse meat you wish to put into a pasty is beginning to go bad, or if it has any worms in it, boil water with vinegar and salt and give the venison or coarse meat a boiling in it; then you take it out and let it drain.[4.4]

When the meat has been prepared as has been described, lard it frequently with lardoons that are more or less the size and length of your little finger, depending on the quality of the meat. It is proper for those lardoons to have steeped some time in a little vinegar seasoned with salt. Before sticking them into the meat, sprinkle them with ground pepper or mild spices.

If the meat is thick and half a foot long or more, like a round of veal or a guinea fowl or something else, slash it, or cut it up into rounds of about four fingers' width, but in such a way that all of the skin or underside remains whole. By means of those deep slashes all parts of the meat can be larded easily, which cannot be done without the slashes. Besides, the meat remaining whole, it would be more difficult to cook. And the pasty's sauce could not penetrate into the meat without a great deal of difficulty were the meat not slashed as has been described.

Some people set any beef and mutton they wish to bake in a pasty to steep for two or three hours in verjuice seasoned with salt and pepper or spices, and with some fine herbs; that has to be done as soon as the meat is pounded with the rolling pin and is larded. When the meat is removed from the pickling, the pasty should be made up as follows. When the flesh is ready to be put into a pasty, season it carefully with salty spice[4.5] in such a way that the spice adheres to the meat and coats it all around. If it is a fowl or some other meat which is hollow, sprinkle it on the inside

---

[4.4] The advice in this paragraph is remarkable. In older recipe collections, compiled in aristocratic milieux and describing the best of refined, upper class dining, we might reasonably assume that the question of tainted meat would never arise. It didn't in medieval cookery manuals; it didn't for La Varenne in the household of the Marquis d'Uxelles. However, for the author of the *Pastissier françois*, a proportion of whose readership may very well have occupied a somewhat lower station in French society, there was a realistic possibility both that such spoilage was unavoidable and that the spoiled meat could not merely be discarded.

[4.5] See Recipe II,2.

as well. And make a couple of slashes on the thighs and on the back before sprinkling it with spice.

When the meat is seasoned, put it on one of the ends of the crust of dark or white pastry dough,[4.6] whichever you prefer. That crust should be a good inch thick, and long enough to make the whole pasty. When you have set the meat on one end of the dough, stick a few whole cloves into its upper side, then garnish it with slices or "bandages"[4.7] of lard. On top of all of the other things you can add a few bay leaves as well. In addition, you put on fresh butter which is spread out as is said in the previous recipe.

You need a quart and a half of flour, or close to a half-bushel, to put a hare into a pasty, or a good guinea fowl or four ducks. You also need about two pounds of butter. And if you want the crust to be fine,[4.8] you can put in up to two and a half or three pounds of butter — but when the crust is so rich,[4.9] it will be apt to burst in the oven.

If that pasty is of venison or some other flesh that isn't fat,[4.10] you need more lard and butter than if the meat was fat. For example, to do up a hare, you need a half pound or nine ounces[4.11] of fresh butter to put on the hare, and a pound and a half, or at the very most two pounds, of lard to lard it, as much for the actual larding as to cover it. If the flesh in the pasty is not dry nor so lean — for example if it were a guinea fowl or a leg of mutton — a good three ounces of fresh butter would be enough to put on that meat; and be sure to lard it well.

[4.6] For these doughs see Chapter I, above. With the meat set on one end of the dough and the other, as we shall see, lifted over it, the pasty or "pie" will be a very large turnover.

[4.7] Properly, "plasters" (*emplastres*) of lard, represented as a curative dressing for the meat.

[4.8] As mentioned earlier, the term *fine* when applied to dough or pastry refers to the composition of the pie-shell dough, its relative "richness" as determined normally by the amount of butterfat in it. By extension, "fineness" in dough is related to the thinness of a crust and, consequently, to both its edibility and its fragility as a pie shell.

[4.9] *grasse*, because of the butter.

[4.10] Game animals were considered to be generically less fat than any domestic counterpart.

[4.11] *une demie livre ou 3 quarterons*: in Chapter VI the author has informed us that his pound (as of butter) has thirteen ounces.

Note that there are pastry chefs who sometimes use clarified lard instead of butter to make their pie crusts.

Finally, when the meat is wholly seasoned with all of the ingredients, and is garnished, too, with butter on top, you fold over the end of the crust that is free, with the edge of its dough moistened to refresh it, and you seal the side-wall. When the edge is sealed, you shape it as you like. Then you gild the pasty.[4.12]

Sometime afterward[4.13] it is put in the oven. The oven should be almost as hot as in the previous recipe to cook these pasties, which are sufficiently cooked in two hours provided they are not exceptionally big and large. When they have cooked and cooled, you stop up the holes in the top with a little dough — after the pasty has been in the oven a little while, do not forget to make a hole or two in its covering so that it doesn't burst.

5. How to Make a Royal Pie, for eating warm

Get a good leg of mutton, remove its skin, its bones and its ligaments. Then pound the flesh so as to tenderize it; then chop it up very finely, and as you chop it you season it with salty spice.

When that flesh is perfectly chopped up, you make up the pastry with dark dough,[5.1] giving it a thickness of two good finger widths or of two inches depending on the size of the pie. And make it so it is high. Coat the bottom and around the inner side-wall with slices of lard. Also put a handful of finely chopped beef fat on the bottom. Then put the chopped meat into the pie and, in season, chestnuts: of those you can put in as many as you like, half-roasted. When the meat is in the pie, you add in a handful of finely chopped beef fat, and about half a pound of beef marrow which is cut into bits the size of a walnut. Cover all that mixture with a few slices of lard. Finally, you cover the pie with dark dough a finger thick. Make a hole in the centre of the lid.

That pie should be in the oven about 20 or 24 hours. The oven should be stopped up during that time, so that it will give a heat sufficient to bake

---

[4.12] See Chapter III for this sort of golden glazing.

[4.13] The printed text reads *quelque temps après*. Marnette differs, showing "immediately after."

[5.1] That is, with some proportion of rye flour. See Recipe I,1.

the pie. The pie should be drawn out of the oven from time to time so as to pour into it either sauce or bouillon if it is needed.

Take the bones and skin that you have removed from your leg of mutton, break up the bones roughly and boil them in water along with the skin for about an hour and a half, without salt. When that bouillon is made and is boiled away so that only about a pint is left, you use it in the following way. When the Royal Pie has been in the oven about four hours, you take it out and, with a funnel, you pour about a cup of that hot bouillon into it. Then you put the pie back into the oven. At the end of another two or three hours, you take it out again and check whether it wants any sauce so that you can again add the aforesaid bouillon. And you do the same thing from time to time for up to 15 or 16 hours. Then once again you take the pie out of the oven and take off its cover in order to garnish it with hard-boiled[5.2] egg yolks cut in half, and also to put in mushrooms, coxcombs, rooster kidneys and other tidbits. You can also put in a small clove of garlic and a dash of vinegar. To sharpen the sauce, spice up those tidbits.

Then you put the pie back in the oven and you leave it there about three hours to finish cooking. Manage that in such a way that the sauce has boiled away enough before taking the pie out of the oven. Maintain the fire in the oven constantly so that the heat is just strong enough to bake the pie without burning it.

When the pie is baked, before serving it to the table you remove the clove of garlic you put in. Then you put the cover back on so as to serve that pie covered. And if it is not eaten up all at once, you can reheat it in the oven until it is all finished.

6. How to Make a Pie and a Tourte of Capon, Breast of Veal, Squab, Larks and other things, for eating warm

Make up your pastry crust, which should be of fine dough. Make it of a size and height proportionate to what you want to put in it, and do it so that the centre of the bottom is a little thicker than the rest of the crust. Cover the bottom with a little chopped beef fat, and marrow if you

---

[5.2] The text does not actually indicate how these eggs, qualified as *durs*, are to be hardened. Recipe XXXIII,11 implies that they might be hardened by being set by the fire rather than by being boiled. Hot coals are always available in kitchen, while boiling water may not be.

have any, or else you put lard there chopped so fine that the bits are the size of peas.

Then you get the meat you want to put into the pie: it should previously have been washed in hot water, and it should also have been wiped and not still be damp. If it is breast of veal, you can plump it[6.1] a little in water that is almost boiling. When the meat is dried, you cut it into chunks the width of two fingers, and you cut the ribs in two.

If it is a capon or some other fowl or game bird that you want to put into your pie, you have to flatten the belly, break the big bones, make some slashes on the belly, remove the neck, the wing-ends and the legs. Place the meat in the pie. Then you season it with salty spice, and afterwards garnish the pie with a bit of butter and a few slices of lard. You can also add in some tidbits, asparagus stalks, artichoke bottoms, hard egg yolks either whole or quartered, mushrooms, verjuice mash, finely chopped parsley and also some quenelles;[6.2] and on top of those things you put your slices of lard and your butter. Then, the pie being filled, you cover it over and band it round with paper[6.3] to strengthen the crust and prevent it from bursting.

Make a hole in the centre of the top. Then gild the pie and put it in the oven. Give it a heat similar to what must be given to platter pies, as we shall say in the next recipe.[6.4] These pies should be cooked enough

---

[6.1] *la faire blanchir ou revenir*: the two verbs are synonymous here. See in Recipe 13, below, *chair de veau . . . qui soit blanche, c'est a dire qui soit cuite plus qu'a demy*. This involves a preliminary parboiling procedure which is not primarily a "whitening" *per se* but rather, as the author clarifies, a "plumping": the standard verb for "to plump" is *faire revenir*.

[6.2] These are the *andoüillettes* which the contemporary English translator of the *Cuisinier françois*, I. D. G., glosses as "balls, or roundish small peeces of minced flesh well seasoned." Eggs provide the adhesion in the mixture. While normally this "flesh" was veal, on lean days a spiced hash of fish could be also be used. In La Varenne's kitchen the paste was rolled into balls or mini-sausages; these were kept on hand to be used to lend flavour and as a garnish in a wide variety of dishes.

[6.3] One or several strips of buttered paper are wrapped around the circumference of the pie to lend strength and to hold everything firmly. The procedure was quite common whenever a baking dish was not used, when a fine, frangible (and edible) dough was chosen for the shell, and when the contents of the pie were relatively mobile. The procedure is more explicitly described in the following Recipe 8.

[6.4] Actually, in Recipe 8, below. Marnette translates the term *pastéz d'assiete* as "your Pasties, which are to bee served up hot to Table."

in about an hour and a half, more or less depending on the size of the pie and depending, too, on the degree of heat in the oven.

You can make this pie in a tourtière with a puff-pastry crust, mainly if you fill it with squab.

7. How to Make a Pasty with Sweet Sauce

If you wish to make one of those Pasties with Sweet Sauce, you draw it to the mouth of the oven when it is half-cooked and you set a funnel into the hole in the centre of the pastry top and into it pour a glassful — or as much as is necessary depending on the size of the pie — of very sweet hypocras,[7] or else of melted butter in which sugar has been dissolved along with a little cinnamon, more or less of the one and the other according to the size of the pie. Put the pie back in the oven and finish baking it.

8. How to Make a Platter Pie[8.1]

Get (for instance) close to a pound of veal or fresh pork or mutton or beef; a round of veal is the most suitable flesh for making these pies. Also get a pound of beef fat which is fresh, or else the marrow, and chop them up finely together. When they are coarsely chopped, you season them with salt and spice, then you finish chopping them up. Along with the meat and the fat you can also chop up some scallions or parsley. When the meat is minced, you add in the white and yolk of a raw egg, or only the white, and you mix that into the hash with a wooden spatula so as to bind the mixture better. Into it you can put pinenuts and currants if you wish.

Then you make up a circular shell of fine pastry, and you half-fill it with your hash; flatten out the meat mixture and press it out against

---

[7] The traditional beverage known, after the Greek physician Hippocrates (*c.* 460–*c.* 375 BC), as *hypocras* or *vinum hippocraticum* was composed of red wine and an indeterminate but broad variety of spices. See a recipe for it in *The French Confectioner*, Recipe IV,1.

[8.1] *Pasté d'assiette*: see also Recipe V,82 in *The French Cook*. Because such pies are made up and baked without the support of an encompassing oven dish or tourtière, they can be served directly, as is and hot, to the table on such a serving receptacle as a platter. According to Cotgrave and Huguet (Edmond Huguet, *Dictionnaire de la langue française du seizième siècle*, Paris: Didier, Champion, 1925), they were used as hors d'œuvres at the beginning of a meal.

the shell. Then over it you put asparagus or mushrooms, quartered hard egg yolks, a few slices of beef palate. As well, if you have any you can put sweetbreads, pistachios and any other tidbits you can get; among those tidbits you can also put a few pieces of beef marrow and half-roasted chestnuts. In verjuice season you can put in about a dozen mashed verjuice grapes, more or less according to the size of the pie. Then you finish off filling the pie with your hash, and you press it down somewhat on the tidbits. If you make a very tall pie, you can do several layers in it, both of chopped meat, seasoned as directed above, and of tidbits.

Cover your pie over and gild its top after having made a little hole at the tip of the peak[8.2] of the lid. If the crust of your pie is very fine and quite tall, you put a band of coarse paper around the body of the pie. That band should be cut to the height of the wall,[8.3] and should be greased with good fresh butter on the side that is against the crust; then a cord is put around that strip so as to bind it to the pie.

When the pie is garnished, filled and covered, you can put it in the oven. There is no need for the oven's heat to be nearly so great as for cooking larger pies. These pies should be cooked enough in a good half hour, provided they are not very large and provided the oven heat is right for them. Depending on whether these pies are bigger or smaller, they will need more or less time to cook.[8.4]

You can make one of these pies in a tourtière, and make the crust of puff pastry.

9. How to Make a Minced Veal (*Gaudiveau*) Pie[9.1]

Minced Veal Pies should be made with meat from round of veal or

---

[8.2] The French term used here, *la pointe du chapiteau*, indicates that the pastry lid of the platter pie, the upper crust, is conical in shape. See the next recipe.

[8.3] *Il faut que cette bande soit découpée par le bord.* The intention seems to be that that paper be trimmed as it is held against the irregular height of the pie's wall. Marnette understands *une bande de gros papiers* as "a stay of gray course paper," and writes only that "this said stay must be *fastened* to edge of your Pastie" (my italics).

[8.4] Even though the author gives a range of baking times, the half-hour average time suggests that platter pies are relatively small in genre.

[9.1] See also Recipes V,81 and XIV,7 in *The French Cook* for this *Pasté de gaudiveau*. Properly the meat mixture called *gaudivaux* makes use of only veal along with a variety of condiments. Marnette calls the *pasté de gaudiveau* "a Cockney ovall minced Pie."

with some other flesh chopped with the fat and seasoned like that of platter pies. That is why a Minced Veal Pie is different from a platter pie only in that platter pies are round and topped with a cone of pastry,[9.2] whereas Minced Veal Pies are flat, open and oval-shaped.[9.3] There is another peculiarity of Minced Veal Pies, and that is that they are moistened and seasoned with a white sauce made from verjuice and egg yolk mixed together;[9.4] with that sauce a Minced Veal Pie is moistened as it is baked, then the pie is put back in the oven for about another eighth of an hour for the sauce to thicken. You have to make the meat of a Minced Veal Pie adhere to its crust, and for that reason you have to press it with your fingers, mainly along the side-wall so that its dough is firm.

When you have laid in the first layer of meat, it is covered with asparagus stalks and other tidbits, among which you can, in their season, put half-roasted chestnuts,[9.5] and verjuice mash when you have any; then you can grate a little nutmeg on the tidbits. You cover those tidbits with a layer of meat that has been chopped and seasoned as has been said, and after you have pressed the meat a little on the tidbits, you set up the side-wall. You can reinforce that with a band of dough[9.6] which you stick onto its inside, and you do it in such a way that it protrudes a little onto the meat.[9.7] You have to cut out that side-wall of dough that will touch the meat of your pie, adding in a few quenelles which you have made from your chopped meat for that purpose. You can grate a little nutmeg on the pie when it is ready to be put in the oven.

Bake the pie and, when it is almost done, you take it out to the mouth of the oven in order to pour into it the white sauce of which we

---

[9.2] *ronds & couverts en pointe.*

[9.3] Cotgrave gives secondary and tertiary glosses in his definition of the French term *goudivaux* (see Appendix 2, below, *s.v.* pie): "A kind of open Pie . . . Also, a figure in carving, like that pie; or, a long painted Ovall."

[9.4] The composition of this so-called white sauce is confirmed in Recipe 16, below. The inappositeness of its name raises questions, although the sauce is in fact one of the most common preparations in La Varenne's kitchen.

[9.5] The text offers a choice here between varieties of chestnut, *chastaignes ou marrons*, the first being ordinary, the second cultivated and larger.

[9.6] Marnette translates this *bande de paste* as a "shoulder of paste."

[9.7] . . . *en sorte qu'elle deborde un peu sur la chair.* This reinforcement seems to be designed as a sort of interior horizontal buttressing.

have spoken above in this recipe. Then you finish off baking the pie.

You can also make one of these pies in a tourtière, using puff pastry for the crust.

10. A Tidbit Pie

To make a Tidbit Pie, you use chopped and seasoned meat in the same way as for a Minced Veal (*Gaudiveau*) Pie or else a platter pie. But you have to put less chopped meat into the Tidbit Pies; rather you put in many tidbits, and fat and marrow between the layers of tidbits. The top of the filling is garnished with quenelles of the same chopped meat, then a little nutmeg is grated over them. Finally the pie is covered and put in the oven.

11. How to Make a Tidbit Tourte

Make a Tidbit Pie in a tourtière. The crust should be of puff pastry.

12. Another Way to Make a Tourte of Chopped Meat

Get veal or capon or whatever other good boiled meat you like. Remove the skin, the ligaments and the bones, then chop up that flesh finely and grind it afterwards in a mortar. Add in a little fresh cheese and the same amount of old cheese that has been grated or cut up very small; also add in about six well beaten eggs and as much beef marrow as is needed, or hog's fat which has been cut up small. Mix all those things together and season them with fine salt and with a small quantity of spice mixture or ground cinnamon.

When your mixture is ready, in a tourtière you set out a shell of puff pastry. Fill it sufficiently with your filling or mixture, then cover it with a dough lid. Make a little hole in the centre. Bake this tourte as is needed.

13. Cardinal's Pies

In a little tourtière or a white metal mould,[13.1] spread out puff pastry to a thickness of about a quarter *écu*, and let it overhang all around. Fill the shell sufficiently with veal or flesh of fowl, raw or else blanched — that is, flesh that has been more than half-cooked — chopped up very small along with the same quantity of beef marrow or beef fat. That mixture should be seasoned with salty spice; you can mix in pinenuts and currants and a few bits of hard egg yolks.

[13.1] Marnette translates *un moule de fer blanc* as "a white lattin square Pie-pan."

When the pie is filled, you cover it neatly with a crust of puff pastry, then you bake it.

Some people put sugar into this sort of pie, and also put in some sweet sauce[13.2] when it is half-cooked. If these pies are small, you can cook them in a little copper oven.[13.3]

14. An English Pie

Get a very tender young hare which is dressed; remove all the pluck, too. Cut off the head and the legs, flatten the belly, also pound the flesh of the young hare to make it tenderer. Make little slashes that are rather long and deep on the back and thighs; or else you can cut your young hare up into pieces. Then lard the flesh with little lardoons.

When the young hare is prepared in that way, you make a pastry shell of a large enough size, giving it a thickness of two good fingers. Set it on a sheet of paper, and on one of the ends of that shell you make a bed of beef marrow or fat, or of finely chopped lard; that bed or layer should be as long and as wide at the young hare, the bed of fat also being seasoned with salty spice. Then you lay the young hare on the bed of fat with its belly down, and if you have cut the hare into pieces you have to set them all back into their proper place. Then the hare is seasoned on top with salty spice; you also put chopped marrow and fat on the hare, then tidbits such as currants, well washed pinenuts, and candied lemon peel, very finely cut up or finely sliced; also add bits of beef marrow, mushrooms, pistachios, and sweetbreads if you have any, blanched cock's combs, hard egg yolks, either whole or quartered, and capers if there are any. Those tidbits should be mixed, and seasoned with a little salty spice. When they are laid out on the young hare, you cover it with a thin layer of finely chopped fat. You again put on top a few small slices of lard, then you spread lengthwise about half a pound of good fresh butter which must be put on the mixture; on top of the butter add a good big handful of powdered sugar.

When the pie is filled, you cover it with the other end of the pastry sheet that is still free. When it is sealed and well fashioned, it has to be

---

[13.2] See Recipes 3 and 7, above, and 17, below, for possible compositions of this sweet sauce.

[13.3] The name of these *petits fours* will eventually designate the small items usually baked in them.

gilded on top, then put into the oven on a sheet of paper. Take care that you don't break it.

After the pie has been in the oven for half an hour, you make a hole in the centre of its upper crust so that it doesn't burst. You give it fire as for a Turkey-Cock Pie.[14.1] This pie can be cooked in two good hours.

Some people soak half a grain of musk in a drop of rosewater and pour it into this pie while baking it, but the odour of musk is disagreeable to most women, and others;[14.2] for that reason it is better not to put any in.

When this pie is baked, you take it out of the oven and gradually spread some sugar glazing[14.3] on the crust with a knife or with the back of a silver spoon. That glazing should be almost as thin as a sheet of paper. As soon as the pie is glazed with that, you put it back in the mouth of the oven for about an eighth of an hour to dry the glazing. The heat must be extremely slight so the glazing remains white: if the oven is too hot, the glazing becomes russet-coloured. Just as soon as the glazing has dried, the pie has to be taken out of the oven and served as promptly as you can, so the pie won't get cold and the glazing dissolve.[14.4]

15. A Swiss Pie

Make up a platter pie with *pâte brisée*, making the crust a good finger thick. On its bottom spread a handful of veal chopped with fat, then fill the pie with a young hare or rabbit that has been cut up into pieces. Season that meat with salty spice, adding in a quantity of chestnuts, a scallion or a shallot, either crushed or cut up, and tidbits if you have any. Then on top of that put a handful of veal chopped with fat, and six or seven veal quenelles, then half a pound of butter, four ounces of marrow and four ounces of chopped beef fat, then a few slices of lard on the whole composition.

When the pie is made up, you cover it with a lid of puff pastry the thickness of a little finger; gild the lid and make a hole in its centre. Then

---

[14.1] The reference to heat at the end of Recipe 4, above, is not particularly helpful.

[14.2] For this last phrase Marnette is less vague: " ... and some Males too."

[14.3] For the composition of this *glace de sucre* see Chapter V.

[14.4] The original text has, *de peur que ... la glace ne se fonde*. As the pie cools, the hardened film of sugar glazing is apt to absorb enough humidity to "melt".

you have to band the pie round about with buttered paper the height of the pie, and tie the paper with a cord to hold it in place.

Put the pie into the oven on a clean sheet of paper, and give it a moderate hearth as for a cake. It takes about two hours to cook.

16. A Giblet Pie[16]

Giblets of fowl have to be well picked over and cleaned. The necks are cut up, wings, gizzards, livers, from which you take out the gall — wash all those things carefully two or three times in water, then drain them. You can also cut up the pluck of a suckling piglet or of a lamb, after having taken out the bitter part — that is to say, the gall; that pluck has to be washed after being cut up. Then those pieces have to be put into a very clean terrine and seasoned with salty spice, parsley and finely chopped lard. You can add in mushrooms and verjuice mash when there is any, or midribs of chard or asparagus or cut up artichoke bottoms.

When that mixture is ready, set up the shell or crust of the pie. It is proper for it to be of fine dough — make it two quarter-écus thick more or less depending on the size of the pie. Then it is filled with the seasoned giblets and offal we have mentioned. Then on those giblets are put a few slices of lard and a good chunk of fresh butter, the amount depending on the size of the pie, which is flattened out.

Put a lid of dough on the pie and gild it. If necessary, band it with a strip of paper greased with butter. Make a hole in the centre of the lid and put the pie in the oven. When it is baked, a little white sauce, composed of egg yolks thinned with a little verjuice, is poured into it with a funnel. Put the pie back into the oven a while for the sauce to thicken.

17. Italian Platter Pie of Puff Pastry

Set up your puff pastry making it an inch thick. Then cover its bottom with a handful of veal chopped with fat. Then add three partridges or three old doves with their feet, wings and neck cut off, their belly crushed, larded with a few lardoons across their flesh as in a venison-type pie.[17.1]

---

[16] *Un Pasté de Requeste.* Nicolas de Bonnefons's *Pastez de Requeste* are made with squab giblets: . . . *des Abbatis de Pigeonneaux, à sçavoir les Aisles, Testes, & Iusiers, que les Patissiers ostent des Pigeonnaux qu'ils mettent en Paste pour le Bourgeois* (*Delices de la campagne,* Amsterdam, 1661, 234).

[17.1] See Recipe 2, above.

Then you season them with salty spice.[17.2] Also put in skinned chestnuts, pinenuts, currants — of each of those a small handful — three hard egg yolks cut in half, a little ground cinnamon, six ounces of sugar, a slice of lemon, mushrooms, and tidbits if you have any. Instead of partridge and doves you can use some other meat in this pie — for instance, rabbit cut up and well interlarded.

To enrich the meat in this pie, you add onto all of those ingredients a handful of veal chopped up with marrow or fat, six or seven veal quenelles, half a pound of butter, chopped fat and marrow — of each of those four ounces — with a few slices of lard on top. Cover the pie with a lid of puff-pastry dough the thickness of a little finger or thereabouts. Gild the lid and make a hole in its centre.

You have to band this pie all about with buttered paper which is the height of the pie, and bind that paper with a cord to keep it in place.

Put the pie in the oven on a sheet of white paper and give it a mild hearth as for a cake. It takes about two and a half hours to bake this pie. When it is almost done, you take it out of the oven and through a funnel in the hole in the lid you pour a sweet sauce made of four ounces of sugar and close to a cup of wine, along with a little ground cinnamon. Put the pie back in the oven for about half an hour to thicken the sweet sauce.

18. To Make Little Spanish Pies

Make fine dough, for one and a half cups of flour[18.1] adding four egg yolks. When that dough is ready, you set up the shells for little platter pies the thickness of two sheets of paper or of a testoon,[18.2] more or less depending on their height. You fill them with the following hash.

Very finely chop up the white of a capon, four ounces of fresh pork, three ounces of mutton, two veal sweetbreads,[18.3] fat lard, good beef

---

[17.2] See Recipe II,2.

[18.1] *un litron de farine.* A dry measure of volume, a *litron* would amount to roughly the same as La Varenne's twelve-ounce pound or three-quarter of a modern pound. Marnette's equivalent is "one pinte of flower." The amounts here merely establish a ratio of eggs-to-flour and of course are not specific quantities for these pie shells.

[18.2] The *teston*, was a thin silver coin. We have to bear in mind that even by the seventeeth century ordinary paper was still relatively bulky.

[18.3] Here the text reads *deux ris ou fagoües de veaux*: both *ris de veau* and *fagoües de veau* are names for the same thing, the animal's pancreas. Marnette, not always very accurate or faithful in his translation, writes merely "two Calves kidneys."

marrow, beef fat — of each of those three ounces — a little chives or onion, a lot of mushrooms, some salt, of mild spice whatever you like; and chop up all those things together. Fill your shells with that hash. Then you have to cover your pies with puff-pastry dough, [made] with clarified lard.[18.4] Gild that upper crust. Then you bake those little pies.

19. To Make Little Princess Pies

Get sweet dough[19.1] and from it make little shells as thin as possible; they must be built up in little tourtières as if you were making little Cardinal's Pies.[19.2] Fill these pies with roast or boiled meat that is very delicate, such as capon white meat chopped very finely with good beef marrow, and seasoned with salty spice. You can add in blanched tidbits, mushrooms cooked in butter, and similar things.

When the little pies are filled, they are covered with the same dough. Then you bake them. They take a moderate hearth, and will be done in less than a quarter of an hour.

20. To Make a Venison Pie[20.1] with Carp or some other Fish, for eating cold

Get a fine carp or some other large fish and, if it has scales, scale it, then clean it out. Some fish, such as eel, have to be skinned. When the fish has been gutted, the gills can be removed — those are the fish's lungs.[20.2]

When the fish is readied, you make deep slashes on its back, then lard the fish with whale lard[20.3] or with strips of eel; on meat days you

---

[18.4] In Recipe 4, above, the author mentions that some pastry chefs use clarified lard, *sain doux*, instead of butter to make their pie crusts.

[19.1] See the *paste de sucre* in Recipe I,6.

[19.2] See the *Pastés à la Cardinale* of Recipe 13, above.

[20.1] *pasté en venaison*. In Recipe 2, above, see the note about a venison-*type* of pie. Like a chunk of venison, a fish will now be wrapped whole and baked *en croûte*.

[20.2] This explanation may seem strange, even superfluous. However, the French term, *ouyes*, "ears," perpetuated a very old designation of a fish's gills; in the Middle Ages and Renaissance they were called *oreilles*. Whether Marnette understood the word *ouyes* or not, he adds his own urgent warning: "You may also take out its lungs, which is nought to bee eaten either boyled, baked or stewed."

[20.3] This being a fish pie would make it suitable for serving on lean days provided *all* of its ingredients were lean. Here the lard, normally pork fat, has to be changed. Incomprehensibly Marnette writes, "Lard you fish with lard made of her wings …."

can lard the fish with the [pork] lard used to lard meat.

Do not [forget to] remove the milt [and] any eggs that are found in the fish's belly.[20.4]

When your fish is quite ready, you set out a sheet of pastry that is two or three fingers thick. If it is a large fish that you wish to put *en croûte*, the sheet has to be of a sufficient length and width. Then on one end of it you lay down a layer of fresh butter which is proportionate to the length of the fish; then you sprinkle it with salty spice. You lay out your fish on the butter, then you sprinkle your salty spice into the belly and outside of the fish; put a layer of butter into the belly, as well as a layer on top and, on that, a few bay leaves. You can can put the milt or the eggs alongside the fish, and spice them. Salt your pie sensibly. When it is seasoned, the pie must be closed, and for that fold or turn back the end of the crust that was left bare.

Then gild this pie, with lean gilding if it is in Lent.[20.5]

Put the pie into the oven. When it has been there for about half an hour, you make a little hole in the top of the crust, then you put the pie back into the oven to finish baking it. It takes a good three hours to bake one of these fish pies if it is large. When you judge that it is baked, you take it out of the oven and, by means of a little stick slid gently into the pie through the hole in the upper crust, you check whether the sauce is covering the fish; if it looks as if the sauce is too boiled away,[20.6] as often happens, you melt butter, which has to be seasoned with your salty spice, and pour it into the pie by means of a funnel in order to increase the sauce.

One day after this pie is cooked, you stop up the hole in the pie's lid with a little dough.[20.7]

[20.4] Marnette has, "You must not forget to take out of your fish the Milters, and Rows which you shall find in their bellies." This removal is standard practice in preparing a fish: see the beginning of Recipe 23, below. Since both milt and roe do appear later as optional ingredients in both this and the next recipe, it seems that the text here of the French edition — *ne pas oster les laites ou laictances* — is clearly in error.

[20.5] For this alternative in which hen's eggs are replaced, see Chapter III.

[20.6] *paroist estre trop courte*; properly, "seems too reduced."

[20.7] To the end of the recipe Marnette adds, "And thus your said Pie will keep for a good while, till such time as you shall have occasion to eat it.

21. How to Make a Fish Pie, covered or open, for eating warm

Get whatever fish you like, such as a carp, eel, tench or red mullet, clean it and prepare it as we directed in the previous recipe, except that you don't need to lard it.

Some people think it is appropriate to scald or plump the fish in hot water[21.1] when the fish is dressed, particularly if it is slimy,[21.2] such as tench or eel are, before putting it into the platter pie, which pastry chefs do, because if you put a raw fish into a pie it will make the pie burst.

When the fish is readied, a shell of fine pastry or puff pastry has to be made up, and made proportionate in length and height to the size of your fish, for normally fish pies are made in an oval shape. Nevertheless, note that normally the crust of these pies is not made so fine, that is, not as much butter is used, primarily when it is intended that these pies be open, because the crust would collapse[21.3] too easily and the sauce would be lost. That crust should be about the thickness of two or three *piastres* or 58-sous coins.[21.4] Note, therefore, that you should not make the dough of these fish pies so fine, and that good pastry chefs knead it with warm water so that it is firmer. And when the shell is set up to make an open fish pie, you should leave it exposed to the air for an hour or two to harden up before putting the fish into it.

You have to proportion the size of your shell to the size of the fish you want to lay within it. When the pastry shell is solidified, you put a layer of fresh butter on the bottom. Sprinkle that with salty spice, then lay your fish down on it. You should have made cuts into the thickest part of its flesh. If the fish is in slices and if the shell is made oval shaped,

---

[21.1] In later editions the long passage that begins here with the words *dans de l'eau chaude* and continues through the next five paragraphs to the words *humectée par le beurre fondu* ("moistened with the melted butter") was somehow removed and printed in the preceding recipe immediately after the directions about removing the fish's milt and eggs.

[21.2] The term *glaireux* refers to the oily, mucous coating on the surface of certain fish. It is that substance, high in protein, that yields a jelly when it is concentrated. In older French *glaire* is egg white.

[21.3] In the text: *renverseroit*, properly "fall over". The sense is clearly that this thinner, richer dough might burst.

[21.4] Literally *piastres ou pieces de cinquante huict sols*. The equivalent is "two or three half crowns at least," according to Marnette.

the slices must be set back in their proper arrangement. Put a layer of butter into the fish's belly as well, and another layer on top. Season with salty spice. Along side the fish you can put its eggs or milt, sprinkling them with salty spice. Then into the pie you can add pinenuts, currants, mushrooms, capers, asparagus, bits of artichoke bottoms or other such things if you have them, and verjuice mash. Some people also put in oysters that have been plumped in boiling water. [Take care] that your pie is not oversalted.

Then, if the crust is fine and you are afraid it might collapse in the oven when it is moistened with the melted butter, the pie has to be banded on the outside; a double band of paper can also be put on the inside before filling the pie.[21.5] Those bands should be of paper that is doubled up and well greased with butter, and they should be tied on the outside with two or three rounds of cord.

Put your pie into the oven and be careful that the crust doesn't collapse one way or the other; if it should subside in some place, it should be set back up again with the oven shovel. When this pie is half-baked, you draw it out to the oven's mouth to replace butter and mashed verjuice grapes; or else you put about two ounces of skinned, ground almonds into it, or almond milk made with a little verjuice. Return the pie into the oven.

These open fish pies can be baked in an hour and a half, or there-abouts, provided they are of a moderate size.[21.6]

Note that if you wish to put a whole eel into pastry, and to make an open pie with it, it must be rolled around and its backbone cut every four inches or so: if you don't break its backbone it will straighten out as it cooks, and in straightening it could break the crust and spoil it; that is why it is better to cut it up into slices of whatever length you like.

These fish pies can be made covered. For that you need to make a sheet of fine dough long enough and wide enough to make up your pie all of a single piece, like a venison-type pie.[21.7] When that sheet is ready, on one end of it put a layer of fresh butter, season that with spice, and lay

---

[21.5] There is no mention later of this inner band being removed.

[21.6] A possible serving garnish for an open fish pie is mentioned in Recipe XXI,3.

[21.7] See Recipe 2, above.

out the prepared fish. When the pie is completely filled, you cover it with the end of the shell that is left bare. Then a hole is made in the centre of the top, as was directed in the paragraph on venison-type pies.

Note that sometimes round pies or platter pies are made with fish. These pies should be covered, and likewise what is put inside is cut up into slices.

22. Pies of Deboned, Chopped Fish

Get as much fine, butter-enriched dough[22.1] as is needed, like that for platter pies or Minced Veal (*Gaudivaux*) Pies. Build up your little shells or crusts as for Cardinal's Pies[22.2] or for three-sous-sized platter pies. If you are making platter pies, the crust has to be a little thicker in the centre of the bottom.

When the shells are set up, you fill them first with a thin layer of fresh butter. Then the pie is half-filled with minced carp or some other fish, and seasoned as we shall suggest below. Then on that hash you put a bed of lean tidbits — for example, a few pieces of artichoke bottoms or parboiled asparagus, or milt or carp tongues cooked in court bouillon, or half-roasted chestnuts. Outside of Lent you can add in hard egg-yolk halves;[22.3] if it is a meat-day, you can mix in a few pieces of beef marrow.

When the pie is filled with tidbits, you add in yet another chunk of butter; and if you don't put any tidbits into this pie, you mustn't omit putting butter on the first layer of minced fish. After that you finish off filling the pie sufficiently with fish hash, on top of which you again put a little bit of butter. If the pies are built up round like platter pies, a pastry lid is added in the shape of a cone;[22.4] it must be pierced at its top, and then gilded.

[22.1] *paste fine estoffée.* The same verb *estoffer* is used in Recipe 2, above; it refers to the addition of butter-fat to a "fine" pastry dough.

[22.2] See Recipe 13, above.

[22.3] It is to be noted that eggs are forbidden during Lent but apparently not on other lean-days outside of Lent. The detailed subtitle of the *Pastissier françois* includes a promise to show *le moyen d'apprester toute sorte d'œufs pour les jours maigres*: "the way to prepare every sort of egg dish for lean-days." See Chapters XXIX and XXXII.

[22.4] The author has written *en façon d'une piramide*, which term seems to suppose a square base. Marnette translates "like unto a pinacle."

Put these pies into the oven, and give them a hearth as for little platter pies.[22.5]

If you make open minced-fish pies, when they are baked you can add in a sweet sauce: if it is a meat-day, you can put in the stock of a mutton leg or of some other roast meat, or else a white sauce of raw egg yolks mixed with verjuice. Then the pie has to be put back in the oven a short while for it to take on the flavour of the sauce, and for the sauce to thicken. But these minced-fish pies are difficult to manage if they are on the large size; that is why it is easier to make tourtes with puff-pastry dough.[22.6]

23. How to Debone Fish and to Prepare a Good Fish Paste as a Pie Filling

To make a fish paste, you need first of all to scale the fish if it needs it, then skin it — that is to say, take off its skin — then gut the fish's belly by removing its bowels and all that is there, whether eggs or milt, and blood. Then you debone it — that is to say, you need to separate the flesh from the bones; the more that small bones are found in with the fish's flesh, the more attentive you have to be in deboning it. You can do that by lifting a fish's flesh — for example, that of a carp — in a slab with a knife; but because that way of deboning a fish is difficult, and given that the fish's flesh is completely raw, it is better to debone the fish in the following way.

When the fish is cleaned and gutted, it must be plunged into almost-boiling water and left to steep there for a length of time that depends on how thick it is. It is time to take it out of the water when you you can easily detach the flesh from the bones, and that way it is easy to debone the fish. However, to the extent that the water takes away some of the flavour of the fish, it is better to cook the fish in a court bouillon. After it has half-cooked in the court bouillon, so that it takes on its flavour, it is easy to separate the fish's flesh from its bones.

When you have drawn the fish's flesh away from its bones, you put it on a table and add to it a little parsley, some salt, mushrooms cut into

---

[22.5] In Recipe 8, above, we were told that for platter pies the oven heat need not be as high as for a large pie. The baking time mentioned there is relatively short: half an hour.

[22.6] This is the *paste feuilletée* whose recipe is given in Recipe I,4.

pieces, and a little spice. If you like sweet things, you can add in currants and well-washed pinenuts. Everything has to be chopped up together. When the hash is ready, the pies are filled with it as has been directed.

If you have any filling left over, you can put it into a bowl with butter and an onion, or a whole scallion, and cook it. While it is cooking, turn it over from time to time. You can also add in capers, a little court bouillon if you have any and, as it finishes cooking, a little verjuice.

When the hash is cooked and the sauce is done and tasting good, you remove the onion or scallion, and you grate a little nutmeg over the hash if it so happens that you have put in no spice at all. On the hash you can stick sippets of fried bread. A little German Sauce[23.1] would also be good in a hash, if you haven't put in any court bouillon.

To dress up[23.2] a fish paste even more, you can chop up yolks and whites of hard-boiled eggs with the fish hash. Or else you can put into it the stock of a mutton leg or of some other good meat.

If you wish to make quenelles of fish, get minced fish before it is cooked in butter, and moisten it with a little egg white or verjuice or white wine; then squeeze that hash in your hand to bind it like quenelles; then cook them like hash [as above]. Some people cook the fish paste before making pies; but when the hash is cooked, it is too runny because of the sauce.

24. To Make Little Oil-Dough Pies with Fish Paste

Get dough made with oil,[24.1] and make up little shells in little tour-tières — provided you wouldn't rather make little raised pies.

When the shells are set up, you fill them with a hash of carp or pike or perch or sole or of the flesh of any other good fish, cooked in court bouillon. That flesh should be chopped up well with parsley and pinenuts and a few adequately desalted anchovies. You can also add in mushrooms

---

[23.1] There is no recipe for this *Sauce d'Alemagne*, either here or in *The French Cook*. A German Broth (*Brouet d'Allemagne* was popular in earlier French cooking: see *The Viandier of Taillevent*, ed. Scully (Ottawa: University of Ottawa Press, 1988), Recipe 22; the *Menagier de Paris*, ed. cit., §108 (and its lean version, made with eggs, §127); and Chiquart, *On Cookery*, ed. cit., Recipes 2 and 7.

[23.2] The verb here, *déguiser*, "disguise," has interesting implications.

[24.1] See Recipe I,5, above.

cooked in butter. All those things must be chopped up well together, and the mixture seasoned with salty spice.[24.2]

When that hash is chopped very finely, you add in good, clarified oil in moderation, as is directed in the paragraph on Oil Dough.[24.3] When the hash is ready, the shells are filled, then the pies are covered with lids of oil dough. Then gild them and cook the pies, your heat being moderate. Those who don't like oil can use butter in these pies, instead of putting in oil.

Chapter VIII

Consecrated Breads

1. How to Make Consecrated Bread[1.1]

If you wish to use half a bushel of wheat flour[1.2] to make consecrated bread, you must first get an amount of about two chicken's eggs of free leaven,[1.3] and put about a third of your flour on a very clean table. Make a well — that is to say, a hole — in the centre of the flour, put the leaven in it and moisten the leaven thoroughly with hot water, working it with your hands; then you mix your flour with the leaven that has dissolved in the water, adding whatever water is required in order to knead that dough

---

[24.2] For this variety of the common blend of mild spices, see Recipe II,2, above.

[24.3] That is, again, Recipe I,5, above.

[1.1] *un pain benist*. This "bread" is properly flat, round "wafers." The kitchen of a noble household may well have been called upon to provide such wafers to be consecrated in the Mass. We may also understand that the *pâtissier* in a private household of the time used such a recipe as this and the next one to make a delicate table bread for his master's meals.

Rather than "Consecrated Bread" the English translator Marnette interestingly uses the term "March-Pain Wafer." A secondary sense of this old term for marzipan is, according to the *Oxford English Dictionary*, anything that is delicious or exquisite. The reason for Marnette's avoidance of a literal translation of the French title may lie in Cotgrave's gloss of *Pain benist* as "Holie-bread, used in Popish Churches."

[1.2] In Chapter VI we are told that a half-bushel of flour should weigh six pounds or a little more; further, in Recipe 4, above, the half-bushel contains roughly one and a half quarts of flour.

[1.3] *franc levain*. This leaven is a sour wheat paste that is in a state of fermentation, a sourdough. Towards the end of this recipe beer foam (barm) or brewer's yeast are mentioned as alternative leavening.

until it is very smooth; it should end up quite soft. When the dough is kneaded enough, so that it has no lumps in it, you cover it carefully and keep it warm in a place without any draughts or cold, just as if it were to make bread.

If it is summer, leave the dough like that for two or three hours, so that the leaven or dough can work sufficiently; but if it is a cold time of year, like winter, you need five or six hours for the leaven to work.

Check on the dough from time to time, and when you see that it is swollen and sort of fissured on top, you put the rest of your half-bushel of flour on a table. Make a big hollow in its centre and put a little warm water there in which you have melted two ounces of salt, then three ounces of fresh butter;[1.4] also put all of your dough into the same hollow and mix everything together and reduce it to a dough that should not be as soft as the first dough. Punch and knead all of the dough well, then turn it over like a large loaf of bread, and cover it straight away so it doesn't get cold and darken.[1.5]

Leave all of your dough like that for about half an hour. Then set it out lengthwise,[1.6] or else put it on a pastry board that has been floured so that the dough doesn't stick to its surface. Then form up your consecrated breadloaf, which has then to be gilded on both the inner and outer sides. You have also to prick consecrated bread inside and out with a sharpened stick so that it doesn't swell up. When the consecrated bread is fashioned, you set it onto a peel that is big enough, taking care not to break the loaf, and put it into the oven.

It takes a short half-hour to bake a loaf of consecrated bread from a half- bushel of flour. The oven should be a little less warm than to bake a loaf of coarse bread. You can tell whether a loaf of consecrated bread

---

[1.4] Rough equivalences only, here: *un demy carteron* and *un quarteron* for the salt and butter respectively, bearing in mind that these "quarters" are of a twelve-ounce pound. It is perhaps interesting to recall that the word *ounce* derives from the same source at the English word *inch*: Latin *uncia*, meaning the twelfth part of something. Troy measure today perpetuates the system of twelve ounces to the pound.

[1.5] *afin qu'elle ne se morfonde, & ne se hasle pas.* Marnette seems uncertain about the second verb and puts "that it may not take cold, and become flaggy."

[1.6] *vous la dresserés en long.* Marnette has "You may make it into a rowl [roll]." A loaf of consecrated bread is somewhat elongated, like a stubby modern baguette, rather than a round mound.

is done by the same means as we shall describe you can see that bread is done.[1.7]

Note that many pastry chefs use brewer's yeast or beer foam[1.8] for the consecrated bread they make instead of putting in leaven, because brewer's yeast prepares the dough and makes it rise more promptly; it makes their products more attractive, too, and makes them more delicate, even though less wholesome.

Note, too, that if you make a large loaf of consecrated bread you have to beat[1.9] the dough with a big chunk of wood that pastry chefs call a bat.

2. A More Delicate Consecrated Loaf, that in Paris is called "cousin", and in other places people call a "cantel".[2.1]

Make up your leavening as we said in the previous recipe with the third of your half-bushel of fine flour; when it has risen or is ready, you put the rest of your half-bushel of flour on the pastry table or table and make a well in its middle. Heat half a pint of water — or rather milk,[2.2] so that that consecrated bread or cantel is finer and more delicate; into the milk you dissolve two ounces of salt and twelve ounces of butter,[2.3] then you pour that into the centre of the flour. You also add half a pound of soft, non-skimmed cheese;[2.4] and, if you wish, you can also add in three

---

[1.7] There seem to be no such hints in *The French Pastry Chef*.

[1.8] *leveure ou escume de bierre* here, as opposed to the *franc levain* that has been specified earlier.

[1.9] The author's term here is *broyer*. Normally that verb means to grind or reduce to powder, but here the context clearly indicates that the chef is collapsing the risen dough with something more powerful, a "bat" or *broye*, than merely his fist. Marnette writes merely, "rowle your paste with a great wooden Rowling pin."

[2.1] Marnette is rather free with his handling of this rubric: "To make a March-Pain far more delicate, which is usually at Paris, called a Cousen or Nephew, and in other places it is called a Kindnesse or a Contril." While the *Oxford English Dictionary* attests to *cantle* in English usage, only a form *cantel* could properly be related to La Varenne's *chanteau*.

[2.2] The author has overlooked a difficulty. The *chopine* of water weighing roughly sixteen ounces, and the *chopine* of milk weighing roughly twenty-four ounces, the quantity of liquid here will vary according to the choice allowed.

[2.3] *une livre de beurre*.

[2.4] *fromage mol non ecresmé*: that is, cheese made from whole milk, from which the butter fat has not been removed: "not uncreamed," as Marnette puts it.

or four eggs mixed with a little milk. Put in the leaven, too, and knead everything together carefully.

When you have worked and kneaded all the dough well, you turn it[2.5] as was said in the previous recipe, then you cover it over and let it sit for about half an hour. Then from it you make a cantel or a consecrated loaf, which has to be gilded and pricked, and finally put in the oven.

Note that this fine consecrated bread takes longer to bake because its dough is richer.

Chapter IX

Tourtes

1. How to Make a Pastry-Chef's-Cream Tourte

Make up a shell of fine or puff-pastry dough,[1.1] and set it out in a tourtière.

Note that it is good for copper tourtières to be tinned on the inside so that the pastry of baked dishes doesn't stick to the tourtière and doesn't absorb anything bad[1.2] from the copper. The bottom of tourtières should also be flat without any bumps, so that the bottom of the baked dish doesn't stick to the bottom of the tourtière.

Note, too, that, if the baked item is not of puff pastry, a bit of butter has to be spread with the thumb inside the tourtière, to grease it lightly so that the baked dish doesn't stick to the tourtière as it bakes. The inside of the tourtière has to be greased also when you use it for a baked dish that has no crust, such as a Bread Omelet.[1.3] If the crust of a baked dish is made of puff pastry, there is no need to grease the bottom of the tourtière with butter; rather it is enough to sprinkle it lightly on the inside with a pinch of wheat flour so the shell won't stick to the tourtière.

[2.5] The loaf of bread for consecration is formed into a roll.

[1.1] For the *paste fine* and *paste de feuilletage* see Recipes I,3 and I,4, respectively.

[1.2] While Marnette tries to cover all bases with "any ill or offensive sent or taste," the author's phrase, *aucune mauvaise qualité*, is in fact broader and is likely intended to include any dangerous physical properties thought to be in the nature of copper.

[1.3] For the *Aumelette au pain, ou ratton*, see Recipe XXXIII,22.

When the tourtière is lined with its pastry shell, you must set (for example, for a tourte of moderate size) some three ounces[1.4] of good fresh butter in a dish[1.5] on the fire to melt. When it has melted, you add into it about the amount of three eggs of Pastry Chef's Cream[1.6] and a good handful of sugar, a little ground cinnamon and extremely little rosewater. You can add in currants, pinenuts and small slices of candied lemon peel. All of that has to be blended together. Then it is filled into the shell, which should be about two testoons thick.[1.7] When the tourte is filled enough, it is garnished on top with strips of dough.

It takes about a quarter of an hour to bake this tourte. When it is cooked, or nearly, it is taken out of the oven and sprinkled with sugar, then it is put back a little for the sugar to glaze. Then you take it out again and at that time you can sprinkle it with a few drops of rosewater.

Note in general that, if you want to use pinenuts or currants, they must be cleaned and washed before being put into a baked dish.

Note, too, that if you bake in the oven a tourte or any other pastry dish that is done in a tourtière, you should sometimes set the tourtière on coals.[1.8] And note, too, that if you bake a pastry dish in a tourtière on hot coals rather than in the oven, the upper edge of the pastry must be below that of the tourtière, and the tourtière must be covered with a suitable lid[1.9] on top of which coals, more or less hot depending on the size and thickness of the pastry dish, are set: for there has to be heat over

---

[1.4] Because the author has said explicitly that his pound (of butter: see Chapter VI) has thirteen ounces, the *quarteron* here would weigh one-quarter of that.

[1.5] The vessel known as a *plat* is clearly concave, a dish. Throughout his work the preposition regularly associated with this word is *dans*: "*in* a dish."

[1.6] This *cresme de pastissier* is found in Recipe IV,1.

[1.7] Or the thickness of four sheets of (seventeenth-century) paper. In Recipe VII,18 the thickness of the *teston* is equated to two sheets of (very coarse) paper. In English coinage Marnette's equivalent is "about half a crown."

[1.8] The translation here is literal. Because of the next sentence, though, the intended meaning must be that any such tart or pie in a tourte pan, prepared for baking in an oven, "should sometimes" (*il faudra quelquefois*) be baked on coals on a hearth. In Recipe IX,7 a tourte is set on hot coals within an oven. In any case the sense is clearly that these are alternative procedures, even if the author doesn't specify exactly what the conditions determining the "sometimes" are.

[1.9] In Chapter VI the author has told us that pastry chefs normally use a tourtière with a lid.

and under the tourtière when a bit of pastry is being baked in a tourtière by the fire, without putting it in the oven.

2. Another Very Delicate Cream Tourte

Lightly grease a tourtière with a little good fresh butter, then fit the tourtière with a shell of fine or puff pastry. Then fill that shell sufficiently with fine Pastry Cream.[2] You can add in some very good fat lard, an amount of one or two eggs, that has been grated with a rasp or a knife. You can also add in candied lemon peel cut up into little bits. Then you have only to fashion the top of the tourte with little strips of dough. Then bake it.

When this tourte is baked, you sprinkle it with sugar and put it back a short while in the oven, then wash it lightly with a few drops of rosewater before serving it.

3. A Beef-Marrow Tourte

Get four ounces of beef marrow and work it with your fingers into little pieces of about the size of small hazelnuts. Add in roughly the same amount of ground sugar and two egg yolks, a little pinch of salty spice,[3.1] pinenuts, currants, and finely chopped lemon peel; also put in biscuit or macaroon, or skinned ground almonds, and about a chicken's-egg amount of breadcrumbs. Mix all of that together with a spatula or spoon. When that mixture is ready, you fill a shell in a tourtière with it, then you band your tourte tightly on top[3.2] or else you cover it a sheet of dough that has cut-outs in several places.

Bake your tourte. When it is done, you sprinkle it with sugar and put if back briefly in the oven.

4. A Lard Tourte

Grate fat lard with a knife or a rasp, or merely chop it up very small; you can steep it a while in clean water. Then you measure out four ounces of it, and add to it roughly the same amount of ground sugar and two egg

---

[2] The recipe for *cresme fine de Pastisserie* is in IV,2.

[3.1] Directions for this spice mixture are given above in Recipe II,2.

[3.2] That is, with strips of pastry set closely together to form an upper crust.

yolks, a pinch of salty spice, about a third of a lemon peel[4] and also about the amount of an egg of white bread in very fine crumbs, or else of macaroon, or only about the same amount of skinned almonds ground with a little rosewater — or else instead of one of those things you can put in a good spoonful of Pastry Chef's Cream, because it is good in all sorts of tourtes. Mix all of those things together. Again, you can add in a few currants and pinenuts. When that mixture is ready, you put enough of it into a tourtière that has its shell. Then you finish off fashioning your tourte, and finally you bake it. When it is done, you sprinkle it with sugar and put it back in the oven a short time. When you take it out again, you sprinkle a few drops of rosewater on it.

5. A Veal-Kidney Tourte

When a loin of veal is roasted, you take the kidney along with the fat that is on it, chop it up very small and season it as for the Beef-Marrow Tourte;[5] into that mixture you can add a spoonful of fine Pastry Chef's Cream. With the mixture fill a tourtière fitted with its shell and cover it over with a sheet of dough with cut-outs. Then bake your tourte. When it is done, put on some sugar and then a few drops of rosewater as in the previous recipe.

You can make a tourte with veal tongue in the same way as with veal kidney.

6. An Egg Tourte

Fit your tourtière with a shell of fine or puff pastry, then in the shell spread a handful of powdered sugar. Cut about a score — more or less, depending on how many you need — of hard-boiled egg-yolks in half. Arrange those yolk halves on the layer of sugar and, when the layer of yolks is set out, you stick a whole clove into about five or six of them; then you sprinkle the layer of yolks with a little powdered cinnamon. Add in as much as you like of candied lemon peel; you can also add in some pinenuts and some currants. Onto that mixture put a good handful of

---

[4] The term that is used here, *le tiers d'une fueille d'escorce de citron*, seems to indicate that in seventeenth-century kitchens lemon peel was kept on hand, likely in a dry or candied state. See candied lemon peel in Recipes 6, 9 and 15, below. In Chapter IX of the *French Confectioner*, see Orange Zests.

[5] Recipe 3, above.

sugar and a good chunk of fresh butter — for instance, two ounces[6] of butter — spread out and laid on the sugar.

Cover the tourte with small strips of dough, then bake it like the other tourtes. When it is done, sprinkle it with sugar and put it back in the oven a little longer. When it comes out again, it should have a few drops of rosewater sprinkled on it.

7. An Herb Tourte

Get two handfuls of mild herbs such as chard or lettuce or mallow or spinach. Remove their ribs, then wash the herbs and give them a boiling in boiling water so as to tenderize them.[7.1] Then take them out of the water and squeeze them in your hands or between two plates so as to remove the water from them.

Chop those herbs very small or grind them in a mortar. Then you put an amount of about two eggs of that purée into a bowl, along with the quantity of about one egg, or a little more, of good fresh butter, already melted; add in a good handful of powdered sugar — you can put in more sugar. Season that mixture with a small pinch of mild spices and the same amount of powdered cinnamon, along with a small pinch of salt. You can also put in about the amount of a hen's egg of fine, white breadcrumbs, the same amount of very dry biscuit or else two macaroons, or else a few sweet almonds, skinned and ground in the mortar. Also add in about the third of a lemon peel[7.2] cut into small bits, and about the amount of two eggs of Pastry Chef's Cream. You can also add a raw egg yolk, or else the amount of an egg of good soft cheese that is made with unskimmed milk;[7.3] you can also put in a few pinenuts and currants, mainly in winter and during Lent. Mix all those things carefully together with a wooden spatula or with a spoon.

When that mixture is quite thick, you fit a tourtière with a shell of fine or puff pastry about two testoons thick, then you fill the shell sufficiently

---

[6] *un demy quarteron.*

[7.1] *... afin de les mortifier.* This term is normally applied to the hanging of game animals. Marnette inserts his own interpretation: " ... to mortifie them, that is, to take the earthy sent and taste from them."

[7.2] This lemon peel is probably understood to be candied. The qualification is not explicitly mentioned in a number of these tourte recipes.

[7.3] *bon fromage mol qui ne soit pas escresmé.* See this ingredient also in Recipe VIII,2.

with your mixture. Finish off the top of the tourte with small strips of dough. You can crimp the upper edge of the tourte if you like, or mark a pattern on it.

Put the tourte into the oven, and from time to time put some coals under it; it can be baked in a short half-hour. When it is almost done, it has to be taken out of the oven and sprinkled with a good handful of sugar and a few drops of rosewater, then put back in very briefly. When you take it out for the last time, you sprinkle it again with a handful of sugar.

8. A Root Tourte

Get skirret roots, scrape and clean them, and cook them in water until they are sufficiently parboiled. Then take them out of the water and grind them in a mortar; you can also strain them through a sieve so as to leave only the core.[8] When you get the amount of about two eggs of those ground roots, or of their core, you have to put it into a bowl with half that amount of white bread or macaroon, together with a two-eggs-amount of Pastry Chef's Cream, two handfuls of sugar, a little rosewater, some salt, some cinnamon, spices to taste, as well as some pinenuts, some currants and some lemon peel. Mix all that together with about an egg's amount, or a little more, of melted fresh butter. When the mixture is ready, you lay it down in a tourtière fitted with a shell of fine or puff pastry. Cover the tourte with strips of pastry and bake it. When it is done, or almost, it has to be sprinkled with a handful of sugar and with a few drops of rosewater, then put back into the oven for a short while. Then you take it out and sprinkle it with sugar again. Then it is done.

9. A Tourte of Raw Fruit

Fit your tourtière with a shell of fine or puff-pastry dough. Into that put a layer of sugar, then fill it with seeded red currants or with verjuice mash or with ripe cherries or with halved apricots or with peeled and, optionally, pitted plums. If you want to put whole apricots into a tourte, you have to peel them. Add in a bit of butter, a little powdered cinnamon, a few small slices of candied lemon peel and a handful or more of sugar, depending on the size of your tourte.

---

[8] *la moüelle*, literally, the marrow.

Then you cover over the tourte with a sheet of pastry, whose middle you can slice; then you gild it[9] and put it into the oven. When it is baked, you sugar its top and put it back a short while in the oven; then it is done.

10. A Tourte of the Flesh of Pumpkin, Gourd or Melon

Get the pulp of a pumpkin or gourd or melon, cut it into pieces about the size of a walnut, half-cook it over a low fire in the juice it will exude, being careful to turn the pieces over from time to time so they won't burn. If you want to spare yourself some work, you can put a little water with the pulp of that fruit so it will cook more quickly and easily, although that is a little less tasty.

When your pumpkin is half-cooked, it has to be taken out and let drain thoroughly; or else you squeeze it in your hand or in a linen cloth to remove the moisture from it. Then you pound it or squash it with a spoon.

Instead of preparing pumpkin or the pulp of a gourd or melon in the way we directed, you can get some that is still raw and pound it, then half-cook it in some meat bouillon or water. When it is half-cooked, as if it was to be fricasseed in butter or oil, you put it through a strainer or a coarse cloth or a sieve so as to remove its strings.

When the pumpkin is prepared, you put it into a bowl or small basin. Add in a good five ounces or more of sugar,[10.1] a pinch of spices or of powdered cinnamon and a little salt. You can also put in some pinenuts, currants, lemon peel[10.2] cut small and Pastry Chef's Cream, or else some white breadcrumb or macaroon or crushed biscuit, or an egg's amount of sweet almonds, skinned and carefully ground in the mortar. You can also put in some cheese freshly made from unskimmed milk. Into that mixture add as much melted fresh butter as is necessary, or some marrow or pork fat cut up into small pieces. If it is a meat-day, instead of putting Pastry Chef's Cream into that tourte you put a few raw egg yolks.

Mix all of those things together and thicken them as for a pie filling; if you have difficulty in making the mixture thick, you add in a few spoonfuls of milk in order to blend it better.

---

[9] Chapter III gives a recipe for this.

[10.1] *un bon quarteron & demy de sucre ou encore plus.*

[10.2] In the previous recipe, as well as in Recipes 6 and 15, this lemon peel was preserved, *i.e.* candied.

When the mixture is ready, an adequate amount of it has to be laid into a tourtière that is fitted with a pastry shell. Then that tourte has to be covered with a sheet of pastry, and your baked-dish gilded and baked. When it is done, you sprinkle its top with sugar[10.3] and throw a few drops of rosewater over that.

11. An Apple Tourte

Fit up a tourtière with a pastry shell, then put down a layer of sugar on that and fill it with peeled and cored apples or pears, chopped quite small or sliced, mixed with some pinenuts and some currants, and with some lemon peel if you like. Sprinkle that mixture with a little powdered cinnamon; add in as well whatever amount of powdered sugar you like and a chunk of fresh butter — for a medium-sized tourte about the size, say, of a walnut. Cover the tourte just like any other fruit tourte,[11] and put it into the oven when it is gilded. When done, sprinkle it with sugar and put it back briefly into the oven.

12. A Tourte or Pie or Chausson[12.1] of Apples, Pears or Other Raw Fruit

Make up the crust into whatever size and shape you like, then put a layer of sugar inside, lay in some peeled, cored and quartered apples or other fruit, add a chunk of fresh butter and some small amount of powdered cinnamon and green aniseed; instead of butter you can put some marrow in these fruit tourtes or pies. You can also put in some pinenuts, and currants or damascene raisins[12.2] or prunes, and some lemon peel sliced

---

[10.3] The text erroneously reads *vous la poudrerez par dessus avec beurre.*

[11] Recipe 13, below, indicates that directions for cutting an opening or openings in the upper crust may have been omitted here, or perhaps at the corresponding place in the next recipe, 12.

[12.1] Unfortunately, the last sort of pasty, a *chosson* (so spelled), is not expressly described in this recipe or elsewhere. Cotgrave, at the beginning of La Varenne's century defined a *chausson* only as "a litle hose; also a socke." Today we might say that the shape of this type of turnover resembled a bootee. There is no mention of using a pie plate or tourtière to contain this pasty. Even in La Varenne's day it was probably a turnover; the end of this recipe mentions covering over only the tourte or pie.

[12.2] In the text: *du raisin de Corinthe ou de Damas.* Cotgrave glosses *Raisins de Damas*, or raisins, as "the best, and greatest kind of Raisins of the Sunne." Cotgrave's phrase, "of the sun," identifies the fruit as sun-dried, or damson perhaps merely dried.

small. You can also sprinkle the top of that mixture with powdered sugar. Cover that tourte or pie over and put it in the oven.

13. A Jam Tourte

Fit your tourtière up with a pastry shell. Put a little powdered sugar onto the bottom of that shell, then spread out your jam[13.1] in the shell; you can add a little finely cut lemon peel and, on top too, a little sugar and a little rosewater. Cover your tourte with a sheet of dough whose centre is cut out as we suggested in the recipe for the Apple Tourte.[13.2] gild the top of the tourte and put it into the oven, baking it quickly because there is only the crust to cook. When it is done, sugar its top, then put it back into the oven a short while. Having taken it out again, you can again sprinkle it with a little sugar.

14. Another Tourte Made Like a Jam Tourte

Get fruit that has been dried in the oven or in the sun and boil it in water to soften it — fruit like prunes or dates or damascine raisins; you can add in sugar. When the fruit is soft enough, the pits and seeds have to be removed, then you grind the fruit or else you extract its pulp with a sieve; to that add some sugar, a little flour and a very little ground cinnamon. Mix everything together, then fill your shell with it. You finish off this tourte like the one in the previous recipe.

15. A Frangipane Tourte[15.1]

On the pastry table[15.2] set out a good twelve ounces of fine flour and a moderate amount of salt; the flour has to be moistened in a cool place

---

[13.1] Directions for preparing a wide variety of *confitures* or "jams" — that Marnette terms "comfits" — are provided in *The French Confectioner*. See particularly Chapter XI, "Moist Confections" (*Confitures liquides*) in that work.

[13.2] In Recipe 11 for Apple Tourte the ending, in which such a direction for cut-outs in the upper crust might have been read, seems to be a little confused.

[15.1] Nowdays the cream filling known as frangipane is usually composed of cream, ground almonds & sugar; this *franchipanne* uses pistachios rather than almonds. It is a variety of the *cresme de pastissier*: see Chapter IV, above. The whole tourte may be compared with La Varenne's version in *The French Cook* at Recipes VIII,64 and XXI,37.

[15.2] This is the pastry chef's *tour à paste*, first mentioned in Recipe I,2. It was presumably so called not because of a round or elevated form but because of its structural solidity.

with enough egg white to reduce it to a soft dough as for puff pastry.[15.3]
When that dough is ready, you let it sit a very short while so that it is
more manageable. Then you roll it out on the table, making it as thin as
you can.[15.4]

Just as soon as the dough is rolled out, you grease the bottom of
a tourtière with clarified lard. One end of the dough is set in there
to make a shell.[15.5] The shell[15.6] has to be greased with lard and the
dough folded over on top, and that fold of dough again greased with lard;
and a fourth layer of dough is made, whose top is not to be greased.
When the fourth layer — that is, the fourth sheet of dough — is formed,
you put into [the tourte shell] as much as is necessary of the following mixture,[15.7] which should be ready when you begin to make up the
tourte.

Into a skillet put three cups of very fresh milk cream, unbeaten; add
four egg yolks, a small pinch of salt and two pinches of fine flour. Mix
all of that together and boil it on the fire for almost half an hour, stirring
the mixture continuously until it is as thick as cooked gruel. When the
mixture is cooked, it is poured into a bowl and, when half-cooled, you add
in twenty-five pistachios that have been skinned in hot water like almonds,
then well pounded or coarsely ground in a marble mortar as if they were

---

[15.3] *paste molle comme du feuilletage*: "as for layering."

[15.4] The thinness of this sheet of dough is crucial because, as the next paragraph explains,
the pastry crust will consist of four layers of it, each separated from the next by a
coating of lard as in puff-pastry dough. See Recipe I,4. The flaky pastry crust is
potentially appetizing enough to be eaten.

[15.5] The length of the entire sheet of thin dough must be more than four times the diameter
of the tourtière and allow for the depth of its sides which have also to be covered.
Folding the sheet of dough back upon itself twice will quadruple the crust's thickness.
The procedure described in *The French Cook* uses six separate pieces of dough laid
on top of one another to form each of the lower and upper crusts.

[15.6] La Varenne writes *cette abesse* but may mean only the upper surface of the first *half*
of the length of the sheet of dough. When the dough is folded the first time grease
will then be between the first and second layers of the final shell and between the
third and fourth.

[15.7] This is the frangipane filling. The recipe that follows can be compared with those
for the various versions of Pastry Chef's Cream in Chapter IV.

for making macaroon. Also add in a good five ounces[15.8] of powdered sugar, a pinch of beaten cinnamon, a slice or leaf of candied lemon peel that has been picked into small bits, some twenty good pinenuts and a good pinch of currants. As well, at the same time you can add in a little ambergris and musk[15.9] moistened in a small half-spoonful of orange-blossom water or rosewater, and the amount of half an egg of squashed beef marrow. Mix all of those things together and fill the tourte sufficiently with them.

When the tourte is full enough with the mixture, the dough has to be folded four times over the filling to make the cover; grease the upper surface of each layer of dough. Then the edge of the tourte is trimmed;[15.10] and you have to crimp it, or take it in your two thumbs, to try to stick the layers of dough together so they are sealed, so the filling doesn't escape. The edging of the tourte can also be fashioned however you wish — for instance, battlemented.[15.11]

The two uppermost leaves of the cover have also to be sliced without touching the ones beneath: that has to be done with a knife or a penknife,[15.12] making small slits that shouldn't penetrate deeper than the second layer of the cover so that the filling doesn't run out.

The tourte has to be gilded on top and put into the oven on a few coals that are not white hot. Make sure the tourtière is quite level and upright. It takes almost an hour to bake that oven-dish, which swells up almost six inches.

When that tourte is baked and taken out of the oven, you sprinkle sugar on top and a few drops of rosewater or of orange-blossom water; then it is put back into the oven's mouth so that it glazes — that takes eight minutes.[15.13] Then it is ready to serve.

[15.8] *un bon quarteron & demy.*

[15.9] Usually these two flavourings are alternatives: the conjunction here should perhaps have been "or".

[15.10] Because of the irregular shape left by the multiple folding of the layers of dough.

[15.11] To the possibility of such crenellations Marnette adds the option of "pinked works."

[15.12] The *canif* was quite literally a pen-knife, designed with a short, pointed blade for sharpening quill pens, those normally being the tough pinion feathers of a goose.

[15.13] This precision in the measurement of time may surprise the modern reader but is

Chapter X

A Feuillantine

Put the amount of two eggs of Pastry Chef's Cream[x.1] into a bowl, along with four ounces of powdered sugar, a raw egg yolk, a pinch of currants, the same of pinenuts and of candied lemon peel cut up very very small, one or two macaroons[x.2] ground up very finely, a little ground cinnamon and some good rosewater. You have to mix all of those things together with a spatula or a silver spoon, and add in a few drops of orange-blossom water or of lemon juice — little is needed of either.

Alternatively, instead of all those ingredients, you can make up the mixture with only Pastry Chef's Cream, white breadcrumbs or ground biscuit, a few currants, sugar, a little cinnamon and a few drops of lemon juice.

When all of that is mixed together, you make two sheets of puff pastry the size and thickness of a small platter. Put one of the sheets of dough on a sheet of paper, and onto that dump the mixture, spreading it out a little with the spatula. Then you moisten the edges of the pastry and cover it with the other sheet of dough. You have to seal the edges of the two shells carefully together in the manner of a pie.[x.3] Then put the feuillantine into the oven to be baked in half an hour or so.

When this baked dish is almost done, sprinkle it with sugar, and sprinkle a few drops of rosewater, or preferably of orange-blossom water. Then it is put back in the oven a short while to make the sugar glaze over. When it comes out of the oven for the last time, it should be sprinkled again with sugar.

A feuillantine can be made up and baked in a tourtière. You can also make little ones of it, and of whatever size you like.[x.4]

---

more apparent (in our translation) than real: the text has, here and elsewhere, "a half of a quarter of an hour," a rough approximation.

[x.1] Recipe IV,1.

[x.2] See Chapter XXVII.

[x.3] See the next chapter, on various *tartes*. Like the *pâté* the *feuillantine* is generally double-crusted. A generation or so later, Richelet provides useful confirmation of this: "*Feuillantine*. Piece de patisserie entre deux abaisses, qui est feuilletée, & garnie de blanc de chapon roti, & haché, de pâte de macarons, de farce à la crème, d'écorce de citron hachée bien menuë avec sucre & autres assaisonnemens"; "*Pâté*. C'est une piece de patisserie composée d'une abaisse & d'un couvercle . . . ."

[x.4] Marnette becomes voluble at this point, adding: " . . . and you may serve them up

Chapter XI

Pies and Flans[xi]

1. How to Make Pies[1.1]

Make up your crust, whose dough should not be as fine as for making a tourte. Make it the thickness of a testoon at the most, proportionate to the size of the pie, and do it in such a way that the centre of its bottom is a little thicker than the rest.

When the crust has dried,[1.2] you fill it with Pastry Chef's Cream[1.3] or jams or fruit or cheese, which filling has to be seasoned with sugar, currants, pinenuts, cinnamon or mild ground spice, fresh butter and other ingredients as if it was for making a tourte.

When the pie is filled, you band it on top with a few strips of dough; then it is sugared and put into the oven. When it is baked, you sprinkle it again with sugar, and sprinkle it, too, with a few drops of rosewater.

Tarts[1.4] are made in the same way.[1.5]

2. Cheese Pie[2.1] or Flan

Get roughly two handfuls of soft, non-skimmed cheese, roughly a two-

---

to the Table piping hot severally, or joyntly, according as you have company and occasion; all which depends on the will of those who are to spend [consume] them as aforesaid."

[xi] Chapter XI has no title.

[1.1] Marnette translates *des tartes* here as "small tarts of all sorts." "Small" seems to be the operative word, distinguishing a *tarte* ("pie") from a *tourte* ("tourte"), the latter being larger. The author notes that the pie in Recipe 5, below, *resemble à une petite tourte ou escuelle renversée.*

[1.2] *ressuyée*: Marnette also agrees on "dried", although the French author likely meant "consolidated" as well. The auther uses a verb to this effect in Chapter XIII: *Mettés cette crouste à l'air durant quelque temps, afin qu'elle se seche & se rafermisse.* In none of the five recipes of this chapter is there any mention of a baking vessel in which pies and flans are to be formed. The thinness of the crust and fluid nature of the fillings point to some sort of dish unless these *tartes* are indeed on the diminutive side.

[1.3] See Chapter IV.

[1.4] *petites tartelettes* in the text.

[1.5] Marnette adds, "to be eaten hot."

[2.1] Cheese cake might be a more recognizable name for this preparation.

walnut amount of dry, rather low-fat cheese[2.2] which is either squashed or grated or simply cut into very small pieces, along with salt to taste, and about four ounces of good, unsalted, melted butter. Add in the white and yolk of one or two eggs. Mix all of those things together and work them all thoroughly smooth. If the mixture is too thick, add in a little cold water; but if the soft cheese that you use is very soft and gives off a whey, you shouldn't put any water into the mixture, but rather that whey should be drained off because the mixture would turn out too runny. Reduce the mixture to the consistency of a gruel that is well cooked and as thick as glue. You also have to add in an egg's amount of fine flour or white breadcrumbs.

Fill the pie with the mixture or filling and put it in the oven. When it is baked, you can sprinkle it with sugar.

Note that good pork fat can be used in place of butter to make Cheese Pies.

3. Another Finer Cheese Pie, which is called a Lover's Pie[3]

Beat two or three egg yolks with a handful of powdered sugar and, when they are well mixed, pour them into the shell or crust set out to make the pie. Spread out the first mixture, then on top of that put as much as is necessary of the cheese filling and the other ingredients suggested for making the Plain Cheese Pies. With the pie sufficiently filled, bake it. When it is almost done, sprinkle sugar and a little rosewater on it, put it back into the oven to finish baking it and to make the sugar glaze.

4. Another Sort of Cheese Pie

Set up your shell and, when it has dried or firmed up, put into it a layer of good dry cheese — for example, a good Angelot;[4.1] of it you need to put in about the depth of a good finger's thickness, or of a thumb or more, and this cheese should be cut into little pieces or squashed with a

---

[2.2] This *fromage sec un peu affiné* may be a cheese made from milk that has been partly skimmed by having some of its butterfat separated from it. See also Recipes XIV and XV,7. In Recipes VIII,2 and IX,7 the cheese is specified as being from unskimmed milk, having therefore a high fat content.

[3] Marnette freely interprets the title of the French *Tartes d'amy*: "Other sorts of Tarts and Cheese-Cakes which are made of a finer stuff or dough, and are usually the good Wives Tart, or a Tart for a friend in a corner."

[4.1] Cotgrave recognizes the existence of this cheese, but without describing it.

press.[4.2] On top add an optional amount of good fresh butter and a few beaten egg yolks. Bake the pie. In Picardy it is called a pimpled pie[4.3] and it makes wine taste good.

This pie is more delicate if you mix together the eggs, butter, cheese and the rest of the seasoning to make them into a filling with which the shell is filled. Moreover, instead of dry cheese it is better to use two sorts of soft cheese in it, one of which is a little fresher than the other.

5. Another Cheese Pie or Flan

Get a carefully weighed half-pound of fat cheese that is still soft but fully dried, and squash it on the table. Then add in a good two-thirds cup[5.1] of good fresh, thick cream, a small pinch of parsley leaves chopped very fine, three egg yolks and a bit of salt; mix everything well together. When that mixture is reduced to a very smooth filling, pour it into a shell of fine pastry the thickness of a good two testoons and as big as a trencher-plate; on that filling put two ounces of good fresh butter broken into small bits. Cover the filling with an upper shell of very fine, very thin pastry; moisten its edges with a little water and seal them together tightly, making a cord[5.2] shaped however you like. This pie looks like a small tourte or an upside-down bowl. The cover has to be gilded. In its centre make a medium-sized slit[5.3] in the shape of a cross in order to let the contents of the tourte breathe, and it is proper to raise the points of that opening. Bake the pastry-dish, which takes a good half-hour or thereabouts.

[4.2] Marnette: "in a Morter." The printer set *escachoy*, a word normally spelled *escachoir*: Parisian pronunciation of the time tended to drop a final *r*; see also *bouchoy* in Recipe XXV,1.

[4.3] Marnette reads this word, *une boutonnée*, in the sense of reserved, reticent, buttoned-up, but for some reason in the negative: "Now in the Province of Picardy such like Tarts are called, unbuttoning Tarts, for they cause men to relish a cup of Wine very well." In eating a buttoned-up pie, he suggests, you become *un*buttoned. The bits of cheese will leave a bumpy surface on the pie. Several centuries before, the *Menagier de Paris* distinguished between the culinary use of the terms *larder* and *boutonner*: the first was when lard was stuck into a foodstuff, the second when cloves were inserted. (Ed. Brereton and Ferrier, p. 173, §12.) *Cf.* the Dimpled Cake (*Gasteau verollé*) of Recipe XV,7.

[5.1] This is the *posson* or *poinçon*, almost exclusively a measure of milk.

[5.2] This *cordon* is the appearance of a crimped seal between the upper and lower crust. Marnette calls it a "ruffe."

[5.3] In the text the word *ouverture* erroneously has an initial *c*: *couverture*.

Chapter XII

Rattoons

1. To make Rattoons[1.1]

On the pastry table put (for instance) three-quarters of a pound[1.2] of fine flour, a good three ounces[1.3] of butter if you have any, about half an ounce of salt, and a cup or so of warm water. Work everything together and reduce it to a very smooth dough; it should be quite soft. Put that dough on some buttered paper and shape it like cakes;[1.4] make them two testoons thick and more or less the size of a small trencher-plate, whatever you like, raising up the rim a little. The rattoon must be gilded and[1.5] filled a little with the Cheese Pie filling.[1.6] Then you bake them.

2. Another Sort of Rattoon

Get three or four full spoonfuls of fine wheat flour or of rice flour; moisten that with milk so that the mixture is as thick as well cooked gruel, adding in a little finely ground salt. You can also mix in one or two egg yolks, or a macaroon[2.1] or a spoonful of skinned, well ground almonds — though it is not necessary to add either macaroon or almonds or egg yolks.[2.2]

With the mixture ready, in a rather large skillet or a medium-sized tourtière[2.3] you melt an egg's amount of good fresh butter and, when that

---

[1.1] This pasty had been prepared for French tables since the Middle Ages. At the beginning of the seventeenth century Cotgrave defined a *raston* as "a fashion of round, and high Pie, made of butter, egges, and cheese." Though formerly merely a cheese-cake, the sense today of *raton* is a "pastry with a cream cheese basis" (*New Larousse Gastronomique*).

[1.2] *un litron*: see Chapter VI.

[1.3] *un bon quarteron*: a pound of butter is of thirteen ounces.

[1.4] Chapter XV will be devoted to these *gasteaux*.

[1.5] The edition shows "or" here: *dorer ou remplir*. The cheese filling seems necessary.

[1.6] Recipes XI,2 and following.

[2.1] See Chapter XXVII.

[2.2] " ... save only to give it a better taste," comments Marnette.

[2.3] The tourtière of La Varenne's day is a relatively shallow, round, flat pan with a side of about an inch — two finger-widths, he says in Chapter XIII — high that slopes outward. For the depth of a tourtière see also Recipe XV,1.

is melted, half-browned and very hot, pour into it the above-mentioned mixture in such a way that it spreads evenly in the skillet or tourtière and is no thicker than your little finger or so. Let the rattoon cook slowly over a moderate fire without covering it, and watch from time to time that its bottom doesn't burn. When it is coloured on top and browned[2.4] enough, turn it over so the other side can cook. When it is done, you set it out on a trencher-plate and sprinkle the top and bottom with sugar.

Chapter XIII

A Dariole[xiii.1]

Into a basin or a bowl put (for instance) three ounces[xiii.2] of fine flour, and the white and yolk of two eggs. Blend those together with a spatula or spoon, slowly pouring in a little milk, and salt to taste — though little is needed. Mix that flour or mixture well [to a consistency] as if you were making gruel. When the mixture is quite smooth, add in three cups of milk, blending it well into the other ingredients as if you intended to make gruel. And if you do not have enough cow's milk or any other sort of animal milk, almond milk can be used — in which case a little more flour should be put in.

With the mixture ready, a shell is set into a tourtière and, with the tourtière in the oven, you fill it with enough of the above-mentioned mixture; then the dish is baked. When done and removed from the oven, the filling is sliced with a cross without touching the crust, then into that slit is put about the amount of a walnut of good unsalted butter and a good

---

[2.4] The term *rissolé* refers to the colour of the deep-fried turnover.

[xiii.1] Cotgrave's gloss of *darioles* is "small pasties filled with flesh, hearbes, and spices, mingled, and minced together." We have to assume that the English dictionary-maker was describing a somewhat different *dariole* current back at the beginning of La Varenne's century. FitzGibbon describes a modern dariole: "A small French cake cooked in a dariole mould" — which is further described as "a small cyclindrical mould . . . ." "The mould is lined with pastry and filled with *frangipane* cream [see Recipe IX,15] mixed with chopped almonds and flavoured with a liqueur. That is baked in the oven and, when cooked, the cakes are turned out and sprinkled with sugar."

[xiii.2] Calculating the equivalence of *la quatriesme partie d'un litron* is a little awkward. The author's own note at the end of Chapter VI, above, states that a *litron* of flour "should weigh three *quarterons*" — that is, three-quarters of a pound, this pound being of 16 ounces because it weighs flour.

quarter- pint of powdered sugar along with a little rosewater. Afterwards put your dariole back into the oven so that the butter and sugar can melt and the pastry absorb their flavour — which happens quite quickly. Then it is taken out of the oven.

In case you don't have a tourtière, you need to get a bit of dough that is not so fine to make up a rather large shell in the shape of a pie; make its sides about a good two finger-widths high. Set the crust in the open for a while for it to dry out and strengthen. Then, when you want to finish the dariole, into the bottom of the shell put a small walnut's amount of fresh, unsalted butter. Put the shell into the oven to strengthen it. Then, of the above-mentioned filling, pour into the shell about a quarter of what is needed to fill it; then after a little while as much again is poured in; then some time later it is filled up with enough of the same above-mentioned mixture or filling.

It takes about a good half-hour to bake a dariole or pie that has three cups of milk. When that dariole is baked, you can add on some butter, sugar and rosewater, as has been said above,[xiii.3] or else you can merely sprinkle it with sugar and a little rosewater.

Chapter XIV

Talmouses[xiv.1]

Get (for example) about two fistfuls of soft cheese, fresh and from un-skimmed milk, a good handful of fine flour, an egg, both white and yolk,

---

[xiii.3] That is, into the cross cut into the surface of the custard.

[xiv.1] Cotgrave glosses the French dish *Talmouse* as "a Cheese-cake; a Pie, or cake made of egges, and cheese." This genre of pasty had been known since at least the fourteenth century. In the *Menagier de Paris* (ed. Brereton and Ferrier), a talmouse is to be served in the second course of a meat dinner (p. 178), and in the fourth course of a meat supper (p. 180). In Savoy in 1420 Chiquart was making and serving *les tartres, les talmouses, les flaons de creme de lait* (ed. cit., Recipe 6). Today FitzGibbon expands a little on this: "*Talmouses*. Small French tartlets with a variety of fillings which always have cheese as a base. The baking tins are lined with a *pâte brisée* or chou pastry and are usually filled with a cheese soufflé mixture, or spinach mixed with cheese, then baked in a slow oven . . . ." Ménage relates the origin of the name *talemouse* or *talmouse* to the softness of the thing: "C'est . . . par antiphrase qu'on a appellé *talemouse* ou *casse-museau* cette tarte farcie de fromage, dans laquelle au contraire le nez s'enfonce bien avant lorsqu'on la mange." Gilles Ménage, *Dictionnaire étymologique de la langue française*, ed. A.F. Jault, 2 vols. (Paris: Briasson, 1750; repr. Geneva: Slatkine, 1973); II, 510b; modern editions of Littré's dictionary agree with Ménage.

and some salt to taste; you can add in the quantity of about an egg of skim-milk cheese,[xiv.2] dry and chopped small or grated with the grater. Mix those things together, wrap the mixture in a shell of fine pastry and give it the shape of a three-cornered talmouse.[xiv.3] Glaze the talmouse and put it in the oven.

Note that talmouses should not be fully filled because the mixture in them swells and would escape in baking.

Chapter XV

Sponge Cakes[xv]

1. To make an Excellent Sponge Cake in a Tourtière

Get two small cream cheeses, freshly made and without salt — each should weigh about ... ;[1.1] put them into a bowl or a little basin and squash them with a spoon. Then you add to them almost a good three ounces[1.2] of good unsalted, melted butter; then add in three or four eggs,

---

[xiv.2] *fromage affiné*, which Marnette interprets merely as "old".

[xiv.3] The direction to form a *talemouse qui a trois cornes*, literally "three-horned", is a little strange when no other talmouse is described among these recipes. The pastry resembles a turnover whose angles are perhaps made more pointed.

[xv] The chapter has no title, but Recipes 1–4 and 6 deal expressly with varieties of *gasteaux mollets*, literally "soft cakes". Marnette calls the first example merely "an excellent great Cake" and others "soft Tarts or Cakes." A modern equivalent of the plainest sort of *gasteau* might be a scone made of white flour; all of the recipes are for versions of that. A mould or cake pan is used only in Recipes 1 and 3; generally the very thick batter of these cakes lets them bake unsupported on buttered paper.

The French term *gasteau* has a long history in the forms *gastel* and *guastel*. The *Viandier* of Taillevent refers to *des gastiaulx blans ou aultre pain blanc* (Recipe 176). A Picard variant of the pronunciation, *wastel*, was in use in England already by 1194; it can be found in many later-medieval English recipe collections and for that period it is glossed by the *Oxford English Dictionary* as "Bread made of the finest flour; a cake or loaf of this bread." In the 1700s Ménage supposed an interesting etymology: "*Gâteau*. Parce que sa figure est vaste & étendue, étant plus applati que le reste des pains, il fut ainsi appellé, de *vastellum*, formé de *vastus*"(!)

[1.1] *sic*: the text shows suspension points here, as if the author had forgotten to insert a specific weight, or else the typesetter could not read a handwritten figure. See also the same curious negligence in Recipe XXI,1 where the weight of cream cheeses is again left unspecified. Marnette makes no reference to the weight of the small cheeses in either recipe.

[1.2] Butter, we are told in Chapter VI, is measured in pounds of thirteen ounces, so that

both yolks and whites, which need to be blended one after the other into that mixture, and little by little you mix in three small spoonfuls of fine flour, or else half a loaf of white bread, thoroughly crumbed,[1.3] or else a small egg's amount of finely grated biscuit; add in a finely-crushed macaroon and two or three full spoonfuls of powdered sugar — that is, about an ounce of sugar. Season the mixture with a little very fine salt. Then the filling has to be tasted, to see whether it is salted enough: it takes little salt. That filling should be more or less of the consistency of gruel that is fed to children: if you think it is too thick, a small spoonful of milk or water can be mixed in to make it more runny.

When the filling is seasoned, the inside of a tourtière has to be greased with a little bit of fresh butter, then the above-mentioned filling is poured into the tourtière until it is evenly about a finger's thickness deep; stir the tourtière a little so that the filling spreads evenly inside. Then the tourtière is put into the oven or onto the coals — in this latter case you have to cover the tourtière with a lid on which you must put hot ash as well as coals, and you do it in such a way that there is not more heat concentrated in one place than in another. If the tourtière is covered with a lid, it is removed from time to time to see whether the sponge cake is baking, and whether it is darkening more in one area than in another: some of the coals have to be removed from the area that is too dark.

If the cake swells up much while it is baking, so that it touches the lid of a covered tourtière, that is an indication that the fire is too hot or that the cake is too thick; then you have to decrease the heat or pull the tourtière out of the heat a little, and leave it uncovered a short while to let the cake breathe so it will shrink down. Then the tourtière is covered again with its lid, with some coals on top, and you put the tourtière back on the hot ash to finish the baking. It takes about three quarters of an hour to bake one of these sponge cakes gently.[1.4]

When the sponge cake is baked enough, it is put on a large trencher-plate. Sprinkle its top with sugar. It is good either warm or cold.

---

this *bon quarteron de bon beurre*, or quarter-pound, would weigh something a little better than three ounces.

[1.3] The qualification here is *bien desliés*.

[1.4] *à loisir*: literally in a leisurely manner.

If you bake this cake in an oven, the tourtière should not be covered: it bakes more easily like that, and you can make it deeper — for example, it can be made a good inch deep, or a little more, depending on the height of the sides of the tourtière.

Note that into the mixture or filling of this cake you can add two ounces of sweet almonds, skinned and well ground, instead of a macaroon. You can also put in an ounce of good, coarsely ground pinenuts, mainly if you do not want any macaroon in the mixture; you can also add in a little lemon peel[1.5] or apricot paste, or some other similar dry confection.[1.6] But those ingredients are not at all necessary because this sponge cake is still excellent even without almonds or pinenuts or candied lemon peel; besides, it is easier to make.[1.7]

2. Sponge Cake[2.1] without Cheese

On a table or in a basin or wooden bowl set out about a pound and a half[2.2] of fine flour; make a well in its middle — that is, a rather large cavity in the middle of the flour — into which you put about a pound of beaten, fresh, unsalted butter[2.3] — the butter can be worked with your hands to soften it if it is too firm; also put in about two cups of milk cream, using wine measure rather than milk measure because [otherwise] there would be too much of it;[2.4] then add in close to an ounce of ground salt, and also break in four fresh eggs.

Note that all of the milk cream should not be put in at once: it is enough for you first to pour in about one-half or two-thirds of the two cups.

[1.5] Several lines later the author will say that this is *candied* lemon peel.

[1.6] For examples such a *confiture seiche*, and directions for their preparation, see *The French Confectioner*, Chapter XII.

[1.7] " . . . and less expensive," Marnette frugally notes.

[2.1] Again, *Gasteaux mollets*: literally "Rather Soft Cakes."

[2.2] *deux litrons*: probably a little more than three pints, although Marnette, who tends to be inconsistent in his equivalents, writes "about two pints of flower." The same amount of flour is used to make the cake in Recipe 4, below.

[2.3] We recall that in Chapter VI the author tells us that his pound of butter has thirteen ounces.

[2.4] In Recipe IV,1 the author warns that the *chopine* used by dairy merchants is considerably larger — by roughly 50% — than the normal measure. A *chopine* of milk or cream, using dairy measure, would amount to three cups.

Blend and work all those things together, putting in some milk cream from time to time to moisten the mixture, until you can no longer feel any lumps or clots in the dough,[2.5] and until the dough is firm enough to stand up on some paper in the shape of a sponge cake without spreading out or collapsing much anywhere when it is set up like a cake.

When you think that dough is good and ready, it should be tasted so as to judge whether it is properly salted. Then it is put in lumps or handfuls on some buttered paper. Make up your cakes, making them about a thumb-width thick or a little more, and the size of an average trencher-plate, more or less as you like. Then they are gilded on top.

Put the sponge cakes in the oven. It takes about three-quarters of an hour to bake them enough. The oven's hearth should be roughly as hot as for baking Bourgeois bread,[2.6] or some other sort of moderately sized loaf: for if the oven is not hot enough, the sponge cakes will not brown; contrarily, if the oven is too hot, the cakes will not bake well inside.

3. Another Sponge Cake without Cheese, that should be made in a tourtière

Into an earthenware pot or a large bowl put twelve ounces[3.1] of fine flour; mix in eight eggs, a spoonful of good brewer's yeast,[3.2] then a good three ounces[3.3] of butter, or a little more, melted on the fire along with two-thirds of a cup[3.4] of milk. Blend those ingredients together well and season the mixture with ground salt. Taste it and, if it is salty enough, it has to be covered with a warm cloth and set close to the fire so that it is exposed to only a little gentle heat. Leave it by the fire for about an hour so that the mixture swells and rises.

[2.5] Despite modern usage, throughout this chapter, I translate the very thick cake batter that is called *paste* as "dough".

[2.6] According to Cotgrave, *pain bourgeois* is "crible bread betweene white and browne; a bread (that somewhat resembles our wheaten, or cheat) a loafe whereof is to weigh, when tis baked, 32 ounces."

[3.1] *un litron.*

[3.2] See Recipe VIII,1 where the author has advised that for some pastry chefs this *leveure de bierre* has certain advantages over ordinary baker's *franc levain*.

[3.3] Again, *un bon quarteron.*

[3.4] *un posson*, roughly five and a half ounces: see Chapter VI. In Recipe 5 we are told that both the butter and the milk must be hot.

When the mixture has swollen, you melt about two ounces[3.5] or less of good unsalted butter in a rather large tourtière, then you pour in the mixture or filling; then the tourtière is covered with its lid. Put heat below and above, and bake the cake. It takes about three-quarters of an hour or more to bake one of these sponge cakes thoroughly.

When the cake is done, it can be eaten just as it is. Alternatively, as soon as the cake is baked and removed from the tourtière, the top is cut away from the bottom with a knife or a thread through the soft inside. You turn the top over in order to coat the soft part of the cake with good melted butter which has to be poured into it; then add on some powdered sugar and a little rosewater or cinnamon water.[3.6] Then set the two halves of the cake back on one another. Let the cake sit a while by the fire so that[3.7] it doesn't get cold before being eaten.

Note that this sponge cake is quite thick, that is why a part of the soft inside can be removed leaving only the two crusts still with a little of the soft inner part, like a *poupelin*.[3.8]

4. Another Sponge Cake without Cheese, called "Egg Bread" by the Flemish

Into a basin or on a table put a pound and a half[4.1] of fine flour; break in two eggs, add over six ounces[4.2] of fresh butter which you have melted and heated on the fire along with two-thirds of a cup of milk; into that mixture also put in a silver spoonful of good thick brewer's yeast, more rather than less, and some salt to taste. All those things have to be mixed and worked together to reduce them to a very cohesive dough; as the dough is kneaded, it is sprinkled from time to time with a little flour.

When the dough is thoroughly kneaded, it is firm. Then you shape it like a loaf of bread[4.3] and set it on a sheet of paper; cover it with a very

---

[3.5] *un demy quarteron.*

[3.6] A recipe for Cinnamon Water can be read in *The French Confectioner* at IV,16.

[3.7] " . . . so that," Marnette inserts here, "the Sugar and rose-water may soak in, and that . . . ."

[3.8] See below, in Chapter XVII, a recipe for this variety of bap or bun.

[4.1] Or twenty-four ounces: *deux literons* (spelled thus), a *litron* being three-quarters of a sixteen-ounce pound.

[4.2] *une demie livre.*

[4.3] In La Varenne's day a loaf is of course a round mound.

warm serviette. The dough has to be set quite close to the fire, yet not too close or the side that is too close to the fire will harden.

You leave that dough in gentle warmth until it has risen enough: it takes about five quarter-hours for it to rise. When is has risen enough and begins to form a crust[4.4] or to split a little, you fashion it like a cake.[4.5] Its top needs to be gilded. Then you put the cake in the oven.

The oven's hearth should be almost as hot as for baking a medium-sized loaf of bread. It takes about half or three-quarters of an hour to bake it. When it is taken out of the oven, you can sprinkle it with sugar and with a few drops of rosewater before serving it to the table — though that is not necessary.

5. A Lady Lucia Cake[5.1]

On a table set out twelve ounces of fine flour. In it make a hollow, into which you put eight egg yolks and two egg whites and half an ounce of ground salt; add in nine ounces of good fresh butter that you have melted in a bowl on the fire, along with two or three ounces[5.2] of milk — or rather of milk cream; the milk and the butter have to be very hot and almost boiling when they are put into the mixture; and also put in what is left at the bottom of the bowl. Work all of those substances together until the mixture or dough has almost cooled; then it is left to cool for a good half-hour for it to firm up.

In the meantime you prepare the following leavening; begin it a good quarter-hour after the dough is made up. To make that leavening, on the table you set out four ounces of fine flour; in it make a well, and put into that two ounces of good thick yeast;[5.3] add in a little hot milk or cream

---

[4.4] *elle commencera à s'escailler*: literally, "to scale."

[4.5] In subsequent recipes a "cake" is either one inch high (Recipes XV,5 and 9, and XVII) or two inches high (Recipes XV,7 and 8). In Recipe 10, below, a knife is used for a cake-shaping operation. There the perimeter of the dough is cut in order to form up the cake.

[5.1] Marnette has his own name for this *Gasteau à la Dame Lucie*: "A Tart or Cake according to Mistris Susanna the Dairy-maids manner."

[5.2] This is a *posson* of milk. Marnette translates this quantity as "a quarter of a pint."

[5.3] The term used here is *leveure*, rather than *levain* or *franc levain*. Normally the term applies to a beer foam or brewer's yeast, as distinct from a sour dough leaven. See Recipe VIII,1, where we're told that it works in dough more quickly and produces more attractive results.

— enough to reduce those ingredients to a very cohesive and quite soft dough as they are thoroughly worked on the table. When the dough is kneaded enough, you form it up like a small loaf of bread and let it sit like that for about eight minutes or until the leavening[5.4] has swollen enough and begins to split or form a crust on top. That leavening has to be kept in a slightly warm place.

As soon as the leavening begins to split or to crust on top, you mix it into the above-mentioned dough, working everything well together. Then you shape all of that dough, doing it like a loaf of bread. Put it on a sheet of paper and form it like a cake, making it a good inch thick; gild it. Let it sit for about a good hour if it is in summer, or two hours in winter, putting it in a place that is not cool.

When the cake is ready for the oven, you shape its side and slash its top deeply with a knife's point — the knife should be used before, as the cake is being put in the oven. It needs quite a gentle heat, and let it bake slowly; it is baked in a short hour. Do not remove it unless it is quite dry inside, so that it doesn't break.

6. Sponge Cakes with Cheese

Get an amount of two-handfuls of cheese, freshly made and creamy, and season it with finely ground salt; also into that add half a pound of good unsalted butter and two eggs. If the cheese is on the dry side — that is, a little too dried out and consequently less moist than it should be to make these cakes — a little water should be put into the mixture to help it bind; close to three-quarters of a pound[6] of flour should also be added in. Work all that with your hands to blend it all well together. When the mixture is ready, grease a sheet of paper and on it lay out the dough in order to fashion a cake, which you make two fingers thick. Gild it on top and put it in the oven. It can be baked in less than half an hour.

[5.4] Here the author's word is *levain*, as it is twice at the beginning of this paragraph. The yeast is making the leaven which will then in turn be used in the recipe.

[6] *un litron.*

7. A Dimpled Cake[7.1]

Make up some dough as we directed for the Sponge Cake with Cheese, spread it out on the paper in the shape of a cake and make it a good two inches thick. Then, with your hands, raise up the edge all around, three fingers high, as if you intended to make up a pie;[7.2] press down the middle of that cake a little with your hand.

Then you get about three ounces of skim-milk cheese, depending on your taste, and cut it into pieces about the size of little dice; they have to be set out on the cake and, as they are spread around on its top, they have to be pressed or flattened by hand to make them sink into the cake a little. Afterwards, among those bits of cheese, you have also to scatter a good three ounces of good unsalted butter, cut into small pieces; add onto that one beaten egg. Then raise up the edging of the cake and bend it inwards.

This cake should be baked in half an hour or so. Give it a hearth-heat as for other baked-dishes.

Those who really like cheese make these cakes double: for that you make two shells, one-finger thick,[7.3] and on the lower one you make a layer of small flat blocks[7.4] of fine cheese; then the other shell is put on top and the two are joined snugly together. This cake is finished off as we directed above.

[7.1] The bits of cheese leave a bumpy surface on this cake. In its name, the qualification *verollé* refers literally to the appearance left by the pox on skin. An earthy translation of the term might be "pustuled". Marnette writes "knobbed or kertled." In his *Delices de la campagne* Nicolas de Bonnefons briefly describes the making of similar *Gasteaux verolez*. He begins: "You must get some of the dough of the Milanese Cake [cf. the following recipe in the *French Pastry Chef*], spread it out rather flat and, before baking it, put little chuncks of fine cheese and butter on it . . . " (Paris: Pierre Des-Hayes, 1654, Book I, Ch. XVII, p. 32; published with the *Jardinier françois* of Bonnefons; 8th edn., Paris, Anthoine Cellier, 1666). See also the description of the Pimpled Pie (*une boutonnée*) in Recipe XI,4, above.

[7.2] We should understand "pie-shell" here. Two paragraphs later the author will indeed write of *abesses*, "shells".

[7.3] Rather like a double-crusted pie, this "cake" now, alternatively, has two thinner "shells" from the same amount of dough.

[7.4] The original term, *billeté*, will be glossed by the author later, in Recipe XX,3: " — that is, cut into small pea-sized pieces." Literally the word means "cut as a billet", as in heraldry.

8. A Milanese Cake[8.1]

On a table set out eighteen ounces[8.2] of fine flour and make a hollow in the middle of it; into that put a pound of good butter, neither salted nor hard, and also break in two or three eggs; add in the amount of a fistful of good soft cheese, creamy and freshly made, and some salt to season the mixture. All that has to be worked well and reduced to a dough by adding in a little water.

When that dough is sufficiently worked, you spread it out in the shape of a cake on some paper that has been greased with butter; it is made about a good two inches thick.[8.3] You can also fashion the edge. Gild your cake on top once or twice and slash it, too, with a knife; it can be pricked here and there. It can be baked thoroughly in a good half-hour.

If you want the cake to be very dry and crumbly, it should be left to dry out fully in the oven.

Kings' Cakes are made like the Milanese ones, but they are made less fine; moreover, pastry chefs put brewer's yeast in them.[8.4]

9. An Almond Cake

On a table, set out (for instance) a good three-quarters of a pound, or a little more, of fine flour; make a hollow in its middle and put close to half a pound of powdered sugar in the hollow, spreading it out; to that add half a pound of skinned sweet almonds, beaten or ground in a marble or stone mortar; also put in some five ounces[9.1] of good, unsalted butter; add in a little fine salt — that is, about the amount of a little hazelnut — and two or three egg yolks, and a little rosewater. Work all that together and, if the dough seems too thick to you, you can add in a little good rosewater.

[8.1] See a version of this *Gasteau de Milan* also in both Nicolas de Bonnefons, *Delices de la campagne* (Paris: Pierre Des-Hayes, 1554), Book I, Ch. 16; and the *Art de bien traiter* (1674), Part V, Ch. 7, of L. S. R., reproduced in *L'Art de la cuisine française au XVIIe siècle* (Paris: Payot & Rivages, 1995), p. 235.

[8.2] *un litron et demy.*

[8.3] According to Bonnefons, the dough of a *gasteau de Milan* begins as a thin square and "like a napkin" is folded over twice, to keep a square, rolled out, and that repeated four times.

[8.4] See Recipe VIII,1 for the advantages and drawbacks of this optional use of brewer's yeast.

[9.1] *un quarteron & demy.*

When the dough is ready, it has to be spread evenly in the form of a cake on buttered paper. Make this cake about a good inch thick, and slash its top as if you were marking out a certain number of parts.

Occasionally this cake is gilded on top, but it is better to put it into the oven without gilding it. It takes a gentle heat; it is baked and dried enough at the end of an hour or slightly more.

If this cake is not gilded, it has to be glazed with sugar when you take it out of the oven: for that, just as soon as it is baked and out of the oven, a Sugar Glazing,[9.2] no thicker than a sheet of paper, has to be spread over it, then you put it back for a little while in mouth of the oven to dry the glaze. Then it is done.

As soon as it comes out of the oven, the warm cake can be stuck with some candied cinnamon sticks and some pieces of candied lemon peel — which have to be stuck in immediately while the glazing is hot.[9.3]

10. A Puff-Pastry Cake

Spread out some puff pastry on ungreased paper, making the dough about a finger or a thumb thick; with a knife cut all around the dough so as to shape it round like a cake. Gild its top and put it in the oven; it is baked and dried out in an hour or so.

Chapter XVI

Flamiches[xvi.1]

On a very clean table set out about a pound and a half of good fat cheese, slightly salted and made a few days before, like two or three days but no more than ten or twelve days before; squash the cheese by hand or with a wooden pestle, working it until there are no more lumps; then you add to it about eighteen ounces of good unsalted butter, two ounces or so of

---

[9.2] For this coating, see Chapter V, above.

[9.3] For the candied cinnamon, see *The French Confectioner*, Recipe XV,5; for the candied lemon peel, see the same work, Chapter IX.

[xvi.1] Cotgrave describes the composition of this sort of cake: as in the present text it is "made of butter, cheese, flower, and yolkes of egges; after baking glazed over with sugar, and rosewater"; he gives no equivalent English name. No exact English equivalent existed either for Marnette: "Refined Cakes or Tarts, in French called *Flemiches*." Their composition suggests that the name may derive in some way from "flan".

ground salt and eight or nine eggs. Work all those things together until they blend well as if it were a very soft dough or a pie-filling. Then that has to be spread out on the table; pour into it about a glassful of cold water so as to moisten or thin the mixture even more and to lighten it, almost as if it were beaten eggs.

Then you get about a quart of fine flour and spread about two-thirds of it over that mixture, mixing and blending the two together; then, holding back only a handful or two of the flour, all the rest of it is similarly added in. With the mixture reduced to a very smooth dough, it has to be sprinkled with a little flour and worked gently two or three times over the space of a good eight minutes. Then the dough has to be rolled out a little once or twice with the wooden pestle, then it is gathered into a mound again and let sit and develop itself again for about eight minutes or more.

Then the dough is spread out again lengthwise and cut to make cakes of whatever shape and size you like, making them two or three fingers thick more or less, depending on their size. These cakes are set on some paper greased with a little good butter, then an edge is fashioned all around each.[xvi.2] Slash, then prick and gild their tops.

Then bake the cakes; it takes about half an hour to bake them perfectly. They need a hearth about as hot as for baking medium-sized loaves; keep the oven stopped up so as to brown them more. Look at the cakes from time to time while they are in the oven to keep them from burning, and bake them slowly — that is why they shouldn't have too intense a heat. Don't remove them from the oven until they have dried out enough.

[xvi.2] *Puis on les façonnera tout autour du bord.* The instruction in *façonner* is ambiguous: it may have to do with adding a decorative motif (a crenellation, for instance, as in Recipe IX,15 where the chef is working with a tourte shell of pastry) or, as Marnette reads it, merely "raise their borders round about." The more likely sense seems the latter: "Form a higher outer edge on them."

Chapter XVII

A *Poupelain*[xvii.1]

Get about a fistful of cheese curds — that is, creamy cheese that has just been made that day — put them into a bowl and smooth them out, adding a pinch of flour to them. That done, two eggs are broken into that mixture, along with a good handful of fine flour and a little ground salt; then everything has to be blended together with the wooden spatula.

When the mixture is ready, you set it on some buttered paper; spread it out to about a finger thick in the shape of a cake. Then you put it in the oven; the hearth has to be hot; this cake is baked in half an hour. Then it has to be taken out of the oven and sliced across to open it and separate the two crusts, whole, from one another; you set them out apart from one another in a basin or some other suitable vessel in which there is a sufficient quantity of good melted, unsalted butter; the butter has to be clarified, as will be explained later.[xvii.2] The lower crust has to be dipped into the butter first, and a little afterwards taken out and let drain; then the upper crust of the *poupelain* is dipped into the same butter.

When the two crusts have drained, the upper and lower surfaces have to be sprinkled with sugar, and a little rosewater sprinkled as well on their inner sides; you can also garnish the inner side of the lower crust with

---

[xvii.1] According to Cotgrave, *popelins* are "soft cakes made of fine flower ... like our Welsh Barrapyclids." Marnette likewise resorts to a comparison: " ... a Poupelain as they call it in French, or a puff Cake, like a Pumpion." In Chapter XIX Marnette refers back to this recipe as for "Composition Cakes." See also Recipe XXIX,5.

A similar recipe for this "cake" is given by Nicolas de Bonnefons in his *Delices de la campagne* (Paris, 1654): *Les Poupelains se font de la mesme Paste* [as is used for *Petits choux*], *& se tirent fort plats, puis se mettent au Four sur du papier bœuré; estans cuits, on les couppe par moitiées, & on les trempe par dedans de bœure fondu bien clarifié, leur en donnant autant qu'ils en peuvent boire, puis on les poudre de Sucre, & on les remet au Four pour les secher; en les tirant on y degoute de l'Eau rose, & on les rejoint, les poudrant encore de Sucre par dessus; puis on les sert promptement pendant qu'ils sont en leur grande chaleur, car ils se ramoliroient par trop, s'ils estoient rechauffez.*

The dough for the *Petits choux* and the *Poupelains* is made with eggs "with half of the whites removed," flour, soft cheese and salt. (Book II, Ch. XXXVI.) The *Cuisinier* of Pierre de Lune (1656) offers a recipe for a stuffed *poupelin*, qualified as being Flemish, which suggests a modern jam-filled doughnut.

[xvii.2] The directions for clarifying butter constitute the whole of Chapter XVIII, immediately below.

small slices of lemon peel. Then cover the lower with the upper crust, which has to be sugared well; then set the *poupelain* back in the mouth of the oven for the sugar to glaze, and also to keep the *poupelain* warm until you want to eat it.

Chapter XVIII

To Clarify Butter

Melt some fresh butter and let it boil gently on a bright fire until it becomes thin and runny[xviii.1] and the "cheese"[xviii.2] falls to the bottom; then the vessel is taken off the fire. Let the butter half-cool so that all the impurities[xviii.3] sinks to the bottom, or else it will be picked up in the scum. The [clarified] butter has to be skimmed very carefully and then poured into pots to be used when you like.

Chapter XIX

Little Cabbages[xix]

The dough for Little Cabbages has to be made like the one for *Poupelins*, it needs only to be a little heavier with flour.

When the dough is made up, it has to be set out on buttered paper in individual globs more or less the size of an egg; make them round, gild them lightly a little, then put them into the oven. The oven hearth, and the oven too, should be properly hot.

When the Little Cabbages are baked, you can slice them in half and dip them in [melted] butter, then do them up as we directed for the *Poupelin*. Otherwise you can cut some Little Cabbages into pieces, put them into a bowl with a little unsalted butter and rosewater, warm them up and eat them like that.

[xviii.1] The single adjective here is *clair*, the consistency of what Indians call ghee. Although not its usual sense, the word may also mean transparent.

[xviii.2] *fromage.*

[xviii.3] *ordure.* Marnette translates "dross and filth."

[xix] These are merely smaller versions of the *Poupelains* of Chapter XVII, what Marnette calls "little Puff-paste Bunns."

Chapter XX
Waffles

1. To make Sugar Waffles

Break three eggs into a basin, add four ounces of powdered sugar and beat them together; then put in four ounces of fine flour or a little more, and mix all that together; then add in a little under two ounces[1.1] of good unsalted butter, melted, and blend it well in the mixture by means of a wooden spatula or spoon. If you think the mixture is too weak — that is, too thin — you have to add in a little sugar and flour to thicken it.

When that mixture is ready, the waffle iron has to be heated on both sides — and don't heat it up so hot that it smokes because then it would be too hot and would burn the waffles. When the waffle iron is hot enough, it has to be opened and about a small egg's amount of your batter put in and spread out a little; then you close the waffle iron gently and set it on the fire, turning it over a little while afterwards so the waffle is cooked on both sides. Then lift it gently out of the waffle iron and immediately cut away any dribbles[1.2] — that is, the edges.

If the waffles stick to the iron, that means that the batter is too thin; in that case a little flour and butter have to be mixed in, and an egg, too.

These waffles are better cold than warm.

2. Milk Waffles, or Cream Waffles

Put three-quarters of a pound of flour in a basin, break two or three eggs into it and mix them together, adding some milk cream or milk, and a pinch of salt; also add in an amount of two eggs of freshly made cream cheese or else simply some soft, creamy cheese, along with three ounces of good melted butter. Even if you put in only two ounces of butter, that is enough provided you put in two ounces of good beef marrow that is squashed very fine.

[1.1] *un demy quarteron.* Butter is measured in a thirteen-ounce pound.

[1.2] Literally, "the slobbers": *baveures.* Equally picturesquely, Marnette translates "the beards." As in previous chapters, *paste* can apply to either a batter or a dough of a whole range of consistencies from runny to stiff and compact enough to make a two-inch-thick casing for a pie.

The finished waffle turned out by his waffle iron is rectangular, longer than wide according to Recipe 3, below.

Mix all that together well and, when the mixture is well blended, the irons have to be put in the fire and the waffles made. These waffles should be eaten while they are still warm.

3. Fine-Cheese Waffles

Put three-quarters of a pound of flour into a basin, break two eggs into it, add in a quarter-pound of melted butter, an egg's amount of soft cheese and a two-eggs' amount of fine cheese, in chunks — that is, cut into small pea-sized pieces; also add in a little ground salt.

All those things have to be mixed together and reduced to a rather soft dough, and if it is too stiff a little cold water should be worked into it — or rather a little milk or milk cream. Knead and work everything together until you have given your dough a good consistency.

Then you set your waffle iron in the fire and heat up both sides of it enough. In the meantime, you should take bits of your dough and flatten each of them as if for a pie-shell that is about the size of the waffle iron and no thicker than a fifty-eight-sous coin[3.1] and longer than wide; when the waffle iron is hot, put one of those leaves of dough into the iron, close it and cook the waffle on both sides.

These waffles have to be eaten while they are still warm rather than waiting for them to cool.

If you are afraid of the fine cheese sticking to the waffle iron, do not put any into the waffle mix; rather, when you have set out the small leaves of dough to make waffles, you put some fine cheese, cut into little bits, onto them — for each waffle there should be about the amount of a big walnut; set those little bits of cheese along the middle of each little leaf and lap the cheese in the leaf;[3.2] then you place each leaf in the waffle iron to cook it first on one side and then on the other, turning the waffle iron over when necessary.

4. Other Excellent Waffles

Get a pint of milk and heat it to a little more than lukewarm in a small kettle; then into a pewter basin or some other vessel you put two

---

[3.1] Marnette has "not much thicker than a peece of Eight, or a Crown."

[3.2] *l'envelopé dans l'abesses*: while the spelling and syntax of the typesetter tends to be hit-and-miss, the sense here is that the cheese is incorporated deeply into the dough just before being flattened out (again) for the waffle iron.

pounds of fine flour, or a little less, and then moisten it with the warm milk.

A dozen egg yolks[4.1] have to be put into a bowl and beaten, then mixed gently into the above-mentioned batter with a large wooden spoon.

Before putting in the eggs, there has to be mixed into the batter a good half-spoonful of runny, good beer yeast,[4.2] that is to say, of beer yeast that is thick. After all those things a good nine ounces of fresh butter is also added into the batter: it is melted in a skillet and, when it begins to boil it is poured into the batter. Add in a small half-handful of fine salt.

Note that as soon as the eggs are in the mixture, it should hardly be stirred any more, and only slightly, because waffles are less light if the mixture is stirred much and energetically after the egg yolks are in it. The mixture has to be set by the chimney corner and covered to keep warm until it has risen or swollen; sometimes it takes two hours for the mixture to rise or swell, which depends on the quality on the yeast.

When the batter has really puffed up, the waffle iron is heated, then it is rubbed with butter; batter is laid on it with a wooden spoon, and at the same time the iron closed. It is turned over and put on the fire; when the waffle is thought to be cooked on one side, you turn the iron over onto its other side.

Cook these waffles carefully, on a bright low fire, with the waffle iron supported on a tripod.[4.3]

[4.1] *demy quarteron de jaunes d'œufs*: the word *quarteron* represents a "quarter" of some basic quantity, normally a pound or, in the case of things that can be counted, one hundred. Here a *demy quarteron* would be the yolks of twelve or thirteen eggs.

[4.2] *égout de bonne leveure.*

[4.3] Following the end of this recipe, the English edition of 1656 by Mounsieur Marnette has inserted a section of three paragraphs headed by a rubric that reads: "The translators additionall observations, concerning Wafers." These amount to further variations on the theme and are interesting enough to reproduce here, with all their capitals and italics.

"You may make your Wafers farre Excellenter and pleasing, or if in case you will go to the charges of grating into the mixture of your said Wafer paste, three or four *Holland* Biscuites, some Rice, or if you please some Naples Biscuit, or Dyer bread, and two penny-worth of Saffron dissolved, which will greatly adde to their tendernesse, pleasantnesse in eating, and delightfulnesse.

"So likewise after your said wafers are baked, you must sprinkle them over with

Chapter XXI

Fritters

1. To make Fritters[1.1]

Get three-quarters of a cup of fine flour, add into it three small cream cheeses — that is, about ... [1.2] — made from unskimmed milk that same day, break three eggs into it and about the amount of an egg of grated or finely chopped beef marrow; blend all that mixture and combine it well, adding in about a cup of white wine, or as much as is necessary; season the mixture with a pinch of fine salt and an ounce of powdered sugar. The mixture or batter should be about as thick as cooked gruel. You can then add in some sliced apple or some grated, finely cut lemon peel.

When the mixture is ready, you must heat up some clarified lard or butter or oil. When it is hot enough, you stir your mixture with a spoon, then take a good amount of it in the spoon and pour it into the lard. As soon as the fritters are cooked, they have to be taken out of the pan, drain them, sprinkle them with sugar if you like, and sprinkle them with a few drops of rosewater or orange-blossom water.

Note that you can make your fritter batter stiffer and give it the consistency of a soft dough by putting in less wine, and that dough can be used for making Donkey's Farts[1.3] — that is, instead of making ordinary fritters you divide your dough into small round pieces the size of little

---

half a spoonfull of good fresh butter, that you must have ready melted at hand for that purpose, and afterwards powder them with good store of Cinamon, and fine powder Sugar smal beaten together, and after all this, sprinkle them again with Rose-water, or Orange flower-water, which will give them a most fragrant rellish.

"And to render them yet better, you may adde unto the said mixture, a quarter of a pound of the best Marrow you can get, sliced small or grated."

[1.1] *La maniere de faire des beignets ou beignetes.* The modern reader should not think of a modern doughnut or holed fritter: the seventeenth century ate whole ones. The author hesitates on the proper form of the relatively old word in French; in the two recipes that follow this one he sticks with the first form, the masculine.

[1.2] The suspension points are in the text, as if either the typesetter or the author intended to verify an actual amount. Cf. the same apparent hesitation or *lapsus* earlier, at the beginning of Chapter XV.

[1.3] The name of this variety of fritter invites speculation. A contemporary and long-standing proverb in French expressed the common consequence of presenting beauty to an unappreciative audience: *Chanter à l'âne, il vous fera des pets*: "Sing to the

hazelnuts and set them to cook in clarified lard or butter or oil until they are browned.

2. Other Fritters called Tourons[2.1]

Cook some rice in milk or in water; it has to be quite thick and, when it has cooled, you grind it, adding, if you like, some skinned sweet almonds which also have to be ground. Put that mixture into a bowl, add in half as much or so of fine flour, a few raw eggs, a little fine salt and white wine or milk as you wish.[2.2] Mix everything together well and blend it into a sort of hash or gruel or batter that is neither too stiff nor too soft. You can also mix in some currants and some grated lemon peel.

Then you heat up some clarified lard or some butter and, when it is hot enough, you take some of the mixture in a medium-sized spoon and pour it into the pan. Cook these fritters on both sides; for that, you turn them in the pan one after the other. When cooked, they are taken out, drained, put into a dish and sprinkled with sugar before eating.

3. Other Fritters

Knead some flour with water and salt, make your batter moderately stiff, roll it out with a rolling pin, cut it into little square pieces or into whatever other shapes you like, then fry them in butter or in clarified lard or oil.

When you have taken them out of the pan, you can sprinkle them with sugar, or else you can use them to garnish a platter of spinach or peas, or an open-faced fish pie, or on some other dish.[3]

---

donkey and he will fart back at you!" These little round airy fritters may be the pastry chef's contribution to the world's lovely things. Compare this recipe with that of the earlier Whore's Farts in *The French Cook*, VIII,41.

[2.1] The French name for this variety of fritter is *Tourron*. Marnette sees the word as a derivative of *tour* and adds his own little gloss: "*Tourrons*, or pointed Fritters, in shape like unto a Turret." The name seems related to that of a modern Spanish confection of nuts. The fifteenth-century Catalan *Libre de totes maneres de confits* (ed. Luis Faraudo de Saint-Germain in *Boletín de la Academia de Buenas Letras de Barcelona*, 19 (1946), 97–134) contains a recipe for a *torro*, a sort of nougat.

[2.2] *à discretion*: this phrase normally applies to an optional quantity of an ingredient, which may still be the sense here.

[3] As at the end of the previous chapter, Marnette here appends "The Translators additionall description how to make excellent Pan cakes, according to the Flemish and Holland Fashion and the which as it seems was omitted in this Treatise":

Chapter XXII
Rissoles

1. To make Rissoles

Get some beef, mutton, pork or veal that is either roasted or boiled, chop it up very small and season it with a little salty spice.[1.1] Then you make little shells of white, moderately-fine dough[1.2] in which you enclose a little of the chopped meat. When your rissoles are fashioned, they have to be fried in some clarified lard that is hot enough for making fritters; when the crust looks yellow on one side in the lard, you turn the rissoles over with a little stick without breaking them. When they are browned[1.3] on both sides, they have to be taken out with a skimmer or a holed spoon.

2. More Delicate, Puff-Pastry Rissoles[2.1]

Get good boiled meat, or rather roasted — if it is not entirely cooked, it is better — for instance, the white meat of fowl or round of veal; if there

---

"Take five Pints of Milk, one quarter of a Peck of flower, eight Eggs two penny-worth of Saffron a whole Nutmeg grated, mix all these together, and beat them well untill you bring them to a sufficient thick body, as of a pudding or thick broath, shred thereunto fifteen or sixteen Pippins, and half a pound of Currans, adde thereunto half a quarter of an ounce of Ginger powdered, stir all these ingredients very well together, and set them in a great earthen pot, either in the chimney corner, or in the passage of an entry where the ayr and wind play through to rise and work, and leave them so working, for at least the space of ten or twelve hours.

"You must observe to put them in a sufficient big vessel, least they chance to work over.

"Having thus well mingled, steeped and worked them, you may bake your Pancakes thereof, as thick or thinne as you please your self in a Frying pan with good fresh butter, over a quick fire.

"Observe that in case you intend to eat your said Pancakes hot, you must make them the thinner, if you keep them to bee eaten cold, you must make them the thicker.

"Observe that in the mingling of your Pancakes, you must not put any butter into them, for that would hinder them baking, and would make them too washy, &c.

"And having thus baked them, you must powder them with sugar and Cinamon powdered, and sprinkle them with Rose-water, or Orange flower-water if you please."

[1.1] See Recipe II,2, above.

[1.2] In the text: *abesses de paste blanche à demy fine*. The author wants only a moderate amount of butter in his rissole dough. See Recipes I,3 and VII,21.

[1.3] The French culinary vocabulary used by La Varenne had a word for that sort of deep-frying: *rissoler*.

[2.1] These baked turnovers are not rissoles in the sense the word had had since it was first used in the Middle Ages for a deep-fried pasty.

is any coarse skin on it, it has to be taken off, then the meat chopped up and put into a bowl with a little salty spice or currants, some pinenuts, a reasonable amount of sugar and a little rosewater; mix everything together.

Then you have to make up some small shells of puff pastry, the thickness of a quarter *écu*. In each shell wrap an amount of a small egg or a walnut of your mixture, more or less as you like, and make up your rissoles; gild them[2.2] and put them in the oven on some paper. These rissoles need to be baked with a gentle heat, as for baking a pie. Let them bake slowly: they need about half an hour to bake if they are small.

When the rissoles are almost done and the crust is browned, they have to be taken out of the oven and the top sprinkled with sugar, then put back a short while in the oven to finish baking them and to glaze the sugar.

Chapter XXIII
Jaw-Breakers

1. To make Jaw-Breakers[1]

You need long pieces of beef marrow, each of which, if possible, the length of a thumb; scald them in water that is almost boiling, then they have to be taken out with a holed spoon and drained a little, then set out on a table and sprinkled as heavily as possible with powdered sugar that is seasoned either with a little salty spice or with a little salt and powdered cinnamon.

Then you immediately make up small shells out of very thin puff pastry; on one end put a bit of marrow a thumb long and, if necessary, you add some more sugar seasoned as directed, then you turn the other end of the shell over the marrow, moistening the edges of the dough so that you can join the two more easily.

When your Jaw-Breakers are made, they have to be fried in some butter or or clarified lard; do not break them open turning them over. When done, they have to be taken out of the oil with a holed spoon, then sprinkled with sugar and eaten right away.

[2.2] See Chapter III.

[1] Properly, perhaps, "Snout-Smashers". Furetière indicates that the term *casse-museaux* is used ironically for a particularly soft and delicate pastry. They are, in effect, varieties of small turnover. See the quotation from Ménage in the note to Chapter XIV, above.

2. Other Jaw-Breakers

Get some soft, creamy cheese that is freshly made, or else some curdled milk, along with some dry cheese cut up quite small, some raw eggs, a little fine flour — or rather some Pastry Chef's Cream[2] — currants, pinenuts, sugar seasoned with salty spice, or only salty spice alone; you can also put in a little finely-chopped cooked meat. Mix all those things together and make a sort of hash of them, adding in a little milk. That hash should be somewhat runny.

Enclose the mixture in small puff-pastry shells and of them make up Jaw-Breakers, which you have to do in butter or clarified lard. Then you sprinkle them with powdered sugar if you like.

Chapter XXIV

Butter Simnels[xxiv.1] or Cracknels

On a table set out six ounces of fine flour,[xxiv.2] make a little depression in its middle, put in about half a glassful of brewer's yeast, adding whatever hot water is necessary, and work everything together, making it into a rather soft dough to use as leavening — for that reason the dough has to be made up into a little loaf and put into a warm place so that it swells or rises quickly; if it is in summer, it can rise enough in eight minutes.

While waiting for the yeast to rise, on a table you set out about three pounds of fine flour,[xxiv.3] make a well in its middle and into that put a pound of unsalted butter that you have previously worked and softened if it is too hard; to that add an ounce or a little more of fine salt and mix that all together, adding in whatever cold water is necessary in order to knead the dough.

---

[2] See Recipe IV, 1. The author's reason for inserting the alternative is not clear. It does not seem to be a correction or amplification.

[xxiv.1] The French name of this sort of wafer, *eschaudez*, reflects the manner of its preparation: the French verb *eschauder* is cognate with the English word *scald*: hot water was poured on the pasty dough in order to make it rise.

[xxiv.2] This step in the recipe covers only the preparation of the "leavening" to be used later with main ingredients.

[xxiv.3] *un quart de fleur de farine*: In Chapter VI we have learned that a quarter-bushel of flour weighs three (sixteen-ounce) pounds.

When that dough is half kneaded, you get your leavening if it is ready — that is, if it has puffed up and risen: it has to be mixed in with your dough as you finish kneading it. When it is sufficiently kneaded, you cut it into pieces which you shape by hand into small loaves which have then to be spread out to form them into simnels.[xxiv.4]

When that is done, you need a kettle or preserving pan on the fire with water that is almost boiling; throw your simnels into it and leave them there until they float up, then they have to be stirred around a little in the water. Then get a skimmer to lift some of that water and you sprinkle or wash your simnels with it. You leave them in the water, though, until they become plump and firmed up: in order to tell when that has happened, you have to take out one of your simnels and handle it to see whether it is firm enough.

When you decide that the simnels are plumped enough, you take them out of the water with a skimmer and set them to drain and cool on a small wicker tray. Then you put them into the oven; ordinary small simnels need only a quarter of an hour to bake. But the oven has to be really hot — that is, it must be as hot as for baking big pies.

If the simnels do not brown enough as they bake, towards the end some burning coals will have to be set on one of the cheeks or sides of the oven so the heat will play right onto[xxiv.5] the simnels.

Note that if you do not put any butter into your simnel mixture, you will be making only Salt-and-Water Simnels,[xxiv.6] which are more highly thought of by some people than Butter Simnels. As for Egg Simnels, they are made just like the Butter ones, but eggs have to be put into the dough: for that, for a quart of flour fifteen eggs have to broken, and only six ounces of butter put in. The dough with which you intend to make Egg Simnels has to be well worked and softer than that for the other sorts of simnel. Note, too, that Egg Simnels need a less intense oven than those that are only the salt-and-water sort, or those with butter.

[xxiv.4] The traditional shape of a simnel is triangular.

[xxiv.5] *se rebatte sur*. La Varenne's oven penetrates into the room: if necessary, additional heat can be applied to the curved exterior of the top and sides. The heat will radiate through the brick or stone of *une de joues ou costé du four*.

[xxiv.6] Marnette calls these "bare and ordinary Simnels."

Chapter XXV

Biscuits

1. To make Plain Pastry-Chef Biscuits[1.1]

Break (for instance) eight eggs into a bowl, beat them as if for making an omelet, add in about two liards-worth of beaten coriander or green aniseed and a pound of powdered sugar; blend those things together a little, then add in a good twelve ounces or close to a pound of fine flour. All that has to be blended together carefully, and beat them until the batter becomes white — the biscuit will be all the finer and better as the batter is beaten more.

When the batter is white from having been beaten, you pour it out into a biscuit mould, which Pastry Chefs call a biscuit tourtière, of white metal;[1.2] before the batter is put into them, their inside has to be greased with fresh, melted butter. Fill your moulds to the top, putting the batter or mixture into them only when the oven is ready and not before; then the biscuits have to be sprinkled on top with very dry sugar and put into the oven right away, far from the coals. You can experiment with one or two biscuits to learn how to make them without too great a loss, for that sort of pastry is hard to do well.

The heat of the oven has to be gentle to bake biscuits, and should be rather like what you have [left] in the oven when bread is a little more than half-baked. The oven has to be left open and the biscuit watched while it is baking because, in the first place, it will swell up, and then, it will brown: that happens in about eight minutes. If the biscuit blackens in the oven, that means that the oven is too hot; that is why the biscuits have to be drawn to the mouth of the oven, so as to let the heat moderate a little. If, on the contrary, the biscuit stays dough-pale in the oven without browning, that means that the oven heat is too mild: in that case the

---

[1.1] Traditionally the *bis-cuit* was the product of a double baking. In the recipes that follow there is no evidence of any survival of that origin.

[1.2] This "mould" is a flat tray in which a number of depressions will hold and form the biscuits, much like a modern madeleine form. Marnette assumes that biscuits are diamond-shaped: "little Lossenges," he says in Recipe 4, below. Referring to the individual depressions in his mould, the author will subsequently write the plural here.

stopper[1.3] has to be set in the oven's mouth, and removed frequently so the biscuit doesn't burn.

When the biscuit has browned and has been in the oven between roughly a quarter and half an hour, or a little more depending on the size of the biscuit, it is taken out. Feel the biscuit gently with your hand and if it pushes back and seems firm without giving way, you can trust it to be baked; take it out of the oven immediately and remove it from its mould or tourtière while it is hot.

2. Queen's Biscuit

Make the dough as in the previous recipe except that you put in fewer eggs because the Queen's Biscuit dough has to be a little more firm; for that, instead of eight eggs (for instance), six are enough.

When the dough is ready, with a wooden spatula you lay it out on some very white paper. You make these biscuits round like little bread buns and sprinkle their tops with sugar.

The Queen's Biscuit has to have a hotter hearth than ordinary biscuit. As soon as the Queen's Biscuit is baked, you take it out of the oven and loosen it from its paper by deftly slipping a thin knife between the biscuit and the paper.

3. Piedmontese Biscuit

It is made with dough similar to that of the Queen's Biscuit; you have only to lay out the dough elongated on the paper, making it about a finger thick, as narrow as possible and a good finger in length. Sprinkle it with sugar and put it into the oven.

This biscuit should be left only a short time in the oven because it bakes quickly, but the oven has to be as hot as for baking Queen's Biscuit. When baked, you loosen it immediately from its paper.

4. Cinnamon Biscuit

Get marzipan dough,[4.1] add in some ground cinnamon, mixing them well together and making the dough firm. Roll it out on the pastry table

---

[1.3] *bouchoy*: the type-setter likely omitted a silent *r* from the end of the word *bouchoir*.

[4.1] A recipe for Ordinary Marzipan is provided at the beginning of the next chapter. In *The French Confectioner*, an entire section of 25 recipes, Chapter XVI, is devoted to various sorts of marzipan.

and do it twice — that is, it has to be spread and rolled out two times on the table; when the dough is rolled out the second time, it has to be spread out with the rolling pin as if you intended to make a pie-shell; it should not be thicker than a fifty-eight-sou coin. Then the dough is cut like little biscuits[4.2] or little squares, and put on some paper.

Give them a very mild hearth heat, as it usually is after bread is taken out; they can then be dried in a warm chamber.

5. Snow-Sugar Biscuits

Clarify a quarter pound of royal sugar[5] and cook it to the consistency of a very thick syrup or of *rosat* sugar. Then into that add two egg whites, whipped to a mousse, beat everything together and spread it out on paper in the form of little biscuits. Give them a very gentle oven.

6. Pistachio Biscuits

Shell some pistachios, then grind them in a mortar and mix them into the mixture for Snow-Sugar Biscuits in order to make a greenish biscuit.

7. Gamby Biscuit[7.1]

Get some puff pastry after it is folded and gone through all of its turns;[7.2] the dough has to be reduced to the thickness of a quarter-écu and cut into whatever shape you like and laid out on paper.

Give the biscuits a very gentle oven; it is quite all right to put them into the oven after taking other pasties out. They take about half an hour to bake. When they are done, they are glazed with Sugar Glazing.[7.3]

8. Lenten Biscuit

You need (for instance) about half a pound of sweet almonds, skinned and ground in the mortar, a pound and a half of powdered sugar and a

---

[4.2] " . . . in the form of little Lossinges," Marnette writes here. Recipe 8, below, suggests also that biscuits are normally "elongated".

[5] Royal sugar is by definition a finer variety of sugar.

[7.1] *Du biscuit de Gamby.* Marnette amplifies: "A Gamby Bisket, that is to say, a crooked form of Bisket, or Kortled Bisket."

[7.2] That is, after it has been rolled and folded the proper number of times.

[7.3] For Sugar Glazing, see above, Chapter V.

small almond's size of tragacanth gum[8.1] that has steeped at length in a spoonful of hot water.

Mix all of that together in a mortar along with a cupful of egg whites, and half a spoonful of lemon juice (or else merely grate up some lemon peel in the amount of half a hazelnut or a nutmeg — the lemon being raw[8.2] and good to eat); all of those things are likewise beaten in a mortar for a good hour; and you should make the paste a little thicker than for marzipan, such that it is difficult to handle and blend well together.

When the paste is like that, it is taken out onto the pastry table and is worked there with a little powdered sugar and flour mixed together. Then spread that dough out with the rolling pin and give it two or three turns — that is, the dough has to be spread and folded two or three times on the table just the same as for puff pastry; finally you flatten it and roll it out evenly, making it the thickness of a fifty-eight-sou coin and you cut it into equal-sized, elongated pieces shaped like meat-day biscuits.[8.3] Then, all at the same time, they are set onto some paper and from there put into the oven that should be as hot as for Cinnamon Biscuit.

Chapter XXVI

Marzipan[xxvi.1]

To make Ordinary Marzipan

Get a pound of sweet almonds, fresh and whole; put them into almost-boiling water and let them steep for about a quarter of an hour off the fire to soften their skin; then skin them and, as they are skinned, they are put into cool water.

With the almonds all skinned, you wash them in one or two changes of water, then set them to drain on a wicker tray or drainboard. That done, you grind them in a marble or stone mortar, gradually adding in a

---

[8.1] The author of *The French Confectioner*, Recipe II,3, assures us that we can buy this *gomme contragan* in any spicer's or druggist's shop.

[8.2] *crud*, "fresh" as distinct from candied and preserved. See the same qualification in Recipes XXVIII,1 and 2.

[8.3] Presumably this shape may be that of any of the preceding biscuits except for the first variety, that makes use of a biscuit mould.

[xxvi.1] See also Chapter XVI in the *French Confectioner*.

small half-glassful of rosewater as you are grinding so they don't become oily. They have to be ground until they are reduced to a very smooth paste and there is nothing left to grind, so that if you handle that paste in your fingers you can't feel any hard, sharp bits. When ground, the almond paste should also be quite firm, which requires that a little rosewater be put in while grinding it.

With the paste made ready like that, you add in some powdered sugar, at the rate of eight or twelve ounces per pound of peeled almonds; mix the sugar well with the almond paste; also add in a fresh egg white. Then with the pestle beat all those things again in the mortar. When the paste is blended perfectly smoothly, take it out of the mortar and put it into a bowl. Then work the paste on a very clean table that should be sprinkled from time to time with powdered sugar instead of flour, to prevent the almond paste from sticking to the table or to your hands.

Split the paste into as many parts as you like and shape them however you like. If you make pies of it, make them about seven or eight sheets of paper thick, and set them on some white paper when they are made up; then set them to more than half dry in an oven whose heat is very gentle — for that heat should be such as to dry out marzipan without burning it; despite this, the hearth should be somewhat warm — so you can put the marzipan in the oven after bread or biscuit has been removed from it.

When the marzipan is baked and dry, take it out of the oven to glaze it — that is, to ice it properly with a Sugar Glazing which has to be spread on the marzipan with the back of a silver spoon or with a knife;[xxvi.2] then it is put back right away into the mouth of the oven to dry out the glazing, which takes eight minutes or so. After that, the marzipan is taken out and, if you wish to prick the top of it with cinnamon sticks or lemon peel,[xxvi.3] that is done as it comes from the oven and before the glazing has cooled, so that you don't break it. Marzipan needs more time to dry out in a warm chamber, but the glazing and the marzipan are all the prettier and whiter that way.

[xxvi.2] This Sugar Glazing and the manner of its application have been described earlier, in Chapter V.

[xxvi.3] Though the text does not say so here, both of these garnishes, the *canela* (as distinct from *canelle*) and the *escorce de citron*, are candied: see Recipe XV,9.

Chapter XXVII

Macaroon

Get some almonds, as is directed in the chapter on Marzipan,[xxvii.1] then you grind them and reduce them to a very smooth paste. For one pound of almonds (for instance), add in as much again of powdered sugar and four egg whites; mix those together, adding in a little rosewater, and beat them right away in the mortar to make the paste very smooth, though it has to be rather soft.

When the paste is ready, lay out chunks of it apart from one another on some white paper; those chunks should be somewhat long with the shape of a macaroon,[xxvii.2] and sprinkle them on top with some fine sugar. Then put them into the oven to dry out until they are quite firm to the touch on top. The heat of the oven should be gentle, as in the chapter on Marzipan, yet the hearth should be somewhat hot so as to swell the paste and make it puff up.

Macaroon should be in the oven a little longer than marzipan since it is thicker: macaroon can be left until it is thoroughly dry, or until the oven has cooled. Nevertheless, good Pastry Chefs do not leave their macaroon in the oven that long in case it browns: they take it out before it is wholly dried out, but then they keep it warm on top of the oven for twenty-four hours for it to dry out slowly without losing its whiteness.[xxvii.3]

Chapter XXVIII

Lemon Buns[xxviii]

1. To make Lemon Buns

Into a mortar put four ounces of powdered royal sugar; to that add in an egg white and a little lemon juice and two hazel-nut's amount of

---

[xxvii.1] That is, the preceding one, Chapter XXVI. In Recipe IX,15 the author implies that pistachios are appropriate for making macaroons; he also indicates there that a marble mortar should be used for the grinding.

[xxvii.2] Marnette writes, " . . . in the shape of a chesnut."

[xxvii.3] Marnette adds, " . . . which is all the beauty of your said Macaroons."

[xxviii] These *pains de citron* are fantasy "buns" only, and the *paste* of which they are made is not the flour-based dough that one would expect in this book on pastry.

finely-grated raw lemon peel. Beat everything together and blend it all well so that the paste is very thick and can barely still be handled.

Then you break that paste into chunks the size of a walnut, make them round in your hands working them with powdered sugar,[1.1] then flatten them out and arrange them on some white paper. Then you put them in the oven at mid-oven — that is, they shouldn't be set too far into the oven;[1.2] give them a gentle heat similar to what is needed for baking macaroon; and don't stop up the oven. It takes about a quarter of an hour to bake them.

Take the Lemon Buns out when the sugar has fused well and is firm.

2. Other Lemon Buns

You have to make up your paste as in the previous recipe except that you put in twice the amount of raw lemon peel. When the paste is ready, you break it into chunks of about the size of half a walnut, squeeze them between your fingers, then put them on some paper and bake them like the other Lemon Buns.

Chapter XXIX
Egg Dishes

1. Egg Pie

Make up some dough with a little flour and salted water, or use a finer dough;[1] roll it out, cut it into pieces and turn up the edges of each piece, forming as many small pies. Break a fresh egg in each one of those shells, season each with salt, sugar and a little ground cinnamon, then cover each with an upper crust. Cook these pies moderately in some very hot butter, taking them out before the egg is very hard.

2. Egg Pot Pie[2.1]

Make an omelet seasoned with salt, chives and parsley, or other finely chopped herbs. Then you chop up the omelet and put it into a pot with

---

[1.1] A coating of sugar is to remain on the outside of the buns.

[1.2] *il ne faut pas les mettre trop avant dans le four.* Marnette adds an explanation: " . . . For if you should put them quite into the bottom of the Oven, they would bee subject to burn."

[1] That is, a dough containing some amount of butter. See Recipe I,3.

[2.1] The *pasté en pot*, in which the baking dish replaces a pastry shell entirely, looks very much like an old-fashioned pottage. Furetière has a definition of the genre: "*Pasté* some clear pea purée and some butter or oil; season that with salt and spices moistened with some verjuice; in summer red currants can be added. After boiling everything a while, add in some hard-boiled egg yolks stuck with whole cloves; you can also put in fried onion. Serve it hot. You can stick some fried bread[2.2] on top.

3. Egg Cake or Tourte

Into a tourtière put about an egg's amount of fresh butter; while that melts, break five or six eggs, to them add some salt, a large egg's amount or a little more of fine, white breadcrumbs, or two spoonfuls of fine flour. Beat everything fully together, then add in two or three spoonfuls of cream or milk, a small pinch of spices or ground cinnamon; again beat your eggs a little and pour them into the tourtière when the butter has melted and half browned. Cover the tourtière with its lid, on which you put hot ash and a few coals to cook the tourte on all sides. Serve it hot; you can grate some cheese over the top, or some sugar, and add on a few drops of rosewater.

4. Apple Egg Tourte

Into a bowl put the amount of two eggs, or a little more, of the soft part of a baked apple;[4.1] to that add two spoonfuls of powdered sugar, two small spoonfuls of fine flour, five or six eggs and some salt to taste. Stir everything together until the flour is fully blended with the rest of the ingredients, and pour that mixture into a tourtière or skillet or bowl in which you have spread an egg's amount, or a little more, of fresh butter.[4.2] Cover the tourtière, set it on a little fire and cover the lid with a few coals as well. After a quarter-hour or a little more you open the tourtière to see whether the cake is baked and whether it is darkened enough top and

---

en pot, ou *hochepot*, est un ragoust bourgeois fait de bœuf dans un pot, qui luy tient lieu de croust: c'est la nourriture ordinaire des Flamans"; and likewise, Richelet: "*Pâté en pot*. C'est de la viande hachée [here instead, eggs] & assaisonnée comme si on la vouloit mettre en pâte, & qu'on fait cuire dans un pot." This particular version of the dish, with its use of herbs, pea purée, verjuice, and fried onion, has a distinctly medieval air to it, that of the old *hochepot* (hotch-potch or, simply, stew).

2.2 Marnette calls this *pain frit*, "Sippets."

4.1 *moële*: literally, "marrow." The apple is said to be *cuite*, "cooked," which could be either boiled or baked.

4.2 Should we understand "*melted* fresh butter"?

bottom. If it is done enough, you have only to set it out on a trencher-plate to serve it to the table. You can put some sugar on it and some rosewater, and prick it with the odd piece of candied lemon peel.

Instead of the soft part of apples, to make a cake you can use some pumpkin or melon flesh, or that of some other fruit that has been cooked.

5. Beaten Eggs in the Form of a Cake or *Poupelain*[5.1]

Break (for instance) four or five eggs, putting the whites aside in one bowl and the yolks in another; with a little handful of reeds or with little sticks beat the whites until they froth up; also beat the yolks a little. Then into a medium-sized skillet or a tourtière you put almost two eggs' amount of good fresh butter and, when it has melted and browned, you have to beat the whites again a little, adding to them two good spoonfuls of powdered sugar and some salt to taste. When the butter is half-browned, put into it a small bit of toast or the upper crust of a loaf of bread, that crust being round and roughly half the size of a hand; immediately afterwards pour in the yolks, then add the whites on top.

Cook those eggs on a few hot coals; they are done shortly and burn easily. Give them colour in the same way as the Milk Eggs,[5.2] then you set them out on a trencher-plate and sprinkle them with sugar.

6. Eggs like Fritters

Get some costmary or catmint, some balm, some tansy and some parsley — of each two or three sprigs — and some very tender bugloss in the same amount as all the others; you can add in some scallions and lettuce; chop up all of those herbs very small. Then beat (for instance) six or eight eggs as if it were for making an omelet; to them add the chopped herbs and some salt to taste. Then melt some good butter in a pan or a large bowl and, when the butter is half-browned, take your beaten eggs with quite a large spoon and pour spoonfuls of them into the butter in a quantity enough to make three or four fritters of a hand's size or so. When they have cooked enough, take them out. Make as many of them

---

[5.1] See Chapter XVII, above.

[5.2] The reference may be to Recipe XXX,4, below, where eggs are coloured by means of a hot fire shovel. The same procedure is to be used for the omelet in Recipe 11 of the present chapter and in XXXIII,10.

as you like, but they have to be eaten quite hot. Some people grate some sugar[6] on top.

7. Other Eggs Like Fritters or Macaroons

Boil some eggs until they are hard, then chop them up with some parsley and a little chives and thyme; season that hash with salt, blend it with some egg whites or with raw yolks; then you make little balls of them[7] shaped like egg-sized quenelles, or like macaroon, or like whatever else you like. Fry them or cook them a little in some half-browned butter in the chafing dish or in a pan. Then take them out and sprinkle them with a little nutmeg, and with salt if there's any need.

8. Other Eggs Like Fritters

Break four eggs; to them add some salt, beat them and make an omelet. As soon as it is half-cooked, chop it up along with a handful of parsley browned on a fire shovel,[8] add in half an ounce of currants and almost as much pinenuts; bind that hash with a raw egg and a little flour. Then make little balls of it, or pieces of whatever shape you like. Cook the balls in some half-browned butter as in the previous recipe; then take them out of the butter to dry, and sprinkle them with sugar and with salt if need be. Eat them before they cool.

9. Egg *Bisque*

Into a large dish put a layer of good sliced cheese between two layers of sops or slices of toast dried by the fire; moisten them with pea purée or with some other lean bouillon that has been seasoned with butter and salt. Simmer all that a while over a low fire. Then the pottage has to be garnished with coarsely-chopped parsley.

Then you add in some eggs poached in water or prepared some other way, whether whole or not; between the eggs you can place gobs of carp milt, or some little fried fish such as smelt or gudgeon, or some sippets of fried bread; add in some capers and mushrooms, or whatever other

---

[6] " ... and Cinamon," Marnette adds.

[7] The typesetter has put *vous enserez de petites pelottes* — undoubtedly another blunder: *vous en ferez* .... The similarity between the letter *f* and the long *s* had long given rise to misreadings by scribes and type-setters.

[8] *amorty sur une pesle de feu.* In traditional cookery parsley was often "fried" in a dry pan before being incorporated into a mixture.

lean tidbits you have that are well cooked and seasoned; some people put in currants and boiled prunes. Season the whole thing with a few whole or coarsely broken cloves or with some other spice such as ginger. Then slowly you add in as much purée as is needed, or some other lean bouillon,[9.1] and put the dish back on the fire for a while, watching that the bread doesn't stick to the bottom. Verjuice can be added to this *bisque*, or else some Green Sauce;[9.2] some people put wine in it.

When the *bisque* is ready and tasting good, grate some nutmeg onto it, or some bread crust, and serve it.

10. Egg Civet

Heat up some good oil, break some eggs into it and take them out before the yolk has hardened very much; then put them in a dish. To them add a sauce made of onions sliced in rounds and fried in oil, everything being seasoned with salt and verjuice. Grate a little nutmeg on it.

11. Herb Omelet[11.1]

Into a silver dish or something else that is not too big, put (for instance) eight egg yolks. If it is a meat-day, mix the yolks with about a cup of good meat bouillon made without herbs; instead of bouillon you can use cream or milk; add in a little pinch of fine salt and two finely-crushed macaroons; the same amount of grated biscuit can also be put in; add in as well three or four spoonfuls of the juice of pears ground in a mortar with some rosewater; also put in two ounces of powdered sugar. Pour that mixture into a dish in which there is about a walnut's amount of good melted butter.

Let the bottom of the Herb Omelet set while the dish is on the fire. When the omelet itself has half-set, add in an ounce of candied lemon peel, grated or cut into extremely little bits; into it also add an ounce of peeled and ground pistachios. Let the Herb Omelet set wholly over a moderate fire. Then you give it a little colour with a red-hot shovel.[11.2]

[9.1] The printer has set *d'autre boüillon maigre bien beurré*. Marnette shows, "any other lean porridge, that is to say, porridge made without flesh in it."

[9.2] See *The French Cook*, Recipe VII,2.

[11.1] This recipe can be compared with the one that is included in the *The French Cook*, VIII,99.

[11.2] The *French Cook* resorts to this procedure frequently. See Recipe III,11, for instance, in that work.

The dish is taken off the fire and the Herb Omelet is stuck with little slices of candied lemon peel; sugar it on top.

Chapter XXX

Various Ways of preparing Eggs: scrambled, poached or cooked in water[xxx]

1. First Way

Boil some water, then break some eggs one after the other and dump them separately[1] into it. When they are moderately cooked and not yet hardened, take them out. They can be used to garnish an herb pottage or whatever other sort of pottage you like. These eggs can also be served up by themselves with various sauces. Sometimes they are poached in milk or in sweet wine.

2. Second Way

In a dish put four scrambled or poached eggs. Season them with salt; you can grate cheese on top.

3. Third Way

Some of these eggs can be put in a dish,[3.1] adding to them a little salt and sprinkling them with sugar or with the odd drop of rosewater or verjuice or lemon or orange juice; you can also add a little ground cinnamon or cinnamon water.[3.2]

4. Fourth Way

Alternatively, you can put the eggs in a dish in which there is a little good melted butter; season them with salt and, optionally, sugar; if you

---

[xxx] This rubric applies to the whole final section of the *Pastissier françois*, Chapters XXX to XXXIV. As far as this present Chapter XXX is concerned, given that the next chapter, XXXI, is devoted explicitly to uses for hard-boiled eggs, we may consider that the eggs to be dealt with now are considered to be "soft".

[1] That is, without letting them touch one another.

[3.1] Despite the word being *plat*, this vessel was somewhat concave or dished. The author regularly writes, as here, *dans un plat*.

[3.2] *The French Confectioner* contains a recipe for Cinnamon Water at IV,16. In several subsequent recipes for eggs that same preparation is suggested as an alternative garnish to rosewater.

don't put in any sugar, nutmeg will not be at all bad. These eggs can be coloured before they are put into the dish by holding a very hot fire shovel or pan over them for a while.[4]

5. Fifth Way

Sometimes Green Sauce[5] is put on eggs; and they are kept on the fire for a while. Season them with salt and nutmeg.

6. Sixth Way

Or else you can brown some butter in a pan, then cook some chopped onion in it; season that with finely ground salt and pepper. When the onion is cooked, add a dash of vinegar and immediately pour the sauce on the poached eggs. Some people add a little nutmeg. Note that if the eggs are arranged in the dish in the shape of a fish, they are called a Salmon of Eggs[6]

7. Seventh Way

In browned butter cook some chopped onion; when it is done, add in a sauce made of vinegar and mustard mixed together. It is seasoned with salt and poured over the eggs.

8. Eighth Way

Alternatively, brown some butter, then add in a sauce consisting of sweet mustard[8.1] or of grape mash mixed with some wine,[8.2] or of hypocras. Take the pan off the fire straight away without boiling that sauce, and pour it over your eggs. Instead of browning the butter in the pan it is enough to melt it in a dish, then to add in the hypocras or sweet mustard mixed as directed; then the poached eggs are put into that. Grate some sugar on top.

---

[4] See this procedure in Recipe XXIX,11 also, as well as in Recipe 10, below.

[5] See *The French Cook*, Recipe VII,2.

[6] *un Saumon d'œufs.*

[8.1] No recipe is given for this *moustarde douce*. It may well be simply a mixture of mustard with wine or hypocras.

[8.2] This grape confection, called *raisiné*, is essentially the medieval *rappée*, a mash of fresh grapes. By La Varenne's day it was common as a spread on bread, or could be preserved in thickened form by boiling and straining.

9. Ninth Way

You can stew some herbs and put them into a dish and arrange the eggs on top, along with a few added sippets of bread fried in butter, or slices of omelet. Grate nutmeg or sugar on top.

10. Tenth Way

You can also melt some good butter in a dish over a moderate fire; then you break some eggs and, after removing the white, you put the whole yolks into a bowl and pour them, one after the other, into the melted butter. When the butter begins to boil, remove the dish from the fire. A little ground cinnamon can be added on top.[10]

Chapter XXXI

Various ways of preparing Hard-Boiled Eggs

1. First Way

Into a dish put a piece of butter, some vinegar or verjuice and a little salt. When the butter melts, add in three hard-boiled egg yolks, broken.[1] mix them into the sauce. Then the dish has to be garnished with hard-boiled eggs cut in halves or quarters; grate a little nutmeg or bread crust on top of them.

2. Second Way

Brown some butter in a pan; to it you can add some chopped parsley or scallions. When that is cooked, pour it into a dish, after seasoning it

---

[10] Marnette appends another extensive note: "The Translators additional description how to poach or butter a dish of Eggs without any butter at all":

"Beat as many Eggs as you please into a good large silver dish, whites & yolks together, after which set your said dish over a Chafing-dish of hot charcoals throughly lighted, putting nothing more into the said dish unto your eggs, but stir them continually with a silver spoon, that so they may not become hard, nor stick to the dish; and when they are enough poached to your fancy, take them off from the said Chaffingdish, and adde unto them a good quantity of Orange juyce, well seasoning your said eggs with salt, and if you please yourself, powdering them with good store of sugar and cinamon, not forgetting to put grated or shredded Nutmeg into them, as you are a straining of them, and before you pour your Orange juyce upon them.

"Observe, that this kind of buttering, or poaching of Eggs without butter is least offensive to the pallate, and less nauseous to the stomack, which is oftentimes overcharged by the adding of butter to these kind of dishes and junkets."

[1] *qui soient écachez*: presumably the yolks are crumbled coarsely.

with salt and pepper; then put in some hard-boiled egg halves. You can mix in some mustard or make a Sauce Robert.[2] Boil that sauce a little before serving the eggs.

3. Third Way

Occasionally hard-boiled eggs, cut in half, are simply fried. Occasionally, too, they are dipped in flour that has been moistened with wine or milk, then they are [deep-]fried like fritters. After removing them from the butter, put them into a dish and sprinkle them with salt; add in some vinegar or lemon juice or a sweet sauce;[3] ground cinnamon can also be put on.

4. Fourth Way

These eggs can be served with the sauces suggested for the poached eggs.[4]

5. Fifth Way

Again, you can put halved eggs into a dish and season them with a white sauce made in the pan with raw egg yolks and some verjuice, or white wine, mixed together, all of that seasoned with salt and a small quantity of spices or ground-up fine herbs; then pour all of it over your eggs.

Chapter XXXII

Egg Dishes

1. Portuguese Eggs

You can fricassee hard-boiled eggs or fry them in a pan, as follows. First of all, in some butter you need to fricassee some finely chopped parsley or onion or scallions. When the parsley or onion is half-cooked, add in some hard-boiled eggs sliced in rounds; to that you can add a

---

[2] This *sauce à robert* is used in recipes for Loin of Pork (V,56) and for Hake (XVI,80) in *The French Cook*. It is also mentioned for use with an omelet in Recipe XXXIII,24, below. The sauce known as Barbe Robert had a very long history and is described in medieval recipe collections. Its principal ingredients are onions, mustard and vinegar.

[3] A standard Sweet Sauce is composed of wine, sugar and cinnamon. See Recipes VII,3 and 17.

[4] Chapter XXX.

handful of mushrooms, peeled, washed and cut up. Season everything with salt, and fricassee it well in the pan, towards the end adding in some vinegar. When these eggs are chopped up in the dish, you can grate some nutmeg on top; garnish them, too, with sippets of fried bread which you lard as in a Carp Hash;[1.1] you can also embellish that fricassee with slices of raw lemon.

Sometimes some onion or some parsley is half-fricasseed in good butter, then some hard-boiled eggs, sliced in rounds, are added in. A short time before you take them out of the pan, you add a sauce that is composed of mustard mixed with verjuice or vinegar and seasoned with salt.[1.2] After you have stirred them around once or twice in the pan on the fire, you have only to set them out; you can grate a little nutmeg on top.

2. Stuffed Hard-Boiled Eggs

Get mild herbs, such as lettuce, purslane, beet greens, borage, sorrel, parsley or chervil, and a little thyme; remove their stems; if you want the mixture to be very tasty, include a lot of parsley or chervil and a few chives. When the herbs are clean and washed, they have to be chopped up; season them with salt and a little cloves or pepper; along with the herbs can also be chopped up some very clean mushrooms that are already cooked and well seasoned; some people even add in some finely cut up cheese.

Pour that mixture into a pan and cook it in some half-browned butter or in some other grease or oil. When it is half-cooked, some people add in some currants or pinenuts — which is not at all necessary, salt being a sufficient seasoning. When it is cooked, you put in hard-boiled egg yolks chopped into small bits, and stir it around the pan once or twice more. Then you set it out in a dish and garnish it on top with hard-boiled egg halves. Occasionally their yolk is removed and combined with the mixture; when cooked, the whites are filled with some of the mixture before setting them out on the rest of the mixture. Occasionally, instead of putting the whites onto the mixture, it is thought enough merely to stick sippets of bread into it, or little dough cakes fried in butter. A little nutmeg or bread crust can be grated on top.

[1.1] A recipe for Carp Hash is found in *The French Cook* at XVI,11, although there is no mention of either sippets or larding in that recipe.

[1.2] See this same mixture in Recipe XXX,7.

3. Sorrel Eggs

Many people are content to cook sorrel or barberry, with their stems removed, in a dish or in a pan: put in some good butter and some salt to taste; to that you can add some pepper or spices. With the mixture cooked, set halved or quartered hard-boiled eggs in it. Sometimes a white sauce is made with raw egg yolks blended with a little verjuice or water and mixed with the sorrel when it is cooked; then the eggs are added. You can grate nutmeg on top.

Chapter XXXIII

Various ways of making Omelets

1. First Way: a Plain Omelet

Get (for instance) half a dozen eggs, break them separately on a trencher-plate, then beat them together in a dish, adding in some fine salt and the odd drop of water or milk. Melt some butter in a pan and, when it has browned, pour in the beaten eggs and let them cook more or less depending on whether you want to have a moist[1.1] omelet or a dry one. For want of butter, you can use oil or some other grease to make these eggs and any other sort of omelet.

If you want an omelet to be green, you have only to put some Green Sauce[1.2] into the eggs when they are beaten, or else you can serve some along with the omelet; ordinarily, though, people prefer a dash of vinegar.[1.3] You can serve some mustard, whether ordinary mustard or sweet mustard; in that case, it is proper to serve the omelet rolled up like a large sausage and split at each end, which ends must be turned outwards.[1.4]

[1.1] The adjective here, *baveuse* (literally, "slobbery") applies to an omelet that is not fully cooked — perhaps "flabby or limber", as Marnette writes; perhaps "soft" or "runny".

[1.2] See *The French Cook*, Recipe VII,2.

[1.3] " ... but the usual custom," writes Marnette, "is to eat your Omelet with a little vinegar, and some powder sugar."

[1.4] The text is not too clear: *fenduë par les deux bouts, qu'il faut escarter un peu loin* [this word should undoubtedly be *l'un*] *de l'autre*. What the author intends is better explained later, in the recipe for Egg-and-Fish-Hash Omelet (Recipe 19 in this chapter): there the text adds that the cut ends are to be bent out "in the form of a star".

2. Celestine Omelet[2.1]

Break a dozen or a score or so of eggs, season them with salt and beat them; you can add fine crumbled white bread and some chopped parsley or[2.2] some powdered sugar; also put in some thinly sliced good fresh butter, enough to properly fricassee such a quantity of eggs in a pan.[2.3] While all that is being beaten together, into a very clean frying pan put a pound of good olive oil or butter and heat it until it boils, and right away pour it out of the pan; without wiping the pan, you immediately put in the beaten eggs seasoned with salt and butter as has been said. Let them cook, stirring them only in the middle gently with a stick that is rather large and flat at its end, or with the point of a knife, so that the eggs set better. When the omelet is half-cooked, turn it over with a trencher-plate or a fish-turner to finish its cooking and to keep it from sticking to the pan and burning; move the pan often.[2.4]

When this omelet is set out, you can sprinkle it with sugar and a little rosewater and cinnamon water.[2.5] This omelet can easily be made in a covered tourtière with high sides.

3. Crackling Omelet[3.1]

Beat (for instance) six eggs and season them with salt. Melt butter in a pan and into it pour the beaten eggs all at once; immediately afterwards add in some sippets or some fried fine breadcrumbs — you have to spread out the one or the other all around the pan while it is on the fire.[3.2] When the omelet is cooked and you are ready to turn it out into the dish, do it in such a way that the fried bread is on top. Some people fry some parsley to

---

[2.1] Marnette: "An Omelet according to the Celestines or the Saints fashion."

[2.2] The type-setter's *ou* is questionable.

[2.3] This butter goes into the egg mixture. Pierre de Lune's *Omelette à la Célestine* (*Le cuisinier*, ed. cit., p. 406) specifies little chunks of butter here.

[2.4] Nicolas de Bonnefons adds that the finished *Omelette à la Celestine* roughly two fingers thick. *Delices de la campagne* (1661), 163–64.

[2.5] See *The French Confectioner*, Recipe IV,16.

[3.1] In French, *Aumelette cretonneuse*: *cretons* are cracklings or greaves, the crisp residue left after frying fat.

[3.2] The peculiarity of this Crackling Omelet is that it contains numerous crisp bits in the tender substance of the egg.

garnish the top with it as well, and sometimes a little vinegar is splashed there, too, in much the same way as Pastry Chefs put rosewater on pies.

4. Apple Omelet

Pare three or four apples, cut them in rounds, fricassee them in a pan in four or five ounces of fresh butter, with as much sugar as you like. When they are cooked, you can pour over them seven or eight beaten eggs, seasoned with salt. Stir the pan often to keep the omelet from sticking and burning. When you slide the omelet into the dish, do it so that the apples are enclosed within it. Then sprinkle it on top with sugar.

When the apples have cooked, it is easier to take them out of the pan and put them to dry on a platter; then you go ahead and make a slightly moist omelet and, when it is cooked enough, you can wrap the apples quickly in it; then grate some sugar on top. Some people are content to put fricasseed apples on a trencher-plate and cover them with a moist omelet which they then sprinkle with sugar.

5. Stylish Omelet[5]

Beat some eggs and salt them, add in some pinenuts, currants and finely chopped candied lemon peel. With the butter melted and half-browned in the pan, pour in the eggs, scrambling them well. Dish up this omelet as soon as it is moderately well done; it can be rolled like a large sausage. Grate some sugar over it; on top you can also add a few drops of rosewater or of cinnamon water.

6. Lemon-Peel Omelet

Beat some eggs with a little milk; you can add in a little candied lemon peel, grated very finely, and some salt to taste; and make the omelet.

7. Bacon Omelet

Get the fat part of a quarter-pound or so of fat bacon, remove the rind and cut the fat into little bits about the size of a hazel-nut; melt it in the pan. When it begins to dry out, add in six or seven beaten eggs, salted if need be.

---

[5] While the author doesn't specify which style he is referring to in his expression *à la mode*, Marnette has his eye on his English readers: "An Omelet according to the newest mode, Oxford Cates, or the Covent Garden guise."

8. Another Way

Break six or seven eggs; to them add about two ounces of finely cut fat bacon and some salt if need be. Beat everything together and pour it into a pan in which there is as much half-browned butter or melted marrow as is necessary, and cook the omelet.

9. Cream Omelet

Break six eggs; to them add three or four spoonfuls of cream and some salt to taste. Beat everything together well and pour it into half-browned butter. Cook this omelet [only] moderately.[9]

10. Another Cream Omelet

Melt about three ounces of butter in a pan, then into it pour half a dozen eggs, beaten and properly salted. When they have set, add in about a quarter cup of good cream. When the omelet has cooked and is set out, grate some sugar over it; you can also add some rosewater. The cream must not boil; therefore, if the omelet is not cooked enough when the cream is put in, it can be coloured by heating a red-hot shovel.

11. Herb Omelet

Chop up some mild herbs such as lettuce, sorrel, borage, bugloss or mallow; remove their stem and, when they are thoroughly chopped up, they have to be beaten with eggs, adding in some salt and, if you want your omelet to be sweet, some currants. Melt some butter and, when it is hot enough, pour in the eggs. When the omelet is set out, grate some sugar over it. If you want this omelet to be very tasty, put more salt and spice in it.

12. Parsley Omelet

Break some eggs, add in some finely chopped parsley leaves and some salt; beat your eggs and make your omelet. [Alternatively,] you can chop up one or two handfuls of parsley coarsely and fry it in some butter, then to that add six or seven beaten eggs seasoned with salt.

13. Chive Omelet

Chop up some chives and beat them with some eggs seasoned with salt. You pour them into some half-browned butter or some oil and make an omelet of them.

---

[9] Marnette has: " . . . Your said omelet to bee very well fryed; and strew it with Sugar and Cinamon if you please."

14. Chicory-Stuffed Omelet

Get some white chicory and simmer it in boiling water — wild chicory can be used; take it out of the water after a short while, drain it, then chop it up small; season it with salt. You can also add in half-cooked mushrooms cut into small bits. Cook it all in some butter, then take it out and mix it with some beaten eggs to make an omelet right away — it should not be over-cooked. Set it out, grating some nutmeg or sugar on top.

15. Cheese Omelet

While butter is melting in your pan, cut up some cheese very small and beat it together with eggs; add in some salt to taste, and pour all of it into some half-browned butter to make the omelet.

16. Cucumber Omelet

Get whatever quantity of an omelet is neeeded and chop it up small; you can add in some pinenuts and currants, or an herb mixture or some well-seasoned, cooked fish hash, or some carp milt that is already cooked; along with each of those things you can also put some finely chopped, half-cooked mushrooms; blend all of that with a few raw egg whites or yolks. Then fill large cucumbers with the mixture after hollowing them out and emptying them. When they are filled, the entrance hole has to be plugged again.

Peel the cucumbers and cook them between two dishes or in a tourtière, seasoning them with butter and salt. When the sauce[16.1] is almost done, add in a little verjuice or vinegar if need be, or some fish sauce.[16.2] Grate some nutmeg and breadcrumbs over their top, or else put on some sugar, depending on the nature of the filling or hash that is in the cucumber. Instead of sauce, a very thin, moist omelet can be made to wrap a stuffed cucumber in, when it is cooked and ready to eat.

A cucumber can be stuffed with veal kidney, this being cooked and chopped together with its fat and egg yolks, pinenuts, currants, salt, and

---

[16.1] *sausse.* This must be an error, perhaps for *farce,* "stuffing, filling," a word that is found a little further on. The end of this paragraph indicates that it is the cooking of the cucumbers (and their contents) that the chef keeps his eye on.

[16.2] This *sausse de poisson* may be some standard fish sauce (at the cook's option), or more likely a fish bouillon. *Cf.,* too, the *jus de mouton* in the next recipe.

so forth. When it is cooked, between two dishes or in a pan, it is finished off as is directed above.

17. Turkish Omelet[17.1]

Get the flesh of a saddle of hare or of some other venison,[17.2] chop it up small with a little fat bacon, some pistachios or pinenuts or almonds or filberts or skinned hazel-nuts, or else with some macaroons or roasted, shelled chestnuts, or some bread crust cut into pieces like chestnuts; season that hash with salt, spice and a few fine herbs. If the meat is raw, you need some butter or marrow or good fat cut very small, and, when it has melted in a pan, dump in the meat, chopped and seasoned with the above-mentioned ingredients, and set it to cook.

Then melt some butter in a pan and make an omelet. When it is half-cooked, add in the hash; when it is fully cooked, take it out of the pan with a skimmer or a trencher-plate without breaking it, and receive it in a dish in such a way that the hash is upwards. Then you sprinkle the omelet with mutton drippings[17.3] or those of some other roasted meat, and grate nutmeg on top. Some sippets of fried bread can be added, and some cut-up lemon slices.

If the hare flesh or other venison is roasted, all you have to do is chop it up and season it, as has been said, then make the omelet. When it is half-cooked, add in the hash, then finish off the omelet. For want of venison, you can use a hash of ordinary meat.

18. Veal-Kidney Omelet

Get the kidney of a loin of veal; after it is roasted, chop it up with its fat and season it with salt, spices and a little thyme or some other fine herbs; you can also add in little fricasseed bread crusts or cooked mushrooms or peeled pistachios. Then make an omelet; when it is half-cooked, dump in the hash. When the omelet is fully cooked, set it out in a dish and add nutmeg or sugar on top.

[17.1] The printed text has *Aumelette à la Truque* but undoubtedly represents, originally at least if not in seventeeth-century culinary usage, the modern word *turque*: Turkish.

[17.2] *venaison* — that is, game or game meat.

[17.3] *jus de mouton* is readily available in La Varenne's kitchen, mutton being most commonly roasted. See also Recipes VII,2 and 23, and its frequent use in *The French Cook*.

19. Egg-and-Fish-Hash Omelet or Tourte[19.1]

Get some flesh of carp or some other well-deboned fish, and some blanched carp milt, adding in some salt and pepper or some spice and, if you wish, mushrooms; make a hash; you can also add in pinenuts, currants and candied lemon peel cut up very small. Cook it all in some butter in a pan or tourtière. When the fish hash is cooked, make a well-seasoned omelet; when it is half-cooked, dump in the hash drained of its sauce. When the omelet is fully cooked, it has to be rolled, set out on a platter and split at both ends which you turn outwards like a star,[19.2] with sugar grated over it and sprinkled with rosewater if you like.

20. Stuffed Omelet

Make up a mixture of mild herbs and hard-boiled egg yolks, salted; into that you can also chop some half-cooked mushrooms or some currants. Put the mixture onto a trencher-plate or into a dish and cover it with a moist omelet.[20]

21. Asparagus Omelet

Get some asparagus stalks that are tender and small, break them into little pieces and half-cook them in some browned butter in a pan; then onto them pour some beaten eggs, salted, and make your omelet. Some people parboil the asparagus in salted water and, after removing them from the bouillon and draining them, put them into the pan with the beaten eggs. With the omelet made up and set out, onto it put a dash of vinegar or verjuice. Sometimes some well-washed, cut-up mushrooms can be used: they are done[21] between two dishes on the fire, then they are pressed and the moisture that comes out of them is used to sprinkle on the omelet, on which nutmeg can also be grated.

[19.1] The text reads, *Aumelette ou tourte aux œufs, & hachis de poisson.* The edition of Lyon, 1680, p. 354 has: *Aumelette en tourte aux œufs* . . . : Omelet as a tourte with eggs . . . .

[19.2] The same decorative presentation has been used earlier, in the recipe for a Plain Omelet (Recipe 1, above).

[20] This resembles the facile alternative procedure of which the author seemed a little contemptuous at the end Recipe 4, above.

[21] *on les fait faire*: "stewed," writes Marnette.

22. Bread Omelet, or Rattoon[22.1]

Beat (for instance) four fresh eggs with five or six spoonfuls of milk, adding in some salt and about the size of an egg or a little more of fine, white breadcrumbs, or else a full silver spoonful of flour, that has to be wholly blended with the eggs by beating them together. Then they are poured into the butter to make the omelet, which has to be turned over once; use plenty of butter. When the omelet is cooked, you can cut it into long slices like biscuits[22.2] or into whatever other shapes you like. Add on sugar and a little rosewater.

If you do not turn this omelet over in the pan, but leave it soft on one side, it will be just as good.

These eggs can be cooked in a medium-sized skillet of yellow copper that has a high rim, or in a small tourtière,[22.3] in order to do a sort of cake of them, and to make it far better.[22.4] In addition, you add two or three spoonfuls of powdered sugar into the eggs, beat them well and pour them into the tourtière or skillet where there is a chicken egg's amount, or a little more, of good fresh, half-browned butter. Cook these eggs gently over a low fire; if the bottom sticks, you can loosen it with a spoon. These eggs can be done without any milk. When they have set all around, expose them to the fire or cover them with a very hot shovel to firm up their top. Then you set out the cake on a trencher-plate; you can garnish it with some sugar.

23. Eggs in the Mirror[23]

In a platter with the back of a spoon, spread out about an egg's amount of good butter, then into it break five or six eggs and season them with very fine salt; then you put about six spoonfuls of good cream onto the white of the eggs and add in a little salt. Cook these eggs and colour them with a hot shovel, yet without hardening the yolks.

[22.1] *Ratton.* In the Middle Ages a similar preparation was known as a *raston.* See a variety of other Rattoons in Chapter XII. Marnette renders the title of this present recipe as, "An Omelet only made with flower, in the form of an Egge-tart."

[22.2] " . . . like your Naples Bisket," says Marnette.

[22.3] See a mention of a similar procedure in Recipe IX,1

[22.4] *plus excellent*: "more excellent and pleasing," writes Marnette.

[23] These eggs are not scrambled; the name of the dish evokes the image of the setting for the yellow yolks, although Marnette interprets the *Œufs au miroir* freely by writing, "An Omelet called in French a Miroir, that is, a dainty, light, thin, and clear Omelet."

24. Eggs in Browned Butter

Brown some butter in a pan; break some eggs into a dish and, without beating them, pour them into the butter and season them with fine salt. When they have cooked, set them out in a dish and sprinkle them with hot vinegar,[24.1] and grate a little nutmeg on top. A Sauce Robert[24.2] can be added to these eggs, which some people call Milanese Eggs.

25. Eggs with Milk

Beat (for instance) five or six eggs; add in some very fine salt, about half a pint of good milk, which has to be poured in gradually, and blend the eggs with a part of the milk as you add in a spoonful of powdered sugar. Pour that mixture into a dish which is set on a pot full of boiling water or on a chafing-dish, and in which there should be a chicken's egg amount of good melted butter; when the eggs-and-milk mixture is poured in, you must cover the dish with another bowl and leave the eggs to cook gently without stirring them.

When the eggs are cooked enough, they have to be coloured by means of a very hot shovel, which helps to finish off cooking them on top. Then they are taken off the heat and sugar is grated over them; you can also add a few drops of rosewater or cinnamon water.

After they are cooked, if these eggs are kept a while before being served moisture forms — mainly when the milk is not of very good quality. You can prevent that moisture from forming by blending a little flour with the milk that goes into them. If you cook them on a vessel full of boiling water, they will be much more delicate and will form less moisture, and the dish will not melt;[25.1] all that has to be done is to mind the fire while the eggs cook.[25.2] They will be even more delicate if you do them with some cream, and if you put in only a few or no egg whites, but they will take more of them. Sometimes finely chopped parsley leaves are put into Eggs with Milk: stir them in as the eggs and milk are being mixed. They

---

[24.1] *vinaigre qui ait passé par la poësle.*

[24.2] See Recipe XXXI,2. According to Marnette's wording it is the use of the Sauce Robert that makes this "omelet" into Milanese Eggs.

[25.1] This is the only mention we find of the danger of such a culinary contre-temps.

[25.2] The author seems to be writing for a cook or pastry chef in a kitchen where the personnel doesn't include menials to tend the fires.

will be good even though there is no sugar in them; and sometimes Eggs with Milk are made without putting in any butter.

Chapter XXXIV

Various sorts of Egg "Marmalade"[xxxiv]

1. Verjuice "Marmalades" or Verjuice Scrambled Eggs without Butter

Break (for instance) four eggs and beat them; add in some salt and four spoonfuls of verjuice. Put that on the fire and scramble it gently with a silver spoon until the eggs have sufficiently set; then take them off the fire and scramble them a little more until they set fully. In the same way you can make scrambled eggs with lemon or orange juice, but you mustn't put in too much, mainly of orange juice, since otherwise they would have to stay on the fire longer and that will give them a rather bitter flavour.

2. Verjuice Scrambled Eggs with Butter

Melt some butter in a dish or pan. Beat (for instance) four eggs with some verjuice, add some salt, pour them into the butter and stir them until they set and thicken. Grate a little nutmeg on top; you can also add sippets of fried bread.

Otherwise put some fresh butter and some good honey into an earthenware bowl on the fire. While the butter is melting, break half a dozen egg yolks or as many as are needed, and to them add about half a glass of verjuice for half a dozen yolks with no whites; season them with salt and beat all that together as if it were for making a yolk omelet. Pour the mixture into the butter and keep stirring it with a spoon until it has thickened.

3. Verjuice-Mash Scrambled Eggs

Cook some verjuice mash in butter, then get some eggs beaten with verjuice and seasoned with salt, pour them into the butter and scramble them until they are cooked. Then grate a little nutmeg on top.

[xxxiv] This chapter, entitled *Diverses manieres de Marmelades*, continues to examine the different ways in which eggs can be prepared. In seventeenth-century French cookery a *marmelade* of eggs described the lumpy texture of scrambled eggs. This genre of preparation stands as distinct from the omelet (of the previous chapter) with its relatively smooth consistency.

Other [Verjuice] Scrambled Eggs. Mix (for instance) four eggs with a little verjuice, and cook them as you scramble them. When they are half-cooked, add in about two spoonfuls of mushroom stock or sauce that has been carefully prepared;[3] add in a little salt and finish cooking the eggs.

4. Scrambled Eggs with Meat Bouillon

Break (for instance) four fresh eggs and mix them with about six spoonfuls of consommé[4] or some other meat bouillon with no herbs in it; spoon the bouillon in; you can add a little verjuice and some salt to taste. Cook that over a moderate fire until it is half-set, then take the dish off the fire. You can grate a little nutmeg on it, or some bread crust.

5. Cream Scrambled Eggs

Beat four eggs in a dish along with two spoonfuls of cream, salted; you can also put in a little candied lemon peel that is grated or finely cut. Pour that mixture into another dish where there is some melted butter; cook it gently, stirring until it is sufficiently set.

6. Cheese Scrambled Eggs

In a dish melt about an egg's amount of butter. Into another dish break three eggs and beat them as for an omelet, adding in about a small walnut's amount of cheese cut up into small bits. When the butter is melted, pour the eggs into it and cook them over a moderate fire, constantly scrambling them with a spoon until they are half-set; then take them off the fire. Keep them covered with a trencher-plate so they don't cool, and serve them promptly. If the cheese is not very salty, add in as much salt as is needed while you are mixing the eggs.

7. Scrambled Eggs with Chicory

Cut some tender white chicory very small and put it between two dishes or in a tourtière over a low fire so that it exudes its moisture, then drain it carefully and cook it in some butter and salt. When it is well cooked, beat some eggs as if for an omelet, and pour them into the butter where the chicory is; it takes (for example) five or six eggs to make up a medium-sized dishful, and the more eggs, the better it all is. If you put in

---

[3] The preparation of this *jus ou sausse de champignons* is described in Recipe XI,1 of *The French Cook*.

[4] This a meat broth, but concentrated by having been boiled down. Marnette has "Gelly".

only the yolks, it will take more of them. Scramble everything together, and grate some nutmeg on it. When it has all set sufficiently and the eggs are more or less firmed up together, stop stirring; they have only to be covered and left on the fire a short time more to finish off cooking.

8. Cucumber Scrambled Eggs

Peel some cucumbers, parboil them in water, then take them out to drain; then you cut them into thin slices and put three or four handfuls of them into a pan where there is close to three ounces of half-browned butter, seasoned with fine salt and pepper; fricassee them. When they are done enough, pour in three or four egg yolks mixed with a little verjuice, and stir everything together in the pan. When the eggs are cooked enough, set it all out in a dish; you can grate nutmeg on top.

9. Green-Sauce Scrambled Eggs

Break (for instance) four eggs and beat them a little as if for making an omelet; season them with salt and a little pepper and spice, adding in about an egg's amount of breadcrumbs or much the same amount of fine flour. Beat that mixture well, adding in the same quantity of Green Sauce[9] as there is of eggs. Then pour the mixture into a dish where there is about an egg's amount of fresh butter that is very hot and half-browned; cook these eggs gently, scrambling them with a spoon until they are sufficiently cooked.

10. Another "Marmalade" of Scrambled Eggs

Mix the whites and yolks of six eggs with about six spoonfuls of rosewater or of plain water; add in some salt along with a crushed macaroon and a walnut's amount of fine, white breadcrumbs, or two macaroons alone, and about half a leaf of candied lemon peel, either grated or chopped into small bits. Pour that mixture into a dish where there is about an egg's amount of good, very hot butter; let the eggs cook, turning them from time to time with a spoon as you do other scrambled eggs.

When this "Marmalade" has cooked enough, without letting it dry out too much, take it off the fire.

When these eggs are half-cooked, a spoonful or two of hypocras or of Malmsey or Spanish wine can be added into them; then scramble them

---

[9] For this very common preparation see *The French Cook*, Recipe VII,2.

and finish cooking them gently. These eggs are more pleasant to eat cold than hot. When they are cooked, they can be set into a shell of fine pastry[10] and a tourte made of them.

11. Almond Scrambled Eggs

Get a very thin biscuit or two, separate their top from their bottom and dry them out by the fire. Likewise harden (for instance) four eggs, then remove their yolks, crush them with a spoon in a bowl, add in three other raw yolks, two ground macaroons or else a good egg's amount or a little more of skinned almonds that are fully ground with a little rosewater, two spoonfuls of sugar and some salt to taste; mix everything together. You can add in some candied lemon peel, cut up very small.

Taste the mixture and, if you think it is well seasoned, put it on a low fire and scramble it with a spoon. When it is quite hot, add in some of the pieces of biscuit dried by the fire, the size of a quarter-écu or so, push them a little into this "marmalade" so that they are covered but also so that they can easily be extracted with a fork.[11]

12. Other Scrambled Eggs

Season mushrooms well, or agaric, and cook them; a few broken asparagus stalks can be added in. When the mushrooms or agaric are ready to serve, break three or four eggs over them and scramble them and cook them with the rest until they are sufficiently set.

13. Polish Eggs

Steep white bread crumb in some meat bouillon, then grind it in a marble mortar and put it into a dish; break twelve or more eggs, to them add a little salt and, little by little, five or six spoonfuls of bouillon; then put in some candied lemon peel, grated or only sliced very thinly. Pour that mixture into a dish where there is some fresh butter, melted and half-browned; cook these eggs gently, scrambling them until they set. Instead of meat bouillon, milk can be used to do these eggs.

---

[10] See Recipe I,3. A "fine" pastry dough contains butter, can be made relatively thin and is often eaten together with the pie's filling.

[11] The use of a fork at table is to be noted.

14. Darling Eggs[14.1]

Get (for instance) ten fresh egg yolks, put them into a platter with as many spoonfuls of consommé or of herb-free and de-greased meat bouillon — spoon that gradually into the yolks, stirring continuously so as to blend the yolks fully with the bouillon; then you add in about two to four ounces of powdered sugar and an ounce of candied lemon peel, grated or cut into small, extremely tiny bits; let everything blend together about a half an hour, after having added in a little salt if you think your bouillon is not salty enough. Then into another bowl you have to put about four spoonfuls of rosewater along with half an ounce of sugar, bring them only briefly to a boil, then pour in the eggs, seasoned as was directed; cover the platter, cook them gently, like Eggs with Milk,[14.2] or else you can turn them over with a silver spoon like Eggs in Verjuice.[14.3] When they've set, take the dish off the fire. Then, when they have cooled a little, you put an ounce of powdered sugar on top, and sometimes also a small amount of musk dissolved in rosewater or cinnamon water. Eat these eggs half-cooled, although they are good cold, too.

15. Huguenot Eggs[15]

Break four or five eggs and put them with the drippings of a joint of mutton or of some other roast meat, scramble them together on the fire; add in some salt or some verjuice or lemon or orange juice; sometimes well-cooked, seasoned mushrooms are also put in. As soon as the eggs are sufficiently set, they have to be taken off the fire; keep them covered a short while. Then grate a little nutmeg on them; sometimes a little powdered ambergris and sugar are put on.

In that same way you can make scrambled eggs with a sauce of asparagus or chicken or fish — after having deboned it.

[14.1] This is literal: the dish's name is *Œuefs mignons*. Marnette interprets: "Exquisite, and Courtly, buttered Egges."

[14.2] Recipe 25 of the previous chapter.

[14.3] Recipes 1 and 2 of the present chapter.

[15] *Œufs à la buguenotte*: an obvious blunder by the type-setter of this edition; it is likely that a previously used lower-case *b* was erroneously dropped into the *h* compartment. Marnette does not translate this title, but tries to clarify it: "The Fifteenth and last manner of stirring of Eggs, called in French a la Hugenotte, or the Protestants manner." For the essential importance of the mutton dripping to this dish see Gédéon Tallemant des Réaux, *Historiettes*, ed. Antoine Adam, 2 vols. (Paris: Gallimard, 1961), II, p. 251 and n. 7.

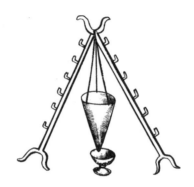

The French Confectioner

**in which is taught how to make all sorts of confections, dragées,
liqueurs and pleasant beverages, along with
the Way of Folding Table Linen,
and of making all sorts of shapes with it.**

Preface: To the Reader

If you wish to get the best from this book, always be very careful whenever you cook any sugar. When I say that sugar is "cooked coarse smooth, or fine smooth, or coarse pearl, or fine pearl,"[1] the fine is the least cooked, the coarse is the most cooked. When I say "cooked to a jelly,"[2] that is when the sugar is mixed with decoctions[3] or fruit juices. Jelly is made when, taking up syrup in a spoon and pouring it off, it falls in big globs and doesn't flow like syrup does.

Take care that the bottles into which you put your pleasant beverages are very clean, and stop them up carefully, too. Keep your Italian Waters[4] as cool as you can, and make them up only as you need them. Do not put your syrups in too dry a place, to keep them from candying.[5]

The whisk I speak about for your creams and milk dishes should be made of cleanly peeled birch or of peeled young elm branches; make it the thickness of a thumb and bind it with its ends cleanly cut.

The salads in which I put no seasoning are served with vinegar and sugar.

---

[1] *cuit à lisse gros, à lisse menu, à perle grosse, à perle menu.*

[2] *cuit en gelée*, as in Recipe X,1 and throughout that chapter.

[3] In the author's terminology a decoction is the watery juice extracted from a fruit when it has been boiled in water, perhaps also with sugar. In a certain way it is the counterpart of a meat broth.

[4] Recipes for these are found in Chapter IV, Section b.

[5] *de crainte qu'ils ne candissent.* For the candying of fruit, see Chapter XIV.

You can give an amber or musk flavour to any praline by means of prepared musk and amber.[6] With the same musk and amber you can also flavour your marzipans, even the glazed ones.

You can colour your conserves with prepared colours whenever you cannot get fruits:[7] for example, instead of pistachio, you can use a juice of beet greens,[8] and instead of pomegranate, you can use barberry.[9] You can also use amber and musk.

The fruits and flowers that you blanch should be stored in a dry place.

You can colour your sugar pastes however you want with prepared colours.

Clean the straw carefully onto which you take out your oranges and lemons; you can also take them out onto wicker trays or a fine brass grill.

You can garnish your compotes with candied lemon peel, Cherries with Ears,[10] pistachios, pomegranate seeds, chestnuts, Brignol plums, and so forth.

I did not write down the sugar necessary for the confections in each recipe for fear of making things too long. But if you want to do them well, for each one put in the same weight of sugar as of fruit, except for cherries and quince. For cherries, put in twelve ounces of sugar for every pound of cherries; they can, though, be done with even less sugar, putting in only half a pound for each pound of fruit. For quince, put in twenty ounces of sugar for every pound of fruit.

For oranges and lemons you cannot put in too much — they have to swim in sugar; any syrup that is left over can be used in conserves, in pralines, in compotes of pears and with green walnuts.

For dry confections also put in a pound for a pound. After having removed them from the stove,[11] put them into boxes of pine or whatever,

---

[6] For this procedure, see Chapter I, immediately below.

[7] Colourants are dealt with in Chapter II.

[8] See the author's directions for extracting a green colouring from *poirée* in Recipe II,1.

[9] See the same alternative mentioned in Recipe VII,18; there the berry is "powdered".

[10] For this particular confection, *cerises à oreilles*, see Recipe XII,6.

[11] This *estuve* is a relatively small warming chamber, built or placed adjacent to a larger oven, not in itself heated but taking its warmth from that oven. In the *French Pastry*

always separating each of them with paper to keep them from spoiling. Store them in a dry place. Take care to change the paper often, at least until no more syrup oozes from them and the paper is no longer dampened. You can use the left-over syrup in moist confections and in fruit pastes, mixing together equal amounts of sugar and syrup.[12]

Put fruit pastes also into boxes, and change their paper often. With them too use the same weight of sugar as of mashed fruit[13] to make your pastes; you can do them with twelve ounces or half a pound of sugar.

Keep your candied preparations in a dry place. With Genoa pastes, put in half a pound of sugar for a pound of mashed fruit.

Keep your white salt in a dry place.

Keep your basins, or the skillets in which you make your confections, very clean. They should be of red copper, the skimmer and spoon of the same copper, or of silver.

The oven for cooking your marzipans should be of iron or of red copper. That is not to say that you could not do them in a pastry or bakery oven, for want of the other.[14]

Chef it is used to dry biscuit; throughout the *French Confectioner* it is solely used likewise to dry confections.

[12] A series of recipes for various fruit and flower pastes is found in Chapter XIII, below.

[13] The French term *marmelade*, here and throughout *The French Confectioner*, designates an unsweetened strained compote of cooked fruit. See Chapter XIII in general. At the risk of confusion we shall use the English word "marmalade" rather than "mashed fruit".

[14] The "ovens" of which the author writes here were those common varieties available to a confectioner or pastry chef in the seventeenth century. The iron (or red copper) oven, appropriate and preferred for marzipan, was portable. It sat on coals, perhaps over coals on legs; the heat within it could be regulated fairly closely by the intensity and proximity of the heat radiating from the coals, which if need be could also be strewn on top of or heaped around it. In Recipe XVI,7, for instance, the confectioner varies the source of his heat in this oven from bottom to top at different stages of making the same dish.

The *four de pastissier ou boulanger* was the traditional stone or brick construction that was either built into or through the wall of a kitchen or bakery; alternatively it could, bee-hive shaped, semi-cylindrical or rectangular, be free-standing. Its interior was heated to a desired temperature by means of embers which were usually shovelled out before the food to be baked was placed into it. This later type of oven had the drawback of offering only a slowly dying heat, appropriate, though, for most types of baking.

The French Confectioner

or

How to make all sorts of confections, liqueurs and pleasant beverages

Chapter I

Preparing Musk and Amber[i]

Put the musk or amber into a small cast-iron mortar and grind it well with the pestle, itself also of cast iron. Add in a little powdered sugar. After having ground this well, put it into some paper for use with whatever you wish.

Chapter II

Prepared Colours

1. Prepared Beet Greens for making a Green Colour

Get very green beet leaves, remove their stalks, wash them well and pound them in a mortar; then put them into a cloth to extract their juice. Put this into a dish, bring it to a boil and pour it through a sieve or a serviette; take what is left on the serviette to use in your pastes and conserves.

2. Prepared Cochineal

Get an ounce of cochineal, half an ounce of alum, half an ounce of mineral crystal[2] and grind it all together well in an cast-iron mortar. When you wish to use it, mix it with a little verjuice or with wine spirit and put it through a cloth filter, and use the juice.

3. Tragacanth Gum[3]

You can find this at spicers' and apothecaries' shops.

4. Lily Flower

In summer get some lily flowers, remove the yellow stamens that are inside and dry them. Reduce them to powder when you want to use them.

---

[i] These seem to be among the author's preferred flavouring agents.

[2] According to Richelet *cristal mineral* is a compound of highly purified saltpeter (potassium nitrate) and flowers of sulphur. See also Appendix 1 a).

[3] This substance was also more popularly known as "gum dragon".

Chapter III

Cooking Sugar

1. Clarifying Sugar and Brown Sugar

Put your sugar or brown sugar into a basin or skillet and boil it. Put some eggs into a terrine or some other vessel — that is, the whole egg, both whites and yolks, or the whites alone, if you prefer, but either is good; beat them with a small whisk and a little water until they are all frothy. Put a part of this into your sugar as it begins to boil, stirring it with the skimmer, then skim it and put in some more beaten egg whites and skim it. Continue like that until the sugar is quite clear and clean; filter it through a straining bag or a cloth. It can be kept as long as you like provided it is cooked smooth.[1.1]

For twenty-five pounds of brown sugar you need about three pints of water[1.2] to dissolve it and three eggs to clarify it, and three cups of water with the eggs in order to whisk them together. Before straining your sugar, make sure it is cooked smooth.

2. Cookings of Sugar: Smooth

The first is to the "smooth" stage,[2] which is reached when the syrup begins to thicken. Taking it with your finger and putting it on your thumb, it no longer flows but remains round like a pea.

3. Cooked to the Pearl Stage[3.1]

The second cooking is when, taking it with a finger and putting it on your thumb and spreading your thumb and finger, it stretches into a small thread. When you can draw out a big one the length your hand, that is called cooked to the "coarse pearl" stage.[3.2]

[1.1] *cuit à lisse*: for this cooking stage, see the next recipe.

[1.2] *pintes d'eau*: according to La Varenne (the *French Pastry Chef*, Chapter VI), a *pinte* of water or wine weighs about thirty-one ounces.

[2] *la première* [*cuisson*] *est à lisse*.

[3.1] *cuit à perle*.

[3.2] *à perle grosse*: literally "large pearl".

4. Cooked to the Feather Stage[4.1]

This cooking has several different names: some people say "to the blowing stage",[4.2] others "to the spatula stage",[4.3] others "to the pink stage",[4.4] others "to the feather stage"[4.5] — at which I shall leave off. You can tell it has been reached by putting a spatula in and then shaking the sugar in the air and it flies off like dry feathers without any stickiness;[4.6] or else dip a skimmer into the sugar, blow through it until the sugar flies off in leaves. This is the cooking stage for conserves and tablets.

5. Cooked to the Burnt Stage

This cooking is seen when, dipping your finger in cool water, then into the sugar and again into cool water, the sugar breaks cleanly like a glass without sticking together;[5.1] you can do the same test with a little stick. This is the cooking stage for large Lemon Biscuit,[5.2] for Caramel and for Twisted Sugar or Pennets.[5.3] It is the final cooking stage for sugar.

[4.1] *cuit à la plume.* According to the *Encyclopédie* (XV, 617b) a century later, *sucre à la plume* is much as is set out here: "C'est le sucre qui a atteint le quatrième degré de cuisson. On l'éprouve avec l'écumoir ou la spatule, comme le sucre à souffler, & toute la différence qui s'y rencontre, c'est que le sucre à la plume étant un peu plus poussé de chaleur, les bouteilles [surface bubbles] qui sortent de la spatule, en se secouant, sont plus grosses; & même dans la grande plume, ces bouteilles sont si grosses & en si grande quantité, qu'elles semblent liées les unes aux autres. ... Les Confiseurs emploient [le sucre à la plume] pour leurs massepains."

[4.2] *à soufle.*

[4.3] *à l'espatule.*

[4.4] *à rosard.* In the fourteenth century *sucre rosart* was a confection made with the distillate rosewater: see the *Menagier de Paris*, ed. Jérôme Pichon, 1846; repr. Geneva (Slatkine), 1970; Vol. II, p. 275: "Pour faire de sukere rosart en plate."

[4.5] *à la plume.*

[4.6] *comme des plumes seiches sans gluë.* Nowdays the masculine word *glu* is birdlime; in the seventeenth century Furetière defined it as "Composition visqueuse. En Surie [Syria] on en fait avec des prunes de Sebesten." Here in the feminine it is an abstract word for stickiness, adhesiveness or adhesion. See the same word in the next recipe.

[5.1] *comme un verre sans gluë.*

[5.2] Recipe XVI,13 mentions a lemon marzipan in the shape of a biscuit.

[5.3] *du sucre tors, ou penide.* Recipes VII,15, 16 and 17 make use of sugar so cooked. Diderot's *Encyclopédie* (XV, 618a) traces the process for arriving at this stage of cooked sugar: "*Sucre tors,* en latin *penidum saccharum*: on le prepare de la maniere suivante. On fait dissoudre telle quantité de sucre que l'on veut; on le clarifie avec un

Chapter IV

Cordials and Italian Waters[iv.1]

a. Cordials

1. Hypocras[1.1]

Get some good wine and put it into some sort of good clean vessel that will not give off a bad taste. Into it put some sugar or brown sugar, a little cinnamon, some ginger the amount of a hazelnut, two spikes[1.2] of long pepper, twelve whole cloves, some nutmeg, or two leaves of mace, and a rennet apple, peeled and sliced in rounds; let everything steep for about half an hour, covered. Then half-grind a dozen sweet almonds and put them into your straining bag when your sugar has dissolved and you are ready to strain your hypocras; put in a little orange-blossom water and

---

blanc d'œuf; on le coule, & on le fait épaissir peu-à-peu; quand il forme de grosses bulles, on le retire du feu jusqu'à ce qu'elles disparoissent; on le verse ensuite sur une planchette qu'on doit avoir frottée avec de l'huile d'amandes douces. Lorsqu'il est un peu refroidi, on le prend avec un crochet & avec les mains saupoudrées d'amidon; enfin après lui avoir donné la forme convenable, on le garde pour l'usage." Elsewhere (XII, 301b) the *Encyclopédie* repeats this recipe, concluding " . . . on la paîtrit avec les mains comme la pâte; & pendant qu'elle est encore chaude, on la tire en petits bâtons retors comme des cordes" — it is drawn out into little twisted sticks like bits of rope. Still elsewhere (XI, 632b) we are told that *sucre tors* is drawn out into strands that are very fine or coarse, long or short, most often twisted, but always white.

Nostradamus's ch. 28 is devoted to detailed instructions on making *"penites*, which we call *succre panys."*

[iv.1] The title for this whole chapter, of which the series of Italian Waters (Chapter IV b) is apparently intended to constitute a subset of recipes, is *Breuvages délicieux*: "Tasty Beverages". N. Audiger (*La maison reglée*, 1692) offers an extensive set of directions for making *eaux et liqueurs à la mode d'Italie* that includes recipes for Rossoli, Populo and Angelique. That Book IV of his work begins with a disquisition on distilling. See p. 538 f. in *L'art de la cuisine française au XVIIe siècle* (Paris: Payot, 1995).

[1.1] Hypocras was a digestive beverage that had been well known, and drunk, throughout Europe since the high Middle Ages. It was commonly used also as an ingredient in cooking. Still in Audiger, *La maison réglée* (Paris: N. Le Gros, 1692), there are recipes for Hypocras as well as for Rosolio, Populo and Angelica. See *L'art de la cuisine française au XVIIe siècle*, ed. Gilles and Laurence Laurendon (Paris: Payot, 1995).

[1.2] These *brains* (modern *brins*) are the aments or sprigs, the catkin-like formations of long pepper.

strain it along with your almonds, straining them three or four times. If you wish to give it an amber and musk flavour, grind your amber and musk in a small mortar with a little powdered sugar and put it into some cotton or hemp cloth and attach this to the bottom of your straining bag and pass the hypocras over the top. Should you wish to keep it more than eight days, don't put in any apple nor lemon. For two pints of wine, it takes about a pound and a half of sugar, two grains of amber and a grain of musc.[1.3]

2. Rosolio[2]

Get good wine spirits and put them into a very clean bottle or a vessel that is narrow at the top. Into it also put six grains [weight] of crushed white pepper, two grains of long pepper, two leaves of mace, a little cinnamon, twelve whole cloves, a hazelnut amount of ginger — everything should be in the right proportions — three pinches of aniseed and coriander which are ground. Stop the bottle up tightly and let the contents infuse for twenty-four hours in a cool place, then filter it through a straining bag as for hypocras; while straining, add in some lemon juice. Cook your sugar to the feather stage, then take it off the fire and add in your wine spirits and filter it once again through the straining bag. It needs much more amber and musk than the hypocras; for one pint of wine spirits, it takes three pounds of sugar.

3. *Populo*

Make the same mixture as for the Rosolio. Cook a pound of sugar to the feather stage; put in a cup of wine spirits, after having filtered them, and let it cool; put in a half-pint of good clear white wine, a rennet apple, peeled and sliced in rounds, and a little orange-blossom water. Filter it through the straining bag like the Rosolio. Do not forget to flavour it well with amber and musk.

[1.3] The *grains* here are a measure of weight.

[2] This *rossoly* — in modern French *rossolis* — is a cordial, whose primary function, like that of the hypocras of the preceding recipe and the *populo* of the following, is to promote digestion. Nicolas de Bonnefons deals briefly with the mixed drink in a chapter entitled *Du Rossolis, Populo, Aigre de Cetre, Malvoisie, & autres Boissons precieuses* stating that all are made with fine sugar and *bonne Eau de Vie, ou esprit de Vin* — that is, distilled wine (*Delices de la campagne*, Paris: Pierre Des-Hayes, 1654; Amsterdam: Jean Blaev, 1661; Book II, Ch. XLVII, p. 76).

4. Angelica

Get a pint of blanquette or Scipion wine,[4.1] put in a pound of royal sugar,[4.2] a little ground aniseed and coriander, a rennet apple and a lemon, peeled and sliced in rounds, three or four pieces of lemon peel, a little powdered galingale and a little orange-blossom water.[4.3] Let all that infuse for half an hour without heating it, then pass it through the straining bag along with ambre and musk as for the hypocras.

5. Burnt Wine[5]

Get a silver pitcher or a new earthenware crock and into it put a pint of good wine, a pound of sugar, a little mace, some long pepper, cloves, a sprig of laurel and two sprigs of rosemary. Have a big coal fire and put your crock in the middle of it with the flames all around; when it is boiling strongly, set fire to it with a paper spill. When the fire inside dies, take the crock down off the fire. It is drunk hot.

6. Wine of the Gods

Pare some rennet apples and the same number of lemons, and slice them in rounds. Get a basin or a dish and in it form a layer of apples and lemons; on this put a layer of powdered sugar, and repeat for as much as you want to make of it; pour good wine over the top until it is soaked. Cover the dish and leave it all to infuse for about two hours; then pass it through the straining bag like hypocras.

7. Alexandrian Sorbet

Get a round of veal, remove its fat carefully, cut the meat up into pieces and cook it in three pints of water until this boils away to half a pint. Strain the water through a cloth; take the broth, combine it with two pounds of sugar, boil it to the feather stage and take it off the fire. Put into it half a pint of lemon juice and pour it into glass flasks. This potion

---

[4.1] Perhaps wine from Cyprus, much prized in the seventeenth century. See Appendix 1, *s.v.* wine.

[4.2] This *sucre royal* is a double-refined sugar. It is used in mixtures that are not to be heated.

[4.3] Audiger's recipe for *Angelique* begins with a half ounce of the herb angelica. See note 1.1, above.

[5] *vin bruslé*. The Dutch equivalent, *brande wijn*, would become the word "brandy". According to Furetière that phrase was current in French in the form *brandevin* to designate a distilled *eau de vie*. The beverage in this recipe is still a wine.

can be kept provided it is well stoppered and stored in a dry place. When it is to be used, two spoonfuls of it should be taken and put into a glass and the glass filled with cool water, and pour this back and forth several times into another one.

8. Cedar Eagle

Get twenty-five big lemons, cut them lengthwise, remove their cores and seeds; very gently cut out the area where the juice is and put it in a new earthenware crock. Boil two pounds of sugar to the feather stage and, when it is cooked, put your pot on a big coal fire; pour your cooked sugar into it and let it boil until the syrup is cooked to the pearl stage. It can be kept and is used in the same way as the Sorbet.

9. Lemonade[9.1]

Get a pint of water and into it put half a pound of sugar, the juice of six lemons and two oranges, the peel of half a lemon and [half] an orange that you have pressed; blend[9.2] the water well in two very clean vessels, pouring it back and forth several times from one into the other, and strain it through a white serviette.

10. Orangeade

It is made in the same way as the Lemonade, except that it doesn't take any lemons.

b. Italian Waters[iv.2]

11. Raspberry Water

Get very ripe raspberries, press them and strain them through a cloth, putting the juice in a glass flask or bottle without a lid. Set that in

---

[9.1] "*Cette boisson est toute contraire aux precedentes; [rossolis, populo, etc.] car au lieu que les autres eschauffent, celle-cy rafraichit*" (Bonnefons, *Delices de la campagne*, 1661, 80).

[9.2] The term that the author uses here, and in several further instances where a mixture is poured repeatedly between vessels in order to mix it thoroughly, is *battez*, literally "beat". A modern equivalent might be *frappez*.

the sun for three or four hours, then draw off the juice very gently so as not to stir up the dregs which are on the bottom. Mix a cup of juice with a pint of cool water and half a pound of sugar, blending it well between two vessels; when the sugar is dissolved, strain it through a serviette. It is drunk as cool as possible.

Cherry Water, Pomegranate Water and Red-Currant Water are made the same way.

12. Apricot Water

Get very ripe apricots, remove their pits, cook them in very clean water, let the water cool and strain it through a serviette. For a pint of water add in a quarter-pound of sugar. This is drunk like Raspberry Water.

13. Jasmine Water

Get a pint of water, add in a quarter-pound of royal sugar, a handful of jasmine blossoms and set everything to infuse together for half an hour. Blend them in two vessels, then strain the mixture through a serviette.

Orange-Blossom Water and White-Musk-Rose-Blossom Water are made like that of Jasmine.

14. Barberry Water

Get barberry berries, bring them to a boil in a little water and strain them. Take that juice and combine a cup of it with a pint of water and four ounces of sugar. Blend it all well between two vessels, and strain it through a serviette.

15. Coriander Water

Grind up some coriander and put it into a pint of cool water with four ounces of sugar and let them steep until the water takes on all of the flavour. Strain it.

Aniseed Water, Orange Water and Lemon Water are made the same as Coriander Water.

16. Cinnamon Water

Boil a pint of water together with half an ounce of broken-up cinnamon. When removed from the fire, add in four ounces of sugar, let it cool and strain it.

Chapter V
Refreshing Syrups

1. Violet Syrup

Separate the violet petals from their buds and pound them in a mortar. Cook some sugar to the feather stage, remove it from the fire and into it put your violets, stirring them with the sugar, and strain this through a serviette. For a pound of sugar you need four ounces of cleaned violet petals.

2. Violet Syrup by Infusion

Get a new, big-bellied earthenware crock, put four ounces of cleaned violet petals into it in half a pint of water, stop it up tightly and let it simmer on some coals for twenty-four hours. Strain the violets through a serviette and press them. Take the decoction that drains through, boil it with a pound of sugar until the syrup is cooked to the pearl stage; remove it and store it in a glass flask or bottle, stopping it up when it has cooled.

Borage Syrup, Bugloss Syrup[2.1] and Pale-Rose Syrup[2.2] are made in the same way as Violet Syrup.

3. Cherry Syrup

Get two pounds of very ripe cherries and remove their stems and pits; boil them in a cup of water until all their juice is out,[3] then strain this through a serviette. Take a quarter-pint of this juice, combine it with a pound of sugar and boil this until the syrup is cooked to the pearl stage; this should be done over a hot fire. Then take it down and store it away.

[2.1] In 1557 the physician Nostradamus specified the use of only bugloss bark, for this syrup: "To confect bugloss bark, which the Spanish call *lingua bovina* [ox tongue], which is a cordial confection preserving a person from becoming hectic or dropsical (*hydropicque*), and keeps a person happy and cheerful, dispels all melancholy, rejuvenates a man, delays aging, brings good colour to the face, maintains a man in health, restrains an irascible (*cholerique*) man from quarrelling."

[2.2] *roze pasle*: is this flower a pink or a carnation? Nostradamus calls the preparation only *syop rosat* (ch. 29), and directs: "Get red roses of the sort that are cerulean in colour (*qui ont la couleur cerulée*), partaking of both white and red, which we call *color saraceus*, which is a rosy pink (*incarnat*). Get 900 of them ... ." He qualifies that syrup as *laxatif*, declaring that "an ounce of it will work marvellously and without violence, so that it can be given to a pregnant woman of any age at any time in her first or last months without any danger whatever."

[3] *jusqu'à ce qu'elles ayent jetté toute leur eau*: "until they have exuded all of their moisture."

4. Apricot Syrup

Get very ripe apricots, peel them and remove their pits. Put very clean little sticks on the bottom of a basin, arrange a layer of apricots on the sticks, then a layer of powdered sugar, and repeat this until you have as much as you want to make of it; cover them over and put them in the cellar for a night. If you want to keep the syrup that has fallen into the basin, draw it off and boil it until it has cooked to the pearl stage.

You can use the apricots to make tourtes[4.1] or marmalades.[4.2]

5. Verjuice Syrup

Crush verjuice grapes and draw off the juice, put it into an open glass bottle and set it in the sun. Do not stop it up in any way; keep it filled. When the verjuice is clear, cook a pound of sugar to the feather stage and put a cup of verjuice into it. Draw it off and store it away.

6. Quince Syrup

Grate a very ripe quince, press the gratings in a serviette or a press, take the juice that comes through, put it into a glass flask and put this in the sun or in a warm place. When the juice is clear, cook a pound of sugar to the feather stage, take it off the fire and into it add four ounces of the juice. Draw it off and store it away.

7. Mulberry Syrup

Get fifty mulberries that are still only red, and boil them with a cup of water. When they are cooked, strain them through a serviette and press them. Take the juice and boil it with a pound of sugar until it is cooked to the pearl stage. Draw it off and store it away.

8. Apple Syrup

Pare apples, slice them in rounds, remove their seeds and do them up as with the Apricot Syrup, but do not cook them.

[4.1] See the *French Pastry Chef*, Recipe IX,9. The author is speaking of the fruit that remains, not the syrup that has been made from it.

[4.2] Various recipes in Chapter XIII indicate that the term *marmelade* can be applied to a wide variety of pared, seeded and boiled fruit that has been put through a strainer, and before this mash has been sweetened.

9. Pomegranate Syrup

Pick the seeds out carefully, press them, draw off their juice and put this in a glass bottle in a warm place. When the juice is clear, cook a pound of sugar to the feather stage, take it off the fire and put a cup of pomegranate juice into it. Draw it off and store it away.

10. Lemon Syrup

Cook a pound of sugar to the feather stage. Get four ounces of lemon juice and put it into the sugar away from the fire. Draw it off and store it away.

Chapter VI
Pralines

1. Pralines

Cook a pound of sugar almost to the feather stage; into it put a pound of sweet almonds along with their skins, and stir; when you see that the sugar is cooked to the feather stage, take it off the fire and let it cool, stirring continuously to make the almonds take on the sugar. When they have cooled, put them on a table, remove the sugar that has not been taken up by the pralines and set it aside. Put the pralines back into the confectioner's bassin[1.1] in which they cooked on the fire, stirring them continuously with the spatula. When they exude moisture,[1.2] put in the remaining sugar and stir them to coat them with it. And when they exude moisture, take them off the fire and stir them until they have cooled. Replace them again once or twice on the fire to redden them, stirring continuously, and take them off each time they begin to exude moisture. You can flavour them with amber and musk.

2. Lemon Pralines

Get some lemon zests and cook them in water, and confect them as you are directed in the treatise on lemon and orange zests.[2.1] When the

---

[1.1] This *bassine* (as distinct from a *bassin*) was defined by Cotgrave in 1611 as a particularly deep bassin or "posnet", specifically used by confectioners; in Recipe XV,1 we are told that it is (or can be) of red copper or silver, two-handled and flat-bottomed. Its use is called for fairly frequently in this work.

[1.2] *lors qu'elles jetteront leur jus*

[2.1] See Chapter IX, below.

sugar is cooked to the pearl stage, put in the zests and take them off the fire, stirring them well so they are covered with sugar. Turn them out onto straw.[2.2] Similarly with oranges.

3. Violet Pralines

Cook half a pound of sugar to the feather stage, take it off the fire and into it put about three ounces of cleaned violet petals and a pound of pralines,[3] stirring everything all together with the spatula. Turn them out on straw.

4. Rose and Broom[4] Pralines

Get some rose petals and cut them up very small; make pralines with them like the Violet ones.

Chapter VII
Conserves

1. Orange-Blossom Conserve

Clean the petals of orange blossoms of their bud and cut them up into small bits. Cook some sugar to the feather stage, take it off the fire and put in your orange blossoms, stirring with a spoon or spatula. Set this out on some paper when it begins to cool.

2. Moist Orange-Blossom Conserve

Clean the orange blossoms of their bud and boil the blossoms in water; take them out and put them into cool water, drain them and pound them in a mortar. Cook some sugar to the feather stage, take it off the fire, put in your orange blossom and mix it all together; put it into a glazed or stoneware crock and let it cool before covering it. For half a pound of orange blossoms you need a pound of sugar.

3. Conserve of Orange-Blossom Water

Cook some sugar to the feather stage, take it down off the fire, put a little orange-blossom water[3] into it and set it out on some paper.

[2.2] This straw matting (*la paille*) seems to be in common use for the purpose of drying candied fruits.

[3] *sic.*

[4] There is no explicit reference to these *genests* in the following recipe.

[3] See directions for making this in Recipe IV,13.

4. Conserve of Pomegranate Seeds

Clean very red pomegranate seeds. Make a paper case of a size to hold the sugar you want to use, and put the pomegranate seeds into this. Cook some sugar to the feather stage and pour it into the drum over the pomegranate seeds. When it begins to cool, cut it into strips[4] with a knife.

5. Pistachio Conserve

Clean the pistachios in hot water and put them into cold water; drain them and crush them in a mortar. Cook some sugar to the feather stage, take it off the fire and put the pistachios into it, mixing them in well. Set them out on some paper.

6. Another Pistachio Conserve

Clean some pistachios and cut them into pieces. Cook some sugar to the feather stage and put some pistachios into it. Set them out on some paper.

7. Lemon-Juice Conserve

Cook some sugar to the feather stage, take it off the fire and put some lemon juice into it. Set it out on some paper.

8. Lemon-Grating Conserve[8]

Grate a lemon into some water, strain the gratings through a cloth and dry them. Cook some sugar to the feather stage and mix in the gratings. Set it out on some paper.

9. Rose Conserve

Get powdered Provins rose petals[9] and moisten them with a little lemon juice. Cook some sugar to the feather stage, remove it from the fire and put the roses into it. Set that out on some paper.

10. Violet Conserve

Clean the violet petals of their buds, crush them in a mortar and strain them through a cloth in order to extract the juice. Cook some sugar to the feather stage, remove it from the fire, put your violet juice into it and stir. Set it out on some paper.

---

[4] *coupés-la par bande.*

[8] *rapure de citron.* See also *The French Cook*, Recipe Confections,6.

[9] The text doesn't mention petals but only *des roses de Provins en poudre.* In *The French Cook* the directions for making Rose Conserve (Recipe Confections,5) are rather more detailed.

11. Marbled Violet Conserve

Do this the same way as the previous one and, after putting in the violet juice, put in a little lemon juice and it will become multi-coloured.

12. Marbled Conserve

Get some dried apricots, some dried cherries and some very freshly candied lemon peel[12] and cut them up into small pieces. Cook some sugar to the feather stage, put the fruit into it and set it out. You can also make it with all sorts of fruit and with blossoms of a variety of colours.

13. Cherry Conserve

Get very ripe cherries, remove their pits and stems, boil them a little in some water, drain them well and cut them up. Cook the sugar to the feather stage, take it off the fire and put your cherries in it. Set them out.

14. Cherry-Juice Conserve

Get some slightly unripe cherries, extract their juice and do it like the previous ones. Red currants and raspberries are done like the cherries.[14]

15. Caramel

Cook some sugar to the burnt stage,[15.1] take it off the fire and put in a little amber.[15.2] Rub some sweet-almond oil on a marble slab or a platter, dump your caramel on it in small chunks as for a conserve,[15.3] turning it out with a spoon.

16. Twisted Sugar[16.1]

Cook some sugar to the burnt stage, take it off the fire and dump it onto a marble surface that you have rubbed with sweet-almond oil; also

---

[12] *écorce de citron confite bien verte.*

[14] Recipe IV,11 similarly uses only the juice of cherries, red currants and raspberries.

[15.1] See Recipe III,5.

[15.2] See Chapter I.

[15.3] This *caramelle* is not properly a *conserve* because there is no fruit or flower petals being candied.

[16.1] See Recipe III,5. This *sucre tors* is really a sort of taffy drawn out and twisted into a shape that anticipated the modern licorice ropes or nibs. One of several past participles of the verb *tordre*, "to bend, twist," *tors* applied normally to strands of something that are twisted together.

rub your hands with this oil, and work the sugar well. Get iron hooks to draw it and pull it. Set it out like twisted marzipan.[16.2]

17. Pennets

They are made the same way as the Twisted Sugar.[17]

18. Ham Slices

Cook some sugar to the feather stage and divide it among three vessels; into one of those put some lemon juice, into another some Provins roses, and into the third some powdered cochineal, or else some pomegranate juice or ground-up barberry berries. On some paper make a layer of the white and two layers of red, and repeat until the sugar is the thickness of a ham. Cut it into slices to look like slices of ham.

Chapter VIII

How to Blanch Fruits and Flowers

1. To Blanch Fennel, Cherries, Currants, etc.

Get bunches of fennel when they have dropped their flowers or are dry. Put some egg whites into a dish with a little orange-blossom water, steep the bunches of fennel in it, then sprinkle them with powdered sugar until they are completely white. Dry them by the fire or in the sun.

2. Dry Fennel[2]

Get sprouts or sprigs of fresh, very tender fennel, boil them in a lot of water and, when they are cooked, put them into cool water, then drain them well. Cook sugar to the pearl stage, put your fennel into it and boil it with a hot fire until the sugar is cooked to the feather stage. Take it off the fire and turn the fennel out onto some straw.

[16.2] There is no *massepain tortillé* in this book or among any of La Varenne's recipes. See, however, the note to Recipe XVI,5.

[17] By the eighteenth century the *Encyclopédie* (XII, 301b) defines a pennet as incorporating barley water and consequently having enhanced medicinal properties: "*Penide, ou sucre d'orge*, en Pharmacie, c'est une préparation de sucre que l'on compose en la faisant bouillir avec une décoction d'orge, jusqu'à ce qu'elle devienne cassante ou fragile . . . ."

[2] *Fenouil au sec.* This recipe and several subsequent ones (Recipes VII,3, X,15 and X,18) are for "dry" confections and anticipate those that will be outlined in Chapter XII.

3. Dry Roses

Get rose hips, remove the green part, leaving the stem, boil them two or three times, then put them in cool water. Confect them. Turn them out the same as fennel.

Chapter IX

Oranges and Lemons

1. Whole Oranges and Lemons[1]

As carefully as you can, remove the peel of the oranges, put it in cool water and the oranges in some other water. Boil the water in which the oranges are, divide the oranges into segments and set them to cook, boiling them for half an hour. Take them out and put them into cool water. With a small steel spoon squeeze out their juice, remove their peel and the seeds from inside. Cook sugar to the pearl stage; drain the oranges, boil them in the sugar over a hot fire until the sugar is cooked to the feather stage. Take the oranges off the fire and let them sit a while, then turn them out onto some straw and let them dry before taking them up. For twenty-five oranges you need about six pounds of sugar.

2. Orange Rings

Peel the oranges as you did the whole oranges and slice them into rounds half a finger thick, put them into cool water. Boil water; drain the orange rings, remove the core of the rings, and cook them in the water. When they are done, take them out and put them into cool water. Confect them like the Whole Oranges, and separate them as you turn them out onto straw.

3. Orange Fingers[3.1]

Peel the oranges as you did the other ones, putting them, as you do each one, into some cool water; cut them into quarters, cut away the inside, and clean them with a knife. Cut them into strips like lardoons and, as you do each one, put it into cool water. Boil some water; drain

---

[1] The word "whole" means "uncut" here because, unlike the next two recipes, the oranges are only separated into segments. Despite the "Lemons" in the title, they are not dealt with here but only in Recipe 5.

[3.1] *tailladins*.

the orange strips and put them into the water and cook them. Again put them into cool water, then confect them like the ones before. Turn them out onto straw with small forks.[3.2]

4. Orange Zests

Take the zests or peelings which you remove,[4.1] boil them in a lot of water for about eight minutes,[4.2] then take them out and put them into cool water, boiling them four successive times, each time putting them into cool water. Drain them and confect them like oranges. Set them out onto the straw in the shape of little rocks.

5. Lemon Segments

Peel the lemons as the oranges, split them into segments,[5.1] clean away their cores and, as you do each one, put it into cool water. Boil some water and put the lemon segments into it, taking them out when they begin to soften and putting them in cool water. Confect them like oranges[5.2] and turn them out on straw, separating them from one another.

Lemon Fingers are made the same as those of oranges.[5.3]

6. Lemon Pulp

Get large lemons or limes and peel them like oranges; with a knife remove the fruit in pieces as long and as broad as you can and the thickness of an *escu blanc*; as you do each one, put it into cool water. Cook them in water, then confect them as the Lemon Segments. Set them out on the straw without them touching one another.

The fruit of citron and ballotin[6] can be confected in the same way as lemon.

[3.2] At this point the type-setter has added the phrase *en forme de petits rochers*, accidentally borrowed from the end of the following recipe.

[4.1] In the preceding recipes.

[4.2] *environ demy quart d'heure.*

[5.1] The author speaks of "quartering" the peeled fruit, but in Recipe 1 the oranges are split "by their end" — into segments, clearly.

[5.2] That is, by following the procedure of Recipe 1, nominally for Whole Oranges *and Lemons*.

[5.3] Recipe 3.

[6] Even into the nineteenth century there was some hesitation whether this fruit should be classified as an orange or a lemon. In their *Histoire naturelle des orangers* (Paris: Mme Herissaut le Doux, 1818), A. Risso and A. Poiteau describe the tree and fruit

Chapter X

Confections not available from Confectioners' Shops[x]

1. Rennet-Apple Compote

Get some rennet apples, pare them, cut them into quarters, remove their core, putting them, as you core each one, into cool water. Cook them in some water and some sugar on a hot fire. When the apples are done, take them out, set them to drain on a platter or on the edge of a dish;[1.1] set them out on a platter. Finish off cooking your syrup, boiling it until it is cooked down to a jelly;[1.2] as it begins to cool, spoon it onto the apples. For six apples you need a pint and a half of water and twelve ounces of sugar.

2. Calvi-Apple Compote

Get very red Calvi apples, quarter them, split the peel into strips,[2] core them and cook them as for the Rennet-Apple Compote, not putting in as much water but putting in a cup of wine.

---

as follows: "*Limonier balotin. Limone Balotino.* Foliis ovalibus, obtusis, acutisque, serratis, crassis: fructu magno, subrotundo, basi apiceque depresso, coronato, mammâ obtusâ terminato; cortice crasso; pulpâ acidâ." Though not well enough known to be dealt with by other botanists of the time — it is not mentioned for instance by Giorgio Gallesio, *Pomona italiana ossia Trattato degli alberi fruttiferi* (Pisa: Niccolò Capurro, 1817–31) — it was grown in the latitude of Paris: Risso and Poiteau continue, "Les fleurs se développent à Paris vers le commencement de juin. ... Le fruit est gros, arrondi, déprimé à la base et au sommet, d'un jaune foncé, à surface assez lisse, terminé par un mammelon écrasé, ... ; la peau est épaisse, blanche intérieurement, spongeuse, d'une saveur douce; la pulpe, moins jaune que la surface du fruit, est divisée en douze loges, et contient un suc abondant d'un acide agréable. ... On trouve de fort beaux individus de cet arbre dans l'Orangerie de Versailles et dans celles de Paris où on ne le connaît que sous le nom de *Balotin*. Le Suc de ses fruits est d'un acide très-agréable" (pp. 169–70). Two large colour illustrations of the *Citrus Limonum Balotinum*, branch, leaves, flowers and fruit, whole and in cross-section, are presented in Tables LXXIX and LXXX.

[x] We may speculate upon the reasons why the confections in this chapter were not "commercially viable": low popularity, hence insufficient demand; exceptional expense of the ingredients; complexity of the procedures involved.

[1.1] On the edge, presumably, so that, a dish being slightly concave, excess moisture will drain to its centre.

[1.2] This *cuit en gelée* is not one of the "cooking stages" of sugar that the author has outlined in Chapter III. He does, however, describe it in the very first paragraph of his Preface to the Reader.

[2] This peel is merely sliced but not removed: see the next recipe.

3. Another Rennet-Apple Compote

Cut some rennet apples into quarters, core them and cook them in half a pint of water with half a pound of sugar. When all the syrup is gone and they begin to bake[3] on the bottom, place a platter on top and tip them over onto it in the same way as you turn over a cheese. Arrange them with the peel upwards.

4. Compote of Whole Apples

Get rennet apples, slash the skin and cook them like quartered apples. Leave a little syrup with them and serve them whole.

5. Rennet-Apple Jelly

Peel rennet apples, cut them into pieces, remove their seeds, cook them in water, put them into a serviette and squeeze them well. Take the apples' decoction and boil it with some sugar on a hot fire until the syrup is cooked.[5] For a pint of decoction you need a pound of sugar.

6. Pomegranate Jelly

Make the Rennet-Apple Jelly and, when it is almost cooked, put in some very red pomegranate seeds which you have cleaned. Let them boil a little and strain them through a cloth.

7. Chestnut Compote

Roast some chestnuts on the coals, shell them and flatten them, then put them into a silver dish with some apricot syrup,[7] or some other sort of syrup, and a little Spanish wine; boil them. When you want to serve them, put a plate on top and tip them over on it like a cheese.

8. Lemon Compote

Peel lemons, cut them into rounds and remove their seeds; bring them to a boil in some water, remove them and put the into cool water. Cook some sugar to the coarse pearl stage,[8] drain the lemons and put them into it to boil until the syrup has cooked to a jelly. Set them out on a platter.

---

[3] *rostir.*

[5] The remaining steps in the procedure for making a jelly are merely implied.

[7] For this preparation see Recipe V,4.

[8] This particular "pearl" stage is defined in Recipe III,3, above.

9. Orange Compote

Do this like the lemon one, but don't cook it in water.[9]

10. Lemon-Pulp Compote

Peel lemons, remove their pulp in slices and, as you do, put it into cool water; boil some water and boil your lemon pulp in it, then put it back into cool water. Cook some sugar to the pearl stage, put the lemon pulp into it until the syrup is cooked to the coarse pearl stage. Set it out on a platter, adding on some lemon juice as you serve.

Orange-Pulp Compote is done the same way.

11. Pear Compote

Peel some pears and cook them on a hot fire with lots of water; when they are cooked, put them into cool water. Drain them and confect them in water, and sugar them.[11] Put on some lemon juice when serving.

12. Another Pear Compote

Peel some milady's-thigh pears or some other variety of pear and put them into an earthenware pot in water along with sugar and a little wine and cinamon. Let them boil until there is hardly any syrup left.

13. Compote of Pears in Orange Juice

Cook some big pears on the coals or under a cooking bell, peel them or[13] split them into quarters, core them and boil them with sugar in a little water. When the syrup is completely reduced, add in some orange juice and take them out.

14. Barberry Compote

Remove the stems and the seeds of the barberry, boil the fruit in water with some sugar, cooking the syrup to the pearl stage, then take it out.

---

[9] The negative is emphatic — *ne la faites point cuire à l'eau.* The sense is likely that in their preliminary treatment the oranges are to be even less boiled ("not at all cooked") than the lemons.

[11] *& les confisez avec de l'eau, & les sucrez, mettez du jus* .... The procedure intended here is to be similar to what is outlined in Recipe 1, above, where a "decoction" of the fruit's sweet, watery juice is to be reduced to a jelly. Compare this with the next recipes.

[13] *sic.*

15. Dry Chestnuts

Cook chestnuts on the coals and shell them. Cook some sugar to the feather stage and take it off the fire; put the chestnuts into it and stir them around. When the sugar begins to cool, take them out and put them on straw.

16. Glacé Chestnuts[16.1]

Make a glazing of some orange-blossom water and some sugar, as is directed in recipe for Glacé Marzipan.[16.2] Cook some chestnuts on the coals, shell them, flatten them, glaze them on one side and cook them with the upper part of the oven;[16.3] then turn them over on their other side, glaze them and cook them the same way.

Glacé Brignol plums, cherries and peaches are done the same way as the chestnuts.

17. Glacé Apricots

Get dry candied apricots and glaze them the same way as the chestnuts.

18. Dry Pistachio Compote

Clean pistachios in hot water, then put them in cool water. Drain them, dry them. Set them out to dry like the chestnuts.[18]

19. Quince Jelly[19]

Cut quinces into pieces and boil those well in some water; put them into a cloth and squeeze them well. Take the decoction that comes through

---

[16.1] In the *Confiturier françois* published with the pseudo-*Cuisinier françois* in Lyon by Jacques Canier, 1680, p. 408, this recipe does not have a separate rubric but continues the text of Recipe 15.

[16.2] See Recipe XVI,4, below.

[16.3] The text has ... *les faites cuire avec le dessus du four.* Apparently the heat is to be applied particularly against the upper surface of the metal chamber, so that the glazed upper side of the flattened chestnuts will be exposed to the heat radiating from it.

[18] "Set them out," that is, after having coated them with sugar which has been cooked to the feather stage. The reference is to Recipe 15, above.

[19] A century earlier, in 1557, Nostradamus recorded three recipes for *gelée de coings* (chapters 15–17), the first of which he qualifies as being "of a sovereign beauty, goodness, flavour and excellence fit to be set before a King, and which will stay good a long time." The rubric of the two succeeding recipes is, each one, even more laudatory.

the cloth and put it with sugar — a pound of sugar for every pint of liquid; cook it over a low fire, keeping it covered. When it is cooked, take it and set it out.

20. Thin Cotignac

Do this the same as for Quince,[20] and put it into pine boxes. You can add in a little cochineal to make it redder.

21. Thick Cotignac

Pare some very ripe quinces, cut them into pieces, cook them well in some water, then put them through a very fine strainer and take up what has gone through. Cook some sugar to the pearl stage with [some] water in which the quince was cooked.[21] Boil the quince over a low fire until everything is cooked to a jelly; put this away in pine boxes. For a pound of marmalade use a pound of sugar.

22. Quince Marmalade

Do this the same way as the Thick Cotignac, but do not cook it as much, and put it into glazed or earthenware pots, covering it with paper when it has cooled.

23. Apple Marmalade

It is done the same way as the quince one.

24. Apple Cotignac

Do it as the quince one, cooking it over a hot fire and without covering it.

Chapter XI
Moist Confections[xi]

1. Fresh Apricots

Peel the apricots and, as you peel each one, put them into cool water. Heat up some water and put the apricots into it; add in a little vinegar

---

[20] Presumably this reference is to the preceding recipe for Quince Jelly. The *codignat* of Nostradamus (ch. 21) likewise follows other recipes for confecting quince.

[21] The original text is faulty: *faites cuire du sucre à perle avec de l'eau dans laqu'elle aurons cuit les coings.* Nothing is ever said about what to do with the strained quince juice.

[xi] Recipes for confections of a drier consistency, "candy" as we might classify them, will be treated in the next chapter.

and, keeping them covered, boil them until they are plump.[1.1] Remove them from the fire, let them cool in the water, then take them out and put them into cool water. Cook some sugar to the pearl stage, drain the apricots and put them into it, cooking them over a hot fire until the syrup is cooked to the coarse pearl stage,[1.2] then take them out. If they are to be stored, do not cook the sugar so much before putting them into it.

2. Almonds

Cook ash or pearl-ash[2] in some water, put in the almonds and leave them there until they can be skinned under your thumb; take them out, skin them with your fingers and put them into some cool water. Confect them like the apricots.

3. Gooseberries[3]

Remove their flower, their stem and the seeds inside. Cook them and confect them like the apricots.

4. Cherries with their Pits

Get very ripe cherries and remove their stem. Cook some sugar to the feather stage, put the cherries into it and boil them over a hot fire for a quarter of an hour, take them off the fire and let them cool.[4] Then put them back again on the fire again and cook them until the syrup is cooked to the coarse pearl stage. Then remove them.

5. Raspberries

Get some raspberries that are not too ripe, remove their stem and put them in a terrine. Cook some sugar to the feather stage, pour it on

---

[1.1] In this context the words *vert* and *verdir* (see Recipes 11, 23 and 25 below) refer to fleshiness, a state of having swollen with moisture. The belief seems to be that such a condition will render fruit more ready to absorb sugar.

[1.2] See Recipe III,3, above.

[2] Cotgrave glosses these *cendres gravelées* as "ashes made of the burnt lees, or dregs of wine," and *gravelée* alone as "tartar, old lees of wine." The substance is in fact a crude sort of potash, a potassium compound. The alkaline solution will soften the almond shells by breaking down the lignins; the residual enzymes from the wine yeasts might also help to degrade the shells. See the use of pearl-ash with apricots in *The French Cook*, Recipe Confections,1.

[3] *groseilles vertes*: "green currants."

[4] That is, the cherries and the sugar are to be let cool together (as in several of the next recipes), then later returned to the boil.

the raspberries and put them into a stove in a dry place for half a day. Boil them over a moderate fire until the syrup is cooked to the pearl stage.

6. Red Currants

Remove the currants' stem. Cook some sugar to the feather stage, put the currants into it and, skimming them, let them cool. Finish cooking them, cooking the syrup to the pearl stage.

7. Apricots with their Pits and Skins

Get the apricots as they begin to ripen, remove their stem and puncture them in places with a knife. Warm up some water, put the apricots into it but do not boil them; take them out as they froth on the water, put them into cool water and drain them. Cook some sugar to the pearl stage, put the apricots into it, let them boil for eight minutes, then take them off the fire and let them cool; finish them on a hot fire, cooking the syrup to the coarse pearl stage.

8. Mulberries

Get some slightly red mulberries and remove their stem. Cook some sugar to the feather stage, put the mulberries into it and, after skimming them, let them cool. Then boil them again until the syrup is cooked to the pearl stage.

9. Pitted Apricots

Remove the pits from the apricots, prick them, then confect them like the other fruit.

10. Peeled Apricots

Peel the apricots as delicately as you can and, as each is peeled, put them into cool water. Blanch them in water and confect them like the other things.

11. Imperial Plums

Get the plums as they begin to ripen. Heat up water, put the plums into it after pricking them with a knife point, add in a little vinegar and keep them covered; heat up the water but do not boil it. When they begin to become plump, take them off the fire and let them cool in their water; keep them covered. When they've cooled, take them out and put them into cold water. Cook some sugar to the feather stage; drain the plums, put them into the sugar and cook them over a hot fire. After skimming them, take them[11] off the fire and let them cool. Finish boiling them over a hot fire until the syrup is cooked to the gross pearl stage. Take them out and store them away.

12. Peeled Imperial Plums

Peel the imperial plums as delicately as you can, putting each as you do it into cool water. Cook them and confect them the same as the others.

13. White *Perdrigon* Plums

Get the white perdrigon plums while still slightly green; plump them and confect them the same as the Imperials.

14. Peeled *Perdrigon* Plums

Peel the plums and put them as they are peeled into cool water. Plump them and confect them the same as the others.

15. Red *Perdrigon* Plums

Cook them in boiling water and, as they cook, take them out and put them into some cool water. Cook some sugar to the feather stage; after draining the plums, put them into it; cook them over a moderate fire; after skimming them, let them cool. Finish them on the same heat and cook the syrup to the pearl stage; remove them.

16. Red Damson Plums

They are confected the same as the perdrigon plums. Every sort of plum can be confected in one or the other of these two ways: those that are to be served, like the imperial plums; and those that are to become red,[16] like the red perdrigon plum. The white ones can can also be done like the red perdrigon plum, but cook them in the sugar over a hot fire.

17. Russet Pears

Get very ripe russet pears, cook them in a lot of water and, when they are cooked, put them into cool water; peel them very delicately and put them back into some cool water. Cook sugar to the smooth stage,[17] put

---

[11] The plums and the sugar.

[16] *qui se doivent rougir:* clearly this *rougir* is an error, perhaps for a verb such as *serrer*, "to put away, store away."

[17] *à lisse:* see the definition of this cooking stage of sugar in Recipe III, 2, above.

the pears into it and cook them over a moderate fire; you can add in some cloves and some dry orange peel. Let them cool. Finish them the same way [as already described], cooking the syrup to the pearl stage. Remove them.

18. Muscadelle Pears

Do them the same way as the russet pears, but cook them on a hot fire and do not add in any cloves or orange. Every sort of pear can be confected in the same way; cook the white ones with a hot fire.

19. White Walnuts

Get some very tender green walnuts and skin them down to the white so that no green is left; as you do each one, put it into cool water. After piercing them through with a larding-needle, cook them over a hot fire in a lot of water; let them boil until a pin that you prick them with does not stick; take them out, put them into cool water and stick them with cinnamon, cloves or candied lemon peel. Cook some sugar to the smooth stage, put the walnuts into it, cook them over a hot fire, then let them cool. Finish off their cooking, doing the syrup to the pearl stage; remove them.

20. Green Walnuts

Get very tender green walnuts, skin them, pierce them, cook them and confect them like the other sorts.

21. Apricot Peaches

Boil them in some water until the skin begins to fall off, then take them out and put them into some cool water; remove their skin and set them to drain. Also cook some sugar to the pearl stage, put the fruit into it, cook it over a hot fire, then let them cool. Finish off their cooking until the syrup is cooked to the coarse pearl stage, then you take them out.

22. Alberge Peaches

Get some alberge peaches[22.1] and put them into cool water. Cook some sugar to the pearl stage; drain the peaches and put them into the sugar and, when the syrup is almost cooked to the pearl stage, take them off the fire, put them into a terrine and let them sit for twenty-four hours. Put them back on the fire, cook the syrup to the coarse pearl stage and remove them.

[22.1] *alberges.*

In the same way you can confect melocoton peaches,[22.2] mirabelle plums, and all the clingstone peaches[22.3] — that is, peaches whose pit adheres to the flesh. If you confect any of these, they have to be recooked every two months, or whenever the syrup begins to become runny.[22.4]

23. Corbeil Peaches

Get some peaches that are not quite ripe, skin them, remove their pit, put the fruit into cool water and plump them the same as the imperial plums. Confect them in the same way.

24. Muscat Grapes

Get muscat grapes as they begin to ripen and remove their seeds. Cook sugar to the feather stage, put the grapes into it, cover them and let them sit. When they have cooled, put them back on a moderate fire, cook the sugar to the pearl stage, then draw off the confection. Skinned muscat grapes are done the same way.

25. Verjuice Grapes

Get the verjuice grapes as they begin to ripen, remove their seeds, putting them, as you do so, into cool water. Heat up some water and put the verjuice grapes into it and, keeping them covered, cook them over a low fire until the grapes have recovered their plumpness. Take them off the fire, let them cool, remove them and put them into cool water. Cook the sugar to the feather stage, drain the verjuice grapes, put them into the sugar and cook this over a hot fire; the syrup should be cooked to the pearl stage. Remove them.

26. Quince

Get very ripe quince, pare them, split them into quarters and, having cored them, put the fruit into cool water. Boil some water, put the quince into it; take them out when they have softened a little, putting them back into cool water. Cook some sugar to the smooth stage and, having drained

---

[22.2] *mirlicotons.*

[22.3] *pavies.*

[22.4] The author wrote *commence à se décuire*: until the syrup "begins to uncook." Furetière defined the verb *decuire* as: "Perdre la cuisson. Il se dit particulierement des conserves & des syrops, lors qu'ils se liquefient trop à faute d'une suffisante cuisson, & qu'ils sont en danger de se corrompre."

the quince, put them into the sugar and, keeping them covered, cook them over a low fire; you can add in a little cinnamon. Cook the syrup to a jelly,[26] then the confection has to be taken out.

Chapter XII

Dry Confections[xii]

1. Angel Throat[1.1]

Get fully extended romaine lettuce, remove the leaf and the skin[1.2] very delicately and put it into cool water. Boil some water and put the leaves into it and cook them until they cannot be lifted with a pin stuck into them. Take them out, put them into cool water, then take them out, drain them and put them into a terrine that is long enough to hold them. Cook some sugar to the pearl stage and pour it over them. Then put them into a stove[1.3] for two days. After that pour the syrup gently into a confectioner's bassin,[1.4] cook it again to the pearl stage and pour it over the lettuce leaves; put them back into the stove for two more days. Then put them into the confectioner's bassin with the syrup and boil them until the syrup is cooked to the pearl stage. Put them into stoneware crocks

---

[26] *en gelée*: this cooking stage is not defined as a cooking stage for sugar, but is described in the author's Foreward to the Reader. We have seen references to jellied fruit in certain recipes of Chapter X.

[xii] In each of the recipes of this chapter, the normally "moist" confection (of the sort described in the previous chapter) undergoes a "drying" operation, normally in a stove (*étuve*). In this operation, the fruit is thoroughly dried of the syrup in which it has been candied. Recipes 2 and 4 make the distinction between the moist and dry versions explicit.

[1.1] While Nostradamus does not give his recipe for *laictues confites en succre* as picturesque a name as this *Gorge d'ange*, his procedure for its preparation is quite similar. See his book on *Confitures liquides* of 1557, ch. 7. To his recipe he appends directions for clarifying the sugar to be used should it not be white but *cassonnade* — that is, he writes, *le succre qui est noir*.

[1.2] *la peau*. What the cook is preparing the short stem or heart alone of each "leaf". Nostradamus calls it the *tige* and describes it as an index finger in breadth and a finger in length.

[1.3] *mettés à l'étuve*. The small metal chamber known as a "stove" was warmed by a few coals or merely by its close proximity to a bakery oven; it offered a means to dry a foodstuff slowly.

[1.4] *bassine*. See the note to this word in the recipe for Pralines, VI,1.

and put them away. When you want to use them, take them out and dry them in the stove.

In the same way you can confect cabbage broccoli and sprigs of elderberry.

2. Green Apricots, Dry

Do them the same way as the moist ones.[2] After they have sat for eight days in the syrup, take them out, drain them and set them out on some tin sheets or on slates, taking care to turn them over; then dry them the stove.

Green almonds can be confected in the same way.

3. Green Currants

Seed them and do them the same as green apricots.

4. White Walnuts

Do them the same as for the moist ones.[4] When you need to use them, drain them and dry them; turn them out onto tin sheets or slates.

5. Cherries with their Pits

Get very ripe cherries, leave on the stems, boil them a short while[5] in a little water and drain them. Cook some sugar to the feather stage, put the cherries in it and boil them for eight minutes; then put them in a terrine and leave them there for eight days. After this you put them into the confectioner's bassin and cook the syrup to the small pearl stage, put them back into the terrine. When they have cooled, drain them, set them out on slates, then dry them in the stove, being careful to turn them over.

6. Cherries with Ears[6]

Remove the cherries' stem and pit, confect them in the same way as walnuts and dry them in the stove.

---

[2] Dealt with in Recipe XI,1.

[4] In Recipe XI,19.

[5] The text, here and in XIII,3, reads that the cherries are to be boiled for "twenty boils": *vingt bouillons*. The phrase "a single boil" (*un seul bouillon*) is common and means that the foodstuff should merely be brought to a boil. Here "twenty boils" seems to indicate a longer but still brief period.

[6] This and the next preparation involve an important step which, curiously, is not mentioned. The cherries and apricots are split in two, pitted and confected. Then, to make the appearance of "ears" they are set out with each half overlapping the other.

7. Apricots with Ears[7.1]

Get apricots just as they are beginning to ripen, pit them and, having skinned them very delicately, put each as you do them into cool water. Then warm up some water, put them into it, taking them out as they float up on the surface; put them back into cool water, drain them, and then put them into a terrine. Having cooked some sugar to the small pearl stage, pour it over the apricots and let them sit for a day; then pour the syrup very gently into a confectioner's bassin, cook it again to the pearl stage and then pour it over the apricots. Continue to recook the syrup like that five or six times and, when the apricots have taken on sugar enough, let them sit for eight days. Drain them and dry them in the stove, being careful to turn them over often and to changer their paper[7.2] until they are dry.

8. Apricots with their Pits

Remove the skin[8] of the apricots and confect them like the others.

9. Corbeil Peaches

Get peaches that are slightly green, skin them, pit them, confect them and take them out like Imperial plums.[9]

10. Imperial Plums

Get slightly green plums as they are beginning to ripen and pierce them in three or four places with a knife. Heat up some water, put them into it and cook them without boiling them; add in a little vinegar and cover them over, leaving them until they begin to plump up. Take them off the fire and let them cool in their water. Then take them out, put them into cool water, drain them, put them into a terrine and finish them like the apricots.

[7.1] For the name of this confection, see the note to the previous recipe.

[7.2] *les retourner, & les changer de fueille*, this being the sheet of paper on which they are sitting in the stove. See the general advice on pastry-making that the author offers the reader at the beginning of his book, specifically about frequently changing this paper.

[8] *Ostez les noyaux*. Clearly either this direction or the name of the recipe is in error. In the previous chapter the corresponding pair of recipes for apricots deal with those with their skin but without pits (Recipe XI,9) and those with pits but without skin (Recipe XI,10).

[9] That is, of the following recipe.

11. Peeled Imperial Plums

Skin the plums, putting each as you do them into cool water. Finish them the same as the others.

12. Lilevert[12] and Perdrigon Plums

They are done the same as the Imperial plums.

13. Blanquette Pears

Get thoroughly ripe blanquette pears, cook them in a lot of water over a hot fire, take them off when they begin to soften and put them into cool water. Pare them, putting each as you do them into more cool water, core them and put them into a terrine. Cook some sugar to the smooth stage, pour it over the pears and let them sit for a day. Pour the syrup into a confectioner's bassin and cook it to the pearl stage; continue recooking the syrup for eight days, the last time putting the pears into the syrup and cooking it to the pearl stage. Put the pears back into the terrine and leave them there for eight days. Drain them of their syrup, set them out and dry them in the stove.

Muscadelle pears and russet pears can be confected the same way.

14. Quartered Pears

Cook them in water and put them into cool water; peel them, split them in four, core them and confect them the same as the blanquette pears.

15. Muscat Grapes

Get muscat grapes just as they begin to ripen, remove their seeds and put the fruit into a terrine. Cook some sugar to the pearl stage, pour it over the muscat grapes and finish them like the apricots.

16. Peeled Muscat Grapes

Remove their skins and seeds, and confect them like the previous ones.

17. Verjuice Grapes

Plump verjuice grapes in water just as for the moist confection[17.1] and confect them like the dry muscat grapes.[17.2]

---

[12] Properly these *prunes de lilevert* should be spelled *de l'Isle vert*.

[17.1] Recipe XI, 25, above.

[17.2] Recipe 15, above.

18. Quince

Get very ripe quince, split them into quarters, pare and core them, cook them in a lot of water and take them out as they are cooked, putting them into some cool water. Drain them, put them into a terrine and finish them like the blanquette pears.

19. Quartered Apples

Get rennet apples, quarter them, pare and core them, cook them in water and put them into cool water; drain them, put them into a terrine and confect them like the blanquette pears.

Chapter XIII

Pastes

a. Fruit and Flower Pastes[xiii]

1. Apple Paste

Get rennet apples, peel and core them, cook them in water, drain them and put them through a strainer or sieve. Take the marmalade that comes through and dry it in a skillet on the fire, stirring continuously to keep it from burning. When it is quite dry and no longer sticks to the skillet, add in some powdered sugar and stir it again a little. Take it off the fire and set it out on tin sheets or slates and dry it in the stove; when it is dry on one side, turn it over onto the other by lifting it with a knife, and put it onto other sheets and dry it [in the stove]. When it is dry, take it and put it into pine boxes with some paper.

2. Apricot Paste

Get apricots, pit them, cook them in water and put them through a strainer or hair sieve. Take the marmalade and do with it the same as for apples.

3. Cherry Paste

Get very ripe cherries, remove their stems and pits, boil them a short while, take them out and drain them. Strain them like the apples.

[xiii] In the *Confiturier françois* that was published together with the *Cusinier françois* in Lyon, 1680, this chapter has a slightly different rubric: *Les pastes de fruits de fleurs*.

4. Raspberry and Red Currant Paste

This is done[4] the same as with apples.

5. Peach Paste

Get peaches that are not quite ripe, peel and pit them; cook them in water and strain them. Do them as with apples.

6. Muscat Grape Paste

Get them when they are not quite ripe, take out their seeds and put them through the strainer. Take the marmalade and make the paste the same as with apples.

7. Verjuice Grape Paste

Remove the seeds of the verjuice grapes, plump them in water as for confecting them moist sort,[7] and strain them. Do them like the Apple Paste.

8. Quince Paste

Get very ripe quince, pare them, split them into four and core them. Cook them in some water, drain and strain them. Finish them like the apple sort.

b. Counterfeit Pastes[xiii]

9. Cherry, Raspberry, Currant Pastes

Take some apple marmalade and give it a red colour with prepared cochineal or with *sinabre*. Make the paste like the apple sort.

10. Counterfeit Apricot Paste

Take some apple marmalade and give it a yellow colour with prepared lily blossoms.[10]

---

[4] In the singular: *Elle se fait*. Two different pastes are likely intended.

[7] Recipe XI,25.

[xiii] The qualification *contrefaite* or "mock" in this rubric is a term of very long standing in the European culinary vocabulary. Traditionally it identified a preparation that was not what it seemed, such as grains of "rice" made of flour (*The Vivendier*, Recipe 49), or a "cheese," *ricotta contrafatta*, made of ground almonds, sugar and rosewater (*The Neapolitan Recipe Collection*, Recipe 168). For the present series of recipes the term refers to the way colourants or a special mould are used to play a joke on a confectioner's patron or clients.

[10] See this preparation in Recipe II,4.

11. Plum Paste

Take some apple marmalade and give it a green colour with prepared beet greens. Make the paste like the apple sort.

12. Violet Paste

Clean some violet petals of their buds and grind them in a mortar. Take some apple marmalade and mix the violets into it. Make the paste in the same way as the apple sort.

You can make pastes from all sorts of flowers in the same way.

13. Genoese Paste

Get very ripe quince and boil them whole. When they are cooked, take them out and put them in cool water; peel them, put the flesh of the quince through the strainer and take the marmalade. Cook some sugar to the feather stage[13.1] and, having taken it off the fire, put the marmalade into it, stirring it well with a spatula or spoon. Then put it into a terrine and let it cool. Set it out, putting a tin mould of the shape you want to give it, on a slate and put the paste into the mould filling it out fully. Lift the mould, smooth out the paste,[13.2] carve its top surface or make a branch design on it. Dry it in a stove. When it is dry on one side, turn it over, flipping it from one slate to another, and dry its other side. When you want to make use of it, get some gold leaf, cut this up into pieces and gild your paste here and there: slightly moisten the spot you want to gild and apply the gold to it.

Chapter XIV

Candying Fruits and Flowers

1. Candied Oranges

Get dry-confected oranges.[1.1] Cook some sugar to the pearl stage and almost to the feather stage, and put it into a terrine; stick a pin into each

---

[13.1] The phrase used in the text to describe this cooking stage of sugar is *cuire à soufle*. The particular term *à soufle* has not been used by the author since he mentioned it in Recipe III,4 as one of the several phrases in current use to describe the "feather" stage of cooking sugar.

[13.2] The text has *faites la paste bien unie*: the cook should smooth out any irregularities and fill in any air holes or cracks.

[1.1] See Recipe IX,1.

orange [segment], tie the end of a thread to the pin and tie the thread to sticks that you put within[1,2] the terrine; put the oranges into it so that they all soak and they touch neither the bottom nor the sides nor one another. Put them in the stove and leave them there for four or five days, then take them out.

2. Candied Apricots

Get some dry-confected apricots,[2] tie them and candy them the same as the oranges.

3. Candied Fennel

Get some dry sprigs of fennel, tie them by their stem and candy them the same as the oranges. You can candy all sorts of fruit the same way.

4. Candied Violets

Put violets along with their stems into a terrine. Cook some sugar to the pearl stage and almost to the feather stage and pour it over the violets. When this has cooled, put them in a dry place, cover them and leave them for eight days; take them out and set them to dry on some straw. Do not put them in a stove.

5. Candied Orange Blossoms

Get buds of orange blossoms and candy them in the same way as the violets.

6. Candied Borage Blossoms

Candy them the same as the violets. You can candy all sorts of flowers in the same way, except for roses.

7. Candied Rose Hips

Get some rose hips, boil them a dozen times in fresh water, drain them well and candy them the same as the oranges.

[1,2] *au dedans de* — rather than "across the top of." It seems that these sticks are to be wedged tightly across the inside of the terrine, but still at some distance above the level of the syrup. They are not to be dislodged or moved by the bubbling of the syrup.

[2] Recipe XII,2.

Chapter XV

Dragées

It must be noted that to make dragées there are two different cookings of sugar: one is called "to the pearl stage" and the other "to the smooth stage" — as they are explained for the cooking of the sugar in the Treatise on Confections;[xv.1] that is why people speak of "pearled dragées" and "smooth dragées".[xv.2]

For all sorts of dragées you need to have a great confectioner's bassin, of red copper or silver, with two handles and flat-bottomed, suspended in the air by two cords at about waist-height; beneath this you put a fire basket[xv.3] or a terrine with a moderate fire in it to make the pearled dragées.

You have to have a red-copper utensil shaped like a funnel — whose spout is the size of an aglet of a lace — which you hang in the air above the middle of the confectioner's bassin and into which you put the syrup when you need it.

1. Pearled Almond Dragées

Get some whole sweet almonds, clean them carefully of their dust and dirt, put them into the confectioner's bassin and dry them a little on the

---

[xv.1] Above, in Chapter III at Recipes 3 and 2, respectively. The reference to the *Treatise on Confections* is strange and seems to suggest that this present chapter on dragées originated apart from the *French Confectioner*.

By the seventeenth century dragées were one of the oldest confections in Europe. Generically they had evolved from being merely a glob of candied, spiced sugar in late-medieval pharmaceuticals. Both sugar and spices possessed the humoral property of moderate warmth (sugar also being moist and spices generally being dry); physicians commonly prescribed either to help a patient's stomach fully "cook" the food he or she had ingested. In combination, in the form of dragées, these drugs constituted an ideal but strictly medical function of "stomach-closer" or digestive, and were taken, and graciously served to guests, at the conclusion of a meal. The practice of coating a seed or nut with such candied, spiced sugar grew over the years until by La Varenne's time "dragée" meant a candied almond.

[xv.2] The next two recipes deal with *amandes perlées* and *amandes lisées*. For the first the syrup is still liquid enough to run through the confectioner's funnel.

[xv.3] Richelet describes a *rechaud* as an "*instrument de cuisine qui est de terre, ou de métal, dans quoi on met du feu pour rechaufer ou tenir chaud quelque ragoût, ou pour faire cuire quelque chose entre deux plats. Le bon réchaut est fait de fer de cuirasse & composé d'un corps, de trois piez, d'une grille, d'un fond, d'une fourchette & d'un manche.*"

fire. Put some syrup in the funnel, being careful to stir the bassin and turn the dragées in it so they take on the sugar evenly; sometimes you can also stir them by hand and separate them if any of them are sticking together. Stop the syrup from time to time and let them sit and dry out. You can make them as large or as coated with sugar as you like by carrying on in the same way.

2. Smooth Almond Dragées

Prepare the almonds and dry them in the confectioner's bassin. In a spoon get syrup cooked to the smooth stage, about a cup at a time, and pour it into the bassin, stirring the almonds around frequently with your hand and letting them sit occasionally. You can coat them with as much sugar as you like by carrying on the same way.

3. Smooth Pistachio Dragées

Get broken, carefully cleaned pistachio nuts, put them into the confectioner's bassin and at the same time put in sugar that has been cooked to the smooth stage. Do them like the Smooth Almonds. You can also make Pearled Pistachio Dragées by doing them the same as the Pearled Dragées, but they shouldn't be dried out in the bassin. The sugar has to be poured at the same time.

4. Milanese Cinnamon-Stick Dragées

Get good fresh cinnamon, cut it into small pieces like lardoons and put them into the confectioner's bassin; put some sugar, cooked to the pearl stage, into the funnel. Do them like the Pearled Almond Dragées.

5. Pearled Orange Dragées

Get some oranges that are good for confecting, remove their peel thinly from on top, cut each orange into four, core it and cut it up into small pieces like lardoons; cook them in water. Confect them dry; take them out onto some straw and make sure all the pieces are separate. Put them into the confectioner's bassin and do them like the Pearled Almond Dragées.

6. Sugared Peas[6.1] or Verdun Aniseed Dragées

Get good, very sweet anise, clean it carefully, remove all its stems

---

[6.1] This *pois sucrez* is a descriptive, alternative name for the end result of this recipe — like the *anis de Verdun* — rather than an ingredient. See the same reference to peas in Recipe 10, below.

and, when it is well cleaned, put it into the confectioner's bassin and dry it a little; finish the aniseed the same as the Smooth Almond Dragées. If you wish to make larger ones, you have only to let them get larger.[6.2]

7. Pearled Coriander Dragées

Get fresh coriander, pick it over and clean it carefully, and put it into the confectioner's bassin. Do them the same as the Pearled Almond Dragées.

8. Fennel-Seed Dragées

Get fennel seed, green and very sweet, and do it the same as the Verdun Aniseed Dragées.

9. Smooth Apricot Dragées

Get some dry-confected apricots or some apricot paste[9] and pound this in a mortar with a little orange-blossom water; make it up into little balls the size of a pea and flatten them with your fingers like a lentil; leave them somewhat dry. Make dragées of them like the Smooth Almond Dragées.

10. Lemon-Pulp Dragées

Take some lemon pulp drawn out dry and make dragées of it the same as the apricot ones. You can give an amber and musk flavour to the pastes as you pound them in the mortar.

11. Melon-Seed Dragées

When melons are good, the seeds of the best should be stored away and kept in a dry place. When you want to make dragées, they have to be dried in the confectioner's bassin. Make the dragées with syrup cooked to the smooth stage the same as the Smooth Almond Dragées.

12. Cucumber-Seed Dragées

In cucumber season their seeds should be stored away and kept in a dry place. When you want to make dragées, the seeds' skin has to be taken off and the inner kernel used. Make the dragées the same as the Melon-Seed ones, but they shouldn't be dried out in the confectioner's bassin.

[6.2] That is, by coating them with additional baths of sugar.

[9] See Recipes XII,2 and XIII,2 respectively.

13. Pumpkin-Seed Dragées

Pumpkin-seed dragées are made also in the same way as those with cucumber seeds. In the same way you can also make dragées of all sorts of fruits or fruit pastes.

You can give an amber and musk flavour to any dragées by putting musk and amber into the confectioner's bassin with the last coating of sugar you give them.

Chapter XVI

All sorts of Marzipan

1. Plain Marzipan

Marzipans and biscuits are described in the *French Pastry Chef*. Clean sweet almonds in hot water and put them into cool water. Drain them well, grind them in a mortar with a wooden pestle, being careful to moisten them quite often with ordinary water, with orange-blossom water or with some other sort, so that the paste doesn't have an oily taste. When they are fully ground so there are no coarse pieces left in the paste, cook some sugar to the feather stage and put your almonds into it; mix them well and dry the mixture on a moderate fire, being careful to stir it well with the spatula to prevent it from burning on the bottom. When it begins to dry out and not to stick on the skillet, take it out. You can serve it hot or dish it up whatever way you want; it can also be served cold. If your paste is too dry, pound it again in the mortar with some egg white and make it as soft as you like. When your marzipan is set out, bake it in the oven[1] with a moderate fire above and below. You can use this paste for several sorts of marzipan. A pound of almonds takes twelve ounces of sugar.

2. Royal Marzipan

Take some of that marzipan paste and make it up into rings.[2.1] Put some egg whites into a platter and dip your rings in it, then dredge them in some powdered sugar, coating them well, and set them on some paper.

---

[1] Throughout this chapter on marzipans what the confectioner will be using is the small iron or red-copper oven mentioned in the author's Preface to the Reader.

[2.1] In several of the recipes below, the reader is told to make use of "the syringe" in order to make rings of marzipan.

Bake them with a hot fire above and a moderate fire below,[2.2] not taking them off the paper until they have cooled.

3. Round Royal Marzipan

This is done like the previous sort, but into each ring must be put some paste the size of a hazelnut: this paste is made with egg whites and some powdered sugar, stirred well with a spoon gradually until it is fairly workable; do take care to stir it well.

4. Glacé Marzipan

Take some plain marzipan paste and make it up into rings or whatever shape you want. Then make a glazing with some orange-blossom water and some powdered sugar: get some orange-blossom water, put some sugar into it and mix them well together until this glazing is slightly thick. Dip one side of your marzipan into it, put it on some paper and bake it with a moderate heat applied to the top of the oven. When it has baked, let it cool, then dip the unglazed side [into the glazing] and bake it as before.

5. Marzipan Pie[5.1]

Take some plain marzipan paste and make it up into a pie[5.2] of whatever size you want; dry it in the oven. Into it pour some glazing you have made with orange-blossom water,[5.3] and bake it with a moderate heat on the top of the oven.

6. Glazing for Marzipan Pies

Get an egg white, put some powdered sugar in it and mix it well; add in a little lemon juice and add in sugar until the glazing is rather

---

[2.2] It is the small metal oven that is to be used and not the big baker's oven.

[5.1] Already in the middle of the fifteenth century *The Neapolitan Recipe Collection* (Ann Arbor: University of Michigan Press, 2000) had a *Torta de marzapane* (Recipe 180). A century later, in 1557, Nostradamus published a similar preparation in French (*Tartre de massapan*, ch. 27) which, he wrote, "Hermolaus Barbarus called 'martial loaves', which are used as medicine."

[5.2] *la dressés en tarte*. In this short series of recipes for "pies" the marzipan appears to be used to make shallow cake-like confections which may be glazed and served as such, or else shells that are filled with a variety of other things. Furetière's gloss (*s.v. massepain*) indicates that a *tarte de massepain* is normally, or can be, "twisted" and glazed: *glacé, tortillé*.

[5.3] The making of this sort of glazing follows in the next recipe.

stiff. You can also use glazing made with orange-blossom water and sugar.

7. Orange-Blossom-Marmalade Pie

Get some marzipan paste and with it make up your pies to the size you want; bake them with the bottom of the oven and not the top. Fill them with orange-blossom marmalade and glaze their top, baking the glazing with the upper part of the oven.[7]

8. Apricot-Marmalade Pie

It is made like the previous sort, except that apricot marmalade has to be put in. You can make pies with any sort of marmalade.[8]

9. Apricot Marmalade

Get dry, pitted apricots and pound them in the mortar with some orange-blossom water; add in some powdered sugar until the paste is workable. You can make it up however you like, and bake it in the oven with fire above and below. You can also make pies and shells of it.

10. Marzipans of Cherries, Apples, Plums and Peaches[10]

Any sort of marzipan can be glazed; bake the glazing with the top of the oven. You can also give the marzipan a musk or amber flavour.

11. Orange or Lemon Marzipan

Get confected oranges and grind them up well in a mortar; add to that twice as much Plain Marzipan paste, blending[11] all of this well together. Make it up as you like; bake it in the oven. You can glaze it.

---

[7] *avec le dessus du four* seems to indicate that the pie should be placed next to oven's roof. In the preamble to this book see the author's recommendation that "the oven for cooking your marzipans should be of iron or of red copper."

[8] The term *marmelade* is applied to any sort of compote or mash, usually boiled, strained and unsweetened, of fruit or flowers. See, for instance, Recipes X,21–24 and Chapter XIII.

[10] These fruit-flavoured varieties of marzipan are presumably made by mixing each fruit with Plain Marzipan, as in Recipe 11.

[11] The verb in the text is *pelez-les*, indicating that a shovel-like utensil, perhaps a sort of spatula of wood, is used for the mixing.

12. Marzipan Shaped like a Biscuit

Take the same paste and spread it out with a rolling pin, cut it in the form of a biscuit; do[12] one side of it with a knife and bake it with the top of the oven. When this has cooled, glaze it on the other side and bake the glazing with the top of the oven.

13. Moist Marzipan

After cleaning them, grind some sweet almonds in the mortar, moistening them with some orange-blossom water. When they are well ground, add in the same amount of powdered sugar and some grated fresh lemon peel. Make the marzipan up like a bun or in the form of a biscuit and shape it with a knife; bake it with a low heat on the top of the oven. When cooled, glaze it on the other side and bake it the same way.

14. Curled Marzipan

Grind cleaned almonds and, when they are well ground, for one pound of almonds add in three egg whites and grind the almonds well; slowly add in some powdered sugar until the paste is workable. Load this paste into the syringe and make it up into rings on some paper; bake it with the top of the oven and a moderate heat. When it has cooled, turn it over. It has to be taken off the paper while it is warm.

15. Puffed Marzipan

Grind twenty-five very well-cleaned sweet almonds, moistening them with orangle-blossom water. When the almonds are well ground, add in six egg whites and grind them again; gradually put in some powdered sugar until the paste is workable. Load the paste into the syringe and set it out as rings on some paper; bake it in the oven, where it takes more fire above than below.

16. Jasmine Paste

Get some jasmine blossoms — for example a handful — grind them in a mortar with a little tragacanth gum, and gradually add in some powdered sugar until the paste is workable — you'll need at least a pound of it.

---

[12] *façonnez* — that is, give it a form, an appearance, perhaps a design. Only the other side will be glazed.

You can use a syringe or else work it out.[16] Dry it by the fire or in a stove.

17. Orange-Blossom Paste

This is done the same way.

18. Puffed Paste

Soak some tragacanth gum in orange-blossom water, strain it through a cloth and beat it well in a mortar; gradually put in some powdered sugar until you have made a very workable paste; pound it thoroughly. Spread it out on a table with a rolling pin to the thickness of a *escu blanc*. Make a glazing of some orange-blossom water and some powdered sugar and glaze your paste. Cut it up however you like on some paper and bake it in the oven with a moderate heat above and below.

19. Sugar Shell

With this same paste you can make all sorts of shells and crusts. Do not glaze them. Bake them by the fire.

20. Whore's Farts[20]

Put some egg whites in a mortar and a little orange-blossom water, beating them well; gradually put in some powdered sugar and make up a workable paste. With this paste make small balls the size of a walnut. Put these on some paper and bake them in the oven.

21. Glazed Whore's Farts

Make balls of the same paste and dip them in some egg whites, then dredge them in some powdered sugar. Remove them onto some paper and bake them in the oven.

22. Lemon Paste

This is made with the same paste as the previous sort and by putting lemon gratings into it.

23. Musk Pastilles

Take some of the paste of which the Whore's Farts are made and make some balls of it the size of peas. Put them on some paper and

---

[16] *filler*: "to spin." The image is of strands of wool being spun into a thread.

[20] Compare the name of these delicacies, *Pets de putain*, with that of the fritters in Recipe XXI,1 of *The French Pastry Chef*: *pets d'asne*, "Donkey's Farts."

bake them in the oven with a moderate heat. Mix some musk into your paste.

24. Red Musk Pastilles

Redden your paste with some cochineal or powdered sandalwood.

25. Green Musk Pastilles

Make your paste green with some juice of beet greens.

How to Fold all Sorts of Table Linen
and to make all sorts of shapes with it[*]

1. How to Pleat Linen[1.1]

To fold linen well you have to know how to pleat it and ruffle it correctly. "Pleated and beaten" means to lay out a very white, very smooth, very tighly pleated napkin[1.2] on a very clean table or on a very smooth piece of cardboard that is used only for that purpose. After laying out the napkin there, you have to take it crosswise between the [longer] hems and pleat its lower part, making the folds as small as you can; press them as firmly as you can between your fingers. This is called "folded in cross-billet fashion". You can use it for marking place settings or for hand-washing.

---

[*] This mini-treatise has clearly been appended to the work on confections, following as it does a general alphabetized index to the contents of that work, and the words *Fin de la Table du Confiturier*.

   The illustrated exposition of Mattia Giegher, *Trattato delle piegature*, "Treatise on Linen Folding," (translated in Appendix 6, below) provides a little help in grasping the processes described in the present *Maniere de plier toutes sortes de linge de Table*. The marginal illustrations reproduced here are drawn from Giegher's *Trattato*.

[1.1] Throughout this chapter the modern reader should bear in mind that the table napkins common in La Varenne's day were somewhat larger in size as well as of somewhat thicker and coarser fabric than what we might easily imagine used for the purpose today. A fair amount of strength and energy was required to give the linen the shapes that the author describes in these directions. On the other hand, though, the linen seems to have been stiff enough to retain the folds, pleats, curls and ruffles that are formed in it, as well as the various shapes eventually given to it.

[1.2] *une serviette … bien unie & bien fermée*. The napkin used in this chapter can generally be assumed to be rectangular: ¶ 32 directs how to adapt this rectangle for a folding procedure that must begin with a square; ¶ 31 seems to suggest that a napkin is normally twice as long as it is wide. In only the last two paragraphs is a square napkin, or one that has been squared, expressly meant to be used. The actual dimensions of the common napkin are, however, open to speculation. We should understand them to have been very generous in modern terms — likely greater than a yard or metre in length — so as to allow some of the more extensive folding that is described in this treatise.

When the pleats are tightly together and touching one another, you can shape it into a heart by folding it at the middle and then joining the two ends together at the middle, about four fingers[1.3] in length, then roll the napkin towards the point that will be the heart.[1.4] Or else you can fold it in two or three, or leave it out its full length.

2. How to Ruffle[2.1] a Napkin

When you have pleated the napkin very smoothly and squeezed it very tightly, it has to be ruffled with the finger tips as finely as possible, beginning in the middle [and working outwards], or at one of the ends and working to the other. Care has to be taken to press the folds against one another and to keep them smooth. You can use this sort of folding to make several sorts of place setting by arranging it in different shapes on the bread.[2.2]

3. Folded in a Band

Take a napkin crosswise by the hems and fold it about the width of a thumb; make another fold which goes beyond the hem again by a thumb [an inch]; again make a fold of the same width on the other side,[3] and keep on doing the same for the whole length of the napkin, keeping the fold as smooth as you can. Afterwards, turn the napkin over with your hand and fold it in three by bringing each end towards the middle, then

---

[1.3] This unit of measurement is standard: a "finger" always refers to a finger-width. A similarly "handy" measure was the "thumb"[-width] or *pouce*, an inch.

[1.4] *le cœur.*

[2.1] The verb here is *friser* as distinct from the *plisser* of the previous paragraph. The napkin-folder must master two basic "folds", mentioned in the author's very first sentence: pleating and ruffling, *plisser & friser*. What the author intends by the latter is a gathering of the already-pleated fabric in a series of alternating ridges, so that its appearance takes on the herringbone look described by Matthia Giegher and named by him *spinapesce*.

[2.2] This bread would be a relatively small circular mound of table bread to be broken apart for personal consumption during a meal. There are, however, other loaves mentioned below where the chef is to use *un gros pain long*. Likewise, when the author speaks of a "small" loaf, we may imagine table bread with the form and size of a semi-spherical bun.

[3] These directions are not entirely explicit. It seems that the full pleat between each reverse fold is to be roughly two inches in width.

fold it across the middle. In this way you can make several different place settings.

4. Folded as a Melon

Take a napkin folded in bands, but at each end leave close to half a foot unfolded. Take the napkin again crosswise and pleat it with very fine pleats.[4.1] When setting it on the bread, tuck the two unfolded ends under the bread.

5. A Ruffled Melon

Fold the napkin the same as the previous one and, when it is pleated, take each of the pleats in it one after the other again, lifting them upwards with the point of a pin or a larding-needle. Arrange it on the bread the same way as the other.

6. Double Sea-Shell

Take a napkin, fold it crosswise at the middle and fold one of the halves in bands, leaving at least six fingers unfolded at the end. Then turn it over to the other side and fold this the same. Take the napkin crosswise and pleat it very finely, pressing the pleats tightly. Open the two ends of the napkin that are not folded in bands, put in a loaf of bread and turn the napkin over its full height on the loaf;[6] the two ends should be beneath.

7. Ruffled Double Sea-Shell

Fold the napkin in bands and pleat it the same as the previous one, drawing out the inward folds as in the Ruffled Melon. Set it out on the plate the same as the other one.

8. Plain Sea-Shell

Take a napkin lengthwise, fold about a foot of the napkin under and fold the rest in bands up to six fingers from the hem. Take the napkin crosswise and pleat it very closely. Get a loaf of bread and tuck the two ends of the napkin under it and turn the sea-shell over on the loaf. You can ruffle it the same as the other one.

[4.1] Beginning five inches in from one end and ending five inches before the other.

[6] The banded, pleated napkin is tipped so that the "sea-shell" is standing on the loaf of bread.

9. Ox's Hoof

Fold a napkin lengthwise in three, take the two corners and bring them together making a point in the middle of the napkin. Turn the napkin over and take the two ends and join them together in the middle so that two corners are made on the two sides of the napkin. Join the two corners together very evenly, refold the napkin across its middle. Then open two of its ends, putting the bread inside and put the ends under the bread. Turn the napkin over on the bread and take out one of the corners on the bottom of the plate.[9]

10. As a Cock

Fold a napkin crosswise in two so that the two hems touch; beat it crosswise as tightly as you can and ruffle it very finely. Open the napkin up to within a finger of its middle, again squeezing the folds as hard as you can. Put a large loaf of bread under the middle of the napkin so that the ridge[10.1] of the napkin is in the middle of the loaf. By one of the ends or at the ridge you draw out the head and beak of the cock, which you lift upwards. You can make a comb and wattle on it with some red broadcloth or serge, and its eyes with some red seeds which you can stick on with white wax or some moistened tragacanth gum.[10.2] At the other end of the ridge you draw out the tail, which you lift upwards; on each side of the napkin you form its wings which you lay out properly alongside.

11. The Pheasant

You make the pheasant the same way as the Cock, but you do not make any comb on it and you mark its head and neck with lit-tle flowers of appropriate colours, sticking them on with moistened tragacanth gum. You lengthen its tail and wings more than for the Cock, and keep them straighter.

12. The Hen

You make the Hen the same way as the Cock, but do not make its comb as red or as big, nor its head so raised, and the tail lower down and bigger.

---

[9] The Ox's Hoof will have a splayed base.

[10.1] *l'areste*: the bone or backbone; here, the spine along the fold of the napkin.

[10.2] In some of the pseudo-creatures to be formed from folded napkins, the appendages and details depend extensively upon glue and scrap bits of colourful fabric.

13. Brooding Hen in a Bush

You fold the napkin the same as for the Cock, and you put a large loaf of bread into it. You make the bush with the edges of the napkin which you turn around about the loaf in swirls the size of a fist, here and there making thorns stick out. And make the head and tail [of the Hen] stick out from under the bush.

14. Hen with its Chicks

You fold the napkin the same as for the Cock and set it up on a loaf of bread. You draw out the Hen's little ones from the edges of the napkin and make them come out from under its wings, its stomach and its tail. You can also make some of them on its back. Be careful to form its beak and eyes well.

15. The Chicken

The Chicken is done the same as the Cock, but it calls for a small loaf of bread and hardly any comb, and its tail is not very tall.

16. The Capon

The Capon is done the same as the Cock, but it has to have a bare comb.

17. Two Chickens in a Pie

Fold a napkin crosswise in three and pleat it lengthwise. Ruffle it as finely as you can, then open out the two ends to within a finger of the folds. Under each fold you put a round loaf of bread and you form the edges of the napkin like the edges of a pie. Over those you make the heads of the chickens stick out of the folds that are on the bread.

18. Four Partridges

Fold a napkin crosswise in four, beat it over its length and ruffle it up very finely. Open it to within a finger of the folds and put a small loaf beneath each fold. Form the beak, the tail and the wings of a partridge right on the ridge of each loaf.

19. A Dove Brooding in a Basket

Fold a napkin in the same way as for the Cock, open it and put a loaf of bread beneath the folds. Make the shape of the basket with the edges of the napkin, draw out the dove's head and tail right on the ridge above the basket, with the wings alongside.

20. Turkey Hen

Fold the napkin of the Turkey Hen the same as for the Cock. Put a large loaf of bread beneath it, raise the head a little higher and keep the neck big. Put a bit of red taffeta on its beak, scatter little flowers of different colours on its head and neck. You can make its tail in a round like the peacock's,[20] but do not raise it up so high.

21. The Tortoise

Beat a napkin crosswise, ruffle it very finely and put a round loaf of bread under its middle. Draw out a head from the middle of one of the hems and the tail from the other; draw out the four feet from the four corners of the napkin.

22. The Dog with a Collar

One foot in from one of the hems of the napkin make a band[22.1] an inch wide; beat the napkin over its length and ruffle it, except for the band which you raise up with folds the same as the Ruffled Double Sea-Shell,[22.2] with which you make the collar. Put a large, long loaf beneath its belly and a Queen's loaf[22.3] in its head, which you raise up a little. Draw out the four feet from the four corners of the napkin.

23. Suckling Piglet

Fold the napkin the same as for the Dog, but do not make any bands. Make the head rather long and lower it down, putting a somewhat large loaf of bread in the head and a long one beneath the belly.

24. The Hare

Beat the napkin crosswise and ruffle it very finely. Put a long loaf under the napkin to form the belly, and a small loaf to form the head. Make the four feet with the four corners of the napkin, and keep it as long as you can.

---

[20] Surprisingly there is no effort here among these various folded fowl to represent a peacock.

[22.1] This "band" appears to be a narrow strip of fabric which has been raised by means of a downward fold at each edge.

[22.2] See ¶ 7, above.

[22.3] This particular sort of loaf, a *pain à la reine*, is similar to a modern brioche, a rich bread of relatively small and round shape, suitable also for giving form to the Carp's head of ¶ 28.

25. Two Rabbits

Fold the napkin the same as for the Hare, putting two long loaves beneath it and making a break[25] in the napkin between the two loaves. Don't make the bodies as long as for the Hare, nor the head as large. You can turn one head one way and the other another way.

26. The Hedgehog

Fold a napkin crosswise in bands[26] that are an inch wide, beat it and raise up all of the folds the same as for the Ruffled Sea-Shell. Put a round loaf of bread beneath it, making your napkin quite round. Draw out the four feet from the corners of the napkin, and make a small head.

27. The Pike

Make a band a half-foot wide across the width of the napkin. Bring the hem up to touch the edge of the band, beat the napkin over its full length and ruffle it. In place of the band make about four fingers of ruffling and leave another four fingers without a ruffle; again ruffle another four fingers and, to form the tail, next to the hem leave four fingers without any ruffle. Put a long loaf of bread under the napkin and arrange the edges carefully. Put another loaf into the band which isn't ruffled, from which band you form the mouth.

28. The Carp

Beat a napkin crosswise; ruffle about half a foot of it, leave five or six fingers without rippling, then again ruffle another similar amount, leave another similar a-mount without rippling, and at the end leave two or three fingers without rippling in order to make the tail. Put a long loaf of bread under the napkin to make the body and a Queen's loaf[28] to make the head.

29. The Turbot

Beat a napkin crosswise and ruffle it for up to four fingers at one end. Put a big round flat loaf of bread under the napkin at the end which

---

[25] This *séparation* is not a matter of ripping the napkin in two but merely of hiding the fact that both rabbits are formed from the same napkin.

[26] Compare this with the use of a single "band" for the Dog with a Collar, above, ¶ 22.

[28] As in ¶ 22, this bread is a sort of brioche.

isn't folded and turn it round about the napkin. Make a little head and a little tail.

30. The Brill

The Brill is done the same as the Turbot.[30]

31. The Mitre

Fold a napkin crosswise at its middle, bringing the two [end] hems together. Refold the four corners of the napkin inwards so that they make a point in the middle[31] that is a thumb or so in width. Beat the napkin over its length, make it very fine except at the point that you leave without ruffling. Open the napkin at the point, put a round loaf of bread into the bottom of the napkin and close it up again; raise the point up half-opened. You can put a long loaf in it in order to keep it straight.

32. Holy Ghost Cross

Take a square napkin — or else fold one end over so that it is square — fold the four corners of the napkin towards the centre making sure that they touch snugly and evenly. Turn the napkin over, folding it the same way; turn it over once again and fold it the same way, and the cross is properly formed. You can put a round loaf of bread beneath it.

33. Cross of Lorraine

Fold the napkin the same as the previous one and turn it over onto its other side. Then draw the point in the middle of the napkin back to the outer four points. You can put the round loaf of bread within the cross or on the napkin.

---

[30] We may well wonder whether animated table conversation was generated by an effort to distinguish one's Brill from one's neighbour's Turbot.

[31] This appears to indicate that a standard napkin is twice as long as it is wide.

Appendices

T he first five of the six Appendices here list, in English and alphabetically, the various elements of the cookery found in the *Cuisinier françois*, the *Pastissier françois* and the *Confiturier françois*. Appendix 6 is a translated excerpt from Mattia Giegher's *Trattato delle piegature*.

1. Ingredients
   a) Plants
   b) Land and air creatures
   c) Water creatures
2. Preparations
3. Procedures
4. Kitchen equipment
   a) Fixtures
   b) Recipients, vessels
   c) Implements, utensils, materials
   d) Fuel
5. Weights and Measures
   a) Weights
   b) Volume measures (liquid and dry)
   c) Quantities
   d) Sizes, distances
   e) Time
   f) Heats

In these Appendices references indicate the work, chapter and recipe number (if there is one). The works are identified by the following *sigla*:   Cook = *The French Cook*

Confections = the concluding chapter in *The French Cook*: Sundry Sorts of Dry and Moist Confections

Pastry Chef = *The French Pastry Chef*

Confectioner = *The French Confectioner*

Linen = the chapter titled "How to Fold all Sorts of Table Linen" which is appended to *The French Confectioner*.

Where no recipe number appears after the Roman numeral identifying a chapter, the head word is not found in a particular recipe: either there are no numbered recipes in that chapter or else the term is found here and there throughout the chapter. Where a zero appears rather than a recipe number (*e.g.* XXI,0), the reference is to a passage at the beginning of a chapter, usually preliminary to the first recipe proper. The various paragraphs in the treatise on linen folding are indicated with a ¶ before their number. A number following the word "passim" indicates an approximate frequency of a commonly used term.

The French names of the named dishes or preparations as they are found in the three books are printed in bold type. Whether generic or particular, if such names are primarily the name of a determining ingredient they will be found in Appendix 1. Ingredients, in the entry for that particular ingredient; otherwise they appear in Appendix 2. Preparations.

Words that La Varenne used in feminine or plural forms for reasons of context or syntax may be represented here in the masculine singular. Similarly verbs generally appear in the infinitive.

The following reference works, identified in these Appendices by the *siglum* that is indicated in each case, have proved useful.

Acad: *Le Grand Dictionnaire de l'Académie Françoise*, 2nd edn., 2 vols. (Paris: Jean Baptiste Coignard, 1695).

Cotg: Randle Cotgrave, *A Dictionarie of the French and English Tongues* (London: Adam Islip, 1611; facs. reprod. Columbia: University of South Carolina Press, 1950). In his translation of the *Cuisinier françois*, I.D.G. depends much upon Cotgrave.

DEI: Carlo Battisti and Giovanni Alessio, *Dizionario Etimologico Italiano*, 5 vols. (Florence: Barbèra, 1975).

Delices: Nicolas de Bonnefons, *Les delices de la campagne* (Amsterdam: Jean Blaev, 1661; first publ. 1654).

DMF: Algirdas Julien Greimas and Teresa Mary Keane, *Dictionnaire du moyen français. La Renaissance* (Paris: Larousse, 1992).

DuCange: Charles du Fresne, Sieur DuCange, *Glossarium mediæ et infimæ latinitatis*, suppl. D.P. Charpentier, nouv. éd. Léopold Favre (Niort, 1883–87; repr. Paris, 1937–38).

Encyc: Denis Diderot, Jean le Rond d'Alembert, *Encyclopédie ou Dictionnaire raisonné des sciences, des arts et des métiers* (Paris: Briasson, David, Le-Breton, Durand, 1751 ff).

Escoffier: August Escoffier, *The Escoffier Cook Book. A guide to the fine art of cookery* (New York: Crown Publishers, 1969)

FEW: Walter von Wartburg, *Französisches Etymologisches Wörterbuch* (Leipzig, Berlin: Teubner, 1934 ff).

FitzG: Theodora FitzGibbon, *The Food of the Western World* (New York: Quadrangle/The New York Times Book Co., 1976).

Fur: Antoine Furetière, *Dictionnaire universel* (LaHaye & Rotterdam: Arnaut & Reinier Leers, 1690). Furetière's glosses seem often to be inspired by what he has read in La Varenne.

Godefroy: Frédéric Godefroy, *Dictionnaire de l'ancienne langue française* (Paris: F. Vieweg, 1881–1902; repr. Vaduz: Kraus, 1965).

Huguet: Edmond Huguet, *Dictionnaire de la langue française du seizième siècle* (Paris: Didier, Champion, 1925).

I.D.G.: *The French Cook. Prescribing the way of making ready of all sorts of Meats, Fish and Flesh, with the proper Sauces, either to procure Appetite, or to advance the power of Digestion. Also the Preparation of all Herbs and Fruits, so as their naturall Crudities are by art opposed; with the whole skil of Pastry-work.* Together with a Treatise of Conserves, both dry and liquid, *a la mode de France.* ... Written in French by Monsieur De La Varenne, Clerk of the Kitchin to the Lord Marquesse of *Uxelles,* and now Englished by *I. D. G.* (London: Charles Adams, 1653). At the end of his preliminary material and just before the beginning of his first chapter, La Varenne's English translator has provided a brief glossary of terms which he has left in their original French form or which, though translated, are explained.

Larousse: Pierre Larousse, *Grand Dictionnaire Universel* (Paris, 1875).

Marnette: *The French Pastery-Cooke. The Perfect Cook being the most exact directions for the making all kind of Pastes, with the perfect way teaching how to Raise, Season, and make all sorts of Pies, Pasties, Tarts, and Florentines, &c. now practised by the most famous and expert Cooks, both French and English.* ... *by Mounsieur Marnettè* [*sic*] (London: Nath. Brooks at the Angel in Cornhil, 1656). The title page shows also the spellings Angell, Cornhill and Brooke.

NLG: Prosper Montagné, *New Larousse Gastronomique* (London: Hamlyn, 1977).

OCF: Alan Davidson, *The Oxford Companion to Food* (Oxford: Oxford University Press, 1999).

Pegolotti: Francesco Balducci Pegolotti, *La Pratica della Mercatura*, ed. Allan Evans (Cambridge, Mass.: Mediæval Academy of America, 1936).

RDH: Alain Rey, *et al.*, *Le Robert Dictionnaire historique de la langue française*, 2 vols. (Paris: Dictionnaires Le Robert, 1992).

Rich: P. Richelet, *Dictionnaire françois, contenant les mots et les choses, plusieurs nouvelles remarques sur la langue françoise: ses expressions propres, figurées & burlesques, la prononciation des mots les plus difficiles, le genre des noms, le regime des verbes: avec les termes les plus connus des arts & des sciences. Le tout tiré de l'usage et des bons auteurs de la langue françoise* (Geneva: Jean Herman Widerhold, 1680; repr. Geneva: Slatkine, 1970).

TLL: *Thesaurus linguæ latinæ*, 10 vols. (Leipzig: Teubner, *c.* 1900).

TLF: *Trésor de la langue française*, 16 vols. (Paris: CNRS, Gallimard, 1971– 1994).

Tobler: Adolf Tobler & Erhard Lommatzsch, *Altfranzösisches Wörterbuch* (Berlin: Weidmann, 1915– ; repr. and currently Wiesbaden: Steiner, 1955–).

Tré: *Dictionnaire universel françois et latin contenant la signification et la définition tant des mots de l'une et l'autre langue, avec leurs différens usages, que des termes propres de chaque Etat & chaque Profession … vulgairement appellé Dictionnaire de Trévoux*, 3 vols. (Trévoux, 1704); many subsequent editions including, in 6 vols., Paris: Delaune, 1743.

1. Ingredients

We append here a listing of everything handled in La Varenne's kitchen, whether an edible ingredient or (occasionally) something separated from a foodstuff and discarded as non-edible. We indicate as well the French term used in La Varenne's text. Where appropriate, we offer a tentative description of a foodstuff as the author probably knew it.

This Appendix 1 is in three divisions: a) Plants, minerals; b) Animals, fowl (and their products); c) Water creatures.

If the name of a dish or a preparation incorporates the name of an ingredient, it will normally be found in this Appendix 1, in bold typeface, in the entry for that ingredient. Otherwise the names of generic preparations and specific dishes (*e.g. pottage* and **Queen's Pottage**) will be found in Appendix 2, below.

a) Plants, minerals

agaric, St. George's agaric (*Tricholoma sævum*), Cook XIV,25, 28; XIX,1, 3; XXI,6, 15, 17, 21; XXX,38; Past XXXIV,12 *mousserons*; *Delices*, 111: "*C'est une petite espece de Champignons tous blancs qui ne viennent qu'au mois de May, cachez sous la mousse (d'où ils ont pris leur nom)*"; Fur: "*Champignon*. "Les meilleurs champignons sont les mousserons, qui viennent aux premieres pluyes d'Avril, qui ne sont point dommageables"; Cotg: "*Mouscheron*. A mushrome, or Toad-stoole"; see also mushroom

almonds, Cook III,11 (passim 58); Confectioner XI,2; XVI,14 *amandes, amendes*; sweet almonds, Pastry Chef IV,2, 3; IX,7, 10; XV,1; XXI,2; XXV,8; XXVI,0; Confectioner IV,1; VI,1; VII,15, 16; XV,1, XVI,1, 13, 15 *amandes, amendes douces*; Almond Cake Pastry Chef XV,9 **Gasteau aux amendes**; see also cake, confections, dough, dragées and tourte in Appendix 2 and to clean in Appendix 3
—— almond bouillon, almond broth, white bouillon, Cook III,6, 13; XV,7,

12, 28, 40, 42; XXV,0, 2, 10, 19, 25 *bouillon (blanc) d'amandes*; a recipe for the preparation, Cook XXIV,4; see also bouillon (white)
—— almond purée, Cook XV,33 *purée d'amandes*; almond paste, Pastry Chef XXVI,0 *paste d'amandes*
—— almond milk, Cook XV,58; XXIX,3; Pastry Chef XIII,0 *laict d'amandes*
—— almond cream, Cook XXX,46 *crême d'amandes*; see also tourte in Appendix 2
—— almond oil, Confectioner VII,15, 16 *huile amende*

alum, Confectioner II,2 *allun*

amber, ambergris (a flavouring agent), Cook VIII,18; IX,66; Confectioner Preface; I,0; IV,1, 2, 4; VII,15; XV,13 *ambre*; Cook IX,79; Pastry Chef IX,15; XXXIV,15 *ambre gris*; see Pegolotti, *s.v. ambra*; see also to flavour in Appendix 3

anise, aniseed, Cook V,8; IX,0; XXIII,7; Confections,65; Confectioner IV,4, 15; XV,6 *asnis, anis*; Verdun Anise, Confectioner XV,6, 8 **(Pois sucrez ou) Anis de Verdun**; Cotg: "*Anis*. The

Sauce, Cook XIX,20 **Asperges à la sauce blanche**; Creamed Asparagus, Cook VIII,88; XIX,21 **Asperges à la cresme**; Asparagus in Green Peas, Cook XXVIII,31 **Asperges en pois verds**; see also omelet, Appendix 2

balotin: see lemon

barberry, Confectioner Preface; IV,14; VII,18; X,14 *(grains d', pepins de l')espine-vinette, épine-vinette*; Cotg: "As *Espine benoiste*. The Barberrie-tree"; Fur: "L'*espine-vinette* est un petit arbre qui porte des fruits rouges fort astringents"; see also compote, waters in Appendix 2

—— barberry juice, Cook Confections 49 *jus d'epine-vinette*

bay, bay-laurel, Cook V,66; VI,18; XIV,2; XVI,83; XXI,1; XXII,2, 3, 5, 6, 12, 14, 15; XXIII,7; Pastry Chef VII,1–4, 20 *(feuille(s) de) laurier*; sprig of bay, laurel Confectioner IV,5 *branche de laurier*

beet greens: see chard

beetroot, Cook VIII,29; XX,9; XXII,7; XXVI,76; XXX,1–3 *bettes-raves*; Cotg: "*Bette-rave*. A kind of delicate red Parsenip, which, boyled, yeelds a sweet vermillion sap"; I.D.G.: "Red beets, or red parsnips" (XXII,7)

biscuit, Cook VIII,79; XV,22; Pastry Chef IX,3, 7, 10; X; XV,1; XXV (passim); XXVI; XXIX,11; XXXIV,11; Confectioner XVI,1 *biscuit*; *RDH*: "Depuis le XVIIe siècle le mot s'applique aussi à un gâteau sec fait avec des œufs, de la farine et du sucre" (1660); see also Appendix 2

blossoms: see orange

blanquette: see pears, wine

borage, Cook XV,1; Pastry Chef XXXII,2; XXXIII,11; Confectioner V,2; XIV,6 *bouroche, bourache*; see syrup, Appendix 2

—— borage blossoms, Confectioner XIV,6 *fleurs de bouroche*; Candied

Borage Blossoms, Confectioner XIV,6 **Fleurs de bouroche candie**

bouquet: see fennel, herbs, sage

bread (as an ingredient), Cook (passim) *pain*; see also varieties of bread in Appendix 2

—— coarse bread, Cook III, 43; Pastry Chef VII,1, 2 *gros pain*; Cotg: "*Gros pain*. Course browne bread"; Marnette: "houshold bread," "brown bread or Rye bread"

—— white bread, Cook V,8 *pain blanc*

—— bread crust, Cook III,43; XV,1, 25, 52, 55; XX,17, 18; XXIX,1; Pastry Chef *entameure (de pain), croute*; crust, especially grated crust, Cook V,4, 51 (passim 23) *chapelure (de pain)*; Cotg and I.D.G.: "*Chapelure*. Chippings of bread"; Fur: "Partie qu'on retranche des crousts de pain quand on le chapele";

—— crustless (loaf of) bread, crumb, breadcrumbs, Cook III,10 (passim 39) *mie (de pain)*; Cotg: "*Mie de pain*. The crumme, or pith of bread"

—— fried bread, Cook V,31; XV,17, 24, 47; XXV,14, 16; XXIX,2 *pain frit*

—— toast, pieces of toast, Cook VI,20; VII,4; VIII,46 (passim) *rosties, roties*; Cotg: "*Rostie*. A toast"; Rich: "Petit morceau de pain qui est délié & coupé en tranche, qu'on fait sécher devant le feu, ou sur le gril sous lequel il y a de la braise & qu'on trempe en suite dans du vin, ou dans quelque liqueur"; burnt bread, Cook XXVII,0 *pain bruslé*

broccoli, cabbage broccoli, Cook XXIX,9; Confectioner XII,1 *brocolis, brocolis de choux*; La Varenne: "Ce sont de rejettons de choux verds"

broome, Confectioner VI,4 *genests*; Cotg: "*Genest*. Broome; (especially that kind therof which is called, Bastard Spanish Broome)"

bugloss, Cook XV,1; Pastry Chef XXIX,6; XXXIII,11; Confectioner V,2 *buglose*; see syrup, Appendix 2

butter: see section b) below

or *Marons*. They are the biggest kind
of chestnuts"; Cotg: "*Chastaigne*. A
Chesnut"; see compote, glacé preparations in Appendix 2

chicory, endive, Cook III,2, 33; IV,7;
XV,1, 46; XXII,10; XXX,13 *chicorée,
chichorée*; see also marmalade, omelet
in Appendix 2

—— white chicory, Cook III,2, 33; IV,6;
XX,16; Pastry Chef XXXIV,7 *chicorée,
cichorée blanche*; White Chicory Cook
XX,16 **Chicorée blanche**; see the note
in Cook III,2

—— wild chicory, Pastry Chef XXXIII,14
chichorée sauvage

chippings: see crust

chives (*Allium Schoenoprasum*) or welsh
onion, scallion, (*Allium fistulosum*)
Cook IV,2 (passim 90); Pastry Chef
VII,8, 15, 23; XXIX,6; XXXI,2;
XXXII,1 *siboule(s)*; Pastry Chef VII,18;
XXIX,2, 7; XXXII,2; XXXIII,13 *ciboulette*; Cotg: "*Ciboule*. A Chiboll,
or hollow Leeke"; I.D.G.: "*Chibols*.
They are sives, or young small greene
onions"; Fur: "*Ciboule*. Petit oignon
qui a peu de teste, qu'on mange en
salade, & dont on fait des sauces. *Ciboulette*. Petite ciboule servant aux
mêmes usages". The translation of *siboule* and *ciboulette* is problematic.
Occasionally (as in Cook V,72, XVI,18,
XX,5 and XXVI,85) when it is stuck
with cloves, or wherever a recipe specifies one, two or three *siboules*, the bulb
is clearly being used and "scallion"
or "spring onion" is the most likely
modern sense. Often the leaves seem
called for by a recipe (as in Cook II
and V,2 where they compose a *bouquet*
along with parsley and thyme, or in
Cook XV,39 where La Varenne writes,
"fine herbs, such as parsley, *siboules*,
thyme"); in those places "chives" would
be a reasonable rendering of the author's intentions. Cotgrave (quoted
above) implies that in 1611 the interest in a *siboule* is only in its tubu-
lar, leek-like leaves. An illustration

in Furetière (*s.v. brin*) reads, "Il faut
mettre deux ou trois brins de ciboulette
dans cette salade." Cf. onion, garlic;
see also shallots; and omelet, Appendix
2.

choke: see artichoke

cinnabar: see vermillion

cinnamon, Cook VIII,79; XIX,16; XX,13;
XXIV,4; XXVI,87; Confections,25; Pas-
try Chef II,1; VII,1–3, 7, 12, 17; IX,1,
6–12, 14, 15; X; XI,1; XV,3; XXIII,1;
XXV,4, 8; XXIX,1, 3; XXX,3, 10;
XXXI,3; XXXIII,2, 5, 25; XXXIV,14;
Confectioner IV,1, 2, 16; X,12; XI,19,
26; XV,4 *canelle*; pieces of cinna-
mon, Cook XVII,17 *canelles*; Marnette:
"Mace"; see waters in Appendix 2

—— candied cinnamon (sticks), Pastry Chef XV,9; XXVI; Confectioner
XV,4 *canella, canela*; Fur: "*Cannelat*.
Morceau de cannelle entouré de sucre,
qui forme une espece de dragée"; see
also candied foods, Appendix 2

citron (*Citrus medica*), Cook Confections,22; Confectioner IX,6 *ponsif, pon-
siere*; Cotg: "*Poncille*. The Assyrian
Citron; a fruit as big as two big Ley-
mons; and of a verie good smell, but of
a faint-sweet, or wallowish taste; *Poncire*. A Pome-Citron"; *NLG*: "*Poncire*:
Genre de citron presque sans jus mais à
peau très épaisse que l'on confisait"

cloves, whole cloves, Cook XIX,16;
XX,11; XXIII,7; Confections,25; Pastry Chef II,1; VII,1–4; IX,6; XXIX,2,
9; XXXII,2; Confectioner IV,1, 2, 5;
XI,17, 19 *clou(s,x) de girofle, clou(s,x)
de giroffle* (the word *girofle, giroffle* is
never found alone); Cook III,1 passim
57); Confectioner XI,18 *clou, cloux*;
used for sticking into onions (Cook
V,46, passim), into scallions (Cook
V,72; XVI,18; XX,5; XXVI,85), into
tuna (Cook XVI,83), etc.

cochineal, a scarlet or crimson dye derived from a particular dried, pulver-
ized insect, Confectioner II,2; XIII,9;

fruit: mashed fruit, Confectioner Pref *marmalade*

galingale (grated) (*Cyperus longus*), Confectioner IV,4 *(poudre de) cypre*; Cotg: "*Cyprés*. The Cyprus tree; or Cyprus wood; Cypere; Cyperus, or Cypresse, Galingale (a kind of reed)"; *Cyperus longus* is the scientific name of galingale

garlic, Cook V,29; VIII,46; XIV,2; Pastry Chef VII,5 *ail*

ginger, Cook V,8; Pastry Chef II,1; XXIX,9; Confectioner IV,1, 2 *gingembre*

gold leaf, Confectioner XIII,13 *or en feüille*

gooseberries: see currants, above

gourd, Pastry Chef IX,10 *courge*

grapes, Cook XXII,40 *raisins*; see also Grape Confection in Appendix 2

—— currants, Cook XIV,36; Pastry Chef VII,3 (passim 28) *raisin de Corinthe*; Cotg: "*Raisin de Corinthe*. Currans, or small Raisins"; Fur: "Le *raisin de Corinthe* est un raisin delicieux & sucré dont le grain est fort menu & pressé, & la grappe sans pepins"; see also the entry for currants (red, green), above

—— Damascus raisins (sun-dried), Pastry Chef IX,12, 14 *raisins de Damas*; Cotg: "*Raisins de Damas*. The best, and greatest kind of Raisins of the Sunne" [i.e. sun-dried grapes: raisins]; Fur (*s.v. Raisin*): "Le *damas* est un excellent raisin à manger, dont la grappe [bunch] est fort grosse & longue, le grain tres-gros, long & ambré, qui n'a qu'un pepin. Il y en a de blanc, & de rouge"

—— muscat grapes, Confectioner XI,24; XII,15, 16, 17 *muscat*; Cotg [adj. only]: "*Cerise muscate*. The Muske (a delicate) cherrie; Raisin muscat: the Muscadine Grape, or Muscadine Raisin"

—— verjuice grapes, Cook III,31 (passim 98); Confections,18, 19; *verjus*; Confectioner V,5; XI,25 *verjus*; Cotg: "*Verjus*.

Veriuyce; especially that which is made of sowre, and unripe grapes; also, the grapes whereof it is made"; *Delices*, 74: "*La Bicane blanche, ou Bourdela est le meilleur Raisin à faire Verjus*"; see also verjulce, below

—— verjuice mash, Cook XVII,7; XVIII,3; XX,5; Pastry Chef VII,6, 8, 9, 16, 20; IX,9; XXXIV,3 *verjus de grain, en grain*; Pastry Chef VII,21 *verjus en grain*; Pastry Chef VII,21 *verjus pilé*; Cotg: see above; Marnette: "Verjuyce in the Grape"; see also verjuice, below

gratin, Cook XX,2 *gratin*; Cotg: "The remnant of childrens pap, left in, or sticking to, the bottome of the skellet wherein it was boyled"; *RDH*: "Partie d'un mets qui s'attache au fond d'un récipient et qu'il faut gratter, racler pour le détacher" (1564); I.D.G.: "*Grattin*. It is that which doth sticke to the bason or pipkin, when pappe is made; or else a kind of skin which gathereth about, or at the top of the pappe, when it is sodden enough"

gum, gum arabic, Cook Confections,31 *gomme*; Cotg: "*Gomme*. Gumme Arabicke; comes from the shrub Acacia, the Ægyptian thorne"

—— tragacanth gum, gum dragon Cook Confections,51, 52, 53; Pastry Chef XXV,8; Confectioner II,3; XVI,16, 18; Linens 10, 11 *gomme adragan, gome adragant, gomme contragan*; Marnette: "Gum cantraga"; Cotg: "*Sang de dragon*. Dragons-blood; is not (as ignorant people imagine) the bloud of a Dragon crusht to death by an Elephant, but the Gumme of the Dragon tree opened, or bruised in the dog-daies; also, Bloudwort, red Patience, bloudie Patience (an hearbe)"; the term *adragant* is a corruption of the Greek and Latin *tragacantha*, literally "goat's thorn"; for a description and the commerce of this, see Pegolotti, p. 376, *s.v. draganti*

legumes, *legumes*; I.D.G.: "They are all kinds of pot hearbs, as also any fruit growing in a garden, as cowcombers, artichocks, cabbidge, meloens, pompkins, &c"

lemon, Cook III,5 (passim 114), Confectioner IV,1 (passim) *citron*; lemon slice, piece, Cook III,1; V,41 (passim); Pastry Chef VII,17; XXXII,1; XXXIII,17 *tranche, morceau de citron*; Lemon Salad, Cook VIII,34; XXX,42 **Salade de citron**; Lemon Loaves, Pastry Chef XXVIII,1, 2 **Pains de citron**; Lemon Preserve, Cook Confections,6 **Conserve de citrons**; Lemon Marzipan, Confectioner XVI,11 **Machepains de citrons**; Cotg: "A Citron, Pome-Citron"; see also biscuit, candied foods, compote, confection, dragées, fingers, pastes, pralines, preserve, syrup, waters in Appendix 2

―― balotin, Confectioner IX,6 *ballotin*; *Encyc* (II, 48b): "*Balotin*. Terme de Jardinage, espece de citronnier"; Larousse: "*Balotin*. Bot. Variété de citronnier"; FitzG: "The *Citrus Balontinum* is a kind of orange tree with leaves that have serrated edges. The fruit is not unlike a lemon and is used in the same way"

―― lemon pulp, Confectioner IX,6; X,10 *chair de citron*; Lemon Pulp (confection) Confectioner IX,6 **Chair de citron**

―― lemon juice, Cook III,36 (passim); Pastry Chef I,6; X; XXV,8; XXVIII,1; XXX,3; XXXI,3; XXXIV,1, 15; Confectioner IV,2, 7, 9; VII,7, 9, 11, 18; X,10, 11; XVI,6 *jus de citron*

―― lemon peel, zest, Cook V,21 (passim); Pastry Chef VII,3, 14; IX,1–4, 6–13, 15; X; XV,9; XVII; XXI,1, 2; XXV,8; XXVI; XXVIII,1, 2; XXIX,4, 11; XXXIII,5, 6, 19; XXXIV,5, 10, 11, 13, 14; Confectioner Preface; IV,4; VI,2; VII,12; XI,19; XVI,13 *escorce,*

écorce, ecosse, zestes de citron; lemon-peel gratings, Cook Confections,6; Confectioner VII,8; XVI,22 *rapure de citron*; Confectioner X,8 *la peau des citrons*; candied lemon peel, Pastry Chef VII,3 (passim); Confectioner Pref *escorce de citron confit*

―― a lemon lardoon, Cook Confections,25 *un lardon de citron confit*

lentils, Cook XXV,44; XXVI,84 *lentilles*; Confectioner XV,9 *nantille*

lettuce, Cook III,17, 25, 27; VIII,96; XV,1, 15, 46, 52; XX,4; XXII,5; XXV,13; XXIX,1, 16; XXX,43; Pastry Chef IX,7; XXIX,6; XXXII,2; XXXIII,11; Confectioner XII,1 *laictuë(s), laittuës, letues*; Rich: "Sorte d'herbe froide, humide & rafraichissante dont il y a de plusieurs sortes"; Lettuce Pottage Cook XXV,13 **Potage de laittuës**; Stuffed Lettuce Pottage, Cook XV,15 **Potage de laictuës farcies**

―― head lettuce, Cook VIII,96; XXII,5 *laitues pommees*; Cotg: "*Laictue pommée*. Cabbage Lettuce, loafed Lettuce, headed Lettuce"

―― romaine lettuce, leaf lettuce, Confectioner XII,1 *letuës romaines montées*; Rich: "*Laituë Romaine* qui est la meilleure de toutes"

lily stamens (a yellow colourant), Confectioner II,4; XIII,10 *brains jaunes, fleurs de lys (preparées)*

lime, Confectioner IX,6 *limon*

macaroon: see Appendix 2

mace, Confectioner IV,1, 2, 5 *(feuilles de) massis*; Fur: "*Macis*. Escale ou écorce rouge, qui est l'enveloppe de la noix muscade, quand elle est meure. Les Hollandais entre leurs espisceries font grand trafic de macis, qui est une droque des plus estimées."

mallow (common) (*Malva sylvestris*), Pastry Chef IX,7; XXXIII,11 *mauves*

marigold blossom, Pastry Chef III *fleur de soucy*

marjoram, Cook Confections,38 *marjolaine*

mash: see apples, cherries

marzipan, orange preparations, pastes, pie, preserve, waters in Appendix 2

—— orange blossoms, orange-blossom water, Cook VIII,34, 38, 66, 79, 80, 82; XIX,10; XXI,31, 37; XXX,26; Confections,11, 14, 30, 31; Pastry Chef IX,15, X; XXI,1; Confectioner IV,1 (passim) *(eau de) fleur(s) d'orange*; orange blossom buds, Confectioner XIV,5 *fleur d'orange en bouton*; Candied Orange Blossoms, Confectioner XIV,5 **Fleurs d'orange candie**; Orange-Blossom Paste, Confectioner XVI,17 **Paste de felurs d'orange**; Moist Orange-Blossom Conserve, Confectioner VII,2 **Fleur d'orange liquide**; Conserve of Orange-Blossom Water, Confectioner VII,3 **Conserve d'eau de fleurs d'orange**; see also pie in Appendix 2

—— orange juice, Cook V,42 (passim); Pastry Chef XXX,3; XXXIV,1, 15; Confectioner IV,9; X,13 *jus d'orange*

—— orange peel, zest, Cook V,21 (passim); Confectioner VI,2; IX,1; XI,17 *escorce, écorce, zeste(s), la peau d'orange*; Orange Zests (confections), Confectioner IX,4 **Zestes d'orange**

—— orange pulp, Confectioner X,10 *chair d'orange*

—— balotin: see lemon

orchil, archil (a colourant from a lichen), Cook Confections,13 *tourne sol*; Fur: "*Tournesol*, est . . . une poudre bleuë qui sert à colorer l'empois [starch], qui aide à blanchir le linge. . . . L'urine recente & l'eau de vie rougissent le tournesol"

orris powder, Cook Confections,13 *poudre d'Iris*; Cotg: "*Iris de Florence*. The Flowerdeluce of Florence, whose root yeelds our Orice powder"; this plant is the orris (*Iris germanica*, var. *florentina*)

parsley, Cook II; III,43 (passim 158); Pastry Chef VII,1 (passim 30) *persil*

—— parsley root, Cook III,2; XXV,21 *racine de persil*

parsnip, Cook XV,37; XX,6; XXV,32; XXVI,79; XXIX,5; XXX,15, 16 *panets*; Cotg: "*Panaiz*. A certaine root thats lesse, and ranker, then the ordinarie Parsenip; otherwise resembling it, and oft mistaken for it"; see also carrots

paste (of fruit, nuts), Confections,10, 25 (passim) *paste*

pastry: see dough in Appendix 2, below

Pastry-Chef's Cream: see Appendix 2

peaches, Confectioner X,16; XVI,10 *pesches, peches*; see also pastes, Appendix 2

—— apricot peaches, Confectioner XI,21 *avant péches*; Cotg: "*Avant-Pesche*. Th'Avant-peach, or hastie peach; russet on one side, and red to the Sunne-ward, yet bigger than th'ordinarie red Peach; it comes timely, and eats delicately; and therefore some call so, the greatest kind of Abrecock [apricot]" (the *OED* glosses *hasty* as "ripening early"); Fur: "*Pesche*. La premiere & la plus hastive est l'*avantpesche* musquée, qui est blanche & petite, douce et sucrée"

—— clingstone peaches, Confectioner XI,22 *pavies*; Cotg: "*Pavie*. A bastard Peach, or fruit like a Peach"; clingstone peaches (small), Confectioner XI,22 *alberges*; Cotg: "*Alberge*. A kind of small Peach"; Fur: "*Pesche*. L'*alberge* est jaune dedans & dehors, de mediocre grosseur, d'excellent goust, un peu platte; *Alberge*. Espece de pesche precoce, & qui vient devant les autres, qui est jaune et ferme: en Latin *Persicum minus, alberga*"; glossed in *DMF*

—— melocoton peach, Confectioner XI,22 *mirlicotons*; Cotg: "*Mirelicoton: mirecoton*. The delicate yellow Peach, called a Melicotonie"; Fur: "*Mircoton*. Fruit qui est une espece de péche. Il vient de l'Espagnol *mirlicotones*"; this fruit is the result of a peach grafted on a quince

—— Corbeil peaches, common peaches, Confectioner I,23; XII,9 *pêches de Corbeil*; Cotg: "*Corbeil*. The name of a

IX,15; X,18; XV,3; XXV,6; XXIX11; XXXIII,17, 18; Confectioner Preface; VII,5, 6; X,18; XV,3 *pistaches*; Pistachio Cream, Cook XXX,47 **Cresme de pistaches**; see also biscuit, compote, confection, dragées, preserves Appendix 2

plums (fresh), Cook Confections,16; Pastry Chef IX,9; Confectioner XIII,11 *prunes*; Plum Paste Confectioner XIII,11 **Paste de prunes**

—— brignol plums, Cook III,15; XXV,28; XXVIII, 24; Confectioner Preface; X,16 *brugnolles, prunes de brugnoles, brignolles*; Cotg: "*Brignon*. The name of a excellent plum, whereof there be two kinds, a bigger and a lesse"; I.D.G.: "*Brignols*. They are a kind of plummes which grow beyond Sea"; Fur: "*Brignole*. Espece de prune excellente qu'on seche, & qu'on envoye à Paris de la ville de Brignolles en Provence. La *prune de brugnolle* est une espece de perdigon qui a la chair jaune, & est bonne cruë, seche, & en marmelade"; see glacé preparations, Appendix 2

—— imperial plums, Confectioner XI,11, 12; XII,10, 11 *prunes imperiales*; Fur: "*Prune Imperiale* est la plus grosse de toutes les prunes, & qui est d'une figure oblongue"

—— perdrigon plums, Confectioner XII,12 *prunes de perdrigon*; white perdrigon plum Confectioner XI,13, 14, 16 *perdrigon blanc*; red perdrigon plum Confectioner XI,15 *perdrigon rouge*; Cotg: "*Perdigonne*. The name of an excellent plumme"

—— red damson plums, Confectioner XI,16 *prunes de Damas rouges*; Cotg: "*Prune de Damas*. A Damson, or Damask Plumme"

—— lilevert plums, Confectioner XII,12 *prunes de lilevert*; Fur: "La *prune d'Isleverte* est tres-longue, & menuë,

qui demeure toûjours verte. Elle est fort estimée"

—— myrobalan, cherry, mirabelle plums, Confectioner XI,22 *mirabolans*; Cotg: "*Myrabolan*. An East-Indian Plumme called, the Myrobalan Plumme, whereof there be divers kinds distinguished by severall names . . . "; FitzG: "*Myrobalan* (*Rosaceæ*), the name given to varieties of plum indigenous to the East Indies but now grown widely in Alsace and Lorraine, and to a lesser extent in other parts of France where they are known as *mirabelles*"

—— prunes, Cook XXVI,88; XXVIII,23; XXX,24; Pastry Chef IX,12, 14; XXIX,9 *pruneaux*; Tours prunes, Cook XXVI,88 *pruneaux de Tours ou communs*; Cotg: "*Pruneau*. A Prune; or a little Plumme"; Fur: "*Pruneau*. Prune sechée au Soleil. On estime les pruneaux de Tours, qui sont faits de grosses prunes"

pomegranate (seeds), Cook V,28 (passim 35); Confectioner Preface; IV,11; V,9; VII,4; X,6 *grenade, grains de grenade*; see also jelly, preserve, salad, syrup, waters Appendix 2

—— pomegranate juice, Cook Confections,12; Confectioner V,9; VII,18 *jus de grenade*

pumpkin, Cook XV,19, 20; XX,5; XXI,33; XXV,17, 18; XXIX,7; XXX,31; Pastry Chef IX,10; XXIX,4; Confectioner XV,13 *citrouille, citroüille*; pumpkin seed, Confectioner XV,13 *graine de citroüille*; Cotg: "*Citrouille*. A Citrull; a Citrull Cowcumber, or Turkish gourd; a kind of great Melon, in colour, and forme resembling a Citron"; Fur: "Le plus gros de tous les fruits qui rampent sur la terre. Il est de figure cylindrique & oblongue"; Pumpkin Pottage, Cook XV,19, 20; XXV,17, 18; XXIX,7 **Potage de citrouille, citroüille (au beurre, au laict)**; Pumpkin Tourte, Cook XXI,33 **Tourte de citroüille**

purslane (*Portulaca oleracea*), Cook VIII,96; XXII,4; XXIX,1 *pourpier*

sorrel, Cook III,23; XV,1, 25, 27, 47, 54; XVI,25, 49; XVII,1, 6, 8; XVIII,17, 19; XXV,25; XXIX,1; Pastry Chef XXXII,2, 3; XXXIII,11 *oseille, ozeille*; sorrel juice, Cook XVIII,19 *jus d'ozeille*

spices, spice mixture, Cook IV,2 (passim 16); Pastry Chef II,1 (passim 25) *espice, espisse, episse*; see also to spice, Appendix 3

—— mild spices, Pastry Chef II,2; VII,2–4, 18; IX,7; XI,1 *epice, espisse douce*; Mild Spice Mixture of Pastry Chefs, Pastry Chef II,1 **Espice douce des Pastissiers**

—— prepared spice (for sausage: pepper, cloves, salt, ginger), Cook V,8 *epice preparé*; Pastry Chef II,1 *episse composée*

—— salty spice, Pastry Chef VII,4, 5, 7, 13–17, 19, 20, 24; IX,3, 4; XXII,1, 2; XXIII,1, 2; XXXI,5 *episse, espice salée*; Salty Spice, Pastry Chef II,2 **Episse salée**

spikes: see pepper

spinach, Cook XXI,29; XXVI,85; XXVIII,28; XXX,19; Pastry Chef IX,7; XXI,3 *espinars, espinards*

spirits: see wine, below

stamens: see lily

starch: see flour

strawberries, Cook V,10; XXI,40; Confections,14 *fraises*

sugar, Cook III,15 (passim 130); Pastry Chef I,6 (passim 75); Confectioner (passim) *sucre*; see also the varieties or stages of "cooked" sugar in Appendix 2, and sugar in Appendix 3; see also dough in Appendix 2

—— powdered sugar, confectioner's sugar, Cook Confections,3, 4, 9, 11–14, 31–33, 46, 47, 64, 65; Pastry Chef I,6 (passim 31) *sucre en poudre*

—— finely powdered sugar, Cook Confections,64, 65 *farine de sucre*; Pastry Chef XXVII,0 *sucre fin*

—— brown sugar, Confectioner III,1; IV,1 *castonnade*; Cotg: "*Cassonade.*

Powder Sugar; especially, such as comes from Brasile"; Fur: "*Cassonade ou Castonade.* Sucre qu'on ameine & qu'on vend en poudre ou en gros morceaux, qui n'a pas eu sa derniere preparation par laquelle on le durcit & on le met en pain. On tient que la *cassonade* sucre mieux que le sucre raffiné & mis en pain; mais elle fait bien plus d'escume"; the French word is believed to derive from *casser: casson,* "something broken" — that is, crude sugar in pieces

—— musk sugar, Cook XIX,5 *sucre musqué*

—— rose sugar, Pastry Chef XXV,5 *sucre rosat*; Rich: "C'est un composé de roses & du sucre"; Encyc: "*Sucre rosat,* parmi les Epiciers, est un sucre blanc, clarifié & cuit dans de l'eau rose"; Tobler (VIII, 1472), *FEW* (X, 481b): *sucre rosart*

—— royal sugar, Pastry Chef XXV,5; XXVIII,1; Confectioner IV,4, 13 *sucre royal (en poudre)*; Fur: "Le *sucre royal,* ou *sucre fin,* est le plus épuré & le plus blanc, lequel ne se dissout point dans de bon esprit de vin bien rectifié"; *Encyc:* "*Sucre royal.* C'est en termes de Confiserie, ce qu'il y a de plus dur & de plus fin en fait de sucre: on le clarifie en Hollande où l'on a l'art de le faire meilleur qu'ailleurs"

syrup: see Appendix 2

tansy, Pastry Chef XXIX,6 *tenesie*

thyme, Cook III,9, 43; IV,13; X,4; XV,10, 33, 39; XVI,18, 25, 91; XVIII,1 *thim, thin*

tidbits: see subsection b), below

toast: see bread

truffles, Cook III,6 (passim 68) *trufles, troufles*; I.D.G.: "*Trouffles, or Truffles.* They are a kind of Mushrum"

turnip, Cook III,4, 18, 45; IV,10; V,14, 24, 51; XV,4, 6, 21, 37, 48, 49; XX,12; XXIII,4, 19, 40; XXVI,77; XXIX,4 *navet*; a smaller tuber than the usual

de vin n'est autre chose que de l'eau de vie plusieurs fois rectifiée ou distillée"

—— wine lees, dregs, Cook IX,0; Confectioner IV,11 *lie de vin*

yeast: see leavening

zest. see lemon, orange, peel

b) Animals, fowl (and their products)

animal, Pastry Chef XIII *animal*

bard, Cook III,5, 24, 31; VI,56; VIII,73 *barde (de lard)*; I.D.G.: "It is a sheet of lard or bacon"; see also lard, lardoon and to bard in Appendix 3

beef, Cook V,0, 14, 20, 27, 29, 31, 53, 54, 85; VIII,102; XI,0; XIV,12; Pastry Chef VII,4, 8; XXII,1 *bœuf*; [Plain] Piece of Beef, Cook V,31 **Piece de bœuf [au naturel]**; Piece of Beef in the English or Chalon Fashion, Cook V,14 **Piece de bœuf à l'Angloise ou Chalonnoise**; Daube of a Piece of Beef, Cook V,27 **Piece de bœuf à la daube**; Piece of Beef as a Fool's Bauble, Cook V,29 **Piece de bœuf à la marotte**; Stylish Beef, Cook V,53 **Bœuf à la mode**; Braised Beef, Cook V,54 **Bœuf à l'estoffade**; see also veal

—— breast of beef, Cook V,14 *poitrine de bœuf*

—— leg of beef, Cook III,39, 43 *trumeau de bœuf*; Pottage of a Leg of Beef, Cook III,39 **Potage de trumeau de bœuf**; Pottage of Leg of Beef with Bread Fingers, Cook III,42 **Potage de trumeau de bœuf au tailladin**; Fur: "*Trumeau*. C'est la cuisse du bœuf, la partie qui est au dessus de la jointure du genou en montant"

—— short rib (of beef), Cook VI,52 *alloyau* Cotg: "*Aloyau de bœuf*. A short rib of beefe, or the fleshie end of the rib, divided from the rost, and rosted; a little piece of (rosted) beefe having a bone in it"; Rich: *Aloiau.* "Piece de beuf qu'on léve sur la hanche

qu'on rôtit ordinairement, ou qu'on met en ragoût"

—— beef tongue: see ox tongue, below

—— palates, beef palates, Cook III,16, 35; V,4, 13, 14, 15, 20, 49, 98; XIV,6, 11, 24, 28; Pastry Chef VII,8 *palets, palais de bœuf*; Rich: "Ce mot se dit des hommes & des animaux, & veut dire la partie supérieure du dedans de la bouche"

—— beef gut, Cook V,11 *boyau de bœuf*

—— (beef) kidneys, Cook V,13 *roignons*

—— cow's udder, Cook VIII,16 *tetine de vache*

—— beef marrow, Cook III,38; IV,8, 9; V,77, 78, 80; VIII,38; XIV,28–30; Pastry Chef VII,2, 3, 5, 6, 8, 10, 12–15, 17–19, 22; IX,3, 5, 8, 10, 12, 14, 15; XX,2; XXI,1; XXIII,1; XXXIII,8, 17 *moële, moëlle, moësle, moüelle, moüeille (de bœuf)*; Marrow Tourte, Cook V,77; XIV,30 **Tourte de moëlle**; Marrow Fritters, Cook VIII,38 **Baignets de moëlle**

—— beef grease, Cook IV,1, 6; IV,8, 9; V,49, 69, 74, 75, 79, 82, 83, 84; VI,49; XIV,3, 6, 11, 13, 17, 31; Pastry Chef VII,5, 6, 8, 13–15, 18 *graisse de bœuf*

—— beef stock, Cook XI,2 *jus de bœuf*; this recipe directs on the making of it

—— ox tongue, beef tongue, Cook V,17; VI,53; VIII,53, 57 *langue de bœuf*; Fresh Ox Tongue, Cook VI,53 **Langue de bœuf fraische**; [Salted] Ox Tongue, Cook VIII,57 **Langue de bœuf**; Ox Tongue in Ragout, Cook V,17; VIII,53 **Langue de bœuf en ragoust**

birds, fowl (in general), Pastry Chef VII,4, 6 *oyseaux*; river birds, water fowl, Cook I *oiseaux de riviere*; large birds, Pastry Chef VII,4 *gros oiseaux*; Cook II; XIII,2; Pastry Chef VII,4, 13, 16 *volaille*; see also turkey

—— liver, Pastry Chef VII,16 *foyes (de volaille)*; see also poultry

blackbirds, Cook XIV,20 *merles*; Cotg: "A Mearle, Owsell, Blackbird"

blood, Cook VI,5; XXII,15 *sang*

boar, Cook V,66, 67; VI,44; VIII,93;
XIV,4; Pastry Chef VII,4 *sanglier*;
young wild boar, Cook I; V,0; VI,18
francs marcassins; Shoulder or Loin of
Boar, Cook VI,44 **Espaule ou longe de
sanglier**; Shoulder of Boar in Ragout,
Cook V,66 **Espaule de sanglier en
ragoust**; see also Appendix 2
—— boar venison, boar "bacon", Cook
VI,44 *la venaison, qu'on appelle communement de lard*
bouillon (passim) *bouillon*; see also almond (white) bouillon, herb bouillon
in Appendix 1 a); meat bouillon, below; fish bouillon, Appendix 1 c); sauce
(white sauce), Appendix 2; and, as a
measure of cooking time, Appendix 5 e)
brain, Cook IV,8 *cervelle*
breast: see beef, mutton, veal
brisket, Cook IV,11, 12, 13; V,1; XIV,6
brichet
buntings, ortolans, Cook I; VI,29; VIII,52
ortolans
butter, Cook III,16 (passim 358); Pastry
Chef I,1, 4 (passim 200) *beurre, beure*;
Butter Tourt, Cook XXI,28 **Tourte de
beurre**; Melted Butter, Cook XXII,1
Beurre fondu; Salted Butter, Cook
XXIII,7 **Beurre salé**; see also to butter
(Appendix 3, below)
—— clarified butter, Cook VIII,38 (passim 17) *beurre affiné*
—— browned butter, Pastry Chef
XXXIII,24 *beurre noir*; see also to
brown in Appendix 3
capon: see poultry
cheese, Cook III,14, 49; VIII,38, 42, 48;
XVII,14; XIX,9; XX,1; Pastry Chef
VII,12; 10; XI,1; XII; XV,2–4, 6–8;
XVIII; XX,2; XXIX,3, 9; XXX,2;
XXXII,2; XXXIV,6 *fromage*; Eggs
with Cheese, Cook XVII,14 **Œufs au
fromage**; see also whey, below; flan,
omelet, pie, pottage, ramekin in Appendix 2
—— cream cheese, Pastry Chef XV,1;
XX,2; XXI,1 *fromage à la cresme*;

creamy cheese, cheese from whole,
unskimmed milk, Pastry Chef VIII,2;
IX,7, 10; XI,2; XIV; XV,6, 8; XVII;
XXI,1; XXIII,2 *fromage qui ne soit pas
écremé, fromage non écremez*; Pastry
Chef XI,5; XVI *fromage gras*
—— fat-free, skim-milk cheese (made
from skimmed milk), Pastry Chef XI,2;
XIV; XV,7 *fromage affiné, ecremé*;
Pastry Chef XV,7; XX,3 *fromage fin*
—— dry cheese, Pastry Chef XI,2, 4;
XXIII,2 *fromage sec*
—— angelot, a dry (salted) cheese, Pastry Chef XI,4 *de bon fromage sec, par
exemple d'un bon angelot*; *Delices*,
183; Cotg: "*Angelot*. The cheese
called, an Angelot"
—— cheese curds, Cook XIX,9; XX,1;
Cook XIX,9 *fromages à petits choux,
j'entends fromage blanc & mol*; Pastry
Chef XVII *fromage à petits choux, ce
sont des fromages non écremez qui
sont faits du jour mesme*; white cheese,
Cook XXVIII,31 *fromage blanc*; fresh
cheese, Pastry Chef VII,12; IX,10; XV,6
fromage frais (fait); soft cheese, Pastry
Chef VIII,2; IX,7; XI,2, 4; XIV; XV,8;
XX,2, 3; XXIII,2 *fromage mol*
chicken: see poultry
cock, cockscombs, cockerels: see poultry
consommé, a reduced meat broth, Pastry Chef XXXIV,4 *consommé*; Rich:
"*Consommé*. Bouillon qui est fait de
viandes délicates & nourrissantes, telles
que sont le veau, le mouton, le chapon;
& qu'on donne aux malades pour les
nourrir un peu"; see also to boil down,
in Appendix 3
cracklings, Cook VIII,13; X,3 *cretons*;
Cotg: "The crispie peeces, or mam-
mockes, remaining of lard, that hath
beene first shred, then boiled, and then
strained through a cloth, &c"; *TLF*:
"Morceau de panne de porc frite"
cream (of milk), Cook VIII,66 (passim
38); Pastry Chef IV; XV,2; XX,3;
XXI,1 (passim 40) *cresme, creme (de
lait)*; Confectioner Pref *cresmes*; see

also Appendix 2 for preparations called creams

curlew, Cook I *courlis*; Cotg: "*Courlis*. A Curlue"

cutlets: see mutton

dairy products, Confectioner Pref *laictages*; see also butter, cheese, cream, milk, whey

deer; see also stag

—— fallow deer, buck, Pastry Chef VII,4 *dain*; Rich: "*Daim*. Sorte d'animal sauvage qui est un peu plus grand que le chevreuil, & qui a quelque raport avec le cerf, hormis qu'il n'est ni si gros, ni de même couleur que le cerf"

—— deer, roe-buck, Cook V,13, 51, 67; VI,28, 47, 48; VIII,13, 14, 15 *chevreuil*; Loin of Roe-Buck in Ragout, Cook V,51 **Longe de chevreuil en ragoust**; Rich: "Bête fauve qui ressemble au cerf, excepté qu'il est plus-petit, qu'il s'aprivoise bien plus-aisement & qu'il ne fait point de mal de son bois"

—— doe, Cook V,13; VI,46, 47; XIV,25 *biche*; Fur: "Femelle du cerf qui n'a point de bois sur la teste"

—— deer fawn, Cook I; VI,46 *faon de biche*; VI,47 *faon de chevreuil*

—— deer haunch, Cook V,67 *cuisseaux de chevreuil*; Haunch of Roe-Buck, Cook V,67 **Cuisseaux de chevreuil**; Rich: "*Cuissot*. Ce mot se dit en parlant de cerf. C'est la cuisse d'un cerf pour mettre en pâte"

—— deer liver, Cook VIII,13, 14 *foie de chevreuil*

—— deer udder, Cook VIII,15 *tetine de chevreuil*

delicacies, Cook VIII,2 *menus droits (de cerf)*: Fur: "On appelle chez les Rotisseurs, *du menu*, les foyes, bouts d'ailes, gesiers et autres choses dont on fait des ragousts & des fricassées"; Rich: "*Menus droits*. Terme de chasse. Ce sont les oreilles du cerf, les bouts de sa tete, le mufle, les dentiers, le franc boiau & les neuds"; Fur: "*Droit*, en

termes de Chasse, signifie la part de la beste deffaite qui appartient au Veneurs, ou aux chiens"; Cotg: "*Menus droicts*. All vailes [mod. sl. 'perks'], or fees belonging to an officer; and particularly, the head, feet, skin, and intralls of a slaughtered beast, or all such parts as a Cooke, or yeoman of the slaughterhouse, reserves for himselfe"; see also giblets

doe: see deer

dotterel: see plover

dove, Cook III,1; V,4, 33; Pastry Chef VII,4, 17 *pigeon*; Pottage of Dove with Green Peas, Cook III,28 **Potage de pigeons aux poix verts**; Half Bisque [of Large Dove], Cook III,48 **Demie bisque**

—— squab, young dove, Cook III,1, 17, 22; IV,1, 4, 5, 13; V,1, 6, 9, 56; VIII,9, 58, 100, 101; XIV,6, 11, 28, 32–34; Pastry Chef I,3, 4; VII,6 *pigeonneau, pigeonneaux (de voliere)*; Squab Bisque, Cook III,1 **Bisque de pigeonneaux**; Squab Pottage, Cook III,17 **Pottage de pigeonneaux**; Pottage of Roast Squab, Cook III,22 **Potage de pigeonneaux rostis**; Pottage of Stuffed Squab, Cook IV,4 **Potage de pigeonneaux farcis**; Squab in Ragout, Cook V,6 **Pigeonneaux en ragoust**; Fricasseed Squab, Cook V,44 **Pigeonneaux fricassez**; Squab Tourte, Cook V,78, XIV,28 **Tourte de pigeonneaux**; Rich: "Jeune pigeon"

—— squab liver, Cook V,6 *foyes (de pigeonneaux)*

—— wood-pigeon, Cook I; VI,33 *ramier, pigeon ramier*; Garnished Pottage of Wood-Pigeon, Cook III,9 **Potage de ramiers garny**; I.D.G.: "Stockdove"

—— young wood-pigeon, Cook I *ramereaux*

—— rock-dove, Cook VI,13 (*Columba livia*) *bizet*, common pigeon; Cotg: "A kind of small Stockedove, or Quest, resembling a Partridge, but much worse meat"

les pieds,) ... ; Cotg: "*La petite oye.* The giblets of a Goose"; Pastry Chef VII,16 *requeste, Pasté de Requeste*; Cotg: *Requeste d'un Oye.* The Goose giblets"; see also mutton, pork, poultry; and pie in Appendix 2

goat kids, Cook I; XIV,25 *chevreaux*

goose, Cook III,25, 26, 29; V,33, 34; Pastry Chef VII,4 *oye*; domestic goose Cook VI,37 *oye privée*; fat goose (for salting, with peas) Cook I *oye grasse pour saler aux poix*; Pottage of Salted Goose in Pea Purée, Cook III,26 **Potage d'oye sallée à la purée**; Goose in Ragout, Cook V,34 **Oye en ragoust**; Daube of Goose, Cook V,33 **Oye à la daube**; see also giblets

—— goslings Cook I; III,23, 24, 25; IV,11, 26; VI,17; XIV,26 *oysons*; Pottage of Gosling with Peas, Cook III,23 **Potage d'oyson aux poix**; Pottage of Stuffed Gosling, Cook IV,11 **Potage d'oyson farcis**

—— gosling liver Cook VI,17 *son foie*; see also giblets

—— wild goose Cook VI,36 *oye sauvage*

grease: see lard

Guinea fowl: see turkey

ham: see pork, and ham, pie, Appendix 2

hare, Cook V,23, 83, 84; XIV,3; Pastry Chef VII,4; XXXIII,17 *lievre, liévre*; Hare Civet, Cook V,23 **Civé de liévre**; saddle of hare, Cook VI,43; Pastry Chef XXXIII,17 *rable de lievre*; Saddle of Hare, Cook VI,43 **Rable de liévre**; Cotg: "*Rable.* The chine, or parts about the chine, of a Deere, &c."; Fur: "*Rable.* Partie de l'animal qui est vers les reins entre le train de devant [forequarters] & celuy de derriere [hindquarters]. Il ne se dit gueres que des liévres, lapins & autre gibier semblable, dont on sert le *rable*, comme la plus delicate partie"; see also Escoffier, §1812

—— young hare, leveret, Cook I; V,84; VI,5; XIV,3; XXI,0; Pastry Chef VII,14,

15 *levraut, levreau, levreaut, levreaux (de janvier)*

haslets: see Appendix 2

heron, Cook I; VI,42 *hairon, heron*

hock (veal): see veal

joint: see mutton

kidneys, Cook XIV,16 *roignons*; see also beef, mutton, poultry, veal

knuckle (of a leg), Cook III,46; IV,6, 10; V,12, 28, 72; VI,54; XIV,27 *manche (d'épaule)*; Fur: "Le devant [forequarters] est le manche de l'épaule"; see also mutton, veal (hock)

lamb: see mutton

lard, fat, grease (pork), bacon, Cook III,3 (passim); Pastry Chef VII,1 (passim) *lard*; Pastry Chef IX,10; XI,2; XXXII,2 *graisse (de porc)*; its application is described as a "bandage" (*emplastre de lard*) in Pastry Chef VII,4; Lard Tourte, Cook V,76 **Tourte de lard**; Rich: "Graisse de porc qui n'est battüe, ni fondüe, mais que l'on bat, & que l'on fond quand on veut faire du saindoux pour faire des bignets"; I.D.G.: "*Lard.* It is fat bacon; *Meane Lard.* They are slices of lard, of a middle sise; *Great Lard.* They are big slices of lard"; Cotg: "*Lard.* Lard, fat Bakon, the fat of Bakon, or of Porke; also, a Flitch of Bakon"; see also pork, bard, and to lard in Appendix 3

—— solid (unsalted) pork fat (in a slab), Cook V,8, 9, 11 *panne de porc (frais)*; Cook V,10 *panne de lard*; Pastry Chef VII,12 *panne de porc*; Cotg: "*Panne de gresse.* A leafe of fat"

—— medium lard, Cook III,9 (passim) *moyen lard*

—— coarse lard, Cook III,3 (passim) *gros lard*

—— lardoon, finger of lard, Cook III,15 (passim 12); Pastry Chef VII,3, 4, 14, 17; Confectioner IX,3; XV,4, 5 *lardon*; I.D.G.: "*Lardons.* They are small long slices of Lard"; Rich: "Petit morceau de lard qu'on met entre les ailes de la lardoire lorsqu'on veut piquer la

Mutton, Cook XIV,2 **Pasté de membre de mouton**; Cotg: *"Un membre de veau, de mouton, &c.* A joynt of Veale, Mutton, &c."*; Fur: *"Un membre* de mouton, c'est une esclanche, une épaule"*; Cook V,27; Pastry Chef VII,5 *éclanche, esclanche (de mouton)*; Cotg: *"Esclanche de mouton.* A leg of Mutton (cut large with the whole bone at it)"; Rich: "C'est ce qu'on apelle dans les provinces *gigot de mouton.* C'est la cuisse du mouton qu'on fait rôtir, ou qu'on met en ragoût"; Cook III,46; V,12, 13; XIV,27; Pastry Chef VII,4 *manche (d'espaules)*; Pottage of Shoulder Knuckle in Ragout, Cook III,46 **Potage de manches d'espaules en ragoust**; Shoulder Knuckles *à l'Olivier*, Cook V,13 **Manches d'espaules à l'Olivier**; Shoulder-Knuckle Pie, Cook XIV,27 **Pasté de manches d'espaules**; Shoulder of Mutton in Ragout, Cook V,49 **Espaule de mouton en ragoust**; see also knuckle

—— sheep's feet *pieds de mouton*: Sheep's Feet in Ragout, Cook V,41 **Pieds de mouton en ragoust**; Fricasseed Sheep's Feet, Cook V,70 **Pieds de mouton fricassez**

—— cutlets (of mutton), Cook V,52; VI,50, 55 *costellettes*

—— sirloin (of mutton), Cook VI,50 *haut costé*; Cotg: *"Haut costé.* A surloyne"

—— mutton tail *queuë de mouton*: Plain Mutton Tail, Cook V,31 **Queuë de mouton au naturel**; Mutton Tail in Ragout, Cook V,20 **Queuë de mouton en ragoust**; Roast Mutton Tail, Cook V,30 **Queuë de mouton rostie**

—— mutton stock, drippings, Cook III,1 (passim 12); Pastry Chef VII,2; XXXIII,17 *jus de mouton*; Cook IV,4; V,39; VI,52; VIII,84, 87, 97; Pastry Chef VII,23; XXXIV,22, 23 *jus d'éclanche de mouton, jus d'un membre de mouton*

—— mutton tongue, Cook V,19, 60, 71; VIII,89–91; XIV,24; for salting Cook XXIII,3; Mutton Tongue in Ragout, Cook V,19; VIII,89 **Langue de mouton en ragoust**; Larded Mutton Tongue, Cook VIII,90 **Langue de mouton piquée**; Grilled Mutton Tongue, Cook VIII,91 **Langue de mouton sur le gril**; Roast Mutton Tongues Cook, V,71 **Langues de mouton rosties**; Fried Mutton Tongue in Ragout, Cook V,60 **Langue de mouton fritte en ragoust**; Fried Mutton Tongue in Ragout with Fritters, Cook V,60 **Langue de mouton fritte en ragoust & begnest**; Roast Mutton Tongues, Cook V,71 **Langues de mouton rosties**; Mutton-Tongue Pie, Cook XIV,24 **Pasté de langues de mouton**

—— ram's kidneys, Cook III,19; VIII,97; XIV,6; XXIII,5 *roignons de belier, bellier*

—— lamb, Cook I; III,31; IV,9; V,13, 25, 69; VI,15; VIII,24; XIV,23 *agneau, aigneaux*; Lamb in Ragout, Cook V,25 **Agneau en ragoust**

—— lamb's head *teste d'agneau*; Pottage of Deboned, Stuffed Lamb's Head, Cook IV,9 **Potage de testes d'agneaux desossées farcies**; lamb's tongue, Cook VIII,24; lamb's lung, lights, Cook IV,9 *mouts d'agneau*; lamb's liver, Cook IV,9 *foye d'agneau*; lamb's offal, pluck, Cook III,31; IV,9; VIII,24 *abatis (d'agneau)*; Pottage of Lamb Offal, Cook III,31 **Potage d'abatis d'agneaux**; Pastry Chef VII,16 *fressure d'un aigneau*; La Varenne (Cook VIII,24): "Abbatis d'agneaux. Prenez les pieds, les oreilles & la langue . . . "; I.D.G.: *"Abbatis, or Abatis.* They are the purtenances of any beast *viz.* the feet, the eares, the tongue, &c. They are also the gibblets of any foule *viz.* the neck, wings, feet, gisard, liver, &c"; see also pork, giblets

offal: see mutton

palets: see beef

Whole Suckling Piglet, Cook VI,40 **Cochon de laict au naturel**; Stuffed Piglet, Cook V,69 **Cochon farcy**; Pottage of Piglet, Cook III,37 **Potage de cochon de laict**; Daube of Piglet, Cook V,32 **Cochon à la daube**; Piglet in Ragout, Cook V,37 **Cochon en ragoust**

—— piglet offal, Cook III,37 *abatis (de cochon)*; Pastry Chef VII,16 *une fressure de cochon de laict*; see also mutton, giblets

poultry; see also giblets, turkey, waterhen

—— (poultry) liver, Cook VIII,63; Pastry Chef VII,16 *foyes (de volailles)*; see also pullet, below

—— chicken, Cook III,5 (passim); Pastry Chef XXXIV,15 *poulet*; Marinated Chicken, Cook V,12; VIII,23; XXIII,4 **Poulets marinez**; Stewed Chicken, Cook V,62 **Poulets à l'estuvée**; Pottage of Chicken Garnished with Asparagus, Cook III,5 **Potage de poulets garny d'asperges**; Pottage of Chicken with Cauliflower, Cook III,20 **Potage de poulets aux choux-fleurs**; Pottage of Chicken in Ragout, Cook III,21 **Potage de poulets en ragoust**; Pottage of Chicken with Green Peas, Cook III,27 **Potage de poulets aux poix verts**; Pottage of Chicken with Rice, Cook III,41 **Potage de poulets au riz**; Pottage of Stuffed Chicken, Cook IV,3 **Potage de poulets farcis**; Fricasseed Chicken, Cook III,19; V,43 **Poulets fricassez**; Chicken in Ragout in a Bottle, Cook V,86 **Poulet en ragoust dans une bouteille**

—— grain-fed chicken, perhaps spring chicken, Cook I; VI,10 *poulets de grain*; Fur: "On appelle *poulets de grain* les poulets qu'on esleve au printemps, & qu'on nourrit de grain"

—— pullet, Cook I; V,1, 7; VII,14, 56 *poularde*; pullet liver, Cook V,7 *foyes de poulardes*; Pullets in Ragout, Cook V,7 **Poulardes en ragoust**; Fur: "Jeune

poule engraissée"; Rich: "Poule jeune et grasse, *poularde*"

—— Norman neutered pullet Cook I *poularde chastrée de Normandie*

—— capon, Cook III,2 (passim 34); Pastry Chef VII,6, 12 *chapon*; barnyard and chicken-run capons, Cook I *chapons de pallier et de cluseaux*; capon white meat, Pastry Chef VII,18, 19 *blanc de chapon*; capon liver, Cook V,81; XIV,7 *foie de chapon gras*; capons, young, Cook I *chaponneaux*; capon stock, Cook XIII,1 *jus de chapon*; Capon with Cress, Cook VI,39 **Chapon au cresson**; Capon with Oysters, Cook V,58 **Chapon aux huistres**; Pottage of Capon with Rice, Cook III,40 **Potage de chapon au riz**; Pottage of Stuffed Capon, Cook IV,1 **Potage de chapons farcis**; Pie of Deboned Capon, Cook V,80 **Pasté de chapon desossé**; capon tourte, Pastry Chef VII,6 *tourte de chapon*

—— cock, Cook VIII,5; Pastry Chef VII,5 *coq*; cock's kidneys, Pastry Chef VII,5 *rognons de coq*

—— cockscombs, Cook I; III,1, 5, 8, 10–12, 38; V,75; VII,9, 63; XIV,6, 28, 31, 35; XXI,0; XXII,15; Pastry Chef VII,5, 14 *crestes (de coq)*

—— cockerels, Cook III,14; IV,2; VI,14 *estudeaux*; Cockerel Pottage, Cook III,14 **Potage d'estudeaux**; Pottage of Stuffed Deboned Cockerel, Cook IV,2 **Potage d'estudeaux desossez farcis**; Cotg: "*Hestoudeau*. A Cockerell, or great Cocke chicke; also, a Caponet; and in some few places (wherein any sort of yong, big, or well-grown pullein is termed thus) a Pullet"

quail, Cook III,8; VI,6; XIV,18 *caille*; Pottage of Marbled Quail Cook III,8 **Potage de cailles marbrées**; young quail, Cook I; VI,23 *cailleteaux*

rabbit, Cook I; VII,3; Pastry Chef VII,4, 15, 17 *lapin*; young rabbits Cook I; III,30; V,55; VI,19; VII,3; XIV,14 *lapreaux*; Pottage of Young Rabbit, Cook III,30 **Potage de lapreaux**;

Young Rabbit in Ragout, Cook V,55
Lapreaux en ragoust

rails (*Rallidæ rallinæ*), Cook I; VI,21; VII,4 *ralles*

ram's kidneys: see mutton

rennet, Cook Confections,41 *prezure*; Cotg: "*Presure*. The rennet wherewith milke, imployed in cheese-making, is curded"; Fur: "*Presure*. C'est un certain acide qu'on trouve dans l'estomach des veaux. . . . C'est de la presure qu'on se sert ordinairement pour faire cailler le lait"

ribs (of animal), Cook V,26; XVI,52 *costes*; see also beef (short rib)

rind (of bacon): see pork

rock-dove: see dove

roe-buck: see deer

saddle: see hare

saveloy: see Appendix 2

scoter: see duck

short rib: see beef

shoulder blade, spatula, patella (unspecified animal), Cook V,72 *pallete*; Cotg: "*Palette du genouil*. The knee bone, or panne; the whirlebone of the knee"

sirloin: see veal, mutton

slime: see Appendix 1 c), below

snipe, Cook I; VI,31, 32; VII,7 *beccassine*; see also woodcock

spareribs: see pork

squab: see dove

stag, Cook VIII,2; Pastry Chef VII,4 *cerf*; see also delicacies

stock (meat juice): see capon, mutton, veal

swallow, sea-swallow, Cook I *hirondelle de mer*

sweetbreads: see veal

teal: see duck

thiastias (a wildfowl similar to the white-tail, *q.v.*), Cook VI,41

thrush, Cook I; III,35; VI,20; VII,4; VIII,22 *mauviettes, moviettes*; Pottage

of Small Thrush, Cook III,35 **Potage de moviettes**; Cotg: "*Mauvis*. Thrush"
—— large thrush, throstle, Cook I; VI,30; V,5; VIII,101 *grive*; Cotg: "The great Thrush called a Fieldfare, or Feldifare; also, the Throstle"

tidbits, Cook III,5 (passim 25); Pastry Chef I,3 (passim 16) *beatilles*; Rich: "Toutes sortes de petites choses délicates qu'on met dans les pâtez, dans les tourtes, comme sont les crêtes de coq, des ris de veau, &c."; Fur: "Petites viandes delicates dont on compose des pastés, des tourtes, des potages, des ragousts, comme ris de veau, palais de bœuf, crestes de coq, trufles, artichaux, pistaches, &c."; *Acad*: "Menuës choses delicates & propres à manger que l'on met dans les pastés, & dans les potages; comme ris de veau, crestes de coq, foyes gras, &c."; I.D.G.: "They are all kinds of ingredients, that may be fancied, for to be put together into a pie, or other wise *viz*. Cock's combes; stones or kidnies, sweet breads of veale, mushrums, bottoms of hartichocks, &c"; I.D.G.: "*Beatilles of pullets*. They are the gibblets." These "tidbits" are probably to be cooked (perhaps sautéed) before being used as a garnish, or precooked in some way (see Cook III,19) before entering a preparation; see also omelet, pie, pottage Appendix 2

tongue: see beef, mutton, pork, veal; and carp in Appendix 1 c)

tread (of an egg), Cook XVII,12 *germe*

tripe *gras double*: Fat Tripe in Ragout, Cook V,42 **Gras double en ragoust**; Cotg: "*Le gras double*. The fat tripe; or, that part of the paunch which yeelds the fattest, and thickest tripes"; see also cod

turkey, *Meleagrididæ*, Pastry Chef VII,4 *volaille d'Inde*; turkey hens (perhaps Guinea hens), Cook I; V,1 *poules d'Inde*; Cotg: "*D'Inde*. A Turkie Henne"; turkey cocks (perhaps Guinea cocks), Cook I; Pastry Chef VII,14 *cocqs d'Inde*; Cook I *dindons*; Cotg:

"*Coq d'Inde.* A Turkie Cocke"; see pie, Appendix 2. Guinea fowl, *Numida mealeagris*, from West Africa had originally been called "turkey" up to the previous century; from 1498 on, however, American turkeys were raised domestically in Spain and then throughout Europe, and the French qualification *d'Inde* and the English name "turkey" was generally transferred to them.

—— young turkey (perhaps Guinea chicken), Cook I; IV,13; V,1, 9, 22, 36, 65; VI,11; XIV,6 *poulets d'Inde*; year-old turkey-cocks Cook I *dindons de l'année*; Pottage of Stuffed Young Turkey, Cook IV,13 **Potage de poulet d'Inde farcy**; Young Turkey with Raspberries, Cook V,1 **Poulet d'Inde à la framboise**; Daube of Young Turkey, Cook V,22 **Poulet d'Inde à la daube**; Young Turkey in Ragout, Cook V,36 **Poulets d'Inde en ragout**; Fur: "*Dindon.* Jeune coq d'Inde"

—— Giblets of Young Turkey, Cook V,65 **Abbatis de poulets d'Inde**

—— turkey chicks (perhaps Guinea chicks), Cook VI,24 *dindonneaux*; Fur: "*Dindonneau* est un jeune dindon, lors qu'il est frais esclos [hatched], & qu'il n'est queres plus gros que le poing"

tortoise, Cook III,36, VI,4; XV,9; VIII,77; XIX,25; XXV,7; XXVIII,9 *tortuë*; Pottage of Tortoise, Cook III,36 **Potage de tortuës**; Rich: "Il y a plusieurs sortes de *tortuës*: il y a des tortuës de terre, des tortuës d'eau & des tortuës de mer"

turtledove, Cook I *tourterelles*; Cook VI,4 *tourte*; Cotg: "*Tourterelle.* A Turtle, or Turtle Dove; *Tourte.* A Turtle Dove"

udder: see deer, beef

veal, Cook IV,2 (passim); Pastry Chef VII,15 *veau*; Fricassee of Veal, Cook V,46 **Fricassée de veau**; Veal Tourte Cook V,79; XIV,31 **Tourte de veau**; Veal Pie, Cook XIV,17 **Pasté de veau**; veal stock, Cook XIII,1 *jus de veau*; see also beef, pluck, above

—— breast of veal, Cook III,34; IV,7; V,15, 50; VI,49; XIV,10; Pastry Chef I,3; VII,6 *poitrine, poictrine de veau*; Braised Breast of Veal, Cook V,15 **Poictrine de veau à l'estoffade**; Fried Breast of Veal, Cook V,50 **Poictrine de veau fritte**; Stuffed Breast of Veal, Cook VI,49 **Poictrine de veau farcie**; Pottage of Breast of Veal, Cook III,34 **Potage de poictrine de veau**; Pottage of Stuffed Breast of Veal, Cook IV,7 **Potage de poitrine de veau farcie**

—— minced veal, veal paste, minced-veal mixture, Cook IV,2 (passim 12) *gaudiveaux, godivaux*; I.D.G.: "*Gaudiveaux.* They are forced meat of veale, that is, meat of veale minced, seasoned, and wrought into small long peeces like chitterlings"; *RDH*: "Un hachis de viande utilisé comme farce"; see also pie, quenelle, Appendix 2, and Escoffier, §198

—— round of veal, fillet of veal, Cook III,7; V,47, 73; VI,49; VIII,15; XIV,17 *ruelle de veau*; Confectioner IV,7 *rouelle de veau*; Round of Veal in Ragout, Cook V,47 **Ruelle de veau en ragoust**; Cotg: "*Rouelle de veau.* The broad end of a leg of Veale, cut round, and divided from the knuckle"; Rich: "*Rouelle.* Ce mot se dit en parlant de chair de veau: c'est une partie de la cuisse du veau coupée en rond"

—— shoulder of veal, Cook V,48; VI,58 *espaule de veau*; Shoulder of Veal in Ragout, Cook V,48 **Espaule de veau en ragoust**

—— loin of veal, Cook V,4, 14, 38; VI,34; VIII,46; Pastry Chef IX,5; XXXIII,18 *longe de veau*; Loin of Veal in a Marinade, Cook V,4 **Longe de veau à la marinade**; see also tourte, Appendix 2

—— sirloin (of veal), Cook V,26 *haut costé*; Sirloin of Veal in Ragoust, Cook V,26 **Haut costé de veau en ragoust**; Cotg: "*Haut costé.* A surloyne"

—— veal hock, knuckle, Cook III,33; IV,6; V,3; VIII,26 *jarret, jaret de veau*;

Pottage of Knuckle of Veal, Cook III,33 **Potage de jaret de veau**; Pottage of Stuffed Knuckle of Veal, Cook IV,6 **Potage de jarets de veau farcis**; Cotg: "*Jarret*. The hamme, or hough"; Fur: "*Jarret de cheval*, est la jointure du train de derriere [hindquarters] qui assemble la cuisse avec la jambe. On dit aussi, un *jarret* de bœuf, un *jarret* de veau, qui est propre à faire des bouillons"; see also knuckle

—— calf's head, Cook III,44; IV,8, 9; V,63 *teste de veau*; Pottage of Fried Calf's Head, Cook III,44 **Potage de teste de veau fritte**; Pottage of Deboned, Stuffed Calf's Head, Cook IV,8 **Potage de teste de veau desossée farcie**; Fried Calf's Head, Cook V,63 **Teste de veau frite**

—— calf's feet, Cook IV,8; V,41; VIII,26 *pieds de veau*; Calf's Feet in Ragout Cook V,41 **Pieds de veau en ragoust**; Fricasseed Calf's Feet, Cook V,70 **Pieds de veau fricassez**

—— calf's entrails, Cook V,10 *fraises de veau*; Cotg: "*Fraise*. A calves chaldern"

—— calf's sweetbreads, Cook III,1, 10; IV,5; V,6, 15, 20, 28, 69, 75, 80, 81, 86; VIII,10–12, 52, 58; XIV,6, 17, 28, 35; XXI,0; Pastry Chef VII,14, 18 *riz, ris de veau*; Rich: "Sorte de petites parties de la gorge du veau qui sont fort délicats & dont on se sert dans les ragoûts & dans de certains pâtez"; *RDH*: "Terme de boucherie (1583)" with the same sense as *risée de veau*; Cook III,3; Pastry Chef VII,8, 18 *fagouës, fagoües*; Cotg: "*Fagouë*. A certaine kernell under the kannell bone (in men slender, thicke in beasts)"; Veal Sweetbread Tourte Cook XIV,35 **Tourte de riz de veau**

—— veal kidney, Cook VIII,46; XIV,17; Pastry Chef IX,5; XXXIII,16, 18 *roignon (de veau)*

—— veal liver, calf's liver, Cook V,40, 61, 64; VI,59 *foye de veau*; Calf's

Liver in Ragout, Cook V,61 **Foye de veau en ragoust**; Fricasseed Veal Liver, Cook V,40 **Foye de veau fricassé**; Larded Calf's Liver, Cook V,64 **Foye de veau picqué**

—— veal tongue, calf's tongue, Pastry Chef IX,5 *langue de veau*

venison: see game

waterhen (young), Cook I, VI,38 *poulette d'eau*

whey, Pastry Chef XI,2 *petit laict*; Fur: "On appelle *lait clair*, ou *petit lait*, cette serosité qui le sepa re du caillé par l'acide"

white-tails, Cook VI,41 *cus blancs, ou thiastias*; Cotg: "*Cul blanc*. The bird called a Whittaile"

woodcock, Cook I; VI,32, 41; VII,5 *becasse, beccasse*; Pottage of Roast Woodcock, Cook III,47 **Potage de beccasses rosties**; see also snipe

—— woodhen, Cook I, VI,2 *genillotte (de bois)*: Cotg: "*Gelinote, gelinote de bois*. The pied, or peckled Pheasant, or wood Henne; somewhat rounder bodied, and much daintier meat, then an ordinarie Henne"; Cotg glosses the word *genillette* as a Savoyard term for "a Henne"; young woodcock, Cook I *beccasset*

wood-pigeon: see dove

c) **Water creatures**

anchovy, Cook XV,55; XVI,17, 22; XVII,13; Pastry Chef VII,24 *anchois, anchoix*

barbel (*Barbus barbus*), Cook XVI,28–32; XXVI,21; XXVII,35 *barbeaux*; Cotg: "The river Barbell"; in modern usage the *barbel de mer* is the red mullet

bream (probably the freshwater bream, *Abramis brama*, similar to the carp), Cook XVI,12; XVIII,19; XXVII,30 *bresme*; Cotg: "*Brame*. A Breame. *Brame de mer*. The sea Breame (called so at Paris, where it is ordinarie) also, the Guilt-head, or Goldennie (and divers other fishes of that kind are also called so by the inhabitants of the sea coasts"

brill (*Scophthalmus rhombus*), Cook XVI33; XVIII,2; XXI,6; XXVI,22; XXVII,2, 3 *barbuë*; Cotg: "*Barbuë*. A kind of lesse Turbot, or Turbot-like fish, called by some, a Dab, or Sandling"; the turbot is scientifically called a *Scophthalmus maximus*

burbot (*Lota lota*), Cook XV,40; XVI,16, 17, 88; XVIII,25, 26; XIX,15; XXI,21, 23; XXVII,24, 25; XXVIII,17, 30, 32 *lotte, [lothe, lotthe]* (*Lota lota*) (a freshwater cod)

—— burbot liver, Cook XV,8; XIX,15; XXI,21; XXVIII,17, 32 *foye de lotte*; Burbot Liver Tourte, Cook XXI,21 **Tourte de foyes de lottes**

carp, Cook XV,2–8, 10, 13, 14, 33; XVI,6–11, 32, 39, 60, 72, 73, 91; XVIII,27, 28; XIX,16, 24; XXI,0, 1, 4, 12, 13, 24; XXIV,1; XXV,2, 5, 6; XXVI,0, 5–8, 10; XXVII,22, 23, 33; XXVIII,29; Pastry Chef VII,20–24 *carpe*; Carp *au bleu*, Cook XVIII,27 **Carpe au bleu**; *Encyc* (II, 284b): "*Poisson au bleu.* C'est une façon d'accommoder le poisson en le faisant cuire avec ses écailles"; see also pike

—— milt carp, Cook XVIII,27 *la meilleure sorte de carpe est laitée*; carp milt, Cook XV,6, 31; XVI,61, 88, 93; XIX,13; XXI,22; XXV,23; Pastry Chef VII,22 *laitances de carpes*; Pastry Chef XXIX,9; XXXIII,16, 19 *laite, laites de carpe*

—— carp tongues, Cook XVIII,28; Pastry Chef VII,22 *langues de carpe*

chub (*Leuciscus cephalus*), Cook XVI,22–24; XXVI,18, 19; XXVII,36 *vilain*; Cotg: "*Vilain.* The Chevin, or Pollard fish (called so because it feeds upon nothing but filth)"; Godefroy: "*Villain.* Poisson, le meunier [miller's thumb, bull-head; chub]"

cod, Cook XVI,68–71, 77; XVIII,18; XXI,11; XXVI,54–56; XXVII,29

morue; cod tripe, Fricasseed Cod Tripe, Cook XVI,77; XXVI,64 **Tripes de morue fricassées**

crawfish (sea crustacean, *Palinurus vulgaris*), perhaps also spiny lobster (also of the family *Palinuridæ*), Cook XVI,58, 59; XXVI,44, 45 *langouste*; Crawfish in a White Sauce, Cook XVI,59 **Langouste en sauce blanche**; Cotg: "*Langouste.* A kind of Lobster that hath undivided cleyes, a long beake (or beard) and prickles on her backe"; Fur: "*Langouste de mer*, est un petit poisson que quelques-uns appellent *dragon marin*, ou *cheval marin*, en Latin *hippocampus*, ainsi nommé à cause de la ressemblance qu'il a avec les chenilles des herbes des champs, estant long d'environ six doits, & à cause qu'il a la teste & le col ressemblant au cheval, ayant neantmoins un bec long & creux comme un flageolet. Son corps est basty de petits cercles & rondeaux cartilagineux & pointus . . . "; see also lobster

crayfish (freshwater crustacean, *Astacus fluviatilis*, freshwater lobster), Cook XV,2, 4, 30, 40; XXI,25; XXIV,1; XXV,1; XXVIII,33, 34 *escrevisses, ecrevisses*; crayfish juice, stock, Cook XV,30 *jus d'ecrevisses*; Cotg: "*Escrevisse.* A Crevice, or Crayfish; (By some Authors, but not so properly, the Crab-fish is also tearmed so.)"; Fur: "Poisson testacée, espece de cancre. Il y a des escrevisses de riviere, & des escrevisses de mer. ... Manege le derive de l'Anglois *crab-fish*, qui signifie escrevisse"; Rich: "Poisson couvert de coque, qui naît aux rivieres qui coulent des montagnes & aux eaux frêches"

cuttlefish (*Sepia officinialis*), Cook XVI,78; XXVI,65 *seiches*; Fricasseed Cuttlefish Cook XVI,78 **Seiches fricassées**; Cotg: "*Seiche.* The Sound, or Cuttle fish"

2. Preparations

If the name of a dish embodies in it the name of a specific ingredient, that dishname (with the usual reference to the instance or instances of its appearance in one of La Varenne's works) will normally be found in Appendix 1, Ingredients. For instance, *pottage* and **Queen's Pottage** will appear here in Appendix 2, Preparations, whereas **Hops Pottage** will appear in Appendix 1, Ingredients, in the entry for *hops*. The names of particular prepared dishes in La Varenne's work are normally written with a capital.

Also included in this section are terms associated with a specific genre of preparation, such as pottage.

Alexandria: see sorbet

almonds: see cake, confections, dough, dragées, tourte, below; and almonds in Appendix 1

Angelica (a cordial), Confectioner IV,4 **Angelique**; Fur: "*Angelique*. Une espece de boisson, qui est un hypocras fait de Coindrieu, ou d'autre vin exquis" [Elsewhere Furetière classifies Coindrieu along with muscat as a sweet dessert wine.]

Angel Throat (a dry confection), Confectioner XII,1 **Gorge d'ange**

baked dishes, Pastry Chef I,3, 4; V,0; IX,1; X,0; XI,5; XIII,0; XV,7; XVII,0 *pieces de four*

Basque: see pie

batter: see dough

bauble, a fool's bauble, Cook V,29, 83; XIV,13 *(à la) marotte*; Godefroy: "*Marotte*. Poupée, tête de poupée"; Fur: "Un baston au bout duquel il y a une petite figure ridicule en forme de Marionette coiffée d'un bonnet de différentes couleurs"

Bayonne ham: see ham

beverages, delicious beverages, Cook IV,1–10 *breuvages delicieux*; see also waters

Pupton, Cook V,75 **Poupeton**; *Delices*, 250: "... *une espece de Pasté que l'on appelle Pourpeton, tout semblable à la Tourte de Beatilles, reservé que le hachis se paistrit avec œufs cassez, & se dresse dans une Terrine, au lieu que la Paste se met dans la Tourtiere*"; see the recipe called "A French Pupton of Pigeons" in Hannah Glasse, *The Art of Cookery, made Plain and Easy* (first published 1747) (Totnes, Devon: Prospect Books, 1995), p. 45; Cotg: "*Poupette*. Sorte de bouillie"

Biscuit, Cook Confections,46; Pastry Chef XXV **Biscuit**; see also Appendix 1

—— Snow-Sugar Biscuits, Pastry Chef XXV,5, 6 **Biscuit de sucre en neige**

—— Cinnamon Biscuit, Pastry Chef XXV,4 **Biscuit de canelle**

—— Plain Pastry-Chef Biscuits, Pastry Chef XXV,1 **Biscuit commun de Pastissiers**

—— Lenten Biscuit, Pastry Chef XXV,8 **Biscuit de Caresme**

—— Gamby Biscuit, Pastry Chef XXV,7 **Biscuit de gamby**; Marnette: "a crooked form of Bisket, or Kertled Bisket"

—— lemon biscuit (large), Confectioner III,5 *grand biscuit de citron*

—— Lenten Biscuit, Pastry Chef XXV,8 **Biscuit de charnage**

—— Queen's Biscuit, Pastry Chef

XXV,2 **Biscuit à la Reyne**
—— Piedmontese Biscuit, Pastry Chef
XXV,3 **Biscuit de Piedmont**
—— Pistachio Biscuits, Pastry Chef
XXV,6 **Biscuits de pistaches**
—— Savoy Biscuit, Cook Confections,65
Biscuit de Savoye; a sort of sponge
cake; see *OCF, s.v. Savoy*
bisque, Cook III,48 *bisque*; Fur: "Potage
exquis fait de plusieurs pigeons,
poulets, beatilles, jus de mouton, &
autres bons ingrediens qu'on ne sert
que sur la table des Grands Seigneurs.
Ce mot en ce sens vient de *bis cocta*,
parce que la *bisque* se faisant de
plusieurs beatilles, il en faut faire
plusieurs cuissons separées et reïterées,
avant que de loy donner la derniere
cuisson et perfection. On appelle *demi-
bisque*, celle qui se fait à moindre frais,
et où on ne met que la moitié des ingredients de la precedante"
—— Egg Bisque, Pastry Chef XXIX,9
Bisque aux œufs
—— Squab Bisque, Cook III,1 **Bisque
de pigeonneaux**
—— Half Bisque [of Large Dove], Cook
III,48 **Demie bisque**
Boar's Head, Cook VIII,93–95 **Hure de
sanglier**; *Delices*, 291: "*La Hure* [*de
sanglier*] *se sert toute entiere sur la
Table des Grands*"; Cotg: "*Hure*. The
head of a Beare, Wolfe, wild Boare, or
any other savage, and dangerous beast";
see also salmon jowl
bouillon: see Ingredients, above, 1 b)
—— white bouillon: see sauce (white
sauce). below
braised (meat) Cook V,15, 54, 57 *(cuit à
l')estoffade*; *TLF*: "*Estouffade*. Manière
de faire cuire très lentement et dans
leur vapeur certaines viandes"; see also
to braise in Appendix 3
—— Braised Breast of Veal, Cook V,15
Poictrine de veau à l'estoffade
—— Braised Beef, Cook V,54 **Bœuf à
l'estoffade**
—— Braised Partridge, Cook V,57 **Perdrix à l'estoffade**

bread, loaf of bread *pain*; see also sippet,
below, and bread as an ingredient in
Appendix 1
—— bourgeois bread (coarse), Pastry
Chef XV,2 *pain bourgeois*; Cotg: "*Pain
bourgeois*. Crible bread betweene white
and browne; a bread (that somewhat resembles our wheaten, or cheat) a loafe
whereof is to weigh, when tis baked, 32
ounces"; Huguet: "*Pain bourgeois.
Pain fait d'une farine fine*. ... Le
pain dit Bourgeois, et celuy nommé
de Chapitre, suivent le molet, n'estans
differens par entre eux qu'en la figure, le Bourgeois s'eslevant plus en
rondeur que celui de Chapitre, qui est
plus pressé, plus plat"; Tré: "*Pain de
chapitre*. Du pain qu'on distribue par
chaque jour à chaque Chanoine. Il est
de fine fleur de farine bien pétrie, et
d'une consistence assez ferme. Il étoit
autrefois broyé, & avec peu de levain"
—— bun(s), small loaf, loaves of bread,
Cook III,10; XV,23; XXIX,8; Linen
¶¶13, 15, 18, 24 *petit(s) pain(s)*
—— cantel, Pastry Chef VIII,2 *(pain
benist ou) chanteau*; Fur: "On appelle ... *chanteau*, une grosse piece de
pastisserie formée en long, & de même
que la bordure du pain benit, qu'on
fait faire pour envoyer à ses parens &
amis, à cause que celuy qu'on a ren-
voyé de l'Eglise n'y peut pas suffire: &
parce qu'on le fait de paste plus fine,
on l'appelle autrement *cousin*, à cause
qu'on l'envoye à ceux qui touchent de
plus prés, ou qu'on aime le mieux";
Rich: "Gros morceau de pain benit
qu'on donne à celui qui doit faire le
pain benit"; Cotg: "*Chanteau*. A gob-
bet, lumpe, crust, or cantell of bread,
&c."
—— consecrated bread, holy bread, Pastry Chef VIII,1, 2 *pain benist*; Tré:
"Un pain qu'on offre à l'Église pour le
bénir, le partager avec les Fidèles et le
manger avec dévotion"; Rich: "C'est

du pain que le Prétre benit & qu'on coupe par morceaux pour le distribüer aux fidelles durant une Messe solannelle"; *RDH*: "Pain excellent"

—— consecrated bread (variety of), Pastry Chef VIII,2 *cousin: un pain benist & plus delicat, lequel on appelle à Paris du cousin; & en d'autres endrois on le nomme un chanteau*; Rich: "*Cousin*. Terme de paticier. Pain benit, meilleur & plus délicat que les pain-benits ordinaires & où il entre du beurre, des œufs & du fromage"; Fur: "*Cousin*, signifie un chanteau long qu'on faisoit cy-devant, quand on rendoit le pain benit, pour en envoyer des parts aux parents & aux amis, parce que le chanteau de l'Eglise ne suffisoit pas, & n'estoit pas si bien estoffé, ni si delicat. On faisoit honneur à ses amis en leur envoyant du *cousin*"

—— *flamiches*, a fine bread, Pastry Chef XVI *flamiches*; Cotg: "*Flamiche*. (In Paris, and thereabouts they call so) a kind of better bread then ordinairie, reserved for the Maisters, and Mistresses own mouthes; as also, a cake made of butter, cheese, flower, and yolkes of egges; after baking glazed over with sugar, and rosewater"; *FEW* (III, 600a): a form *flamique* is attested in the NE in the 12th c., and in modern Namur *flamitche* is a "tarte ordinaire, faite de pâte de pain et semée de sucre et de beurre."

—— Queen's loaf, Linen ¶¶ 22, 28 *pain à la reine*; Fur: "[Les Boulengers] mettent du sel & de la levure de biere au *pain à la Reine*"; see the quotation *s. v. leavening* in Appendix 1; Ronald Sheppard and Edward Newton, *The Story of Bread*, London (Routledge & Kegan Paul), 1957, p. 155, describe "Queen's Bread or brioche" as small and "very rich, the liquid content of the dough consisting almost entirely of eggs"

Burnt Wine (a cordial), Confectioner IV,5 **Vin bruslé**; Fur: "*Vin bruslé* est celuy qu'on fait bouillir avec du sucre"

cake (a dough mixture that has caked), Cook Confections,31, 53, 64; Pastry Chef VII,15, 17; XII; XV (passim); XVI; XVII; XXIX,3–5; XXXII,2; XXXIII,22 *gasteau, gâteau*; Fur: "*Gasteau*. Pastisserie faite avec du beurre & de la farine. ... Les Picards l'appellent encore *watel*"; Rich: "*Gâteau*. Morceau de pâte qu'on étend où l'on met du sel & du beurre, & qu'on fait quelquefois cuire au feu & ordinairement au four"; see also Fish Cake, below

—— sponge cake, Pastry Chef XV *gasteau mollet*; sponge cake called Egg Bread by the Flemish, Pastry Chef XV,4 *lequel gasteau les Flamans nomment du* **Pain aux œufs**

—— Almond Cakes, Cook Confections,49 **Gasteaux d'amendes**

—— Cakes of Cherries, Apricots, Pistachios and Almonds, Cook Confections,31 **Gasteaux de cerises, d'abricots, de pistaches, & d'amandes**

—— Dimpled Cake, Pastry Chef XV,7 **Gasteau verollé**; Fur: "*Verolé*. Qui a la grosse verole [pox]"

—— Egg Cake or Tourte, Pastry Chef XXIX,3 **Gasteau ou tourte aux œufs**

—— Kings' Cakes, Pastry Chef XV,8 **Gasteaux des Roys**

—— Lady Lucia Cake, Pastry Chef XV,5 *Gasteau à la dame Lucie*

—— Milanese Cake, Pastry Chef XV,8 **Gasteau de Milan**

—— Pistachio Cake, Cook Confections,53 **Gasteau de pistaches**

candied foods, Cook XX,11 *confit*; Confectioner Pref *candi*; Fur: "*Sucre candi*. Une preparation de sucre qui se cristalise: ce qui se fait en le fondant jusqu'à six ou sept fois"; see *Encyc*, XV, 615b and Supplément II, 199a; see also confection, preserve, below, and to candy, to preserve in Appendix 3

—— Candied Apricots, Cook XXI,40 *abricots confits*; Confectioner XIV,2

Abricots candis

—— candied lemon, lemon peel, Cook VIII,78, 79; XVII,17; XX,5; XXI,25, 29, 40 *escorce de citron confit, un lardon de citron confit*

—— Candied Borage Blossoms, Confectioner XIV,6 **Fleurs de bouroche candie**

—— Candied Cucumbers, Cook XX,11 **Concombres confites**

—— Candied Fennel, Confectioner XIV,3 **Fenouil candi**

—— Candied Oranges, Confectioner XIV,1 **Oranges candies**

—— Candied Orange Blossoms, Confectioner XIV,5 **Fleurs d'orange candie**

—— Candied Raspberries, Cook Confections,54 **Framboises confites**

—— Candied Rose Hips, Confectioner XIV,7 **Boutons de rose candie**

—— Candied Violets, Confectioner XIV,4 **Violette candie**

capital, Cook XVI,91; Pastry Chef VII,2, 8 *chapiteau*; I.D.G.: "Chapiteau. It is any worke set over the lid of a pie"

caramel, Cook Confections,50; Confectioner III,5; VII,15 *caramel, caramelle*; Fur: "*Caramel*. Drogue que les Apothicaires preparent pour le rheume, qui consiste particulierement en du sucre fort cuit"; from the Italian *caramello* and *caramella*

Cardinal; see also Mazarin, *s.v.* creams

—— Cardinal's Leg of Mutton, Cook V,2 **Membre de mouton à la Cardinale**

—— Cardinal's Pie, Cook V,85; XIV,12; XXI,13; Pastry Chef VII,13, 19, 22 **Pasté à la Cardinale, Cardinalle**; see also pie, below

caudle (of milk), Cook VIII,64 *chaudeau (de laict)*

cedar eagle (a cordial), Confectioner IV,8 *aigle de cedre*

Chalon: see beef in Appendix 1 b)

chausson (var. of turnover) (of apples, pears), Pastry Chef IX,12 *chosson (de pommes ou de poires)*; the French word

chausson is literally a slipper or sock; *Acad*: "Il se dit, par analogie, d'une Sorte de pâtisserie qui contient de la marmelade, de la compote ou des confitures, et qui est faite d'un rond de pâte replié sur lui-même"; *RDH*: "Une préparation de pâte renfermant des fruits, une compote" (1783)

Cinnamon Water: see waters

civet: see egg dishes

claret, Cook Confections,38 *clairet*; Fur: "On a appellé autrefois *clairet*, l'hypocras ou vin composé avec des espiceries. Les Allemands l'appellent encore *claret*, les Espagnols *clarea*, & les Auteurs modernes *claretum*"

colourants; see also to brown, to gild, Appendix 3

—— green (chard juice), Confectioner II,1; XVI,25 **Poirée preparée, jus de poirée**

—— red (cochineal), Confectioner II,2 **Cochenille preparée**; vermillion (cinnabar), Confectioner XIII,9 *sinabre*

—— yellow (lily stamens), Confectioner II,4 **Fleur de lis**

—— red, blue (orchil, archil), Cook Confections,13 *tourne sol*

Combalet: see tourte

compote, Confectioner Pref *composte, compote*; Fur: "*Compote*. On le dit . . . de la cuisson des fruits ou confitures qu'on veut manger proprement [neatly]"; see also glacé preparations

—— Apple Compote, Cook Confections,56; Confectioner X,1, 3, 4 **Composte de pommes**; Compote of Whole Apples, Confectioner X,4 **Pommes entieres**; Calville-Apple Compote, Cook Confections,57; Confectioner X,2 **Composte de pommes de Calvil, Compote de calvis**; Rennet-Apple Compote, Cook Confections,56; Confectioner X,2 **Compote de reinette**

—— Barberry Compote, Confectioner X,14 **Compote d'espine-vinette**

—— Chestnut Compote, Confectioner X,7, 15 **Compote de marons, Marons**

Muscat, Muscats sans peaux, Verjus, Verjus liquide, Verjus sec; see also Grape Confection, below

—— Lemons, Whole, Cook Confections,23 **Citrons entiers**

—— Mulberries, Confectioner XI,8 **Mures**

—— Oranges, Cook Confections,24 **Oranges**; Orange Blossoms, Confectioner VII,2 **Fleur d'orange liquide**

—— Peaches: Avant Peaches, Clingstone Peaches, Corbeil Peaches, Confectioner XI,21, 22, 23; XII,9 **Avant péches, Alberges, Péches de Corbeil**

—— Pears: Russet Pears, Muscatdelle Pears, Blanquette Pears, Confectioner XI,17, 18; XII,13, 14 **Poires de rousselet, Poires muscadelles, Poires de blanquette**

—— Pistachios (a dry confection), Confectioner X,18 **Pistache au sec**

—— Plums: Imperial Plums, Peeled Imperial Plums, White *Perdrigon* Plums, White *Perdrigon* Plums, Peeled *Perdrigon* Plums, Red *Perdrigon* Plums, Red Damson Plums, Lilevert, Plums Cook Confections,16; Confectioner XI,11, 12, 13, 14, 15, 16; XI,10, 11, 12 **Prunes liquides de toutes sortes, Prunes imperiales, Prunes imperiales sans peau, Perdrigon blanc, Perdrigon sans peau, Perdrigon rouge, Prunes de damas rouges, Prunes de lilevert**

—— Quince (moist & dry), Cook Confections,37; Confectioner XI,26; XII,18 **Coins (secs), coings**; Cook Confections,55 **Coins liquides**

—— Raspberries, Confectioner XI,5 **Framboises**

—— Roses, Cook Confections,14; Confectioner VIII,3 **Roses, Rozes au sec**; Rose Hips Cook, Confections,21 **Boutons de roses secs**

—— Strawberries, Cook Confections,49 **Fraises**

—— Walnuts: White Walnuts, Green Walnuts, Cook Confections,25; Confec-

tioner XI,19, 20; XII,4 **Noix blanches, Noix vertes**

consommé: see Ingredients, Appendix 1 b)

cotignac, Confectioner X,20, 21, 24 *cotignac*; Thin Cotignac, Confectioner X,20 **Cotignac clair**; Thick Cotignac, Confectioner X,21 **Cotignac espais**; Cotg: "*Cotignac*. Codinniack; preserve, or Marmalade of Quinces"; Fur: "*Cotignac*. Confiture ou paste de coins. Le bon cotignac se fait à Orleans. Cotignac se dit aussi de la paste ou gelée de quelques autres fruits"

—— Apple Cotignac, Confectioner X,24 **Cotignac de pommes**

—— Orleans Cotignac, Cook Confections,48 **Cottignac d'Orleans**; I.D.G.: "Marmalat of Quinces of Orleans"; see Furetiere's statement, above

course, serving, Pastry Chef XXI,3 *mets*; Cotg: "*Mets, més*. A messe, course, or service of meat"; Fur: "*Mets*. Ce qui est bon à manger, qu'on a preparé pour servir sur la table"; see also entremets

court bouillon, Cook XVI,23 (passim 40) *court bouillon*; Tré: "manière de faire cuire certains poissons, comme les carpes, les saumons, les brochets: ce qui se fait avec du vin, du laurier, du romarin, du sel & des épices; après quoi on les sert à sec dans une serviette, ou on les mange avec du vinaigre. On appelle demi court-bouillon, la même manière de les apprêter, mais on les sert avec un peu de la sauce où ils ont été cuits"; Rich: court-bouillon, vin, laurier, romarin, sel, poivre & orange, où l'on fait bien cuire du poisson; *TLF* (6,368a): same [ingrs. & purpose only, no desc.]

—— half court bouillon, Cook XVI,10 (passim 8) *demi court bouillon*

cracknel, Pastry Chef XXIV *craquelin*; Cotg: "A Cracknell, made of the yolke of egges, water, and flower, and fashioned like a hollow trendle"

creams, foods prepared with a cream: asparagus, Cook VIII,88; XIX,21;

eggs XVII,9, 16; mushrooms XIX,2; XXX,37; morels XXX,46; see also omelet, tourte (Frangipane)

—— Cooked Cream, Cook Confections,40 **Cresme cuite**

—— English Cream, Cook Confections,41 **Cresme d'Angleterre**

—— Lenten Cream, Pastry Chef IV,3 **Cresme pour le Caresme**

—— Mazarin Cream, Cook VIII,83 **Cresme à la Mazarine**; named perhaps in honour of Cardinal Giulio Mazarini (1602–61), an Italian prelate who in 1642 became prime minister of France

—— Pastry-Chef's Cream, Pastry Chef IV; (passim) **Cresme de pastissier**; Pastry Chef IX,2 *creme de pastisserie*

—— Cream of Pistachios, Cook VIII,18; XXX,47 **Cresme de pistache**

—— Cream Tourte, Cook XXI,35 **Tourte de cresme**; Little Musk Cream Tourte Cook XXVIII,27 **Petite tourte de cresme musquée**

—— Whipped Cream, Cook Confections,39 **Cresme foüettée**

Dariole, Pastry Chef XIII **Dariole**

daube (a stewed, braised treatment), Cook V,21, 22, 27, 32, 33 *(à la) daube*; Rich: "*Daube*. Certaine maniere d'aprêter la viande avec des choses qui relévent le goût de la viande & révaillent l'apétit"; etymological dictionaries trace *daube* in French back to only 1642 and derive it from the Italian *addobbo*, "a seasoning"; see beef, goose, mutton, pork (piglet), turkey in Appendix 1

decoction, Confectioner Preface; IV,7; V,2; X,5, 19 *decoction*

Donkey's Farts (variety of fritter), Pastry Chef XXI,1 **Pets d'asne**; spherical doughnuts whose dough is the size of hazel-nuts (La Varenne)

dough, pastry dough, Cook (passim 130) *pâte*; see also paste in Appendix 1

—— coarse dough (of oatmeal, buckwheat, barley), Pastry Chef VII,2 *paste gru*; Cotg: "*Grus*. A gruell"; Fur:

"*Gruau*. ... Ce mot vient de *grutellum*, diminutif de *grutum*. ... En quelques lieux on dit *gruel* & *grut*: & on le prend aussi pour toutes autres choses pilées grossierement, c'est à dire, reduittes en grains"

—— fine dough, Cook V,77 (passim 36); Pastry Chef IX,6, 9 *paste fine*; recipe in Cook XXI,0; semi-fine dough, Cook XIV,37 *pâte à moitié fine*

—— dark dough, Cook V,29 (passim 13); Pastry Chef I *paste bise, bize*; Cotg: "*Pain bis*. Rye bread, course bread, browne bread"; recipe in Cook XXI,0

—— feuilleté dough, puff pastry, Cook XIV,28 (passim 15); Pastry Chef I,4; VII,9, 11–13, 15, 17, 22; IX,1, 6, 9; X; XV,10; XXII,2 *paste feuilletée*; Pastry Chef VII,8 *crouste feuilletée*; half-feuilleté dough, *pâte brisée*, a short pastry dough, Pastry Chef I,4; VII,3; VII,15 *paste demy fueilletée*; Marnette: "*demi feuilleté*: Half leaved Paste or Dough"; Cook XV,45; Pastry Chef VII,3, 17, 18; IX,1, 2, 7, 8, 15; XXIII,2; XXV,7, 8 *paste, crouste, abesses de fueilletage*; I.D.G.: "puft paste"; Cotg: "*Gasteau fueilleté*. A cake of puffe-past"; recipe in Cook XXI,0; see also rissoles

—— hot water dough, Cook XXI,0 *pâte d'eau chaude*

—— oil dough, Pastry Chef I,5; VII,24 *paste à l'huile*

—— spun pastry, spun dough, Cook VIII,42–44; XIX,11; XXVIII,10 *pâte filée*; see to spin, Appendix 3

—— sweet dough, Pastry Chef I,6; VII,19 *paste de sucre*; semi-sweet dough, Pastry Chef I,6 *paste à demy sucre*

—— sheet, leaf, layer of dough, Pastry Chef IX,3, 5, 9, 10, 13; IX,15; X *fueille de paste*; Pastry Chef IX,15 *fueillet de paste*

—— pastry shell, crust, Cook V,77 (passim); Pastry Chef I,3 (passim); Confectioner XVI,9, 19 *abaisse, abbaisse,*

XXXIV,10 **Marmelade aux œufs brouillez**

—— Milanese Eggs, Pastry Chef XXXIII,24 **Oeufs à la Milanoise**; an alternative name for **Oeufs au beurre noir**

—— Mirror Eggs, Cook XVII,3 **Oeufs au miroir**; Creamed Mirror Eggs, Cook XVII,16 **Oeufs au miroir de cresme**

—— Poached Eggs, Cook XVII,8; Pastry Chef XXIX,9; XXX,0, 2, 6, 8; XXXIV,4 **Oeufs pochez à l'eau**

—— Polish Eggs, Pastry Chef XXXIV,13 **Œufs à la polonnaise**

—— Portuguese Eggs, Cook VIII,79; Pastry Chef XXXII,1 **Oeufs à la portugaise**

—— Salmon of Eggs, Pastry Chef XXX,6 **Saumon d'œufs**

—— Scrambled Eggs, Cook XVII,15 **Oeufs brouillez**; see also marmalade, below

—— Sliced Fricasseed Eggs, Cook XVII,7 **Oeufs fricassez en tranches**

—— Snowy Eggs, Cook VIII,83; XVII,19 **Oeufs à la neige**

—— Sorrel Eggs, Cook XVII,6 **Oeufs à l'ozeille**

—— Stuffed Eggs, Cook XVII,1 **Oeufs farcis**

—— Threaded Eggs, Cook VIII,81; XIX,4 **Oeufs filez**

—— Eggs with Verjuice, Cook XVII,12 **Oeufs au verjus**

England, English: see cream, pie; and beef in Appendix 1 b)

entrée, Cook V,0; VIII,16, 53; X,4; XV,54; XVI,0; XVII,0; XVIII,11, 30; XX,0, 20; XXI,12; XXVI,0; XXX,0 *entrée*; Cotg: "*L'entrée de table.* The first course, or, the meat thats first served up, at table"

entremets, Cook II; VIII; X,4; XIX,0, 4, 6; XX,26; XXI,40; XXVIII,0 *entre mets, entre-mets, entremets*; Cotg: "*Entremets.* Certaine choice dishes served in between the courses at a feast, or banquet"; Fur: "*Entremets.* Plats de

ragoust qu'on met sur la table entre les services, & particulierement entre le rost & le fruit"; Rich: "Tous les petis ragoûs [*sic*] & autres choses delicates qui se servent aprés les viandes, & immédiatement devant le fruit"; see also course

epigramme: Veal Hocks *à l'épigramme*, Cook V,3 **Jarets de veau à l'épigramme**; *RDH*: "Épigramme d'agneau. Côtelettes ou poitrine braisée, panée et cuite sur le gril"; Larousse: "*Epigramme d'agneau.* (Art culin.) Ragoût au blanc, dans lequel on fait entrer quelques parties intérieures de l'animal"; *NLG* cites a supposed origin of the culinary sense "towards the middle of the eighteenth century"

false, counterfeit (qualifying a preparation), Confectioner XIII,9–11 *contrefait*

Feuillantine, Pastry Chef X **Feuillantine, Feuillentine**; Fur: "On appelle à Paris *feuillantine*, une espece de pastisserie feuilletée faite en forme de tarte ou de tourte de viande hachée, sucre & cresme"; Marnette: " . . . a Fueillentine, or Puff-paste"

fingers (of bread), Cook III,38, 42 *tailladins*; pastry fingers, Cook XV,44, 45; XXV,38 *tailladins feuilletés*; Lemon Fingers, Confectioner IX,5 **Tailladins de citrons**; Orange Fingers, Confectioner IX,3 **Orenges en tailladins**; Pottage of a Leg of Beef with Bread Fingers, Cook III,42 **Potage de trumeau de bœuf au tailladin**; Capon with Bread Fingers, Cook III,42 **Chapon au tailladin**; La Varenne (Cook III,38): "*tailladins, c'est à dire des morceaux de pain de la longueur & grosseur d'un doigt en forme de lardons*"; *cf.* a strip, Confectioner X,2 *taillade*; see to slash, Appendix 3

Fish Cake (a dish of compressed fish), Cook XVI,72, 73; XXVI,57 **Soupresse de poisson**; *Delices*, 318: "*Avec du Saulmon salé, du Hareng soret, des Tanches, & autres Poissons desossez,*

garnish, garnishing, trimming(s), Cook III,14 (passim 27) *garniture*; see also tidbits, Appendix 1 b); garnishing salad: see salads

gaudivaux: see pie (Minced Veal)

Genoa, Genoese: see pastes

German Sauce: see sauce

gilding, Pastry Chef III; V; VII,20 *doreure*; Pastry-Chefs' Gilding, Pastry Chef III,0 **Doreure des Pastissiers**; Cotg.: "A gilding"; Marnette: "varnish," "wash"; see also to gild in Appendix 3; cf. glazing, below

glacé preparations; see also glazing, below; to glaze, Appendix 3
—— Glacé Apricots, Confectioner X,17 **Abricots glassez**
—— Glacé Brignol Plums, Confectioner X,16 **Brugnolles glacées**
—— Glacé Cherries, Confectioner X,16 **Cerises [glacées]**
—— Glacé Chestnuts, Confectioner X,16 **Marons glassez**; see also compote
—— Glacé Marzipan, Confectioner XVI,4 **Machepain glacé**
—— Glacé Peaches, Confectioner X,16 **Pesches [glacées]**

glazing, Cook XXI,40; Confections,9, 31, 34; Pastry Chef V; VII,14; IX,1, 15; XV,9XVII; XXV,7; XXVI; Confectioner X,16; XVI,4–7, 10, 12, 18 *glace, glace de sucre*; Marnette: "*glace*, sugared Ice, or Frost"; see also to glaze, Appendix 3

grape confection, Pastry Chef XXX,8 *raisiné*; Cotg: "*Raisiné*. A confection of grapes, made thicke, and eaten with bread, as honie; or as *Raisinnée*; *Raisinnée*: a sauce, or confection of delicate, blacke, and ripe grapes, first pressed betweene the hands; then boiled with water and salt; and then strained, & put into earthen vessells, where it will harden like a Marmalade, and keepe verie long"; Fur: "Raisiné est une preparation de raisin qu'on fait avec du vin doux, qu'on fait cuire & reduire à la moitié, pour le conserver."

On l'étend sur du pain pour le gouster des enfans" [FitzG: grape jam]

grape mash: see Appendix 1 a)

gruel, porridge (of wheat, rice), Cook VIII,42; XXI,35 *bouillie, boulie*; Wheat Flour Porridge, Cook XX,2; XXX,22 **Bouillie de fleur de bled, de farine**; Porridge of Rice and Strained Almonds, Cook XXX,23 **Boulie de ris & d'amendes passées**; children's gruel, Pastry Chef XV,1 *bouillie qu'on donne aux enfans*; Cotg: "*Boulie*. Pap, or broth, for children"; I.D.G.: "pap"

ham, gammon, smoked or cured ham:
—— Mayence Ham, Bayonne ham, Cook IX **Jambon de Mayence**; Pastry Chef VII,1, 2 *jambons de Mayence ou de Bayonne*; Tré: "*Jambon de Maience*. C'est une préparation de jambons, qui se fait en les salant, avec du salpêtre pur, & en les pressant dans un pressoir à linge huit jours. Après quoi on les trempe dans l'esprit de vin [distilled wine], où il y aura des grains de geniévre pilés et macérés, & ensuite on les met sécher à la fumée du bois de geniévre"; the article in Tré goes on to explain that this treatment of ham was that practiced in Westphalia, but was so named because such hams sold well at a fair in Mayence.
—— Ham Slices (variety of preserve, mock ham), Cook Confections,10; Confectioner VII,18 **Tranches de jambon**
—— fish ham, fish gammon, Cook XVI,73; XIX,24; XXVI,58 *jambon de poisson*; Cotg: "*Jambon*. A gammon"

hash, (seasoned) minced meat or fish, Cook III,11, 38; V,72; XXI,18; Pastry Chef VII,8, 18; XXIX,7, 8; XXXIII,17, 18 *achis, hachis*; Cotg: "*Hachis*. A hachey, or hachee; a sliced gallimaufrey [see the next word], or minced meat"; see also stuffing
—— meat hash *achis de chair*; Minced Roast Meat, Cook,V,72 **Achis de viande rostie**; Minced Raw Meat, Cook V,74 **Achis de viande crue**; Minced

marzipan, pastes, preserve, syrup, waters

—— Lemonade (a sweet beverage), Cook Confections,36; Confectioner IV,9, 10 *limonade*; cf. Italian *limonata*

Lent, Cook I,0; XXI,0; XXV,25; XXVI,0; XXVII,0; XXVIII,0; XXIX,3; 11, 12; XXX,0; Pastry Chef III; IV,3; VII,20, 22; IX,7 *Caresme, Charesme*; see also fish days, meat days

liaisons: see thickeners

loaf: see bread

logate: see mutton, Appendix 1b

Lucia: see cake

macaroni, Pastry Chef XXIX,7 *macaroni*

macaroon, Cook XV,44; XXI,39; Confections,47; Pastry Chef IV,3; IX,3, 4, 7, 8, 10, 15; X; XII,6; XV,1; XXVII; XXVIII,1; XXIX,7, 11; XXXIII,17; XXXIV,10, 11 *macaron*; Cotg: "*Macarons*. Macarons; little Fritter like Bunnes, or thicke Losenges compounded of Sugar, Almonds, Rosewater, and Muske, pounded together, and baked with a gentle fire; also, the Italian Macaroni; lumps, or gobbets of boyled paste serued up in butter, and strewed ouer with spice and grated cheese"; Fur: "Patisserie faite de sucre, de farine & d'amandes, taillée en petit pain plat, & de figure ovale"; the origin of the word is in the Italian *macarone*, "quenelles"

marmalade: scrambled eggs, Pastry Chef XXXIV **Marmalades**; a mash of fruit cooked with sugar Confectioner Preface; V,4; X,21; XIII (passim); XVI,8 *marmelade*; Fur: "*Marmelade*. Paste confite, à demi liquide, faite de la chair des fruits qui ont quelque substance, comme les prunes, les coins, les abricots; ... de la bouillie"; the word derived in French in the sixteenth century from the Portuguese where *marmelada* was specifically a quince jam; see also Cotignac, egg dishes

—— Almond Scrambled Eggs, Pastry

Chef XXXIV,11 **Œufs brouillez aux amandes**

—— Cheese Scrambled Eggs, Pastry Chef XXXIV,6 **Œufs brouillez au fromage**

—— Cream Scrambled Eggs, Pastry Chef XXXIV,5 **Œufs brouillez à la cresme**

—— Cucumber Scrambled Eggs, Pastry Chef XXXIV,8 **Œufs brouillez aux Concombres**

—— Darling Eggs, Pastry Chef XXXIV,14 **Œufs mignons**

—— Green-Sauce Scrambled, Eggs Pastry Chef XXXIV,9 **Œufs brouillez à la sausse verte**

—— Huguenot Eggs, Pastry Chef XXXIV,15 **Œufs à la buguenotte** (*sic*)

—— Polish Eggs, Pastry Chef XXXIV,13 **Œufs à la Polonnaise**

—— Scrambled Eggs with Chicory, Pastry Chef XXXIV,7 **Œufs brouillez avec cichorée**

—— Scrambled Eggs with Meat Bouillon, Pastry Chef XXXIV,4 **Œufs brouillez avec bouillon de viande**

—— Verjuice-Mash Scrambled Eggs, Pastry Chef XXXIV,3 **Œufs brouillez au verjuis de grain**

—— Verjuice Scrambled Eggs without/with Butter, Pastry Chef XXXIV,1, 2 **Œufs brouillez au verjus sans/avec beurre**

—— Apple Marmalade, Cook Confections,58; Confectioner X,23; XIII,9–12 **Marmelade de pommes**

—— Apricot-Marmalade Pie, Confectioner XVI,8 **Tarte de marmelade d'abricots**

—— Orange-Blossom-Marmalade Pie, Confectioner XVI,7 **Tarte de marmelade de fleurs d'orange**

—— Quince Marmalade, Confectioner X,22 **Marmelade de coings**; quince marmalade, Confectioner XIII,13 (in the preparation **Paste de Gennes**)

marzipan, Cook XXI,40; Confections,30; Pastry Chef I,4; V; XVI; XXV,4, 8; XXVI; Confectioner Preface; XVI

Fur: "*Aumelette*. Oeufs brouillés & fricassés en la poësle"

—— Apple Omelet, Pastry Chef XXXIII,4 **Aumelette aux pommes**

—— Asparagus Omelet, Pastry Chef XXXIII,21 **Aumelette aux asperges**

—— Bread Omelet, Pastry Chef XXXIII,22 **Aumelette au pain**

—— Celestine Omelet, Pastry Chef XXXIII,2 **Aumelette à la celestine**

—— Cheese Omelet, Pastry Chef XXXIII,15 **Aumelette au fromage**

—— Chicory-Stuffed, Omelet Pastry Chef XXXIII,14 **Aumelette farcie avec chichorée**

—— Chive Omelet, Pastry Chef XXXIII,13 **Aumelette à la ciboulette**

—— Crackling Omelet, Pastry Chef XXXIII,3 **Aumelette cretonneuse**

—— Cream Omelet, Cook XVII,10; XIX,8; Pastry Chef XXXIII,10 **Omelette de cresme, Aumelette à la cresme**

—— Cucumber Omelet, Pastry Chef XXXIII,16 **Aumelette aux concombres**

—— Deer-Liver Omelet, Cook VIII,14 **Foye de chevreuil en omelette**

—— Egg Omelet, Pastry Chef XXXIII,19 **Aumelette (ou tourte) aux œufs**

—— Ham Omelet, Cook VIII,76 **Omelette de jambon**; Bacon Omelet Pastry Chef XXXIII,7, 8 **Aumelette au lard**

—— Herb Omelet, Cook VIII,99; Pastry Chef XXIX,11 **Arbolade, Herbolade**; Pastry Chef XXIX,11 *herbolade*; Pastry Chef XXXIII,11 **Aumelette aux herbes**; I.D.G.: "*Arbolade*. It is a kind of French Tansie"; Marnette: "a Tansie"

—— Lemon Peel Omelet, Pastry Chef XXXIII,6 **Omelette à l'escorce de citron**

—— Parsley Omelet, Cook XVII,11; Pastry Chef XXXIII,12 **Omelette de, au persil**

—— Plain Omelet, Pastry Chef XXXIII,1 **Aumelette simple**

—— Stylish Omelet, Pastry Chef XXXIII,5 **Aumelette à la mode**

—— Turkish Omelet, Pastry Chef XXXIII,17 **Aumelette à la Truque**; *Encyc* (XI, 467a): "Il y a différentes especes d'omelettes, comme omelettes farcies, omelettes au sucre, omelettes aux pois verds, omelettes à la turque, &c."; in 17th-c. Italian, *trucco* was a form of *turco* (*DEI*)

—— Stuffed Omelet, Cook XVII,18; Pastry Chef XXXIII,20 **Omelette farcie, Aumelette à la farce**

—— Tidbit Omelet, Cook VIII,9 **Omelettes de beatilles**

—— Veal-Kidney Omelet, Pastry Chef XXXIII,18 **Aumelette au roignon de veau**

orange preparations: see candied foods, compote, confection, dragées, fingers, pastes, pie, preserve, waters

—— Orangeade, Confectioner IV,10 **Orangeade**

—— Orange Rings, Confectioner IX,2 *oranges par anneaux*

—— Orange Zests, Confectioner IX,4 **Zestes d'orange**

—— Whole Oranges (confections), Confectioner IX,1 **Oranges entiers**

Orleans: see cotignac

panada, a bread pudding for the sick, Cook XIII,4, 5 *panasde*; Cotg: "*Panade*. A Panado; crummes of bread (and currans) moistened, or brewed with water"; Fur: "*Panade*. Espece de souppe ou de potage fait de pain cuit, & imbibé dans le jus de viande, qu'on donne aux malades qui ne peuvent pas encore digerer la viande, & aux personnes delicates, qui en prennent le matin en guise de bouillon pour s'engraisser"; perhaps a Provençal or north-Italian word: cf. Venetian *panada* (*DEI*)

VII,2, 24 *pasté dressé*; Raised Pie of Eel Hash, Cook XXI,18 **Pasté dressé d'achis d'anguille**

——— : Apricot Marmelade Pie, Confectioner XVI,8 **Tarte de marmelade d'abricots**

——— : Basque Pie, Pastry Chef VII,2 **Pasté à la Basque**

——— : Cardinal's Pie, Cook V,85; XIV,12; XXI,13; Pastry Chef VII,13, 19, 22 **Pasté à la Cardinale, Cardinalle**; I.D.G.: "pie after the Cardinal's way"; Marnette: "pie after the Cardinals manner"

——— : Cheese Pie, Pastry Chef XI,2, 3, 4, 5 **Tarte au fromage**

——— : Egg Pot Pie, Pastry Chef XXIX,2 **Pasté en pot aux œufs**; see note in Pastry Chef XXIX,2

——— : English Pie, Cook V,84; VI,3; Pastry Chef V; VII,14 **Pasté à l'Angloise**; *Delices*, 42: "*Il se fait de mesme que la Rissole; reservé que dans le hachis de Volaille, l'on y mesle ou le Porc frais, ou le gigot de Mouton, ou le Liévre, & autres chairs selon l'appetit d'un chacun*"

——— : Giblet Pie, Pastry Chef VII,16 **Pasté de requeste**; Fur: "*Requeste. On dit proverbialement, qu'une chose est de requeste, pour dire, qu'elle est rare, qu'on a de la peine à en avoir. ... On appelle aussi pastez de requeste, de petits pastez de viande froide, et faits du menu des volailles*"; see also giblets Appendix 1

——— : Marzipan Pie (glazed), Confectioner XVI,5, 6 **Tarte de machepain**

——— : Minced Veal Pie (an oval, open pie), Cook V,81; XIV,7; Pastry Chef VII,9, 10, 22 **Pasté de gaudivaux**; Cotg: "*Godiveaux, Goudivaux. A kind of open Pie, made of minced veale, butter, hearbs, and spice, baked together, and afterwards hard yolks of egs put on the top of it*"; Fur: "*Godivaux. Espece de pasté qui se fait de veau haché &*

d'andouillettes avec plusieurs autres ingrediens & ragousts, comme asperges, culs d'artichaux, palais de bœuf, jaune d'œufs, champignons, etc"; Rich: "*Godiveau. Sorte de pâté de chair de veau, où il y entro dos culs d'artichaux, & des champignons, qui est découvert, & fait en ovale*"; Marnette: "A Cockney ovall minced Pie"; see also minced veal, Appendix 1b

——— : Mutton-Tongue Pie, Cook XIV,24 **Pasté de langues de mouton**

——— : Orange-Blossom-Marmalade Pie, Confectioner XVI,7 **Tarte de marmelade de fleur d'orange**

——— : pimpled pie, Pastry Chef XI,4 *une boutonnée*; Cotg: "*Boutonné. Buttoned; budded; cauterized; set thicke with pimples, or pockie botches*"; Marnette: "unbuttoning Tarts"

——— : Princess Pies (small), Pastry Chef VII,19 **(petits) Pastés à la Princesse**

——— : Royal Pie, Pastry Chef VII,5 **Pasté royal**

——— : Spanish Pies, Pastry Chef VII,18 **(petis) Pastez à l'Espagnolle**

——— : Swiss Pie, Pastry Chef VII,15 **Pasté à la suisse**

——— : Tidbit Pie, Pastry Chef VII,10 **Pasté de beatilles**

——— : turkey-cock pie, Pastry Chef VII,14 *pasté de coq d'Inde*

——— : Turkish Ham Pie, Pastry Chef VII,3 **Pasté de jambon à la turque**

——— : Venison Pie, Cook VIII,3; XIV,1, 6, 9, 14, 26; XXI,0; Pastry Chef VII,2, 4, 17, 20, 21 **Pasté de, en venaison**

Piedmont, Piedmontese: see biscuit

place setting, Linen ¶¶ 1, 2, 3 *couvert*; Fur: "*Couvert*, signifie ... la nappe, la couverture de la table, & encore plus particulierement ce qui sert à chacun des conviez, comme l'assiette, la serviette, la cuiller, le couteau, & la fourchette"

Polish: see egg dishes

populo (a cordial), Confectioner IV,3 **Populo**; Fur: "*Espece de liqueur ou de* rossolis fait avec de l'eau de veau, & peu d'eau de vie"; see also Rosolio

porridge: see gruel

Portuguese: see egg dishes

pottage, Cook III,0, 2 (passim 240) *potage*; Rich: "Bouillon du pot, soit gras, ou maigre, qu'on verse sur des soupes de pain [sops] coupées fort proprement & qu'on sert ensuite au commencement du dîner"; see also the major ingredients of various pottages in Appendix 1 (*e.g.* squab)

—— Healthy Pottage, Cook III,2; XX,4; XXIX,1 **Potage de santé**

—— Jacobin Pottage, Cook III,13 **Potage à la Jacobine**

—— Jacobin Cheese Pottage, Cook III,49 **Potage à la Jacobine au fromage**

—— Queen's Pottage, Cook III,11, 12; XV,7; XXV,5; XXIX,11 **Potage à la Reyne**

—— Princess Pottage, Cook III,12; XV,8, 57; XXV,6; XXIX,13 **Potage à la Princesse**

—— Profiterole Pottage, Cook III,10; XV,23; XXV,23; XXIX,8 **Potage de profiteolles**

—— Stewkettle Pottage, Cook III,43 **Potage de marmitte**

—— Tidbit Pottage, Cook III,19 **Potage de beatilles**

poupelain, a sort of bap, Pastry Chef XV,3; XVII; XIX; XXIX,5 *poupelain, poupelan, poupelin, paupelain, paupelin*; Cotg: "*Popelins.* Soft cakes made of fine flower, kneaded with milke, sweet butter, and yolkes of egges; and fashioned, and buttered, like our Welsh Barrapyclids"; Fur: "*Poupelin.* Piece de four, pâtisserie delicate faite avec du beurre, du lait & des œufs frais, pastrie avec de la fleur de farine. On y mêle du sucre & de l'écorce de citron"; Marnette: "Pumpion, Pompion Tart"

pralines, Confectioner Preface; VI,1 *praslines*; Rich: "*Pralines,* ou amendes à

la praline. Ce sont des amendes rissolées dans du sucre, amendes qu'on fait bouillir dans du sucre jusques à ce qu'elles soient un peu séches & qu'elles croquent [crunch] sous la dent"; the cook of the Marshal of Plessis-Praslin (1598–1675) invented this sort of candy

—— Broom Pralines, Confectioner VI,4 **[Praslines de] genests**

—— Lemon Pralines, Confectioner VI,2 **Praslines de citrons**

—— Orange Pralines, Confectioner VI,2 **[Praslines] des oranges**

—— Rose Pralines, Confectioner VI,4 **[Praslines] de roze**

—— Violet Pralines, Confectioner VI,3, 4 **Praslines de violets**

preserve, Cook XXX,2 (passim 10); Confectioner Preface; VII (passim) *conserve(s)*; preserved food (in general) Cook Confections,2 (passim) *en conserve*; Cotg: "*Conserve.* ... A Conserve, as of Roses, Violets, &c."; Fur: "*Conserve.* Confiture seche qui se fait avec du sucre de plusieurs pastes, ou fruits, ou fleurs, &c. pour les rendre plus agreables au goust"; see also candied foods, Caramel, Ham Slices, Sugar Wreath, Twisted Sugar, and to candy, to preserve in Appendix 3

—— Cherry Preserve, Confectioner VII,13 **(Conserve) de cerises**

—— Cherry-Juice Preserve, Confectioner VII,14 **(Conserve) de jus de cerise**

—— Fruit Preserve, Cook Confections,9 **Conserve de fruits**

—— Lemon-Grating Preserve, Cook Confections,6; Confectioner VII,8 **Conserve de citrons, de rapure de citron**; Lemon-Juice Preserve, Confectioner VII,7 **(Conserve) de jus de citron**

—— Marbled Preserve, Confectioner VII,12 **Conserve marbrée**

—— Orange-Blossom Preserve Confectioner VII,1 **Conserve de fleurs d'oranges**; Moist Orange-Blossom Preserve Confectioner VII,2 **(Conserve) de fleur d'orange liquide**; Preserve of Orange-Blossom Water Confectioner VII,3 **Conserve d'eau de fleurs d'oranges**

—— Pistachio Preserve, Cook Confections,8; Confectioner VII,5, 6 **Conserve de pistaches**

—— Pomegranate Preserve, Cook Confections,7; Confectioner VII,4 **Conserve de (grains de) grenade**

—— Rose Preserve, Cook Confections,5; Confectioner VII,9 **Conserve de roses**

—— Violet Preserve, Confectioner VII,10 **Conserve de violette**

—— Marbled Violet Preserve, Confectioner VII,11 **Conserve de violette marbrée**

Princess: see pies, pottage

profiterole, Cook III,10; XV,23; XXV,23; XXIX,8 *profiteolles*; Fur: "*Profiterole*. Ce mot se disoit autrefois d'une paste cuite sous les cendres. Maintenant les Cuisiniers font encore des potages de *profiteroles* avec de petits pains dégarnis de mie, sechez, mitonnez, & garnis de beatilles"; a diminutive of the word *profit*; *RDH*: the original sense of the word (1542) was the "petit profit, petite gratification que reçoivent les domestiques. Ce mot s'est spécialisé dans le vocabulaire culinaire, désignant d'abord une pâte cuite sous la cendre (1549)"; see also pottage

pudding: see sausage

puffed (*souflé*): see marzipan, pastes, sugar ; see to puff in Apprendix 3

Queen's bread: see bread

Queen's Pottage: see pottage

quenelle (of veal or fish, a ball of seasoned minced meat or fish and eggs used primarily as a garnish), Cook V,80; XV,3, 14; XVI,42; Pastry Chef VII,6; 9, 10, 15, 17, 23; XXIX,7 *andouillette, endouillette, andoüillette*; Pastry Chef VII,18 *andouillettes de veaux*; Fur: "*Andouillette*. Petit ragoust que font les Cuisiniers avec de la chair de veau hachée & des œufs, dont ils

garnissent les potages & les pastés, & dont ils font des entrées de table"; I.D.G.: "*Andouillets*. They are balls, or roundish small peeces of minced flesh well seasoned"; Marnette: "Small sausages"; see also sausage, see also Escoffier, §205

ragout, piquant sauce, zesty sauce, a manner of preparing by means of this, Cook III,21 (passim 144) *ragoust, ragoût*; I.D.G.: "*Ragoust*. It is any sauce, or meat prepared with a haut goust, or quicke or sharp taste"; Rich: "C'est un assaisonnement que le cuisinier fait, qui pique, qui chatouille & réveille l'apétit"; Tré: "Sauce, assaisonnement pour donner de l'appétit à ceux qui l'ont perdu, ou pour le reveiller; ou pour le châtouiller. Lat. *Condimentum, conditura*"; *FEW*: derived from the verb *ragouster*, "réveiller le désir, la passion de qn."

ramekin (variety of prepared dish, not the modern vessel), Cook VIII,46–51; XXVIII,20 *ramequin*; I.D.G.: "It is a kind of toste"; Fur: "*Ramequin* est une espece de ragoust que font les goinfres pour se provoquer à boire, & est fait de fromage étendu sur une rostie assaisonnée avec du sucre, du poivre, ou autre espicerie"

—— Cheese Ramekin, Cook VIII,48 **Ramequin au fromage**

Rattoon, Pastry Chef XII; XXXIII,22 **Raton, Ratton**; Cotg: "*Raston*. A fashion of round, and high Tart, made of butter, egges, and cheese"; Marnette: "Rattoone, or round Puff-paste Tart"; Fur: "*Raton*. Espece de pâtisserie platte faite de paste avec du fromage ou de la cresme cuite, dont les enfans sont fort friands"

rissoles, deep-fried turnovers, Cook VIII,36, 37; XVI,42; XXVIII,29; XXX,26; Pastry Chef XXII,1, 2 *rissoles (feuilletées)*; Cotg: "*Rissolle*. Mushrome thats fashioned like a Demie-circle, and growes cleaving to

trees; also, a small and delicate minced
Pie, made of that fashion"; Fur: "*Rissole*. Sorte de pâtisserie faite de viande
hachée & espicée, enveloppée dans de
la paste deliée. On l'appelle aussi *oreille de Parisien*, parce qu'elle est faite
en forme d'une oreille"

rosette: see pastry

Rosolio (a cordial), Confectioner IV,2
Rossoly; Fur: "*Rossolis*. Une liqueur
agreable qu'on sert à la fin du repas,
qui aide à la digestion. Elle est composée d'eau de vie bruslée, de sucre, de
canelle, & quelquefois parfumée"; *DEI*:
"*Rosolio* è il fr. *rossolis*, mentre la nos-
tra voce [*rosoli*] è passata inalterata in
fr."; the Italian drink was a mixture of
alcohol, sugar and rose essence

roux: see sauce, below

royal: see cake (Kings'), marzipan, pie in
this Appendix; and sugar in Appendix 1

salads, Confectioner Pref *salades*; as a
salad (of cucumber, lettuce, asparagus, chicory, cabbage), Cook VIII,92;
XVI,82; XX,11; XXII,3, 5, 8, 10, 12;
XXVI,70; *(en) salade, sallade*; Jowl,
or Sandwich, of Salmon in a Salad,
Cook XVI,82 **Hure, ou entre-deux de
saumon à la sallade**; Cotg: "*Salade*.
A Sallet of hearbes, &c"; Fur: "*Salade*.
Espece d'entremets qu'on sert sur la
table pour accompagner le rosti. Il est
composé d'ordinaire d'herbes crües,
assaisonnées avec du sel, de l'huile &
du vinaigre. On y met quelquefois des
œufs durs & du sucre"
—— Boiled Salad, Cook XXX,43 **Salade
cuite**
—— garnishing (of a salad), Cook III,39
fourniture; Fur: (*s.v. Salade*. ... Une
salade d'herbs, de laituës, de celeri, de
chicorée, d'estragon & d'autres menuës
herbes, qu'on appelle de la *fourniture*";
"*Fourniture*. Des menuës choses qui
accompagnent celle qui est principale";
his illustration of this sense is "Avec

cette salade de laituës il faut de la *four-
niture* ou de menuës herbes, comme
estragon, cerfeuil, ciboulette, &c."
—— Lemon Salad, Cook VIII,34;
XXX,42 **Salade de citron**
—— Pomegranate Salad, Cook VIII,92
Salade de grenade

sauce *sauce*; Fur: "*Sauce*. Liqueur dans
laquelle on fait cuire plusieurs sortes de
mets; ou qu'on prepare, quand ils sont
cuits, pour les faire trouver de meilleur
goust"
—— butter, browned butter: see russet
sauce, below
—— German sauce, Pastry Chef VII,23
sauce d'Alemagne
—— green sauce, Cook V,23, 69; VII,2,
9; XVI,9, 49 *sauce verte*; Fur: " ...
qui est de l'oseille pillée"
—— pepper sauce, Cook V,5, VII,1 (passim 22) *poivrade*; Cotg: "*Poyvrade*. A
seasoning with, or sauce made of, Pepper"; Rich: "Sauce avec du vinaigre &
du poivre"
—— red sauce, Cook XXI,25 *sauce
rouge*; see also russet sauce
—— russet sauce, roux (of browned butter or lard), Cook XVI,44, 64, 65, 67,
75, 81, 83; XVII,8; XVIII,3; XXI,20
(implicit); XXVI,50, 69; XXX,4 *sauce
rousse*; browned butter, Cook XVI,75;
XVII,1; XX,1; XXX,6 *beurre roux*;
sort of preparation that involves browning in flour, fat, Cook III,16; XV,51
au roux; Rich: "*Roux, rousse*. Ce mot
se dit du beurre fort chaud & presque
rouge [russet]"; Cotg: "*Roux*. Reddish,
ruddie, red-Deere colour, a ruddie or
sad yellow, Lyon tawnie"; contemporary dictionaries gloss *roux* only as a
noun identifying a colour or as an adjective, as in Furetière's illustration:
"Les bonnes fritures se font au beurre
roux." See also red sauce, above; and
to brown, Appendix 3
—— Sauce Robert, Cook V,33, 56;
VI,44; XVI,23, 86; XVIII,17; Pastry Chef XXXI,2; XXXIII,24 **Sauce
Robert, Sauce à Robert**; Rich: "C'est

une sausse avec des oignons, de la moutarde, du beurre, du poivre, du sel & du vinaigre qu'on met ordinairement avec du porc frais rôti"; Fur: " . . . avec de l'oignon & de la moustade"; see also Escoffier, §52

—— short sauce (boiled away, reduced, condensed), Cook V,24 (passim 29) *sauce courte*; *TLF* (6,365a): "court 4. Qui ne s'étend pas assez; sauce courte: Qui manque de fluidité, trop épaisse"

—— Sweet Sauce, Cook III,32; V,71; VI,5, 12, 47, 53; VIII,86; XVI,48, 81; XXV,28; XXVI,35, 69; XXVII,8; Pastry Chef VII,3, 17; XXXI,3 *sauce, sausse douce*; Fur: " . . . avec du vin & du sucre"

—— white sauce, white broth, white bouillon (of eggs or egg yolks and verjuice), Cook XIV,5 (passim 26); Pastry Chef XXXI,5 *sauce, sausse blanche*; Cook III,31 *bouillon blanc*; *cf.* to glaze, Appendix 3

sausage, Cook III,3; V,8, 9 *saucisse*; see also quenelle, saveloy

—— large sausage, Cook V,10; Pastry Chef XXXIII,1, 5 *andouille, andoüille*; Large Sausages Cook V,10 **Andoüilles**; Cotg: "*Andouille*. A linke, or chitterling; a big hogges gut stuffed with small guts (and other intrailes) cut into small pieces, and seasoned with peper and salt"; I.D.G.: "*Andouilles*. They are the great guts of porke, or beef, filled up with thinne slices of tender meat, or small guts of porke well seasoned with peper, salt, fine hearbs, &c. Some doe call them Chitterlings"

—— Sausages of Partridge White-Meat, Cook V,9 **Saucisses de blanc de perdrix**

—— grey pudding, Cook V,64 *boudin gris*

—— White Pudding, Cook V,8, 9 **Boudin blanc**; Fur: "*Boudin*. Boyau de porc empli de son sang & de sa graisse, dont on fait un mets bon à manger: celuy-là s'appelle *boudin*

noir; mais le *boudin blanc* est le même boyau rempli de blanc de chapon, de lait & autres ingrediens"

Saveloy, Cook V,11 **Servelats**; Cotg: "*Cervelat*. An excellent kind of dry saucidge that resembles our blacke pudding, but that it is somewhat thicker, and shorter; and is eaten could [cold] in slices"; Rich: "Petit saucisson rempli de chair hachée & fort épicée que vendent les charcutiers de Paris"; I.D.G.: "*Cervelats* [and *Servelast*]. They are a kinde of saucidges made beyond sea"

—— Eel Saveloy, Cook XVI,51; XIX,12; XXVIII,13 **Servelats, Servelast d'anguille**; XXVI,37 **Anguille en cervelact**

Savoy: see biscuit

season, seasons, Cook I; VI,0; seasonal herbes, Cook IV,6 *herbes selon la saison*; seasons: of vine leaves, Cook VI,6, 23, 29, 32 *feuilles de vignes en la saison*; of flowers, Cook VI,0; VIII,0; XVIII,22 *fleurs de la saison*; of vinegar, Cook VIII,1 *vinaigre . . . s'il est en saison*; of verjuice, currants, Cook VIII,54, 75, 89 *dans la saison, verjus ou groseilles*; of chestnuts, Pastry Chef VII,5, 9 *la saison des marrons*; of cucumbers, Confectioner XV,12 *la saison des concombres*; of (fresh) verjuice mash, Pastry Chef VII,8 *la saison de verjus de grain*

—— spring, Cook VI,29, 32 *printems, printemps*

—— summer, Cook VI,32; Pastry Chef VIII,1; XV,5; XXIV; XXIX,2; Confectioner II,4 *esté*

—— autumn, Cook VI,32 *automne*

—— winter, Cook III,2, 23; V,71; VI,32; Confections,56; Pastry Chef VII,3; VIII,1 *hyver*

shell, pie shell: see dough

simnel, wafer, Pastry Chef XXIV *eschaudez*; Cotg: "*Eschaudé*. A kind of Wigg, or Symnell, fashioned some-what like a Hart; a three-cornered Sym-nell"; Fur: "Gasteau fait en forme de triangle ou de cœur avec de la paste *es-chaudée*, de l'eau, du sel, et quequefois avec du beurre et des œufs. On mange le Jeudy Saint des *eschaudés benits*"; Rich: "Sorte de petit gateau fait de fine fleur de froment, d'œufs, de beurre & de sel, que les paticiers vendent deux liards"

sippets (of bread, fried bread), Pastry Chef XXXIII,17 *mouillettes (de pain frittes)*; Pastry Chef VII,23; XXIX,9; XXXIII,3 *appreste, apreste de pain frit, pain en appreste*; Fur: "*Mouil-lette*. Petit morceau de pain long & menu preparé pour tremper dans des œufs à la coque [soft-boiled eggs]"; Rich: "*Aprête*. Morceau de pain délié & coupé en tranches avec lequel on mange un œuf molet"

Snow Paste: see paste

sorbet, Alexandrian Sorbet (a cordial), Confectioner IV,7, 8 **Sorbet, façon d'Alexandrie, sorbec**; first attested in 1553, a borrowing from the Italian *sorbetto*

Spanish: see pie, fritters, Tourons

stewed foods, dishes, Cook XVI,54 *es-tuvées*; Cook XV,31; XVI,14, 17, 28, 45, 50, 85 *à l'estuvée, en estuvée, en façon d'estuvée*; see also to stew in Appendix 3 and stove in Appendix 4
—— Stewed Barbels, Cook XVI,32 **Bar-beaux à l'estuvée**
—— Stewed Burbot, Cook XXVI,13 **Lotte à l'estuvée**
—— Stewed Carp, Cook XVI,6; XXVI,5 **Carpe(s) à l'estuvée**
—— Stewed Chicken, Cook V,62 **Poulets à l'estuvée**
—— Stewed Chub, Cook XVI,24 **Vilain à l'estuvée**
—— Stewed Dace, Cook XVI,27 **Soies à l'estuvée**
—— Stewed Eel, Cook XVI,50; XXVI,38 **Anguille à l'estuvée, en**

façon d'estuvée; Stewed Sea Eel, Cook XVI,54; XXVI,40 **Anguille de mer à l'estuvée**; Sea Eel Fried and Stewed Cook XXVI,41 **Anguille de mer fritte à l'estuvée**
—— Stewed Herrings, Cook XXVI,72 **Harans à l'estuvée**
—— Stewed Lamprey, Cook XXVI,36 **Lamproye à l'estuvée**
—— Stewed Salmon, Cook XVI,14; XXVI,11 **Saumon à l'estuvée**
—— Stewed Shad, Cook XVI,45 **Alloze à l'estuvée**

stewed fruit: see compote

stock (juice extracted from a foodstuff), (passim) *jus*; stock (liquid basis for broth, etc.), Cook XV,10 *fonds*
—— beef stock, juice, Cook XI,2 *jus de bœuf*; see also beef in Appendix 1
—— mushroom stock, juice, Cook XI,1 *jus de champignons*
—— mutton stock, juice, Cook XI,2 *jus de mouton*; see also mutton in Ap-pendix 1

Strawberries (formed of coloured marzi-pan), Cook Confections,49 *en forme de fraises*

stuffing, filling, hash, Cook IV,3 (passim) *farce*; Cotg: "A Pudding, Haggas, Liv-ering; any stuffing, in meats"; I.D.G.: "It is any thing made up for to stuffe any meat with"; I.D.G.: "Hash. It is minced meat"; Marnette: "pudding"; see also to stuff in Appendix 3, below

sugar; see also sugar in Appendix 1, and to sugar in Appendix 3
—— sugar paste, Confectioner Pref *paste de sucre*
—— Pennet, a piece or stick of bar-ley sugar, Confectioner III,5; VII,17 **Penide, Peneide**; Cotg: "*Penide*. A Pennet; the little wreath of sugar taken in a cold"; Fur: "Terme de Pharma-cie, est une preparation de sucre cuit avec une decoction d'orge jusqu'à un certain degré, aprés quoy il est long-temps manié tant avec la main qu'avec

des crochets jusqu'à ce qu'il devienne blanc"

—— Twisted Sugar, Confectioner III,5; VII,16,17 *sucre tors*; Cotg: "*Tors*. . . . Wrested, wrinched, wrung; bowed, crooked, wried, awrie"; see *Encyc* (XI, 632b and XV, 618a)

—— various stages in cooking sugar (see also stages in cooking syrup, below):

– burnt stage, Confectioner III,5 *à brusle* (perhaps in error for *bruslé*)

– smooth stage, Confectioner Preface; III,2 *à lisse*

– pearl stage, Confectioner III,3 *à perle*; coarse pearl stage, Confectioner Pref *à grosse perle*; fine pearl stage, Confectioner Pref *à perle menu*

– feather stage, Cook Confections,5–9, 19; Confectioner III,4 *à plume*; see *Encyc*, XV, 617b

– pink stage, Confectioner III,4 *à rosard*; same as feather stage

– blowing stage, Confectioner III,4; XIII,13 *à soufle*; same as feather stage

– spatula stage, Confectioner III,4 *à l'espatule*; same as feather stage

– to a jelly, Confectioner Preface; X,1 *en gelée*

Swiss: see pies

syrup (often mentioned as an ingredient): Cook VIII,79 (passim); Cook Confections,15 (passim); Pastry Chef V; XXV,5; Confectioner Preface; III,2 (passim 60) *syrop*

—— Refreshing Syrups Confectioner V **Syrops rafraichissants**

—— various stages in cooking syrup (see also stages in cooking sugar, above):

– pearl stage, Confectioner IV,8; V,2; X,10, 14; XI (passim); XII,1, 13 *(cuit) à (grosse) perle, à perle menu*

– smooth stage, Confectioner XV,2, 11 *cuit a lisse*

– cooked to a jelly, Confectioner X,8 *cuit en gelée*

—— Apple Syrup, Confectioner V,8 **Syrop de pommes**

—— Apricot Syrup, Confectioner V,4

Syrop d'abricots

—— Borage Syrup, Confectioner V,2 **Syrop de bourache**

—— Bugloss Syrup, Confectioner V,2 **Syrop de buglose**

—— Cherry Syrup, Cook Confections,33; Confectioner V,3 **Syrop de cerise**

—— lady's bedstraw syrup (as an ingredient), Cook Confections,50 *syrop de capilaire*; *Encyc*: "*Sirop de capillaire*. C'est de l'*adiantum fructicosum brasilianum*, C.B.P. qu'on fait le sirop de capillaire, qui est très-adoucissant; on peut lui substituer le capillaire commun. . . . Le meilleur est celui qui nous vient de Montpellier. . . . Le sirop de capillaire est très-vanté; il possede toutes les vertus de cette plante: on l'emploie dans les maladies de poitrine: on le mêle dans la tisane ordinaire, dans les émulsions, dans le thé, pour les rendre plus adoucissans"

—— Lemon Syrup, Confectioner V,10 **Syrop de citron**

—— Mulberry Syrup, Confectioner V,7 **Syrop de mures**

—— Pale Rose Syrup, Confectioner V,2 **Syrop de roze pasle**

—— Pomegranate Syrup, Confectioner V,9 **Syrop de grenade**

—— Quince Syrup, Confectioner V,6 **Syrop de coins**

—— Raspberry Syrup, Cook Confections,35 **Syrop de framboise**

—— Verjuice Syrup, Confectioner V,5 **Syrop de verjus**

—— Violet Syrup, Confectioner V,1, 2 **Syrop de violette**

talmouse, Pastry Chef I,3; XIV *talemouse, thalemouse*; Pastry Chef XIV **La maniere de faire des thalemouses**; Cotg: "*Talmouse*. A Cheese-cake; a Tart, or cake made of egges, and cheese"; Marnette: "Cheese-Cakes"

tart, tartlet, Pastry Chef XI,1 *petite tartelette*; Fur: "*Tartelette*. Petite tarte qu'on donne ordinairement aux enfans à leur gouster, quand on leur veut donner quelque friandise"

thickeners, liaisons, Cook V,31 (passim 27) *liaisons*: almonds Cook X,1; bread, breadcrumbs, sieved bread crust Cook III,4; V,40; VI,52; carp or eel flesh, butter Cook XXVI,0; eggs, verjuice, Cook V,70; raw eggs III,49; V,1, 45; egg yolks, verjuice Cook V,42; XVI,89, 90; egg yolks V,34; eggs, flour Cook XXIII,4; flour Cook III,45; IV,5; V,57; dry-fried (?) flour, starch, Cook XXV,20, 40; flour sautéed in lard Cook V,1; X,3; mushrooms Cook X,2; XIV,35; truffles Cook X,4; XIV,55; veal sweetbreads, meat stock, mushrooms Cook VIII,52; see also to thicken, Appendix 3

Threaded Eggs: see egg dishes

tidbits: see omelet, pie; and in Appendix 1 b)

Tourons, Pastry Chef XXI,2 **Tourrons**; perhaps influenced by the Neapolitan (and Catalan) *turrone* and Lombard *torón*, a mixture of almond paste and honey, the word deriving from the verb *turrar*, "to roast" (*DEI*)

tourte, Cook V,76 (passim 50) *tourte, tourtre*; Cotg: "*Tourte*. The made-dish which we call a Florentine"; Rich: "Il faut dire *tourte* & non pas *tourtre* pour dire une piece de four qu'on fait cuire dans une tourtiere & qui est faite de pigeonneaux, de béatilles, de moêle, ou de fruits"; I.D.G.: "It is a kind of a great cake"; see also pie, tart — the distinctions between *tourte, tarte* and *pasté* being moot

—— Almond Cream Tourte, Cook XXX,48 **Tourte de cresme d'amendes**

—— Apple Tourte Cook XXI,36 **Tourte de pommes**

—— Beef-Marrow Tourte, Pastry Chef IX,3 **Tourte de moüelle de bœuf**

—— Combalet Tourte, Cook Confections,33 **Tourte à la combalet**; in the shape of a small boat; *DEI*: "*Comballo*. Battello tutto d'un pezzo"

—— Cream Tourte, Cook XXI,35 **Tourte de cresme**; Little Musk Cream Tourte, Cook XXVIII,27 **Petite tourte de cresme musquée**

—— Egg Tourte, Pastry Chef IX,6 **Tourte aux œufs**

—— Frangipane Tourte (with a filling of frangipane cream), Cook VIII,64; XIV,37; XIX,7; XXI,37; XXVIII,12; Pastry Chef IX,15 **Tourte de franchipane, franchipanne**; *DEI* glosses *frangipane* as a "profumo d'ambra o zibetto in origine profumo per guanti; dal nome del marchese Muzio Frangipane, introdotto con Caterina dei Medici," the word being used in France from 1588 (and reintroduced into Italy only in the 19th c.; *TLF*: "*Frangipane*. 2. Crème pâtissière parfumée aux amandes . . . ; Pâtisserie garnie de cette crème"; see also note in Cook VIII,64

—— Herb Tourte, Cook XXX,12; Pastry Chef IX,7 **Tourte d'herbes**

—— Jam Tourte, Pastry Chef IX,13 **Tourte de confiture**

—— squab tourte, Pastry Chef I,4 *tourte de pigeonneaux*

—— Veal-Kidney Tourte, Pastry Chef IX,5 **Tourte de roignons de veau**

Turk, Turkish: see omelet, pie

Twists: see fritter

Twisted Sugar: see sugar, above

Verdun Anise: see pea dishes

waffle, wafer, Pastry Chef XX *gauffre*; Fur: "*Gauffre*. Une menuë piece de pastisserie faite de fleur de farine, d'œufs & de sucre, & cuitte entre deux fers treillissez [hatched] comme de petits carreaux"; Marnette: "Wafer"

—— Sugar Waffles, Pastry Chef XX,1 **Gauffres au sucre**

—— Milk or Cream Waffles, Pastry Chef XX,2 **Gauffres au laict ou à la cresme**

—— Fine Cheese Waffles, Pastry Chef XX,3 **Gauffres au fromage fin**

waters, potions, cordials; see also beverages
—— savoury water, waters, Cook VIII,37, 41, 42, 65, 79, 81–83; XIX,5; XXI,28, 31, 32, 34 *eau, eaux de senteur*
—— Italian waters, Confectioner Preface; IV b *eaux d'Italie*
—— Aniseed Water, Confectioner IV,15 **Eau d'anis**
—— Apricot Water, Confectioner IV,12 **Eau d'abricots**
—— Barberry Water, Confectioner IV,14 **Eau d'espine-vinette**
—— Cherry Water, Confectioner IV,11 **Eau de cerise**
—— Cinnamon Water, Pastry Chef XXXIII,2; Confectioner IV,16 **Eau de canelle**
—— Coriander Water, Confectioner IV,15

Eau de coriande
—— Jasmine Water, Confectioner IV,13 **Eau de jasmin**
—— Lemon Water, Confectioner IV,15 **Eau de citron**
—— Orange(-Blossom) Water, Confectioner IV,15; VII,3; IX,15; X; XXI,1; Confectioner IV,1, 3, 4; VII,3; VIII,1; X,16; XV,9; XVI,18, 20 **Eau (de fleur) d'orange**
—— Pomegranate Water, Confectioner IV,11 **Eau de grenade**
—— Raspberry Water, Confectioner IV,11 **Eau de framboise**
—— Red-Currant Water, Confectioner IV,11 **Eau de groseille**
Whore's Farts (Glazed), Confectioner XVI,20, 21, 23 **Pets de putain (glacez)**
Wine of the Gods, Confectioner (a cordial) IV,6 **Vin des dieux**

3. Procedures

This section groups verbs (and the odd gerund) having to do with actions in La Varenne's kitchen. These actions are effected by the cook in the course of his work, or describe what a foodstuff does as it is being prepared.

to bake, roast, Confectioner X,3 *rostir*

to band, wrap (a pie shell) around with (paper) strips, Cook *bander*; Cotg: "To bind, swaddle, swath, tye with bands, fasten with strings"; I.D.G.: "make a brimme about it" (XXI,29)

to bard (place strips of pork meat across a roast), Cook V,17, 49, 57, 58; VI,6, 29, 39, 44, 60, 68; VIII,61, 102; XIV,15; Pastry Chef VII,2 *barder*; VI,6 *barder d'une bande de lard*; Rich: "*Barder*. Terme de rotisseur: couvrir d'une barde de lard, quelque volaille, ou quelque oiseau"; I.D.G.: "It is to lay a sheet of lard about, or upon any meat"; I.D.G.: "*Barde*. It is a sheet of lard or bacon"; bard with greased paper Cook VI,8; bard with pastry Cook VIII,78; bard with vine leaves Cook VI,9, 23, 32; see also to lard

to be strong, be noticeable, stand out (in flavour), Cook XV,49; XVI,17 *paroitre*

to beat (a napkin, with a flat bat), Linen ¶¶1, 27 *bastonner, bâtonner*

to blanch, plump, Cook Vi,1 (passim) *blanchir*; I.D.G.: "To Whiten. It is to steep in water, either cold or hot, for to make plump, or white, or both"; in this acceptation the verb *blanchir* has the rather general sense of preparing a foodstuff for cooking: the action may clean or plump or seal, or all three; see also to gild, to glaze, to plump, to sear

—— in hot (or warm) water, Cook VIII,68–70; XIX,19; XXI,20, 23; Confections,62 *les jettés dans l'eau boüillante pour les blanchir*; Cook III,1

(for squab): *faites les blanchir, c'est à dire, mettez les dans un pot avec de l'eau chaude, ou du bouillon du pot, & les couvrez bien*; Pastry Chef VII,13: *chair ... qui soit blanche, c'est a dire qui soit cuitte plus qu'a demy*; Marnette (translating the same passage): "let [the flesh] be perboyled; that is to say, let it be above half boyled"; *Acad*: "*Blanchir de la viande. C'est la mettre dans l'eau tiede pour la faire revenir*"

—— in cool water, Cook III,14, 34, 37, 46; IV,3–5, 8; V,3, 12, 65; VIII,11, 74, 97; XIV,23; XV,15; XX,11, 17; XXII,2, 3, 5, 12; XXV,35, 41 *blanchir dans l'eau fraische*; Cook III,27 (for lettuce) *que vous aurés fait blanchir, c'est les mettre dans l'eau fraische*

—— in milk (for white pudding), Cook V,9 *boudin blanc, que vous ferez blanchir ... avec du laict*

—— in almond (or crayfish) bouillon (for tidbits), Cook XV,40 *les blanchissez avec du bouillon d'amandes, ou autrement avec du bouillon d'escrevisses*

—— over a flame: see to sear

to blend *destremper*; Cotg: "To soake, steepe, moisten, water, season, or lay in water; soften, or allay, laying in water; to make fluide, liquid, or thinne"

to boil away *esbouillir, ébouillir*; Rich (refl.): "Ce mot se dit parlant de sausse & de bouillon, & signifie se consumer, se reduire à peu de sausse, ou de bouillon"; Cotg: "To boyle throughly; to boyle to the diminution of the liquor thats in boyling; to overboyle, or boyle almost dry"

to boil down (a liquid), Cook XV,1 *consommer*; Fur: "*Consommer*, se dit ... d'une coction extraordinaire, qui fait une entiere dissolution des parties [*e.g.*] Il faut faire *consommer* la viande pour faire de la gelée"; see also consommé in Appendix 1 b)

to braise, Cook III,39; V,3 *estoffer*; literally, to cook over the coals (in a fire basket) Confectioner X,13 *cuire à la braise*; see also to stew; and braised in Appendix 2

to break up (dough) *broyer*; Rich: "Casser menu"; see also to squash

to brown, toast *se hasler*; Rich: "*Hâler*. Devenir bazané, devenir noir à cause de l'ardeur du Soleil"; to brown (as butter, flour or another foodstuff in a pan), Cook V,1, 39, 50; XVI,64; XVII,1, 4; XXI,14; XXVI,86; XXIX,8 *roussir*; Cook III,16; XV,51 *(mettre) au roux*; to brown (in fat) Cook XVIII,14; Pastry Chef XII,2, 6; XXI,1 XXII,1 *rissoler*; Cotg: "*Rissoller*. To frie a thing untill it be browne; *Rissolé*. Fried throughly, or browned all over in the frying"; Fur: "*Rissoler*. Cuire les viandes ou autres mets jusqu'à ce qu'on leur donne une couleur rousse"

to build up, set up (a pie shell), Cook V,80 (passim) *dresser*; to build up, compose (a dish with ingredients), fill (a shell) Confectioner XVI,7 *emplir*; see also to fill

to butter, coat with butter, Cook XIX,24 *ébeurrer*

to candy, candied, Confectioner Preface; XIV (passim) *candir, candi*; Cotg: "*Se candir*. To candie, or grow candide, as sugar after boyling"; Fur: "*Candir*. Terme de Confiseur, qui se dit des confitures dont le sucre s'épaissit & se glace sur la surface des vaisseaux"; see candied preparations in Appendix 2

to chill, become chilled, cold, Pastry Chef VII,14; VIII,1; XV,3 *se morfondre*;

Rich: "*Morfondre*. Gagner du froid"; Cotg: "*Se morfondre*. To take cold, catch cold, get a cold"

to chop (passim) *hacher*; see also hash, Appendix 2

to clean, skin (almonds, pistachios, orange blossoms, violets, etc.), Cook XIV,32; XXI,31; Pastry Chef IX,8; Confectioner V,2 (passim) *monder*; Cotg: "*Mondé*. Cleaned, made cleane; also, pruned; picked, pilled"; see also to peel, and *cf.* Escoffier, §2338

to coat with blood, Cook VI,5, 45 *enseigner*

to consolidate (dough), Pastry Chef I,4 *se restuire*; Cotg: "*restuyer*. To sheath, or shut up, againe"; *estuyer*. To sheathe, case; cover with, put into, shut up in, a sheath, or case"

to cook (passim) *cuire*, usually *faire, mettre, laisser cuire*; also without a causative auxiliary: Cook V,15 *ensorte qu'ils se melent & achevent de cuire*; Cook XVI,52 *noir a force de trop cuire*; Cook XVII,14 *en telle quantité que vous jugerez pouvoir cuire*; Cook XVII,17; Pastry Chef XV,2; Confectioner XI,15 *cuiront*; Cook V,64 (passim 6); Pastry Chef IV,2 (passim 5) *en cuisant*; Cook V,50; XVII,14, 17; Pastry Chef IX,10; XII,6; XXXIII,25 *cuise, cuisent*; Pastry Chef VII,1 *afin que ce pasté puisse cuire*; Pastry Chef XXII,2 *ces rissoles veulent cuire à feu doux*

to crease *plisser*; Cotg: "*Plisser*. To plait, fould, lap up, or one within another"

to crimp (the rim of a pie shell), mark (that rim) with a fork or other instrument, Pastry Chef IX,7 *fraiser, friser*; Cotg: "*Frizer*. To frizle; crispe; curle (as water blowne on by a gentle wind), ruffle, braid"; to mark a (diagonal) pattern on a pastry edging Pastry Chef IX,7 *viteler*; Gode: "*videller*. Repriser" [perhaps, by extension, to trace a mark like an overcast stitch]; "*Viteller*. Canneler avec les dents d'une fourchette les bords d'une pâte à tarte" (Laurendon, *L'art de la cuisine française au XVIIe siècle*)

to crush: see to squash

to darken, become dark, Pastry Chef VIII,1 *se hasler*

to debone, remove bones from, Cook XV,14, (passim) *desosser*; see also to fillet

to desalt, remove the salt from, Cook IX *dessaller*

to dip, dredge, Cook XV,25 (passim 9); Confectioner XVI,4 *tremper*; Cotg: "To dip; moisten, wet, soake, steepe; season, temper, supple in liquor, &c"; see also to steep

to disintegrate (said of flesh falling apart or away from bones), Cook XVIII,1 *decharner*

to draw off, draw out (a cooked fruit from a pot, from syrup) *tirer*; to draw out to dry, Confectioner XV,10 *tirer au sec*

to dress (a carcass), gut (a fish), remove viscera from, Cook III,14, 30 (passim) *habiller*

to dry, to put in the sun, Cook Confections,12, 14, 51; Pastry Chef IX,14; Confectioner IV,11; V,5, 6; VIII,1 *mettre (secher) au soleil*

to enrich, fortify, Cook V,72; XIV,6, 8, 16; XXI,0, 6; XXVIII,29; XXX,26 *nourir, nourrir*

to enrich (pastry dough with butter, pie with fat), Pastry Chef I,2; VII,2 *estoffer*

to eviscerate (carcass); gut, clean (fish); draw (fowl), Cook V,6 (passim 32) *vuider, vider*

to fill (a pie shell), make up, garnish, trim *garnir (une abaisse)*; Rich: "Pourvoir de tout ce qui est nécessaire. Assortir, meubler, ajuster"; Confectioner XVI,7 *emplir*; see also to build up

to fillet, to debone (fish), Cook XV,3 4 *decharner*

to flavour:

—— with amber, Confectioner Preface;

IV,1, 3; VI,1; XV,10, 13; XVI,10 *ambrer*

—— with musk, Cook VIII,26; XIX,5; XXI,35; XXVII,27; Confectioner Preface; IV,1, 3; VI,1; XV,10, 13; XVI,10 *musquer*; Cotg: "*Musquer*. To bemuske, to perfume with Muske"

to fold, Cook XVII,18; XIX,3 *ployer*; Linen (passim) *plier*; Cotg: "*Ployer*. To plie, bow, bend; also, to arch, or vault; also, to fould. *Plier*. To fould, plait; plie, bend, bow"; to fold in the shape of a heart, Linen ¶ 1 *plier en cœur*; to fold in bands, Linen ¶ 3 *plier par bande*; to fold in cross-billet fashion, Linen ¶ 1 *plier en baston rompu*; see also to pleat

to fricassee, Cook III,5; V,42, 55 (passim 85); Pastry Chef IX,10; XXXII,1, 2; XXXIII,4, 18; XXXIV,8 *fricasser*; Cotg: "*Fricasser*. To frie"; Rich: "*Fricassée*. C'est couper quelque viande ou des œufs, &c. en morceaux, l'assaisonner & la faire cuire avec son assaisonnement"; Fur: "*Fricasser*. Cuire promptement quelque mets, soit dans la poësle, soit dans un chauderon, avec un assaisonnement convenable"; see also fricassee, Appendix 2

to froth up (of boiling fruit), Confectioner XI,7 *mousser*

to funnel, Cook V,8, 9, 11 *entonner*; see also funnel, Appendix 4

to fry, Cook III,44 (passim 140); Pastry Chef XXII,1 (passim 22) *frire, faire frire*; to fry in hot butter *mettre au roux*; see also to sauté

to gild, give a golden colour to (for serving), Cook V,84; XIV,2, 3, 31; XV,6 (with butter); XVI,89–91, 93; XXI,0, 13; XXVII,0; XXVIII,29 (with butter); Pastry Chef III (passim 39); Confectioner XIII,13 *dorer*; generally by means of eggs, to produce a yellowish coating; Marnette: "to burnish"; I.D.G.: "*To endore*. It is to wet, or daube with some liquor, as one doth a pie or cake before is be put in the oven"; see also gilding (*doreure*), Appendix 2; to glaze, below

to glaze (for serving), Cook XV,13 (passim) *blanchir*; by means of egg whites, Cook VIII,83; egg whites and sugar, Cook Confections,62; sugar, Cook XXI,40; Confections,4, 31; Pastry Chef V; XXI,3; XV,9; XXII,2; XXV,7; XXVI; Confectioner Preface; X,16, 17; XVI,7, 10–13, 18, 19 *glacer*: this produces a clear *glace*; egg yolks, Cook XV,54; egg yolks and verjuice, Cook IV,9; XV,29, 34, 35, 38, 50; XVI,52, 77; egg yolks and vinegar, Cook IV,6; see also to blanch, to gild, above; *cf.* sauce, white sauce (*sauce blanche*) and glazing (*glace*) in Appendix 2

to grate (lemon, etc.), Cook III,20; VIII,27, 29; XXI,30; Confections,6, 13; Pastry Chef VII,9 (passim); Confectioner V,6 (passim)*rasper, raper*

to grill, Cook VIII,56, 95 *griller*; Grilled Pork Tongue in Ragout Cook VIII,56 *Langue de porc grillée en ragoust*; see also grill, Appendix 4

to grind, pound (in a mortar), Cook III,23 (passim 40); Pastry Chef IX,10; XXI,2; XXVI *piler (dans un mortier)*

to hang (a newly killed animal before butchering it), Cook Cook V,7; VI,24, 34, 46, 51; XIV,2; Pastry Chef VII,4, 5; IX,7 *mortifier*; Cotg: "*Mortifier*. To mortifie, or make tender, flesh thats to be eaten"; Rich: "Ce mot se dit de la *viande* & signifie la laisser un peu faisander; la laisser tant soit peu corrompre pour l'atendrir"; Marnette: "to mortify"; see also to tenderize

to infuse, Confectioner IV,6 *infuser*

to interlard: see to lard

to keep, set aside (for later use), Cook VIII,93; X,0; Confections,10 *conserver*; to (prepare) for keeping, Confections,2 (passim) *(cuire) en conserve*

to knead, Pastry Chef I,2; IX,7; XX,3 *fraiser*; Rich: "*Fraiser*. Terme de patissier. C'est bien manier la pâte";

Cook XVI,68; XXIII,7; Pastry Chef I,1, 2; VIII,2 *pétrir, paistrir*; to work (dough), Pastry Chef I,2 (passim) *manier*; Cotg: "*Pestrir*. To knead; to worke, settle, or soften (as dough) with the hands"

to lard, insert pork fat into (a meat), Cook III,26 (passim 57); Pastry Chef VII,4 (passim) *larder*; Cotg: "*Larder*. To lard; to sticke, season, or dresse with lard; also, to pricke, or pierce, as with a larding pricke"; Rich: "Piquer de la viande avec une lardoire & y laisser le lardon"; I.D.G.: "It is to sticke any meat with slices of lard"; to lard with eel, Cook XXI,6; XXV,40; with eel, carp, Cook XV,48; XXI,0, 1; with cloves, Cook Confections,25; to lard Cook III,7, 15 (passim) *piquer, picquer*; Rich: "*Piquer*. Terme de cuisinier & de rotisseur: c'est larder d'un certain sens"; Cotg: "*Piquer*. To pricke, pierce, or thrust into"; see also to bard, to stick

—— to interlard, Cook VI,52; Pastry Chef VII,17 *entrelarder, entre-larder*

to lay down (a pastry shell), Cook VIII,78; XXI,28,37 *foncer*; Cotg: "*Foncer*. To head a peece of Caske; to set a bottome, or head, into any such vessell"; see also to build up

to make russet coloured: see to brown

to marinate, Cook V,4, 19; VIII,23, 74; XVI,5, 15, 52, 87; XVIII,14, 22; XX,11; XXI,0; XXII,11; XXIII,6; XXV,28; XVI,52, 87 *mariner*; Marinated Tuna Cook XVI,83 *Ton mariné*; Fried and Marinated Tench Cook XVI,5 *Tanches frittes & marinees*; Marinated Chicken Cook V,12; VII,23; XXIII,4

to moisten, mix (into), Cook VIII,64; XX,1; XXI,0, 37; Confections,10; to steep (in order to remove salt), Cook XIV,9 *détremper*; Cotg: "*Destremper*. To soake, steepe, moisten, water, season, or lay in water; soften, or allay, by laying in water; to make fluide, liquid, or thinne"; see also to steep

to parboil, Pastry Chef VII,22; IX,8; XXXIII, 21; XXXIV,8 *parbouillir*

to pare: see to peel

to peel, pare, skin (fruit, nuts), Cook V,69; Confections,1; (passim); Pastry Chef IV,2 (passim); Confectioner Preface; IV,3 (passim) *peler*; Fur: "*Peler* se dit aussi des fruits ou des arbres, quand on oste delicatement la pellicule ou l'écorce qui les couvre. On pele des fruits pour les confire"; see also to clean

to peel (away), remove, pick over (pomegranate rind), Cook VIII,92, (artichoke leaves), Cook VIII,71; Pastry Chef VII,16 *éplucher, esplucher*; Cotg: "*Esplucher*. To picke, or cull, as pease, &c; to plucke, or teyse, as Roses, Wooll, &c"; see also to polish, to shell, to pare, and peelings in Appendix 1

to pleat, put (a series of) crease(s) into (linen), Linen (passim) *plisser*; Cotg: "*Plisser*. To plait, fould, lap up"; see also to fold

to pluck (feathers), Cook VI,10 (passim 12) *plumer*

to plump, refresh (fruit, meat in water), Confectioner XI,11, 13, 14, 23; XII,10, 17; XIII,1 *verdir*; Cook Confections,1, 16, 18 *taverdir*; Pastry Chef VII,6, 20, 21 *revenir*; see also to blanch, to rise

to polish (rice, remove the bran coat from), Cook III,40 *éplucher*; Fur: "*Esplucher*. Oster l'ordure, la vermine de quelque chose, en retrancher ce qu'il y a de mauvais"; see also to pick out, shell, to peel

to preserve, candy, pickle (with salt, vinegar), Cook XX,11; XXII,40; Confectioner VI (passim) *confire*; to make a dry confection Confectioner XV,5 *confire au sec*; Cotg: "*Confire*. To preserve, confect, soake, or steepe in; also, to season, relish, or give savor unto"; see also to candy, above, and preserve in Appendix 2

to press, squeeze (in a press), Cook III,23; VIII,26, 75; XI,2; XIII,1; XV,39; XIX,6; XXIV,1; Confections,7; Pastry Chef IX,15; XXVIII,2 *presser*; press between two plates, Cook VIII,75; Pastry Chef IX,7 *presser entre deux assiettes*; squeeze between two spoons, Cook Confections,56 *espreindre entre deux cuilliers*; see presse in Appendix 4

to project, jut out, protrude, overlap, Pastry Chef VII,9, 13; Linen ¶ 3 *deborder*; Rich: "Aler au delà du bord"

to puff up, Confect XVI, 15, 18 *soufler*; Acad: "*Soufflé* s'emploie aussi comme nom masculin, en termes de cuisine, pour désigner une crème, une purée, etc., qui se gonfle à la cuisson"

to put away, store away (in larder for later use), Cook VIII,27; Confectioner V,2, 3, 5–7, 9, 10; X,21; XI,11; XII,1; XV,11, 12 *serrer (dans un lieu frais, sec)*

to remove seeds (from), Cook XII,2 *greneler*

to ruffle, ripple, put a wave in (a napkin), Linen ¶ 2 *friser*; Cotg: "*Frizer*. ... To curle (as water blowne on by a gentle wind), ruffle, braid"

to rise (as dough rising with yeast or in hot water), Pastry Chef VIII,2; XXIV *(faire) revenir, renvenir*; Cook XXI,0 *nourir*; Cotg: "*Revenir*. To swell, rise, or increase, as dough by leavening, or flesh by parboyling"; see also to plump

to roast, Cook III,4 (passim) usually *faire, mettre rostir*; occasionally without a causative verb: Cook VI,59 *à mesure qu'il rostira*, V,58 *lorsqu'il rostit*, XVI,68 à mesure qu'elle rostit; Cook Cook IV,4; XXV,40 (passim) *cuire, mettre, rostir à la broche, donner un tour de broche*; see also spit, Appendix 4

to sauté, brown, Cook V,13; VIII,50 (passim) *passer, passer par la poêle*; I.D.G.: "*To Passe in the panne*. It is to frie a little, or to parboile in the frying panne"; see also to brown

to scald, Cook III,17 (passim 19)
échauder; Rich: "Brûler avec de l'eau
chaude. Peler avec de l'eau chaude";
Cotg: "*Eschauder*. To scald, or cast
hot liquor upon"

to scale, Pastry Chef VII,20 *ecailler*; Cotg:
"*Escailler*. To skale, or pull the skales
of"

to scrape, scrape smooth, Cook V,31
raser; Cook V,8 (passim) *ratisser*

to sear, Cook VI (passim) *blanchir sur le
feu*; Cook VI,1 (for pheasant) *faites le
blanchir sur le feu, c'est à dire refaire
sur le gril*; see the notes in Cook VI,1
and 46; see also to blanch

to season, make savoury, (passim) *saison-
ner, assaisonner*; Cotg: "*Assaisonner*.
To season, temper, make savourie, give
a good tast unto"

to set, congeal (of eggs, as in an omelet),
(passim) *prendre*

to set up: see to build up

to shell, cull (mussels), Cook XV,29;
(crayfish) XV,2; (peas) XXIV,2
éplucher; Rich: "Ce mot se dit proprement des herbes. C'est oter, & séparer
les méchantes herbes & qui ne peuvent
être utiles de celles qui sont bonnes
& qui servent"; Cotg: "*Esplucher*. To
picke, or cull, as pease, &c."; see also
to peel, to polish

to shovel, mix in, Confectioner XVI,11
peler

to simmer, steep, Cook I,4 *mittonner*;
Rich: "Terme de cuisinier: faire bouillir fort-doucement sur de la cendre
chaude"; I.D.G.: "*To stove or soak*.
It is to cause to boil very softly before,
or over the fire, that so the juice or
liquor may be imbibed, or drunk in by
degrees, to the end that the potage, or
sauce, may be well allayed, of a good
consistence"; Confectioner V,2 *infuser*

to skewer, fasten with a skewer, Cook
VI,49 *brocheter*

to skim, Cook III,27, 33; XVI,71; Confections,39; Pastry Chef XVIII; Confectioner III,1; XI,6, 8, 11, 15 *escumer*

to skin (an animal, fish), singe off (an animal's hair), Cook V,69; VI,40; VIII,63;
peler; Pastry VII,23: *il faut ... le
peler, c'est-à-dire oster la peau*; Rich:
"Oter le poil, oter la peau; arracher
l'écorce"; see also to clean, to peel

to slash, gash, Cook X,4 *taillader*; Cotg:
"*Taillad é*. Cut, slashed, gashed, slit,
launced, incisioned"; Pastry Chef VII,4
entailler, faire une entaille; see also to
slice

to slice into, slit, make slits in *inciser*
Cotg: "To cut into, to make an incision; to launce, open, slit; also, to
carve, grave, intayle"; Cook XVI,87;
XVIII,5 *ciseler, cizeler*; Cotg: "*Ciseler*.
To carve, or grave with a chisell; also,
to clip, or cut with sizars"; see also to
slash

to spice (add spice to food), Pastry Chef
VII,5, 20 *espisser*

to spin (dough), Cook VIII,42; XVI,16
filer; Cotg: "*Filer*. To twist, spin, draw
out threads; also, to ... prolong, extend in length"; Fur: "*Filer*, se dit neu-
tralement des choses onctueuses qui
s'espandent en longs filets continus"

to squash, crush, break down, Pastry Chef
XVI; XXXI,1, 11 *escacher, écacher*;
Cotg: "*Escacher*. To squash; beat, batter, or crush, flat; to thrust, presse,
knocke, squeeze, hard or close together"; Fur: "*Escacher*. Presser, ap-
platir, froisser, écraser"; see also to
press, and press in Appendix 4

to squeeze: see to press

to steep, soak, Cook III,14 (passim 26)
tremper (intransitive); Cotg: "To dip;
moisten, wet, soake, steepe; season,
temper, supple in liquor, &c"; see
also to dip; to steep (in order to remove salt), Cook XIV,9 *détremper*;
Cotg: "*Destremper*. To soake, steepe,
moisten, water, season, or lay in water;
soften, or allay, by laying in water; to
make fluide, liquid, or thinne"; see also
to moisten

to stew, Cook XV,31; XVI,17 *cuire, mettre, accommoder, servir à l'estuvée, en estuvée*; Confections,3 *mettre secher à l'estuvée*; Fur: "*Estuvée*. Sorte de cuisson et de preparation de viandes, qui se fait d'ordinaire entre deux plats, ensorte que la sausse qui bout y soit comme estouffée"; Cotg: "*Estuvé*. Soaked, bathed, stued, washed in warme liquor"; *TLF*: "*à l'étuvée*. (Avec une) cuisson des aliments en vase clos, en utilisant la vapeur d'eau qui s'en dégage"; cooking process between two dishes, Cook III,21; V,76; VIII,2, 75; XIV,29XV,10, 33; XVI,66; XVII,1, 6; XX,5; XXII,11; XXV,28; XXVI,85; Pastry Chef XXXIII,16, 21; XXXIV,7 *mettre, fondre, mittonner, cuire, blanchir, jetter (son) eau entre deux plats*; to stew under a cooking bell, Confectioner X,13 *cuire à la cloche*; see also stewed foods in Appendix 2; and bell (cooking bell), and stove in Appendix 4

to stick (an onion with whole cloves), Cook III,43 (passim 35) *piquer, picquer* (a scallion with cloves), XVI,18; XX,5; (salmon with cloves), XVI,13, 14; (turnip with cloves), XV,37; (cabbage with cloves), XXII,12; (lettuce with cloves), XXII,5; (tuna with cloves), XVI,83; see also to lard

to stir, Cook VIII,17; XVI,69, 90; XVII,12 *tourner*; to stir, work together Confectioner XVI,11 *peler*; Fur: "*Peler*. Labourer legerement"; see also to turn

to strain, Cook XV,2, 3, 5, 7–10; XX,5; XXI,31; XXX,23; Confectioner IV,3 *passer*; Cook III,25, 28 *(vos poix entiers ou) passés, passer (des poix en purée)*; Rich: "*Passer*. Couler quelque liqueur au travers d'une chose"; Cook III,27; VIII,7, 9; XV,20; XX,19; Confectioner X,21 *passer dans une passoire*; Cook XVII,2 *passer par un couloir*; Pastry Chef I,6 *passer par un saz*; Cook X,1–4; XI,1; XIII,3; XV,34;

XXIV,4 *passer par l'estamine*; Cook VIII,102; XV,43; XXI,25; XXIV,1; Confectioner II,1, 2; IV,7, 11 *passer dans (par) un linge*; Confectioner IV,1, 2, 4, 6 *passer dans une chausse*; Cook Confections 27, 29, 58 *passer dans un (gros) tamy*; Cook Confections,48, 56; Confectioner IV,9, 12–14 *passer dans une serviette (en double)*;

to stuff, farce, Cook V,69 (passim 72) *farcir*; Cotg: "To stuffe, cramme, fill up; to franke, to feed"; I.D.G.: "It is to stuffe, or fill up any meat"

to sugar, put sugar in, add sugar to, Cook VIII,46 (passim); Pastry Chef IX,6 (passim); Confectioner VIII,1 *sucrer*; also (passim) *poudrer du sucre, rasper du sucre*

to sun: see to dry

to tenderize (meat, by beating), Pastry Chef VII,5 *mortifier*; (by steeping in vinegar) Cook VI,39 *amortir*; browned, dried (parsley on a hot fire shovel), Pastry Chef XXIX,8 *amorty*; Fur: "*Mortifier*. Alterer un corps naturel, le rendre plus tendre, plus mol. [*e.g.*] On *mortifie* la chair en la frappant avec un baston"; see also to hang

to thicken, Cook V,1 (passim 120); Pastry Chef I,2, 4, 6; VII,8, 9, 17; XV,4–6; XVI,0; XXV,8; XXVII,0 *lier*; see also thickeners, Appendix 2

to thin, dilute, draw out, combine, mix, blend, Cook III,49; IV,5 (passim); Pastry Chef III; IV,0; XX,2; XXXI,3 (passim); Confectioner XVI,1, 4, 6 *delayer, délayer, deslayer, dilayer*; Cotg: "*Delayer*. To macerate, allay, or soften, by steeping, &c; also, to make thin"; Rich: "Détremper avec du lait, ou de l'eau"; Rich: "Détremper, méler quelque chose de liquide avec une autre chose pour n'en faire qu'un corps"; to thin, draw out, make fine, Cook III, 11, 12 *delier*; Cotg: "*Delier*. To make thin, small, fine, slender; to lessen, extenuate, or minish"

to trim (away), Pastry Chef IX,15 *roigner*

to truss, truss up, (fowl) *trousser*

to turn (spit: transitive), Cook V,1;
XVI,39 *tourner*; see also to stir, and
spit in Appendix 4

to turn (a sauce: intransitive) Cook
VIII,86; XVIII,21; XVI,16: "c'est-à-
dire, qu'elle vienne on huile" *se tourner*

to use a syringe, Confectioner XVI,16
seringuer

to warm (dough), take the chill off
dégourdir; Cotg: "*Desgourdir*. To un-
benumme; to quicken, revive, resolve a
thing that is benummed, or stiffe with
cold; also, to supple; to make, or wax
nimble, gentle, plyant"; Rich: "Oter
l'engourdissement"

to wash, Pastry Chef IX,2; XXIV
bassiner; Cotg: "*Bassiner*. To bath,
wash, or heat in warme liquor"

to work: see to knead

4. Kitchen Equipment for Handling, Cooking and Serving

We list here the hardware of La Varenne's cookery. The list is divided into a) fixtures; b) receptacles, vessels (pots, pans, dishes); c) utensils, materials (fabrics, straw); d) fuel.

For articles of silver, see dish, spoon and (in Appendix 5d) coins.

a) Fixtures

cellar (a cool storage place), Cook IX,0; XXIII,7 *cave*

hearth: see heats in section f)

oven, Cook V,15 (passim 20) Pastry Chef *four*; pastry or bakery oven, Confectioner Pref *four de pastissier ou boulanger*; of copper, Pastry Chef VII,13 *four de cuivre*; Confectioner Pref *four de fer ou de cuivre rouge*; Pastry Chef VI *de petits fours particuliers*; see also stove

—— oven stopper, Cook VIII,83; XXVI,87 *couvert, couvercle de four*; Pastry Chef XXV,1 *bouchoy* (likely a misprint for *bouchoir*; Larousse: "*Bouchoir*. Plaque de fer dont on ferme la bouche d'un four")

pastry table, Pastry Chef I,2; XXV,4 (passim) *le tour, le tour à paste*; Rich:

"Terme de patissier: c'est une sorte de table grande & épaisse sur quoi on travaille en patisserie"; Marnette: "pastry table", "kneading board or Table" (Pastry Chef I,4); *Encyc* (XVI,456a): "*Tour*. Terme de Pâtissier. Ils donnent ce nom à une forte table qui a des bords de trois côtés; c'est sur cette table qu'ils paîtrissent leur farine & tournent leur pâte, soit pour ce qu'on appelle des *pains bénits*, soit pour faire des croûtes, des pâtés, tourtes & autres pieces de *four*"; see also pastry board in section c), below

press (for pressing to extract juice), Cook IX,0; XI,2; Confectioner V,6 *presse*

salting-tub, salting-vat, Cook XXII,12 *salloir*; Cotg: "*Salloir*. A salting, or sowcing tub, or table"

stopper: see oven

stove (located contiguous to heat source), Cook Confections,2, 3, 16; Pastry Chef XXV,4; XXVI,8; Confectioner Preface; XI,5; XII,1, 2, 5–7, 13; XIII,1, 13; XIV,1, 4; XVI,16 *estuve, etuve*; Ric: "*Étuve*. Lieu échauffé par des fourneaux"; Cotg: "Stove, hot-house, hot-bath"; still in modern French: *TLF* 8,309b: "Récipient destiné à maintenir les mets au chaud, à chauffer les plats"; this was not a baker's oven but a relatively small container made of iron or red copper (Confectioner Pref) — with a removable lid (Cook XXVI,86) — which could be placed in or on the coals

warm chamber: see stove

b) Receptacles, vessels

basin, Cook XVI,33, 70; XVIII,20, 27, 28; XXI,16, 24; Confections,48; Pastry Chef IX,10; XIII; XV,1, 2, 4; XVII;

XX,2–4; Confectioner Preface; IV,6; V,4 *bassin*; of red copper, Confectioner Pref; of tin, Pastry Chef XX,4; see also to wash, Appendix 3

 —— confectioner's basin, deep basin, Confectioner III,1; VI,1; XII,1, 5, 7, 13; XV,0–7, 11–13 *bassine*; of red copper or silver, flat-bottomed, two-handled: Confectioner XV,0; Cotg: "*Bassine*. A deepe, or bason-like, and footlesse, posnet, used most by Conservers, or Comfet-makers"

bell, cooking bell (for pears), Confectioner X,13 *(cuire à la) cloche*; Cotg: "A little Bell-resembling vessell, wherein Peares are ordinarily stewed, or sodden"; Fur: "*Cloche* se dit de certains vaisseaux & utenciles qui ont la figure d'une cloche. On fait cuire des fruits sous une cloche de fer qu'on fait rougir"

biscuit mould: see mould

bowl (wooden), Pastry Chef XIII; XV,2 *jatte (de bois)*; Cotg: "*Jate, Jatte*. A Bowle, a Mazer"; Pastry Chef IV,0 (passim30) *escuelle*; glazed earthenware bowl, Pastry Chef V *escuelle de fayance*; Cotg.: "A dish; *Escuelle à oreillons*. A porrenger"; Marnette: "Porrenger"

boxes (of pine), Cook Confections,48; Pastry Chef II,1; Confectioner Preface; X,20, 21; XIII,1 *boettes, boëtes (de sapin)*

case, coffer (of paper), Confectioner VII,4 *quaisse de papier*; Cotg: "*Quaisse*. A square woodden chest, such as Armour, or Marchandise is carried in"; Fur: "*Caisse*. Vaisseau fait de menuës planches de sapin ou autre bois leger, pour transporter des marchandises"

 casserole, Cook XV,51, XVI,33, 34, 37; XVIII,1, 7, 26; XXVI, 23; XXVII,3 *castrolle*; defined by La Varenne in Cook XVIII,28

as "une piece faite en façon de grande tourtiere, comme une espece de lechefritte"; Rich: "*Casserole*. Maniere de plat de cuivre étamé, de fort petit bord, & bien plus creux que les plats ordinaires, propre à faire des fricassées, ou des ragoûts"; see this word also in Appendix 2

cauldron, kettle (of bronze), Cook XVI,6, 10; Pastry Chef XX,4 *chaudron, chauderon (d'airain)*; Cotg: "*Chaudron*. A kettle, or cauldron; Looke *Chauderon*": "*Chauderon*. A Cauldron, or kettle"; Rich: "Vase de cuivre jaune ou rouge servant à la cuisine"; Cook V,66; VI,44; IX,0; XIII,2; XVI,14, 71, 75; XX,17; XXII,1 *chaudiere*; Cotg: "*Chaudiere*. A great cauldron, or kettle"; Rich: "Grand vase de métal propre à la cuisine"; see also kettle

crock, earthenware pot, Cook III,13; VIII,26; XV,1; XXII,9; Pastry Chef XV,3; Confectioner IV,5, 8; X,12 *pot de terre*; stoneware crocks, pots, Confectioner XII,1 *pots de grais*; glazed (earthenware) pot, Confectioner VII,2; X,22 *pot de fayance*; see also pot, terrine; and pie, Appendix 2

dish, a slightly concave or dished plate, Cook III,1 (passim 95); Pastry Chef IX,1 (passim 47); Confectioner II,1 (passim 5) *plat*; silver dish, Pastry Chef XXIX,11; Confectioner X,7 *plat d'argent*; Cotg: "*Plat*. A Platter; or great Dish"; Rich: "*Plat*. Sorte de vaisselle qui est creusée, qui a des rebords, & qui est faite de métal, de faiance ou de terre dans quoi on sert le potage & la viande sur table"; a *plat* is dished, allowing two of them to contain a foodstuff that is cooking (*e.g.* Cook III,21); see also plate; and to stew, Appendix 3

dish-warmer: see fire basket

double boiler, Cook XXX,35 *pot double*

dripping pan, Cook V,14, 58, 71; XVI,60, 70; XVIII,20, 28 *lechefritte*

earthenware dish: see pot, terrine

fern glasses: see glasses

fish pan, fish kettle, Cook XVIII, 27 *poissonniere*; defined by La Varenne in Cook XVIII,27; Cotg: "A long Panne to seethe fish in"

glass, Cook XVII,17; Pastry Chef VII,7; Confectioner IV,7 *verre*; fern glasses (made of glass made with fern) Cook XVII,17 *verres de fougère*; Fur: "*Fougere*. Petite herbe qui croist dans les bois, & elle sert principalement à faire du verre, aprés qu'on l'a reduite en cendre, à cause de la quantité du sel alkali qu'elle contient"; for glass see also bottle, flask

kettle, stew-kettle Cook III,43; V,50, 86; XIII,5 *marmite, marmitte*; see also cauldron

mould, biscuit mould (of tin), Cook Confections,65; Pastry Chef VII,13; XXV,1; Confectioner XIII,13 *mousle, moule à biscuit, moules de fer-blanc, tourtiere à biscuit (de fer blanc)*

pan, frying pan, Cook III,4 (passim 140); Pastry Chef XXI,1 (passim 40) *poesle, poële*; preserving pan, Pastry Chef XXIV *poesle à confiture*; Cotg: "*Paelle*. ... A footlesse Posnet, or Skellet, having brimmes like a Bason; a (little) Panne"; see also skillet

pitcher (silver), Confectioner IV,5 *aiguiere (d'argent)*

plate, a flat serving platter, trencher-plate, Cook V,71 (passim 34); Pastry Chef X,0 (passim 14); Confectioner VII,15

(passim 7); Linens ¶7 *assiette, assiete*; silver plate, Cook Confections,7 *assiette d'argent*; Platter Pie, Cook V,82; XIV,11 *Pasté d'assiette*; Cotg: "*Assiette*. A trencher-plate"; Rich: "Instrument de table, rond, de métal, de terre, ou de bois, sur quoi on mange & coupe ses morceaux"; an *assiette* is flat, allowing dough to be rolled out on it (*e.g.* Cook XXI,37); *cf.* platter, dish

platter: see plate

pot (probably iron) Cook II (passim 90); Pastry Chef XXIX,2; XXXIII,25; XXXIV,13 *pot*; pot, large-bellied, brass kettle Cook XIII,2; Confectioner V,2 *cocquemart, coquemare, coquemar*; Cotg: "*Coquemart*. A brazen pot, or chafer, having a cover"; I.D.G.: "*Coquemare*. It is a long brasen pot"; see also bell, crock, double boiler, terrine

ramekin: see Appendix 2

skillet, small pan, Cook VIII,18, 26, 42, 81; XV,29; XVI,3, 6, 33, 52; XVII,8, 9; XVIII,7; XXV,43; Confections,26, 29; Pastry Chef IV,1; IX,15; XII,6; XX,4; XXIX,4, 5; XXXIII,22; Confectioner Preface; III,1; XIII,1; XVI,1 *poëlon, poeslon, poëslon, poislon*; of red copper, Confectioner Pref *poëslons de cuivre rouge*; of brass, Pastry Chef XXXIII,22 *poëslon mediocre de cuivre jaune*; Cotg: "*Poeslon*. A Skellet, or Posnet; also, a little Frying-panne"; Fur: "*Poeslon*. Terme diminutif de *poesle*"; I.D.G.: "pipkin"; Marnette "skillet"

splints, wooden, Cook V,69 *éclisses de bois*

stoneware: see crock

terrine (a round, earthenware dish with slightly sloping sides), Cook III,46; V,1, 5, 14–16, 20, 25, 36, 47, 54, 59; VI,44; XXIII,7; Confections,39; Pastry Chef VII,16; Confectioner III,1; XI,5, 22; XII,1, 5, 7, 10, 1315, 18, 19; XII,13; XIV,1, 4; XV,0 *terrine*; Rich: "C'est un ouvrage de terre qui a le bord rond, qui est creux, qui n'a ni piez, ni anses & qui depuis le haut jusques au fond va toujours en étrecissant"; see the [implied] depth of a *terrine* in Confectioner XIV,2; see also crock

tourtière, torte pan, Cook III,7; V,73; VIII,64; XVI,93, XVII,2; XVIII,28; XXI,17; XXVI,87; Confections,31; Pastry Chef VII,8 *tourtiere*; of copper, tinned inside, Pastry Chef IX,1 *tourtieres de cuivre ... estamées par dedans*; Rich: "Piece de baterie de cuisine d'argent, ou de cuivre étamé, ronde, creuse d'environ trois doigts, avec des rebords hauts d'autant & qui vont en talus [sloping], quelquefois avec trois pieds, quelquefois sans piez, & quelquefois aussi avec un couvercle, servant aux bourgeois & aux patissiers pour faire des tourtes"; I.D.G.: "*A Tourte- panne*. It is a panne made of purpose for to bake a tourte in"; Marnette: "Tart pan"; the *Encyclopédie* of Diderot and D'Alembert shows a *tourtière* which is quite shallow and has sloping sides, looking much like a modern pie-plate.

trencher-plate: see plate

vessel(s), Cook Confections,41; Pastry Chef XVII; XVIII; XX,4; XXXIII,25; Confectioner III,1; IV,1, 2, 9, 11, 13, 14, 18 *vaisseau*; Cook Confections,41 *vaisselle*; silver vessel, Cook Confections,5 *vaisselle d'argent*

c) Utensils, materials

bags (leather, for keeping spices), Pastry Chef II,1 *bourses de cuir*

basket, Linen ¶ 19 *panier, pannier*

bottle (glass), Cook V,86; XIII,2; Confectioner IV,11; V,2, 5, 9 *bouteille de verre*

brass grill: see gril

bristles, pig's bristles (brush of), Pastry Chef III *(une brosse ou ballet de) soye de porc*

brush, Pastry Chef III; VII,1 *brosse*; see also bristles, feather

cardboard, Linen ¶ 1 *carte*; Fur: "*Carte*, signifie ... un corps fait de plusieurs feuilles de papier collées ensemble, ou de papier haché, mouillé, reduit en bouillie, rassemblé & seché dans une presse"

chafing dish: see fire basket

cloth, Cook III,11 (passim 17) *linge*; rag Cook XVI,51; XVIII,27 *torchon*; Cotg: "*Torchon*. A rubber, a wiper, a shooe-clowt"; I.D.G.: "a clout"; a large cloth, Cook XVI,71; XVIII,18 *nappe, nape*; Cotg. "*Nappe*. A table-cloth"; see also filter, cotton, hemp

colander (for breadcrumbs), Cook XVII,2 *couloire*; Cotg: "*Couloire*, as *Couloir*. A cullander"; see also

filter cone (of paper), Cook VIII,79 *cornet*; I.D.G.: "*Cornet*. It is a Coffin of paper, such as the grossers doe put and wrap fruit, or spices in"

cotton (cloth), Confectioner IV,1 *du cotton*

draining board, Pastry Chef XXVI *égoutoir*; Rich: "*Egoutoir*. Morceau de bois long d'environ trois piez, gros comme le bras, avec des rangs de chevilles de part & d'autre, sur quoi on met égouter la vaisselle"

faience: see bowl, pot

feather (for whipping egg whites, applying a glaze), Cook VIII,83; Pastry Chef III *plume*; bunch of feathers, cluster Pastry Chef III *ballet de plumes*; see also sugar: feather stage, in Appendix 2

filter, sieve, strainer (coarse, fine; of cloth, hair, metal), Cook X,1–4; XI,1; XIII,3; XV,34, 55; XXIV,4; Pastry Chef IX,10 *estamine*; Fur:

"*Estamine*. Petit estoffe fort mince, travaillée quarrément comme la toile. Estamine se dit aussi d'un morceau d'estoffe claire [light, thin] dont les Apothicaires & autres se servent pour passer ou filtrer leurs medecines ou autres liqueurs. On a aussi appelé estamine, les bluteaux [bolting-cloth] ou sas deliez fait de crin [horsehair] ou d'autre estoffe"; Cook Confections,5, 27, 29, 58; Confectioner II,1; XIII,1 *tamy, tamis, gros tamy, tamy delié*; hair sieve Confectioner XIII,2 *tamis de crain*; Pastry Chef I,6 *saz*; cloth, linen filter, Cook III,11 (passim 16); Confectioner II,2; III,1 *un linge*; coarse linen filter Cook Confections,43; Pastry Chef IX,10 *gros linge*; washing cloth, wash filter Cook XVIII,25 *(laver entre deux) linges*; Cotg: "*Tamis*. A searce, or boulter; (also, a strayner) made of haire"; Fur: "*Tamis*. Sas, vaisseau rond au milieu duquel il y a un tissu de toile de crin, ou de soye, par lequel on passe des drogues pulverisées, ou qu'on veut monder & espurer pour en retirer le plus delié"; Cotg: "*Sas*. A ranging sive, or searce"; Fur: "*Sas*. Tamis, utencile de figure cylindrique, qui a au milieu une toile ou reseau de crin, par les trous duquel on passe les poudres qu'on veut avoir fort deliées. [*e.g.*] On passe la farine au sas dans les huches, et il sert de blutoir"; Marnette: "*Sas*. A hair or ranging sieve"; see also colander, napkin, straining bag, and the sub-entry (cloth) immediately below

fire basket, chafing dish, dish-warmer

 (a metal pan or basket holding hot coals over which a dish with food can be set), Cook VIII,65, 75; XV,9; XVI,18; XX,11, 15, 16, 19; Pastry Chef XXXIII,25; Confectioner XV,0 *réchaut, rechaud*; Cotg: "*Rechault*. A chafing-dish; also, hot coales, or embers (used sometimes

in stead, or for want, of a Chafing-dish)"; Rich: "Instrument de cuisine qui est de terre, ou de métal dans quoi on met du feu pour rechaufer, ou tenir chaud quelque ragoût, ou pour faire cuire quelque chose entre deux plats. Le bon réchaut est fait de fer de cuirasse & composé d'un corps, de trois piez, d'une grille, d'un fond, d'une fourchette & d'un manche"

fish-turner, spatula, Pastry Chef XXXIII,2 *friquet*; Cotg: "A little slice, or scummer, to turne fish in a frying-pan"; see also spatula

flask (glass), Confectioner IV,7, 11; V,2, 6 *phiole (de verre)*

fork, Pastry Chef XXXIV,11; Confectioner IX,3 *fourchette, fourchetes*

funnel, confectioner's funnel, Cook XVI,90; Pastry Chef VII,2; Confectioner XV,1 *entonnoir*; a red-copper funnel-like implement, Confectioner XV,0 *un outil de cuivre rouge en façon d'entonoir*; see also to funnel, Appendix 3

grater (for lemon, etc.), Pastry Chef IX,2, 4; XIV *raspe*

grill, Cook V,8 (passim 34) *gril*; brass grill (a tray of fine brass wires), Confectioner Preface *fils d'arechal*; Fur: "*Archal*. Fil de leton passé par la filiere"; see also to grill, Appendix 3

hemp (cloth), Confectioner IV,1 *filasse*

hooks (iron), Confectioner VII,16 *crochets de fer*

iron, cast iron: see wafer, mortar, pestle

knife, Pastry Chef IV,2; V; VII,14, 23; IX,2, 4, 15; XV,3, 5, 8, 10; XXV,2; XXVI; Confectioner VII,4; IX,3, 6, 7, 11; XII,10; XIII,1; XVI,13 *cousteau, couteau*; see also pen knife larding-needle, Confectioner XI,19; Linens

¶ 5 *lardoire*; Cotg: "A larding sticke, or pricke"; Har.

marble slab, Confectioner VII,15, 16 *une pierre de marbre*

mortar (of stone, marble), Cook III,23 (passim 19); Pastry Chef I,6 (passim 15); Confectioner II,1 (passim) *mortier (de marbre ou de pierre)*; cast- iron mortar Confectioner I; II,2 *mortier de fonte*; see also pestle, below; to grind, Appendix 3

mould, pan (of white metal, for baking pies), Pastry Chef VII,13 *moule (de fer blanc)*

napkin, serviette (passim) *serviette, linge*; used when serving a preparation, Cook V,84 (passim 20) *serviette*; used for straining, Cook XIX,16; Confections,42, 44, 45, 48 *serviette*; Fur: "*Serviette. Linge de table qu'on met sur chaque couvert pour manger proprement, pour étendre sur ses habits, & s'en essuyer les mains & la bouche.* [*e.g.*] *Quand on lave les mains c'est un service honnête de presenter la serviette*"; see also filter (cloth); to ruffle, Appendix 3
—— various folds: folded in a Band, Linen ¶ 3 *Plié par bande*; a Melon, Linen ¶ 4 *Plié en melon* a ruffled Melon, Linen ¶ 5 *Melon frisé*; double Sea-Shell, Linen ¶ 6 *Coquille double*; ruffled Double Sea-Shell, Linen ¶ 7 *Coquille double & frisée*; plain Sea-Shell, Linen ¶ 8 *Coquille simple*; Ox's Hoof, Linen ¶ 9 *Pied de bœuf*; a Cock, Linen ¶ 10 *En coq*; the Pheasant, Linen ¶ 11 *Le faisant*; the Hen, Linen ¶ 12 *La poule*; Brooding Hen in a Bush, Linen ¶ 13 *Poule qui couve dans un buisson*; Hen with its Chicks, Linen ¶ 14 *Poule avec ses poussins*; the Chicken, Linen ¶ 15 *Le poulet*; the Capon, Linen ¶ 16 *Le chapon*; Two Chickens in a Pie, Linen ¶ 17

Deux poulets dans un pasté; Four Partridges, Linen ¶ 18 *Quatre perdrix*; a Dove Brooding in a Basket, Linen ¶ 19 *Un pigeon qui couve dans un panier*; Turkey Hen, Linen ¶ 20 *Poulet d'Inde*; the Tortoise, Linen ¶ 21 *La tortue*; The Dog with a Collar, Linen ¶ 22 *Le chien avec un collier*; Suckling Piglet, Linen ¶ 23 *Cochon de laict*; the Hare, Linen ¶ 24 *Le lievre*; two Rabbits, Linen ¶ 25 *Deux lapins*; the Hedgehog, Linen ¶ 26 *Le herisson*; the Pike, Linen ¶ 27 *Le brochet*; the Carp, Linen ¶ 28 *La carpe*; the Turbot, Linen ¶ 29 *Le turbot*; the Brill, Linen ¶ 30 *La barbuë*; the Mitre, Linen ¶ 31 *La mitre*; Holy Ghost Cross, Linen ¶ 32 *Croix de Saint Esprit*; Cross of Lorraine, Linen ¶ 33 *Croix de Lorraine*

paper (sheet of, band of), Pastry Chef VII,2 (passim 45); Confectioner Pref (passim 28) *(fueille, fueillet, bande de) papier*; see also cone, cardboard, above; and case, in section b)

pastry board (wooden), Pastry Chef VII,2; VIII,1 *rondeau (de bois)*; Cotg: "*Rondeau de pastissier. A round and flat board whereon Pastissiers doe raise their Pastry Chef and Pies*"; Rich: "*Deux petits ais* [planks] *colez & chevillez* [pegged] *ensemble, coupez en rond, large d'environ deux piez & grans d'autant. Ais large & façonné en rond dont les patissiers de Paris se servent pour mettre leurs patisseries lorsquelles sont faites*"; see also pastry table, in section a), above

peel, oven shovel, Pastry Chef VII,21; VIII,1, 2 *pesle, pelle a four*; Cotg: "*Paelle. A shovell; a fire-shovell; also, a Peele wherewith bread, &c, is set into an oven*"; see also shovel

pen knife, Pastry Chef IX,15 *canif*; Cotg: "*Canif. A pen-knife*"

pestle, Pastry Chef I,6; XXVI *pilon*; wooden pestle, Pastry Chef XVI *bistortier*; Confectioner XVI,1 *pilon de*

bois; cast-iron pestle, Confectioner I
pilon de fonte; Cotg: "*Bistortier*. A
rolling pin, or pestle, of wood"

pin, Confectioner XI,19; XII,1; XIV,1;
Linens ¶5 *espingle, epingle*

press, squasher (to crush cheese), Pastry Chef XI,4 *escachoy* (likely a misprint for *escachoir*; in the same book see *bouchoy*, "oven stopper," *s.v.* oven, above); Cotg: "*Escacheur*. A squasher; a beater, or crusher of things flat; a thruster, presser, or squeezers of things, hard or close together"; see to squash, Appendix 3

rod, wooden skewer, Cook XVI,76;
XVIII,29 *verge*; see also stick, whisk

rolling pin (wooden), Pastry Chef I,2, 4;
VII,4; XXI,3; XXV,4, 8; Confectioner
XVI,12, 18 *un rouleau (de bois)*; see
also stick

sausage filler, made of copper or white
metal, Cook V,8 *boudiniere*

serviette: see napkin

shovel, fire shovel, Cook III,11, 13, 49;
VIII,48, 50, 66 (passim 18); Pastry
Chef XXIX,8, 11; XXX,4; XXXIII,10,
22, 23, 25 *pesle, paisle, pelle (de feu,
du feu)*; see also peel

sieve: see filter

skewer, Cook VI,31, 40; VIII,11; XV,39
brochette; see also spit, and to skewer
in Appendix 3

skimmer, a holed instrument, Cook Confections,26; Pastry Chef XXII,1; XXIV;
XXXIII,17; Confectioner Preface; III,1,
4 *escumoir, écumoir, ecumoire*; of red
copper or silver (Confectioner Pref)

slate, Confectioner XII,2, 4, 5; XIII,1, 13
ardoise, ardoises

spatula (of wood), trowel, Pastry Chef V;
VII,8; IX,3, 7; X; XIII; XVII; XX,1;
XXV,2 *gâche, gache (de bois)*; Rich:
"Terme de patissier. Petit instrument
de bois, long d'un bon pié, large &

délié par le bout d'embas, dont les
patissiers se servent pour manier leurs
farces"; Cotg: "*Gasche*. An Oare, or
Scull to row with"; Cook Confections,5,
6; Confectioner III,4; VI,1, 3; VII,1;
XIII,13; XVI,1 *espature, espatule, epatule*; I.D.G.: a "wooden slice"; Cotg:
"*Espatule*. A (Chirurgions, or Apothecaries) little slice"; Fur: "L'*espatule*
de bois sert aux Apothicaires à remuer
leurs syrops & autres drogues qu'ils
preparent"; see also fish-turner

spit, Cook III,4; IV,4; V,1; 4, 14, 51, 64,
69; VI,4, 13, 16, 20, 26, 45, 46, 48, 49,
51–53, 59; VII,5; VIII,56 XVI,41, 61;
XXV,40, XXVI,47 *broche*

spoon Cook XVII,15; XIX,10; Confections,1, 9, 56; Pastry Chef IV (passim); Confectioner IX,1 (passim) *une
cuiliere, cuilliere, cuilier, cuillier,
cuiller, cueiller, cueillier, cueilliere*;
steel spoon, Confectioner IX,1 *une
cuilier d'acier*; red copper or silver
spoon, Confectioner Pref *cuilliere de
cuivre ou d'argent*; silver spoon, Pastry
Chef IV,2; V; VII,14; X; XV,4; XXVI;
XXXIII,22; XXXIV,1, 14; Confectioner
Pref *une cuillier, cueillier, cuilliere,
cueilliere d'argent*; see the note in the
Pastry Chef IV,2

stick, rod, bat, Cook V,14; Pastry Chef
VII,20; XIX,5; XXII,1; XXXIII,2;
Confectioner V,4; XIV,1 *baston*; Pastry Chef VII,2 *des bastons de fagots*;
see also rod, rolling pin, whisk, and
rosemary in Appendix 1

strainer: see filter

straw, Cook Confections,4; Confectioner
Pref (passim) *paille*

strainer, sieve, Cook III,23, 26; VIII,42,
65, 79, 81; XV,20; XX,19; XXI,33;
XXV,18; Confectioner X,21; XIII,1, 2,
6, 13 *passoire*; I.D.G.: "A straining
panne. It is a panne made much after
the forme of a warming pan, but that it
is without a lid or cover, and that it is
round at the bottome, and full of small

holes cullender-like"; see also colander, filter, napkin

straining bag (for liquids), Cook VIII,26, 27, 29; XIX,16; Confections,38; Confectioner III,1; IV,1–4, 6 *chausse*; Fur: "*Chausse*, est ... une piece de drap ou d'estamine, ou même de papier gris sans colle, qui aboutit en pointe comme un capuchon, qui sert aux Chymistes, aux Apothicaires & autres pour filtrer & clarifier les liqueurs. [*e.g.*] On passe l'hypocras, l'eau de blanc d'œuf par la chausse"; see also filter, napkin

string, Pastry Chef VII,8, 15, 17, 21 *ficelle*

syringe, piping bag, Confectioner XVI,14, 15 *seringue*; Fur: "*Seringue*. Instrument qui sert à compresser l'air ou les liqueurs. Il est composé d'un cylindre concave & d'un piston qui l'emplit exactement, son mouvement fait sortir avec violence par un trou qui est à l'extremité, l'air ou la liqueur qui y est enfermée"; see also to use a syringe, Appendix 3

thread, Pastry Chef XV,3; XXX,6; Confectioner XIV,1 *fil*

tin sheets, white-metal sheets, Confectioner XII,2, 4; XIII,1 *feuilles de fer blanc*

tripod, Pastry Chef XX,4 *trepied*

vine leaves, Cook VI,6, 9, 23, 29, 32; VIII,95 *feuilles de vignes*

waffle iron, wafer iron, Pastry Chef XX *gauffrier*

whisk, of (cleanly peeled, slender) birch or elm branches, Confectioner Preface; III,1 *balet ... fait de bouleau ...,*

ou branches d'ormeau; feather whisk Pastry Chef III *ballet de plumes*; Cook Confections,39 *verges*; Cotg: "*Balet*. A beesome, or broome"; Fur: "*Balai*. Utencile de mesnage qui sert à amasser & à oster les ordures, à tenir les maisons nettes & propres. On fait des *balais* de menuës branches de bouleau [birch] liées ensemble au bout d'un baston. On en fait aussi de genest [genista, broom], de jonc [reeds], & de plumes pour nettoyer les tableaux & les meubles."

wicker mat, tray, Pastry Chef VII,2; Confectioner Pref *claye*; Rich: "Ouvrage de vanier, qui est plat, qui est long de 4 ou 5 piez, plus ou moins, & large d'environ 3 ou 4, & quelquefois davantage selon les choses dont on a besoin"; Cotg: "A hurdle, or lattice of (Ozier) twigs, &c"; small wicker mat, tray Pastry Chef XXIV; XXVI *clayon*; Fur: "*Clayon*. Ouvrage d'osier fait en rond, dont se servent particulierement les Pâtissiers pour porter leurs pains benits, & leurs autres pâtisseries. On s'en sert aussi dans les cuisines pour faire égoutter les mets qu'on fait cuire dans de l'eau"

d) Fuel

coal, Cook V,28; Confectioner IV,5, 8 *(feu de) charbon*

coals, live coals, embers, Cook V,13 (passim); Pastry Chef VII,1 (passim); Confectioner X,7 (passim) *braise, braize*; Pastry Chef IX,1; XV,1; XXIX,3, 5; Confectioner V,2 *cendre (chaude)*

firewood (in bundles), Pastry Chef VII,2 *fagots*

5. Measures

a) Weights

ounce, Cook Confections,5, 27, 36, 38; Pastry Chef II,1 (passim); Confectioner II,2 *(une, deux, trois, quatre, douze, treize) once(s)*; half an ounce, Pastry Chef I,4; Confectioner II,2; IV,16 *une demie once*

pound (of butter: 13 ounces; of flour: 16 ounces), (passim) *livre*: Pastry Chef VI: *"Remarquez, que quand nous parlerons du mot de livre, par exemple d'une livre de beurre, nous entendons parler de la livre qui pese treize onces, ou deux marcs des Orfevres, & ainsi des autres poids ... proportion"*; Cotg: *"La livre des Espiciers, Grossiers, &c.* Contains but 12 ounces; (whereas our Grocers pound containeth 16). *La livre marchande.* Containes in some places 14, in others 18, but in the most 16, ounces"; Fur: *"Livre. Une mesure du poids des corps graves qu'on pese, qui est differente selon les lieux. Celle d'Avignon, de Provence & de Languedoc est de 13 onces. La livre de Paris est de 16 onces, celle de Medecine 12."*

—— light pound (of butter, dough, sugar, quince, etc.: 13 ounces), Cook V,8, 84; VIII,27, 79; XIV,13; XIX,16; XXI,0; XXIII,1 Confections,10, 38, 46, 47, 65; Pastry Chef I,4 (passim 70); Confectioner Pref (passim) *une livre, quatre livres, quinze livres*

—— pound (of flour: 16 ounces), Cook XXI,0 *quatre livres*

—— half pound (of sugar, almonds, etc.: 6 ounces), Cook III,32; V,84; VIII,79; XIV,3; XVI,31; XXI,40; Confections,33, 53, 58; Pastry Chef I,1 (passim) *une demye livre*

—— quarter pound (of sugar, etc., 3 ounces; of flour, 4 ounces) *quarteron,*

carteron; Cook XXI,40; Confections,39, 47, 53, 56; Pastry Chef I,6; IV,2; Confectioner IV,8; IX,1; (passim 60) *un quarteron, carteron (d'amandes, beurre, chair, citrons, farine, fromage, graisse, mouelle, oranges, pistaches, sucre)*; see Pastry Chef VI: *"Le litron ou seizieme partie d'un boisseau de fleur de farine doit peser trois quarterons, c'est ... dire douze onces"*; Cotg: *"Quarteron. A quarter of a pound; also, a Pinte, or little Quart; also, the halfe of an Emine"*; see also section c), below

—— one-eighth of a pound, two ounces Cook VIII,26; Pastry Chef VII,3; IX,6; XI,5; XIII; (passim) *demy quarteron (de beurre, lard, leveure, oeufs, jaunes d'oeufs, pignon, raisin de Corinthe, sel, sucre)*; see also section c), below

—— five ounces, Cook Confections,56; Pastry Chef IX,10, 15; XV,9 *un quarteron & demy*

—— nine ounces, "three-quarters of a pound" (of sugar, butter), Cook Confections,35, 42, 44; Pastry Chef VII,4; XV,5; XX,4; Confectioner Preface; X,1; XVI,1 *trois quarterons*; Pastry Chef XXVI *une demie livre ou trois quarterons (de sucre)*

—— twelve ounces (of flour), Cook Confections,46, 65; Pastry Chef VI (see the text, above); IX,15; XV,5; XXV,1 *trois quarterons*

—— fifteen ounces, "a pound and a quarter" (of sugar), Cook VIII,26; Confectioner Pref *cinq quarterons (de sucre)*

grain, one-480th of an ounce, Confectioner IV,1 *un grain, deux grains*; Cook Confections,38 *un grain de musque*; several grains, Pastry Chef VII,8; IX,15; Confectioner IV,2 *six grains, une douzaine de grains, une vingtaine de grains;*

Cotg: "The foure and twentieth part of a pennie-weight"; Fur: "Le *grain* est la vingt-quatriéme partie du denier. Il y a 480 *grains* à l'once"; see also d) sizes (a grain), below

dram, Pastry Chef VI *gros*; Cotg: "*Gros.* A Dramme, or the eight part of an ounce, of Gold, or Silver; of other wares, the 32 part of an ounce; or, the 256 part of a pound"

a macaroon's weight (of ground almonds), Cook XXI,29 *le poids d'un macaron*

b) Volumes (liquid and dry)

Note: In the *French Pastry Chef Chef* (IV,1) La Varenne points out that dairy merchants have their own definition of a *chopine*, which amounts to a pound and a half of milk.

bushel (of flour), Pastry Chef I,1; VI *boisseau (de farine)*; Pastry Chef VI: "*Remarqués que quand nous parlerons d'un boisseau de farine, nous entendons parler de la farine qui est sans son & que le boisseau de cette farine doit peser douze ... treze livres ou environ*"; Cotg: "*Boisseau.* The (French) bushell; (and the 12 part of a *Septier*) is somewhat lesse than our London pecke, & a halfe; for a *Boisseau* of wheat weighes 20 pounds; our pecke of wheat meale, 14"; Marnette: "a Peck and a half"

—— half bushel (of flour), Pastry Chef I,2, 3; VI; VII,4; VIII,1, 2 *demy boisseau (de farine)*; Pastry Chef VI: "*Remarqués ... que le demy boisseau doit peser six livres ou un peu plus*"; Marnette: "three quarters of a peck"

—— quarter bushel *quart de boisseau*; Pastry Chef VI: "*Remarqués ... que le quart de boisseau doit peser trois livres ... bon poids*"; Pastry Chef VI; XVI; XXIV; *quart (de boisseau) (de fleur de farine)*; Pastry Chef VII,4 *un quart & demy, ou approchant d'un*

demy boisseau de farine; Rich: GET QUOTE "grain measure"

—— eighth bushel, Pastry Chef I,4 *un demy quart (de fleur de farine)*

"litron" (generally a measure of flour) *litron*

—— 12 ounces in weight, 3/4 of a (16-ounce) pound (of flour), Pastry Chef I,5; VI; VII,18; XII; XIII; XV,2, 3, 6, 8, 9; XX,2, 3; XXI,1 *litron, literons*: "*Le litron ou seizieme partie d'un boisseau de fleur de farine doit peser trois quarterons, c'est ... dire douze onces*"; Cotg: "*Litron.* A measure (most commonly) of wood, containing somewhat more then our pinte, and used by the Retailers of Salt, Pulse, Millet, Rapeseed, &c."; I.D.G.: "It is a measure of one pinte, or a little more"; Rich: "*Sorte de mesure qui est de la grandeur d'une chopine, où l'on vend les choses qui ne sont pas liquides, comme sel, chatégnes*"

—— six ounces (of flour), Cook XIX,9; Pastry Chef IV,0, 3; XXIV *demy litron*

—— quarter-pint (roughly), four ounces (of flour), Pastry Chef XIII *la quatriesme partie d'un litron (de farine)*

quart *pinte*

—— of water, juice, wine, vinegar: 31 ounces by weight, four cups, one quart (Imperial measure: three cups, three-quarters of a quart), Cook V,33, 66; VI,44: XIII,3; XVI,40; Confections,27 (passim); Pastry Chef VII,5; Confectioner III,1; IV,1, 4, 5, 7, 9, 11–16; XX,5, 19 *pinte*; Pastry Chef VI: "*Remarquez que quand nous parlerons d'une pinte, que c'est de la pinte selon la mesure du vin de Paris, qui tient la pesanteur de deux livres moins une once ou environ d'eau, & environ la mesme pesanteur de vin*"

—— of milk: 47 ounces by weight, six cups, one and one-half quarts (Imperial measure: less than five cups, one and one-third quarts), Cook V,8; Confections,39; Pastry Chef XX,4 *pinte de lait*; Pastry Chef VI: "*Remarqués que quand nous parlerons d'une pinte de laict, que la pinte doit peser trois livres moins une once ou environ, & les autres mesures a proportion*"; see also eighth-pint, below

"chopine" *chopine*; Pastry Chef VI (& Richelet): "*La chopine est la moitié d'une pinte*"; see also Pastry Chef XV,2; Cotg: "*Chopine*. A Chopine; or the Parisien halfe pint; almost as big as our whole one; (at S. Denis, and in divers other places about Paris, three of them make but one pint)"

—— of water, wine: 16 fluid ounces, two cups, one pint, Pastry Chef VIII,2; Confectioner IV,3, 7; V,2; X,3 *une chopine d'eau, de vin*

—— of milk: 24 fluid ounces, three cups, one and one-half pints, Cook XXI,40; Pastry Chef IV,0, 2, 3; IX,15; XIII; XV,2; XXXIII,25 *une chopine de lait, de cresme* (except in Pastry Chef XV,2); Cook Confections,39 *chopine de cresme*

—— a quart (of wine), Cook XIX,16; Confectioner X,1 *trois chopines de vin, d'eau*; = 48 oz

septier (of liquids): two cups, sixteen fluid ounces

—— one cup, a half-pint, eight fluid ounces (of water, bouillon, wine, juice), Cook III,32; XVI,3; Pastry Chef I,2; VII,5, 17; XII,1; XXI,1; XXIX,11; Confectioner IV.3, 11, 14; V,3, 5, 7, 9; X,2; XV,2 *un demy-septier*; Cotg: "*Demi septier de vin*. Is but the halfe of a *Chopine*, or a quarter of the French pint"

—— a quarter cup, two fluid ounces (of water), Pastry Chef I,5 *le quart d'un demy septier (d'eau)*

—— three cups, one and a half pints (of water), Confectioner III,1 *trois demy septiers*

poisson, poinçon, posson

—— (normally) of milk: 2/3 cup, 5 1/2 ounces; 1/8 of a "milk" pint, Pastry Chef VI; XI,5; XV,3–5; XXXIII,10 *poinçon, posson (de laict)*; Pastry Chef VI: "*Le poinçon de laict, c'est ... dire la huictiesme partie d'une pinte de laict, ... la mesure des Laitieres, doit peser cinq onces & demie & trois gros ou environ*" [a *pinte* of milk therefore weighs roughly 47 oz]; Cotg: "*Posson*. The quarter of a *Chopine*; a little measure for milke, verjuice, and vinegar, not altogether so big as the quarter of our Pint"; Rich: "*Poisson*. Mesure qui tient la moitié d'un demi-setier & dont on se sert pour mesurer quelque sorte de liqueur comme le lait"

a cupful, Pastry Chef XXV,8 *une coupe*

a glassful, Cook Confections,56, 59; Pastry Chef I,4; VII,4; XVI *un verre, une verrée*; half a glassful, Pastry Chef XXIV; XXVI; XXXIV,2 *un demy verre*

a spoonful, Cook V,28; XI,2; XIII,1; Pastry Chef XV,1 (passim) *une cueillerée*; half a spoonful (of runny yeast), Pastry Chef XX,4 *une demy cueillée*

a handful (of strawberries, parsley, pistachios, almonds, sorrel, pearl-ash, sugar, salt), Cook V,1 (passim); Pastry Chef XIV *une poignée*

a fistful, Pastry Chef XI,2; XIV; XV,6, 8; XVII *(comme le, les deux) poing(s)*

a dash (of verjuice, vinegar, white wine), Cook III,4 (passim) *un filet (de verjus, vinaigre, vin blanc)*

a drop (of vinegar), Cook VI,53 *une pointe (de vinaigre*; Cook XV,48 *une goutte (de vinaigre)*

an egg-amount, Pastry Chef VIII,1; IX,2–4 (passim 31) *la grosseur d'un œuf (de poule), comme un petit œuf*; Pastry Chef VIII,1 (passim) *(la grosseur de) deux, trois œufs*; half an egg's amount (of marrow) Pastry Chef IX,15 *(comme la moitiée d'un œuf (de moëlle)*

a walnut-amount, Pastry Chef VII,5 (passim 13); Confectioner XVI,20 *(la grosseur d'une) noix* an almond-amount, Pastry Chef XXV,8 *une petite amande* (of *gomme contragan*)

a hazel-nut-amount, Pastry Chef IX,3; XV,9; XXI,1; XXVIII,1; XXXIII,7; Confectioner IV,1, 2; XVI,3 *(la grosseur d'une) noisete, noisette(s)*; Cotg: "A small nut, or hasel nut; also, a Filbeard"

a pea-amount, Pastry Chef VII,6; XX,3; XXI,3; Confectioner III,2; XV,9; XVI,23 *(gros comme un, des) pois, poix*

a sprig (of elderberry, laurel, rosemary), Cook V,66 *baston*; Confectioner IV,5; XII,1 *branche*; sprouts or sprigs (of fennel), Confectioner VIII,2 *jettons ou branches*; Cotg: "*Jecton*. A shute [shoot], sience, twig, sprig"

a small amount, speck, pinch (as of salt), Cook III,1 (passim 10) *brin*; Confectioner VIII,2 *brain*; Cotg: "*Brin*. A (little) slip, or sprig, of an hearbe, &c; also, a corne of salt; and more generally, any small substance, deale, or bit of a thing. *Brain*. The branch of a tree"; Fur: "*Brin*, se dit . . . des menus jets [sprouts] des herbes, des joncs, des cheveux, & de tout ce qui des racines pousse"; see also a macaroon's weight in 5. a), above

c) Quantities

fifty, Confectioner V,7 *un demy-cent*

twenty-five (or twenty-six) of eggs, nuts, Cook VIII,26; Confections,53 *un quarteron*; Cotg: " . . . A quarterne (or the fourth part) of an hundreth"; "good measure" (Pastry Chef VI) normally implied increasing an amount by one unit; I.D.G. uses the term "quartern"; see also pound in section a) above

a dozen (or thirteen), Cook VIII,65, 76, 79; XIX,16; Pastry Chef VII,2, 3, 8; XXXIII,2; Confectioner IV,1; XIV,7 *une douzine*; Cook VIII,26 *demy quarteron*; Cotg: "*Demi quarteron*. The halfe of a

Quarteron"; Cook VIII,26: "*les blancs de demi quarteron d'oeufs*"
—— a half dozen, Pastry Chef XXXIII,1, 10; XXXIV,2, 14 *une demie douzaine*

d) Sizes, distances

coins (diameter)
—— ecu, Pastry Chef XXXIV,11 *la grandeur d'un quart d'escu*
—— testoon, a silver coin roughly 1 1/8 in or 28mm in diameter, minted from Louis XII (1498–) to Henri III (– 1589), Cook XV,23 *la largeur d'un teston*; Cotg: "*Teston*. "A piece of silver coyne worth xviii d sterling"; Richelet writes that by La Varenne's day the *teston* was passing out of use: "Les testons sous Henri IV [r. 1589–1610] eurent encore beaucoup de cours & ils n'ont commencé à n'être plus dans le commerce que du règne de Louis XIII, en 1641."
coins (thickness)
—— ecu, Confectioner IX,6; XVI,18 *l'espaisseur d'un escu blanc*
—— quarter ecu, Cook Confections,10; Pastry Chef I,3; VII,13; XXII,2 *l'épaisseur d'un quart d'ecu*; Pastry Chef VII,16 *l'espoiseur de deux quarts d'escu*; Pastry Chef I,3 *l'espoiseur de trois ou quatre quarts d'escu*
—— piastre Pastry Chef VII,20; XX,3 *l'epaisseur de deux ou trois piastres*; Cotg: "*Piastre*. A Turkish coyne worth about iiij s sterl."
—— a thirty-sou coin, Pastry Chef I,3 *l'epoisseur . . . d'une piece de trente sols*
—— a fifty-eight-sou coin, Pastry Chef VII,20; XX,3; XXV,4, 8 *l'épaisseur d'une piece de cinquante huict sols*
—— testoon, Cook Confections,53, 58; Pastry Chef VII,18 *l'espoisseur, espaisseur d'un teston, de deux testons*; same thickness as two sheets of paper, Pastry Chef VII,18
—— silver Louis, Pastry Chef I,4 *l'espoisseur d'un Louis d'argent d'un escu*

coins (value, price)

—— sou: a pennyworth, Cook Confections,53 *pour un sol*; three-penny (pies) Pastry Chef VII,22 *(pastés d'assiette) de trois sols*

—— two liards worth, Pastry Chef XXV,1 *pour deux liards*; Cotg: "A brazen coyne worth three *deniers*, or the fourth part of a *sol*"; Fur: "Monnoye qui vaut trois deniers, faite de la même matiere que les sous. Elle a cours encore dans le Lyonnais & dans le Dauphiné"

thumb length, Pastry Chef XXIII,1 *longueur du pouce*

thumb width, inch, Pastry Chef I,1, 4; VII,1, 2, 4, 5, 17, 21; XI,4; XV,1, 2, 5, 7–9, 10; Confectioner Preface *(l'espoisseur d'un, deux, quatre) pouce(s), l'epoisseur de deux bons pouces*

finger width(s), Pastry Chef VII,2, 5, 6, 14, 15, 17, 20; XI,4; XIII; XV,1, 6, 7; XVI; XVII; XXV,3; Linen, ¶¶ 1, 6, 8, 10, 17, 18, 27–29 *le, deux ou trois, travers, espoisseur, du, d'un, doigt, de deux, trois, quatre, cinq, six, doigts*

—— every four fingers, finger widths, Pastry Chef VII,4 *de quatre doigts en quatre doigts*

—— length and/or width of little finger, Pastry Chef VII,4; XII,6 *gros & longs comme le, le travers du, petit doigt*

—— half a finger width, Confectioner IX,2 *l'epaisseur d'un demy doigt*

thickness of two sheets of paper, Pastry Chef VII,18 *l'espoisseur de deux fueilles de papier*

a grain of wheat (of rennet), Cook Confections,41 *la grosseur d'un grain de bled (de prezure)*; a peppercorn Cook III,5 *un grain de poivre*; a grain of salt Cook VIII,78; XIX,5 *un grain de sel*; see also a) weights (grain), above (grain)

e) Times

hour (passim) *heure(s)*; Pastry Chef VII,5 *vingt ou vingt quatre heures*

fifteen minutes, Pastry Chef IV; VII,19; XXVI; XXVIII,1; XXIX,4; Confectioner IX,4; XI,4 *quart d'heure*; forty-five minutes, Pastry Chef XV,1–4 *trois quarts d'heure*; seventy-five minutes, Pastry Chef XV,4 *cinq quarts d'heure*; twelve minutes Cook Confections,58; Pastry Chef VII,9, 14; IX,15; XV,5; XVI; XXIV; XXV,1; XXVI; Confectioner IX,4; XI,7; XII,5 *un demy quart d'heure*

a boil, a boiling, Cook III,26; VIII,5, 98; X,1; XIV,9; XV,32; XVI,71; XVIII,17; XXI,35; XXV,40; XXVI,86; XXVIII,29; Confectioner II,1; IV,14; V,4; VII,2; X,8 *un bouillon*; Cook Confections,2, 16 *un bouillon ou deux*; Confections,35; Confectioner VIII,3 *deux ou trois bouillons*; Confections,1, 20 *4 ou cinq bouillons*; Confections,16 *cinq ou six bouillons*; Pastry Chef XXXIV *une demie douzaine de bouillons*; Confections,18 *sept ou huict gros bouillons*; Confections, 21 *huict ou dix bouillons*; Confections,21, 25, 63 *dix ou douze bouillons*; Confectioner XIV,7 *une douzaine de bouillons*; Confectioner XII,5; XIII,3 *vingt bouillons*. Compare this French word *bouillon* with the English *walm* and *warm* meaning a "bubbling" and used in the same sense: Karen Hess, "Amendments to the Robert May Glossary," *Petits Propos Culinaires* 55 (May 1997), 29.

time, times (number of repetitions), Cook III,4; V,70; XXV,40; Confections,29, 33; Pastry Chef XXV,7, 8; XXXII,1, 2 *tour, (cinq ou six) tours (de broche, de poesle)*

f) Heats

warm oven, hearth, Pastry Chef VII,15,
17, 19, 24; XXV,4 *l'âtre doux*; hot
oven Pastry Chef XV,2, 4; XVI; XVII;
XIX; XXV,2; XXVI; XXVII *l'âtre*

chaud; relatively warm, hot: Pastry
Chef VII,2, 22; XV,7 *un peu moins
chaud que si c'estoit pour cuire de
gros pain*; *leur donnés l'atre comme
aux petis pastés d'assiette*

6. Mattia Giegher, *Treatise on Linen Folding*

Mattia Giegher's *Treatise on Linen Folding* (*Trattato delle piegature*) affords a glimpse of the techniques that had been developed in Italy for the folding of linens for refined noble and bourgeois tables. The work was bound with two others by the same author under the collective title *The Three Treatises* (*Li tre trattati*) and published in Padua by P. Frambotto in 1639.

The material of the *Trattato delle piegature* is itself set out by either the author or the printer in three parts: illustrations, a preamble, and a description of the various figures that can be formed by folding napkins; these shapes are shown in the illustrations. We make use of a few of Giegher's illustrations to illuminate our French version of napkin folding. Some of the preamble of Giegher's treatise is worth translating here for the emphasis it places upon the need for a formal mastery of such abilities. Some of the various procedures seems to have been commonplace and were probably in the mind of the French author of the *How to Fold all Sorts of Table Linen* (*Maniere de plier toutes sortes de linge de Table*) appended to the end of the *French Confectioner*.

> Having several times been entreated by my learned lords to round out my books on the *Trinciante* and the *Scalco*, I was clearly obliged to fulfill their fair and reasonable request. [. . .] On copper plates I have had various ways of folding napkins or serviettes etched, adding to them a brief, succinct explanation both to help the reader better understand and to assist the memory of those who will be learning the art from me.

> It seems to me not unreasonable to accord foremost place to this treatise [on linen folding] over the others given that napkins are the first things to be readied for the table. [. . .] [In this book] is shown firstly an easy and efficient way of folding and stocking any table linen to be used on formal occasions, along with many other refinements such as the following shapes with their identifying numbers clearly indicated. Then there follows an image of the table all set, with its sideboard, the wine stewards' station — two of the latter if the banquet is large, in the judgement of the Steward or whomever is responsible. Next are instructions on how the first folds should be made in table linen and napkins in order to form plain pleated linen and herringbones; that is, the first folds making plain pleats, mostly in four and in six layers, and table cloths similarly. The herringbone pattern in napkins is then done, in four, in three and in two — and even singly, which is done the same way as with those napkins that are to be rectangular. The names of all those things will be seen in the abovementioned copper plates.

> Besides that, how flames or blackbirds are made, not only [in napkins] for each animal — for example, the Salamander, etc. — but also in the table cloths.

The first [plate] shows a picture of hands — that is, how they ought to turn up to make the first folds; and the other hands show the way of making the herringbone, leaving a part of the plainly pleated linen without beating on it, so that it can be seen how it is being folded, and the other is beaten upon; alongside can next be seen where everything has been beaten down, so that both can be seen distinctly. The same will be likewise be done with the herringbone, from which will be formed the principal animals, of which mention will be made a little further on. Likewise with the above-mentioned things, into which there is no reason to go so as not to be tiresome, because I trust the memory of those who are learning from me. There will then be a castle, with its two guards, an artillery piece, and also a fully equipped ship. And these things can be set out in the centre of a table, or on a sideboard, or wine cabinet, or wherever. Not only those, but many others: for instance, pyramids, large fowl such as ostriches, peacocks, swans, maybe Hercules, centaurs, and other ingenious things, and fanciful things, as if [for instance] a hunt made of serviettes was taking place on the table; and many other inventions which I haven't had illustrated, thinking that, for anyone who takes pleasure in honouring a magnificent and solemn banquet, it is enough for me to have hinted at them.

In setting the table great care has to be taken that those folded linens are distributed and set out properly: that is, if local custom is such that two people are at the head of the table, there must be two fine plainly pleated linens or else two with herringbone folds; if only one person is there, then it will be proper to put only one of those folded figures there. Then for the rest from place to place you can alternately put a herringbone and a plain pleated linen around the whole table. . . .

It is further to be noted that there are some sorts of plain pleated linens that, when they are opened out, can be set in various ways over bread; that can be done likewise with certain herringbone folds. In sum, each person's judgement will show him the thing to do that will turn out right and honourable.

The names of the figures illustrated here [on the etched plates]: The first illustration of the hands shows their position over the first folds. The second illustration of those hands indicates how to begin the herringbone. The third illustration of the same hands instructs on the positioning of the fingers in order to work easily and well.

Hereafter, the numbered illustrations [on the fourth plate, using plain-pleated linen]:

#1. The first [image] shows table linens such as are the first to be set out and spread on the table. No mention need be made of round ones because not just those are appropriate there, but also salt holders, knives, forks, spoons, bread, serviettes over the bread, and toothpicks.

#2. The second shows plain pleated linen for making mechanisms, Lilies and Mountains that will be at the beginning, and those will be [folded] in four.

#3. The Fan in two ways, which will be [folded] in six and in four. The Saints are similar, then the Double Crown in six.

#4. The Cloaks, in four and in six. All should be plainly pleated linen, though.

#5. The Twelve Mountains, in four, lengthwise because almost all the preceding are crosswise.

#6. The Quadrangles, at the sign Q [in the illustration this folded napkin forms the head of the figure called the Dragon, #12, below].

#7. The Hills, in four.

#8. The Ship, in two.

#9. Covers for the great lords' bread baskets and carving boards, in four.

#10. The Mitre.

#11. The Turkey.

#12. The Dragon.

#13. The Roses, and the Rosemary with the Maltese Cross, in four.

#14. The Twin Fish.

#15. The Pope's Crown.

And all those things are in some places called "triumphs".

The fifth and sixth plates bear similar representations of objects that the skillful Italian linen folder could make out of herringbone-pleated fabric: eagle, dog, lion, beaver, tortoise, bear, pelican, salamander (with crown), and various birds and fish. It is unfortunate that at the time the state of print-making was such that in many if not most instances it is very difficult to understand just what one is looking at or exactly how a sheet of fabric should be folded to make it.